ARISTOTLE ON 1

Aristotle's theory of truth, which has been the most influential account of the concept of truth from Antiquity onwards, spans several areas of philosophy: philosophy of language, logic, ontology, and epistemology. In this book, the first dedicated to this topic, Paolo Crivelli discusses all the main aspects of Aristotle's views on truth and falsehood. He analyses in detail the main relevant passages, addresses some well-known problems of Aristotelian semantics, and assesses Aristotle's theory from the point of view of modern analytic philosophy. In the process he discusses most of the literature on Aristotle's semantic theory to have appeared in the last two centuries. His book vindicates and clarifies the often repeated claim that Aristotle's is a correspondence theory of truth. It will be of interest to a wide range of readers working in both ancient philosophy and modern philosophy of language.

PAOLO CRIVELLI is Fellow and Tutor in Classical Philosophy at New College, Oxford. He has published articles on Plato's logic and epistemology, Aristotle's philosophical logic, and Stoic logic.

ARISTOTLE ON TRUTH

PAOLO CRIVELLI
University of Oxford

CAMBRIDGE
UNIVERSITY PRESS

CAMBRIDGE UNIVERSITY PRESS
Cambridge, New York, Melbourne, Madrid, Cape Town, Singapore, São Paulo

Cambridge University Press
The Edinburgh Building, Cambridge CB2 8RU, UK

Published in the United States of America by Cambridge University Press, New York

www.cambridge.org
Information on this title: www.cambridge.org/9780521823289

First published 2004
Reprinted 2006
This digitally printed version 2007

A catalogue record for this publication is available from the British Library

ISBN 978-0-521-82328-9 hardback
ISBN 978-0-521-03647-4 paperback

To the memory of my father
Renzo Crivelli
and to my mother
Katherine Lester Crivelli

Contents

Acknowledgements *page* ix
Notes on the text x
List of abbreviations of titles of Aristotle's works xi

Introduction 1
1 An overview of Aristotle's theory of truth 1
2 Methodology 39

PART I BEARERS OF TRUTH OR FALSEHOOD

1 States of affairs, thoughts, and sentences 45
1 States of affairs 46
2 Thoughts 62
3 Sentences 72

2 Truth conditions for predicative assertions 77
1 Universals 78
2 Truth and falsehood in *de Interpretatione* 1 82
3 Affirmative and negative predicative assertions 86
4 Assertions about individuals *vs* assertions about universals 89
5 Truth and the categories 95

3 Truth conditions for existential assertions 99
1 Existential assertions concerning simple items 100
2 Non-composite substances 116
3 Singular existential assertions concerning material substances 121

PART II 'EMPTY' TERMS

4 Truth as correspondence 129
1 A correspondence theory of truth? 129
2 The Liar 139

5 'Vacuous' terms and 'empty' terms 152
1 'Vacuous' subjects or predicates 153
2 'Empty' subjects or predicates 158
3 One assertion *vs* many assertions 163

PART III TRUTH AND TIME

6 Truth and change 183
1 Different truth-values at different times 183
2 Truth and relatives 189
3 How far is truth from change? 194

7 Truth and Determinism in *de Interpretatione* 9 198
1 The modal attributes and theses involved in *Int.* 9 199
2 Close textual analysis of *Int.* 9 200
3 Alternative interpretations 226

Appendix 1 *Metaph.* Θ 10, 1051^{b}1: the text 234
Appendix 2 *Metaph.* Θ 10, 1051^{b}2–3: the text 238
Appendix 3 *Int.* 7, 17^{b}16–18: the text 239
Appendix 4 The two-place relations in Aristotle's definition of truth 254
Appendix 5 Aristotle's theory of truth for predicative assertions: formal presentation 258
Appendix 6 The failure of Bivalence for future-tense assertions: formal presentation 266

References 284
Index of names 313
Index of subjects 319
Index of passages 321

Acknowledgements

Many friends and colleagues helped me to shape my views on many of the issues addressed by this study, and alerted me to points where improvement was desirable. Early drafts of parts of the book were presented in Cambridge, Clark, Edinburgh, Florence, Liverpool, Oxford, and Pisa. Among the individuals who in various ways helped me to bring this project to completion, I should like to mention Francesco Ademollo, Francesco Adorno, Fabrizio Amerini, Sylvia Berryman, Susanne Bobzien, Ettore Casari, Walter Cavini, David Charles, Francesco Del Punta, Paolo Fait, Michael Frede, Gabriele Galluzzo, Richard Gaskin, Katerina Ierodiakonou, Fred Miller, Peter Milne, Ben Morison, Massimo Mugnai, David Robinson, Gonzalo Rodriguez-Pereyra, Theodore Scaltsas, Annamaria Schiaparelli, David Sedley, Bob Sharples, Robin Smith, Christopher Strachan, John Thorp, Tim Williamson, and an anonymous referee for Cambridge University Press. The responsibility for the remaining shortcomings is of course mine alone.

Notes on the text

'LSJ' abbreviates the Liddell, Scott, Jones Greek–English lexicon.

I refer to Aristotelian passages by the line numbers as they are printed in Bekker's original edition: these in some cases differ from the 'Bekker lines' of widespread editions (e.g., 101^b38 of Ross's edition of the *Topics* is 101^b39 of Bekker's original edition). Similarly, I follow Bekker's numbering of the chapters within each book of the *Nicomachean Ethics*.

For Greek authors I use LSJ's standard abbreviations. For authors other than Aristotle, I normally use the critical editions on which LSJ relies. For Latin authors, I employ abbreviations which are easy to decode and I use standard critical editions.

'Cf.' at the beginning of a footnote indicates that the passages subsequently referred to express views close to those formulated in the portion of the main text to which the footnote pertains. If I disagree with an author, I say so explicitly (I never use 'cf.' to refer to one or more passages that formulate views with which I disagree).

I use quotation marks for three purposes: (i) to mention linguistic expressions, e.g. the word 'dog' is a noun; (ii) to indicate that a certain linguistic expression is being used in some special or unusual sense, e.g. Homer is a 'philosopher'; (iii) to quote a portion of text from some author, e.g. Aristotle says that 'sentences are true in the same way as the objects' (*Int.* 9, 19^a33). I use double quotation marks ("and") only when what would otherwise be occurrences of single quotation marks would be embedded within single quotation marks.

Abbreviations of titles of Aristotle's works

APo.	*Posterior Analytics*
APr.	*Prior Analytics*
Cael.	*de Caelo*
Cat.	*Categories*
de An.	*de Anima*
Div. Somn.	*de Divinatione per Somnia*
EE	*Eudemian Ethics*
EN	*Nicomachean Ethics*
GA	*de Generatione Animalium*
GC	*de Generatione et Corruptione*
HA	*Historia Animalium*
Insomn.	*de Insomniis*
Int.	*de Interpretatione*
Long.	*de Longaevitate*
MM	*Magna Moralia*
Mem.	*de Memoria*
Metaph.	*Metaphysics*
PA	*de Partibus Animalium*
Ph.	*Physics*
Po.	*Poetics*
Pol.	*Politics*
Pr.	*Problems*
Rh.	*Rhetoric*
SE	*Sophistici Elenchi*
Sens.	*de Sensu*
Somn. Vig.	*de Somno et Vigilia*
Top.	*Topics*
Xen.	*de Xenophane*

Introduction

The study of truth is a central part of the philosophical tradition we have inherited from classical Greece. Aristotle played an important role in developing and sharpening the debate in this area and on many issues that are connected with it. I have two primary goals: to offer a precise reconstruction of all of Aristotle's most significant views on truth and falsehood and to gain a philosophical understanding of them. In this introduction I first offer an overview of Aristotle's theory of truth and then discuss the methodology I adopt in pursuing my primary goals.

I AN OVERVIEW OF ARISTOTLE'S THEORY OF TRUTH

Why an overview? Aristotle speaks about truth and falsehood in passages from several works, mainly the *Categories* (chapters 4, 5, 10, and 12), *de Interpretatione* (chapters 1–9), *Sophistici Elenchi* (chapter 25), *de Anima* (chapter 3.6), and the *Metaphysics* (chapters Γ 7, Δ 7, Δ 29, E 4, and Θ 10). Truth and falsehood are not the main topic of these works: their discussions of truth and falsehood are asides. Reconstructing an Aristotelian theory of truth and falsehood on the basis of such asides poses complicated problems of various sorts. To help readers to keep their orientation through the many bifurcations of the arguments addressing these problems, I decided to offer a concise but precise map of the territory – an overview of Aristotle's theory of truth. References to the passages from Aristotle's works that substantiate the attribution of a certain view to him, and an examination of the relevant secondary literature, will be found in the chapters that follow this introduction.

Universals. To expound Aristotle's theory of truth, I need to present some of his views on universals and signification. I begin with universals.

Luckily, it is not necessary to embark on the daunting task of a complete exposition of Aristotle's views on universals. Aristotle is to this extent a realist about universals: in his view, universals are objects whose nature is neither mental nor linguistic (they are neither concepts nor linguistic expressions). He believes that every universal exists when and only when[1] it holds of some individual or other that at some time or other exists.[2]

Let me spend a few words explaining why the phrase 'at some time or other' is needed. According to Aristotle, some universals sometimes hold of individuals that do not exist then, but exist at other times. For example, Aristotle seems to think that at any time the universal poet[3] holds of all and only those individual human beings (including those who at that time do not exist) who by that time have authored some poem. In particular, Aristotle would probably grant that although Homer does not exist now, the universal poet holds now of Homer. It is because of universals of this sort that the phrase 'at some time or other' is needed.

Aristotle is likely to believe that every universal is everlasting, i.e. exists always. Hence he is likely to be committed to the view that every universal at all times holds of some individual or other that at some time or other exists – in short, that all universals are always instantiated. This of course leaves the possibility open that every individual that at some time or other exists and of which a certain universal holds at one time could be other than every individual that at some time or other exists and of which the same universal holds at a certain other time – in short, the possibility remains that some universal could be instantiated by different individuals at different times.

Signification. I now move on to expound some of Aristotle's views on signification. Aristotle thinks that some utterances of certain noun-phrases and certain adjectival phrases signify a single universal: e.g. he would grant that some utterances of 'man' signify the universal man and that some utterances of 'white' signify the universal white. He also thinks that some utterances of certain noun-phrases signify a single individual: e.g. he would grant that some utterances of 'Socrates' signify Socrates, the Athenian philosopher executed in 399 BC. However, he believes that some utterances of certain

[1] I use 'when and only when' in a strictly temporal sense, i.e. as equivalent to 'at all and only the times at which'.

[2] I use 'to hold of' to express the relation of a universal to its instances. Following Aristotle's lead, I sometimes use 'to be predicated of' to express this same relation.

[3] I normally refer to a universal by simply using a linguistic expression that signifies it (if this linguistic expression is a phrase, I hyphenate it); I avoid referring to a universal by italicising, or enclosing in quotation marks, a linguistic expression that signifies it. For example, I normally refer to universals by means of expressions like 'the universal poet' or 'the universal man-who-authored-a-poem'; I avoid referring to universals by means of expressions like 'the universal *poet*' or 'the universal "poet"'.

noun-phrases and some of certain adjectival phrases signify neither a single universal nor a single individual: e.g. he would concede that some utterances of 'walking white man' or 'walking, white, and tall' signify neither a single universal nor a single individual (he would claim that each of these utterances signifies many universals which do not coalesce in a single universal).

What can be true or false? Having presented Aristotle's views on universals and signification that are necessary to understand his theory of truth, I am in a position to begin addressing the main themes of the latter. Let me start with Aristotle's conception of the bearers of truth or falsehood.

According to Aristotle, items that are true or false are of three main kinds: sentences, thoughts, and certain objects whose nature is neither mental nor linguistic. The sentences that are true or false are sentence-tokens, utterances, events of speech that occur over relatively short portions of time. Similarly, the thoughts that are true or false are thought-tokens, either mental events that occur over relatively short portions of time or thinker-individuated mental states.

For Aristotle, events of perceiving and imagining also are true or false. Events of perceiving and imagining fall under none of the three kinds I just mentioned: they are neither thoughts, nor sentences, nor objects whose nature is neither mental nor linguistic. Since Aristotle's views on the truth and falsehood of events of perceiving and imagining are somewhat isolated from the rest of his reflection on truth and falsehood, in this introduction I shall say nothing more about them.

A puzzling view. A particularly puzzling part of Aristotle's theory of truth is his view that among items that are true or false there are objects (I sometimes use 'object' to mean 'object whose nature is neither mental nor linguistic': I trust that the context will make it clear whether a given occurrence of 'object' is to be understood in this narrow sense). On this point Aristotle's theory of truth is radically different from some modern ones: modern philosophers are ready to acknowledge that certain thoughts or sentences are true or false, but some of them would jib at the suggestion that some objects are true or false.

These objects that are true or false occupy a central position in Aristotle's theory of truth. What are they? What roles do they play in Aristotle's theory of truth?

What are the objects that are true or false? Aristotle distinguishes two kinds of objects that are true or false: composite objects and simple objects.

Some composite objects that are true or false are states of affairs.[4] A state of affairs, which is an object, is composed of two further objects: one of the objects of which it is composed is a universal, the other is either a universal or an individual. A state of affairs is true when and only when the objects of which it is composed are reciprocally combined in the relevant way; it is false when and only when the objects of which it is composed are reciprocally divided in the relevant way.[5] For example, the state of affairs that Socrates is seated is composed of the universal seated and of the individual Socrates; it is true when and only when the universal seated is combined in the relevant way with Socrates, i.e. when and only when Socrates is seated; it is false when and only when the universal seated is divided in the relevant way from Socrates, i.e. when and only when Socrates is not seated. Again, the state of affairs that every diagonal is commensurable is composed of the universal commensurable and of the universal diagonal; it is true when and only when the universal commensurable is combined in the relevant way with the universal diagonal, i.e. when and only when every diagonal is commensurable; it is false when and only when the universal commensurable is divided in the relevant way from the universal diagonal, i.e. when and only when some diagonal is not commensurable. Since no diagonal ever is commensurable, the state of affairs that the diagonal is commensurable is never true but always false. Aristotle allows only 'affirmative' states of affairs: among states of affairs there are the state of affairs that Socrates is seated and the state of affairs that every diagonal is commensurable, but there is not a state of affairs that Socrates is not seated nor is there one that not every diagonal is commensurable. In principle, a state of affairs can exist at a time when it is false, i.e. at a time when the objects of which it is composed are reciprocally divided in the relevant way. For example, the state of affairs that Socrates is seated exists at certain times when it is false; again, the state of affairs that every diagonal is commensurable always exists and is always false. The combination that makes a state of affairs true is not to be confused with the composition whereby the state of affairs is composed of further objects. By the same token, the division that makes a state of affairs false does not destroy the composition whereby the state of affairs is composed of further objects (otherwise the state of affairs could not, even in principle, exist at any time when it is false). For example, the state of

[4] 'State of affairs' can be used in several senses. I use it to denote objects of a 'propositional' nature of which it is sensible to say both that they obtain and that they do not obtain at a time.

[5] 'To be combined' and 'to be divided' are technical expressions. I hope that the examples in this paragraph's sequel will provide an intuitive grasp of their meaning. They will be discussed in greater detail later in this introduction.

affairs that Socrates is seated remains composed of the universal seated and of the individual Socrates even when the universal seated is divided from the individual Socrates in such a way as to make the state of affairs in question false. It remains unclear whether in Aristotle's view all states of affairs are everlasting: does Aristotle believe that the state of affairs that Socrates is seated exists both before and after Socrates exists? A state of affairs, as it is conceived of by Aristotle, is best understood as an object corresponding to a complete present-tense affirmative predicative assertion, and as being composed of the objects signified by the assertion's predicate and subject. For example, the state of affairs that Socrates is seated corresponds to the whole present-tense affirmative predicative assertion that is an utterance of 'Socrates is seated', and is composed of the universal seated, which is signified by the assertion's predicate (an utterance of 'seated'), and of the individual Socrates, who is signified by the assertion's subject (an utterance of 'Socrates').

As I said, some composite objects that are true or false are states of affairs. According to Aristotle, material substances (e.g. Socrates and the horse Bucephalus) are composite objects in that they consist of form and matter. Material substances are not states of affairs, but they resemble states of affairs in interesting respects: as for a state of affairs to be true is to be combined, so for a material substance to exist is to be combined, i.e. it is for its form to be combined with its matter; as for a state of affairs to be false is to be divided, so for a material substance not to exist is to be divided, i.e. it is for its form to be divided from its matter. Aristotle perhaps thinks that material substances rank among the composite objects that are true or false, that for a material substance to be true is to exist, and that for a material substance to be false is not to exist. I can use only the cautious expression 'Aristotle perhaps thinks . . .' because the evidence for attributing the position in question to Aristotle is far less than clear cut. However, independently of whether Aristotle does endorse the position in question, at least two differences between states of affairs and material substances are worth noting. First, while some state of affairs exists at times when it is false, no material substance exists at times when it is false (because, according to the position in question, for a material substance to be false is not to exist). Second, although some material substances (i.e. celestial bodies) are everlasting, most are not; on the other hand, Aristotle does not state how long states of affairs exist, but his position might well be that all states of affairs are everlasting.

Since a simple object has no components between which combination or division could obtain, for a simple object to be true cannot be to be combined, nor can for it to be false be to be divided. Rather, for a simple object to be true is simply to exist, and for it to be false is simply not to exist. Aristotle distinguishes two kinds of simple objects: essences and incorporeal substances. Essences are natural kinds (e.g. the kind horse).[6] The remaining simple objects, incorporeal substances, are God and (perhaps) the intellects that move the heavenly spheres.[7] The application of 'true' to incorporeal substances should not arouse wonder: 'true' is one of the epithets traditionally used to speak of God. Both essences and incorporeal substances are everlasting, i.e. exist always. Hence, all simple objects exist always.

The sense of 'true' and 'false' whereby they apply to objects is probably Aristotle's own creation: it is an extension of the ordinary sense of these expressions which Aristotle introduces in order to construct a better theory of truth. It is not, however, completely unconnected with ordinary usage: 'true' can be used (both in Greek and in English) to mean 'real' (as in 'true coin'), and 'real' is connected with 'existent' (although 'real' and 'existent' are used differently, one can employ the phrase 'the contrast between dreams and what is real' to describe the discrepancy between what exists and what someone would like to exist).

Aristotle's views on the nature of the bearers of truth or falsehood can now be conveniently summarised by the following schema:

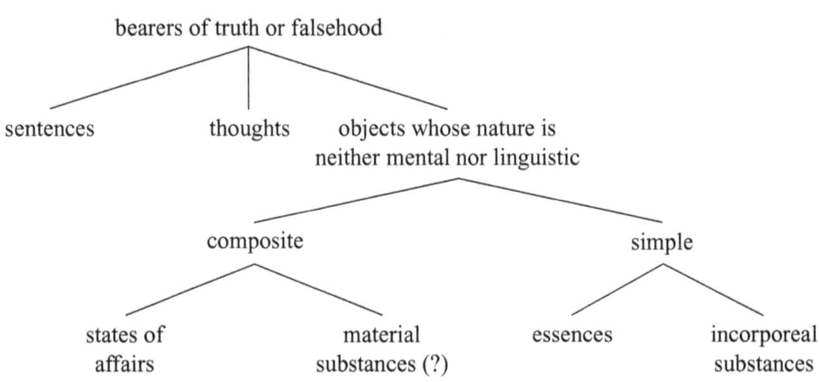

[6] Aristotle's remarks on essence are difficult to understand and are variously interpreted. The view I am attributing to Aristotle here, i.e. that essences are natural kinds, is 'minimal' in that it is compatible with, and perhaps implied by, several of these interpretations.

[7] By 'material' and 'immaterial' I mean 'containing matter' and (respectively) 'not containing matter'. By 'corporeal' and 'incorporeal' I mean 'either containing or mixed with matter' and (respectively) 'neither containing nor mixed with matter'. Thus: Socrates is a material and corporeal substance; Socrates' essence is an immaterial but corporeal substance; God is an immaterial and incorporeal substance.

What roles do the objects that are true or false play in Aristotle's theory of truth? Objects that are true or false play three roles in Aristotle's theory of truth: first, they contribute to explaining what it is to be true or false for items of other kinds which can be such, i.e. for thoughts and sentences; second, they are bearers of modal attributes; third, they are targets of propositional attitudes. In the following subsections I shall examine these three roles in turn.

The first role of objects that are true or false: contributing to explaining what it is to be true or false for thoughts and sentences. As I just said, the first role played in Aristotle's theory of truth by objects that are true or false is to contribute to explaining what it is to be true or false for thoughts and sentences. This role recalls a strategy which is often adopted in modern philosophy of logic, from Frege onwards: that of explaining the truth and falsehood of certain mental states and certain sentences by appealing to the truth and falsehood of propositions (abstract entities whose nature is neither mental nor linguistic). Although there are important differences between Aristotle's conception and the modern strategy, at this stage I would like to call attention to the resemblance.

To expound how objects that are true or false contribute to explaining what it is to be true or false for thoughts and sentences, I must say something about Aristotle's views on thoughts and sentences that are true or false.

Truth-evaluable sentences. Not every sentence is either true or false: some are neither (e.g. prayers). Every sentence that is true or false is an assertoric sentence, or (as Aristotle often calls it) an assertion. But the converse fails: some assertions are neither true nor false (read on to find out which). Assertions coincide with truth-evaluable sentences, i.e. with the sentences with regard to which the question 'Is it true or false?' can be reasonably asked. Note that this question cannot be reasonably asked with regard to certain sentences (e.g. prayers). In the case of some sentences with regard to which the question 'Is it true or false?' can be reasonably asked, the correct answer is 'Neither'. An analogy helps to clarify. Physical objects coincide with colour-evaluable objects, i.e. with the objects with regard to which the question 'What colour is it?' can be reasonably asked. Note that this question cannot be reasonably asked with regard to certain objects (e.g. numbers). In the case of some objects with regard to which the question 'What colour is it?' can be reasonably asked, the correct answer is 'None' (e.g. some transparent objects like crystal balls or diamonds).

Assertions are utterances, i.e. expression-tokens (not expression-types), events of speech that occur over relatively short portions of time.

Truth-evaluable thoughts. Aristotle does not explicitly isolate a class of truth-evaluable thoughts that constitute the mental counterparts of assertions. However, since he regards the spheres of thought and speech as closely analogous, indeed, almost as isomorphic, he is likely to believe that there is such a class of truth-evaluable thoughts corresponding to the class of truth-evaluable sentences, i.e. to the class of assertions.

Some of Aristotle's remarks indicate that he would agree that every belief is a truth-evaluable thought, i.e. a thought with regard to which the question 'Is it true or false?' can be reasonably asked. However, I doubt that Aristotle would claim that every truth-evaluable thought is a belief. Hence, for Aristotle beliefs probably constitute a proper subclass of truth-evaluable thoughts. I guess Aristotle would grant that not every belief is either true or false.

Simple and composite assertions. Aristotle distinguishes two kinds of assertions: simple assertions and composite assertions. An assertion is simple just in case it concerns exactly one object; it is composite just in case it concerns more than one object. Every simple assertion is either affirmative or negative. Composite assertions are equivalent to utterances constructed from several assertions linked by connective particles.

Aristotle concentrates on simple assertions, i.e. assertions that concern exactly one object. He has little to say about composite assertions: he acknowledges their existence, but they remain at the margins of his reflection. He never states that some sentences that are true or false have no assertoric force (like the utterance of 'Socrates is seated' which is a part of an utterance of 'Either Socrates is seated or Socrates is not seated'). Nor does he discuss utterances of 'Either Socrates is seated or Socrates is seated': are they simple (because they concern exactly one object, i.e. the state of affairs that Socrates is seated) or composite (because they are disjunctive)?

Simple beliefs. Aristotle does not explicitly isolate a class of simple beliefs that are the mental counterparts of simple assertions. However, since (as I said) he regards the spheres of thought and speech as closely analogous, he is likely to take such a class for granted: he probably thinks that simple beliefs are those beliefs that concern exactly one object, and that every simple belief is either affirmative or negative.

A general definition of truth and falsehood for simple beliefs and assertions. Having expounded Aristotle's views on thoughts and sentences that are true or false, I am now in a position to address his conception of how objects that are true or false contribute to explaining what it is to be true or false for thoughts and sentences. Objects play this role, in particular, with regard to simple beliefs and simple assertions.

Aristotle's theory of truth and falsehood for simple beliefs and assertions is governed by a general definition of truth and falsehood (henceforth 'DTF'):

DTF Every simple belief, or assertion, concerns exactly one object and is either affirmative or negative. Every affirmative simple belief, or assertion, posits that the object it concerns is true. Accordingly, an affirmative simple belief, or assertion, is true when and only when the object it concerns is true; an affirmative simple belief, or assertion, is false when and only when the object it concerns is false. Every negative simple belief, or assertion, posits that the object it concerns is false. Accordingly, a negative simple belief, or assertion, is true when and only when the object it concerns is false; a negative simple belief, or assertion, is false when and only when the object it concerns is true.

DTF is a *definition* of truth (at least for simple beliefs and assertions). Aristotle does not address the issue of the *criterion* of truth (roughly, the issue of establishing what, if any, reliable ways humans have of discovering truths). Aristotle's silence on the issue of the criterion of truth is remarkable in view of the fact that shortly after his death, with the advent of the Hellenistic philosophical schools of the third and second centuries BC, this issue becomes a hot topic of philosophical debate.

DTF covers at one blow all simple beliefs and assertions, those concerning composite objects as well as those concerning simple ones. It is worthwhile working out the details of Aristotle's account for each case. So, let us examine the forms taken on by DTF with simple beliefs and assertions concerning composite objects and with simple beliefs and assertions concerning simple objects. However, there are two kinds of composite objects: states of affairs and material substances. Let us then study the forms of DTF with regard to simple beliefs and assertions concerning (i) those composite objects that are states of affairs, (ii) those composite objects that are material substances, and (iii) simple objects.

Predicative assertions and beliefs. The simple assertions which concern those composite objects that are states of affairs are predicative assertions; similarly, the simple beliefs that concern those composite objects that are states of affairs are predicative beliefs. Let me first spend a few paragraphs explaining Aristotle's views on predicative assertions and predicative beliefs.

Predicative assertions display a subject–predicate structure (this can be clearly seen in examples of predicative assertions like utterances of the sentence-type 'Socrates is seated' or of the sentence-type 'Socrates is not seated'). Every predicative assertion has at least three parts: the predicate, the subject, and the copula. In every predicative assertion, the predicate signifies a universal, the subject signifies either a universal or an individual, and the copula combines with the predicate to form a predicative expression. Consider a predicative assertion that is an utterance of 'Socrates is seated': the predicate is the part of the assertion that is an utterance of the adjective 'seated' and signifies the universal seated; the subject is the part of the assertion that is an utterance of the name 'Socrates' and signifies the individual Socrates; and the copula is the part of the assertion that is an utterance of 'is' and combines with the predicate to form the predicative expression that is an utterance of 'is seated'. Every predicative assertion is either affirmative (e.g. an utterance of 'Socrates is seated') or negative (e.g. an utterance of 'Socrates is not seated'). Many predicative assertions have further parts over and above the predicate, the subject, and the copula: they contain utterances either of a negative particle (an utterance of 'not', as in an utterance of 'Socrates is not seated') or of a quantifying expression (an utterance of 'every', 'no', 'some', or 'not every', as in an utterance of 'No horse is white'). Many assertions that contain no copula are regarded by Aristotle as equivalent to assertions that do contain one: e.g. for Aristotle an utterance of 'Socrates walks' is equivalent to one of 'Socrates is walking'. Note that in English 'Socrates is walking' is not equivalent to 'Socrates walks'. Aristotle's view, however, is correct with respect to Greek usage: the Greek sentence-type rendered by 'Socrates is walking' is in fact equivalent to that rendered by 'Socrates walks'.

A predicative belief is a belief whose literal linguistic expression would be a predicative assertion. For example, Plato's belief that Socrates is seated is a predicative belief because its literal linguistic expression would be a predicative assertion that is an utterance of 'Socrates is seated'. Every predicative belief has a part that constitutes its predicate (it is about, or concerns, or – as I shall often say – grasps a universal) and one that constitutes its subject (it grasps either a universal or an individual). For example, in Plato's belief that Socrates is seated, the predicate is the part of the belief that grasps the universal seated, the subject is the part that grasps the individual Socrates. Every predicative belief is either affirmative (e.g. Plato's belief that Socrates is seated) or negative (e.g. Simmias' belief that Socrates is not seated). Note that the predicate and the subject of a predicative assertion are utterances, and they *signify* objects; the predicate and the subject of a predicative belief are thoughts, and they *grasp* objects.

Aristotle's classification of predicative beliefs and assertions. Aristotle has a richly articulated classification of predicative beliefs and assertions. Predicative beliefs and assertions divide into two main groups: *singular* and *general* predicative beliefs and assertions. A predicative belief, or assertion, is singular just in case its subject grasps, or signifies, an individual; it is general just in case its subject grasps, or signifies, a universal. Examples of singular predicative assertions are utterances of 'Socrates is seated' and 'Socrates is not seated'. As for general predicative beliefs and assertions, they divide into two subordinate groups: *indeterminate* and *quantified* predicative beliefs and assertions. Examples of indeterminate predicative assertions are utterances of 'A horse is white' and 'A horse is not white'. As for quantified predicative beliefs and assertions, they divide into two subordinate groups: *particular* and *universal* predicative beliefs and assertions. Examples of particular predicative assertions are utterances of 'Some horse is white' and 'Not every horse is white'; examples of universal predicative assertions are utterances of 'Every horse is white' and 'No horse is white'. Aristotle's classification of predicative beliefs and assertions is conveniently summarised by the following schema:

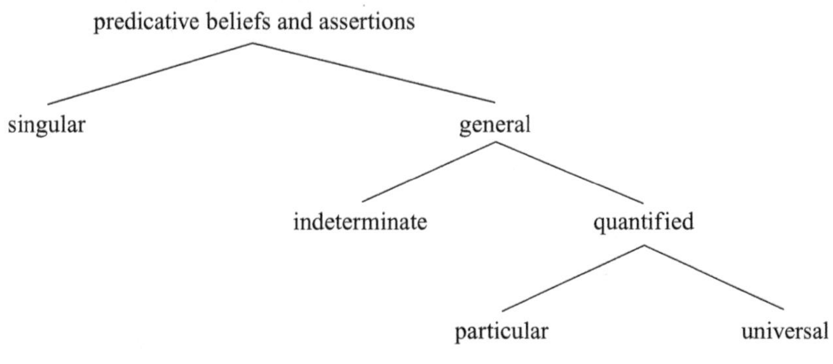

The distinction between affirmative and negative predicative beliefs and assertions cuts across the above classification: every group within this classification is divided into an affirmative and a negative subordinate group. That is, universal predicative beliefs and assertions divide into *universal affirmative* and *universal negative* predicative beliefs and assertions; particular predicative beliefs and assertions divide into *particular affirmative* and *particular negative* predicative beliefs and assertions; similarly with indeterminate and singular predicative beliefs and assertions.

Aristotle has little to say about indeterminate predicative beliefs and assertions. Following his lead, I shall concentrate on universal, particular, and singular predicative beliefs and assertions.

The relationship of predicative beliefs and assertions to states of affairs. Having explained Aristotle's conception of predicative beliefs and assertions, I am now in a position to report his views on how predicative beliefs and assertions are related to states of affairs. Every predicative belief, or assertion, concerns exactly one state of affairs whose two components are, first, the universal grasped, or signified, by the predicate of the predicative belief, or assertion, and, second, the object (a universal or an individual) grasped, or signified, by the subject of the predicative belief, or assertion.

For example, a predicative assertion that is an utterance of 'Socrates is seated' concerns the state of affairs that Socrates is seated, which is composed of the universal seated (signified by the assertion's predicate, an utterance of 'seated') and the individual Socrates (signified by the assertion's subject, an utterance of 'Socrates'). Note that a predicative assertion that is an utterance of 'Socrates is not seated' concerns the same state of affairs: the state of affairs that Socrates is seated. Again, a predicative assertion that is an utterance of 'Every diagonal is commensurable' concerns the state of affairs that every diagonal is commensurable, which is composed of the universal commensurable (signified by the assertion's predicate, an utterance of 'commensurable') and the universal diagonal (signified by the assertion's subject, an utterance of 'diagonal'). Note that a predicative assertion that is an utterance of 'Not every diagonal is commensurable' concerns the same state of affairs: the state of affairs that every diagonal is commensurable.

DTF and predications. In the case of predicative beliefs and assertions, DTF takes on the following form: an affirmative predicative belief, or assertion, is true when and only when the state of affairs it concerns is true, i.e. when and only when the components of this state of affairs are reciprocally combined in the relevant way, i.e. when and only when the universal grasped, or signified, by the predicate is combined in the relevant way with the object (a universal or an individual) grasped, or signified, by the subject. An affirmative predicative belief, or assertion, is false when and only when the state of affairs it concerns is false, i.e. when and only when the components of this state of affairs are reciprocally divided in the relevant way, i.e. when and only when the universal grasped, or signified, by the predicate is divided in the relevant way from the object grasped, or signified, by the subject. A negative predicative belief, or assertion, is true when and only when the state of affairs it concerns is false, i.e. when and only when the components of this state of affairs are reciprocally divided in the relevant way, i.e. when and only when the universal grasped, or signified, by the predicate is divided in the relevant way from the object grasped, or signified, by the subject. A negative predicative belief, or assertion, is false when and only when the state of affairs it concerns is true, i.e. when and only when the components of this state of affairs are reciprocally combined in the relevant way, i.e. when and only when the universal grasped, or signified, by the predicate is combined in the relevant way with the object grasped, or signified, by the subject.

Truth conditions for predications that differ in 'quantity'. Different relations of combination and division are associated with predicative beliefs and assertions that differ in 'quantity' (i.e. by being universal, particular, or singular). I shall first offer an abstract exposition of how different relations of combination and division are called for in an account of true and false predicative beliefs and assertions that differ in 'quantity'; afterwards I shall offer some examples. Here is the abstract exposition:

[a] Every universal affirmative predicative belief, or assertion, posits that the universal grasped, or signified, by its predicate is combined with the universal grasped, or signified, by its subject in such a way as universally to hold of it. Accordingly, a universal affirmative predicative belief, or assertion, is true when and only when the universal grasped, or signified, by its predicate is combined with the universal grasped, or signified, by its subject in such a way as universally to hold of it. A universal affirmative predicative belief, or assertion, is false when and only when the universal grasped, or signified, by its predicate is divided from the universal grasped, or signified, by its subject in such a way as not universally to hold of it.

[b] Every universal negative predicative belief, or assertion, posits that the universal grasped, or signified, by its predicate is divided from the universal grasped, or signified, by its subject in such a way as universally to

fail to hold of it. Accordingly, a universal negative predicative belief, or assertion, is true when and only when the universal grasped, or signified, by its predicate is divided from the universal grasped, or signified, by its subject in such a way as universally to fail to hold of it. A universal negative predicative belief, or assertion, is false when and only when the universal grasped, or signified, by its predicate is combined with the universal grasped, or signified, by its subject in such a way as not universally to fail to hold of it.

[c] Every particular affirmative predicative belief, or assertion, posits that the universal grasped, or signified, by its predicate is combined with the universal grasped, or signified, by its subject in such a way as not universally to fail to hold of it. Accordingly, a particular affirmative predicative belief, or assertion, is true when and only when the universal grasped, or signified, by its predicate is combined with the universal grasped, or signified, by its subject in such a way as not universally to fail to hold of it. A particular affirmative predicative belief, or assertion, is false when and only when the universal grasped, or signified, by its predicate is divided from the universal grasped, or signified, by its subject in such a way as universally to fail to hold of it.

[d] Every particular negative predicative belief, or assertion, posits that the universal grasped, or signified, by its predicate is divided from the universal grasped, or signified, by its subject in such a way as not universally to hold of it. Accordingly, a particular negative predicative belief, or assertion, is true when and only when the universal grasped, or signified, by its predicate is divided from the universal grasped, or signified, by its subject in such a way as not universally to hold of it. A particular negative predicative belief, or assertion, is false when and only when the universal grasped, or signified, by its predicate is combined with the universal grasped, or signified, by its subject in such a way as universally to hold of it.

[e] Every singular affirmative predicative belief, or assertion, posits that the universal grasped, or signified, by its predicate is combined with the individual grasped, or signified, by its subject in such a way as to hold of it. Accordingly, a singular affirmative predicative belief, or assertion, is true when and only when the universal grasped, or signified, by its predicate is combined with the individual grasped, or signified, by its subject in such a way as to hold of it. A singular affirmative predicative belief, or assertion, is false when and only when the universal grasped,

or signified, by its predicate is divided from the individual grasped, or signified, by its subject in such a way as to hold outside it.

[f] Every singular negative predicative belief, or assertion, posits that the universal grasped, or signified, by its predicate is divided from the individual grasped, or signified, by its subject in such a way as to hold outside it. Accordingly, a singular negative predicative belief, or assertion, is true when and only when the universal grasped, or signified, by its predicate is divided from the individual grasped, or signified, by its subject in such a way as to hold outside it. A singular negative predicative belief, or assertion, is false when and only when the universal grasped, or signified, by its predicate is combined with the individual grasped, or signified, by its subject in such a way as to hold of it.

To pin down the above, a definition of the relevant relations of combination and division is called for. A universal *u* is combined with a universal *v* in such a way as universally to hold of it when and only when *u* holds of every individual of which *v* holds. A universal *u* is divided from a universal *v* in such a way as universally to fail to hold of it when and only when every individual of which *v* holds is other than every individual of which *u* holds. A universal *u* is combined with a universal *v* in such a way as not universally to fail to hold of it when and only when *u* holds of at least one individual of which *v* holds. A universal *u* is divided from a universal *v* in such a way as not universally to hold of it when and only when at least one individual of which *v* holds is other than every individual of which *u* holds. A universal *u* is combined with an individual *i* in such a way as to hold of it when and only when *u* holds of *i*. A universal *u* is divided from an individual *i* in such a way as to hold outside it when and only when *i* is other than every individual of which *u* holds.

Some examples will clarify the abstract exposition of the previous subsection.

A universal affirmative predicative assertion that is an utterance of 'Every horse is white' posits that the universal white, signified by the predicate (an utterance of 'white'), is combined with the universal horse, signified by the subject (an utterance of 'horse'), in such a way as universally to hold of it. Accordingly, this utterance is true when and only when the universal white is combined with the universal horse in such a way as universally to hold of it, i.e. when and only when the universal white holds of every individual of which the universal horse holds; the same utterance is false when and only when the universal white is divided from the universal horse in such a way as not universally to hold of it, i.e. when and only when at least one individual of which the universal horse holds is other than every individual of which the universal white holds. Hence, now the utterance of 'Every horse is white' is not true (for it is not the case that the universal white now holds of every individual of which the universal horse now holds), but false (for at least one individual of which the universal horse now holds is other than every individual of which the universal white now holds).

Again, a universal negative predicative assertion that is an utterance of 'No horse is white' posits that the universal white, signified by the predicate (an utterance of 'white'), is divided from the universal horse, signified by the subject (an utterance of 'horse'), in such a way as universally to fail to hold of it. Accordingly, this utterance is true when and only when the universal white is divided from the universal horse in such a way as universally to fail to hold of it, i.e. when and only when every individual of which the universal horse holds is other than every individual of which the universal white holds; the same utterance is false when and only when the universal white is combined with the universal horse in such a way as not universally to fail to hold of it, i.e. when and only when the universal white holds of at least one individual of which the universal horse holds. Hence, now the utterance of 'No horse is white' is not true (for it is not the case that every individual of which the universal horse now holds is other than every individual of which the universal white now holds), but false (for the universal white now holds of at least one individual of which the universal horse now holds).

Predications that differ in category. Different relations of combination and division are associated (not only with predicative beliefs and assertions that differ in 'quantity', but also) with predicative beliefs and assertions that differ in 'category'. There are several versions (or, perhaps, aspects) of Aristotle's theory of the categories. In one of these versions, the categories are predicative relations linking objects. Different categories correspond to different fundamental questions: the category of substance is the predicative relation linking a kind to its subordinate kinds and to its members, and corresponds to the question 'What is it?'; the category of quality is the predicative relation linking a quality to the items it holds of, and corresponds to the question 'What is it like?'; etc.[8] Moreover, there are predicative relations

[8] The question 'What is it?' can be used in a wide range of ways. Within this range we can pick out a sharp question which is truly and appropriately answered by mentioning the kind under which the object referred to by 'it' falls. If someone pointing to Socrates (who, as it happens, is pale) asks 'What is it?', 'It is a man' and 'It is an animal' are true and appropriate answers (they mention the

that are the negative counterparts of those predicative relations that are the categories. Now:

[g] Every affirmative predicative belief, or assertion, corresponding to the question 'What is it?' posits that the predicative relation of combination which is the category of substance links the universal grasped, or signified, by the predicate to the object grasped, or signified, by the subject. Accordingly, an affirmative predicative belief, or assertion, corresponding to the question 'What is it?' is true when and only when the predicative relation of combination that is the category of substance links the universal grasped, or signified, by the predicate to the object grasped, or signified, by the subject. Accordingly, an affirmative predicative belief, or assertion, corresponding to the question 'What is it?' is false when and only when the predicative relation of division that is the negative counterpart of the category of substance links the universal grasped, or signified, by the predicate to the object grasped, or signified, by the subject.

[h] Every affirmative predicative belief, or assertion, corresponding to the question 'What is it like?' posits that the predicative relation of combination that is the category of quality links the universal grasped, or signified, by the predicate to the object grasped, or signified, by the subject. Accordingly, an affirmative predicative belief, or assertion, corresponding to the question 'What is it like?' is true when and only when the predicative relation of combination that is the category of quality links the universal grasped, or signified, by the predicate to the object grasped, or signified, by the subject. An affirmative predicative belief, or assertion, corresponding to the question 'What is it like?' is false when and only when the predicative relation of division that is the negative counterpart of the category of quality links the universal grasped, or signified, by the predicate to the object grasped, or signified, by the subject.

I forgo spelling out the similar descriptions of the truth and falsehood of predicative beliefs and assertions that correspond to other categories.

Here are some examples to clarify the foregoing abstract exposition. An utterance of 'Socrates is a man' is true when and only when the predicative relation of combination that is the category of substance links the universal

universals animal and man), 'It is pale' is true but in most cases inappropriate (in Greek, which is of course the language at issue here, the answer corresponding to the English 'It is pale' would probably be inappropriate in all cases). If, on the other hand, someone pointing to pale Socrates asks 'What is it like?', 'It is pale' is a true and appropriate answer, while 'It is a man' and 'It is an animal' are both true but inappropriate.

man, signified by the predicate (an utterance of 'a man'), to the individual Socrates, signified by the subject (an utterance of 'Socrates'). Again, an utterance of 'Socrates is pale' is true when and only when the predicative relation of combination that is the category of quality links the universal pale, signified by the predicate (an utterance of 'pale') to the individual Socrates, signified by the subject (an utterance of 'Socrates').

In this account, truth and falsehood are parasitical upon the categories because they are defined by mentioning the categories. In Aristotle's view, such parasitism is a reason for leaving truth and falsehood at the margins of metaphysical inquiry, which should concentrate on ontologically fundamental items, i.e. on the categories and their inhabitants.

DTF and existentials concerning material substances. In the case of those composite objects that are material substances, DTF is specified as follows: an affirmative simple belief, or assertion, concerning a material substance is true when and only when this material substance is true, i.e. when and only when this material substance exists, i.e. when and only when its form is combined with its matter. An affirmative simple belief, or assertion, concerning a material substance is false when and only when this material substance is false, i.e. when and only when this material substance does not exist, i.e. when and only when its form is divided from its matter. A negative simple belief, or assertion, concerning a material substance is true when and only when this material substance is false, i.e. when and only when this material substance does not exist, i.e. when and only when its form is divided from its matter. A negative simple belief, or assertion, concerning a material substance is false when and only when this material substance is true, i.e. when and only when this material substance exists, i.e. when and only when its form is combined with its matter.

The above truth conditions make it natural to assume that simple beliefs and assertions concerning material substances should be singular existential beliefs and assertions. Let me spend a few words explaining what I mean by 'existential belief' and 'existential assertion'. An existential assertion is an assertion that consists of an utterance of a name followed by an utterance of a form of 'to exist' or of its negative counterpart 'not to exist' (e.g. an utterance of 'Socrates exists'). Every existential assertion is either affirmative (e.g. an utterance of 'Socrates exists') or negative (e.g. an utterance of 'Socrates does not exist'). An existential belief is a belief whose literal linguistic expression would be an existential assertion (e.g. Plato's belief that Socrates exists). Every existential belief is either affirmative (e.g. Plato's belief that Socrates exists) or negative (e.g. Simmias' belief that Homer does not exist).

The conditions of truth and falsehood for singular existential beliefs and assertions concerning material substances are clearly analogous to those for predicative beliefs and assertions. For example, an utterance of 'Socrates does not exist', which is a singular negative existential assertion concerning the material substance Socrates, is true when and only when Socrates' form is divided from his matter; analogously, an utterance of 'Socrates is not seated', which is a singular negative predicative assertion concerning the state of affairs that Socrates is seated, is true when and only when the universal seated is divided from Socrates in such a way as to hold outside him.

When a material substance does not exist, i.e. when its form is divided from its matter, a singular affirmative existential belief, or assertion, concerning it will be false, and a singular negative existential belief, or assertion, concerning it will be true. The reference to a form and to a portion of matter is secured by passing through a material substance that at some time or other does exist. There is no account of the truth and falsehood of singular existential beliefs or assertions concerning what never exists as a material substance (e.g. my belief that Pegasus does not exist remains unexplained).

DTF and existentials concerning simple objects. In the case of simple objects, DTF takes on the following form: an affirmative simple belief, or assertion, concerning a simple object is true when and only when this simple object is true, i.e. when and only when it exists. An affirmative simple belief, or assertion, concerning a simple object is false when and only when this simple object is false, i.e. when and only when it does not exist. A negative simple belief, or assertion, concerning a simple object is true when and only when this simple object is false, i.e. when and only when it does not exist. A negative simple belief, or assertion, concerning a simple object is false when and only when this simple object is true, i.e. when and only when it exists. Thus, simple beliefs and simple assertions concerning simple objects also are existential beliefs and assertions. For example, an utterance of 'Man exists', which is an affirmative simple existential assertion concerning the natural kind man (an essence, and therefore a simple object), is true when and only when man exists.

Since all simple objects exist always, every affirmative existential belief, or assertion, concerning a simple object is always true, and every negative existential belief, or assertion, concerning a simple object is always false. For example, an utterance of 'Man exists' is always true because the simple object it concerns, the natural kind man, exists always. Aristotle describes thoughts concerning simple objects as unerring: what he means is that all affirmative existential beliefs concerning them are always true. He fails to mention the negative counterpart of this claim, i.e. that all negative existential beliefs concerning simple objects are always false. Note that no corresponding result holds with regard to material substances: since some material substances are not everlasting, some singular affirmative existential beliefs and assertions concerning material substances are sometimes false and some singular negative existential beliefs and assertions concerning material substances are sometimes true.

As I just said, if one has an affirmative existential belief concerning a simple object, and expresses it by an affirmative existential assertion, then one's belief and the assertion expressing it are always true. However, it does not follow that one will be able to understand or define the simple object one is thinking or speaking about. In fact, it does not even follow that one will be able to tell whether one is thinking or speaking about a simple rather than a composite object. However, an everlastingly true affirmative existential belief, or assertion, concerning a simple object can be the starting-point of an inquiry that will eventually lead to understanding or defining that simple object: as this inquiry progresses, one passes from a belief or an assertion 'that it is' to a belief or an assertion about 'what it is'. Beliefs and assertions of these two sorts (i.e. existential beliefs and assertions concerning essences, on the one hand, and beliefs and assertions defining these essences, on the other) are among the indemonstrable premisses (principles) of scientific demonstrations. What I just said applies also to those simple objects that are incorporeal substances (God and, perhaps, the heavenly intellects): even if one has everlastingly true affirmative existential beliefs concerning them, and expresses these beliefs in everlastingly true affirmative existential assertions, it does not follow that one can understand or define them (one can of course begin an inquiry which, if successful, will lead to one's understanding and defining them). Thus, Aristotle's remarks about affirmative existential beliefs and assertions concerning incorporeal substances do not commit him to any form of 'religious intuitionism'.

The second role of true and false objects: bearing modal attributes. As I said, objects that are true or false play three roles in Aristotle's theory of truth. In the preceding subsections I focused on their first role: contributing to explaining what it is to be true or false for thoughts and sentences. Let me now touch upon their second role: bearing modal attributes, i.e. necessity, impossibility, possibility, and contingency. These modal attributes are on a par with truth and falsehood in that they hold of the same items of which truth and falsehood hold: objects, thoughts, and sentences.

Aristotle offers 'statistical' definitions of modal attributes in so far as they hold of objects: an object is necessary just in case it is always true, it is impossible just in case it is always false, etc. (these definitions are called 'statistical' because they turn on how often something is the case). These modal attributes are then transferred from objects to certain beliefs and assertions: e.g. an affirmative (negative) simple belief, or assertion, concerning a necessary object is necessary (impossible). The analysis covers at one blow objects, simple beliefs, and simple assertions of all sorts.

In some passages Aristotle seems to apply his statistical approach to modal attributes of a different sort: to 'diachronic' modalities, i.e. modal attributes with two 'slots for dates', characteristics such as its being at a certain time necessary that something or other should be the case at a different time. For example, he seems committed to claiming that it is now necessary that the state of affairs of there being a sea-battle should be true in 24 hours just in case in the infinite course of time up to 24 hours ago, every time when the total state of the world resembled in relevant respects the total state of the world now was followed 24 hours later by a time when the state of affairs of there being a sea-battle was true. I hope that this example will enable one to understand the following general characterisation of diachronic necessity to which Aristotle seems committed: at t it is necessary that o should be true i later just in case in the infinite course of time up to i before t, every time when the total state of the world resembled in relevant respects the total state of the world at t was followed i later by a time when o was true (where t is a time, i a non-zero interval, and o an object). As we shall soon see, diachronic modalities play a central role in Aristotle's discussion of Determinism.

Aristotle's statistical approach to modalities in terms of time is surprising to modern ears: modern philosophers usually analyse modal attributes differently (e.g. in terms of possible worlds). The surprise slightly eases when one recalls that for Aristotle time is infinite towards the past as well as the future: given that time is thus infinite, it is not unreasonable to postulate that what is possible should be what is true at some time or other.

The third role of true and false objects: serving as targets of propositional attitudes. The third and final role played in Aristotle's theory of truth by objects that are true or false is to serve as targets of propositional attitudes: they are what is believed or disbelieved, desired or shunned, etc. Aristotle is somewhat economical in his assumptions concerning these objects: in the case of states of affairs, which are the most important ingredients in his account of propositional attitudes, he allows only 'affirmative' states of affairs. This metaphysical economy creates some difficulty for the role of states of affairs as targets of propositional attitudes. For it is clear how this theory can analyse 'affirmative propositional attitudes', like an 'affirmative belief' or an 'affirmative desire': e.g. my 'affirmative belief' that this is a sheet of paper can be analysed as my bearing the relationship of believing to the state of affairs that this is a sheet of paper. But it is not immediately clear how this theory can analyse 'negative propositional attitudes', like a 'negative belief' or a 'negative desire': e.g. my 'negative belief' that this is not a wax-tablet cannot be analysed as my bearing the relationship of believing to the state of affairs that this is not a wax-tablet, simply because there is no such state of affairs (for there are no 'negative' states of affairs). Aristotle's solution is to introduce negative counterparts of the ordinary propositional attitudes: thus, alongside belief there is its negative counterpart, disbelief, and alongside desire there is its negative counterpart, shunning. Now my 'negative belief' that this is not a wax-tablet can be straightforwardly analysed as my bearing the relationship of disbelieving to the state of affairs that this is a wax-tablet.

One major problem with this theory is how it can deal with propositional attitudes bearing on complex propositional contents. For example, to analyse my belief that if it is day it is light, the theory should introduce a two-pronged propositional attitude to the states of affairs of its being day and of its being light, while to explain my belief that if it is day it is not night the theory should introduce a different two-pronged propositional attitude to the states of affairs of its being day and of its being night. In general, to account for beliefs expressed by conditionals whose antecedents and consequents are either 'atomic' sentences or negations thereof, the theory should introduce four two-pronged propositional attitudes. For beliefs expressed by conditionals with more complex antecedents or consequents, the theory will need more numerous and complicated multi-pronged propositional attitudes (specifically, the number of n-pronged propositional attitudes must be 2^n). It should be clear that these are pretty cumbersome complications – complications Aristotle never looked into. Aristotle's theorising in this area did not go beyond a vague recognition of some issues, and was driven mainly by the metaphysical concern of keeping down the number of the entities postulated.

Correspondence, time, and Bivalence. In the preceding subsections I expounded Aristotle's ideas on the bearers of truth or falsehood. I focused on his views about certain objects which are neither thoughts nor linguistic expressions, but are, none the less, true or false. In the course of showing how, according to Aristotle, these objects that are true or false contribute to explaining what it is to be true and what it is to be false for beliefs and assertions, I reconstructed Aristotle's views on the truth conditions of beliefs and assertions of various types. In the remainder of this introduction's overview I intend to address three other important issues: first, whether Aristotle can be said to propound a correspondence theory of truth; second, Aristotle's conception of the relation of truth to time; third, his views on Bivalence.

Correspondence-as-isomorphism. Aristotle is often said to propound a correspondence theory of truth. What claim does Aristotle's theory of truth have to being a correspondence theory of truth?

There are various conceptions of what it is to be a correspondence theory of truth. Each different conception introduces different necessary and sufficient conditions for a given theory of truth to be a correspondence theory of truth. According to one of these conceptions – 'the correspondence-as-isomorphism conception', as I shall call it – a theory of truth is a correspondence theory of truth just in case it takes the truth of a belief, or assertion, to consist in its being isomorphic to reality. Specifically, according to the correspondence-as-isomorphism conception, a theory of truth is a correspondence theory of truth for beliefs (assertions) just in case it enjoys the following threefold condition: first, it provides a classification of beliefs (assertions); second, it maps one-to-one the classes of beliefs (assertions) onto characteristics that can hold of the item or items a belief (assertion) is about; third, it states that a belief (assertion) is true when and only when the characteristic on which the class it belongs to is mapped holds of the item or items it is about.

Aristotle's theory of truth surely counts as a correspondence theory of truth according to the correspondence-as-isomorphism conception. In fact, the condition introduced by the correspondence-as-isomorphism conception is met at two levels by Aristotle's theory of truth. First it is met at the theory's most general level, i.e. in DTF, the definition of truth and falsehood for simple beliefs and assertions. DTF relies on a very simple classification of beliefs and assertions: affirmations and denials are the only two classes. These classes are mapped one-to-one onto characteristics that can hold of the objects with which beliefs, or assertions, are concerned: affirmations are mapped on truth, denials on falsehood. An affirmation is true when and only when truth holds of the object with which it is concerned; a denial is true when and only when falsehood holds of the object with which it is concerned.

The condition introduced by the correspondence-as-isomorphism conception is met a second time by Aristotle's theory of truth, at a more specific level: in the definition of truth and falsehood for beliefs and assertions that concern composite objects. Each belief, or assertion, concerning a composite object is then regarded as being about two objects: those of which the composite object it concerns is composed. For the sake of simplicity, I concentrate on predicative beliefs and assertions. One of the two objects a predicative belief, or assertion, is about is a universal (it is grasped, or signified, by the predicate), the other is either a universal or an individual (it is grasped, or signified, by the subject). The definition of truth relies on a classification that introduces six classes of predicative beliefs, or assertions: universal affirmative, universal negative, particular affirmative, particular negative, singular affirmative, and singular negative predicative beliefs, or assertions (again for simplicity's sake, I ignore the more fine-grained distinctions induced by the categories). These classes are mapped one-to-one onto characteristics (binary relations) that can hold of the objects (universals or individuals) that are grasped, or signified, by predicates and subjects of predicative beliefs, or assertions: universal affirmative predicative beliefs and assertions are mapped on the combination of holding universally; universal negative predicative beliefs and assertions on the division of universally failing to hold; etc. A universal affirmative predicative belief, or assertion, is true when and only when the universal grasped, or signified, by its predicate is combined with the universal grasped, or signified, by its subject in such a way as universally to hold of it; a universal negative predicative belief, or assertion, is true when and only when the universal grasped, or signified, by its predicate is divided from the universal grasped, or signified, by its subject in such a way as universally to fail to hold of it; etc.

Correspondence-as-mirroring. As I said, there are various conceptions of what it is to be a correspondence theory of truth, and each different conception introduces different necessary and sufficient conditions for a given theory of truth to be a correspondence theory of truth. We have just seen that Aristotle's theory of truth is a correspondence theory of truth according to one of these conceptions, i.e. according to the correspondence-as-isomorphism conception. However, Aristotle's theory of truth is a correspondence theory of truth also according to a different, stricter conception. This is because Aristotle's theory of truth describes each class of beliefs, or assertions, in such a way that each belief, or assertion, 'mirrors' the characteristic on which the class to which it belongs is mapped. Let me explain what I mean by 'mirroring' here. Consider the two classes of beliefs, or assertions, introduced by

Aristotle's theory of truth at its most general level: affirmations and denials. Affirmations are described as positing that the objects they concern are true, denials as positing that the objects they concern are false. But now, by positing that the object it concerns is true, an affirmation 'mirrors' truth, the characteristic of objects on which affirmations are mapped; and, by positing that the object it concerns is false, a denial 'mirrors' falsehood, the characteristic of objects on which denials are mapped. In general, each class of beliefs, or assertions, in Aristotle's theory of truth is so described that each member of that class posits that the characteristic the class is mapped on obtains. By virtue of this 'mirroring' it assumes with regard to assertions and beliefs, Aristotle's theory of truth counts as a correspondence theory of truth in that a belief, or assertion, is regarded as true when and only when it 'posits its object to be as it is'.

Subjects and predicates are 'non-empty'. I pointed out that Aristotle's theory of truth is a correspondence theory of truth at least in the sense that it takes the truth of a belief, or assertion, to consist in its being isomorphic to reality. I also described the particular form assumed by the idea that truth consists in being isomorphic to reality in the case of predicative beliefs and assertions: a predicative belief, or assertion, is true when and only when a certain relation of combination or division obtains between the objects (universals or individuals) that are grasped, or signified, by its predicate and its subject. This requires that there should be objects of the appropriate kinds that are grasped, or signified, by the predicate and the subject: otherwise the theory would lose one of its toeholds. Since for Aristotle all objects are existent objects, the requirement imposed by his correspondence-as-isomorphism theory of truth entails that in every predicative belief, or assertion, the predicate and the subject grasp, or signify, *existent* objects (universals or individuals), i.e. that both the predicate and the subject are 'non-empty'.

Apparent cases of 'empty' subjects or predicates. But how are those beliefs, or utterances, that seem to be predicative beliefs, or assertions, whose predicate or subject is 'empty', to be treated with regard to truth and falsehood? For example, how are utterances of 'A goat is a goatstag' and 'A goatstag is white' to be treated?

Aristotle's solution is that a thought, or utterance, that seems to be a predicative belief, or assertion, whose predicate or subject is 'empty', really is not a predicative belief, or assertion: it is not even a simple belief, or assertion, but a composite belief, or assertion, in disguise, i.e. a belief, or assertion, which could be accurately formulated as an utterance constructed from several assertions linked by connective particles. Aristotle does not develop this solution in detail: had he done this, he would have realised that it faces serious difficulties.

The laws of the Square of Opposition are valid. The laws of the Square of Opposition are the basic principles which in Aristotle's view govern the logical relations between quantified predicative assertions (i.e. universal or particular predicative assertions). These laws concern quartets consisting of 'coincident' universal affirmative, universal negative, particular affirmative, and particular negative predicative assertions.[9] For example, one of the quartets concerned is that consisting of an utterance of 'Every horse is white', one of 'No horse is white', one of 'Some horse is white', and one of 'Not every horse is white'.

One law of the Square of Opposition is the Law of Contraries: it states that a universal affirmative and a 'coincident' universal negative predicative assertion are never both true (e.g. an utterance of 'Every horse is white' and one of 'No horse is white' are never both true). Another law of the Square of Opposition is the Law of Contradictories: it states that a universal affirmative (negative) predicative assertion is true when and only when any 'coincident' particular negative (affirmative) predicative assertion is not true (e.g. an utterance of 'Every horse is white' is true when and only when any utterance of 'Not every horse is white' is not true, and an utterance of 'No horse is white' is true when and only when any utterance of 'Some horse is white' is not true).

One plausible assumption concerning quantified predicative assertions is that every particular predicative assertion is true only when its subject denotes at least one individual that at some time or other exists (e.g. if at noon on 1 January 1997 no horse exists, then at noon on 1 January 1997 no utterance of 'Some horse is white' or of 'Not every horse is white' is true). It should be noted that the plausible assumption I just mentioned is not among the laws of the Square of Opposition: it is a further principle which has a lot of intuitive plausibility.

The laws of the Square of Opposition, combined with the plausible assumption I just mentioned, encounter difficulties if at some time or other the subject of some quantified predicative assertion denotes no individual that at some time or other exists. For suppose that at a time t the subject of

[9] The adjective 'coincident' here indicates that the subjects of the predicative assertions involved are tokens (utterances) of the same type, and, similarly, the predicates of the predicative assertions involved are tokens (utterances) of the same type.

some quantified predicative assertion denotes no individual that at some time or other exists. Consider a quartet of 'coincident' quantified predicative assertions. By the assumption that every particular predicative assertion is true only when its subject denotes at least one individual that at some time or other exists, both the particular affirmative and the particular negative predicative assertion from this quartet are not true at *t*. Then, by the Law of Contradictories, both the universal negative and the universal affirmative assertion from the same quartet are true at *t*. This consequence conflicts with the Law of Contraries.

As I said in a preceding subsection, Aristotle is committed to the view that in every predicative assertion both the predicate and the subject are 'non-empty'. An important consequence of the 'non-emptiness' of subjects and predicates of predicative assertions is that the Square of Opposition's difficulties evaporate. Assume that in every quantified predicative assertion the subject is 'non-empty', i.e. signifies an existent universal. As I said in the subsection concerning Aristotle's views on universals, Aristotle is probably committed to the view that every universal at all times holds of some individual or other that at some time or other exists. Hence he is probably committed to the view that in every quantified predicative assertion the subject at all times denotes some individual or other that at some time or other exists. But the laws of the Square of Opposition face no difficulty if in every quantified predicative assertion the subject at all times denotes some individual or other that at some time or other exists. The laws of the Square of Opposition only concern genuine quantified predicative assertions: those utterances that seem counter-examples to them, i.e. utterances that seem quantified predicative assertions with 'empty' subjects, are not real counter-examples. They really are composite assertions, and therefore fall outside the realm ruled by the laws of the Square of Opposition.

Singular predications, existence, and time. As we saw, in every singular predicative belief, or assertion, the subject must be 'non-empty', and therefore must grasp, or signify, an existent individual. This requirement is to be understood loosely, as postulating that the subject of the belief or assertion should grasp, or signify, an individual that exists *at some time or other*: the time of the individual's existence can be very distant from that when the belief is held, or the assertion uttered (e.g. although Homer no longer exists you can now have a singular predicative belief that Homer is sick, and you can now have one that Homer is a poet).

The times when the individual grasped, or signified, by the subject exists need not coincide with the times when the whole singular predicative belief, or assertion, is true or false. There is no general law governing the behaviour of all singular predicative beliefs, or assertions, with respect to truth, existence, and time. In particular, it is not required that *every singular* predicative assertion should be true only when the individual signified by its subject exists, nor is it required that *every singular affirmative* predicative assertion should be true only when the individual signified by its subject exists. Different cases behave differently. What determines the behaviour is the predicate, or, more precisely, the universal signified by the predicate. For example, it is because of the nature of the universal sick that a singular affirmative predicative assertion that is an utterance of 'Homer is sick' is true only when Homer exists (for at any time, the universal sick holds only of individuals that exist then). Specifically, since Homer does not exist now, the assertion in question is now false because the universal sick (signified by its predicate) is now divided from Homer (the individual signified by its subject) in such a way as to hold outside him. For the same reason, a singular negative predicative assertion that is an utterance of 'Homer is not sick' is now true. Again, it is because of the nature of the universal poet that a singular affirmative predicative assertion that is an utterance of 'Homer is a poet' is true also at times when Homer does not exist (for the universal poet sometimes holds of individuals that do not exist then). Specifically, although Homer does not exist now, the assertion in question is now true because the universal poet (signified by its predicate) now holds of Homer (the individual signified by its subject).[10] For the same reason, a singular negative predicative assertion that is an utterance of 'Homer is not a poet' is now false. (This distribution of truth-values will never change because the universal poet will always hold of Homer – for it will always be the case that Homer has authored some poem.)

Utterances true at one time and false at another. Aristotle takes the bearers of truth or falsehood, i.e. beliefs, assertions, and objects, to be true or false at times: some of them are always true, others always false, yet others true at one time and false at another. This Aristotelian view that the bearers of truth or falsehood are true or false at times was widespread in Antiquity – in fact, it remained unchallenged.

Assertions, the only sentences that for Aristotle are true or false, are utterances, i.e. expression-tokens, events of speech that occur over relatively short portions of time. Aristotle is therefore committed to claiming that some utterances are true or false at times, and that some of them are even true at one time and false at another. The time when an utterance is produced

[10] Cf. the paragraph to which n. 3 above is appended.

must not be confused with the time or times when it is true or false: an utterance is true or false even at times that are very distant from that when it is produced.

Truth and time in Aristotle and in modern philosophy. From a purely ontological point of view there is nothing unusual in Aristotle's position about utterances, truth, and time: an event can have, lack, acquire, and lose properties at times very distant from when it happens (e.g. the big bang has been unknown for many centuries but is well known now). None the less, modern philosophers disagree with Aristotle about utterances, truth, and time. Modern philosophers claim that no utterance is true or false *at a time*: rather, they say, some truth-evaluable utterances are true and others are false – time does not come into the picture at all.

It is worthwhile examining the motivation behind the modern conception. This is most easily done by considering present-tense predicative assertions, i.e. assertions that are utterances of present-tense predicative sentence-types. Modern philosophers take a present-tense predicative assertion to assert that a certain state of affairs obtains (or fails to obtain) at the time when the assertion itself is produced. Since – modern philosophers say – an assertion is evaluated as true or false by considering what it asserts, a present-tense predicative assertion, which asserts that a certain state of affairs obtains (or fails to obtain) at the time when it is produced, is true just in case this state of affairs does obtain (or fail to obtain) at this time. This modern conception leaves no room for a present-tense predicative assertion being true at a time. By generalising this result, modern philosophers reach the claim that no utterance is true or false at a time.

To see how Aristotle's conception differs from the modern one, let us keep focusing on present-tense predicative assertions. Aristotle would deny that what a present-tense predicative assertion asserts is that a certain state of affairs obtains (or fails to obtain) at the time when the assertion itself is produced. Instead he would claim that a present-tense predicative assertion is temporally indeterminate, i.e. posits the obtaining (or failing to obtain) of a certain state of affairs without specifying any time for its obtaining (or failing to obtain). This is because he regards assertions as expressions of beliefs (this is part of what he means when, at the beginning of *de Interpretatione*, he says that 'utterances are symbols of affections in the soul'), so that the content asserted by an assertion is the same as that of the belief of which it is an expression. Beliefs are states, and a thinker can hold the same belief for a relatively long portion of time. Hence, assertions that are utterances produced during a relatively short period encompassed by the much longer one during which the same belief is held cannot include the time of utterance within their assertoric content. For example, if from 15.00 to 18.00 Plato holds one and the same belief, i.e. the belief that Socrates is seated, the content of this belief cannot be that-Socrates-is-seated-at-16.00 (it cannot be this any more than it is that-Socrates-is-seated-at-17.00). Hence the content asserted by Plato's utterance of 'Socrates is seated' produced at 16.00, being the same as that of the belief Plato held from 15.00 to 18.00, cannot be that-Socrates-is-seated-at-16.00. If present-tense predicative assertions are temporally indeterminate, it is natural to assume that a present-tense predicative assertion should be true when and only when the state of affairs it posits to obtain (or to fail to obtain) does in fact obtain (or fail to obtain). This is clearly brought out by the conditions of truth and falsehood formulated in a preceding subsection: a present-tense predicative assertion that is an utterance of 'Socrates is seated' is true when and only when the state of affairs that Socrates is seated is true, i.e. when and only when the universal seated (signified by the part of the utterance that constitutes its predicate) is combined with Socrates (the individual signified by the part of the utterance that constitutes its subject) in such a way as to hold of him.

Different truth-values at different times do not involve change. According to Aristotle a belief, or an assertion, that is true at one time and false at another does not thereby change: whatever change is involved goes on in the object the belief, or assertion, is about. For example, if an utterance of 'Socrates is seated' is true at one time and false at another, it does not follow that the utterance undergoes any change – it is only Socrates (or, perhaps, the state of affairs that Socrates is seated) that changes. This is probably because truth (being correspondence to the world) is a relational property, and therefore, like other relational properties, is involved at most in a 'mere Cambridge change' that does not count as a genuine change: just as if Socrates is taller than Theaetetus at one time and shorter than him at another, it does not follow that Socrates has changed (because all the change occurred in Theaetetus, who has grown); so if an utterance of 'Socrates is seated' is true (corresponding to the world) at one time and false (non-corresponding to the world) at another, it does not follow that the utterance has changed (because all the change occurred in the world, or in a part of it, be it Socrates, who got up, or the state of affairs that Socrates is seated, which passed from being true to being false).

The fact that an object can have a relational property at one time and lack it at another without undergoing any change is for Aristotle a sign that relational properties are hardly real, i.e. are not genuine properties (acquiring or losing them 'does not make a change'). Aristotle is therefore committed to the view that truth is not a genuine property. In this respect Aristotle's position is close to modern 'minimalist' theories of truth, which also claim that truth is not a genuine property. A fundamental difference, however, remains: in Aristotle's case the idea that truth is not a genuine property is a consequence of his regarding truth as a sort of correspondence to the world, while modern 'minimalist' theories of truth reject the idea that to be true is to correspond to the world.

The failure of Bivalence. Bivalence is the principle that states that every assertion is always either true or false. On at least two important occasions Aristotle seems to reject Bivalence: one is connected with the paradox of the liar (henceforth 'Liar'), the other with future-tense singular assertions.

The Liar. The only passage where Aristotle seems to discuss the Liar is within chapter 25 of *Sophistici Elenchi* (180^a34–180^b7). This passage is obscure: it is not even clear whether it addresses the Liar, and, in case it does, how it reacts to the puzzle. Although these questions cannot be answered beyond doubt, a case can be made for claiming, first, that the passage in question does address the Liar, and, second, that it attempts to solve the Liar by assuming that someone uttering 'I am speaking falsely' (or whatever sentence-type the Liar turns on) is neither speaking truly nor speaking falsely.

A version of the Liar Aristotle could have addressed. There are several versions of the Liar. I shall concentrate on one Aristotle could have addressed.

Let *u* be an utterance of 'I am speaking falsely',[11] let *k* be a time, let *u*'s utterer be an individual, and let speaking-truly and speaking-falsely be universals. Suppose that *u* is the only assertion produced by *u*'s utterer over some period comprising *k*. Also suppose that *u* is a singular affirmative predicative assertion, that the predicate of *u* (an utterance of 'speaking falsely') signifies the universal speaking-falsely, and that the subject of *u* (an utterance of 'I') signifies the individual who is *u*'s utterer. Since *u* is a singular affirmative predicative assertion, by Aristotle's theory of truth we have that *u* is true when and only when speaking-falsely holds of *u*'s utterer. Hence *u* is true at *k* just in case speaking-falsely holds of *u*'s utterer at *k*.

For the argument to develop, the universals speaking-truly and speaking-falsely must be defined: for every time *t* and every individual *s*, speaking-truly holds of *s* at *t* just in case every assertion produced by *s* over any

[11] The same Greek verb can be used to say of a man both that he is speaking falsely and that he is lying.

period comprising t is true at t; for every time t and every individual s, speaking-falsely holds of s at t just in case some assertion produced by s over some period comprising t is false at t. Note that the definition just given requires that speaking-truly should hold of any individual s at any time t such that s produces no assertion over any period comprising t. Thus, speaking-truly holds of a man when he is not speaking at all. In this respect, the universal speaking-truly does not match the meaning we associate with the expression 'to speak truly'.

The final supposition is that for every time t and every individual s, either speaking-truly holds of s at t or speaking-falsely holds of s at t. (If Bivalence holds, this final supposition follows from the last paragraph's definitions.)

First, assume that speaking-falsely holds of u's utterer at k. Then u is true at k. Since u is the only assertion produced by u's utterer over some period comprising k, every assertion produced by u's utterer over any period comprising k is true at k. Hence speaking-truly holds of u's utterer at k. Thus: if speaking-falsely holds of u's utterer at k, then speaking-truly holds of u's utterer at k. But either speaking-truly or speaking-falsely holds of u's utterer at k. Therefore speaking-truly holds of u's utterer at k.

Second, assume that speaking-truly holds of u's utterer at k. Then every assertion produced by u's utterer over any period comprising k is true at k. Since u is the only assertion produced by u's utterer over some period comprising k, u is true at k. Hence speaking-falsely holds of u's utterer at k. Thus: if speaking-truly holds of u's utterer at k, then speaking-falsely holds of u's utterer at k. But either speaking-truly or speaking-falsely holds of u's utterer at k. Therefore speaking-falsely holds of u's utterer at k.

Hence speaking-truly and speaking-falsely both hold of u's utterer at k.

Aristotle's solution for the Liar. Chapter 25 of *Sophistici Elenchi* is concerned with sophistical refutations dependent on the absolute or qualified use of expressions. Sophistical refutations of this kind occur whenever the answerer in a dialectical debate grants that a certain property holds of a certain object in a qualified sense, but is then treated by the questioner as if he had conceded that that property holds of that object without qualification, and thereby finds himself landed with an untenable position. This can happen in various ways. In some cases the answerer grants that one opposite property holds of a certain object in a qualified way while the other opposite property holds of the same object without qualification, but is then treated as if he had conceded that both opposite properties hold of the same object without qualification. In other cases the answerer grants that two opposite properties both hold of a certain object in a qualified way, but is then treated again as if he had conceded that they both hold of the same object without qualification.

A special situation where the answerer can be inclined to grant that two opposite properties both hold of a certain object in a qualified way is that where the two opposite properties 'hold to the same extent' in that the strongest consideration available in support of one opposite property holding of the object is counterpoised by an equally strong consideration in support of the other holding of it. For example, consider a sphere that is exactly half-white and half-black. One can then imagine an answerer in a dialectical debate granting that whiteness and blackness both hold of the sphere in a qualified way because the strongest consideration available in support of whiteness holding of the sphere (a consideration based on direct observation) is counterpoised by an equally strong consideration (also based on direct observation) in support of blackness holding of the sphere. The answerer will however be treated as if he had conceded that whiteness and blackness both hold of the sphere without qualification.

Aristotle regards the case of the Liar as similar. Consider the version of the Liar offered in the last subsection, which turns on an utterance *u* of 'I am speaking falsely'. The first half of that version of the Liar provides the strongest consideration in support of speaking-truly holding of *u*'s utterer at *k*, and is counterpoised by an equally strong consideration in support of speaking-falsely holding of *u*'s utterer at *k*, a consideration provided by the second half of that version of the Liar. One can then imagine an answerer in a dialectical debate granting that at *k* speaking-truly and speaking-falsely both hold of *u*'s utterer in a qualified way. However, he will be treated as if he had conceded that at *k* speaking-truly and speaking-falsely both hold of *u*'s utterer without qualification.

Aristotle's advice in situations of this sort is that the answerer should insist that the two opposites both hold of the same object only in a qualified way, and both fail to hold of that object without qualification. In the case of the sphere that is exactly half-white and half-black, one should insist that whiteness and blackness both hold of the sphere only in a qualified way, and that both fail to hold of it without qualification. Similarly, in the case of the utterance *u* of 'I am speaking falsely', one should insist that at time *k* speaking-truly and speaking-falsely both hold of *u*'s utterer only in a qualified way, and that at *k* both fail to hold of him without qualification. But, now, failing to hold without qualification is failing to hold in the proper sense. Thus, Aristotle's analysis seems to commit him to the view that *u* is sometimes neither true nor false, and therefore to the rejection of Bivalence.

Aristotle's solution leaves him exposed to the Strengthened Liar, which turns on an utterance v of 'This assertion is not true'. The strategy of saying that v is neither true nor false at j (a time within some period over which v is produced), or that it is neither true nor not true at j, leads to disaster: in either case, v is not true at j, and is therefore true at j. Aristotle probably did not realise this difficulty, but it is worthwhile pointing out that his position is not hopeless: certain modern treatments of the Liar, which do not fall prey to the Strengthened Liar, are theories one could imagine Aristotle's position developing into.

Future-tense singular assertions constitute another important and well-known case which, according to Aristotle, shows Bivalence to be false. Aristotle discusses Bivalence and future-tense singular assertions in *de Interpretatione* 9. He confronts certain arguments that assume Bivalence and conclude to Determinism. Since Aristotle regards these arguments as valid but rejects Determinism, he rejects Bivalence. Specifically, he claims that some future-tense singular assertions are sometimes neither true nor false.

Determinism. Determinism is the thesis that for every state of affairs s and every time t, if s is true at t then at every time t' earlier than t it is necessary that s should be true at t, and if s is false at t then at every time t' earlier than t it is necessary that s should be false at t. For example, according to Determinism, if the state of affairs of your being seated is true now then in the whole of the past it was always necessary that this state of affairs should be true now, and if the state of affairs of your being seated is false now then in the whole of the past it was always necessary that this state of affairs should be false now.

Necessity as ineluctability. The necessity mentioned in Determinism is ineluctability: the necessity of what nothing can be done about to change or avoid it. It is a 'diachronic' modality, i.e. a modal attribute with two 'slots for dates': the key formulations are instances of the schema 'At τ it is necessary that α at τ'' (where 'τ' and 'τ'' are to be replaced with designations of times, 'α' with an assertoric sentence-type that does not contain dates), e.g. 'At 13.00 of 1 January 1997 it was necessary that the train should arrive at 13.20 of 1 January 1997'.

The necessity of the present and the past. The advocate and the opposer of Determinism agree that the present and the past are necessary: for every state of affairs s and every time t, if s is true at t then at every time t' not earlier than t it is necessary that s should be true at t, and if s is false at t

then at every time t' not earlier than t it is necessary that s should be false at t. For example, if the milk was spilled (i.e. if the state of affairs of the milk having been spilled was true at some time earlier than now) then it is necessary now (i.e. it is now necessary that the state of affairs in question should be true at that earlier time): nothing can be done now about the milk having been spilled earlier. The two parties therefore agree that the realm of the non-necessary, i.e. of the contingent, is restricted to a part of the future. The disagreement between the two parties surfaces with regard to the extension of this part of the future that constitutes the realm of the contingent: for the advocate of Determinism it is null, for the opposer of Determinism it is inhabited.

A deterministic argument. The most interesting deterministic argument addressed by Aristotle is close to an argument that assumes Bivalence and has Determinism as its conclusion. Before presenting this argument from Bivalence to Determinism, let me give a taste of it by displaying its most characteristic moves. Consider the state of affairs of your opening this book, and let t_O be the time when you first opened this book today. The state of affairs of your opening this book was therefore true at t_O. Let t_I be the time exactly 24 hours before t_O, i.e. the time yesterday exactly 24 hours before when you first opened this book today. Consider an assertion that is an utterance of 'In 24 hours you will open this book'. Since Bivalence holds (by assumption), at t_I this assertion was either true or false. Since 24 hours after t_I, at t_O, the state of affairs of your opening this book was true, at t_I the assertion surely was not false. Hence the assertion was true at t_I. Therefore the state of affairs of the assertion's being true was true at t_I. Hence (by the necessity of the present and the past) at t_I it was necessary that the state of affairs of the assertion's being true should be true at t_I. Therefore at t_I it was necessary that at t_I it should be the case that 24 hours later the state of affairs of your opening this book would have been true. Hence at t_I it was necessary that the state of affairs of your opening this book should be true at t_O.

Having given a taste of it, I am now in a position to present the argument from Bivalence to Determinism. Let s_O and t_O be a state of affairs and a time. Suppose that s_O is true at t_O. Let t_I be a time earlier than t_O. Let i be the exact interval between t_I and t_O. Since Bivalence holds (by assumption), at t_I an assertion that is an utterance of an appropriate instance of 'In ι σ will be true' (where 'ι' is replaced with an expression which signifies i, 'σ' with a name of s_O) is either true or false. Since i after t_I s_O is true, the assertion is not false at t_I. Hence the assertion is true at t_I. Therefore the state of affairs of the assertion's being true is true at t_I. Hence (by the necessity of the present and the past) at t_1 it is necessary that the state of affairs of the assertion's being true should be true at t_1. Therefore at t_1 it is necessary that at t_1 it should be the case that s_0 is true i later. Hence at t_1 it is necessary that s_0 should be true at t_0. Since t_1 was arbitrary, this conclusion can be generalised: at every time t' earlier than t_0 it is necessary that s_0 should be true at t_0. Since s_0 and t_0 were arbitrary, this conclusion also can be generalised: for every state of affairs s and every time t, if s is true at t then at every time t' earlier than t it is necessary that s should be true at t. A parallel argument will establish that for every state of affairs s and every time t, if s is false at t then at every time t' earlier than t it is necessary that s should be false at t. Thus, Determinism is true.

'Aristotle's dream': rejecting Bivalence while accepting Excluded Middle. As I said, Aristotle rejects Bivalence in order to avoid being nailed down to the conclusion of an argument like the one described in the last subsection. Specifically, he claims that certain future-tense singular assertions are sometimes neither true nor false, and he claims that an utterance of 'A sea-battle will take place tomorrow' is sometimes neither true nor false. While rejecting Bivalence, Aristotle in the same breath says things that commit him to accepting Excluded Middle, i.e. to endorsing every instance of the schema 'Either α or it is not the case that α' (where 'α' is to be replaced with an assertoric sentence-type that does not contain dates). His reason for doing so is probably a desire to retain as much as possible of classical logic (as we would call it) while rejecting Bivalence because, in his view, it entails Determinism. Given that Aristotle is committed to accepting Excluded Middle, he is likely to be committed to claiming that every utterance of every instance of the schema 'Either α or it is not the case that α' is always true. Thus, on the one hand, Aristotle claims that an utterance of 'A sea-battle will take place tomorrow' is sometimes neither true nor false; on the other, he seems committed to claiming that an utterance of 'A sea-battle will take place tomorrow or it is not the case that a sea-battle will take place tomorrow' is always true. Some modern logicians mock Aristotle because they take him to be committed to this apparently inconsistent position, which they label 'Aristotle's dream'.

The inconsistency, however, is merely apparent – as I shall argue in the next three subsections.

The history of the universe. Aristotle conceives of the history of the universe as an accumulation of events: new events are added to the stock of earlier ones to constitute the universe 'to date'. At any time, while all of its past and present are given in their full determinateness, not all of its future is yet given. For that time's future is a multiplicity of equally possible developments of the events accumulated until then, and the only part of this future that is already given is what is common to all these alternative developments (this represents what at the given time is already necessary).

The failure of Bivalence. Consider an assertion that is an utterance of 'A sea-battle will take place tomorrow'. Let *t* be a time such that in some but not all possible future developments of the universe at *t* a sea-battle takes place the day after *t*. Then the given assertion is correct at *t* with respect to those possible future developments of the universe at *t* where a sea-battle takes place the day after *t*, but it is incorrect at *t* with respect to the other possible future developments of the universe at *t*, where no sea-battle takes place the day after *t*. Note that the attributes of correctness and incorrectness I just introduced differ from truth and falsehood in an important respect: they are not merely relative to a time, they are relative both to a time and to a possible future development of the universe at that time. Since at *t* there is as yet no fact of the matter as to how the universe will develop the day after *t* with respect to a sea-battle taking place, there are no sufficient grounds for the assertion's being true or false at *t*. For this reason at *t* the given assertion is neither true nor false. Thus, an assertion that is an utterance of 'A sea-battle will take place tomorrow' is sometimes neither true nor false. It is worthwhile emphasising that this conclusion has nothing to do with the impossibility of discovering at *t* what the future will be like: it only depends on the fact that at *t* the future is not yet sufficiently determined as to settle the truth-value of the assertion. In fact, from an epistemic point of view, the past and the present do not differ from the future: as at *t* we do not and cannot know much of what is going to be the case after *t*, so we do not and cannot know much of what was the case before *t* or is the case at *t*.

The validity of Excluded Middle. Consider a disjunctive assertion that is an utterance of 'A sea-battle will take place tomorrow or it is not the case that a sea-battle will take place tomorrow'. Let *t* be a time. Pick a possible future development of the universe at *t*: if it is one where a sea-battle takes place the day after *t*, the given disjunctive assertion is correct at *t* with respect to this possible future development; if it is one where no sea-battle takes place the day after *t*, then again the disjunctive assertion is correct at *t* with respect to this possible future development. Thus, in all cases, the disjunctive assertion is correct at *t* with respect to the chosen possible future development of the universe at *t*. Since this possible future development of the universe at *t* was arbitrary, the disjunctive assertion is correct at *t* with respect to every possible future development of the universe at *t*. This constitutes a sufficient ground for the disjunctive assertion being true at *t*. Since *t* was an arbitrary time, the disjunctive assertion (an utterance of 'A sea-battle will take place tomorrow or it is not the case that a sea-battle will take place tomorrow') is always true.

How good is Aristotle's position on Determinism and Bivalence? In the last three subsections I showed that the claim that an utterance of 'A sea-battle will take place tomorrow' is sometimes neither true nor false and the claim that an utterance of 'A sea-battle will take place tomorrow or it is not the case that a sea-battle will take place tomorrow' is always true are reasonable and reciprocally consistent. These are precisely the claims to which Aristotle seems committed. Hence the solution Aristotle seems to offer to the problems raised by Bivalence and Determinism is coherent and reasonable. To this extent, it is a 'good' solution. However, other philosophers solve these problems differently. Can Aristotle's apparent solution still be regarded as 'good' when it is compared with these alternative solutions?

One of these alternative solutions to the problems raised by Bivalence and Determinism is based on denying that truth and falsehood hold at times. This solution wipes out at one blow all the problems raised by Bivalence and Determinism. But it is not a solution Aristotle could easily take on board because it requires revising a vast amount of his views on truth. Moreover, it goes against the way in which truth and falsehood were ordinarily conceived of in Antiquity: as I said, the idea that the bearers of truth or falsehood are true or false at times was widespread.

Another alternative solution to the problems raised by Bivalence and Determinism is to hold that truth and falsehood belong to a class of properties whose holding of an object at a given time is not simply a matter of what is going on then. A further member of the class of properties in question would be the property of belonging to a world where 24 hours later a sea-battle takes place. It could be defined as the property *P* such that for every object *x*, *P* holds of *x* when and only when a sea-battle takes place 24 hours later. Clearly, this property's holding of a certain object at any given time is not simply a matter of what is going on then. One could then argue that even if the state of affairs of this property's holding of a certain object is true at a certain time, this does not count as something that is present at that time and past shortly later, and therefore falls outside the scope of the principle that the past and the present are necessary. In other words, one could argue that even if the state of affairs in question were true at time t (something in itself already dubious), it would not follow that at every time t' not earlier than t it is necessary that the state of affairs should be true at t. Applying this strategy to the case of truth, one could block the deterministic arguments that derive Determinism from Bivalence, and therefore preserve Bivalence while rejecting Determinism. It is hard to decide whether this alternative solution is superior to the one Aristotle seems to offer, which involves rejecting Bivalence. The main limit of the alternative solution is the difficulty of giving a precise characterisation of the class of those properties whose holding at a given time is not a matter of what is happening only then; the main limit of Aristotle's apparent solution is that it involves giving up an important and intuitively plausible principle of logic.

2 METHODOLOGY

Questioning Aristotle. As I said at the beginning of the introduction, this study has two primary aims: to offer a precise reconstruction of all of Aristotle's most significant views on truth and falsehood and to gain a philosophical understanding of them. Ideally, one should approach a philosopher with a completely 'neutral' attitude, an attitude not 'biased' by specific interests, expectations, or questions. I think, however, that one should honestly admit from the start that such an ideally neutral approach is impossible, and formulate clearly the nature of one's approach to the philosopher one is studying. In the case at hand, my approach involves engaging in a philosophical discussion with Aristotle. I ask him some of the questions about truth which many modern analytic philosophers are interested in. One question I ask Aristotle is: 'What are the bearers of truth or falsehood?' Another question is: 'What are the truth conditions for predicative assertions?' Sometimes I ask Aristotle a further question raised by his answer to one of these questions. One of these further questions is: 'How can your truth conditions for predicative assertions deal with what seem predicative assertions with an "empty" subject or predicate?'

It should be clear how this approach will contribute to achieving one of this book's primary aims, the aim of gaining a philosophical understanding of Aristotle's views on truth: asking Aristotle some of the questions about truth which many modern analytic philosophers are interested in is evidently a way to gain a philosophical understanding of Aristotle's views on truth. But it is not obvious that this approach should contribute to the other primary aim of the book, the reconstruction of all of Aristotle's most significant views on truth and falsehood: one can imagine situations where by asking a philosopher 'analytic' questions about truth one would completely fail to reconstruct that philosopher's most significant views on the matter. However, as it happens, asking 'analytic' questions bears fruit in Aristotle's case: it does allow me to reconstruct almost all of his most significant views on truth and falsehood. Of course, certain aspects of Aristotle's theory of truth come more to the fore than others – but this is unavoidable, I suspect, with any approach. There turns out to be one, and only one, gap: Aristotle's remarks on 'practical truth' (in *EN* 6.2, 1139^{a}26–31) remain unexamined (I decided to forgo addressing them because they are relatively isolated from the rest of his theory).

A good way to understand and appreciate my approach to Aristotle is to contrast it with alternative approaches. For example, one could approach Aristotle by looking at the questions he himself asks, or by examining how his theories grew out of those of his predecessors and developed during his lifetime. I greatly respect these alternative approaches – but I realise and emphasise that they are different from mine.

'Not Aristotle's questions!' The alternative approaches mentioned above highlight some problems for the approach adopted in this study. A problem brought to the surface by the first alternative approach is that by asking Aristotle questions modern analytic philosophers are interested in, one is bound to ask him questions he never dreamt of, perhaps even questions which he lacked the conceptual apparatus to understand or to answer. My strategy with respect to this problem is to look for (not how Aristotle did answer these questions, but) what answers to these questions he is committed to. In pursuing this goal, I apply an empirical methodology: I start from the relevant passages from Aristotle's works, and on their basis I reconstruct the positions he explicitly endorses and those he is committed to. In some important cases, I address in detail philological issues concerning the reading of the text and I take into account the data available from the main witnesses (manuscripts or other sources). Thus, my approach to Aristotle in this study is a combination of a 'philosophically loaded' attitude with a 'historically sensitive' one.

Apparent tensions in Aristotle's position. Another problem for the treatment of Aristotle's thought adopted in this study is brought to light by the second alternative approach. Sometimes there appear to be tensions in Aristotle's views: some things he says seem to be contradictory, or at least pull in different directions. How much coherence should one assume in his work?

My attitude is 'moderately harmonising': I find that my attention is drawn to the common rather than the differentiating traits, and that I tend to try to explain the apparent inconsistencies as *merely* apparent. This, of course, does not mean that I ignore, or try at all costs to explain away, every apparent inconsistency in Aristotle's works. It simply means that I take an apparent inconsistency to be real, and due either to an error or a development in Aristotle's thought, only when it cannot be explained otherwise. It is impossible that Aristotle, however astute he was, would never have made a mistake in discussing issues that still today blunt the sharpest minds, and it is unlikely that he would never have changed his views over thirty or more years of philosophical research. None the less, it seems to be sound to assume that a mistake or a development occurred only when philosophical and philological explanations fail. Part of the reason for proceeding in this way is that the growth of Aristotle's thought is very much disputed among historians.

PART I

Bearers of truth or falsehood

CHAPTER I

States of affairs, thoughts, and sentences

In his commentary on Aristotle's *de Interpretatione* Ammonius asks 'among which of the things that are in any way one should look for truth and falsehood' (17, 29–30). In Aristotle's works there is no formulation of this or of an equivalent question. So, there is a case for doubting that Aristotle ever addressed the problem of what items are bearers of truth or falsehood. However, even if Aristotle never addressed this problem, it is still worthwhile considering what the items are which Aristotle does in fact speak of as true or false. For this result will provide a useful indication for determining what solution Aristotle would have offered for the problem of what items are bearers of truth or falsehood, had he addressed it.

Aristotle applies the word 'true' ('ἀληθής') and its cognates to items of three main kinds: objects (which include states of affairs),[1] mental items (states or acts of believing,[2] knowing,[3] grasping by means of the intellect,[4] perceiving,[5] imagining,[6] etc.), and linguistic items (sentences[7]).[8]

[1] *Cat.* 5, $4^{b}8$–10; 10, $12^{b}5$–16; 11, $14^{a}10$–14; 12, $14^{b}11$–22; *Int.* 9, $19^{a}15$–16; $19^{a}33$; *APo.* 1.33, $88^{b}32$–3; $89^{a}2$–3; *Ph.* 4.12, $222^{a}3$–9; *Metaph.* Δ 7, $1017^{a}31$–5; 29, $1024^{b}17$–21; Θ 4, $1047^{b}12$–14; 10, $1051^{a}34$–$1051^{b}6$; $1051^{b}18$–21; *EN* 3.5, $1112^{a}21$–3; *Rh.* 1.1, $1354^{a}27$–8; 7, $1364^{b}7$–10; [Arist.] *Divis. Arist.* 30, 49, 20–2; 31, 50, 8–10.

[2] *Cat.* 5, $4^{a}26$–8; *Int.* 14, $23^{a}38$; *APo.* 1.33, $88^{b}32$–$89^{a}3$; 2.19, $100^{b}5$–7; *Top.* 4.2, $123^{a}15$–19; *SE* 22, $178^{b}24$–9; *de An.* 3.3, $427^{b}20$–1; $428^{a}3$–4; $428^{a}19$; $428^{b}2$–9; *Metaph.* Θ 10, $1051^{b}13$–14; *EN* 3.4, $1111^{b}31$–4; 4.8, $1124^{b}6$; 6.3, $1139^{b}15$–18; 10, $1142^{b}11$; 7.10, $1151^{b}3$–4; *EE* 2.10, $1226^{a}1$–4; *Protr.* fr. 73 Gigon $306^{b}7$; $306^{b}8$; $306^{b}12$; $312^{a}36$ (= Iamb. *Protr.* 44, 5; 44, 5–6; 44, 9; 59, 13–14).

[3] *APo.* 1.33, $88^{b}32$–$89^{a}3$; 2.19, $100^{b}5$–8; *de An.* 3.3, $428^{a}3$–5; $428^{a}17$–18; *EN* 6.3, $1139^{b}15$–18; 6, $1141^{a}3$–8; 10, $1142^{b}10$.

[4] *APo.* 1.33, $88^{b}32$–$89^{a}3$; 2.19, $100^{b}5$–8; *de An.* 1.2, $404^{a}27$–31; 3.3, $428^{a}3$–5; $428^{a}17$–18; 6, $430^{b}26$–31; 10, $433^{a}26$; *Metaph.* E 4, $1027^{b}27$–8; Θ 10, $1051^{b}22$–33; $1052^{a}1$–4; Λ 9, $1075^{a}5$–10; *EN* 6.3, $1139^{b}15$–18; 6, $1141^{a}3$–8 (cf. *Metaph.* Δ 6, $1016^{b}1$–3; I 1, $1052^{a}29$–31; *Protr.* fr. 73 Gigon $302^{b}36$–8 = Iamb. *Protr.* 34, 17–18).

[5] *Top.* 2.4, $111^{a}14$–20; *de An.* 2.6, $418^{a}11$–16; 3.3, $427^{b}11$–14; $428^{a}3$–4; $428^{a}11$; $428^{b}18$–30; 6, $430^{b}29$–30; *Sens.* 4, $442^{b}8$–10; *Metaph.* Γ 5, $1010^{b}2$–3; $1010^{b}14$–26.

[6] *De An.* 3.3, $428^{a}1$–4; $428^{a}12$; $428^{a}16$–18; $428^{b}10$–17. However *de An.* 3.8, $432^{a}10$–12 seems to presuppose that episodes of imagining are neither true nor false.

[7] *Cat.* 5, $4^{a}23$–6; $4^{b}8$–10; 12, $14^{b}14$–22; *Int.* 1, $16^{a}9$–18; 4, $17^{a}1$–5; 9, $19^{a}33$; *SE* 22, $178^{b}24$–9; *Metaph.* Θ 10, $1051^{b}13$–14.

[8] Aristotle sometimes (*APo.* 1.32, $88^{a}19$–20; *Top.* 8.12, $162^{b}3$–22; *SE* 18, $176^{b}29$–33) applies 'true' and 'false' to arguments.

Section 1 of this chapter focuses on objects, in particular on states of affairs. I examine two passages from the *Metaphysics*. The first, which constitutes the beginning of Δ 29, is the most unequivocal testimony of Aristotle's commitment to states of affairs (I devote some arguments to showing that it is really states of affairs Aristotle is concerned with). The second *Metaphysics* passage is the first part of Θ 10. Aristotle describes states of affairs as being true or false in the strictest, i.e. most fundamental, sense because their truth and falsehood is appealed to in explaining the truth and falsehood of items of other types: an affirmative predicative belief or sentence is true (false) when and only when the state of affairs it concerns is true (false), while a negative predicative belief or sentence is true (false) when and only when the state of affairs it concerns is false (true). The role of states of affairs in Aristotle's theory of truth, however, is not exhausted by their explaining the truth and falsehood of predicative beliefs and sentences: they are also bearers of modal properties and targets of propositional attitudes.

Truth and falsehood of mental items are discussed in section 2 of this chapter. The main witness here is *Metaphysics* E 4. Aristotle claims that every affirmative (negative) predicative belief joins (separates) the objects grasped by its subject and its predicate. This claim can be seen to be consistent with – in fact, a consequence of – Θ 10's characterisation of the truth and falsehood of predicative beliefs in terms of states of affairs.

Section 3 discusses the linguistic items that are bearers of truth or falsehood, i.e. sentences. They are not expression-types, but expression-tokens, i.e. individual utterances.

1 STATES OF AFFAIRS

States of affairs in Metaphysics *Δ 29*. *Metaphysics* Δ 29 discusses the uses of 'false'. The following excerpt from this chapter is the most unequivocal testimony of Aristotle's commitment to states of affairs as bearers of truth or falsehood:

T 1 One way in which what is false is spoken of is by being a false object. This can happen, on the one hand, because it is not combined or it is impossible for it to be composed (the diagonal's being commensurable and your being seated are spoken of in this way, for one of these is false always and the other sometimes, for it is in this sense [*sc.* in the sense of being false][9] that these are non-beings), and, on the other hand, in the case of such items that [. . .] (1024^b17–21)

[9] Cf. E 4, 1027^b29; 1027^b31; Θ 10, 1051^b35–1052^a1.

> Objects are then called 'false' in this way, either because they themselves are not or [. . .] (1024ᵇ24–5)

In T 1 Aristotle offers two, and only two, examples to clarify of what kind the items are which he there describes by using 'object' and 'false'. He names the items which he introduces in these examples by means of the phrases 'the diagonal's being commensurable' (1024^b19–20) and 'your being seated' (1024^b20). What could the items be which Aristotle in T 1 describes by using 'object' and 'false', and names by using 'the diagonal's being commensurable' and 'your being seated', if not the state of affairs of the diagonal's being commensurable and the state of affairs of your being seated? Therefore the items which Aristotle in T 1 describes by using 'object' and 'false' are probably states of affairs. Accordingly, T 1's main point is probably to explain what it is for a state of affairs to be false.[10]

First objection: is T 1 about facts? An objection could be raised. The items which Aristotle in T 1 describes by using 'object' and 'false' could be (not states of affairs, but) facts.[11] Accordingly, T 1's main point would be to explain what it is (not for a state of affairs, but) for a fact to be false (not to obtain).

This objection cannot be ruled out with complete assurance. It is, however, unlikely – for two reasons.

(i) If the objection were correct, Aristotle would be doing something bizarre: he would be beginning his discussion of the uses of 'false' by saying that it applies to certain items whose very nature requires that it should not apply to them – for facts, by their very nature, are true (obtain). To draw an analogy, it would be like beginning a discussion of the uses of the negative expression 'non-quadrilateral' (which in the analogy corresponds to 'false') by saying that it applies to squares (which in the analogy correspond to facts – for the very nature of squares requires that 'non-quadrilateral' should not apply to them).

(ii) One of the items introduced by Aristotle in T 1 to explain what the items are which he there describes by using 'object' and 'false' is 'the

[10] Cf. Alex. Aphr. *in Metaph.* 431, 15–432, 4; Lask (1912), 319–20; Wilpert (1940), 7; de Rijk (1952), 29; Hope (1952), 120; Kirwan (1971/93), 178–9, 199–200; Harvey (1975), 108; Graeser (1978), 449; (1981), 85, 87–8; Schmitz (1985), 115–16; de Rijk (1987), 38; Simons (1988), 112; Sadun Bordoni (1994), 74; Weidemann (1994/2002), 138; de Rijk (1996), 119; Whitaker (1996), 30; Wolff (1999), 49, 61; Modrak (2001), 57.

[11] I use 'fact' in a Russellian sense: every fact, by its very nature, is true (obtains) (cf. Neale (2001), 83–6). Aristotle sometimes seems to use 'object' ('πρᾶγμα') to denote facts: see n. 4 of chapter 4 and the portion of the main text it pertains to.

diagonal's being commensurable' (1024^b19–20). But the diagonal's being commensurable is not a fact.

Second objection: is T 1 about composite things? Another objection could be raised. The items which Aristotle in T 1 describes by using 'object' and 'false' could be (not states of affairs, but) composite things: material substances, which are composed of form and matter (e.g. Socrates), or incidental compounds, which are composed of a universal and some item of which it holds (e.g. Socrates seated). Accordingly, T 1's main point would be to explain (not what it is for a state of affairs to be false, but) what it is for a composite thing not to exist.[12]

This objection also cannot be ruled out with confidence. I have two main reasons for disagreeing with it.

(i) The items Aristotle introduces in T 1 to explain what the items are which he there describes by using 'object' and 'false' obviously are not material substances. Moreover, they are probably not incidental compounds – for they are not designated in the way that is typical of incidental compounds. The proper designation of an incidental compound is a noun-phrase obtained by subtracting the copula from a predicative assertoric sentence-type.[13] Thus, had Aristotle intended to introduce incidental compounds, he would probably have used 'the commensurable diagonal' (the noun-phrase obtained by subtracting the copula from the predicative assertoric sentence-type 'The diagonal is commensurable') and 'you seated' (the noun-phrase obtained by subtracting the copula from the predicative assertoric sentence-type 'You are seated'), not 'the diagonal's being commensurable' (1024^b19–20) and 'your being seated' (1024^b20).

(ii) One of the items Aristotle introduces in T 1 to explain what the items are which he there describes by using 'object' and 'false' is 'the diagonal's being commensurable' (1024^b19–20). If (as the objection we are now considering assumes) T 1's main point were to explain what it is for a composite thing not to exist, then Aristotle would be committed to the view that some item (the diagonal's being commensurable) never exists, and he would be presupposing that 'object' should apply to an item (the diagonal's being commensurable) he is committed to regarding as never existing. But:

(ii.i) Aristotle seems to think that all items are existent items.[14] Therefore one should resist an interpretation of our passage whereby Aristotle turns out to be committed to the view that some item never exists.

[12] Cf. Keeler (1932), 244; Matthen (1983), 125–6; Duminil/Jaulin (1991), 289–90; Ketchum (1998), 322–3; Bäck (2000), 84; Thorp (2001), 10.

[13] Cf. Matthen (1983), 125. [14] Cf. the subsection to which n. 24 of chapter 5 is appended.

(ii.ii) The word 'object' suggests existence. Therefore one should resist an interpretation of our passage whereby Aristotle turns out to be presupposing that 'object' should apply to an item he is committed to regarding as never existing. Objection: 'Some philosophers have claimed that there are objects that never exist.' Answer: 'Let me grant, for the sake of argument, that Aristotle believes both that there are objects that never exist, and that the diagonal's being commensurable is one of the objects that are there but never exist. I am not sure what it exactly is that one is believing when one believes that the diagonal's being commensurable is one of the objects that are there. Whatever it is that one is thereby believing, however, it is enough to commit one to the view that the diagonal's being commensurable is a state of affairs.'

Falsehood and lack of combination. With regard to each of the items which in T 1 he describes by using 'object' and 'false', Aristotle claims that it is false 'because it is not combined or it is impossible for it to be composed' (1024^b18–19). Since these items are probably states of affairs, Aristotle is probably committing himself to the claim that a state of affairs is false just in case it is not combined or it is impossible for it to be combined. But now, if for a state of affairs it is impossible to be combined, then that state of affairs is not combined. Hence Aristotle is probably committing himself to the claim that a state of affairs is false just in case it is not combined.

Only 'affirmative' states of affairs. T 1 suggests that the only states of affairs recognised by Aristotle are 'affirmative' states of affairs.[15] For, suppose that among the states of affairs recognised by Aristotle there were 'negative' states of affairs (e.g. your not walking or the diagonal's not being incommensurable). Then, in explaining what it is for a state of affairs to be false, Aristotle would probably say something which at least suggests that, on the one hand, some states of affairs (i.e. 'affirmative' states of affairs) are false just in case they are not *combined*, and, on the other hand, other states of affairs (i.e. 'negative' states of affairs) are false just in case they are not *divided*. But Aristotle says nothing of this sort. He only says that an object, i.e. a state of affairs, is false 'because it is not combined or it is impossible for it to be composed' (1024^b18–19). Therefore the only states of affairs recognised by Aristotle are probably 'affirmative' states of affairs.

If Aristotle recognises only 'affirmative' states of affairs, this aspect of his theory is remarkable in three ways. (i) It makes the theory ontologically

[15] Cf. de Rijk (1987), 46.

economical (because it does not postulate 'negative' states of affairs). (ii) It suggests an explanation of Aristotle's somewhat obscure claim that affirmations are 'prior' to denials[16] (the reason why Aristotle makes this claim might be that he thinks that there are only 'affirmative' states of affairs, and that they 'correspond' more closely to affirmations than to denials).[17] (iii) It bars the theory from the most natural explanation of sentences about propositional attitudes which employs states of affairs (e.g. if the theory rules out the 'negative' state of affairs of the diagonal's not being incommensurable, then it cannot explain 'Socrates believes that the diagonal is not incommensurable' as saying that the relation of believing obtains between Socrates and the diagonal's not being incommensurable).

It is however worth observing that in the *Categories*[18] Aristotle seems to postulate 'negative' as well as 'affirmative' states of affairs.[19] The conception of states of affairs he seems to present in the *Categories* differs in this respect from the one he seems to endorse in the *Metaphysics*. Given that the *Categories* are probably an early work, I shall assume that Aristotle's conception of states of affairs (as well as of other related ontological matters) underwent a development between the *Categories* and the *Metaphysics*.

The beginning of Metaphysics *Θ 10: objects which 'are' in the sense of being true or 'are not' in the sense of being false.* In the preceding subsections I discussed an excerpt from *Metaphysics* Δ 29 that constitutes the most unequivocal witness of Aristotle's commitment to states of affairs as bearers of truth or falsehood. In this and in the remaining subsections of section 1 I go on to discuss another passage, at the beginning of *Metaphysics* Θ 10, which provides further information about Aristotle's views on the role of states of affairs in his theory of truth and falsehood. It will soon be apparent that this passage contains a rather complex theory.

Metaphysics Θ 10 contains Aristotle's most extensive discussion of truth and falsehood. The chapter divides into three parts: the first (1051^a34–1051^b17) is about the truth and falsehood that concern composite items, the second (1051^b17–1052^a4) is about the truth and falsehood that concern non-composite items, and the third (1052^a4–11) is about the relationship between falsehood and time.

Here is the beginning of the first part of Θ 10:

[16] *Int.* 5, 17^a8–9; *APo.* 1.25, 86^b33–6; *Cael.* 2.3, 286^a25–6 (where, however, Aristotle speaks of positive and privative general terms or concepts, not of affirmative and negative assertions).

[17] Cf. Hennigfeld (1994), 91.

[18] 10, 12^b6–15, cf. 13^a37–13^b1.

[19] Cf. Lask (1912), 297; Ackrill (1963), 110; de Rijk (1987), 34, 55; Simons (1988), 104; Gaskin (1998), 44–5. For a different interpretation of 12^b6–15 see Oehler (1984), 270.

T 2 Given that what 'is' and what 'is not' are spoken of,[20] in some cases with reference to the figures of predication, in others with reference to the potentiality or the actuality of these or to their opposites,[21] and in others by being in the strictest sense true or false,[22] and this [*sc.* to be in the strictest sense true or false], in the case of objects, is to be combined or to be divided,[23] so that he who thinks of what is divided that it is divided and of what is combined that it is combined is right, while he who is in a state contrary to that of the objects is wrong,[24] when is it that what is called true[25] or false 'is' or 'is not'? For it must be investigated what it is that we call this. For it is not because we truly think that you are white that you are white, but it is because of your being white that we who say this are right. (1051^{a}34–1051^{b}9)

At the beginning of T 2 Aristotle says: 'What "is" and what "is not" are spoken of [. . .] by being in the strictest sense true or false' (1051^{a}34–1051^{b}2). He adds: 'This, in the case of objects, is to be combined or to be divided' (1051^{b}2–3). The singular pronoun 'this' at the beginning of the second of these two sentences probably refers to the property, or properties, of being in the strictest sense true or false.[26] Thus, a plausible paraphrase of the second sentence is that according to which it says that in the case of objects, being in the strictest sense true is being combined and being in the strictest sense false is being divided. If this paraphrase is correct, then at least part of what Aristotle is saying at the beginning of T 2 is, on the one hand, that for an object 'to be' in the sense of being true is to be combined, and, on the other, that for an object 'not to be' in the sense of being false is to be divided. That this is indeed at least part of what he is saying is confirmed by three remarks he makes shortly later in Θ 10: at 1051^{b}11–13 he says that '"to be"

[20] Here Aristotle distinguishes three (groups of) senses of 'to be' or 'being': cf. *Metaph.* Λ 2, 1069^{b}26–8; N 2, 1089^{a}26–8. Elsewhere he distinguishes four: see *Metaph.* Δ 7, 1017^{a}7–1017^{b}9 (with Liske (1988), 148–50); E 2, 1026^{a}33–1026^{b}2 (cf. 4, 1027^{b}17–19). Other passages introduce different classifications: see *Metaph.* Z 1, 1028^{a}10–14; Θ 1, 1045^{b}32–4.

[21] The words 'their opposites' mean 'the opposites of the potentiality or the actuality of the figures of predication' ('τἀναντία' at 1051^{b}1 must be construed with 'κατὰ' at 1051^{a}35, and is therefore coordinate with 'δύναμιν ἢ ἐνέργειαν' at 1051^{a}35–1051^{b}1). They allude either to the lack of potentiality and the lack of actuality (cf. Δ 15, 1021^{a}25–6; Rolfes (1904/28), II 239; Tricot (1966), II 521–2) or to the potentiality and the actuality of not being a certain substance (e.g. a man), the potentiality and the actuality of not being of a certain quality (e.g. white), etc. (cf. Θ 8, 1050^{b}8–34; n. 59 of chapter 2; Oehler (1962/85), 175).

[22] For the reading and the translation here see appendix 1. [23] For the reading here see appendix 2.

[24] No English verb-phrase renders adequately 'ἀληθεύειν': some occurrences of 'ἀληθεύειν' require 'to be right', others 'to speak truly'. Similarly, no English verb-phrase renders adequately 'ψεύδεσθαι': some occurrences of 'ψεύδεσθαι' require 'to be wrong', others 'to speak falsely'. Unlike their counterparts in Latin and other European languages, 'ἀληθεύειν' and 'ψεύδεσθαι' are common not only in philosophical but also in non-philosophical contexts (cf. Cavini (1993a), 86).

[25] Here (1051^{b}5) I read 'τὸ ἀληθὲς' with A^b (the reading printed by most modern editions).

[26] I do not attempt a full justification of this claim because it would take too much space (other interpretations are possible).

is to be combined and one, while "not to be" is not to be combined but many'; at 1051^{b}19–20 he says that certain items are such as '"to be" when they are combined and "not to be" if they are divided'; at 1051^{b}33–5 he says that an item of a certain kind 'is true if it is composed, while it is false if it is not composed'.[27]

The beginning of Θ 10 is about states of affairs. Both in T 1 and in T 2 Aristotle speaks of certain items with regard to which he uses the expression 'object'. About each of the items with regard to which in T 1 he uses 'object', Aristotle there says that it is false just in case 'it is not combined or it is impossible for it to be composed' (1024^{b}18–19). About each of the items with regard to which in T 2 he uses 'object', Aristotle there says that for it 'not to be' in the sense of being false is to be divided (see 1051^{a}34–1051^{b}3). But the items with regard to which Aristotle in T 1 uses 'object' are probably states of affairs.[28] It can then be plausibly inferred that the items with regard to which Aristotle in T 2 uses 'object' also are states of affairs.[29]

An alternative to the standard interpretation. The interpretation of T 2 defended in the preceding subsections differs from one that is very widespread among commentators,[30] so widespread that it deserves the title 'the standard interpretation'. The standard interpretation of T 2 depends on translating 1051^{b}2–3 as follows: '[. . .] and this [*sc.* being in the strictest sense true or false, or – as most commentators assume – being true or false] depends, insofar as objects are concerned, on being combined or being divided [. . .]'.[31] The standard interpretation then assumes that the items denoted by T 2's occurrences of 'object' are (not states of affairs, but) individuals and universals which are thought of. The standard interpretation finally assumes that T 2's main claim is, on the one hand, that an affirmative predicative belief is true (false) when and only when the individuals or universals which are thought of are reciprocally combined (divided), and, on the other hand, that a negative predicative belief is true (false) when and only when the individuals or universals which are thought of are

[27] Cf. Thorp (2001), 3.

[28] Cf. the subsection to which n. 10 above is appended.

[29] Cf. Lewinsohn (1911), 201–2; de Rijk (1952), 11–12; Sepich (1953), 107; Lugarini (1955), 105–6; Tugendhat (1966a), 255; Kirwan (1971/93), 178; Wolf (1979), 99; Graeser (1983a), 44; Matthen (1983), 126; Schmitz (1985), 117; de Rijk (1987), 35–6, 45–7; Whitaker (1996), 30, 31; Szaif (1998), 519–20; Crivelli (1999), 54; Wolff (1999), 56; de Rijk (2002), I 130.

[30] For example, Maurus (1668), IV 479–80; Brentano (1889), 7, 18–19; Lukasiewicz (1910a), 19; Ross (1923), 26; (1924), II 275; Burnyeat *et al.* (1984), 154, 156; Mignucci (1994), 147–9; (1996a), 415–17; Galluzzo (1997/98), 50–1; Bäck (2000), 83; Berti (2000), 7–8.

[31] This translation presupposes reading [c] of appendix 2.

reciprocally divided (combined). On the standard interpretation states of affairs do not come into the picture.

Now, the standard interpretation cannot be ruled out with absolute confidence. However, I do believe that the interpretation defended in the preceding subsections is more plausible. At any rate, note that my favoured interpretation in a way encapsulates the standard interpretation. For, as we shall soon see,[32] my favoured interpretation entails the thesis which the standard interpretation regards as T 2's main claim, i.e. the thesis that, on the one hand, an affirmative predicative belief is true (false) when and only when the individuals or universals which are thought of are reciprocally combined (divided), and, on the other hand, a negative predicative belief is true (false) when and only when the individuals or universals which are thought of are reciprocally divided (combined).

States of affairs as composite items. Shortly after T 2 (eight lines later) Aristotle says:

> T 3[33] But then, with regard to non-composite items, what are 'to be' or 'not to be' and truth and falsehood? For they are not composite, so as 'to be' when they are combined and 'not to be' if they are divided, as the log's being white[34] and the diagonal's being incommensurable, nor will truth and falsehood hold still in the same sense as in the case of those. Or, just as truth in the case of these is not the same, so also 'being' [. . .] (1051^{b}17–23)

In T 3 Aristotle contrasts certain items which he regards as composite with others which he regards as non-composite. He offers two examples of those items which he regards as composite: 'the log's being white and the diagonal's being incommensurable' (1051^{b}20–1). They seem to be states of affairs: the state of affairs of the log's being white and the state of affairs of the diagonal's being incommensurable. Thus, Aristotle can be plausibly credited with the view that states of affairs are composite items.[35]

Of what items is a state of affairs composed? Of what nature is the composition whereby a state of affairs is composed of other items? Aristotle does not say. However, his examples suggest a plausible hypothesis about how he would answer these two questions. For, given that the state of affairs of the diagonal's being incommensurable is a composite item, if one asks what items it is composed of, the intuitive answer is that it is composed of

[32] Cf. [6] and [7] below.

[33] 1051^{b}9–17, the passage between T 2 and T 3, will be discussed later as T 6.

[34] Here (1051^{b}20) the witnesses and the earlier editions read 'τὸ λευκὸν ξύλον' (cf. Gohlke (1961), 287; Halper (1989), 289). I adopt the emendation 'τὸ λευκὸν <τὸ> ξύλον', originally proposed by Bywater (1913), 110 and printed by Ross, Tredennick, and Jaeger.

[35] Cf. Wolf (1979), 99–100; Graeser (1981), 87–8.

the diagonal (a universal) and incommensurable (another universal). Again, given that the state of affairs of the diagonal's being incommensurable is a composite item, if one asks of what nature the composition is whereby it is composed of other items, the intuitive answer is that this composition is somehow associated with predication. These considerations about the state of affairs of the diagonal's being incommensurable, mentioned by Aristotle as an example, suggest a plausible hypothesis about how Aristotle would answer the two general questions about states of affairs asked at the beginning of this paragraph: Aristotle would probably say, first, that the items of which a state of affairs is composed are certain individuals and universals which are 'involved in' the state of affairs, and, second, that the composition whereby a state of affairs is composed of these items is somehow associated with predication.

Θ 10 on the truth and falsehood of states of affairs. Two plausible results have been established with regard to Θ 10: (i) the word 'object' denotes states of affairs (although it may denote other items besides); (ii) states of affairs are compounds, and they are composed of further objects (individuals or universals). Therefore when, at the beginning of T 2, he says that 'what "is" and what "is not" are spoken of [. . .] by being in the strictest sense true or false' (1051^a34–1051^b2), and he adds that to be in the strictest sense true or false, 'in the case of objects, is to be combined or to be divided' (1051^b2–3), one claim Aristotle is avowing is probably the following:

[1] For a state of affairs 'to be' in the sense of being true is to be combined. For a state of affairs 'not to be' in the sense of being false is to be divided. For a state of affairs to be combined (divided) is for the objects (individuals or universals) of which it is composed to be reciprocally combined (divided).

Θ 10 on the truth and falsehood of affirmative and negative predicative beliefs. In T 2 Aristotle speaks not only of true and false objects, but also of a thinker's being right and being wrong (see 1051^b3–5). What is Aristotle's view about the relationship between the truth or falsehood of objects, on the one hand, and a thinker's being right or wrong, on the other?

Aristotle says:

> What 'is' and what 'is not' are spoken of [. . .] by being in the strictest sense true or false, and this, in the case of objects, is to be combined or to be divided, so that he who thinks of what is divided that it is divided and of what is combined that it is combined is right, while he who is in a state contrary to that of the objects is wrong. (1051^a34–1051^b5)

Since he is probably applying 'object' to states of affairs, among the claims which Aristotle is making there are probably the following:

[2] In an affirmative predicative belief[36] a state of affairs is thought to be combined. The belief is true (false) when and only when this state of affairs is in fact combined (divided).

[3] In a negative predicative belief a state of affairs is thought to be divided. The belief is true (false) when and only when this state of affairs is in fact divided (combined).[37]

Moreover, Aristotle seems to aver [2] and [3] as a consequence of what he says at the beginning of T 2: note the expression 'so that' at 1051^{b}3. The premisses which it is most natural to supply in order to derive [2] and [3] as consequences of [1] are the following:

[4] In an affirmative predicative belief a state of affairs is thought 'to be' in the sense of being true. The belief is true (false) when and only when this state of affairs in fact 'is' in the sense of being true ('is not' in the sense of being false).

[5] In a negative predicative belief a state of affairs is thought 'not to be' in the sense of being false. The belief is true (false) when and only when this state of affairs in fact 'is not' in the sense of being false ('is' in the sense of being true).[38]

Combination and division of objects. Part of what [1] says is that for a state of affairs to be combined (divided) is for the objects (individuals or universals) of which it is composed to be reciprocally combined (divided). Therefore, since Aristotle probably endorses [1], [2], and [3], he probably endorses also the following:

[6] In an affirmative predicative belief an item *p* is thought to be combined with an item *s*. *p* and *s* are objects (individuals or universals) which are being thought of. The affirmative predicative belief is true (false) when and only when *p* is in fact combined with (divided from) *s*.

[7] In a negative predicative belief an item *p* is thought to be divided from an item *s*. *p* and *s* are objects (individuals or universals) which are being

[36] For mental affirmations and denials see *Int.* 14, 24^{b}1–2 (with Barnes (1993), 49–50); *de An.* 3.7, 431^{a}14–16; *Metaph.* Γ 7, 1012^{a}2–3; *EN* 6.2, 1139^{a}21; 3, 1139^{b}15–18; 10, 1142^{b}13–14.

[37] Cf. de Rijk (1952), 12; Tugendhat (1966a), 255; Kirwan (1971/93), 178; Wolf (1979), 100; Matthen (1983), 126; de Rijk (1987), 35–6, 45–7.

[38] Cf. Joachim (1948), 193–4; Grayeff (1974), 206; de Rijk (1996), 132; Whitaker (1996), 30; Szaif (1998), 519–20; Crivelli (1999), 54.

thought of. The negative predicative belief is true (false) when and only when *p* is in fact divided from (combined with) *s*.[39]

In chapter 3 we shall see that for certain existential beliefs which do not exhibit a predicative structure, Aristotle proposes a theory of truth and falsehood closely parallel to that presented in [1]–[7].

The primacy of the truth of states of affairs. T 2 consists of three clauses. The first (1051ª34–1051ᵇ6) is a long sentence of the form 'Given that . . .' whose brief apodosis (1051ᵇ5–6) is interrogative. The second clause (1051ᵇ6) and the third (1051ᵇ6–9) are sentences beginning with a 'for'. Thus, T 2's second clause probably justifies the question asked in the first clause's apodosis, and the third clause probably justifies the claim made in the second. Since the second clause and the interrogative apodosis of the first are obscure, the most promising approach to the goal of understanding all three clauses is to move backwards from the third: 'For it is not because we truly think that you are white that you are white, but it is because of your being white that we who say this are right' (1051ᵇ6–9). How is this third clause linked to the preceding characterisation of true and false predicative beliefs in terms of the 'being' in the sense of being true and the 'not being' in the sense of being false of states of affairs? A plausible answer can be obtained by considering two other passages that make similar claims.[40]

The first passage is from *Categories* 5:

T 4 It is because the object is or is not that the sentence also is said to be true or false, not because it is able itself to receive contraries. (4ᵇ8–10)

T 4 (which will be discussed again below as part of T 45) can be variously interpreted. On one of its possible interpretations, 'object' means 'state of affairs'. If this is correct, then T 4 is saying that it is because the state of affairs 'is' in the sense of being true or 'is not' in the sense of being false that a predicative assertion is true or false. If this is what T 4 says, then it makes a claim very close to that made by the third clause of T 2, but in a form which mentions states of affairs.

The second passage is from *de Interpretatione* 9:

T 5 [. . .] sentences are true in the same way as the objects [. . .] (19ª33)

T 5 also is ambivalent. However, on one of its possible interpretations, it says that the truth of a sentence 'follows' (i.e. depends on, and in its modal characteristics resembles) that of the corresponding state of affairs.[41]

39 Cf. the references listed in n. 30 above.

40 Cf. Oehler (1962/85), 176–7; Nuchelmans (1973), 34; Hafemann (1998), 91.

41 Aristotle formulates more or less the same view also elsewhere (*Cat.* 5, 4ª34–4ᵇ2; 4ᵇ6–13; 12, 14ᵇ11–22; *Int.* 9, 18ᵇ38–9).

If the suggested interpretations of T 4 and T 5 are correct, some link emerges between the third clause of T 2 and the preceding characterisation of true and false predicative beliefs in terms of the 'being' in the sense of being true and the 'not being' in the sense of being false of states of affairs: when T 2's third clause says that 'it is not because we truly think that you are white that you are white, but it is because of your being white that we who say this are right' (1051^b6–9), it means that it is not because we truly think (or say) that you are white that the state of affairs of your being white 'is' in the sense of being true, but it is because the state of affairs of your being white 'is' in the sense of being true that we who think (or say) that you are white are right. If this exegesis is correct, Aristotle is treating 'You are white' as logically equivalent to 'The state of affairs of your being white "is" in the sense of being true'.

If this interpretation of T 2's third clause is correct, Aristotle is perhaps hinting that the truth and the falsehood of states of affairs are more fundamental than those of predicative beliefs and assertions because they are mentioned in the definitions of the truth and the falsehood of predicative beliefs and assertions (cf. [4] and [5] above). This might be the reason why Aristotle speaks of states of affairs as some of the items that 'are' or 'are not' 'by being in the strictest sense true or false' (1051^b1–2). Aristotle thus seems to have a precisely articulated map of the senses of 'true' and 'false'.[42]

T 2's plan of inquiry. We can now return to interpreting the first and the second clause of T 2. The interrogative apodosis of T 2's long first clause is:

[a] When is it that what is called true or false 'is' or 'is not'?

The second clause of T 2 is:

[b] For it must be investigated what it is that we call this.

On one possible reading of [b], Aristotle means that it must be investigated what the items are which we call this, i.e. what the items are which we call true or false (cf. 'called true or false' in [a]). The reason why this problem

[42] Cf. Brentano (1862), 30–3; (1889), 5–6; Linke (1965), 307; Seidl (1989/91), II 491. If the hypothesis advanced in the main text is correct, an awkward feature of *Metaphysics* Δ 29 can be explained. In Δ 29 Aristotle takes 'false' ('ψεῦδος') to apply to items of three kinds: objects (1024^b17–26), λόγοι (1024^b26–1025^a1), and human beings (1025^a1–13). He mentions neither beliefs nor assertions (the λόγοι of 1024^b26–1025^a1 are probably not assertions, but *definientia* of definitions or descriptions, cf. Kirwan (1971/93), 178 and Vigo (1997), 14). This omission is puzzling because in many other passages he applies 'false' to beliefs and assertions (cf. nn. 2 and 7 above). The omission might be due to the fact that 'true' and 'false' as applied to beliefs and assertions are definable in terms of their application to states of affairs (cf. Modrak (2001), 58).

must be investigated is given in T 2's third clause. As we have seen, the third clause says that the truth and the falsehood of states of affairs are more fundamental than those of beliefs and assertions. For this reason we must be clear about what the items are which we call true or false, i.e. distinguish clearly the kinds of items which are true or false.[43]

As for [a], on its most plausible interpretation Aristotle is asking the question which he could also have formulated by means of the words 'At what times is it the case that what is said to be true or false "is" in the sense of being true or "is not" in the sense of being false?'[44] This interpretation fits well with the emphasis that the sequel of Θ 10 puts on time, but is hard to square with [b]. A connection with [b] might be established by assuming that Aristotle is already hinting that the behaviour of beliefs and assertions with regard to truth, falsehood, and time depends on the behaviour of states of affairs with regard to 'being' in the sense of being true, 'not being' in the sense of being false, and time. More precisely, in [a] Aristotle might be asking at what times a state of affairs 'is' in the sense of being true or 'is not' in the sense of being false because he is assuming that the answer to this question will determine that to the question of when it is that a belief or an assertion is true or false. Then, in [b] he might be pointing out that although 'true' and 'false' apply to states of affairs, beliefs, and assertions, one must not confuse states of affairs with beliefs or assertions.

States of affairs and time. Here is the continuation of T 2 in Θ 10:

T 6 So, if some objects[45] are always combined and it is impossible for them to be divided, and others are always divided and it is impossible for them to be combined, while others admit the contrary states, 'to be' is to be combined and one, while 'not to be' is not to be combined but many. Therefore,[46] with regard to those objects which admit the contrary states,[47] the same belief and the same sentence comes to be false and true, and it is possible to be right at one time and wrong at another, but, with regard to those objects which cannot be otherwise, it [*sc.* the same belief and the same sentence] does not

[43] Different translations of T 2's second clause ('τοῦτο γὰρ σκεπτέον τί λέγομεν', 1051^{b}6) are possible: 'We must consider what we mean by these terms' (cf. Rolfes (1904/28), II 239; Ross (1908), *ad loc.*; Tredennick (1933), I 469; Hope (1952), 197; Warrington (1956), 243; Seidl (1989/91), II 133); 'Concerning this matter we must examine what our position is' (cf. Apostle (1966), 158).

[44] Cf. Bonitz (1842), 35–6; Maier (1896/1936), I 18–19; de Rijk (1952), 8; Oehler (1962/85), 179–80; Grayeff (1974), 207.

[45] 'Objects' ('τὰ πράγματα') is supplied from 1051^{b}5.

[46] At 1051^{b}11–13 the text I translate is '[. . .] ἐνδέχεται τἀναντία, τὸ μὲν εἶναί [. . .] ἀλλὰ πλείω εἶναι. περὶ μὲν οὖν [. . .]'. This is the reading handed down by the main manuscripts, presupposed by William of Moerbeke's translation, and, apart from minor variations in punctuation, printed by most editions.

[47] I take 'ἐνδεχόμενα' (1051^{b}13) as short for 'ἐνδεχόμενα τἀναντία' (cf. 1051^{b}11).

come to be true at one time and false at another, but the same are always true and[48] false. (1051^{b}9–17)

In T 6 Aristotle says that for an object '"to be" is to be combined and one, while "not to be" is not to be combined but many' (1051^{b}11–13). He is probably repeating a point he already made at the beginning of T 2, where, as we saw, at least part of what he was saying was, on the one hand, that for an object 'to be' in the sense of being true is to be combined, and, on the other, that for an object 'not to be' in the sense of being false is to be divided.[49] I previously argued that the items with regard to which Aristotle in T 2 uses the expression 'object' at least include states of affairs,[50] and that what Aristotle meant at the beginning of T 2 was that for a state of affairs 'to be' in the sense of being true ('not to be' in the sense of being false) is to be combined (divided).[51] Therefore this is probably what he means in T 6 at 1051^{b}11–13.[52]

According to the interpretation of T 2 presented in the last two subsections, in that passage Aristotle says that since the truth or falsehood of a state of affairs is the cause of the truth or falsehood of those sentences or beliefs which posit that state of affairs to be true or false, we must investigate the behaviour of beliefs and sentences with regard to truth, falsehood, and time as dependent on the behaviour of states of affairs with regard to 'being' in the sense of being true, 'not being' in the sense of being false, and time. In T 6, which immediately follows T 2, Aristotle carries out at least part of this programme. His analysis moves simultaneously on different levels, depending on the kind of item which is said to be true or false (states of affairs, on the one hand, and beliefs and sentences on the other).[53]

For a state of affairs 'to be' in the sense of being true ('not to be' in the sense of being false) is to be combined (divided). Therefore: states of affairs that are always combined always 'are' in the sense of being true; states of

[48] Here (1051^{b}17) Aristotle seems to use 'and' ('καί') with the value of 'or' ('ἤ'): cf. Bonitz (1848/49), II 410.

[49] Cf. the paragraph to which n. 26 above is appended.

[50] Cf. the subsection to which n. 29 above is appended.

[51] Cf. [1] on p. 54 above.

[52] Cf. [Alex. Aphr.] *in Metaph.* 598, 23–7; Wilpert (1940), 9. Different (but less plausible) interpretations of Aristotle's remark that '"to be" is to be combined and one, while "not to be" is not to be combined but many' (1051^{b}11–13) are possible: (i) an affirmative belief (or sentence) is true (false) when and only when the objects thought (or spoken) of are combined (divided); (ii) for a belief (or a sentence) to exist is for there to be a composition of the objects thought (or spoken) of, i.e. the composition of which those things are ingredients by being thought (or spoken) of in the same belief (or sentence); (iii) for *x to be F* is for *F* to be *combined* with *x* (e.g. for you to be white is for white to be combined with you), while for *x not to be F* is for *F* to be *divided* from *x* (e.g. for you not to be dark is for dark to be divided from you) (cf. Aquinas *in Metaph.* 1900 Cathala/Spiazzi; Oehler (1962/85), 180–1).

[53] Cf. [Alex. Aphr.] *in Metaph.* 598, 10–41; de Rijk (1952), 8–9; Volkmann-Schluck (1979), 265–7; Wolf (1979), 100.

affairs that are always divided always 'are not' in the sense of being false; and states of affairs that at one time are combined and at another are divided, at one time 'are' in the sense of being true and at another 'are not' in the sense of being false. Moreover, an affirmative belief (or sentence) 'is true' when and only when the state of affairs it posits 'to be' in the sense of being true in fact 'is' in the sense of being true; and a negative belief (or sentence) 'is true' when and only when the state of affairs it posits 'not to be' in the sense of being false in fact 'is not' in the sense of being false. Therefore: in the case of states of affairs that always 'are' in the sense of being true or always 'are not' in the sense of being false, the same belief (or sentence) is either always true or always false; in the case of states of affairs which at one time 'are' in the sense of being true and at another 'are not' in the sense of being false, the same belief (or sentence) is true at one time and false at another.

States of affairs and modality. In T 6 Aristotle also uses some modal notions to describe the temporal characteristics of states of affairs: a state of affairs which is always combined is one for which it is *impossible* to be divided (see 1051^{b}9–10); a state of affairs which is always divided is one for which it is *impossible* to be combined (see 1051^{b}10); and a state of affairs which is sometimes combined and sometimes divided is one for which it is *possible* to be in the two contrary conditions (see 1051^{b}10–11). Given that according to Aristotle for a state of affairs 'to be' ('not to be') is to be combined (divided), these remarks suggest that Aristotle endorses a 'statistical' account of the modalities of states of affairs: a state of affairs that always 'is' is one for which it is impossible 'not to be'; a state of affairs that always 'is not' is one for which it is impossible 'to be'; and a state of affairs that sometimes 'is' and sometimes 'is not' is one for which it is possible 'to be' as well as 'not to be'.[54]

Since Aristotle probably endorses a 'statistical' account of the modalities of states of affairs, he probably avers also a 'statistical' account of the modalities of beliefs and sentences: a belief (or sentence) which is always true will be one for which it is impossible to be false; a belief (or sentence) which is always false will be one for which it is impossible to be true; and

[54] For the statistical account of modalities see *Top.* 2.6, 112^{b}1–20; *Ph.* 2.5, 196^{b}10–21; *GC* 2.9, 335^{a}33–335^{b}4; 11, 337^{b}33–338^{a}3; *PA* 1.1, 639^{b}23–4; *Metaph.* E 2, 1026^{b}27–30; Θ 10, 1051^{b}9–17; K 8, 1064^{b}30–1065^{a}6; *EN* 6.3, 1139^{b}22–4. Many commentators take Aristotle to endorse the statistical account of modalities, but there is disagreement on whether it is his only, or most basic, account (see e.g. Trundle (1981), 52–4). I shall later argue that Aristotle endorses a refined version of the statistical account of modalities (cf. the subsection to which n. 38 of chapter 7 pertains).

a belief (or sentence) which is true at one time and false at another will be one for which it is possible to be both true and false. Since the truth and falsehood of beliefs and sentences are consequences of those of the corresponding states of affairs ('It is not because we truly think that you are white that you are white, but it is because of your being white that we who say this are right', 1051^b6–9), the modal properties of beliefs and sentences are also likely to be consequences of those of the corresponding states of affairs.[55] This is part of what Aristotle claims in T 5 (on the interpretation of it suggested above): 'Sentences are true in the same way as the objects.'

Three roles for states of affairs. The texts examined so far make it plausible to distinguish three roles played by states of affairs in Aristotle's philosophy: first, they are bearers of truth or falsehood (for they are true or false); second, they are bearers of modal properties (for they are necessary, contingent, possible, or impossible); third, they are objects of propositional attitudes (for they are the objects of affirmative and negative predicative beliefs).

With regard to the third role, i.e. that of objects of propositional attitudes, Aristotle's view that there are only 'affirmative' states of affairs has a peculiar consequence: that propositional attitudes should come in pairs of contraries. For given that there is nothing like being 'positively' related to a 'negative' state of affairs (because there are no 'negative' states of affairs), the job that would have been performed by being 'positively' related to a 'negative' state of affairs must be taken over by being 'negatively' related to an 'affirmative' state of affairs: hence the need for pairs of contrary ('positive' and 'negative') propositional attitudes. In this respect it is interesting that Aristotle on several occasions[56] draws a parallel between mental affirmations and denials, on the one hand, and pursuing and avoiding on the other: what he has in mind *might* be that pursuing and avoiding are contrary ('positive' and 'negative') propositional attitudes to states of affairs all of which are 'affirmative'. One can also see how in *Metaphysics* Γ 3 Aristotle can argue that nobody could believe a contradiction because 'beliefs in contradictories are contrary' (1005^b28–9), i.e. because someone believing a contradiction would be in contrary states at the same time. If the theory I am attributing to Aristotle is correct, to believe a contradiction is to believe (mentally affirm) and disbelieve (mentally deny) the same state of affairs, and believing a certain state of affairs is contrary to disbelieving that same state of affairs.[57] Thus, although states of affairs within Aristotle's

[55] Cf. Liske (1995), 358; Vigo (1997), 22–5.

[56] *De An.* 3.7, 431^a8–17; *EN* 6.2, 1139^a21–2.

[57] I owe this point to Robin Smith.

philosophy play essentially the same three roles which some modern philosophers attribute to propositions (i.e. being bearers of truth or falsehood, being bearers of modal properties, and being objects of propositional attitudes), they also turn out to be importantly different from propositions in the way they play these roles: for, while there are no 'negative' states of affairs, there are, of course, 'negative' propositions.

2 THOUGHTS

True and false thoughts in Metaphysics *E 4*. In this section I am concerned with Aristotle's views on true and false thoughts. I shall be commenting on *Metaphysics* E 4, which constitutes Aristotle's most thorough exposition of his views on true and false thoughts. E 4 is an extremely compressed chapter on which much has been written. I shall endeavour to show that (contrary to appearances and to what many commentators believe) E 4 is coherent with Θ 10, and that the two chapters present different parts or aspects of one and the same theory of truth and falsehood.

The context. Let me first of all say something about E 4's context. In E 1 Aristotle announces that he is investigating 'the principles and the causes of beings [. . .] *qua* beings' (1025^{b}3–4). At the beginning of E 2 (1026^{a}33–1026^{b}2) he distinguishes four (groups of) senses of 'to be' or 'being': the incidental sense, the veridical sense (whereby 'being' expresses truth), the senses corresponding to the categories, and the senses corresponding to potentiality and actuality.[58] He wants to show that the incidental and the veridical sense can be left aside because they are parasitical. He turns immediately to establishing this result: the rest of E 2 and E 3 discuss what 'is' in the incidental sense, while E 4 addresses what 'is' in the sense of being true. Here is E 4:

T 7 Let us then leave aside what 'is' incidentally: for we have sufficiently determined its nature. As for what 'is' in the sense of being true and what 'is not' in the sense of being false, since they depend on[59] composition and division (and together they are concerned with the apportionment of a contradictory pair: for truth has the affirmation in the case of what is combined and the

[58] Cf. n. 20 above.

[59] I read 'παρὰ σύνθεσιν' (1027^{b}19) with the main manuscripts, ps.-Alexander (*in Metaph.* 456, 31; 457, 20–1; 22; 25–6; 27; 38–9; 458, 4–5), Ross, and Tredennick. Asclepius (*in Metaph.* 373, 32) and more recent MSS have 'περὶ σύνθεσιν', the reading printed by Bekker, Schwegler, Bonitz, Christ, and Jaeger. The idea, expressed here, that truth and falsehood depend on composition and division is picked up later by the remark that 'the cause [. . .] of the latter [*sc.* of what 'is' in the sense of being true] is an affection of thought' (1027^{b}34–1028^{a}1).

denial in the case of what is divided, while falsehood has the contradictory of this apportionment – how thinking together or separately come about, it is another question,[60] but I use 'together' and 'separately' in such a way that what comes to be is not something continuous but a single thing), for falsehood and truth are not in objects,[61] as if the good were true and the bad were immediately false,[62] but in thought, and with regard to simple items and the 'what it is''s they are not even in thought – then[63] what needs to be considered about what 'is' and 'is not' in this sense must be investigated later, but since the connection and the division are in thought, not in objects, and what 'is' in this sense is a different thing that 'is' from the things that 'are' in the strict sense (because thought joins or subtracts[64] either the 'what it is' or that it is such-and-such or that it is so much or something else, whatever it may be),[65] we must leave aside what 'is' in the incidental sense as well as what 'is' in the sense of being true: for the cause of the former is indeterminate, while that of the latter is an affection of thought, and both are concerned with the remaining *genera* of being and do not reveal an outside nature of being. Given that things are so, let these be left aside, and let us consider the causes and the principles of being itself, *qua* being. (1027^{b}17–1028^{a}4)

E 4's promise and its fulfilment in Θ 10. In *Metaphysics* E 4 (= T 7) Aristotle says that 'falsehood and truth are not in objects [. . .] but in thought' (1027^{b}25–7). Thus in E 4 Aristotle regards truth and falsehood as properties of thoughts. At 1027^{b}28–9 he promises to discuss later certain questions[66] 'about what "is" and "is not" in this sense', i.e. about what 'is' in the sense

60 Cf. *de An.* 1.3, 407^{a}6–10; 3.6, 430^{a}26–430^{b}6.

61 At 1027^{b}19–26 my punctuation differs from those of the editions I consulted.

62 Cf. *EN* 3.4, 1111^{b}33–4. Aristotle, however, does think that truth is linked to goodness and falsehood to badness. For truth is a success (a true belief achieved its goal), falsehood a failure (a false belief missed its goal): see *EN* 6.2, 1139^{a}27–9, cf. *de An.* 3.7, 431^{b}10–12; *Metaph.* α 1, 993^{b}19–21; *EN* 3.4, 1111^{b}33–4; 1112^{a}5–7; 4.13, 1127^{a}28–30; 6.2, 1139^{b}12–13; 10, 1142^{b}8–11; *MM* 1.34, 1196^{b}35–6; *EE* 2.4, 1221^{b}29–30; *Rh.* 1.1, 1355^{a}21–2; 1355^{a}37; *Protr.* fr. 73 Gigon 305^{b}25–306^{a}2 (= Iamb. *Protr.* 42, 5–23); Aquinas *in Metaph.* 1230; 1234; 1239 Cathala/Spiazzi; Régis (1935), 67; Tugendhat (1966a), 259–60; Pritzl (1993), 242; Negro (1996/97), 341; Wlodarczyk (2000), 186–7; Modrak (2001), 57. Plato (*Tht.* 194*c*1–3) also thinks that truth is a goal. For 'good' applied to items in the categorial scheme see *Top.* 1.15, 107^{a}3–12; *EN* 1.4, 1096^{a}25–34 (with Ackrill (1972), 207–11); *EE* 1.8, 1217^{b}25–1218^{a}1.

63 The apodosis of the long 'since'–'then' period begins here (cf. [Alex. Aphr.] *in Metaph.* 457, 36–458, 1; Bonitz (1842), 33; (1848/49), II 293–4; (1862/67), 188; Jaeger (1912), 23; Ross (1924), I 365). For 'οὖν' at the beginning of an apodosis see Bonitz (1870), 540^{b}12–25. For a long parenthetical passage separating protasis from apodosis see *Int.* 9, 19^{a}7–22.

64 At 1027^{b}33 I opt for the reading 'ἀφαιρεῖ ἡ διάνοια', attested unanimously by the main manuscripts and printed by Ross. Bonitz, Dübner, Christ, and Jaeger read 'διαιρεῖ ἡ διάνοια' with William of Moerbeke and ps.-Alexander (*in Metaph.* 458, 8–9).

65 Here (1027^{b}32) I read 'ἢ εἴ τι ἄλλο' with E, J, William of Moerbeke, and most editions (cf. E 2, 1026^{a}37). A^{b}, Brandis, and Ross read 'ἤ τι ἄλλο'.

66 There is no inconsistency in Aristotle's programme if he announces, on the one hand, that he will discuss later certain specific but important questions concerning 'being' in the sense of being true and 'not being' in the sense of being false and, on the other, that he will leave aside the systematic

of being true and what 'is not' in the sense of being false.[67] He seems to fulfil this promise in *Metaphysics* Θ 10. Hence Θ 10, and in particular its beginning (1051^a34–1051^b9 = T 2), probably expands on E 4.

The alleged clash of E 4 and Θ 10: (i) the truth of thoughts concerning simple items. Some commentators[68] think that E 4 clashes with Θ 10 and *de Anima* 3.6. For in E 4 Aristotle says that 'with regard to simple items and the "what it is"'s they [*sc.* truth and falsehood] are not even in thought' (1027^b27–8). On the other hand, in the central part of Θ 10 (1051^b17–1052^a4 = T 23) Aristotle commits himself to the claim that thoughts and linguistic expressions concerning non-composite items are true (and cannot be false). Moreover, in the final part of *de Anima* 3.6 (430^b26–31 < T 24) he claims that the 'intellect [. . .] which is of the "what it is" according to the "what it was to be" is true, and it is not something about something'.

However, the clash is merely apparent. For in E 4 Aristotle can be understood as saying that truth and falsehood are not *both* present in thoughts concerning simple items, the ground for this being that thoughts concerning simple items are only true and cannot be false – precisely the contention of Θ 10 and *de Anima* 3.6.[69]

and exhaustive study of 'being' in the sense of being true (cf. Leszl (1975), 216). Alternatively, the appearance of an inconsistency in Aristotle's programme might be dissolved by assuming (with [Alex. Aphr.] *in Metaph.* 458, 10–15, and against Jaeger (1912), 23–4) that Aristotle is merely announcing that he is *provisionally* leaving aside 'being' in the sense of being true. If there is no inconsistency in Aristotle's programme, then the main support for the hypothesis, advanced by Jaeger (1912), 24–5 (cf. Jaeger (1923), 212; Ross (1924), I.XXX; Gohlke (1961), 197, 451), that lines 1027^b25–9 were inserted by Aristotle himself in a later edition of the *Metaphysics* is demolished.

67 I take 'what "is" and "is not" in this sense' ('τὸ οὕτως ὂν καὶ μὴ ὄν', 1027^b29) to mean 'what "is" in the sense of being true and what "is not" in the sense of being false' (cf. [Alex. Aphr.] *in Metaph.* 457, 36–458, 1; Aquinas *in Metaph.* 1233 Cathala/Spiazzi; Bonitz (1848/49), II 294; Ross (1924), II 365; de Rijk (1952), 8). This interpretation is corroborated by the circumstance that shortly later the phrase 'what "is" in this sense' ('τὸ οὕτως ὄν', 1027^b31) surely means 'what "is" in the sense of being true'.
Some commentators (e.g. Schwegler (1847/48), IV 32; Christ (1906), 131; Gohlke (1961), 197; Oehler (1962/85), 171; Luther (1966), 180; Tricot (1966), I 344; Halper (1989), 217) instead take 'what "is" and "is not" in this sense' (1027^b29) to mean 'what "is" in the sense of being true which is appropriate to simple items and essences and what "is not" in the sense of being false which is appropriate to simple items and essences'. Accordingly, they think that the questions Aristotle promises to discuss concern only the 'being' in the sense of being true and the 'not being' in the sense of being false of non-composite items.

68 Ammon. *in Int.* 27, 27–28, 1; [Phlp.] *in de An.* 544, 21–545, 5 Hayduck; Brentano (1862), 33–4; Ross (1924), II 275–6; Wilpert (1940), 10, 13–14; Brandt (1965), 18–19; Hamlyn (1968/93), 142; Reale (1968/93), I 100; Sorabji (1982), 297; (1983), 140; Montanari (1984/88), II 67–8; Vigo (1997), 34.

69 Cf. Ross (1924), I 365; Heidegger (1925/26), 129, 135–6; Harvey (1978), 220; Pritzl (1998), 187–8. Other commentators (Ascl. *in Metaph.* 374, 7–8; Bonitz (1848/49), II 293–4; Jaeger (1912), 23; (1923), 212; de Rijk (1952), 16, 24; Luther (1966), 180; Sillitti (1966), 320–1; Seidl (1971), 181; Volkmann-Schluck (1979), 262; Pritzl (1984), 144; de Rijk (1987), 51; Berti (1990), 113; Fiorentino (2001), 282; Modrak (2001), 65) favour a different reconciliation of E 4 with Θ 10: when in E 4 Aristotle says that 'with regard to simple items and the "what it is"'s they [*sc.* truth and falsehood] are not even in thought

The alleged clash of E 4 and Θ 10: (ii) truth and falsehood holding of thoughts and objects. According to some commentators,[70] E 4's remark 'Falsehood and truth are not in objects [. . .] but in thought' (1027^{b}25–7) clashes with Θ 10's remark 'Being in the strictest sense true or false [. . .], in the case of objects, is to be combined or to be divided' (1051^{b}1–3). For E 4's remark seems to commit Aristotle to

[a] Truth and falsehood do not hold of objects,

while Θ 10's remark seems to commit him to

[b] Truth and falsehood hold of objects

(here and in the rest of this subsection I use 'object' to mean 'object whose nature is neither mental nor linguistic').

However, the clash could be merely apparent. For it could be the case that Θ 10's remark commits Aristotle not to [b], but to

[c] 'Being in the strictest sense true' and 'being in the strictest sense false' hold of objects,

where 'being in the strictest sense true' is a property which not only is distinct from truth but does not even entail it, and, similarly, 'being in the strictest sense false' is a property which not only is distinct from falsehood but does not even entail it. The reconciliation I am suggesting does have some plausibility. For Θ 10's remark is ostensibly about 'being in the strictest sense true' and 'being in the strictest sense false', which can be plausibly taken to be the properties signified by 'true' and 'false' when they are used in some exceptionally strict sense, while E 4's remark is ostensibly about truth and falsehood, which can be plausibly taken to be the properties signified by 'true' and 'false' when they are used in their ordinary sense. Aristotle's position could then be the following: 'being in the strictest sense true' and 'being in the strictest sense false' (the properties signified by 'true' and 'false' in their exceptionally strict sense) hold only of objects (therefore they do not hold of thoughts); truth and falsehood (the properties signified by 'true' and 'false' in their ordinary sense) hold only of thoughts (therefore they do not hold of objects); hence, 'being in the strictest sense true' is not only distinct from truth, but does not even entail it (because the latter fails to hold of some – indeed, all – of the items of which the former holds); similarly,

[διανοίᾳ]' (1027^{b}27–8), what he means is that in the case of simple items truth and falsehood are not even in *discursive* thought (διάνοια), the ground for this being that (as Θ 10 is sometimes taken to claim) they are in a thought of a different kind, i.e. *intuitive* thought (νόησις) (for the distinction between discursive and intuitive thought in connection with truth and falsehood see *Metaph.* Γ 7, 1012^{a}2–5 with Maier (1896/1936), I 21, 79).

[70] Vollrath (1959), 177; Tugendhat (1966b), 405; Fleischer (1984), 27; Schmitz (1985), 116–17.

'being in the strictest sense false' is not only distinct from falsehood, but does not even entail it; 'being in the strictest sense true' and 'being in the strictest sense false' owe their peculiar strictness to their being fundamental (they are fundamental because they are appealed to in defining truth and falsehood);[71] 'being in the strictest sense true' and 'being in the strictest sense false' are theoretical constructs introduced to set up a better theory of truth; the veridical sense of 'to be' and 'not to be' addressed in E 4 is different from, although connected to, the one addressed in Θ 10 (because the veridical sense of 'to be' and 'not to be' addressed in E 4 covers only or mainly the truth and the falsehood that hold of thoughts, while the veridical sense of 'to be' and 'not to be' addressed in Θ 10 covers only the 'being in the strictest sense true' and the 'being in the strictest sense false' that hold of objects). So, it could well be the case that E 4's remark commits Aristotle to [a] while Θ 10's remark commits him to [c], where 'being in the strictest sense true' and 'being in the strictest sense false' bear to truth and falsehood the relationship indicated.[72]

In E 4 Aristotle promises to discuss later certain questions about what 'is' in the sense of being true and what 'is not' in the sense of being false, and he seems to fulfil this promise in Θ 10.[73] As I argued in the last paragraph, what Aristotle does in Θ 10 can be plausibly taken to be to introduce 'being in the strictest sense true' and 'being in the strictest sense false' as properties that hold of objects but not of thoughts, and to define the truth and the falsehood that do hold of thoughts by appealing to 'being in the strictest sense true' and 'being in the strictest sense false' holding of objects. It can then be plausibly inferred that the questions about what 'is' in the sense of being true and what 'is not' in the sense of being false whose later discussion Aristotle promises in E 4 concern precisely this issue, i.e. defining the truth and the falsehood that hold of thoughts by appealing to 'being in the strictest sense true' and 'being in the strictest sense false' holding of objects.

E 4 on the truth and falsehood of affirmative and negative predications. Given that Θ 10, and in particular its beginning (1051^a34–1051^b9 = T 2), expands on E 4, some of the results established above in the analysis of the beginning of Θ 10, and especially [1]–[7], can be used as a guide in the search for a

[71] Cf. n. 42 above and the paragraph it pertains to.

[72] Cf. Heidegger (1926), 168, 305–6; (1930), 87–91; Reale (1968/93), III 311; Seidl (1989/91), I 429; Thorp (2001), 20–1. For different attempts to reconcile the remarks of E 4 and Θ 10 see Aquinas *in Metaph.* 1230–40 Cathala/Spiazzi; Wieland (1962), 194; Luther (1966), 183; Graeser (1981), 88; Halper (1989), 217.

[73] Cf. n. 67 above and the portion of the main text it pertains to.

plausible interpretation of E 4. It is then plausible to assume that when, in E 4, he says that 'truth has the affirmation in the case of what is combined and the denial in the case of what is divided, while falsehood has the contradictory of this apportionment' (1027^b20–3), Aristotle means (i) that an affirmative predicative belief should be assigned the truth-value truth (falsehood) when and only when certain objects (the universal grasped by its predicate and the universal or individual grasped by its subject) of which it thinks that they are combined are in fact combined (divided) (cf. [6] above), and (ii) that a negative predicative belief should be assigned the truth-value truth (falsehood) when and only when certain objects of which it thinks that they are divided are in fact divided (combined) (cf. [7] above).

A proviso is in place here. As we shall see in chapter 3, Aristotle probably thinks that beliefs concerning composite items are not only predicative beliefs, but also existential beliefs about material substances. I leave this aspect of Aristotle's theory for later: for the time being I speak as if for Aristotle beliefs concerning composite items coincided with predicative beliefs.

Affirmative (negative) predications involve joining (separating). In E 4 Aristotle says that 'the connection and the division are in thought, not in objects' (1027^b29–31). He also says that 'thought joins or subtracts either the "what it is" or that it is such-and-such or that it is so much or something else, whatever it may be' (1027^b31–3).[74] By saying this Aristotle probably commits himself, on the one hand, to the claim that in an affirmative predicative belief one item is *joined* with one item, and, on the other, to the claim that in a negative predicative belief one item is *separated* from one item.

What is the joining (separating) involved in affirmative (negative) predications? At the beginning of Θ 10 (1051^a34–1051^b9 = T 2) Aristotle does not explicitly say that in an affirmative predicative belief a person joins one item with one item, nor does he explicitly say that in a negative predicative belief a person separates one item from one item. However, at those points of the beginning of Θ 10 where (having read E 4) one would expect him to say that in an affirmative predicative belief a person joins one item with one item, Aristotle seems to say instead that in an affirmative predicative belief a person thinks of a certain state of affairs that it is combined, i.e. that in an affirmative predicative belief a person thinks of certain objects (the individuals or universals of which the relevant state of affairs is composed) that they are combined; and at those points of the beginning of Θ 10

[74] Cf. *Int.* 1, 16^a9–18.

where (having read E 4) one would expect him to say that in a negative predicative belief a person separates one item from one item, Aristotle seems to say instead that in a negative predicative belief a person thinks of a certain state of affairs that it is divided, i.e. that in a negative predicative belief a person thinks of certain objects that they are divided. The following views (to be compared with [6] and [7] above) can then be plausibly attributed to Aristotle:

[8] In an affirmative predicative belief an item *p* is joined with an item *s*. For *p* to be joined with *s* is for *p* to be thought to be combined with *s*. *p* and *s* are the objects (individuals or universals) which are being thought of. The affirmative predicative belief is true (false) when and only when *p* is combined with (divided from) *s*.

[9] In a negative predicative belief an item *p* is separated from an item *s*. For *p* to be separated from *s* is for *p* to be thought to be divided from *s*. *p* and *s* are the objects (individuals or universals) which are being thought of. The negative predicative belief is true (false) when and only when *p* is divided from (combined with) *s*.[75]

A Platonic view could be the source of [9]. For in the *Sophist* Plato seems to claim, first, that otherness is a cause of division among kinds,[76] and, second, that negative assertions say that certain items are other than certain items.[77] Plato therefore seems committed to the view that negative assertions say that certain items are divided from certain items. This view could be a source of the idea (expressed in [9]) that in a negative predicative belief one item is thought to be divided from one item.

'Thinking together' and 'thinking separately'. Proposition [8] says that for *p* to be *joined* with *s* is for *p* to be *thought to be combined* with *s*; [9] says that for *p* to be *separated* from *s* is for *p* to be *thought to be divided* from *s*. If this is Aristotle's view, some light is shed on an aspect of E 4. At 1027^{b}23 Aristotle speaks of 'thinking together' and 'thinking separately', and these mental acts or states seem to be the same as the joining and the separating of affirmative and (respectively) negative predicative beliefs. If joining two items in an affirmative predicative belief is thinking that they are combined, then it can also be described as thinking of two items together (take 'thinking together' as describing the contents of a single act or state of thinking, i.e. what one is

[75] Cf. Kirwan (1971/93), 198–9. Some commentators (e.g. Kessler (1976), 183) believe that according to E 4 the items joined (separated) in an affirmative (negative) predicative belief are (not objects, but) thoughts.

[76] 253*c*2–3; 256*b*2–3. [77] 257*b*1–257*c*4.

thinking with regard to the things one is thinking of – avoid taking 'thinking together' as expressing a relation that obtains between two ontologically independent acts or states of thinking). Similarly, if separating two items in a negative predicative belief is thinking that they are divided, then it can also be described as thinking of two items separately (take 'thinking separately' as describing the contents of a single act or state of thinking, i.e. what one is thinking with regard to the things one is thinking of – avoid taking 'thinking separately' as expressing a relation that obtains between two ontologically independent acts or states of thinking). This interpretation of the expressions 'thinking together' and 'thinking separately' is confirmed by what Aristotle says immediately afterwards: 'I use "together" and "separately" in such a way that what comes to be is not something continuous but a single thing' (1027^b24–5). Aristotle is pointing out that the expressions 'thinking together' and 'thinking separately' should not be so understood as to presuppose a series[78] of two (or more) ontologically independent thoughts between which the relation of being 'together' or that of being 'separately' obtains.[79]

Combination and division on different levels. In general, to join (separate) is to bring about a combination (division) of some sort. Hence the joining (separating) involved in an affirmative (negative) predicative belief brings about a combination (division) of some sort in the items on which it is performed, i.e. in the objects thought of. But the combination (division) of objects which is brought about by the joining (separating) involved in an affirmative (negative) predicative belief is different from the 'ontological' combination (division) which may concern those same objects and determines the truth or falsehood of the predicative belief: the combination (division) of an object *p* and an object *s* that is brought about by the joining (separating) involved in an affirmative (negative) predicative belief consists in the fact that the 'ontological' combination (division) is *thought* to obtain between *p* and *s*. Of course, the combination (division) of objects that is brought about by the joining (separating) of an affirmative (negative) predicative belief *must* be different from the 'ontological' combination (division) of those objects lest every predicative belief should be true.[80]

78 In *de Aninma* I.3 Aristotle says that thoughts 'are one by continuity like number, not like magnitude' (407^a8–9).

79 Cf. Ascl. *in Metaph.* 374, 1–4; Aquinas *in Int.* 26 Spiazzi; *in Metaph.* 1229 Cathala/Spiazzi; Jaeger (1912), 23; Geyser (1917), 57–8; Brandt (1965), 21–2; Pritzl (1984), 145; de Rijk (1987), 50; Vigo (1997), 4, 11, 19; Pritzl (1998), 181–2, 183.

80 Cf. Tugendhat (1966a), 254–5; (1966b), 405; Pritzl (1998), 181.

Denials also involve joining. In E 4 Aristotle contrasts affirmative and negative predicative beliefs insofar as in an *affirmative* predicative belief one item is *joined with* one item while in a *negative* predicative belief one item is *separated from* one item. However, in some passages he says that both in an affirmative and in a negative predicative belief one item is joined with one item.[81] Why does he say this? At least three answers are possible.

(i) Both the joining involved in an affirmative predicative belief and the separating involved in a negative predicative belief are acts or states in which one item is somehow joined with one item. For the separating involved in a negative predicative belief is not a complete dissolution whereby the things which are being thought of remain totally unrelated, but a particular way to join those things. For example, one wants to distinguish between the separation involved in the belief that no man is an invertebrate, on the one hand, and the separation involved in thinking successively and independently of man and of invertebrate, on the other. The joining involved in both affirmative and negative predicative beliefs amounts to setting or holding the objects which are being thought of in the subject–predicate relation; the joining that is involved only in affirmative predicative beliefs, and is opposed to the separating involved in negative predicative beliefs, occurs when the subject–predicate relation is realised in its affirmative form.[82]

(ii) As in an affirmative predicative belief an 'affirmative' state of affairs is thought 'to be' in the sense of being true, so in a negative predicative belief an 'affirmative' state of affairs is thought 'not to be' in the sense of being false. Thus, both affirmative and negative predicative beliefs involve the joining whereby the 'affirmative' state of affairs with which they are concerned comes to be.

[81] To formulate the claim that both in an affirmative and in a negative predicative belief one item is joined with one item Aristotle uses 'composition' ('σύνθεσις') and 'to compose' ('συντιθέναι') (see *de An.* 3.6, 430^{a}26–430^{b}3; *Metaph.* Γ 7, 1012^{a}2–5) as well as 'interweaving' ('συμπλοκή') (see *de An.* 3.8, 432^{a}10–12; *Metaph.* K 8, 1065^{a}21–3) (cf. Brentano (1889), 18; Maier (1896/1936), I 24–5; Ross (1923), 26; Keeler (1932), 247; Wilpert (1940), 9; Kirwan (1971/93), 199; Miller (1971), 15–16).

Aristotle's claim that both in affirmative and negative predicative beliefs one item is joined with one item fits well with his using the formulae 'one thing about one thing' ('ἓν καθ' ἑνός') and 'something about something' ('τὶ κατὰ τινός') both for denials and for affirmations: see *Int.* 6, 17^{a}34–5; 8, 18^{a}13–14; 11, 20^{b}13; *APr.* 1.1, 24^{a}16–17; 24^{a}29; *APo.* 1.2, 72^{a}8–9; 2.3, 90^{b}33–4; 10, 93^{b}35–7; *SE* 6, 169^{a}7–8; 189^{a}10–11; 169^{a}14; 30, 181^{a}39; 181^{b}23–4; *de An.* 3.6, 430^{b}26–7; *Metaph.* Γ 7, 1011^{b}24 (cf. *Int.* 12, 21^{b}19–20; *APr.* 2.15, 63^{b}35–8; Mignucci (1975a), 32; Cavini (1998), 6).

[82] Cf. Geyser (1917), 57–8; Frege (1918/19), 147–9; Scarpat (1950), 26–7.

(iii) As in an affirmative predicative belief an 'affirmative' item is joined with one item (e.g. in the affirmative predicative belief that Socrates is white, to-be-white, or the thought of being white, is joined with Socrates, or with the thought of him), so in a negative predicative belief a 'negative' item is joined with one item (e.g. in the negative predicative belief that Socrates is not white, not-to-be-white, or the thought of not being white, is joined with Socrates, or with the thought of him).[83]

I suspect that each of these three answers partly explains why Aristotle says that both in affirmative and in negative predicative beliefs one item is joined with one item. In any case, the joining involved in both affirmative and negative predicative beliefs should be distinguished from the joining which is involved only in affirmative predicative beliefs and is opposed to the separating involved in negative predicative beliefs. Aristotle never draws explicitly the distinction between the two types of joining.

Affirmations and denials 'can be called divisions'. In *de Anima* 3.6 Aristotle says that 'all [*sc.* all affirmations and denials] can also be called divisions' (430^b3–4). This remark is baffling. Its most plausible interpretation appeals to the fact that from the start of *de Anima* 3.6 Aristotle is interested in *indivisible* items (cf. 430^a26), which are probably the items thought of by means of simple (indivisible) thoughts which could be obtained from those complex (divisible) thoughts which are affirmative and negative predicative beliefs by dividing them along the joints determined by their subject–predicate structure. It is because this subject–predicate structure of affirmative and negative predicative beliefs is a guide for a possible division of them into simple (indivisible) thoughts that they 'can also be called divisions'.[84]

83 Cf. *de An.* 3.6, 430^b2–3 (with Förster (1912), 175); *de Ideis* fr. 118, 3 Gigon 378^a8–379^a3 (= Alex. Aphr. *in Metaph.* 80, 7–81, 22). In *de Interpretatione* 3 (16^b12–15) Aristotle treats 'does not recover' and 'does not ail' as single expressions: this might be the linguistic counterpart of explanation (iii).

84 Cf. Phlp. *in de An.* 70, 90–71, 99 Verbeke; [Phlp.] *in de An.* 546, 8–9; 548, 11–20 Hayduck; Trendelenburg (1833), 502; Torstrik (1862), 191–2; Trendelenburg (1877), 414–15; Rodier (1900), II 472; Heidegger (1924/25), 186; Wilpert (1940), 8, 14; Vollrath (1959), 22–3, 26–7; Hamlyn (1968/93), 143; Movia (1979), 384; Horn (1994), 110–11; Movia (1996), 285; Vigo (1997), 11–13. Other commentators explain differently Aristotle's remark that both affirmative and negative predicative beliefs 'can also be called divisions'. Some (Them. *in de An.* 109, 33–110, 1; Maier (1896/1936), I 26–30; Hicks (1907), 514–15; Ross (1923), 26; Oehler (1962/85), 156–7) take Aristotle to mean that the thoughts composed by an affirmative or negative predicative belief involve or result from some abstracting or separating away (e.g. abstracting or separating away a form from an image where it is encapsulated) (cf. *de An.* 3.3, 427^b27–9; 7, 431^a16–17; 431^b2; 431^b6–10; 8, 432^a7–14; *Ph.* 1.1, 184^a21–6). Others (Simp. *in de An.* 250, 37–40; Aquinas *in de An.* 750 Pirotta; Maurus (1668), IV 96; Wallace (1882), 275; Heidegger

3 SENTENCES

Utterances as bearers of truth or falsehood. Aristotle probably thinks that every sentence[85] which is true or false is an utterance, i.e. an event which occurs over a relatively short portion of time, i.e. an expression-token and not an expression-type.[86] In the following four subsections I offer four arguments for crediting Aristotle with such a view.

First argument. The idea that every sentence which is true or false should be an utterance, rather than a sentence-type or a statement, agrees with the 'spirit' of some ontological views advanced by Aristotle in the *Categories*. This (admittedly vague) agreement is brought out by a double analogy. Just as, according to the *Categories*, primary substances, which are individuals, are 'prior' to secondary substances, which are the kinds (*genera* and species) of which primary substances are members,[87] so utterances, which are individuals, are 'prior' to sentence-types, which are kinds of which utterances are members;[88] just as, according to the *Categories*, primary substances are 'prior' to the items from other categories, which depend on primary substances because they are in them, so utterances are 'prior' to statements, which depend on utterances because they are the products or results of those

(1925/26), 136–51; Ross (1961), 301; Siwek (1965), 336; de Koninck (1990), 217–18) offer different but less plausible interpretations.

85 'Sentence' here translates 'λόγος'. Between 9.30 and 9.35 Jim produced exactly two utterances, each of which was a token of the type 'I am sleepy'. How many sentences did Jim utter between 9.30 and 9.35? The fact that one might answer both 'One' and 'Two' shows that 'sentence' is ambiguous and can mean both 'sentence-type' and 'sentence-token' (cf. Kneale/Kneale (1962), 49). Thanks to this ambiguity of 'sentence', translating 'λόγος' by 'sentence' does not prejudge the question whether for Aristotle the linguistic items which are bearers of truth or falsehood are sentence-types or sentence-tokens.

86 Cf. Bochenski (1951), 31; Sullivan (1970), 794; Miller (1971), 33; Nuchelmans (1973), 27, 43, 44; Waterlow (1982), 135; Barnes (1993), 49–50; Seel (2001a), 219; Goldin (2002), 240. The idea (here tentatively ascribed to Aristotle) that the linguistic items which are bearers of truth or falsehood are utterances (events, expression-tokens) is apparently avowed by many late-ancient commentators (see Ammon. *in Cat.* 53, 22–4; 60, 10–12; Phlp. *in Cat.* 82, 19–20; Simp. *in Cat.* 118, 19–25; Olymp. *in Cat.* 79, 14–33; Elias *in Cat.* 183, 34–184, 3; anon. *in Cat.* 18, 33–5; Sullivan (1970), 790–800 – the position might originate with Alexander, see Schmidt (1966), 284–5). It is also avowed by Buridan (see Scott (1966), 15) and many medievals (see Spade (1982), 251). Some modern philosophers (e.g. Field (1972), 351–3; Quine (1986), 13–14) endorse it, but others (e.g. Strawson (1950), 162–5; A. R. White (1970), 8, 9–10) criticise it. This idea is close, but not identical, to that, averred by Austin and Strawson, that the bearers of truth or falsehood are statements, which are the products or results of those events that are cases of making a statement (see Austin (1950), 151; Strawson (1950), 162–5). Some commentators (e.g. Bäck (2000), 100) think that for Aristotle the linguistic items which are bearers of truth or falsehood are (not expression-tokens, but) expression-types.

87 *Cat.* 5, 2^a14–19; 2^b29–30.

88 Cf. *Metaph.* Λ 5, 1071^a23–4; M 10, 1087^a20–1.

events that are cases of making a statement, i.e. of utterances.[89] Such a 'priority' of utterances with respect to sentence-types and statements makes them more apt to be bearers of truth or falsehood.

Second argument. In the last part of chapter 5 of the *Categories* (4^a21–4^b19) Aristotle uses systematically 'λόγος' to refer to items of which he says that they are true or false.[90] Shortly afterwards, at the beginning of chapter 6, he uses 'λόγος' to refer to items of which he says that they are quantities.[91] This usage of 'λόγος' strongly suggests that Aristotle would grant that those items of which in the last part of chapter 5 he says that they are true or false and to which he there refers by using 'λόγος' are included among those items of which at the beginning of chapter 6 he says that they are quantities and to which he there refers by using 'λόγος'.[92] To prove that an item of those of which at the beginning of chapter 6 he says that they are quantities and to which he there refers by using 'λόγος' is not composed of parts which have position with respect to one another, Aristotle offers the following argument:

T 8 For none of its parts endures, but once it has been uttered it can no longer be recaptured. So its parts cannot have position, seeing that none of them endures. (5^a33–6)

This argument strongly suggests that Aristotle would grant that those items of which at the beginning of chapter 6 he says that they are quantities and to which he there refers by using 'λόγος' are utterances.[93] So Aristotle would

89 Cf. A. R. White (1970), 16. Objection: propositions and states of affairs are self-subsistent entities which do not depend on utterances. Answer: propositions and states of affairs are not linguistic items and are therefore irrelevant to this subsection's argument.

90 4^a22; 4^b11; etc.

91 4^b23; 4^b32; etc.

92 Waitz (1844/46), I 281, 292 and Bodéüs (2001), 17–21 rightly render the occurrences of 'λόγος' in the last part of *Categories* 5 and in the first of *Categories* 6 by the same word (the Latin '*oratio*' and the French '*discours*'). O'Brien (1978), 29–32 claims that the items of which at the beginning of chapter 6 Aristotle says that they are quantities and to which he there refers by using 'λόγος' are (not sentences, but) words. If O'Brien's claim were correct, then the items of which in the last part of chapter 5 Aristotle says that they are true or false and to which he there refers by using 'λόγος' would probably be (not included among, but) distinct from those of which at the beginning of chapter 6 he says that they are quantities and to which he there refers by using 'λόγος'. O'Brien's argument on behalf of his claim is that the items of which at the beginning of chapter 6 Aristotle says that they are quantities and to which he there refers by using 'λόγος' are there described as consisting of syllables (see *Cat.* 6, 4^b32–7): it is words, not sentences, that consist of syllables. This argument, however, is not conclusive. It might well be the case that the items Aristotle has in mind are sentences, and that his reason for describing them as consisting of syllables is that syllables are the ultimate constituents of sentences and provide him with a ground for saying that sentences are quantities.

93 Cf. Sullivan (1970), 790–1; Heinaman (1981), 300.

probably grant that those items of which in the last part of chapter 5 he says that they are true or false and to which he there refers by using 'λόγος' are utterances. Hence Aristotle probably thinks that those sentences which are true or false are utterances.

Third argument. At the beginning of chapter 3 of *de Interpretatione* Aristotle defines a verb:

T 9 A verb is that [*sc.* that spoken sound significant by convention] which additionally signifies time, none of whose parts is significant in separation, and is always[94] a sign of things said of something else. ($16^{b}6$–8)[95]

At the beginning of chapter 4 he defines a sentence:

T 10 A sentence is a spoken sound significant by convention[96] some part of which is significant in separation.[97] ($16^{b}26$–7)

Shortly afterwards in chapter 4 he says:

T 11 Not every sentence is assertoric, but only that where being true or false is present. ($17^{a}2$–3)

Thus, Aristotle applies 'spoken sound', first, to those items to which he also applies 'verb' (cf. T 9), and, second, to those items to which he also applies 'sentence' and of which he says that they are true or false (cf. T 10 and T 11).

Now, in chapter 3 Aristotle says:

T 12 Verbs said on their own are names and signify something (for the speaker arrests the thought[98] and the hearer pauses), but they do not yet signify whether it is or not. ($16^{b}19$–22)

T 12 is a difficult passage. On its likeliest interpretation, in T 12 Aristotle uses the phrase 'verb said on its own' to denote utterances which are not parts of larger utterances (i.e. of sentences) and really are not verbs but names (because while they 'signify something' – in that the speaker who

[94] At $16^{b}7$ I read 'καὶ ἔστιν ἀεὶ' with B and most editions. Minio-Paluello and Zadro follow other witnesses and read 'ἔστι δὲ'.

[95] Cf. $16^{b}8$–18; *Po.* 20, $1457^{a}14$–18.

[96] At $16^{b}26$ I adopt A's reading 'σημαντικὴ κατὰ συνθήκην', which is printed by Pacius, Bekker, Weise, and Dübner. Most witnesses have 'σημαντική', the reading preferred by Waitz, Cooke, Minio-Paluello, Colli, Montanari, and Zadro. I retain 'κατὰ συνθήκην' because it is required by the back-reference at $17^{a}1$–2 (cf. Montanari (1984/88), I 192; n. 24 of chapter 2).

[97] Cf. *Rh.* 3.2, $1404^{b}26$–7; *Po.* 20, $1457^{a}23$–4.

[98] Whose thought? For Montanari (1984/88), II 242–8 the hearer's, for Weidemann (1994/2002), 179–80 the speaker's. Cf. *Metaph.* Γ 4, $1006^{a}21$–2.

produces one of them brings the hearer to 'pause', i.e. to think for some time in a certain way – they fail to perform the other two jobs that are characteristic of verbs, i.e. the job of indicating that the item signified holds, or does not hold, of the item signified by a close-by name, and the job of indicating when it is that this holding, or not holding, occurs).[99] Thus, in T 12 Aristotle probably applies 'verb' to utterances. (Note that if in T 12 Aristotle were applying 'verb' to expression-types, it would be difficult to make sense of T 12's first sentence: 'Verbs *said on their own* are names and signify something.') So, when he applies 'spoken sound' to those items to which he also applies 'verb', by 'spoken sound' Aristotle probably means 'utterance'.

The upshot of the last paragraph's argument is that when he applies 'spoken sound' to those items to which he also applies 'verb', by 'spoken sound' Aristotle probably means 'utterance'. Hence, when he applies 'spoken sound' to those items to which he also applies 'sentence' and of which he says that they are true or false, by 'spoken sound' Aristotle probably means 'utterance'. So Aristotle probably thinks that every sentence which is true or false is an utterance.

Fourth argument. In *de Interpretatione* and in other works Aristotle speaks of a person who in saying something 'is right' (literally, 'has truth', 'ἀληθεύει') or 'is wrong' (literally, 'has falsehood', 'ψεύδεται').[100] Moreover, to say that somebody is saying something true, he uses 'to say truly' ('ἀληθῶς εἰπεῖν') followed by (a Greek expression which in English would be rendered by) a 'that'-clause.[101] These linguistic facts fit well with the hypothesis that for Aristotle the linguistic items which are true or false are events of saying, i.e. utterances.[102]

Relative truth. Some modern philosophers make the truth of a sentence relative to an interpretation: they claim that 'true' expresses not a property (i.e. a one-place attribute) of sentences, but a relation between a sentence and an interpretation (signification) of the linguistic expressions in the sentence. Usually, the reason why these modern philosophers make such a claim is that they assume that any sentence one might want to evaluate as true or false is not associated with a signification of the linguistic expressions it contains: it is the signification of the linguistic expressions contained in the sentence that determines its being true or false, so much so that the same

[99] Cf. Miller (1971), 17–18; Whitaker (1996), 55, 57–8.
[100] *Int.* 9, 18^a35–7; 18^b7–8; 10, 20^a36; 14, 24^b8; *APo.* 2.19, 100^b6; *SE* 25, 180^b2–5; etc.
[101] *Int.* 9, 19^a4; *APo.* 1.6, 75^a27; 22, 83^a1–2; *SE* 32, 182^a10; etc.
[102] Cf. Wieland (1972), 237.

sentence will be true under one, but not true under another, signification of the linguistic expressions it contains.

Aristotle does not make the truth of a sentence relative to an interpretation. If, as I suggested in the foregoing subsections, for Aristotle every sentence that is true or false is an utterance, i.e. an event which occurs over a relatively short portion of time, then Aristotle is justified in not making the truth of a sentence relative to an interpretation. For he can claim (i) that every sentence one might want to evaluate as true or false, being an utterance, is by its very essence an expression of a certain language (the language which the person who produced the utterance took herself or himself to be speaking on that occasion), and therefore (ii) that every sentence one might want to evaluate as true or false is essentially associated with a signification of the linguistic expressions (utterances) it contains. If Aristotle makes this claim, he is in a position to reply to those modern philosophers who make the truth of a sentence relative to an interpretation because they assume that any sentence one might want to evaluate as true or false is not associated with a signification of the linguistic expressions it contains: he can reply by rejecting their ground, i.e. by asserting that every sentence one might want to evaluate as true or false *is* associated with a signification of the linguistic expressions it contains.

CHAPTER 2

Truth conditions for predicative assertions

This chapter examines what truth conditions for predicative assertions Aristotle is committed to.

Section 1 addresses a preliminary issue: Aristotle's conception of universals. Universals are neither concepts nor linguistic expressions: rather, universals are objects whose nature is neither mental nor linguistic. A universal is an object which is predicated of many things, an individual is an object which is not predicated of many things.

Sections 2–4 concentrate on the truth conditions for singular and quantified predicative assertions (evidence is mainly provided by passages from *de Interpretatione*). Section 2 addresses the discussion of truth and falsehood in *de Interpretatione* 1, where Aristotle alludes to the theory of *Metaphysics* E 4: in an affirmative (negative) predicative belief one object is joined with (separated from) one object. The bulk of section 2 is taken up by a discussion of two objections that could be raised against connecting *de Interpretatione* 1 with *Metaphysics* E 4. Section 3 addresses Aristotle's theory of assertions. Not every sentence is true or false (prayers are neither), and every sentence that is true or false is an assertion (the converse fails). Every affirmative predicative assertion asserts something 'about' something, every negative predicative assertion asserts something 'away from' something. The operation of asserting-about (asserting-away-from) performed by an affirmative (negative) predicative assertion is the linguistic counterpart of the operation of joining (separating) performed in an affirmative (negative) predicative belief. In both cases the operations are performed on objects (not on linguistic expressions or on thoughts). Section 4 expounds the semantic theory of *de Interpretatione* 7. Here Aristotle distinguishes predicative assertions whose subjects signify individuals (i.e. *singular* predicative assertions) from predicative assertions whose subjects signify universals (i.e. *general* predicative assertions). He then contrasts two ways in which a predicative assertion can assert something to hold, or not to hold, of the universal signified by its subject: it can either assert universally that something holds, or does not hold, of this universal (in which case it is a *universal* assertion) or assert non-universally that something holds, or does not hold, of this universal (in which case it is an *indeterminate* assertion). *Particular* predicative assertions (not to be confused with indeterminate predicative assertions) are introduced as the contradictories of universal predicative assertions: all universal predicative assertions are now regarded as affirmative (because they all affirm universality, i.e. they affirm that it is universally that one universal holds, or fails to hold, of one universal), while all particular predicative assertions are now regarded as negative (because they all deny universality, i.e. they deny that it is universally that one universal holds, or fails to hold, of one universal). Such a theory commits Aristotle to different truth conditions for predicative assertions that differ in quantity (i.e. by being universal, particular, indeterminate, or singular): predicative assertions of different kinds assert different relations of combination and division, and it is different relations of combination and division that are appealed to in their truth conditions.

The final section 5 focuses on the last part of *Metaphysics* E 4. It argues that the relevant differences among the relations of combination and division introduced by a predicative assertion have to do not only with the assertion's quantity, but also with the categories: some predicative assertion asserts that it is the combination or division corresponding to the category of substance that obtains between the universal signified by its predicate and the object signified by its subject, another predicative assertion asserts that it is the combination or division corresponding to the category of quality that obtains, etc. This dependence of truth on the categories is a reason for leaving truth at the margins of metaphysical inquiry.

I UNIVERSALS

Universals and individuals in de Interpretatione *7*. A comprehensive examination of Aristotle's views on universals would require a book-length treatment in its own right, which is far beyond what I dedicate to it here. I restrict myself to a succinct discussion of three points: *de Interpretatione* 7's definition of universals and individuals, the ontologically dependent nature of universals, and the everlastingness of universals.

At the beginning of *de Interpretatione* 7 Aristotle defines universals and individuals:

T 13 Of objects some are universal, others individual (and I call 'universal' what is of such a nature as to be predicated of many things, while I call 'individual' what is not such, e.g. man is a universal, Callias an individual).[1] (17^a38–17^b1)

T 13's definitions probably commit Aristotle to the thesis that all universals are objects whose nature is neither linguistic nor mental.[2] To be sure, alternative interpretations of T 13 are possible that do not commit Aristotle to this thesis. For example, T 13 is consistent with the claim that the only objects that are universal are words (the translation should be slightly modified by replacing 'man' with '"man"' – Greek lacked quotation marks). However, a bit of reflection shows that such alternative interpretations are unnatural and implausible.

T 13's definition of a universal turns on the verb-phrase 'is of such a nature as to', which is open to two interpretations: it can mean 'can by virtue of its nature' as well as 'must by its very nature'.[3] On the first interpretation, T 13's definition of a universal leaves the possibility open that some universal could be predicated of nothing, a position Aristotle is commonly taken to reject. On the second interpretation, T 13's definition of a universal entails that every universal is predicated of many things. The second interpretation could be attacked on the ground that it commits Aristotle to the implausible view that a species should become extinct when exactly one of its members is surviving. However, on reflection, the second interpretation does not commit Aristotle to this implausible view: for the position it attributes to Aristotle does not require that a universal should exist at a certain time only if it is predicated *then* of many things. The position attributed to Aristotle by the second interpretation is compatible with the view that a universal exists at a certain time only if it is predicated *then* of at least one thing and *at some time or other* of at least one other thing. What conclusively favours the second interpretation over the first is that in *de Partibus Animalium* I.4 Aristotle says:

[1] Cf. *APr.* I.27, 43^a25–32; *APo.* I.1, 71^a23–4; *SE* 22, 178^b37–9; 179^a8–10; *PA* I.4, 644^a27–8; *Metaph.* B 4, 999^b33–1000^a1; Δ 9, 1018^a1–4; 26, 1023^b29–32; Z 13, 1038^b11–12; 1038^b16; 16, 1040^b25–6.

[2] Cf. *APr.* I.27, 43^a25–32; *APo.* I.11, 77^a5–9; 24, 85^b15–18; Trendelenburg (1836/92), 61; Brentano (1909), 61–2; Ross (1923), 164–5; Graeser (1978), 447–9; Fine (1980), 210–11; Graeser (1983b), 200; Benson (1988), 283; Brakas (1988), 17–19, 56–9, 108–10; Irwin (1988), 78–9; Fine (1993), 25; Upton (1988), 381; Barnes (1995a), 97; Hafemann (1999), 110–11, 112–13; Modrak (2001), 48. Not everyone agrees that for Aristotle universals are non-linguistic and non-mental objects: see e.g. A. C. Lloyd (1981), 1–2.

[3] Cf. Fine (1984b), 39; Irwin (1988), 79–80; Fine (1993), 250. Most commentators (e.g. M. Frede (1978), 55; Fine (1984b), 39; Benson (1988), 283–7; Irwin (1988), 79–80; Devereux (1992), 116) favour the second interpretation, whereby 'is of such a nature as to' means 'must by its very nature', others (e.g. Viano (1955), 30–1; Brakas (1988), 97, 99–100) the first.

T 14 Universals are common: for that which holds of many things we call a universal. (644^{a}27–8)[4]

T 14, which does not contain the verb-phrase 'is of such a nature as to', commits Aristotle to the view that every universal is predicated of many things.

So, the verb-phrase 'is of such a nature as to' in T 13 can be plausibly taken to mean 'must by its very nature'. It is probably indicating that the attribute signified by the immediately following phrase constitutes the essence of a universal. If this is correct, T 13's definition of a universal amounts to the following:

[10] A universal is an object which is predicated of many things.

According to T 13's definition of an individual, an individual is an object which does not satisfy the *definiens* of the definition of a universal:

[11] An individual is an object which is not predicated of many things.[5]

Universals depend on individuals. In *Metaphysics* Z 16 Aristotle says:

T 15 None of the universals exists separately from individuals. (1040^{b}26–7)[6]

I cannot discuss here the issue of what 'separately' means in T 15 and in other comparable passages. My view is that 'separately' here means something like 'independently',[7] and that part of what Aristotle is committing himself to in T 15 is that

[12] Every universal exists when and only when it is predicated of some individual or other that at some time or other exists.[8]

Universals are everlasting. Aristotle does not explicitly say how long universals exist. However, some passages show beyond reasonable doubt that in his view some universals are everlasting, i.e. exist always.

[4] Cf. *Metaph.* Δ 26, 1023^{b}29–32.

[5] For Aristotle's 'negative' definition of an individual as what does not satisfy the *definiens* of the definition of a universal cf. *Cat.* 2, 1^{b}6–9; *APr.* 1.27, 43^{a}32–6; 43^{a}39–40; M. Frede (1978), 54.

[6] Cf. *de An.* 1.1, 402^{b}7–8; *Metaph.* K 2, 1060^{b}20–2; M 9, 1086^{a}31–1086^{b}11; *EE* 1.8, 1217^{b}1–16.

[7] Cf. *Cat.* 2, 1^{a}24–5 (with Oehler (1984), 181; Fine (1985), 164–5); *GC* 1.3, 317^{b}8–11; 317^{b}31–3; *Long.* 3, 465^{b}12–14; *Metaph.* Z 1, 1028^{a}31–4 (with Fine (1984b), 35–6); *EE* 1.8, 1217^{b}1–16 (with Fine (1984b), 37–8); *de Ideis* fr. 119 Gigon 384^{a}12–15 (= Alex. Aphr. *in Metaph.* 98, 19–20); Irwin (1977), 154; M. Frede (1978), 65; Fine (1980), 205–6; (1984b), 33, 34–45, 79; (1985), 159–60; (1993), 51–2, 269. The idea that 'separately' in T 15 and other parallel passages means something like 'independently' is attacked by Morrison (1985), 128–38 and other commentators.

[8] Cf. *Cat.* 11, 14^{a}7–10; Fine (1984b), 77–8; Irwin (1988), 80; Fine (1993), 247, 249, 269. For 'at some time or other' see the subsection to which n. 1 of the introduction is appended.

(i) In *Posterior Analytics* 1.24 he says:

T 16 If there is some single account and the universal is not a homonymy, universals are to no less degree than some of the particulars, but even more, inasmuch as imperishable things are among them, while particulars are more perishable. (85^b15–18)

By saying that 'imperishable things are among' universals (85^b17–18), Aristotle commits himself to the view that some universals never perish.[9]

(ii) Several passages show that according to Aristotle at least some natural kinds exist always. Here is the most explicit passage:

T 17 A kind – of men, animals, and plants – exists always. (*GA* 2.1, 731^b35–732^a1)[10]

Since Aristotle regards natural kinds as universals, he is committed to the view that some universals exist always, i.e. are everlasting.

So Aristotle is committed to the view that some universals are everlasting. Moreover, some remarks he makes seem to commit him to the view that all universals are everlasting. For in *Metaphysics* Z Aristotle makes two connected claims about definitions: first, that whatever is definable is necessary; second, that only universals are definable.[11] By making the first of these two claims Aristotle commits himself to the view that all definable universals are necessary. Since Aristotle believes that whatever is necessary is everlasting,[12] he is committed to the view that all definable universals are everlasting. But now, Aristotle is likely to hold both that every non-definable universal is an ingredient (as *genus* or *differentia*) of some definable universal, and that every universal which is an ingredient (as *genus* or *differentia*) of some definable universal exists at least as long as that definable universal. Since he is committed to the view that all definable universals are everlasting, Aristotle is probably also committed to the stronger view that all universals are everlasting.

Thus, although Aristotle never says that all universals are everlasting, there is some plausibility to the assumption that for him all universals are everlasting.

Universals are always instantiated. Aristotle probably thinks that every universal exists when and only when it is predicated of some individual or

9 Cf. Irwin (1988), 513.

10 Cf. *GC* 2.11, 338^b5–19; *de An.* 2.4, 415^a22–415^b7; *GA* 3.10, 760^a35–760^b1.

11 For the first claim see Z 15, 1039^b27–1040^a7 (cf. 10, 1036^a2–9; *EN* 6.3, 1139^b19–24). For the second claim see Z 10, 1035^b34–1036^a1; 11, 1036^a28–9. Aristotle reports that Plato endorsed claims which are, in fact, very close to these: see *Metaph.* A 6, 987^a29–987^b7; M 4, 1078^b12–17 (with Fine (1984b), 47–51).

12 *EN* 6.3, 1139^b22–4 (cf. n. 54 of ch. 1).

other that at some time or other exists. If, as I just argued, he believes that all universals are everlasting, i.e. exist always, then he is committed to the view that every universal is at all times predicated of some individual or other that at some time or other exists – in short, that all universals are always instantiated.

2 TRUTH AND FALSEHOOD IN *DE INTERPRETATIONE* 1

Joining and separating in de Interpretatione *1.* Here is the second half of *de Interpretatione* 1:

T 18 Just as in the soul some thoughts are neither true nor false while others are necessarily one or the other, so also with spoken sounds: for falsehood and truth have to do with joining and separating. Thus names and verbs by themselves resemble thoughts that are without joining and separating, e.g. 'man' and 'white' when nothing is added: for they are neither false nor true so far, though they are signs of some specific thing (for even 'goatstag' signifies something but is not yet either true or false – unless 'to be' or 'not to be' is added, either simply or with reference to time).[13] (16ᵃ9–18)[14]

T 18 contrasts thoughts that 'are neither true nor false' (16ᵃ10) and 'are without joining and separating' (16ᵃ14), on the one hand, with thoughts that 'are necessarily one or the other [*sc.* true or false]' (16ᵃ11) and do involve joining or separating, on the other. Although T 18 says nothing about the nature of the operations of joining and separating, the parallel with *Metaphysics* E 4 (= T 7) shows that the operation of joining (separating) mentioned in T 18 is the one involved in affirmative (negative) predicative beliefs.[15] Hence in T 18 the thoughts that involve joining (separating) are affirmative (negative) predicative beliefs.

Two objections could be raised against the view that the operations of joining and separating mentioned in T 18 are the same as those mentioned in *Metaphysics* E 4. The first objection claims that there is an important difference between the operations of joining and separating mentioned in

[13] My punctuation of the Greek text here (16ᵃ16–18) is: '. . . ἀληθές πω, σημεῖον δ' ἐστὶ τοῦδε (καὶ γάρ . . . χρόνον).' (cf. *APo.* 1.1, 71ᵃ14–15; Pagliaro (1954), 118; Weidemann (1994/2002), 156; Sedley (1996), 93; Whitaker (1996), 32–3). All the editions I consulted print: '. . . ἀληθές πω. σημεῖον δ' ἐστὶ τοῦδε· καὶ γάρ . . . χρόνον.' (to be translated by '. . . true so far. And there is a sign of this: for even . . . time.').

[14] Cf. *Cat.* 4, 2ᵃ4–10; 10, 13ᵇ10–11; *Int.* 4, 16ᵇ26–8; 5, 17ᵃ17–20.

[15] Cf. Ammon. *in Int.* 26, 23–27, 8; *in APr.* 23, 2–4; Boeth. *in Int. Pr. Ed.* 43, 11–14; *in Int. Sec. Ed.* 48, 21–49, 23; Steph. *in Int.* 6, 22–5; Aquinas *in Int.* 26 Spiazzi; Pacius (1597b), 87–8; (1597a), 61; Waitz (1844/46), I 326; Brandt (1965), 15; Weidemann (1994/2002), 154; Whitaker (1996), 26–7; Vigo (1997), 3.

T 18 and those mentioned in *Metaphysics* E 4: the former are performed on thoughts, the latter on objects.[16] The second objection claims that the theory expounded in T 18 is incompatible with the views about truth and falsehood expounded in *Metaphysics* Θ 10, views that I took to be in the background of E 4.

The following two subsections answer these objections, and thus defend the view that the operations of joining and separating mentioned in T 18 are the same as those mentioned in *Metaphysics* E 4.

Of what kind are the items joined and separated in predicative beliefs? T 18 draws a double analogy: on the one hand, 'names and verbs' (16^a13), which are neither true nor false, correspond to certain 'thoughts that are without joining and separating' (16^a14), which also are neither true nor false; on the other hand, certain linguistic expressions which are either true or false correspond to certain thoughts which involve joining or separating and also are either true or false. Although Aristotle does not explicitly say so, the linguistic expressions which in T 18's analogy are taken to be either true or false are almost certainly predicative sentences.[17]

The exact import of T 18's analogy is unclear. At least two interpretations of it are possible.

(i) Names and verbs which are not parts of sentences are isolated (i.e. not combined with other linguistic expressions in such a way as to compose a predicative sentence). Their condition corresponds to that of thoughts that are isolated (i.e. not combined with other thoughts in such a way as to compose a predicative belief) and are 'without joining and separating'. Then what corresponds to the condition of names or verbs that are combined with other linguistic expressions in such a way as to compose a predicative sentence is the condition of thoughts that are combined with other thoughts in such a way as to compose a predicative belief and do involve joining or separating. Not only the joining involved in an affirmative predicative belief, but also the separating involved in a negative predicative belief is a combination that yields a predicative belief. The joining (separating) involved in an affirmative (negative) predicative belief is performed on thoughts.[18]

[16] Cf. the subsection to which n. 75 of ch. 1 is appended.
[17] Cf. Ammon. *in Int.* 28, 29–31; 29, 18–26; Weidemann (1994/2002), 155.
[18] Cf. Ammon. *in Int.* 26, 12–22; 29, 23–6; Trendelenburg (1836/92), 54; Steinthal (1863/90), I 236; Maier (1896/1936), I 6, 109; Geyser (1917), 52; Ross (1923), 26; Keeler (1932), 244; Brandt (1965), 16–18; Kirwan (1971/93), 198–9; Miller (1971), 12, 45; Seidl (1971), 56; Ringbom (1972), 10; Kessler (1976), 183, 184; Arens (1984), 34; Burnyeat *et al.* (1984), 154, 156; Zanatta (1992), 145; Sadun Bordoni (1994), 65; Whitaker (1996), 29; Caston (1998a), 286; (1998b), 205; Segalerba (2001), 243.

(ii) On the one hand, every predicative sentence is composed of a name or a verb combined with some other linguistic expression, and an affirmative (negative) predicative sentence joins (separates) objects – while a name or a verb neither joins nor separates objects. On the other hand, every predicative belief is composed of a thought combined with some other thought, and an affirmative (negative) predicative belief joins (separates) objects – while the thoughts of which the predicative belief is composed neither join nor separate objects. The joining (separating) involved in an affirmative (negative) predicative belief is performed (not on thoughts, but) on objects.[19]

The most important difference between these two interpretations concerns the nature of the items which are joined (separated) by an affirmative (negative) predicative belief: on interpretation (i) they are thoughts, while on interpretation (ii) they are objects which are being thought of. The following two considerations tell against interpretation (i), and therefore favour interpretation (ii).

First, if interpretation (i) is correct, then Aristotle holds that in a negative predicative belief one thought is separated from one thought, and he also holds that this separation of thoughts is a way to join them (because it is a way to establish some link between them). Given the isomorphism which Aristotle takes to obtain between the sphere of thoughts and that of linguistic expressions, if interpretation (i) is correct then Aristotle should describe the negative sentence 'A goatstag is not' as the result either of separating 'to be' from 'goatstag' or of adding 'to be' to 'goatstag'. But now, at the end of T 18 (16^a15, 17–18) Aristotle describes 'A goatstag is not' as the result of adding 'not to be' to 'goatstag'.[20]

Second, in the other passages where he speaks of affirmative and negative predicative beliefs as being the result of some operation performed on further thoughts, Aristotle mentions combination but ignores separation.[21] This would be surprising if, as interpretation (i) assumes, Aristotle believed that in a negative predicative belief one thought is separated from one thought.

A problem for interpretation (ii) is that it is not clear how the beliefs that correspond to the sentences alluded to at the end of T 18, 'A goatstag is' and 'A goatstag is not', could be taken to involve joining or separating objects. This problem can be plausibly solved by assuming that the beliefs

19 Cf. Boeth. *in Int. Sec. Ed.* 48, 21–49, 23; Pacius (1597a), 61; Brentano (1889), 18–19; Kapp (1942), 50–1; Ackrill (1963), 127; Matthen (1984), 32; Weidemann (1994/2002), 154.

20 In other passages also Aristotle describes a negative sentence as obtained by 'adding' something (a negative expression): see *Int.* 4, 16^b28–30; 5, 17^a11–12; 10, 19^b24–6; 19^b29–30; 20^a35–6; 12, 21^b21–2; 21^b26–33; *APr.* 1.1, 24^b16–18 (cf. Brandt (1965), 19; Smith (1989), 108–9; Barnes (1996), 187–8).

21 *De An.* 3.6, 430^a26–430^b3 (the 'division' mentioned at 430^b3 has probably nothing to do with denial, cf. the subsection to which n. 84 of ch. 1 is appended); 8, 432^a10–12.

corresponding to the sentences 'A goatstag is' and 'A goatstag is not' join or separate the universals goat and stag. After all, the reason why Aristotle discusses the name 'goatstag' is that it comes close to being a linguistic expression that is either true or false. It does so on two grounds: it is 'empty' (hence a candidate for falsehood) and composite (hence resembling predicative sentences, which are composite and are either true or false).[22] Given that Aristotle discusses 'goatstag' partly because this name, being composite, resembles predicative sentences, he can be plausibly taken to hold that the beliefs that correspond to the sentences 'A goatstag is' and 'A goatstag is not' join or separate the universals goat and stag.

In conclusion, interpretation (ii) should be preferred. Hence, in T 18's analogy, the items which are joined (separated) in an affirmative (negative) predicative belief are probably (not further thoughts, but) objects.

The apparent clash of de Interpretatione *1 with* Metaphysics *Θ 10*. In *de Interpretatione* 1 Aristotle says that 'falsehood and truth have to do with joining and separating' (16^a12–13 < T 18). This seems to clash with what Aristotle says in *Metaphysics* Θ 10. For in Θ 10 he says that certain thoughts concerning non-composite items are true, and these true thoughts concerning non-composite items probably involve neither joining nor separating – thoughts that involve joining or separating concern composite items because to join (separate) is to think that a certain composite item 'is' in the sense of being true ('is not' in the sense of being false).

The clash, however, is only apparent. For in *de Interpretatione* 1 Aristotle can be understood as claiming that it is only where joining or separating is present that truth and falsehood are *both* possible. In the case of thoughts concerning non-composite items, it is not the case that truth and falsehood are both possible: as we shall see, if the thought concerning a non-composite item is an affirmative existential belief then it is necessarily true (and therefore cannot be false), while if it is a negative existential belief then it is necessarily false (and therefore cannot be true). So: among the thoughts that involve neither joining nor separating, some are necessarily true (affirmative existential beliefs concerning non-composite items), others are necessarily false (negative existential beliefs concerning non-composite items), yet others are necessarily neither true nor false (concepts). When in *de Interpretatione* 1 he compares names and verbs with thoughts that are neither true nor false and involve neither joining nor separating, Aristotle is comparing names and verbs with a proper subclass of the class of thoughts that involve neither joining nor separating, i.e. with that subclass

[22] Cf. Boeth. *in Int. Sec. Ed.* 50, 1–51, 3; Ackrill (1963), 114; Zanatta (1992), 146.

that consists of concepts. For, within the class of thoughts that involve neither joining nor separating, only concepts are neither true nor false, and therefore fit Aristotle's comparison with names and verbs. Aristotle's comparison is therefore expressed rather misleadingly because it gives the impression that names and verbs correspond to *all* thoughts that involve neither joining nor separating, while they can only correspond to *some* of them, i.e. to concepts.[23]

3 AFFIRMATIVE AND NEGATIVE PREDICATIVE ASSERTIONS

Assertions. Some passages from chapters 4–6 of *de Interpretatione* enable one to spell out an account of the truth and the falsehood of affirmative and negative predicative sentences which can be plausibly attributed to Aristotle:

T 19 Every sentence is significant (not as a tool but, as we said,[24] by convention). However not every sentence is assertoric,[25] but only that where being true or false is present. They are not present in all: e.g. a prayer is a sentence but is neither true nor false.[26] (4, $17^{a}1$–5)

The first single assertoric sentence is the affirmation, next is the denial.[27] (5, $17^{a}8$–9)

An affirmation is an assertion of something about something, a denial is an assertion of something away from something.[28] (6, $17^{a}25$–6)

In Aristotle's view, every assertoric sentence, or assertion,[29] is a sentence. T 19 leaves one with the impression that for Aristotle sentences constitute a *genus* with several subordinate species, among which rank the species assertoric sentence, the species prayer, etc.[30]

Does Aristotle believe that being true or false is the *differentia* that isolates the species assertoric sentence within the *genus* sentence? At $17^{a}2$–3 he says:

[23] Cf. Berti (1994), 125; (1996a), 393.

[24] 4, $16^{b}26$ (with n. 96 of ch. 1) (cf. 2, $16^{a}19$; $16^{a}27$–9).

[25] I render 'ἀποφαντικός', 'ἀπόφανσις', and 'ἀποφαίνεσθαι' by 'assertoric', 'assertion', and 'to assert' (cf. Blank (1996), 178).

[26] Cf. *Po.* 19, $1456^{b}8$–13. In *Int.* 5, $17^{a}11$–12 Aristotle says that 'the account of man is not yet an assertoric sentence' (here 'account' translates 'λόγος', which in other contexts I render by 'sentence').

[27] For single assertoric sentences cf. sect. 3 of ch. 5. For the priority of affirmations over denials cf. n. 16 of ch. 1.

[28] Cf. *Int.* 5, $17^{a}20$–1; 7, $17^{b}38$–$18^{a}4$; *APr.* 1.30, $46^{a}14$–15; 32, $47^{b}3$; 2.15, $64^{a}13$–15; *APo.* 1.2, $72^{a}13$–14; *Metaph.* Γ 6, $1011^{b}19$–20; Θ 2, $1046^{b}13$–15; Fleischer (1984), 15.

[29] Following Aristotle, I treat 'assertoric sentence' ('λόγος ἀποφαντικός') and 'assertion' ('ἀπόφανσις') as synonyms.

[30] Cf. Ammon. *in Int.* 64, 29–30; Anon. *in Int.* 16, 20–17, 3; Pacius (1597a), 69; Textor (1870), 6; DuLac (1949), 163; Xenakis (1957), 539; Weidemann (1994/2002), 191.

'Not every sentence is assertoric, but only that where being true or false is present.' These words are compatible with the claim that being true or false should be the *differentia* which isolates the species assertoric sentence within the *genus* sentence.[31] However, they are also compatible with weaker claims: that being true or false is peculiar to assertoric sentences (i.e. that assertoric sentences coincide with the sentences that are true or false), and that being true or false is present only in assertoric sentences (i.e. that every sentence that is true or false is an assertoric sentence, the possibility being left open that some assertoric sentence might be neither true nor false). Since, as we shall see, Aristotle believes that some assertoric sentence is neither true nor false, he should be taken to be making the weakest of the claims with which his words are compatible: that being true or false is present only in assertoric sentences.[32]

What does an assertion reveal? 'Assertoric' and 'assertion' translate 'ἀποφαντικός' and 'ἀπόφανσις', which are etymologically connected with the verb 'ἀποφαίνω', which means 'to reveal', 'to bring to light'. Some commentators think that the revelation in question is a revelation of reality: to make an assertion, they suggest, is 'to reveal reality in discourse'.[33] This explanation is attractive, but probably wrong. The revelation in question is probably a revelation of the speaker's views: to make an assertion is 'to show what one's opinion really is', 'to make one's views public'.[34] For the *Rhetoric* defines a maxim as 'an assertion [ἀπόφανσις], not about individuals, [. . .] but general, nor about any subject, [. . .] but about those with which actions are concerned [. . .]' (2.21, 1394^a22–5). A parallel passage from the *Rhetoric to Alexander* characterises a maxim as 'a disclosure of one's individual opinion [δόγματος ἰδίου δήλωσις] on general matters' (12, 1430^a40–1430^b1).

'Asserting-about', 'asserting-away-from'. A fundamental idea in Aristotle's account of the truth and falsehood of beliefs is that in an affirmative (negative) predicative belief one item is joined with (separated from) one item. T 19's claim that in an affirmative (negative) predicative assertion one item is

[31] Some commentators (e.g. Ammon. *in Int.* 66, 10–19; anon. *in Int.* 17, 3–5; Aquinas *in Int.* 82–5 Spiazzi; Peter de Rivo *apud* Baudry (1950), 72; Pacius (1597a), 69; Textor (1870), 6; Michelis (1886), 23; Heidegger (1925/26), 128–30) do take these words to mean that being true or false is the *differentia*. Stephanus (*in Int.* 18, 26–35) argues that the phrase 'sentence where being true or being false is present' is not a *definiens* (ὁρισμός), but only a rough description (ὑπογραφή).

[32] Cf. D. Frede (1970), 80–1; Gaskin (1995), 180. Peter de Rivo (*apud* Baudry (1950), 72) suggests a different way of reconciling the characterisation of assertoric sentences as those 'where being true or false is present' with the view that some assertoric sentence is neither true nor false.

[33] Cf. Heidegger (1925/26), 133; Luther (1966), 188.

[34] Cf. Nuchelmans (1973), 26–7.

asserted 'about' ('away from') one item seems to be the linguistic counterpart of this idea.[35] It is therefore plausible to credit Aristotle with an account of the truth and falsehood of predicative assertions which is 'parallel' to his account of the truth and falsehood of predicative beliefs – the parallel consisting in the circumstance that in the account of the truth and falsehood of predicative assertions the operations of *asserting-about* and *asserting-away-from* play a role analogous to that played by the operations of *joining* and *separating* in the account of the truth and falsehood of predicative beliefs. Now, in the account of the truth and falsehood of predicative beliefs, to join one item with one item is to think of those items that they are combined, and to separate one item from one item is to think of those items that they are divided. Thus, in the account of the truth and falsehood of predicative assertions, to *assert* one item *about* one item will be to assert of those items that they are combined, and to *assert* one item *away from* one item will be to assert of those items that they are divided. More specifically, the following views, parallel to [6], [7], [8], and [9], can be plausibly attributed to Aristotle:

[13] In an affirmative predicative assertion the item *p* signified by the predicate is asserted about the item *s* signified by the subject. For *p* to be asserted about *s* is for *p* to be asserted to be combined with *s*. *p* and *s* are the objects (universals or individuals) which are being spoken of. The affirmative predicative assertion is true (false) when and only when *p* is combined with (divided from) *s*.[36]

[35] Cf. Boeth. *in Int. Pr. Ed.* 77, 15–24; 78, 24–79, 6; *in Int. Sec. Ed.* 118, 5–16; 122, 27–123, 22; Aquinas *in Int.* 105 Spiazzi; Waitz (1844/46), I 371; Torstrik (1862), 191; Trendelenburg (1876), 82–3; Vollrath (1959), 22–3; Morpurgo-Tagliabue (1971), 34; Nuchelmans (1973), 27; Brakas (1988), 66–7; Whitaker (1996), 27, 78; Vigo (1997), 3–4; Hafemann (1998), 89; (1999), 110; Fiorentino (2001), 279–80. In the *Sophist* (262*c*12–13) Plato describes what is, in fact, a singular affirmative predicative assertion as combining an object (signified by the name constituting the subject, cf. 262*a*6–8; 262*b*9–262*c*1) with an action (signified by the verb constituting the predicative expression, cf. 262*a*3–5; 262*b*5–6).

[36] I assume that for Aristotle some linguistic expressions signify universals, others individuals. I also assume that for him universals are objects whose nature is neither mental nor linguistic. I therefore also assume that for him some linguistic expressions signify non-mental objects. At the beginning of *de Interpretatione* 1 Aristotle says that 'spoken sounds are symbols of affections in the soul' (16^a3–4), which, in turn, are 'likenesses' (16^a7) of objects. He also says that 'the first items of which these [*sc.* spoken sounds] are signs are [. . .] affections of the soul' (16^a6–7, Minio-Paluello's text). In saying this Aristotle is probably implying that objects are the second items of which spoken sounds are signs. Thus, the theory of signification sketched at the beginning of *de Interpretatione* 1 is at least compatible with the view I assume to be Aristotle's, i.e. that some linguistic expressions signify non-mental objects. Further confirmation comes from *Sophistici Elenchi* 1: 'It is not possible to discuss by bringing in the objects themselves, but we use names as symbols instead of objects' (165^a6–8, cf. Fait (1996), 181–7; Wheeler (1999), 211–12). At *Sens.* 1, 437^a14 Aristotle says that names are symbols without specifying what they are symbols of.

[14] In a negative predicative assertion the item *p* signified by the predicate is asserted away from the item *s* signified by the subject. For *p* to be asserted away from *s* is for *p* to be asserted to be divided from *s*. *p* and *s* are the objects (universals or individuals) which are being spoken of. The negative predicative assertion is true (false) when and only when *p* is divided from (combined with) *s*.[37]

4 ASSERTIONS ABOUT INDIVIDUALS *VS* ASSERTIONS ABOUT UNIVERSALS

Singular, universal, and indeterminate assertions in de Interpretatione *7*. In chapter 5 of *de Interpretatione* Aristotle separates predicative assertions from utterances of other types.[38] Then, in the first part of chapter 7, he produces a classification of predicative assertions:

T 20 Given that of objects some are universal, others individual (and I call 'universal' what is of such a nature as to be predicated of many things, while I call 'individual' what is not such, e.g. man is a universal, Callias an individual), and it must sometimes be of a universal that one asserts that something holds or does not hold, sometimes of an individual, it follows that[39] if one asserts universally of a universal that something holds[40] or does not hold of it, there will be contrary assertions (examples of what I mean by 'to assert universally of a universal' are 'Every man is white' and 'No man is white'), while when one asserts something of universals but non-universally, the assertions are not contrary, though what is being revealed may be contrary[41] (examples of what I mean by 'to assert non-universally of universals' are 'A man is white' and 'A man is not white':[42] man is a universal but it is not as a universal that one[43] uses it in the assertion – for 'every' signifies not the universal, but that one is asserting universally of the universal).[44] (17^a38–17^b12)

37 Cf. Matthen (1984), 29, 34; Vigo (1997), 7.

38 Cf. the portion of ch. 5 where T 38 is discussed.

39 Following Bonitz (1862/67), III 82–3 and Weidemann (1994/2002), 210, I construct 'οὖν' at 17^b3 with 'ἐπεί' at 17^a38 (cf. *APr.* 1.4, 26^b14–20). My punctuation differs from those of all the editions I consulted (it is close to that suggested by Bonitz (1862/67), III 82–3).

40 At 17^b4 I read 'ὑπάρχει τι' with the main manuscripts, Bekker, Waitz, Dübner, Bonitz (1862/67), III 82, Cooke, Colli, Weidemann (1994/2002), 210, and Zadro. Pacius, Buhle, Weise, and Minio-Paluello read 'ὑπάρχει' with other witnesses.

41 Cf. n. 18 of appendix 3.

42 Recall that Greek has no indefinite article: in 'ἔστι λευκὸς ἄνθρωπος' and 'οὐκ ἔστι λευκὸς ἄνθρωπος', translated as 'A man is white' and 'A man is not white', nothing corresponds to the occurrences of 'a'.

43 The subject of 'χρῆται' (17^b11) must be an understood 'τις': cf. *Cat.* 5, 3^b21–2; *Int.* 10, 20^a13–14; *APr.* 2.19, 66^a26; 27, 70^b30–1; Waitz (1844/46), I 289.

44 In my translation, the English

[a] 'Every' signifies that one is asserting universally of the universal

renders the Greek

T 20 divides into two parts. The first (17^{a}38–17^{b}1) contains the definitions of a universal and of an individual that have already been discussed in section 1 of this chapter. The second part (17^{b}1–12) contains a classification of predicative assertions which is based, first, on the type of object the assertion is about, and, second, on the way in which an assertion can be made about a universal.

Singular vs *general assertions.* Aristotle distinguishes two main kinds of predicative assertions: affirmations (denials) where something is asserted to hold (not to hold) of an individual, and affirmations (denials) where something is asserted to hold (not to hold) of a universal. Assertions of the first kind are singular predicative assertions, those of the second are general predicative assertions.

Universal vs *indeterminate assertions.* Aristotle divides the second kind of predicative assertions, i.e. that of general predicative assertions, into two subordinate kinds. He says that there are two ways of asserting that something holds (does not hold) of a universal: on the one hand, one can *assert universally* that something holds (does not hold) of a universal; on the other, one can *assert non-universally* that something holds (does not hold) of a universal.

A predicative assertion of the first subordinate kind is a universal (affirmative or negative) predicative assertion. For example, by producing an utterance of 'Every man is white' one asserts universally that the universal white holds of the universal man (such an utterance is a universal affirmative predicative assertion), while by producing an utterance of 'No man is white' one asserts universally that the universal white does not hold of the universal man (such an utterance is a universal negative predicative assertion).

[b] τὸ πᾶς σημαίνει ὅτι καθόλου (17^{b}11–12).

[b] is elliptical. The interpretation of [b] on which its rendering by [a] relies is based on the fact that [b] occurs again later in *de Interpretatione*, in chapter 10 at 20^{a}9–10, and on the fact that this later occurrence of [b] is followed shortly by a remark which sheds some light on it:

[c] 'Every' and 'no' additionally signify [προσσημαίνει] nothing other than that one affirms or denies universally of the name [ὅτι καθόλου τοῦ ὀνόματος κατάφησιν ἢ ἀπόφησιν] (20^{a}12–14, cf. 19^{b}32).

On the basis of [c], and on the basis of the fact that in T 20 Aristotle mentions twice (at 17^{b}3–4 and 17^{b}5–6) 'asserting universally' and contrasts it with 'asserting non-universally', which he also mentions twice (at 17^{b}7 and 17^{b}9), [b] can be plausibly taken to mean the same as [a]. While T 20 says that assertions are about *universals*, [c] says that affirmations and denials are about *names*. The two claims are compatible, and probably highlight different aspects of the same situation.

An assertion of the second subordinate kind is an indeterminate[45] (affirmative or negative) predicative assertion. For example, by producing an utterance of 'A man is white' one asserts non-universally that the universal white holds of the universal man (such an utterance is an indeterminate affirmative predicative assertion), while by producing an utterance of 'A man is not white' one asserts non-universally that the universal white does not hold of the universal man (such an utterance is an indeterminate negative predicative assertion).

The following view can then be safely attributed to Aristotle:

[15] A singular affirmative (negative) predicative assertion asserts that the universal signified by its predicate holds (does not hold) of the individual signified by its subject. A universal affirmative (negative) predicative assertion asserts universally that the universal signified by its predicate holds (does not hold) of the universal signified by its subject. An indeterminate affirmative (negative) predicative assertion asserts non-universally that the universal signified by its predicate holds (does not hold) of the universal signified by its subject.

Particular assertions. After discussing universal and indeterminate predicative assertions, Aristotle offers the following characterisation of contradictory pairs where one member is a universal predicative assertion:

T 21 I say that an affirmation signifying the <holding, or failing to hold,> universally is contradictorily opposed to a denial signifying the not <holding, or failing to hold,> universally,[46] e.g. 'Every man is white'–'Not every man is white', 'No man is white'–'Some man is white'. (17^{b}16–20)

In T 21 all universal predicative assertions are described as affirmations: every (affirmative or negative) universal predicative assertion affirms universality. Specifically: a universal affirmative (negative) predicative assertion affirms that it is universally that the universal signified by its predicate holds (fails to hold) of the universal signified by its subject. Again, in T 21 the contradictories of universal predicative assertions (which, following traditional terminology, I call 'particular predicative assertions') are described as denying what is affirmed by the corresponding universal predicative assertions: every (affirmative or negative) particular predicative assertion

[45] It is only in the *Topics* and in the *Prior Analytics* that Aristotle uses 'indeterminate' ('ἀδιόριστος') for sentences of this second subordinate kind: see *Top.* 3.6, 120^{a}6–8; *APr.* 1.1, 24^{a}16–22; 2, 25^{a}5; 4, 26^{a}28–30; 26^{a}32–3; 26^{a}39; 26^{b}23–4; 7, 29^{a}27–8; 14, 33^{a}37; 15, 35^{b}15; 16, 36^{b}12; 18, 38^{a}10–11; 19, 38^{b}36; 20, 39^{b}2; 21, 40^{a}1; 27, 43^{b}14 (cf. 1.5, 27^{b}38; 6, 29^{a}8).

[46] At 17^{b}16–18 I read 'ἀντικεῖσθαι μὲν οὖν κατάφασιν ἀποφάσει λέγω ἀντιφατικῶς τὴν τὸ καθόλου σημαίνουσαν τῇ τὸ οὐ καθόλου'. For this reading and its translation see appendix 3.

denies universality. Specifically: a particular affirmative (negative) predicative assertion denies that the universal signified by its predicate universally fails to hold (holds) of the universal signified by its subject. To summarise, in T 21 Aristotle commits himself to the following view:

[16] A universal affirmative (negative) predicative assertion asserts that the universal signified by its predicate universally holds (universally fails to hold) of the universal signified by its subject. A particular affirmative (negative) predicative assertion asserts that the universal signified by its predicate does not universally fail to hold (does not universally hold) of the universal signified by its subject.

Combinations and divisions of different kinds. In chapter 1 of *de Interpretatione* (16ª9–18 = T 18) Aristotle says that the only thoughts that are either true or false are those which involve joining or separating. He is certainly presupposing that in an affirmative (negative) predicative belief one item is joined with (separated from) one item.[47]

Near the end of chapter 7 Aristotle says:

T 22 Clearly a single affirmation has a single denial. For the denial must deny the same thing as the affirmation affirmed, and away from the same thing, either away from an individual or away from a universal (taken either as a universal or not as a universal).[48] I mean, for example, 'Socrates is white' and 'Socrates is not white'. But if something else is asserted away from anything, or the same thing is asserted away from something else, that will not be the opposite denial, but a different one. The opposite of 'Every man is white' is 'Not every man is white'; of 'Some man is white', 'No man is white'; of 'A man is white', 'A man is not white'.[49] (17ᵇ38–18ª7)

T 22 contains a list of contradictory pairs of predicative assertions. In each of the contradictory pairs listed, the first member is an affirmative predicative assertion while the second member is its contradictory denial: 'Socrates is white'–'Socrates is not white', 'Every man is white'–'Not every man is white', 'Some man is white'–'No man is white', 'A man is white'–'A man is not white'. According to Aristotle, in each of the foregoing affirmative (singular, universal, particular, or indeterminate) predicative assertions the universal white, which is signified by the predicate, is asserted

[47] Cf. n. 15 above and the subsection it pertains to.

[48] At 18ª1 I read 'μὴ ὡς καθόλου' with n and Weidemann (cf. 'οὐχ ὡς καθόλου' at 17ᵇ11). Most editors follow B and read 'ὡς μὴ καθόλου'. The reading 'ὡς μὴ καθόλου' would not anyhow enable one to understand the formula as denoting *particular* rather than *indeterminate* predicative assertions: since the last pair of examples at 18ª6–7 consists of indeterminate predicative assertions, 'ὡς μὴ καθόλου' would also have to denote indeterminate predicative assertions.

[49] Cf. *Int.* 6, 17ª25–37.

'about' the object (the individual Socrates or the universal man) signified by the subject, and in the opposite negative (singular, particular, universal, or indeterminate) predicative assertion the universal white, which is signified by the predicate, is asserted 'away from' the object (the individual Socrates or the universal man) signified by the subject. Considerations advanced in previous subsections allowed one to attribute plausibly to Aristotle, on the one hand, the view that for a universal *p* to be asserted 'about' an item *s* is for *p* to be asserted to be combined with *s* (cf. [13] above), and, on the other, the view that for a universal *p* to be asserted 'away from' an item *s* is for *p* to be asserted to be divided from *s* (cf. [14] above). Therefore Aristotle probably believes that in each of the foregoing affirmative (negative) predicative assertions white, the universal signified by the predicate, is asserted to be combined with (divided from) the item (the individual Socrates or the universal man) signified by the subject.

Aristotle can hardly believe that each of the singular, universal, particular, and indeterminate affirmative (negative) predicative assertions mentioned in T 22 asserts white, which is the universal signified by the predicate, to be combined *in the same way* with (divided *in the same way* from) the object (the individual Socrates or the universal man) signified by the subject. Perhaps Aristotle thinks that the combination (division) asserted by a *universal* affirmative (negative) predicative assertion is different from that asserted by a *particular* (or *indeterminate* or *singular*) affirmative (negative) assertion.[50]

Truth conditions for predicative assertions. The nature of some of the relations of combination and division which according to Aristotle are involved in the truth and the falsehood of predicative assertions can be conjecturally reconstructed on the basis of Aristotle's remarks about contradictory pairs where one member is a universal predicative assertion. These remarks make it plausible to assume that Aristotle would avow something like the following theory (which gives truth conditions for universal, particular, and singular predicative assertions):[51]

[17] An utterance *p* that is a predicative assertion is true when and only when the universal signified by (the utterance that is) its predicate bears a certain relation (of combination or division) to the object

[50] Cf. Miller (1971), 29–32. The idea that affirmations of different types involve combinations of different types appears also in Aquinas (*S. Th.* 1^a, q. 85, a. 5, ad 3, cf. Galluzzo (2000), 229–30), but the types of affirmation contemplated by Aquinas are different from those distinguished in the main text above.

[51] Henceforth I ignore indeterminate predicative assertions.

(a universal or an individual) signified by (the utterance that is) its subject. The relevant relation between the universal signified by the predicate and the object signified by the subject depends on what kind of predicative assertion *p* is. If *p* is a universal (particular) affirmative predicative assertion, then it is true when and only when the universal signified by its predicate is combined with the universal signified by its subject in such a way as universally to hold (not universally to fail to hold) of it. If *p* is a universal (particular) negative predicative assertion, then it is true when and only when the universal signified by its predicate is divided from the universal signified by its subject in such a way as universally to fail to hold (not universally to hold) of it. If *p* is a singular affirmative (negative) predicative assertion, then it is true when and only when the universal signified by its predicate is combined with (divided from) the individual signified by its subject in such a way as to hold of (hold outside) it.[52]

Here is a definition of the relations of combination and division appealed to by [17]:

[18] A universal *u* is combined with a universal *v* in such a way as universally to hold of it when and only when *u* holds of every individual of which *v* holds. A universal *u* is divided from a universal *v* in such a way as universally to fail to hold of it when and only when every individual of which *v* holds is other than every individual of which *u* holds. A universal *u* is combined with a universal *v* in such a way as not universally to fail to hold of it when and only when *u* holds of at least one individual of which *v* holds. A universal *u* is divided from a universal *v* in such a way as not universally to hold of it when and only when at least one individual of which *v* holds is other than every individual of which *u* holds. A universal *u* is combined with an individual *i* in such a way as to hold of it when and only when *u* holds of *i*. A universal *u* is divided from an individual *i* in such a way as to hold outside it when and only when *i* is other than every individual of which *u* holds.

Note that the theory presented in [17] is not one which Aristotle himself would have put forward. For [17] gives the truth conditions for predicative assertions of various types, i.e. it indicates necessary and sufficient conditions for a predicative assertion of a certain type being true at any time;

[52] Appendix 5 offers a rigorous presentation of the theory of truth for predicative assertions of which [17] is merely a sketchy presentation. Appendix 4 discusses the two-place relations to which [17] appeals.

but Aristotle never speaks of truth conditions for assertions (or, for that matter, for bearers of truth or falsehood of other kinds) – he never uses an instance of some schema like 'A universal affirmative predicative assertion is true when and only when ϕ'. Within the Aristotelian tradition, the idea of truth conditions for assertions appears explicitly for the first time in the Middle Ages.[53] For this reason I cautiously said that Aristotle would avow the theory presented in [17].

Different perspectives on affirmations and denials. In *de Interpretatione* 7 Aristotle seems to have two different perspectives on the 'quality' of quantified predicative assertions. In the first perspective, a quantified predicative assertion is affirmative (negative) just in case it asserts that the universal signified by its predicate is combined with (divided from) the universal signified by its subject. Thus, in the first perspective, 'every'- and 'some'-assertions are affirmative, 'no'- and 'not every'-assertions are negative. In the second perspective, a quantified predicative assertion is affirmative (negative) just in case it asserts that it is universally (non-universally) that the universal signified by its predicate holds, or does not hold, of the universal signified by its subject. Thus, in the second perspective, 'every'- and 'no'-assertions are affirmative, 'some'- and 'not every'-assertions are negative.

These two different perspectives are perhaps reflected in the lists of contradictory pairs produced to illustrate some general claims about contradictory opposition. In the list at $18^{a}2$–7 'No man is white' is the *second* member of a contradictory pair. This list is so structured that in each of the contradictory pairs mentioned the first member is affirmative, the second negative. Hence, in this list 'No man is white' counts as negative. In the lists at $17^{b}18$–20 and $18^{a}14$–17 'No man is white' is the *first* member of a contradictory pair. Again, both these lists are so structured that in each of the contradictory pairs mentioned the first member is affirmative, the second negative. Hence, in these lists 'No man is white' counts as affirmative.

5 TRUTH AND THE CATEGORIES

The redundancy claim. In the last part ($1027^{b}29$–$1028^{a}4$) of *Metaphysics* E 4 (= T 7) Aristotle argues that the investigation of beings *qua* beings can ignore what 'is' in the sense of being true. He claims that what 'is' in the

[53] One remarkable example occurs in Buridan's *Sophismata* (see Scott (1977), 45), where the '*causa veritatis*' and the '*requisitum ad veritatem*' of a universal affirmative, universal negative, etc. predicative assertion are discussed. However, recall that already in the third century BC, in the philosophical tradition of Megarians and Stoics, a vibrant discussion was going on about the truth conditions for propositions of certain types (see e.g. S.E. *P.* 2.110–12; *M.* 8.265; 428; D.L. 7. 73–4).

sense of being true 'is a different thing that "is" from the things that "are" in the strict sense' (1027^{b}31), i.e. from the things that 'are' in the senses that correspond to the categories. What are his grounds for this claim?

The existential exegesis. According to one answer – call it 'the existential exegesis' – Aristotle is arguing that the things that 'are' in the senses that correspond to the categories are prior 'in respect of nature'[54] to what 'is' in the sense of being true. That is, the conclusion Aristotle aims for is:

[19] If nothing 'were' in any of the senses that correspond to the categories, nothing would 'be' in the sense of being true.[55]

According to the existential exegesis, Aristotle's argument for [19] depends on two premisses:

[20] Whatever 'is' in the sense of being true is a belief.

[21] A belief joins or separates items that 'are' in the senses that correspond to the categories (i.e. it joins or separates either something that 'is' in the sense appropriate to substances, or something that 'is' in the sense appropriate to qualities, or something that 'is' in a sense appropriate to some other category).

Assume [20] and [21]. Suppose that nothing 'were' in any of the senses that correspond to the categories. Then (by [21]) there would be no beliefs (because there would be nothing for a belief to join or separate). Then (by [20]) nothing would 'be' in the sense of being true. Thus, if nothing 'were' in any of the senses that correspond to the categories, nothing would 'be' in the sense of being true, as [19] claims.

The conceptual exegesis. On the second promising answer to the question asked above – call this 'the conceptual exegesis' – Aristotle is arguing that the categories are prior 'in formula'[56] to truth.[57] That is, the conclusion Aristotle is trying to establish is:

[54] Cf. *Cat.* 12, 14^{a}29–35; *Ph.* 8.7, 260^{b}16–19; *Metaph.* Δ 11, 1019^{a}1–4; Z 1, 1028^{a}31–4; *EE* 1.8, 1217^{b}8–16; 1218^{a}4–5; Ross (1924), I 317; G. E. L. Owen (1960), 171; Cleary (1988), 44–6.

[55] Cf. [Alex. Aphr.] *in Metaph.* 458, 7–9; Ascl. *in Metaph.* 374, 12–16; Aquinas *in Metaph.* 1241 Cathala/Spiazzi; Ross (1924), I 365–6; Apostle (1966), 321–2; Reale (1968/93), I 102; Kirwan (1971/93), 199–200.

[56] Cf. *Ph.* 8.9, 265^{a}22–4; *Metaph.* Δ 11, 1018^{b}30–6; Z 1, 1028^{a}31–6; 13, 1038^{b}27–8; Θ 8, 1049^{b}12–14; M 2, 1077^{b}2–4; Cleary (1988), 42–3.

[57] Cf. Maier (1896/1936), I 36; S. Mansion (1946/76), 236; Owens (1951/78), 411–12; Oehler (1962/85), 178–9; Vigo (1997), 26–7.

[22] The definition of truth mentions the categories.

According to the conceptual exegesis, Aristotle's argument for [22] depends on a definition of truth that mentions the categories. The definition prescribes that a belief should be true when and only when the items thought about are related to one another by that predicative relation of combination which is the category,[58] or by that predicative relation of division which is the category's negative counterpart,[59] which the belief posits them to be related by:

[23] A belief is true when and only when either (it joins a universal *p* with an object *s* by positing that *p* stands to *s* in that predicative relation of combination which is the category of substance, and *p* does stand to *s* in this predicative relation) or (it separates *p* from *s* by positing that *p* stands to *s* in that predicative relation of division which is the negative counterpart of the category of substance, and *p* does stand to *s* in this predicative relation) or (it joins *p* with *s* by positing that *p* stands to *s* in that predicative relation of combination which is the category of quality, and *p* does stand to *s* in this predicative relation) or (it separates *p* from *s* by positing that *p* stands to *s* in that predicative relation of division which is the negative counterpart of the category of quality, and *p* does stand to *s* in this predicative relation) or . . .

If [23] is true, it must also be true that the definition of truth mentions the categories, as [22] claims. Therefore [22] follows from [23], and the argument attributed to Aristotle by the conceptual exegesis is valid.

Assessment of the two interpretations. Two considerations favour the conceptual exegesis.

(i) Priority in respect of nature does not justify leaving aside the study of what 'is' in the sense of being true. Consider: the sea is prior in respect of nature to sharks: if there were no sea there would be no sharks, while it is not

58 On the conceptual exegesis, in E 4 the categories are (not the highest *genera* of what exists, but) predicative relations: the predicative relation linking a kind to its subordinate kinds and its members, the predicative relation linking a quality to the items it holds of, etc. For the categories as predicative relations see *APr.* 1.37, 49^{a}6–9; *APo.* 1.22, 83^{a}18–23; *Top.* 1.9, 103^{b}20–39 (cf. Zeller (1921), 261–3; Wagner (1961/62), 89–91; G. E. L. Owen (1965), 82; Kirwan (1971/93), 141; Stough (1972), 270–1; M. Frede (1981), 32–48; (1983), 16–17; Morrison (1992), 22; Anton (1992), 8–16; Patterson (1995), 38; Smith (1997), 74–5). For the categories as highest *genera* see n. 57 of ch. 3.

59 For the negative predicative relations corresponding to the affirmative predicative relations that are the categories see *APr.* 1.37, 49^{a}6–9; *Ph.* 5.1, 225^{a}20–6 (= *Metaph.* K 11, 1067^{b}25–30); *Metaph.* Θ 10, 1051^{a}34–5; Λ 2, 1069^{b}26–8; N 2, 1089^{a}15–19; 1089^{a}26–7 (cf. Apelt (1891b), 108–9; Sillitti (1968), 476; Berti (1983b), 120–2).

the case that if there were no sharks there would be no sea (indeed, the sea existed before sharks did). But, if one for whatever reason were interested in studying both the sea and sharks, such a priority in respect of nature would not justify leaving aside the study of sharks. On the other hand, priority in formula might be thought to justify leaving aside the study of what 'is' in the sense of being true: once one has shown how the notion of truth is to be reduced to the categories, one might feel justified in leaving aside the study of what 'is' in the sense of being true and concentrate on the categories.

(ii) Aristotle remarks that what 'is' in the incidental sense and what 'is' in the sense of being true 'do not reveal an outside nature of being' (1028^a2). Two interpretations of this remark have been offered. On the first, it means that what 'is' in the incidental sense and what 'is' in the sense of being true are not 'outside the mind';[60] on the second, it means that what 'is' in the incidental sense and what 'is' in the sense of being true are not 'external' to the things that 'are' in the senses that correspond to the categories because they mention them in their definitions.[61] The first interpretation is unacceptable: the charge of not being 'outside the mind' could apply to what 'is' in the sense of being true, but not to what 'is' in the incidental sense (there is no trace in Aristotle of the idea that what 'is' in the incidental sense should be mind dependent).[62] The second interpretation fits well the conceptual exegesis.

Although the conceptual exegesis is more plausible than the existential, I suspect that they are both right. On other occasions on which he claims that what 'is' in a certain sense is prior to what 'is' in another, Aristotle argues that more than one type of priority obtains.[63] Such is probably his intention in this case too: he is probably arguing that the things that 'are' in the senses that correspond to the categories are prior to what 'is' in the sense of being true both *in respect of nature* (as required by the existential exegesis) and *in formula* (as required by the conceptual exegesis).

[60] Cf. Aquinas *in Metaph.* 1243 Cathala/Spiazzi; Schwegler (1847/48), IV 33; Brentano (1862), 14, 23, 38, 131; Ross (1924), I 366; Wilpert (1940), 7–8; Owens (1951/78), 310; de Rijk (1952), 8, 34, 56; Reale (1968/93), III 311; Leszl (1975), 215; Graeser (1978), 444; Vigo (1997), 26. The first interpretation is favoured by the parallel passage in *Metaphysics* K (1065^a21–4), which however is probably not by Aristotle.

[61] Cf. [Alex. Aphr.] *in Metaph.* 458, 18–19; Ascl. *in Metaph.* 374, 18–21; Aquinas *in Metaph.* 1243 Cathala/Spiazzi; Bonitz (1848/49), II 294; Natorp (1888), 192; Maier (1896/1936), I 36; Heidegger (1926), 166–7, 304; Kirwan (1971/93), 200; Viano (1974), 351.

[62] Cf. Viano (1974), 351.

[63] *Metaph.* Z 1, 1028^a31–1028^b2; Θ 8, 1049^b4–1050^b6.

CHAPTER 3

Truth conditions for existential assertions

In chapter 2 I sketched a theory of the truth conditions for predicative assertions which can be plausibly attributed to Aristotle. The goal of the present chapter is to attain the corresponding result for existential assertions: to outline a theory of the truth conditions for existential assertions which captures Aristotle's views concerning this subject. Aristotle concentrates on existential beliefs and assertions of two types: those concerning simple items, which are essences and incorporeal substances (i.e. God and, perhaps, the intellects that move the heavenly spheres), and those concerning material substances.[1]

The first two sections of the chapter focus on existential beliefs and assertions concerning simple items. The main witnesses are the middle part of *Metaphysics* Θ 10 and the beginning and the end of *de Anima* 3.6. Section 1 offers truth conditions for existential beliefs and assertions concerning simple items. Simple items are essences and incorporeal substances, all of which are everlasting, i.e. exist always. It follows that every existential affirmative belief, or assertion, concerning a simple item is always true, and every existential negative belief, or assertion, concerning a simple item is always false. Section 2 addresses a scholarly issue: what does Aristotle have in mind when in *Metaphysics* Θ 10 he speaks of 'non-composite substances'? I defend the traditional interpretation, according to which Aristotle has incorporeal substances in mind.

Section 3 addresses the truth conditions for existential beliefs and assertions concerning material substances. Since most material substances are not everlasting, one can refer to a material substance that once existed but does not exist at the time when the belief, or assertion, is evaluated. It follows that an existential affirmative belief, or assertion, concerning a material substance can be true at one time but false at another (in this respect existential beliefs and assertions concerning material substances differ from those

[1] For 'corporeal', 'incorporeal', 'material', and 'immaterial' see n. 7 of the introduction.

concerning simple items). Material substances are composite items: they are composed of form and matter. Material substances therefore resemble states of affairs, which also are composite items. It follows that existential assertions concerning material substances have a lot in common with predicative assertions, which concern states of affairs. An existential affirmation (denial) concerning a material substance asserts that that substance's form is combined with (divided from) its matter, and is true when and only when the combination (division) in fact obtains.

I EXISTENTIAL ASSERTIONS CONCERNING SIMPLE ITEMS

Predicative vs *existential assertions.* Aristotle contrasts in various ways predicative and existential assertions: he distinguishes 'being simply' (εἶναι ἁπλῶς) from 'being something' (εἶναί τι);[2] he opposes knowing that something exists (e.g. that gods exist) to knowing that something is so-and-so (e.g. that the moon is eclipsed);[3] he sets assertions like 'A man is', 'A man is not', etc. apart from assertions like 'A man is just', 'A man is not just', etc.[4]

From composite to non-composite items. After discussing, in the first part of *Metaphysics* Θ 10 ($1051^{a}34$–$1051^{b}17$ = T2 + T6), true and false beliefs and assertions concerning composite items, in the chapter's central part

[2] *APr.* 1.38, $49^{a}37$–8; *APo.* 2.2, $90^{a}3$–5; $90^{a}9$–11; $90^{a}32$–4; *SE* 5, $166^{b}37$–$167^{a}6$; 25, $180^{a}36$–8; *Ph.* 1.3, $187^{a}5$–6 (f's reading); *Metaph.* Z 1, $1028^{a}30$–1 (with Bostock (1994), 57) (cf. *APo.* 2.1, $89^{b}33$; *Metaph.* Z 4, $1030^{a}25$–6; Maier (1896/1936), II.II 282; Ross (1924), I.LXXXIX; (1949), 610; van Bennekom (1986), 1–2; Zaslawsky (1986), 247; Cellluprica (1987), 169; Charles (2002), 112; Thom (2002), 298). On 'ἁπλῶς'–'τι' see *Int.* 11, $21^{a}18$–33; *APr.* 1.38, $49^{a}27$–8; *Top.* 2.11, $115^{b}11$–35; *Rh.* 2.24, $1402^{a}2$–4. Aristotle also distinguishes 'being simply' from 'being particularly' (εἶναι ἐπὶ μέρους) (see *APo.* 2.2, $89^{b}39$; $90^{a}2$ – cf. *SE* 5, $166^{b}38$; Mignucci (1975b), 231; Goldin (1996), 18–19), 'being' (εἶναι) from 'being *this*' (τοδὶ εἶναι) (see *APo.* 1.10, $76^{b}6$), and 'not being at all' (μὴ εἶναι ὅλως) from 'not being something' (μὴ εἶναί τι) (see *Ph.* 1.3, $186^{b}9$–10). Some commentators (e.g. G. E. L. Owen (1960), 165; Kahn (1966), 249, 263) think that Aristotle's contrast between 'being simply' and 'being something' is not between the existential and the predicative use of 'to be'.

[3] *APo.* 2.1, $89^{b}23$–35; 2, $89^{b}36$–$90^{a}23$; 8, $93^{a}16$–20 (cf. 1.1, $71^{a}26$–7). I am following the traditional interpretation of these passages (cf. Grote (1880), 238; Calogero (1927/68), 29; Ross (1949), 609–10; Bolton (1976), 517; Kahn (1966), 264–5; Miller (1971), 59; Mignucci (1975b), 231; Kahn (1976), 326–7; Hintikka (1986), 85; Demoss/Devereux (1988), 134; Upton (1991), 316; McKirahan (1992), 122–3; Barnes (1994), 203–4; Goldin (1996), 17, 41–2, 52–8; Hintikka (1999), 793–4). For a different (but less convincing) reading see Gómez-Lobo (1980) (criticised by Hintikka (1986), 87–9 and Goldin (1996), 17, 52–8). According to Kahn (1973c), 7, the earliest examples in Greek of existential assertions of the form 'There are T's' are from the period of the Sophists, and they always concern the existence of gods.

[4] *Int.* 10, $19^{b}14$–31. Most commentators regard 'A man is', 'A man is not', etc. as existential assertions, and 'A man is just', 'A man is not just', etc. as predicative assertions (see DuLac (1949), 166; Prior (1955/62), 164–5; Ackrill (1963), 142; Mignucci (1975b), 242; Weidemann (1994/2002), 331–2; Whitaker (1996), 135–7; D. Frede (1998), 89).

(1051^b17–1052^a4) Aristotle addresses true and false thoughts and linguistic expressions concerning non-composite items:

T 23 But then, with regard to non-composite items, what are 'to be' or 'not to be' and truth and falsehood? For they are not composite, so as 'to be' when they are combined and 'not to be' if they are divided, like the log's being white and the diagonal's being incommensurable, nor will truth and falsehood hold still in the same sense as in the case of those. Or, just as truth in the case of these is not the same, so also 'being', but truth and falsehood are – well, to touch and to enunciate is true[5] (for affirmation and enunciation are not the same thing), while to be ignorant is not to touch, for it is not possible to err with regard to the 'what it is' except incidentally. Similarly also with regard to non-composite substances,[6] for it is not possible to err. And they are all in actuality, not in potentiality: for they would come to be and cease to be, but now being itself does not come to be or cease to be (for it ought to come to be from something). Thus, with regard to those items which are just what it is to be something and actualities[7] it is not possible to err, but either to think or not to think: however, with regard to them, one does investigate the 'what it is',[8] whether they are such-and-such[9] or not. By contrast, with 'being' as truth and 'not being' as falsehood, one is true if it is composed, while it is false if it is not composed, the other is if it is a 'being' in this sense, while if it 'is not' in this sense it is not.[10] But truth is thinking of these things, while falsehood does not exist, nor does error, but there is ignorance, which is not

5 At 1051^b23–4 I read 'τὸ μὲν ἀληθὲς ἢ ψεῦδος – τὸ μὲν θιγεῖν καὶ φάναι ἀληθές': punctuation apart, this is the reading handed down by the main manuscripts, presupposed by William of Moerbeke's translation, and printed by Ross and Jaeger. Ps.-Alexander (*in Metaph.* 599, 27) and some more recent manuscripts have 'τὸ μὲν ἀληθὲς τὸ δὲ ψεῦδος, τὸ μὲν θιγεῖν καὶ φάναι ἀληθές', the reading printed by Bekker, Schwegler, Bonitz, and Tredennick, and endorsed by Cassirer (1932), 160. Christ's extensive emendation ('τὸ μὲν ἀληθὲς [ἢ ψεῦδος τὸ μὲν] θιγεῖν καὶ φάναι [ἀληθές]') is endorsed by several translators and commentators (e.g. Bonitz (1890), 211; Maier (1896/1936), I 7; Calogero (1927/68), 24). The initial 'μέν' at 1051^b23 is answered by the 'δέ' at 1051^b33 (cf. Ross (1924), II 276; Engelhardt (1953), 40).

6 At 1051^b27 I read 'τὰς μὴ συνθετὰς οὐσίας' with A^b and all the editions I consulted. Variants: 'τὰς συνθετὰς οὐσίας' (J), 'τὰς συνθέτους οὐσίας' (E's first hand, 'μὴ' is added by the second hand). William of Moerbeke's translation also presupposes the absence of 'μὴ'. The readings 'τὰς συνθετὰς οὐσίας' and 'τὰς συνθέτους οὐσίας' are difficult to square with the following 'They are all in actuality, not in potentiality . . .' (1051^b28–30).

7 At 1051^b31 I read 'ἐνέργειαι' with Ross. All witnesses and most editors read 'ἐνεργείᾳ'.

8 At 1051^b32 I read 'τὸ τί ἐστι ζητεῖται' with E, J, and most editions. Christ instead reads 'τὸ ἔστι ζητεῖται' with A^b.

9 At 1051^b32–3 I read 'εἰ τοιαῦτά ἐστιν' with all the main manuscripts and most editions. Ps.-Alexander (*in Metaph.* 600, 34) relies on the reading 'οὐκ εἰ τοιαῦτά ἐστιν', which is adopted by some editors and commentators (Bonitz (1848/49), II 410–1; (1890), 211; Heidegger (1925/26), 177; von Fragstein (1967), 147). For a defence of the reading of the main manuscripts see Maier (1896/1936), I 21; Ross (1924), II 278; Berti (1990), 102; (1992), 85–6; (1993), 22–3; (2000), 14–15.

10 At 1051^b35–1052^a1 I adopt Christ's punctuation: 'εἴπερ ὂν οὕτως, ἔστιν, εἰ δὲ μὴ οὕτως, οὐκ ἔστιν'. Alternative punctuations: 'εἴπερ ὄν, οὕτως ἔστιν, εἰ δὲ μὴ οὕτως, οὐκ ἔστιν' (Ross and most editions); 'εἴπερ ὂν οὕτως ἔστιν, εἰ δὲ μὴ οὕτως, οὐκ ἔστιν' (Bonitz).

like blindness: for blindness is as if one completely lacked the intellectual faculty. (1051^{b}17–1052^{a}4)

Compare the following excerpt of *de Anima* 3.6:

T 24 The thinking of indivisible items concerns items about which there is no falsehood. By contrast, where both falsehood and truth are present there is already some sort of composition of thoughts as if they were a single one – as, in the words of Empedocles, 'where neckless heads of many sprouted' afterwards they were composed by Love, so here too these items which were apart are composed, e.g. incommensurable and diagonal – and, if the thinking concerns the past or the future, by composing and thinking in addition of time. For falsehood always concerns composition: for, even if of something white it thinks that it is not white, it composes non-white.[11] (430^{a}26–430^{b}3)

An affirmation[12] is something about something, as too is a denial,[13] and each one is either true or false. By contrast, not all intellect is such, but that which is of the 'what it is' according to the 'what it was to be' is true, and it is not something about something. However, just as the seeing of a special object is true, but seeing that the white thing is a man or not is not always true, so also with what is without matter. (430^{b}26–31)

T 23 and T 24 are close: T 23's claim that 'it is not possible to err with regard to the "what it is" except incidentally' (1051^{b}25–6) corresponds to T 24's 'intellect [. . .] which is of the "what it is" according to the "what it was to be"' and 'is true' (430^{b}28); T 23's 'non-composite items' (1051^{b}17)

[11] At 430^{b}2–3 I adopt the reading 'ἂν τὸ λευκὸν μὴ λευκὸν τὸ μὴ λευκὸν συνέθηκεν', attested almost unanimously by the manuscripts and printed by most recent editions. Several editors and commentators (Trendelenburg (1833), 92, 502; Roeper (1852), 324, 768; Torstrik (1862), 93; Vahlen (1872), 427–8; Trendelenburg (1877), 84, 414; Maier (1896/1936), I 25; Theiler (1959), 60, 145; Ross (1961), *ad loc.*; Oehler (1962/85), 156) emend the passage.

[12] For 'φάσις' and 'ἀπόφασις' meaning 'affirmation' and 'denial' see Bonitz (1870), 813^{a}19–23. For a different use of 'φάσις' see *Int.* 4, 16^{b}27; 5, 17^{a}17; *de An.* 3.7, 431^{a}8; *Metaph.* Θ 10, 1051^{b}25 (on which cf. n. 52 below and the portion of the main text it pertains to).

[13] At 430^{b}26–7 I read 'ἔστι δ' ἡ μὲν φάσις τι κατά τινος, ὥσπερ καὶ ἡ ἀπόφασις' with Ross (cf. Torstrik (1862), 196–8; Calogero (1927/68), 22–3; Hamlyn (1968/93), 145; Cashdollar (1973), 161; Horn (1994), 115–16). The words 'ὥσπερ καὶ' are only in W: the remaining manuscripts have 'ὥσπερ'. Moreover, 'ἀπόφασις' is Torstrik's emendation: all manuscripts have 'κατάφασις'. The corruption of 'ΩΣΠΕΡΚΑΙΗΑΠΟΦΑΣΙΣ' into 'ΩΣΠΕΡΗΚΑΤΑΦΑΣΙΣ' could easily have occurred.

The text handed down by most manuscripts could be defended if 'φάσις' could be taken to mean 'predicative assertion' (one would then take 'ὥσπερ' to mean 'as for instance': for this usage cf. *APo.* 2.10, 93^{b}36; 11, 94^{b}32; 95^{a}1; 16, 98^{a}36–7; Pacius (1611), 388; Bullinger (1882), 52; Horn (1994), 115–16). Some commentators (e.g. Torstrik (1862), 196; Rodier (1900), II 488; Bodéüs (1993), 233–4) claim that Aristotle elsewhere uses 'φάσις' to mean 'predicative assertion', but their evidence (*Int.* 12, 21^{b}19) is far from clear cut.

correspond to T 24's 'indivisible items' (430^a26).[14] I shall assume that T 23 and T 24 expound essentially the same theory. The bulk of the present section is dedicated to explaining what this theory is.

Beliefs and assertions concerning non-composite items as existential beliefs and assertions. In the central part of Θ 10 (1051^b17–1052^a4 = T 23) Aristotle continues the train of thought of the chapter's first part (1051^a34–1051^b17 = T 2 + T 6): he extends to non-composite items his approach to composite items. Recall:[15] an affirmative (negative) belief, or assertion, concerning a *composite* item posits that this composite item 'is' in the sense of being true ('is not' in the sense of being false), and it is true when and only when the composite item in fact 'is' in the sense of being true ('is not' in the sense of being false). Now, analogously, an affirmative (negative) belief, or assertion, concerning a *non-composite* item posits that this non-composite item 'is' in the sense of being true ('is not' in the sense of being false), and it is true when and only when the non-composite item 'is' in the sense of being true ('is not' in the sense of being false). But there is a difference. For a composite item (like a state of affairs) 'to be' in the sense of being true is for it to be combined, i.e. for its components to be reciprocally combined. However, since a non-composite item lacks components, for it 'to be' in the sense of being true *cannot* be for its components to be reciprocally combined – it must be something different. Aristotle's view seems to be that for a non-composite item 'to be' in the sense of being true is simply to exist, i.e. 'to be there'.[16] This is what Aristotle seems to say near the end of T 23, as the following expansion of my translation shows:

> With 'being' as truth and 'not being' as falsehood, one [a composite item] is true if it is composed, while it is false if it is not composed, the other [a non-composite item] is [exists] if it is a 'being' in this sense [if it 'is' in the sense of being true],[17] while if it 'is not' in this sense [if it 'is not' in the sense of being false] it is not [does not exist]. (1051^b33–1052^a1)

It follows that beliefs and assertions concerning non-composite items are existential beliefs and assertions. Note that this does not imply that every

[14] Cf. the 'simple items' of *Metaph.* E 4, 1027^b27–8.

[15] I am summarising some results of sect. 1 of ch. 2.

[16] Sometimes Aristotle uses 'true' and its cognates to say of something that it exists or that it is real: see *Ph.* 1.8, 191^a25; 8.8, 263^a18; *Cael.* 1.5, 271^b6; 271^b9; 3.1, 298^b13; *Metaph.* A 3, 983^b3; 7, 988^a20; α 1, 993^a30; 993^b17; *MM* 1.1, 1182^a29; *EE* 1.4, 1215^b2; *Rh.* 1.7, 1364^b9; *Protr.* fr. 73 Gigon 304^a20; 304^b13; 310^a27; 310^b14; 310^b20 (= Iamb. *Protr.* 38, 2; 39, 9; 54, 4; 55, 2; 55, 7). Some commentators (e.g. Wilpert (1940), 5) assume that at *Metaph.* α 1, 993^b19–31 'true' and 'truth' mean 'existent' and 'existence', but Bärthlein (1972), 25–33 shows that such an interpretation is questionable.

[17] Cf. *Metaph.* E 4, 1027^b29; 1027^b31; Wilpert (1940), 12; de Rijk (1952), 23.

existential belief or assertion should concern a non-composite item: there may well be existential beliefs and assertions concerning composite items.[18]

An example of an existential assertion concerning a non-composite item. Suppose that for Aristotle the universal man is a non-composite item. The truth conditions for the existential assertion 'Man exists' will then resemble those described by this passage from *Categories* 12:

T 25 Among things which convert as to implication of being, what is in whatever way a cause of the being of the other might reasonably be called 'prior' by nature.[19] And that there are some such cases is clear: for that man is converts as to implication of being with the true sentence about it (for if man is, the sentence whereby we say that man is is true, and this is sure to convert: for if the sentence whereby we say that man is is true, then man is), but the true sentence is in no way the cause of the object's being, while the object seems somehow the cause of the sentence's being true: for it is because the object is or is not that a sentence is called true or false. (14^b11–22)

The interpretation of T 25 raises at least three questions. What do the occurrences of 'object' at 14^b19–21 denote? How should the crucial occurrences of 'to be' be understood? What does the occurrence of 'it' in 'the true sentence about it' (14^b15) refer to? The foregoing subsection's considerations suggest the following (reciprocally connected) answers: the occurrences of 'object' at 14^b19–21 denote those (composite or non-composite) objects that are crucial to the truth or falsehood of assertions concerning them; the crucial occurrences of 'to be' should be understood as expressing the 'being' in the sense of being true discussed in *Metaphysics* Θ 10; the occurrence of 'it' in 'the true sentence about it' (14^b15) refers to the species man. Suppose these answers are correct. Then in T 25 Aristotle first claims that 'among things which convert as to implication of being, what is in whatever way a cause of the being of the other might reasonably be called "prior" by nature' (14^b11–13). He then illustrates this claim by mentioning the species man and the assertion 'Man is': (i) the species man 'is' in the sense of being true, i.e. exists, when and only when the assertion 'Man is' is true (cf. 14^b14–18), (ii) the fact that the assertion 'Man is' is true is in no way the cause of the

[18] My interpretation of Θ 10's central part (= T 23) derives from Brentano: see his (1874/1925), II 54–5; (1889), 20–1; (1914), 164; (1915b), 136; (n.d.), 191. Brentano's interpretation was forgotten by most twentieth-century commentators (there are exceptions: see Calogero (1927/68), 25, 27–9; von Ivánka (1932), 19; Sillitti (1966), 321–4; Sadun Bordoni (1994), 74; Fattal (1996), 434–5, 439–40). In his (1862), 26–7 Brentano favoured a different exegesis of T 23, more in line with the Scholastic tradition (cf. n. 58 below with the paragraph it pertains to; Krell (1975), 82).

[19] This priority 'by nature' ('φύσει') seems different from the priority 'by nature and being' ('κατὰ φύσιν καὶ οὐσίαν') of *Metaph.* Δ 11, 1019^a2–4 (which excludes 'conversion as to implication of being').

fact that the species man 'is' in the sense of being true (cf. $14^{b}18$–19), but (iii) the fact that the species man 'is' in the sense of being true is somehow the cause of the fact that the assertion 'Man is' is true (cf. $14^{b}19$–20). Finally, Aristotle makes a general claim which backs up points (ii) and (iii) of his example: it is because the object 'is' in the sense of being true or 'is not' in the sense of being false that an assertion is true or false, not vice versa (cf. $14^{b}21$–2).[20]

All the non-composite items mentioned in Θ 10 exist always. The non-composite items mentioned by Aristotle in *Metaphysics* Θ 10 are essences and 'non-composite substances'.[21] For Aristotle, essences are natural kinds.[22] Moreover, several passages show that in Aristotle's view at least some natural kinds exist always.[23] So Aristotle can be plausibly credited with the view that essences exist always. As I shall show (in section 2 of this chapter), the 'non-composite substances' mentioned in Θ 10 are probably incorporeal substances, i.e. God and (perhaps) the intellects that move the heavenly spheres. In Aristotle's view, incorporeal substances also exist always. So Aristotle can be plausibly credited with the view that all the non-composite items he mentions in Θ 10 exist always.

Affirmative beliefs and assertions concerning non-composite items are always true. In an earlier subsection I suggested that for a non-composite item 'to be' in the sense of being true is for it to exist. In the last subsection I argued that all the non-composite items mentioned in Θ 10 exist always. If I am right, then all the non-composite items mentioned in Θ 10 always 'are' in the sense of being true. This has two important consequences: first, every *affirmative* belief, or assertion, concerning one of these non-composite items is always true (because it concerns an item that always 'is' in the sense of being true); second, every *negative* belief, or assertion, concerning one of these non-composite items is always false (again because it concerns an item that always 'is' in the sense of being true). I take it that Aristotle is in fact committed to these consequences.

The infallibility of affirmative beliefs concerning non-composite items. As we have just seen, *Metaphysics* Θ 10 can be plausibly taken to commit Aristotle

[20] I disagree with those commentators (Hamlyn (1962), 194; Nuchelmans (1973), 33–4; de Rijk (1987), 34–5; Gaskin (1998), 42–5) who take T 25 to be dealing exclusively with states of affairs.

[21] For essences see $1051^{b}25$–6; $1051^{b}30$–2 (cf. *de An.* 3.6, $430^{b}27$–31; *Metaph.* E 4, $1027^{b}27$–8). For 'non-composite substances' see $1051^{b}27$. In the central part of *de Anima* 3.6 ($430^{b}6$–26) Aristotle discusses non-composite items of other kinds.

[22] Cf. n. 6 of the introduction.

[23] See n. 10 of ch. 2 and the passage it pertains to.

to the claim that every affirmative belief concerning a non-composite item is always true. It is probably this everlasting truth of affirmative beliefs concerning non-composite items that Aristotle has in mind when in Θ 10 he remarks (i) that 'truth is touching' (1051^{b}24), (ii) that 'to be ignorant is not to touch, for it is not possible to err with regard to the "what it is" except incidentally' (1051^{b}25–6), and (iii) that 'truth is thinking of these items' (1052^{a}1). In these three remarks, Aristotle focuses on an essential aspect of affirmative beliefs concerning non-composite items, and he claims that this essential aspect of such beliefs guarantees their everlasting truth. (Aristotle leaves unmentioned the everlasting falsehood of negative beliefs and assertions concerning non-composite items.) Here are some detailed comments on Aristotle's three remarks.

(i) 'Touching' is an essential aspect of every affirmative belief concerning a non-composite item: every such belief must 'touch' the non-composite item it concerns.[24] But this guarantees that the affirmative belief in question should be always true (because the non-composite item it concerns always exists, and therefore always 'is' in the sense of being true). In this sense, 'truth is touching' (1051^{b}24): the everlasting truth of an affirmative belief concerning a non-composite item is guaranteed by that essential aspect of it which is its touching its non-composite item.

(ii) As we have just seen, 'touching' is an essential aspect of every affirmative belief concerning a non-composite item. Not to touch is to be ignorant,[25] i.e. to be in the blank condition of lacking any object to think about.[26] When one has a belief about a 'what it is', i.e. an essence, which is a non-composite item, one cannot err 'except incidentally' (1051^{b}26), i.e.

[24] For the thought–touch comparison cf. *de An.* 2.9, 421^{a}19–26 (where Aristotle claims that the accuracy of touch is proportional to that of thought, cf. Freeland (1992), 234); 3.3, 427^{b}4; 8, 432^{a}1–3; *Metaph.* Λ 7, 1072^{b}20–1; Pl. *Phd.* 79*d*6; *Tht.* 186*d*3–4; 190*c*6–7; 190*d*9–10; 209*a*8; *Smp.* 212*a*4–5; *Phdr.* 273*a*4; *Ti.* 37*a*6; 52*b*2; *Lg.* XII 965*b*4; 969*b*6; Speus. fr. 30 Lang = fr. 35 Isnardi (= Procl. *in Euc.* 179, 18); Thphr. *Metaph.* 9^{b}13–6 (with van Raalte (1993), 456–9); Plot. I, I, 9, 12–14; 5, 3, 10, 43; 5, 3, 17, 24–7; Ross (1923), 25; Rosen (1961), 129–32. Aristotle also compares thought with sight (*Top.* 1.17, 108^{a}11; *de An.* 3.5, 430^{a}14–25; *Metaph.* α 1, 993^{b}9–11; Θ 10, 1052^{a}1–4; *EN* 1.4, 1096^{b}28–9), hearing (*APo.* 1.10, 76^{b}36–8), and perception (*de An.* 1.5, 410^{a}25–6; 3.3, 427^{a}17–29; 4, 429^{a}13–18; 429^{a}23–429^{b}5; 7, 431^{a}8; 8, 431^{b}26–432^{a}3; *EN* 6.12, 1143^{b}5, cf. Pl. *Tht.* 202*b*5–6).

[25] See 'ἀγνοεῖν' at 1051^{b}25 and 'ἄγνοια' at 1052^{a}2, cf. 'μὴ νοεῖν' at 1051^{b}32.

[26] Cf. Maier (1896/1936), I 7, 19–20; Ross (1924), II 279; De Corte (1934), 238; Joachim (1948), 26; Whitaker (1996), 29. At 1052^{a}2–4 Aristotle says that ignorance is unlike blindness because blindness would correspond to having no intellect. The fact that he feels the need to emphasise that ignorance and blindness are different indicates that in his view they resemble each other in important respects – otherwise he would not think that somebody could be tempted to confuse them. The resemblance is probably that ignorance is like not seeing when one can see (in this respect ignorance is unlike blindness, which is the incapacity to see). But the analogy of ignorance with not seeing when one can see suggests that ignorance should be the 'blank' condition of lacking any object to think about. A kindred usage of 'ignorance' was probably displayed in a passage of Aristotle's lost work *On Opposites* reported or summarised in Simplicius' commentary on the *Categories* (390, 19–25 < fr. 625 Gigon 726^{b}9–19).

except insofar as the essence is treated as 'being incidental to' something or something is treated as 'being incidental to' it,[27] i.e. insofar as the essence is treated as a predicate, i.e. as holding of something, or as a subject, i.e. as having something holding of it.[28] The following considerations support this interpretation of the restrictive clause 'except incidentally' at 1051^{b}26.[29]

(ii.i) At the end of *de Anima* 3.6 Aristotle says:

T 26 An affirmation is something about something, as too is a denial, and each one is either true or false. By contrast, not all intellect is such, but that which is of the 'what it is' according to the 'what it was to be' is true, and it is not something about something. However, just as the seeing of a special object is true, but seeing that the white thing is a man or not is not always true, so also with what is without matter. (430^{b}26–31 < T 24)

A '"what it is" according to the "what it was to be"' (430^{b}28) is an essence. Since essences do not contain matter, the phrase 'what is without matter' (430^{b}30–1) probably refers to essences.[30] Hence, T 26 compares the truth or falsehood of a belief concerning an essence with the truth or falsehood of a perception of a special object.

[27] Aristotle sometimes explains what it is for a certain event to happen 'incidentally' by appealing to the circumstance that in it something 'is incidental to' something: see *APo.* 1.19, 81^{b}24–9; 22, 83^{a}1–23; *Top.* 2.3, 110^{b}17–25; *Ph.* 5.1, 224^{a}21–3; *Metaph.* A 1, 981^{a}18–20.

[28] Aristotle sometimes uses 'to be incidental to' ('συμβεβηκέναι' + dat.) as equivalent to 'to be predicated of': see *Top.* 2.3, 110^{b}24–5 (with Brunschwig (1967), 141–2); *SE* 5, 166^{b}28–36 (with Hamblin (1970), 84–6 and Dorion (1995), 233); 6, 168^{a}40–168^{b}2; *PA* 1.5, 645^{a}36–645^{b}2; *Metaph.* A 1, 981^{a}18–20; Z 5, 1030^{b}20–1; N 1, 1088^{a}17–18.

[29] Cf. Fonseca (1577/89), III 668; Suarez (1597), XXVIII; Maurus (1668), IV 480–1; Oehler (1962/85), 214–15; Kessler (1976), 180; Berti (1978), 149; Seidl (1989/91), II 493; Berti (1993), 24–5; Vigo (1997), 39–40; Berti (2000), 12; Charles (2000), 136. Other commentators interpret differently the restrictive clause 'except incidentally' at 1051^{b}26.

According to some (e.g. [Alex. Aphr.] *in Metaph.* 600, 16–17; [Phlp.] *in Metaph.* 39va; Bonitz (1848/49), II 411; Grote (1880), 618; von Fragstein (1967), 147, 148), 'incidentally' here means 'in an improper sense' (cf. *Cat.* 6, 5^{a}38–5^{b}10; *Ph.* 2.3, 195^{b}3–4; *Metaph.* Δ 2, 1014^{a}7–8; I 1, 1052^{a}17–19; Waitz (1844/46), I 442–3). Aristotle is therefore saying that it is only in an improper sense of 'to err' that one can say that it is possible to err about the 'what it is'.

According to other commentators (e.g. Aquinas *in Metaph.* 1908 Cathala/Spiazzi; Maier (1896/1936), I 21; Ross (1924), II 277; Keeler (1932), 245–6; De Corte (1934), 239; Tricot (1966), II 524; Grayeff (1974), 209), 'incidentally' here means 'as a coincidence'. Aristotle is saying that error about a simple item may coincidentally occur because the simple item itself (although simple insofar as not exhibiting predicative composition) is complex insofar as composed of its *genus* and its *differentia*: an error can occur in the attempt to explain the simple item in a definition, but the error cannot be imputed to the thought whereby one 'touches' the simple item, and it is therefore 'incidental' to this thought.

Yet other commentators (e.g. Grayeff (1974), 209; Volkmann-Schluck (1979), 272–4; Burnyeat *et al.* (1984), 159) offer different interpretations which cannot be discussed here.

[30] Cf. Hamlyn (1968/93), 145; Movia (1979), 387; Fattal (1996), 430. Other commentators (e.g. [Phlp.] *in de An.* 557, 9–10 Hayduck; Aquinas *in de An.* 762 Pirotta) take the phrase 'what is without matter' (430^{b}30–1) to refer to intellects, which have no bodily organ (see *de An.* 3.4, 429^{a}18–27), yet others (e.g. Pacius (1611), 388) take it to refer both to intellects and to essences.

Since T 26 compares the truth or falsehood of a belief concerning an essence with the truth or falsehood of a perception of a special object, it is worthwhile considering here, albeit briefly, Aristotle's views on the truth or falsehood of perceptions of special objects. In *de Anima* 2.6 (418^{a}7–25) Aristotle distinguishes several kinds of objects of perception: first he separates objects perceptible 'in themselves' from objects perceptible 'incidentally'; then, within objects perceptible in themselves, he separates 'special' from 'common' objects. A special object can be perceived by only one perceptual faculty. Thus, colours are special objects of perception because they can be perceived by only one perceptual faculty, i.e. sight; similarly with sounds with respect to hearing, odours with respect to smell, flavours with respect to taste, and properties of temperature and solidity with respect to touch.[31] A common object is properly perceived by two or more perceptual faculties[32] collaborating with one another (for this reason it is also described as an object of the faculty of perception as a whole, or 'common perception').[33] Movement, rest, number, figure, and magnitude are among Aristotle's examples of common objects of perception.[34] In a perception of an incidental object one perceives something on the basis of an 'interpretation' of a special object of perception, which one perceives in the strict sense.[35] For example, suppose one sees an instance of whiteness, which is a special object of perception, and 'interprets' it in such a way that one can be described as seeing Diares' son: Diares' son is then an incidental object of perception. (The expressions 'interpretation' and 'interprets' here must be handled with care because the operation involved in perceptions of the sort described is often – though not always – subconscious, while 'interpretation' and 'interprets' tend to be reserved for conscious operations.)[36] Aristotle thinks that some perceptions are true, other false. This view could seem very strange if Aristotle thought that perceptions do not have propositional content. However, Aristotle probably thinks that at least

31 *De An.* 2.6, 418^{a}9–14; *Somn. Vig.* 2, 455^{a}12–15.

32 In several passages (*de An.* 2.6, 418^{a}9–11; 418^{a}16–20; 3.1, 425^{a}27–30; 425^{b}4–11) Aristotle claims that common objects are perceived by *all* perceptual faculties. On one occasion (*Sens.* 4, 442^{b}4–10) he qualifies this claim by saying that common objects are perceived by sight and touch.

33 Cf. Modrak (1987), 63–5, 68.

34 *De An.* 2.6, 418^{a}17–18; 3.1, 425^{a}15–16; *Mem.* 1. 450^{a}9–12; *Insomn.* 1. 458^{b}4–6.

35 Cf. *de An.* 2.6, 418^{a}24–5.

36 In five passages Aristotle uses 'incidental' and 'to be incidental' in talking of perceptions of incidental objects: *de An.* 2.3, 414^{b}6–11; 2.6, 418^{a}8–25; 3.1, 425^{a}13–425^{b}11; 3.3, 428^{b}18–30; *Metaph.* Γ 5, 1010^{b}14–26. Aristotle, however, discusses perceptions of incidental objects also elsewhere: *de An.* 3.6, 430^{b}29–31; *Insomn.* 1. 458^{b}31–3. Other relevant passages are *APr.* 1.27, 43^{a}33–6 and *Metaph.* M 10, 1087^{a}19–20. My interpretation of Aristotle's views on perceptions of incidental objects is close to Modrak (1987), 69–71, 77.

some perceptions do have propositional content. For example, in *de Anima* 2.6 he says that a perception of a special object 'does not err that there is colour nor that there is sound' (418^a15).[37] Again, in *de Anima* 3.3 he says that sight 'is not mistaken that there is whiteness' (428^b21).[38] Aristotle's position is very reasonable: a dog having a perceptual experience involving whiteness can be appropriately described as perceiving that there is whiteness – after all, the purpose of perception is to inform the animal of what is there in the environment. Even when Aristotle expresses himself as if he were saying that a perception is of a 'thing' (e.g. of whiteness), he probably means that one is perceiving that the 'thing' is there.[39] Aristotle believes that perceptions of objects of different types are exposed to error in different degrees: in his view, almost every perception of a special object is true,[40] while perceptions of common and incidental objects are relatively often false.[41] Aristotle probably thinks that perceptions of special objects are false only on those rare occasions when their circumstances are abnormal, e.g. when the perceptual faculty is biased because of a recent intense perception or damaged by illness, or when the medium has distorting effects.[42] Aristotle's main reason for thinking that almost all perceptions of special objects are true is probably that these perceptions are, or are based on, processes of assimilation which in ordinary circumstances are accurate.[43] According to some commentators,[44] Aristotle thinks that perceptions of special objects

[37] Here I take the two occurrences of 'ὅτι' as declarative and I understand an existential 'ἔστι' both after 'χρῶμα' and after 'ψόφος'.

[38] Here I take 'ὅτι' as declarative and I understand an existential 'ἔστι' after 'λευκόν': cf. Everson (1995), 268; Cassin (1996), 286–7; Fattal (1996), 434, 439; Everson (1997), 190.

[39] Cf. Cashdollar (1973), 161–7; Ben-Zeev (1984), 119, 122; Sorabji (1992), 196–203; (1996), 314–15; Cassin (1996), 286–8; Birondo (2001), 62–4. According to other commentators (e.g. Phlp. *in de An.* 88, 68–72 Verbeke) Aristotle thinks that perceptions do not have propositional content, which requires some faculty superior to perception. Note that someone who denies that perceptions might have propositional content could still claim that perceptions were true or false (cf. Block (1961), 8; Ben-Zeev (1984), 119; Caston (1996), 44–5; Charles (2000), 121): one could claim that a vision of whiteness is true just in case the object from which it is produced is white, and, in general, endorse every instance of the schema 'A perception of Φness is true just in case the object from which it is produced is Φ'.

[40] *De An.* 3.3, 428^b18–19. Elsewhere (*de An.* 2.6, 418^a11–16; 3.3, 427^b11–12; 6, 430^b29; *Sens.* 4, 442^b8–10; *Metaph.* Γ 5, 1010^b1–26) Aristotle is more confident – he simply says that perceptions of special objects are true. Once (*de An.* 3.3, 428^a11) he even says that perceptions 'are always true' (is he using 'perception' as a success-expression?).

[41] *De An.* 3.3, 428^b19–25, cf. 2.6, 418^a8–25; 3.1, 425^a30–425^b4; 3, 428^b25–30; 6, 430^b29–31; *Sens.* 4, 442^b8–10; *Insomn.* 1, 458^b31–3; *Metaph.* Γ 5, 1010^b14–26.

[42] Cf. *de An.* 2.9, 421^a9–26; 10, 422^b5–10; 3.4, 429^a29–429^b5; *Insomn.* 2, 459^b5–23; *PA* 2.2, 648^b12–17; *GA* 5.1, 779^b12–780^a25; *Pr.* 31.7, 958^a24–7; 11, 958^b11–15; *Metaph.* Γ 5, 1010^b1–26; 6, 1011^a25–1011^b1; K 6, 1062^b35–1063^a10; *EN* 3.6, 1113^a25–31; 10.2, 1173^b20–5; Kenny (1967), 193; Long (1981), 101; Ben-Zeev (1984), 118; Vasiliou (1996), 127; Charles (2000), 118–19.

[43] Cf. Burnyeat (2002), 45.

[44] E.g. Irwin (1988), 314.

are infallible because an object must have the perceptual quality with which it appears to a perceiver. This interpretation must be wrong: otherwise Aristotle could not avoid the consequence (which, however, he rejects) that perceptions of common objects also are infallible because an object must have the perceptual quality with which it appears to a perceiver.[45] Perceptions of common objects are often false because they require the collaboration of different perceptual faculties: this collaboration can easily go wrong.[46] Perceptions of incidental objects are often false because the 'interpretation' of the special object perceived is flawed. In terms of Aristotle's example, one's perception of Diares' son may well be false because one's 'interpretation' of the instance of whiteness one sees is flawed: Diares' son is not incidentally identical to ('incidental to') the individual that has the whiteness one sees.

There are two aspects to T 26's comparison of the truth or falsehood of a belief concerning an essence with the truth or falsehood of a perception of a special object: first, as almost every perception concerning a special object (e.g. a case of seeing that there is whiteness) is true, so every belief concerning an essence is true; second, as one's perception of an incidental object can be false because the object one perceives incidentally is not incidentally identical to the individual which has the special object one perceives (e.g. one's perception of Diares' son can be false because Diares' son is not incidentally identical to the individual that has the whiteness one sees), so can one falsely think that a certain essence holds of something.[47] Since T 26 is closely connected to the central part of *Metaphysics* Θ 10, T 26's comparison endows with plausibility the suggested interpretation of the restrictive clause 'except incidentally' at 1051^{b}26, i.e. the interpretation according to which this restrictive clause is saying that error with regard to an essence is possible insofar as the essence is treated as holding of something or as having something holding of it.

(ii.ii) A few lines after saying that 'it is not possible to err with regard to the "what it is" except incidentally' (1051^{b}25–6), Aristotle says:

> With regard to those items which are just what it is to be something and actualities it is not possible to err, but either to think or not to think: however, with regard to them, one does investigate the 'what it is', whether they are such-and-such or not. (1051^{b}30–3)

[45] Cf. Block (1961), 3; Vasiliou (1996), 115, 117. [46] *Sens.* 4, 442^{b}4–10, cf. Modrak (1987), 79.
[47] Cf. Phlp. *in de An.* 88, 66–78 Verbeke; [Phlp.] *in de An.* 553, 30–554, 2; 557, 1–6 Hayduck; Block (1961), 2; Moreau (1961), 24; Cashdollar (1973), 161–2, 172; Movia (1979), 313, 387; Charles (2000), 135–6, 138.

This remark makes it plausible to assume that one of the enterprises concerning essence for which Aristotle allows 'incidental' error should be the inquiry into the 'what it is' of 'those items which are just what it is to be something', i.e. the search for a definition of an essence.[48] A definition of an essence is a predicative assertion where the subject is the *definiendum* and the predicate is the *definiens*.[49] It is because of this predicative structure of definitions that the error concerning essence which sometimes occurs in them is described by Aristotle as 'incidental'. One remarkable aspect of Aristotle's position is that having a true existential belief about an essence does not automatically enable one to formulate correctly its definition: despite having a true belief about the essence, one must investigate its essential characteristics (its 'what it is'), and this investigation may well result in a falsehood. This aspect of Aristotle's position fits well with his choice of the image of touching: as touching a thing falls short of grasping it, so referring to an essence in a true existential belief about it does not automatically enable one to define that essence. It is worthwhile observing that this aspect of Aristotle's position seems correct – philosophers keep discussing and disagreeing about the essential characteristics of many items.[50] I suspect, however, that the search for an essence's definition is only one of several cases where 'incidental' error concerning the essence is possible: Aristotle's position on this issue is probably that an 'incidental' error concerning an essence occurs whenever the essence is somehow involved in a false predicative belief (e.g. if I falsely believe that every man is uneducated then I make an 'incidental' error about the essence man, with regard to which I have a true existential belief). Aristotle's mention of the search for the definition of an essence immediately after his mention of an existential belief about an essence fits well with a view he puts forward in the

48 Cf. Oehler (1962/85), 236. For a definition 'revealing' or 'signifying' the essence see *Top.* 1.4, 101^{b}21–2; 5, 101^{b}39; 8, 103^{b}9–10; 7.3, 153^{a}15–16; 5, 154^{a}31–2; *Metaph.* Δ 6, 1016^{a}33–4; 1017^{a}6; 8, 1017^{b}21–2; Z 5, 1031^{a}12; H 1, 1042^{a}17.

49 Cf. the paragraph to which n. 62 below is appended.

50 Cf. Vigo (1997), 32–3. Some commentators (e.g. Sorabji (1980), 218–19; (1981), 243; (1982), 298; Denyer (1991), 204; Galluzzo (1997/98), 54) attribute to Aristotle the view that one cannot err in the search for defining characteristics. The key idea is that what might appear as a mistake in one's search for the defining characteristics of *x* is really a correct step in one's search for the defining characteristics of *y*, which is what one really had in mind: if Mrs Malaprop says that allegories are a certain species of reptile, she is not erring in the search for the defining characteristics of an allegory – rather, she is making a correct step in the search for the defining characteristics of what she really had in mind, i.e. alligators. This position, however, is untenable. It is implausible to say that the definitions proposed by Theaetetus in Plato's homonymous dialogue are correct because they give the defining characteristics (not of knowledge, but) of the items Theaetetus really had in mind. Rather, Theaetetus seems to have made at least three mistakes in his attempt to define knowledge.

Posterior Analytics, i.e. that it is after discovering that something exists that one proceeds to search for what it is.[51]

(iii) 'Thinking of' is an essential aspect of an affirmative belief concerning a non-composite item: in every affirmative belief concerning a non-composite item one must 'think of' that non-composite item. But this guarantees the everlasting truth of the belief (because the non-composite item in question always exists, and therefore always 'is' in the sense of being true): in this sense 'truth is thinking of these items' (1052^a1), i.e. the everlasting truth of an affirmative existential belief concerning a non-composite item is guaranteed by that essential moment of it which is its thinking of its non-composite item.

The infallibility of affirmative assertions concerning non-composite items. When Aristotle says that 'truth is [. . .] enunciating' (1051^b24), what he has in mind is that affirmative existential assertions concerning non-composite items are always true. Aristotle is again focusing on an essential aspect of affirmative existential assertions concerning non-composite items, and he is claiming that this essential aspect of them suffices to guarantee their everlasting truth. 'Enunciation' is the semantic task performed by names within assertions,[52] and is therefore the semantic task performed by the subject of an affirmative existential assertion concerning a non-composite item: in any affirmative existential assertion concerning a non-composite item the subject must 'enunciate' the non-composite item. But this guarantees everlasting truth (because the non-composite item in question always exists, and therefore always 'is' in the sense of being true): in this sense 'truth is enunciating'.

There is no need that all existential affirmative assertions or beliefs should always be true. Aristotle can be plausibly credited with the claim that every assertion (belief) concerning a non-composite item is an existential assertion (belief). This however does not commit him to the converse claim that every existential assertion (belief) should be an assertion (belief) concerning a non-composite item. Since, in Aristotle's view, it is affirmative assertions (beliefs) concerning non-composite items that are always true, Aristotle is not committed to the obviously false claim that every existential affirmative assertion (belief) should be always true: he could consistently acknowledge that some existential affirmative assertion (belief) is sometimes false – but

[51] *APo.* 2.1, 89^b33–5; 2, 89^b36–90^a23; 90^a31–4.

[52] *Int.* 4, 16^b26–30; 5, 17^a17–19 (cf. Torstrik (1862), 196–7; Ross (1923), 60).

he will have to grant that such an existential affirmative assertion (belief) concerns a composite item. Indeed, in the first chapter of *de Interpretatione* (at 16ᵃ16–18) Aristotle considers the assertions 'A goatstag is' and 'A goatstag is not', which he almost certainly regards as (respectively) an everlastingly false existential affirmative assertion and an everlastingly true existential negative assertion.

Aristotle does not even seem committed to the claim that one should be able to tell whether an affirmative existential assertion (belief) concerns a non-composite item: after all, in *Metaphysics* Θ 10, at 1052ᵃ4–7, he acknowledges that one might be unable to tell whether the item with which one's belief is concerned is of an unchanging nature.

No universal being. As we have seen, the thoughts and the linguistic expressions concerning non-composite items discussed in T 23 and T 24 are existential beliefs and existential assertions. This commits Aristotle to the view that being is not a universal.[53] For, if being were a universal (on a par with, say, incommensurable and white), then every existential assertion (belief) would be a predicative assertion (belief) concerning a composite object, i.e. the state of affairs composed of the universal being and of the thing spoken (thought) about. For example, if being were a universal, then the assertions 'Socrates is white' and 'Man exists' should have the same structure: as 'Socrates is white' asserts that the state of affairs of Socrates' being white, a composite object, 'is' in the sense of being true, i.e. asserts that the two components of this state of affairs, the universal white and the individual Socrates, are reciprocally combined, so 'Man exists' should assert that the state of affairs of man's existence, a composite object, 'is' in the sense of being true, i.e. should assert that the two components of this state of affairs, the universal being and the universal man, are reciprocally combined.

The attribution to Aristotle of the view that being is not a universal is hardly surprising: it fits well both with Aristotle's well-known thesis that being is not a *genus*[54] and with his claim that 'one man and an existent man and a man are the same' (*Metaph.* Γ 2, 1003ᵇ26–7).[55] Note, however, that the reason we now have for crediting Aristotle with the view that being is not a universal is particularly strong. For this reason not only enables us to claim that Aristotle rejects a single all-embracing universal, being, attributed by every existential affirmation to whatever it is referring to. It also allows us to

[53] Cf. Brentano (1889), 20; (1914a), 162; (1914b), 128; (1915b), 136.

[54] *APo.* 2.7, 92ᵇ14; *Metaph.* B 3, 998ᵇ22; K 1, 1059ᵇ33–4 (cf. *APo.* 1.32, 88ᵇ1–2; *EE* 1.8, 1217ᵇ33–5).

[55] I follow Jaeger's text. Cf. *Metaph.* I 2, 1054ᵃ16–17.

deny that for Aristotle every existential affirmation attributes some universal or other (possibly different universals for different existential assertions) to what it refers to. For instance, Aristotle cannot coherently endorse a theory of existential assertions which some commentators[56] attribute to him: that every existential affirmative assertion asserts that the item it refers to falls under a certain highest *genus*, where the highest *genus* introduced varies from case to case (in one case it is the category of substance, in another the category of quality, etc.).[57]

Alternative interpretations: (i) non-propositional truth. My interpretation of Aristotle's theory in *Metaphysics* Θ 10 and *de Anima* 3.6 about non-composite items, truth, and falsehood differs from the exegeses offered by most commentators. In this subsection and in the next I discuss two rival exegeses of this area of Aristotle's thought.

The first rival exegesis is very widespread: it is already present in Scholastic authors and is endorsed by most modern commentators.[58] According to this interpretation, in Θ 10 and *de Anima* 3.6 Aristotle distinguishes two senses of 'true'. In its first sense, the most usual one, 'true' applies to items of a propositional sort: assertions, beliefs, and states of affairs. The property expressed by 'true' in this first sense is the property of corresponding to reality, and the contrary of this property is falsehood. In its second sense,

[56] Kahn (1978), 261; Hintikka (1986), 90–2; Grice (1988), 178–82; Hintikka (1999), 787–90.

[57] For the categories as the highest *genera* of what exists see *Cat.* 8, $11^{a}37$–8; 10, $11^{b}15$–16; *APr.* 1.27, $43^{a}29$–30; $43^{a}36$–7; *APo.* 1.22, $83^{b}12$–17; 32, $88^{b}1$–3; 2.13, $96^{b}19$–20; *Ph.* 1.6, $189^{a}14$; $189^{b}23$–4; 5.4, $227^{b}4$–6; 7.1, $242^{b}35$; *de An.* 1.1, $402^{a}22$–5; 1.5, $410^{a}18$–21; 2.1, $412^{a}6$; *Metaph.* Δ 6, $1016^{b}31$–5; 28, $1024^{b}9$–16; I 1, $1052^{b}18$–19; 3, $1054^{b}27$–31; Λ 5, $1071^{a}24$–6 (cf. G. E. L. Owen (1965), 77; (1968a), 108–9; Leszl (1970), 60–6; Brakas (1988), 33–40, 42, 55; Loux (1991), 13; Smith (1997), 74–5; Fraser (2002), 46–7). In one passage (*Metaph.* I 2, $1053^{b}22$–4) Aristotle denies that substance is a *genus*, a claim which raises problems that cannot be addressed here (cf. Brentano (1862), 100–1; Kahn (1978), 251–2; Fraser (2002), 75–81).

[58] Ammon. *in Int.* 27, 28–33; Fonseca (1577/89), III 666; Pacius (1611), 389; Brandis (1835/66), II.II.I 520–1; Bonitz (1848/49), II 409–11; Brentano (1862), 26–7 (cf. n. 18 above); Torstrik (1862), 197; Grote (1880), 618–19; Wallace (1882), 273–4; Dilthey (1883), 197–8; Maier (1896/1936), I 19–20; Joachim (1906), 7, 124; Hicks (1907), 512; Jaeger (1911), 26–7; Lewinsohn (1911), 202–3; Jaeger (1912), 26–7; Ross (1923), 25; (1924), II 225, 275–6, 278; Heidegger (1926), 305–6; Calogero (1927/68), 24; Stenzel (1931), 176–7; Keeler (1932), 244–5; De Corte (1934), 237–8; Wilpert (1940), 10–11; Joachim (1948), 26–7; Owens (1951/78), 412–13; de Rijk (1952), 9–10, 13–14; Engelhardt (1953), 37–8; Tugendhat (1956/88), 57; Reale (1961/67), 161; Aubenque (1962/83), 166; Oehler (1962/85), 182, 218, 241; Apostle (1966), 321; Luther (1966), 180–1, 186–7; Tugendhat (1966a), 256–7; von Fragstein (1967), 146–7; Hamlyn (1968/93), 142; Reale (1968/93), I 101; Seidl (1971), 181–4; Grayeff (1974), 208, 209–10; Engmann (1976), 261; Marx (1977), 7–9; Berti (1978), 144; Apostle (1981), 169, 171; Seidl (1989/91), I 428, II 493–4; Volkmann-Schluck (1979), 286–9; Fleischer (1984), 25–6; Besoli (1985), 9, 41; Frede/Patzig (1988), II 318; Kal (1988), 47; Mignucci (1994), 152–3, 154–5; (1996a), 419–21; Whitaker (1996), 29; Negro (1996/97), 344, 348–50; Vigo (1997), 32; Galluzzo (1997/98), 53–5; Detel (1998), 172; Pritzl (1998), 178, 187–8; Szaif (1998), 521; Fiorentino (2001), 267–8, 275; Modrak (2001), 55, 64–6.

which is somewhat unusual or even deviant, 'true' applies to items which are not of a propositional sort: simple linguistic expressions (subjects and predicates of predicative assertions) and simple thoughts (concepts). The property expressed by 'true' in its second sense is the property of having some object or other as content. More precisely: in the case of a simple linguistic expression, the property expressed by 'true' in its second sense is that of signifying some object; in the case of a simple thought, the property in question is that of grasping some object. The contrary of the property expressed by 'true' in its second sense is (not falsehood, but) lack of content, i.e. the 'blank' condition of a simple linguistic expression which fails to signify any object or of a simple thought which fails to grasp any object ('ignorance').

The main difficulty with the Scholastic interpretation is that it is very hard to see how 'true' could apply to simple linguistic expressions and simple concepts. Simple linguistic expressions and simple concepts are not the type of item to which 'true' naturally applies.

Alternative interpretations: (ii) definitions. According to Silvestrus Maurus, Sorabji, and Berti,[59] the simple items discussed in *Metaphysics* Θ 10 and *de Anima* 3.6 are definitions (sentences consisting of two linguistic expressions, the *definiendum* and the *definiens*) and those thoughts that are their mental counterparts. Moreover, these commentators assume that definitions and their mental counterparts are true (not in a 'secondary' or 'deviant' sense, but) in the 'ordinary' sense. Since for Aristotle definitions are identity statements of a particular type,[60] what he has in mind when he says that a non-composite thought 'is not something about something' (*de An.* 3.6, 430^b27–8 < T 24) is that in such a thought a thing is attributed to itself.[61]

This interpretation faces an objection. For Aristotle a definition is a predicative assertion where the *definiens* is the predicate and the *definiendum* the subject.[62] (ii.i) In the *Topics* (1.4, 101^b11–25) he regards the link between a definition's *definiens* and *definiendum* as one of four ways in which a

[59] Maurus (1668), IV 480–1; Sorabji (1980), 218; (1981), 242; (1982), 298–9; Berti (1993), 28; (1994), 125–6; (1996a), 393–4; Wolff (1999), 55–6; Berti (2000), 10–11, 19, 24–5.

[60] *Top.* 1.5, 102^a5–17; 7, 103^a23–39 (cf. Crivelli (2002), 243–5).

[61] According to Wedin (1988), 125–6, Aristotle distinguishes two kinds of thoughts that cannot be false: acts or states of grasping an item (whose truth consists in being in touch with this item) and acts or states that correspond to the assertion of an item's essence. Thus, Wedin seems to think that both the traditional Scholastic interpretation and the exegesis going back to Silvestrus Maurus are partially correct.

[62] Aristotle's view that a definition is a predicative assertion where the *definiens* is the predicate and the *definiendum* is the subject is compatible with his other view that a *definiens* does not exhibit predicative structure in that in it no *differentia* is predicated of its *genus* (e.g. in the *definiens*

predicate can attach to a subject. He even says: 'It is necessary that whatever is predicated about something should either be predicated in a convertible way or not, and if it is predicated in a convertible way it will be either a definition or something peculiar' (1.8, 103^{b}7–9).[63] (ii.ii) Three passages of the *Posterior Analytics* (1.14, 79^{a}24–9, 2.3, 90^{b}1–7, and 2.13, 97^{b}26–7) presuppose that definitions are universal affirmative assertions. (ii.iii) In *Posterior Analytics* 2.13 (96^{a}32–4) Aristotle indicates that when one is looking for a definition one must first seek every attribute which holds essentially of, but has a larger extension than, the item to be defined, and then form a compound of these attributes that does not extend beyond the item to be defined. Given his view that a definition is a predicative assertion, how could Aristotle claim that (the mental counterpart of) a definition 'is not something about something'? What he could say is that (the mental counterpart of) a definition 'is not *something* about *something different*'. One might attempt to defend the interpretation in question by assuming that the formula 'something about something' ('τὶ κατὰ τινός') has a technical meaning whereby it does not apply to definitions. But even this will not work: in *Posterior Analytics* 2.4 Aristotle, after claiming that 'a syllogism proves something about something' (91^{a}14–15), goes on to consider the consequences of this claim for the question whether the essence can be demonstrated, and has no qualms about the idea that the conclusion of a syllogism might be 'something about something' and none the less be a definition.[64]

2 NON-COMPOSITE SUBSTANCES

Two interpretations of Aristotle's 'non-composite substances'. T 23 mentions, alongside essences, certain 'non-composite substances' ('μὴ συνθεταὶ οὐσίαι', 1051^{b}27). What are these 'non-composite substances'? According to

'biped walking animal', 'walking' is not predicated of 'animal' nor 'biped' of 'walking animal'): see *APo.* 2.3, 90^{b}33–8; *Metaph.* Z 12, 1037^{b}18–21 (cf. Ross (1949), 614–15; Bolton (1976), 523; Barnes (1994), 208; Wedin (1988), 130; Mignucci (1994), 141). In one passage (*Metaph.* H 3, 1043^{b}28–32) Aristotle does seem to assume that a *definiens* exhibits predicative structure in that its *differentia* is predicated of its *genus*.

63 Cf. *Top.* 7.5, 154^{a}36–154^{b}2; *APo.* 2.4, 91^{a}15–16; Mignucci (1975a), 38; (1994), 141; (1996a), 409.

64 There is a passage from *Posterior Analytics* 1.2 (72^{a}20–1) where according to some commentators (e.g. Phlp. *in APo.* 35, 2–13; 37, 7–13) Aristotle says that definitions do not display a predicative structure. However, other commentators (e.g. S. Mansion (1946/76), 138; Ross (1949), 504–5) offer an alternative, and more plausible, interpretation of the passage in question: Aristotle is saying (not that definitions do not display a predicative structure, but) that a definition does not make an existential claim.

the 'traditional' interpretation,[65] they are incorporeal substances, i.e. God and (perhaps) the intellects that move the heavenly spheres; according to the 'modern' interpretation,[66] they are (or at least include) forms of material substances.[67] An assessment of these competing exegeses is best introduced by two points about Aristotle's language.

(i) 'Non-composite'. 'Non-composite' can mean either 'non-composed *with* anything', i.e. 'isolated', or 'non-composed *of* anything', i.e. 'simple'. The notion of non-composition occurs elsewhere in Θ 10's central part: indeed, the passage's main topic is the application of 'true' to non-composite items. But the notion of non-composition occurring elsewhere in the passage is not that of isolation, but that of simplicity.[68] Hence our 'non-composite substances' are probably simple substances. Now, when Aristotle says that a substance is simple, the first thing coming to one's mind is that the substance should not be composed of matter and form: for Aristotle applies 'composite substance' to substances composed of matter and form.[69] Thus, our 'non-composite substances' are probably substances not composed of matter and form.

(ii) 'Similarly also'. Immediately after saying that 'it is not possible to err with regard to the "what it is" except incidentally' (1051^{b}25–6), Aristotle introduces 'non-composite substances' by saying: 'Similarly also [ὁμοίως δὲ καὶ] with regard to non-composite substances, for it is not possible to err' (1051^{b}26–8).

The formula 'similarly also' is common in Aristotle. Its main use is *expansive*: the items it introduces *are not* among those previously discussed.

65 [Alex. Aphr.] *in Metaph.* 600, 25–7; Ascl. *in Metaph.* 6, 20–1; Aquinas *in Metaph.* 1901 Cathala/Spiazzi; Suarez (1597), LIII; Schwegler (1847/48), IV 186, 187; Bonitz (1848/49), II 410; Brentano (1862), 27; (1889), 20; Jaeger (1923), 212; Ross (1924), II 274, 276; Rolfes (1904/28), II 378; Faust (1931/32), I 216, 359; Wilpert (1940), 11; Owens (1951/78), 413–14; Merlan (1953), 158–9; Décarie (1961), 161; von Fragstein (1967), 148; Reale (1968/93), III 464; Grayeff (1974), 208; Aubenque (1962/83), 374–5; (1979a), 79; Wolf (1979), III, 417. Maier (1896/1936), I 7 and Engelhardt (1953), 45 take Θ 10's 'non-composite substances' to include God and the celestial bodies.

66 Jaeger (1912), 25; Oehler (1962/85), 183–4, 221–2; Seidl (1971), 183, 194; Kessler (1976), 181; Marx (1977), 6; Berti (1978), 147–50; Volkmann-Schluck (1979), 274–5; Sorabji (1982), 298–9; Burnyeat *et al.* (1984), 157; Liske (1985), 424; Kal (1988), 126; Seidl (1989/91), I 428; Berti (1990), 115–19; (1993), 25; (1994), 131–2, 134; (1996a), 399–400, 402; Pritzl (1998), 189–90; Berti (2000), 12, 20.

67 Some commentators support neither the 'traditional' nor the 'modern' interpretation: e.g. Mignucci (1994), 150–1 and (1996a), 418–19 takes our passage's 'non-composite substances' to be 'the ontological counterparts of our concepts'.

68 Cf. the 'thinking of indivisible items' in *de Anima* 3.6 (430^{a}26) and the thought of 'simple items' in *Metaphysics* E 4 (1027^{b}27–8).

69 *De An.* 2.1, 412^{a}6–9; *Metaph.* H 3, 1043^{a}30. Aristotle distinguishes three kinds of substance: matter, form, and their compound (see e.g. *de An.* 2.1, 412^{a}6–9; *Metaph.* Z 3, 1028^{b}36–1029^{a}7; 10, 1035^{a}1–2).

For instance, in 'Breathing occurs in all mammals, similarly also with birds' the items introduced by 'similarly also' are not among those discussed previously (birds are not mammals).[70] Another use of 'similarly also' is *restrictive*: the items it introduces *are* among those previously discussed. For instance, in 'Breathing occurs in all mammals, similarly also with whales' the items introduced by 'similarly also' are among those previously discussed (whales are mammals). The restrictive use presupposes either that the items introduced could be expected not to rank among those previously discussed (one could expect whales not to be mammals) or that the items introduced could be expected to lack the property ascribed to those previously discussed (one could expect whales not to breathe).[71]

If the use of 'similarly also' at *Metaph.* Θ 10, 1051^{b}26–7 is expansive, the 'non-composite substances' discussed in Θ 10's central part are not among the items previously discussed, i.e. essences. If instead the use of 'similarly also' at *Metaph.* Θ 10, 1051^{b}26–7 is restrictive, Θ 10's 'non-composite substances' are among the items previously discussed, i.e. essences. In this case, however, 'non-composite substances' could be expected either not to rank among essences or to lack the property ascribed to essences, i.e. the property of being foreign to error.[72]

Assessment of the two interpretations. As for the first point about Aristotle's language, the 'traditional' and the 'modern' interpretation fare equally: Θ 10's 'non-composite substances' may well be (neither God nor the heavenly intellects, which are incorporeal substances not composed *with* matter, but) substantial forms which, though not composed *of* matter, are immersed in (hence composed *with*) it.

The second point about Aristotle's language creates more of a difficulty for the 'modern' interpretation. For suppose the 'modern' interpretation is right. Then Θ 10's 'non-composite substances' are the formal components of 'composite' substances. They therefore are essences in the category of substance. Then they constitute a proper subclass of the essences (the 'what it is''s) mentioned in the preceding sentence (for there are essences not

[70] All the *Metaphysics* occurrences of the formula 'similarly also' which are relevantly similar to the one at hand seem to be instances of its expansive use: see B 2, 996^{b}21; 997^{b}20; 6, 1002^{b}21; Γ 2, 1003^{b}30; 1004^{b}4; Δ 4, 1014^{b}30; 7, 1017^{a}30; 1017^{b}6; 12, 1019^{a}26; Z 1, 1028^{a}22; 17, 1041^{b}27; H 1, 1042^{b}1; Θ 1, 1046^{a}25–6; 3, 1046^{b}32; 1046^{b}35–6; 1047^{a}22; 8, 1050^{a}16; 1050^{a}33; I 2, 1053^{b}26; 1054^{a}1; 6, 1056^{b}3; 7, 1057^{a}26; K 9, 1066^{a}34; Λ 2, 1069^{b}17; 3, 1070^{a}28–9; M 6, 1080^{a}29; 1080^{b}23; 9, 1085^{a}7; 1085^{b}27; N 1, 1087^{b}36.

[71] I know no examples of the restrictive use of 'similarly also' in Aristotle's works.

[72] Discussions of the formula 'similarly also' can be found also in Berti (1978), 147 and Burnyeat *et al.* (1984), 157.

only in the category of substance, but also in other categories).[73] Hence the expansive use of 'similarly also' at *Metaph.* Θ 10, 1051^{b}26–7 is excluded. Aristotle can only have in mind its restrictive use. This presupposes that 'non-composite substances', i.e. essences in the category of substance, could be expected either not to rank among essences or to lack the property just ascribed to essences in general, i.e. the property of being foreign to error. But this presupposition strikes one as odd: any reader who understands enough of Aristotle's jargon to make sense of the expression 'non-composite substances' as denoting the formal components of 'composite' substances will know very well that they are essences, and it is hard to see why such a reader should expect that these essences in the category of substance should have a special reason for lacking the property just ascribed to essences in general, i.e. being foreign to error. No such difficulty arises for the 'traditional' interpretation. For the 'traditional' interpretation can take the use of the formula 'similarly also' at *Metaph.* Θ 10, 1051^{b}26–7 to be expansive: so far Aristotle has shown that essences of things are foreign to error, now he adds that the same holds for incorporeal forms, i.e. God and (perhaps) the heavenly intellects. So the second point about Aristotle's language favours the 'traditional' interpretation over the 'modern'.

An objection raised by some commentators against the 'traditional' interpretation is that it is hard to see why Aristotle should mention incorporeal substances at this point.[74] This objection is easily answered: since Aristotle does believe in incorporeal substances, it is natural that he should mention them in a discussion of non-composite items. Moreover, Aristotle's reason for mentioning incorporeal substances at this point, at the end of book Θ, might be that he is building up the *Metaphysics* towards the treatment of them (in book Λ).

Another objection raised against the 'traditional' interpretation is that human beings do not have a direct and immediate grasp of incorporeal substances (Aristotle himself needs to argue for their existence).[75] This objection can be answered in two ways. First, Aristotle need not be discussing a human epistemic state: he might well be addressing a divine epistemic state. Second, a few lines after our passage (at 1051^{b}32–3) Aristotle clearly says that one's belief in a non-composite item does not require one's ability to articulate its definition. So, even if Aristotle were to claim that human

[73] For items from categories other than substance having essences see *Top.* 1.9, 103^{b}27–37; *de An.* 1.1, 402^{b}16–21; 3.4, 429^{b}10–12; *Metaph.* Δ 6, 1016^{b}1–3; Z 4, 1030^{a}17–27; Berti (1978), 146–7; (1994), 131–2; (1996a), 399; Vigo (1997), 38.

[74] Cf. Mignucci (1994), 150; (1996a), 418.

[75] Cf. Seidl (1971), 183.

beings have an immediate grasp of incorporeal substances, this would not amount to a form of 'religious intuitionism'.

A strength of the 'traditional' interpretation is its ability to explain why Aristotle uses the formula 'being itself' ('τὸ ὂν αὐτό', 1051^{b}29), which has a strong Platonic flavour.[76] If, as the 'traditional' interpretation claims, the 'non-composite substances' of Θ 10's central part are God and (perhaps) the heavenly intellects, Aristotle might be using the formula 'being itself' to suggest a comparison of the role played in his system by God and (perhaps) the heavenly intellects with the role played in Platonic philosophy by the Good and (perhaps) Forms.[77]

Thus, all considered, the 'traditional' interpretation has the edge on the 'modern'.

Properties of 'non-composite substances'. In the last part (1051^{b}28–30) of his discussion of 'non-composite substances', Aristotle indicates some of their properties.

(i) Incorporeal substances are completely in actuality (cf. 1051^{b}30–1).[78] This means that they contain no matter (which Aristotle equates with potentiality and contrasts with actuality).[79] This confirms the previously suggested explanation of why 'non-composite' applies to these substances – it is because they are not composed *of* form and matter.[80]

(ii) The fact that an incorporeal substance cannot come or cease to be is linked to its containing no matter. For all coming to be is 'from' something, i.e. from matter,[81] and matter persists through the process of coming to be, i.e. remains present in what has come to be: thus, only material entities can be the result of coming to be, while 'being itself' (1051^{b}29), i.e. what is

[76] Cf. *Metaph.* B 4, 1001^{a}23; 1001^{a}27; 1001^{a}30; N 2, 1089^{a}3. Aristotle reports that the Platonists use the word 'itself' to compose the name of a form: see *Metaph.* Z 16, 1040^{b}33–4; *EN* 1.4, 1096^{a}34–1096^{b}5; *EE* 1.8, 1218^{a}11.

[77] Elsewhere Aristotle does compare his God with Plato's Good: see *Metaph.* Λ 10, 1075^{a}38–1075^{b}1; 1075^{b}34–7 (with Düring (1966), 221–2). Ps.-Alexander (*in Metaph.* 600, 25–7) identifies the 'being itself' of 1051^{b}29 with 'the simple substance which is above being and moves without being in motion, God worthy of great admiration'. The expression 'above being' ('ὑπερούσιος') used by ps.-Alexander to describe God recalls the expression 'beyond being' ('ἐπέκεινα τῆς οὐσίας') used by Plato to describe the Good (see *R.* VI 509*b*8–10).

[78] Cf. *Metaph.* Λ 6, 1071^{b}17–20; 7, 1072^{a}25–6; 1072^{b}8.

[79] *De An.* 2.1, 412^{a}9; 3.5, 430^{a}10–11; *Metaph.* Λ 5, 1071^{a}8–11; etc. (cf. Oehler (1962/85), 222).

[80] Cf. the subsection to which n. 68 above is appended.

[81] For Aristotle's use of the preposition 'from' ('ἐκ') to indicate matter see *Ph.* 1.7, 190^{b}24–7; 9, 192^{a}31–2; 2.3, 194^{b}23–6; *Metaph.* Δ 2, 1013^{a}24–6; Z 7, 1032^{a}12–14; 8, 1033^{a}25–6; 1033^{b}1–3; 1033^{b}8–9. However, at *Metaph.* Z 7, 1033^{a}19–22 Aristotle observes that on careful examination it is inappropriate to use 'from' to indicate matter.

purely essence or form with no material component, cannot have come to be.[82]

3 SINGULAR EXISTENTIAL ASSERTIONS CONCERNING MATERIAL SUBSTANCES

Aristotle's silence. In the last two sections I discussed Aristotle's views on true and false existential assertions concerning non-composite items. I argued that among these non-composite items there are essences and incorporeal substances. Does Aristotle have views on true and false singular existential assertions concerning material substances (e.g. assertions like 'Socrates exists' and 'Bucephalus does not exist')? If he does have views in this area, what are they?

Aristotle does not explicitly discuss true and false singular existential assertions concerning material substances. My strategy is therefore to attempt to reconstruct what views in this area Aristotle is committed to. The results gained with regard to existential assertions readily translate into points regarding existential beliefs.

Two possible developments. The theory expounded in *Metaphysics* Θ 10 could be developed in two directions. On the one hand, Aristotle might say that material substances are non-composite items alongside essences and incorporeal substances; on the other, he might say that material substances are composite items alongside states of affairs. Some commentators[83] think that Aristotle takes the first direction. However, several passages strongly suggest that he favours the second: he would probably say that material substances are composite items alongside states of affairs.

Matter–form and substance–accident. Aristotle regards the relation of matter to form within a material substance, or 'matter–form relation', as analogous to the relation of a whole material substance to those universals from categories other than substance that hold of it, or 'substance–accident relation'.[84] He does not regard these relations as identical – in fact, when he states that matter and the matter–form compound 'are subjects in different

[82] Aristotle also claims that corporeal forms (forms combined with matter within a material substance) neither come nor cease to be: see *Metaph.* E 3, 1027^{a}29–30; Z 8, 1033^{a}24–1033^{b}19 (with Oehler (1962/85), 218–19 and Liske (1985), 424); 9, 1034^{b}7–16; 10, 1035^{a}28–30; 15, 1039^{b}20–7; H 1, 1042^{a}26–31; 3, 1043^{b}14–16; 5, 1044^{b}21–4; Λ 3, 1069^{b}35–1070^{a}4; 1070^{a}15–17.

[83] E.g. de Rijk (1952), 15–16.

[84] Cf. Leszl (1971), 337; Lewis (1991), 146, 147, 246–8, 259–61.

ways',[85] part of his point is probably that these relations are different. However, for present purposes, what counts is that Aristotle does consider the matter–form and the substance–accident relations as analogous. Here is the evidence for crediting Aristotle with this view.

(i) Aristotle thinks that as a non-substance universal is predicated of a substance, so form is predicated of matter within a material substance.[86]

(ii) Aristotle seems to 'discover' the distinction between matter and form by extending his analysis of qualified coming-to-be (coming-to-be-white and, in general, the phenomenon described by 'to come to be' followed by an adjectival complement) to absolute coming-to-be (birth and, in general, the phenomenon described by 'to come to be' on its own): this is how he introduces the distinction between matter and form in *Physics* 1.7,[87] which is probably one of the earliest texts where it appears.[88]

(iii) Aristotle uses the same technical term, 'compound' ('σύνολον'), for matter–form compounds[89] and for incidental compounds that consist of a substance and a non-substance universal predicated of it.[90]

(iv) In several passages Aristotle draws the analogy explicitly. One such passage is from *Metaphysics* H 4:

> T 27 Those things that are by nature but are not substances have no matter, but substance is what underlies them. For example, what is the cause of an eclipse? What is its matter? For there is none, but the moon is what suffers an affection. What is the cause in the sense of what moves and destroys the light? The earth. Perhaps there is no purpose. And the cause in the sense of form is the account. (1044^{b}8–12)[91]

In T 27 Aristotle says that the moon (a substance)[92] plays in a lunar eclipse (an event) a role analogous to that of matter in a material substance.

Existence, form, and matter. Since Aristotle regards the matter–form relation as analogous to the substance–accident relation, one expects him to believe that for a material substance to exist is for its form to hold of its matter.

85 *Metaph.* Z 3, 1029^{a}2–3; H 1, 1042^{a}26–31 (cf. Θ 7, 1049^{a}27–36).

86 *De An.* 2.1, 412^{a}16–19; *Metaph.* B 1, 995^{b}35; 4, 999^{a}33–4; Z 3, 1028^{b}36–1029^{a}5; 1029^{a}23–4; 13, 1038^{b}4–6; H 1, 1042^{a}26–31; 2, 1043^{a}5–6; Θ 7, 1049^{a}34–1049^{b}2 (cf. Ross (1924), II 164, 257; Leszl (1971), 337; Brunschwig (1979), 148–50; Lewis (1991), 152–3, 266).

87 190^{b}10–17, cf. *GC* 1.4, 320^{a}2–5; *Metaph.* Z 7, 1032^{a}13–25; H 1, 1042^{a}32–1042^{b}3; Λ 1, 1069^{b}3–20; G. E. L. Owen (1966), 148–9; (1978/79), 6; Lewis (1991), 223–8, 245, 248.

88 Cf. Graham (1987), 119, 133–7; Lewis (1991), 245, 247.

89 *PA* 1.1, 640^{b}23–8; *Metaph.* B 1, 995^{b}35; 4, 999^{a}33–4; Z 3, 1029^{a}3–5; 10, 1035^{a}17–21; etc.

90 *Metaph.* M 2, 1077^{b}8–9.

91 Cf. Z 3, 1029^{a}23–4; 13, 1038^{b}5–6; H 2, 1043^{a}4–7 (with Brunschwig (1979), 133–4); Θ 7, 1049^{a}27–36.

92 For the moon being a substance see *Metaph.* Z 2, 1028^{b}8–13 (cf. *APo.* 2.2, 90^{a}12).

This expectation is confirmed by *Metaphysics* Z 17 (1041^{a}10–1041^{b}11). In this passage (on one plausible interpretation of it, an interpretation I shall not endeavour to substantiate here) Aristotle draws an analogy between three cases of knowledge of a thing's existence. The first concerns a lunar eclipse: to know that a lunar eclipse exists is to know that the moon (a substance) has the property of being eclipsed. The second case concerns a house: to know that a house (a substance, perhaps) exists is to know of certain bricks and stones (a portion of matter) that they have a certain form. The third case concerns a man: to know that a man (a substance) exists is to know of a certain lump of flesh and bones (a portion of matter) that it has a certain form.[93]

Aristotle's view that for a material substance to exist is for its form (or essence) to hold of its matter seems connected with another view of his: that a thing's essence is the cause of its existence.[94] It also seems connected with a passage from *Metaphysics* H 2 (1042^{b}15–1043^{a}14) where he distinguishes various 'differences' which by being present in something make it into a certain individual: he associates a signification of 'to be' with each of these 'differences', and he says that for an individual to exist is for its peculiar 'difference' to hold of its matter-like component.[95]

[93] Cf. Charles (2002), 120. At the end of this passage, at 1041^{b}9–11, Aristotle says that the inquiry into simple items must be different from that into the items previously mentioned. Several commentators (Bonitz (1848/49), II 360; Ross (1924), II 225; von Ivánka (1932), 21; Décarie (1961), 151; Grayeff (1974), 208; Aubenque (1979a), 69; Kahn (1985), 326–7; Frede/Patzig (1988), II 318) note that this brief allusion to simple items links *Metaphysics* Z 17 to the central part of Θ 10, where beliefs and assertions concerning non-composite items are discussed.

[94] *De An.* 2.4, 415^{b}12–14 (cf. *GC* 1.3, 318^{b}25; *GA* 2.1, 731^{b}28–30; *EN* 9.4, 1166^{a}4–5; 7, 1168^{a}5–7; *Protr.* fr. 73 Gigon 311^{b}39–40 = Iamb. *Protr.* 58, 11); *Metaph.* Δ 8, 1017^{b}14–16; Z 17, 1041^{a}9–10; 1041^{a}27–8; 1041^{b}8–9; 1041^{b}27–8; H 2, 1042^{b}32–3; 1043^{a}2–4. Aristotle sometimes refers to *x*'s essence by means of the formulae 'to be for *x*' and 'what it was to be for *x*' (see Bonitz (1870), 221^{a}34–9, 764^{b}11–17), formulae which seem to allude to the cause of *x*'s existence (cf. Kahn (1976), 332–3; Loux (1991), 73–5; Bostock (1994), 50; Hintikka (1999), 786; Bäck (2000), 107). However, the formulae 'to be for *x*' and 'what it was to be for *x*' could indicate (not the cause of *x*'s existence, but) the cause for *x* to be *x* (cf. Anscombe/Geach (1961), 24–6, 34–5): e.g. in *Categories* 7 Aristotle seems to identify 'to be for relatives' (cf. 'οἷς τὸ εἶναι' at 8^{a}32 and 'τὸ εἶναι τοῖς πρός τι' at 8^{a}39) with 'to be a relative for relatives' (cf. 'τὸ πρός τι αὐτοῖς εἶναι' at 8^{a}34–5) (cf. *Top.* 5.4, 133^{b}33–6).

[95] Cf. Leszl (1971), 337, 339; Grice (1988), 182; Barnes (1995a), 80–1; Matthews (1995), 236–7; Shields (1999), 234–5; Charles (2002), 121–3. G. E. L. Owen (see his (1960), 165, (1965), 76–7, (1966), 145, and (1978/79), 11–12) interprets differently the passage from H 2: Aristotle would be claiming that for a non-substantial individual to exist is for its peculiar 'difference' to hold of the non-substantial individual itself (not of its matter-like component). The H 2 passage surely can be interpreted as Owen does, and many commentators agree with him (see Cresswell (1971), 98, 106; Ackrill (1972), 210; C. J. F. Williams (1981), 134; Dancy (1986), 65; Hintikka (1986), 86; Upton (1988), 385; Loux (1991), 28, 41, 73; Bostock (1994), 49–50, 52, 254–7; L. Brown (1994), 235; Whitaker (1996), 30–2, 136–7). However, the evidence from other texts makes it more plausible to understand the H 2 passage as claiming that for the non-substantial individual to exist is for its form-like component to hold of its matter-like component.

An account of existential assertions that appeals to form and matter. The considerations of the last subsections show that Aristotle is more likely to regard a material substance as a composite item than as a non-composite item. This result, in turn, makes it plausible to assume that Aristotle would endorse an account of true and false singular existential assertions concerning material substances based on the idea that every such assertion claims that a form is combined with, or divided from, a portion of matter:

[24] A singular affirmative existential assertion concerning a material substance asserts that that substance's form is combined with that substance's matter. Accordingly, it is true (false) when and only when that form is combined with (divided from) that matter.

[25] A singular negative existential assertion concerning a material substance asserts that that substance's form is divided from that substance's matter. Accordingly, it is true (false) when and only when that form is divided from (combined with) that matter.[96]

A singular existential assertion latches on to a form and a portion of matter by passing through a material substance which at some time or other exists. None the less, a singular affirmative (negative) existential assertion concerning a material substance can be false (true) at some time or other, i.e. when the material substance it concerns no longer exists.

Does the form or the matter of a material substance survive forever the material substance's destruction? The form of a material substance is an essence, i.e. a natural kind, and therefore probably survives forever the material substance's destruction.[97] On the other hand, the matter of a material substance is unlikely to survive forever that material substance's destruction. It therefore seems sensible to construct the truth conditions for a singular affirmative (negative) existential assertion concerning a material substance in such a way that they do not require the form or the matter of the material substance concerned to exist when the assertion is false (true). The best way to achieve this result is to characterise the division appealed to by the truth conditions in such a way that the portion of matter and the form in question should be reciprocally divided whenever either of them does not exist:

[26] For every form f, every portion of matter m, and every time t, if f is combined with m at t then both f and m exist at t. For every form

[96] Cf. Leszl (1971), 337–40; van Bennekom (1986), 11–12; Matthews (1995), 236–7.

[97] Cf. the subsection to which n. 21 above is appended.

f, every portion of matter *m*, and every time *t*, *f* is divided from *m* at *t* just in case *m* is other than everything with which *f* is combined at *t*.

Note the asymmetry between singular affirmative existential assertions concerning material substances and affirmative existential assertions concerning non-composite items: a singular affirmative existential assertion concerning a material substance may well be false, when the material substance concerned no longer exists, but an affirmative existential assertion concerning a non-composite item must be always true because the non-composite item it concerns is everlasting, i.e. always exists.[98]

Limits. Propositions [24] and [25] cannot handle singular existential assertions about what never exists, e.g. an utterance of 'Pegasus does not exist'. The singular existential assertions addressed by [24] and [25] are those affirming or denying the existence of a material substance that does exist at some time or other (possibly distant from the time when the assertion is uttered). The singular existential assertions addressed by [24] and [25] are those involving a certain specific use of 'to exist', a use one of the features of which is that the verb can be accompanied by temporal adverbs like 'still' or 'no longer'.[99]

[98] Cf. the subsection to which n. 21 above is appended.

[99] Cf. G. E. L. Owen (1965), 78–9.

PART II

'Empty' terms

CHAPTER 4

Truth as correspondence

Can Aristotle's theory of truth for assertions be regarded as a correspondence theory of truth? Section 1 argues that on certain conceptions of truth as correspondence it cannot, but on at least one other it can. Specifically, Aristotle's theory of truth can be regarded as a correspondence theory of truth in that it can be regarded as taking the truth of an assertion to amount to a relation of isomorphism to reality. In particular: it relies on a classification of assertions, with each class it associates some characteristic that can hold of the items an assertion is about, and it claims that an assertion is true when and only when the characteristic associated with its class holds of the items it is about.

Section 2 addresses Aristotle's reaction to the Liar, which creates a puzzle for correspondence theories of truth like Aristotle's. It is not clear whether Aristotle addressed the Liar, and, in case he did, what version of it he confronted. On the somewhat optimistic assumption that he did address a robust version of the paradox, his solution is that the assertion on which the paradox turns (an utterance of the sentence-type 'I am speaking falsely') is sometimes neither true nor false.

1 A CORRESPONDENCE THEORY OF TRUTH?

Focusing on truth for assertions. The theory of truth we are in the best position to attribute to Aristotle is a theory of truth for assertions (utterances) (it was described in chapters 2 and 3).[1] It is therefore with regard to this Aristotelian theory of truth for assertions that it is worthwhile asking whether it is a correspondence theory of truth. To answer this question, one must first characterise what a correspondence theory of truth for assertions is.

[1] See [17], [24], and [25] on pp. 93–4 and 124 above.

(i) Facts. According to a widespread, 'classical' conception, the hallmark of a correspondence theory of truth for assertions is the claim that an assertion is true (false) just in case there is some (no) fact to which it corresponds.[2] On this conception, Aristotle's theory does not qualify as a correspondence theory of truth for assertions, for it does not mention facts, so that there is no question of assertions corresponding to them.[3] It is also worthwhile noting that although Aristotle sometimes[4] seems to use 'object' ('πρᾶγμα') to denote facts, there appears to be no Greek count-noun which can be used like the English 'fact' in a Greek construction which corresponds word for word to the English 'the fact that . . .'[5]

(ii) States of affairs. According to a second conception, the hallmark of a correspondence theory of truth for assertions is the claim that an assertion is true (false) just in case the corresponding state of affairs obtains (does not obtain). A fact is then defined as a state of affairs that obtains.[6]

This conception provides better prospects for crediting Aristotle with a correspondence theory of truth for assertions: after all, Aristotle does analyse the truth of predicative assertions in terms of states of affairs that 'are' or 'are not' in the sense of being true or false. But a brief reflection shows that Aristotle's views on the relationship between truth and states of affairs do not match the second conception of a correspondence theory of truth for assertions. For Aristotle allows only 'affirmative' states of affairs, so that while an affirmative predicative assertion is true when and only when the corresponding state of affairs 'is' in the sense of being true, a *negative* predicative assertion is true when and only when the corresponding state of affairs *'is not' in the sense of being false* (e.g. 'You are not seated' is true when and only when the state of affairs of your being seated 'is not' in the sense of being false):[7] by contrast, the second conception of a correspondence theory of truth for assertions requires that *every* assertion (*negative* as well

[2] Cf. Russell (1912), 75; Moore (1953), 277; Prior (1967b), 226; David (1994), 17–18; Neale (2001), 86. The correspondence theory of truth advocated by Russell and Moore concerns beliefs, but it can be easily translated into one for assertions.

[3] Cf. David (1994), 18 (*contra* see Ringbom (1972), 12). In Aristotle's remark 'He who is in a state contrary to that of the objects is wrong' (*Metaph.* Θ 10, 1051^{b}4–5), 'objects' denotes not facts but states of affairs.

[4] *APr.* 2.15, 64^{b}10; *GC* 1.8, 325^{a}18; *Ph.* 8.8, 263^{a}17; *Metaph.* A 3, 984^{a}18 (cf. Pritzl (1998), 184).

[5] Cf. Geach (1963), 21. Aristotle's technical expression 'τὸ ὅτι' (*APo.* 1.5, 75^{a}16; 2.1, 89^{b}24; *EN* 1.7, 1098^{b}1; etc.) comes close, but is never followed by a clause expressing the 'content' of 'ὅτι'.

[6] Cf. Boeth. *in Int. Pr. Ed.* 110, 16–18; Tarski (1933), 155; (1944), 118; Chisholm (1966), 103–4; Sommers (1969/70), 267–8; Kirkham (1992), 119; David (1994), 31–4.

[7] Cf. [4] and [5] on p. 55 above (which, however, talk of affirmative and negative predicative *beliefs*, not *assertions*).

as affirmative) should be true just in case the corresponding state of affairs 'is' in the sense of being true.[8]

(iii) Isomorphism. According to a third conception, the hallmark of a correspondence theory of truth for assertions is explaining the truth of an assertion in terms of a relation of 'isomorphism' to reality. Suppose that one has introduced a classification of assertions that singles out n classes $C_1, \ldots, C_n$ of assertions. Suppose, further, that one has established a one-to-one mapping of the classes of assertions singled out by this classification onto certain attributes (properties or relations) $A_1, \ldots, A_n$. One can then set out a correspondence-as-isomorphism theory of truth for assertions by saying that an assertion a is true just in case either a belongs to C_1 and the item (or items) a is about has (or have) attribute A_1 or . . . or a belongs to C_n and the item (or items) a is about has (or have) attribute A_n.

On this correspondence-as-isomorphism conception, Aristotle's theory does rank as a correspondence theory of truth for assertions.[9] In fact, the

[8] However, recall (cf. the paragraph to which n. 18 of ch. 1 pertains) that in the *Categories* Aristotle seems to postulate both 'negative' and 'affirmative' states of affairs. The theory of truth for assertions which most probably accompanies such a conception of states of affairs will claim that an affirmative (negative) assertion is true when and only when the corresponding affirmative (negative) state of affairs obtains. Such a theory would count as a correspondence theory of truth for assertions according to the second conception.

[9] Thus, the widespread view that Aristotle endorses a correspondence theory of truth is vindicated: see Ammon. *in Int.* 20, 32–21, 16; Aquinas *in Int.* 29, 31–2 Spiazzi; *in de An.* 760 Pirotta; Trendelenburg (1836/92), 54–5; (1846), 13–14, 17–18; Bonitz (1848/49), II 409; Brentano (1862), 26, 28–9 (with Krell (1975), 84–6); Steinthal (1863/90), I 246; Ueberweg (1868), 25; Brentano (1874/1925), II 54; Trendelenburg (1876), 78, 83; Dilthey (1883), 197–9; Brentano (1889), 7, 15, 18–19, 24–5 (with Srzednicki (1965), 18); Maier (1896/1936), I 17–18, 34–5, 37–40, 207; Joachim (1906), 124–6; Lukasiewicz (1910a), 20; (1910b), 18; Jaeger (1912), 26; Herbertz (1913), 214–15; Brentano (1914a), 163; (1915a), 219–20; Geyser (1917), 54, 56; Ross (1923), 26; Linke (1924), 407; Calogero (1927/68), 24; Keeler (1932), 247; Popper (1934/59/75), 274; Cooke/Tredennick (1938), 7; Tarski (1944), 117–18; S. Mansion (1946/76), 235–7; Baudry (1950), 8; Scarpat (1950), 24–5; de Rijk (1952), 13; Engelhardt (1953), 41; Viano (1955), 28; Lenz (1957), 773–4; Saunders (1958), 377; Moreau (1961), 22; Reale (1961/67), 161; Oehler (1962/85), 176–9, 245–6; Ackrill (1963), 90, 140; Burrell (1964), 46; Brandt (1965), 14–15; Linke (1965), 307–9; Cahn (1967), 29; Sainati (1968), 213, 225; Tarski (1969), 102–3; D. Frede (1970), 19–20; Abbagnano (1971), 914; Morpurgo-Tagliabue (1971), 32; McKim (1971/72), 103; Patzig (1973), 923; Capozzi (1974), 320–1; Dickason (1976), 20; Graeser (1977), 374; Marx (1977), 9; Graeser (1978), 447; K. J. Williams (1978), 67, 72; Aubenque (1979a), 69; Volkmann-Schluck (1979), 260, 286; M. J. White (1981), 231–2; Bormann (1982), 1; Edel (1982), 242; Seel (1982a), 211; Berti (1983a), 276; Graeser (1983b), 201; Kreiser (1983), 96; Fleischer (1984), 16, 22; Oehler (1984), 222; Craig (1988), 23–4, 32, 236; Hallett (1988), 8; Irwin (1988), 5–6; Donini (1989), 11–12; Halper (1989), 217, 218; Wolenski/Simons (1989), 393; Crivelli (1996), 158–9; Negro (1996/97), 342; Knabenschuh de Porta (1997), 200, 207; Vigo (1997), 7–10, 13–14, 27, 30; Galluzzo (1997/98), 43, 48–9, 58; Pritzl (1998), 177, 180; Szaif (1998), 520–1; K. Taylor (1998), 115; Enders (1999), 8, 118; Hafemann (1999), 130–1; Wolff (1999), 51, 55; Berti (2000), 3, 8–9; Fiorentino (2001), 280–5; Modrak (2001), 4, 55–62.

Some commentators doubt or deny that Aristotle's theory of truth is a correspondence theory of truth: see Adorno (1961), 407; Luther (1966), 182–3, 188; Davidson (1996), 268; Engel (2002), 15–16.

condition introduced by the correspondence-as-isomorphism conception is met at two levels by Aristotle's theory.[10]

(iii.i) Isomorphism with respect to an item corresponding to the whole assertion. In *Metaphysics* Γ 7 Aristotle defines truth and falsehood:

T 28 [That nothing can be in the middle of a contradictory pair, but it is necessary either to affirm or to deny any one thing about one thing] is clear to whoever defines what truth and falsehood are. For, to say that what is is not, or that what is not is, is false; to say that what is is, and that what is not is not, is true. (1011^{b}25–7)[11]

In Γ 8 Aristotle refers back to this definition:

T 29 [. . .] one must argue on the basis of a definition by assuming what 'true' and 'false' mean. But if what is true is nothing but affirming or denying, and what is false too,[12] it is impossible that everything should be false: for it is necessary that the other[13] member of the contradictory pair should be true. (1012^{b}7–11)

T 29 shows that T 28's definition of truth and falsehood is an account of what 'true' and 'false' mean.[14] T 28's definition of truth and falsehood is a premiss of an argument for Excluded Middle. This argument, which is highly compressed, has been variously reconstructed. I shall not discuss it here.[15]

T 28's definition of truth and falsehood can be interpreted in at least four different ways.[16]

According to Heidegger ((1924/25), 127–8, 162–4, 166; (1926), 164; (1927), 226; (1930/31), 138; (1946), 163) Aristotle wavers between a correspondence theory of truth and a conception of truth as 'unconcealedness'. On Heidegger's account of Aristotle's views on truth see Luther (1966), 180; Krell (1975), 90–1; Berti (1990), 101; Vigo (1994), 75; Wolff (1999), 43; Berti (2000), 5, 17–18.

[10] Cf. Wolenski/Simons (1989), 393.

[11] Cf. Pl. *Sph.* 240*d*9–241*a*2; 263*b*4–10; Leal Carretero (1983), 41–3; Szaif (1998), 407. The order of the cases in T 28 matches that at *Int.* 6, 17^{a}26–9: false denial, false affirmation, true affirmation, true denial.

[12] At 1012^{b}8–9 I adopt the reading 'μηδὲν ἄλλο τὸ ἀληθὲς ἢ φάναι ἢ ἀποφάναι καὶ τὸ ψεῦδός ἐστιν', which according to Alexander (*in Metaph.* 339, 18–20) is attested by some manuscript. Editors and commentators prefer different readings or emend the passage.

[13] For 'θάτερον' (1012^{b}11) meaning 'the other' (rather than 'one or the other') see *Int.* 9, 19^{a}22; *Po.* 3.10, 1281^{a}27.

[14] Cf. *Metaph.* Γ 7, 1012^{a}3; 1012^{a}21–4. Aristotle holds that both in scientific demonstrations and in dialectical arguments some of the premisses can be definitions fixing the meaning of terms: for scientific demonstrations see *APo.* 1.1, 71^{a}15–16; 10, 76^{b}15–16; 76^{b}19; 76^{b}20; 2.7, 92^{b}26–8; 10, 93^{b}29–32 (cf. Demoss/Devereux (1988), 134–6; Goldin (1996), 44); for dialectical arguments see *Top.* 2.4, 111^{b}12–16 (cf. Cavini (1998), 7).

[15] Cavini (1998), 7–14 expounds the earlier interpretations of Aristotle's argument and offers a new one.

[16] Cf. Kirwan (1971/93), 117; Graeser (1981), 86; Ledda (1990), 36.

(i) 'To be' is used in the existential sense, whereby it means 'to exist'. The definition can then be paraphrased as follows: 'To say of a thing which exists that it does not exist, or of a thing which does not exist that it exists, is false; to say of a thing which exists that it exists, or of a thing which does not exist that it does not exist, is true.'[17]

(ii) 'To be' means 'to hold of' and is properly applied to universals. The definition can then be paraphrased as follows: 'To say of a universal which holds of something that it does not hold of it, or of one which does not hold that it holds, is false; to say of a universal which holds of something that it holds of it, or of one which does not hold that it does not hold, is true.'[18]

(iii) 'To be' is used in the predicative-elliptical sense, whereby it functions like a schematic expression that could be expanded to 'to be so-and-so'.[19] The definition can then be paraphrased as follows: 'To say of what is so-and-so that it is not so-and-so, or of what is not so-and-so that it is so-and-so, is false; to say of what is so-and-so that it is so-and-so, or of what is not so-and-so that it is not so-and-so, is true.'[20]

(iv) 'To be' is used in the veridical sense, whereby it means 'to be true' or 'to obtain', and is properly applied to states of affairs.[21] The definition can then be paraphrased as follows: 'To say of a state of affairs which in fact "is" in the sense of being true that it "is not" in the sense of being false, or of a state of affairs which in fact "is not" in the sense of being false that it "is" in the sense of being true, is false; to say of a state of affairs which in fact "is" in the sense of being true that it "is" in the sense of being true, or of a state of affairs which in fact "is not" in the sense of being false that it "is not" in the sense of being false, is true.'[22]

17 Cf. Xenakis (1957), 542; Bärthlein (1972), 22; Wolenski/Simons (1989), 393; Davidson (1996), 267; Knabenschuh de Porta (1997), 192.

18 Cf. *Int.* 6, 17^{a}26–30; 14, 23^{b}7–13; *Top.* 2.1, 109^{a}29–30. I know no other Aristotelian passage where 'to be' means 'to hold of' (Bobzien (2002), 372–3 thinks that in *Top.* 2.4, 111^{b}17–23 'to be' does mean 'to hold of', but I find this unconvincing). However, some commentators (e.g. M. Frede (1967), 94–5) take a passage of Plato's *Sophist* (262*e*11–263*b*13) to analyse truth and falsehood by using 'to be' to mean something like 'to hold of'.

19 For 'to be' and 'not to be' used as schematic expressions cf. *Metaph.* Γ 4, 1005^{b}35–1006^{a}1 with 1006^{b}18–22 and Kirwan (1971/93), 89; C. J. F. Williams (1976), 67.

20 Cf. *Int.* 9, 18^{a}39–18^{b}3; 14, 23^{a}40–23^{b}1; 23^{b}4–6; 23^{b}7–8; 23^{b}33–24^{a}3; *SE* 5, 168^{a}9–11; *Cael.* 1.12, 281^{b}8–14; *de An.* 3.6, 430^{b}1–3; *Metaph.* Δ 29, 1024^{b}22–4; Tugendhat (1966a), 251–2; Prior (1967b), 224; Sommers (1969/70), 281–2; C. J. F. Williams (1976), 67; Leal Carretero (1983), 45–65, 87; Fox (1987), 199; Ledda (1990), 35–6, 50.

21 Aristotle does use 'to be' to mean 'is true': see *APo.* 1.1, 71^{a}12–14; 2, 71^{b}25–6 (cf. Mignucci (1975b), 229–30).

22 Cf. Brentano (1889), 24–5, 26–7 (with Srzednicki (1965), 18); Oehler (1962/85), 180–1; Hintikka (1964/73a), 168; Kahn (1966), 253; Kirwan (1971/93), 117; Kahn (1973a), 336; (1973b), 144; Weingartner

On interpretation (i) T 28's definition of truth and falsehood is unacceptably narrow: truth and falsehood would be defined only for existential assertions.[23] The main problem with interpretation (ii) is that there seems to be no other passage where Aristotle uses 'to be' to mean 'to hold of'.[24]

Interpretations (iii) and (iv) also face a difficulty: they cannot accommodate existential assertions – in the case of interpretation (iv), this is because states of affairs are composite items whose 'being' in the sense of being true or 'not being' in the sense of being false accounts for the truth or falsehood only of predicative assertions. To be sure, this defect is less worrying than interpretation (i)'s incapacity to accommodate predicative assertions. For, first, a definition of truth and falsehood is much more limited if it covers only existential assertions than if it covers only predicative assertions. Second, in T 28 Aristotle is in any case interested mainly in predicative assertions: immediately before T 28 one of the formulations of Excluded Middle, which T 28's definition of truth and falsehood is designed to support, is 'It is necessary either to affirm or to deny any one thing about one thing' (1011^{b}24). None the less, it would be desirable to find an interpretation of T 28 that yielded a 'general' definition of truth and falsehood covering all assertions.

Such an interpretation can be obtained by reflecting on the theory of truth and falsehood of *Metaphysics* Θ 10. In this chapter Aristotle distinguishes two kinds of assertions: those about composite and those about non-composite items. The classification generated by this distinction seems to cover existential as well as predicative assertions: every predicative assertion is about a composite object (a state of affairs composed of universals or of a universal and an individual); some existential assertion is again about a composite object (a material substance composed of form and matter); the remaining existential assertions are about non-composite items (essences and incorporeal substances). What it is 'to be' ('not to be') in the sense of being true (false) differs for items of different sorts. Aristotle is able to offer a theory of truth which covers all these assertions at one blow: an

(1978), 187–8; K. J. Williams (1978), 68; Simons (1988), 107–8; Wolenski/Simons (1989), 393; Kirkham (1992), 119–20; Knabenschuh de Porta (1997), 192; Vigo (1997), 8–10; Hafemann (1998), 90–1; Wolff (1999), 51; Modrak (2001), 54.

23 Cf. Wolenski/Simons (1989), 393. Davidson (1996), 267 claims that interpretation (i) does not make T 28's definition of truth and falsehood too narrow because the existential assertions it mentions are those which 'in modern terms' begin with 'there is an *x* such that . . .' or 'it is not the case that there is an *x* such that . . .' Davidson's rescue of interpretation (i) takes universal assertions to be reducible to assertions that begin with 'it is not the case that there is an *x* such that . . .', i.e. to denials of particular assertions. Aristotle, however, seems to do the opposite: he regards particular assertions as denials of universal assertions (cf. the subsection to which n. 24 of appendix 3 pertains). Hence, Davidson's rescue of interpretation (i) fails.

24 Cf. n. 18 above.

affirmative assertion is true (false) when and only when the (composite or non-composite) item it concerns 'is' in the sense of being true ('is not' in the sense of being false), a negative assertion is true (false) when and only when the (composite or non-composite) item it concerns 'is not' in the sense of being false ('is' in the sense of being true). I suggest that Aristotle's definition of truth and falsehood in T 28 expounds this theory. The definition can then be paraphrased as follows: 'To say of a (composite or non-composite) item which in fact "is" in the sense of being true that it "is not" in the sense of being false, or of a (composite or non-composite) item which in fact "is not" in the sense of being false that it "is" in the sense of being true, is false; to say of a (composite or non-composite) item which in fact "is" in the sense of being true that it "is" in the sense of being true, or of a (composite or non-composite) item which in fact "is not" in the sense of being false that it "is not" in the sense of being false, is true.' On this interpretation, T 28's definition of truth and falsehood covers predicative as well as existential assertions. This gives it the edge on the other interpretations, which make Aristotle's definition uncomfortably narrow. Note, however, that even on my preferred interpretation, T 28's definition of truth and falsehood is somewhat limited: for Aristotle recognises also assertions composed of other assertions by means of conjunctions,[25] and T 28's definition is silent about these.

If this reconstruction is correct, Aristotle's theory of truth can be regarded as a correspondence theory of truth based on an isomorphism between the assertion and an object which corresponds to the whole assertion. This correspondence-as-isomorphism theory of truth for assertions relies on a simple classification of assertions. There are just two classes of assertions: affirmations, which assert items 'to be' in the sense of being true, and denials, which assert items 'not to be' in the sense of being false. These two classes of assertions are mapped one-to-one onto precisely two properties that can hold of the item an assertion is about. This mapping is best explained by means of the following diagram (where every item in the left-hand side column mentions a class of assertions, while the item on the same line in the right-hand side column mentions the corresponding property which can hold of the item the assertion is about):

1	asserting 'being' in the sense of being true	'being' in the sense of being true
2	asserting 'not being' in the sense of being false	'not being' in the sense of being false

An assertion is true just in case either it asserts the relevant item 'to be' in the sense of being true and this item 'is' in the sense of being true, or it

[25] *Int.* 5, 17^a8–9; 17^a15–16.

asserts the relevant item 'not to be' in the sense of being false and this item 'is not' in the sense of being false.[26]

(iii.ii) Isomorphism with respect to items corresponding to parts of assertions. The condition introduced by the correspondence-as-isomorphism conception is met again by Aristotle's theory of truth, at a more specific level: in the definition of truth and falsehood for predicative assertions. A predicative assertion is about two objects: one is a universal (signified by the assertion's predicate), the other is either a universal or an individual (signified by the assertion's subject).[27] As in the first account, the correspondence-as-isomorphism theory of truth for assertions relies on a classification of assertions. The second account's classification, however, is more fine-grained than the first's. There are six classes of assertions, and these six classes are mapped one-to-one onto six two-place relations that can hold of the universals or individuals an assertion can be about. The classes of assertions and their mapping onto two-place relations are best explained by means of a diagram (where, as in the previous one, every item in the left-hand side column mentions a class of assertions, while the item on the same line in the right-hand side column mentions the corresponding two-place relation):

1	asserting the combination of universally holding	being combined in such a way as universally to hold
2	asserting the division of universally failing to hold	being divided in such a way as universally to fail to hold
3	asserting the combination of not universally failing to hold	being combined in such a way as not universally to fail to hold
4	asserting the division of not universally holding	being divided in such a way as not universally to hold
5	asserting the combination of holding	being combined in such a way as to hold
6	asserting the division of holding outside	being divided in such a way as to hold outside

(For simplicity's sake, I rely on a simple classification that ignores the distinctions induced by the categories.) An assertion *a* is true when and only when either *a* asserts the universal *p* signified by its predicate to be combined with the universal *s* signified by its subject in such a way as universally to hold of it and *p* is combined with *s* in such a way as universally to hold of it, or *a* asserts the universal *p* signified by its predicate to be divided from the universal *s* signified by its subject in such a way as universally to fail to

[26] Cf. Brentano (1889), 24–5, 26–7 (with Srzednicki (1965), 18 and Wolenski/Simons (1989), 393); Oehler (1962/85), 176–7; Szaif (1998), 520–1.

[27] Cf. [17] on pp. 93–4 above.

hold of it and *p* is divided from *s* in such a way as universally to fail to hold of it, or . . .[28]

Note that the two accounts of truth (the one turning on objects corresponding to complete assertions and the one turning on objects signified by a predicative assertion's predicate or subject) are neither incompatible nor in competition. For the second account can be regarded as a 'sharpening' of the first: the various types of combinations and divisions between objects signified by a predicative assertion's predicate or subject can be regarded as ways in which the state of affairs that corresponds to a complete predicative assertion 'is' in the sense of being true or 'is not' in the sense of being false – recall that for a state of affairs 'to be' ('not to be') in the sense of being true (false) is to be combined (divided).[29]

(iv) Mirror-isomorphism. Aristotle's theory of truth seems to count as a correspondence theory of truth in a different, stricter sense than the ones outlined so far. This is because Aristotle's theory of truth describes each class of assertions in such a way that each assertion 'mirrors' the characteristic on which the class it belongs to is mapped. Consider the first class of assertions in the first type of correspondence-as-isomorphism theory of truth: asserting 'being' in the sense of being true 'mirrors' 'being' in the sense of being true. In general, each class of assertions in Aristotle's theory of truth is singled out by the property of asserting that the attribute on which it is mapped obtains (this can be easily seen in the two diagrams in the last subsections). This circumstance brings it about that Aristotle's theory of truth for assertions counts as a correspondence theory of truth in that it regards an assertion as true when and only when it 'asserts its object to be as it is'.

Aristotle's formulations of his correspondence theory of truth. Many philosophers regard the Latin formula '*Veritas est adaequatio rei et intellectus*' ('Truth is uniformity of thing and mind') as a definition of truth as correspondence. This Latin formula originated in the Middle Ages, and is probably a translation of an Arabic formula created by an unknown medieval Arab philosopher.[30] In Aristotle's works no Greek sentence occurs that could be translated by this Latin formula.[31]

Many philosophers credited with a correspondence theory of truth characterise truth by using some comparative adverb like 'as' or 'in the way'

[28] Cf. Joachim (1906), 124–6; Hallett (1988), 8; Crivelli (1996), 158–9. [29] Cf. [1] on p. 54 above.
[30] Cf. Muckle (1933); Luther (1966), 206–7, 188; Weingartner (1978), 185; Schulz (1993), 36–7.
[31] Cf. Kreiser (1983), 96.

(e.g. 'A true assertion asserts things to be as they are' or '. . . in the way they are'). For instance, in the *Euthydemus* Plato says:

T 30 There are people who speak of things as they are [ὡς ἔχει] [. . .], those who speak the truth. (284*c*9–284*d*2)[32]

Aristotle never characterises truth by employing a comparative adverb, a fact all the more surprising in view of Plato's usage.[33] But other Aristotelian formulations suggest a correspondence theory of truth.

(i) In *Prior Analytics* 2.15, 64^{b}9–10 Aristotle describes the false conclusion of a syllogism as 'contrary to the fact [ἐναντίος τῷ πράγματι]'.

(ii) In *de Anima* 3.3, 427^{a}26–427^{b}6 Aristotle discusses a position of some earlier thinkers: thought is perception and 'like is perceived by like'. He attacks this position by arguing that it entails the absurd consequence that all thoughts should be true – for, obviously, many thoughts are false.[34] He seems to assume that the likeness, i.e. similarity, of a perception (or a thought) to reality entails that the perception (or thought) should be true.

(iii) Aristotle says that knowledge is 'measured' by its object.[35] In saying this he is probably taking issue with Protagoras, who, as Aristotle knew,[36] said that a man is the measure of all things. But what does Aristotle mean by saying that knowledge is 'measured' by its object? Since he thinks that knowledge is true,[37] at least part of what he means could be that the truth of a piece of knowledge consists in its being somehow 'proportionate' to its object, which thereby operates as a sort of 'unit of measurement'.[38]

32 Cf. *Euthd.* 284*d*5; *Cra.* 385*b*7–8, if 'ὡς' at 385*b*7 and *b*8 is the comparative 'as' rather than the declarative 'that'; *R.* v 477*b*10–11; 478*a*6; *Prm.* 161*e*4–5; *Sph.* 263*b*4–5, if 'ὡς' at 263*b*4 is comparative rather than declarative (cf. Crivelli (1990), 92). Alexander (*in Metaph.* 89, 2–6) mentions a Platonic argument for Forms which relies on the assumption that 'what we say truly, this holds', an assumption that could be regarded as a characterisation of truth as correspondence (cf. Wilpert (1949), 46–7). Alexander's report concerns us because its source could be Aristotle's *de Ideis* (it is included in fr. 118, 3 Gigon 382^{a}24–31). According to *Dissoi Logoi* 4.2, a sentence is true 'if things have turned out in the way the sentence is said' (cf. Goldin (2002), 236–7).

33 However see *Po.* 25, 1460^{b}8–11; 1460^{b}32–1461^{a}4; *Metaph.* Δ 29, 1024^{b}21–4; [Arist.] *Divis. Arist.* 31, 50, 8–9. At *Int.* 9, 19^{a}33 Aristotle says that 'sentences are true in the same way as [ὁμοίως . . . ὥσπερ] the objects'. Some commentators (e.g. Trendelenburg (1846), 14; Bonitz (1848/49), II 409; Dickason (1976), 20; Donini (1989), 1; Modrak (2001), 54) regard this remark as a formulation of a correspondence theory of truth. However, what Aristotle has in mind in this passage seems to be something narrower than a correspondence theory of truth: see the subsection to which n. 60 of ch. 7 pertains.

34 Cf. *Metaph.* Γ 5, 1009^{b}12–33.

35 *Metaph.* I 1, 1053^{a}31–5; 6, 1057^{a}11–12.

36 *Metaph.* I 1, 1053^{a}35–6; K 6, 1062^{b}12–14 (cf. 1062^{b}19; 1063^{a}4).

37 See n. 3 of ch. 1.

38 Cf. Fiorentino (2001), 278–9, 281–2.

2 THE LIAR

A version of the Liar. I begin by presenting a version of the Liar that relies on assumptions Aristotle would probably agree to, and therefore constitutes a genuine threat to Aristotle's position.

Let me first of all formulate some definitions and background assumptions – I trust them to be uncontroversial, at least within an Aristotelian framework. Let *u* be an utterance of 'I am speaking falsely',[39] let *k* be a time, let *u*'s utterer be an individual, and let speaking-truly and speaking-falsely be universals. Suppose that *u* is the only assertion produced by *u*'s utterer over some period comprising *k*. Also suppose that *u* is a singular affirmative predicative assertion, that the predicate of *u* (an utterance of 'speaking falsely') signifies the universal speaking-falsely, and that the subject of *u* (an utterance of 'I') signifies the individual who is *u*'s utterer. Since *u* is a singular affirmative predicative assertion, by Aristotle's theory of truth we have that *u* is true when and only when speaking-falsely holds of *u*'s utterer. Since *k* is a time, *u* is true at *k* just in case speaking-falsely holds of *u*'s utterer at *k*.

For the argument to develop, the universals speaking-truly and speaking-falsely must be defined. To this end, suppose that for every time *t* and every individual *s*, speaking-truly holds of *s* at *t* just in case every assertion produced by *s* over any period comprising *t* is true at *t*; analogously, suppose that for every time *t* and every individual *s*, speaking-falsely holds of *s* at *t* just in case some assertion produced by *s* over some period comprising *t* is false at *t*.

The final supposition is that for every time *t* and every individual *s*, either speaking-truly holds of *s* at *t* or speaking-falsely holds of *s* at *t*. Note that if Bivalence holds (i.e. if every assertion is always either true or false), this final supposition follows from the last paragraph's definitions.

First, assume that speaking-falsely holds of *u*'s utterer at *k*. Then *u* is true at *k*. Since *u* is the only assertion produced by *u*'s utterer over some period comprising *k*, every assertion produced by *u*'s utterer over any period comprising *k* is true at *k*. Hence speaking-truly holds of *u*'s utterer at *k*. Thus: if speaking-falsely holds of *u*'s utterer at *k*, then speaking-truly holds of *u*'s utterer at *k*. But either speaking-truly or speaking-falsely holds of *u*'s utterer at *k*. Therefore speaking-truly holds of *u*'s utterer at *k*.

Second, assume that speaking-truly holds of *u*'s utterer at *k*. Then every assertion produced by *u*'s utterer over any period comprising *k* is true

[39] The ancient Liar probably turned on utterances of 'I am speaking falsely' ('ἐγὼ ψεύδομαι') (cf. Alex. Aphr. *in Top.* 188, 19–28; Cavini (1993a), 89, 99), not of 'This assertion is false'.

at *k*. Since *u* is the only assertion produced by *u*'s utterer over some period comprising *k*, *u* is true at *k*. Hence speaking-falsely holds of *u*'s utterer at *k*. Thus: if speaking-truly holds of *u*'s utterer at *k*, then speaking-falsely holds of *u*'s utterer at *k*. But either speaking-truly or speaking-falsely holds of *u*'s utterer at *k*. Therefore speaking-falsely holds of *u*'s utterer at *k*.

Hence speaking-truly and speaking-falsely both hold of *u*'s utterer at *k*.

Refutations. In *Sophistici Elenchi* 1 Aristotle says that 'a refutation is a syllogism together with the contradictory of the conclusion' ($165^{a}2$–3).[40] He means that a refutation is a syllogism[41] together with the assertion contradicting its conclusion, this assertion being the thesis originally endorsed by the answerer in a dialectical debate.[42]

Sophistical refutations. For Aristotle, a sophistical refutation is an apparent refutation.[43] Since a refutation is a syllogism whose conclusion contradicts the answerer's original thesis, there are two main ways in which a sophistical refutation may come to be:[44] either the argument whose conclusion is supposed to contradict the answerer's original thesis appears to be a syllogism,[45] or the conclusion of the argument appears to contradict the answerer's original thesis.

The notion of appearance – as Aristotle understands it with reference to sophistical refutations – has two aspects: falsehood (whatever appears so-and-so is not so-and-so) and delusion (whatever appears so-and-so induces people to believe it to be so-and-so). Since a sophistical refutation mainly comes to be either because the argument at its heart appears to be a syllogism or because the conclusion of this argument appears to contradict the answerer's original thesis, it follows that a sophistical refutation mainly comes to be either because the argument at its heart *is not* a syllogism but *is taken to be* a syllogism, or because the conclusion of this argument *does not* contradict the answerer's original thesis but *is taken to* contradict it. Note that no sophistical refutation is a refutation: 'sophistical' in 'sophistical refutation' has a cancelling effect, like 'fake' in 'fake diamond'.

40 Elsewhere Aristotle says that a refutation is 'a syllogism of the contradictory': see *APr*. 2.20, $66^{b}11$; *SE* 6, $168^{a}36$–7; 9, $170^{b}1$–2 (cf. 8, $169^{b}27$–8; 10, $171^{a}1$–5).

41 Here, as elsewhere in *Sophistici Elenchi*, 'syllogism' denotes not only those arguments with two premisses constructed from three terms which are examined in the *Prior Analytics*, but also other valid arguments (cf. Gobbo (1997), 330–3).

42 Cf. Cavini (1993b), 68–9; Berti (1996b), 61–2; Gobbo (1997), 333–4; Hitchcock (2000), 209.

43 *SE* 1, $164^{a}20$–1; 8, $169^{b}18$–23 (cf. 10, $171^{a}4$–5).

44 *SE* 10, $171^{a}5$–7 (cf. Hitchcock (2000), 209).

45 *Top*. 1.1, $100^{b}23$–5; $101^{a}1$–4; 8.12, $162^{b}3$–5; *SE* 8, $169^{b}18$–23; 11, $171^{b}7$–11; $171^{b}18$–19; 18, $176^{b}31$–3; *Rh*. 2.24, $1400^{b}34$–5.

For Aristotle, what is responsible for the sophistical refutation's argument appearing to be a syllogism or for the argument's conclusion appearing to contradict the answerer's original thesis, is either a feature of language or a move of the questioner's that does not turn on language. Aristotle normally refers to sophistical refutations of a given kind by means of a description that begins with 'dependent on' ('παρά' + accusative): a sophistical refutation is thereby characterised as 'dependent on' the feature of language or the questioner's non-linguistic move that is responsible for its argument appearing to be a syllogism or for this argument's conclusion appearing to contradict the answerer's original thesis.[46]

Expressions used absolutely or with some qualification. Sophistici Elenchi 25 concerns sophistical refutations 'dependent on something being said strictly or in some way, place, manner, or relation instead of absolutely' (180^{a}23–4).[47] Call them 'sophistical refutations dependent on the absolute or qualified use of expressions'.[48]

Sophistici Elenchi 25 contains the only Aristotelian passage that might be (and has been) taken to discuss the Liar.[49] The passage is introduced as follows:

T 31 'Is it possible for the same man at the same time to keep his oath and to break his oath?' 'Is it possible for the same man at the same time to obey the same man and to disobey him?' [. . .] Nor if one keeps one's oath with regard to this or in this way is it necessary that one should keep one's oath (for he who has sworn that he will break his oath, by breaking his oath keeps his oath with regard to this only, but he does not keep his oath). Nor does he who disobeys obey, but he obeys in some way.[50] (180^{a}34–180^{b}2)

[46] I understand the 'παρά' + accusative ('dependent on') construction in Aristotle's formulae 'παρὰ τὴν ὁμωνυμίαν' (4, 165^{b}30), 'παρὰ τὴν ἀμφιβολίαν' (4, 166^{a}6), etc. on the model of 'παρὰ τὴν λέξιν ἐμποιοῦντα τὴν φαντασίαν' (4, 165^{b}25): the 'παρά' + accusative construction introduces the factor on which the production (ἐμποιεῖν) of appearance (φαντασία) depends.

[47] Cf. *SE* 4, 166^{b}22–3.

[48] Arguments dependent on the absolute or qualified use of expressions are discussed by Aristotle also in other passages, both in *Sophistici Elenchi* (4, 166^{b}22–3; 5, 166^{b}37–167^{a}20; 6, 168^{b}11–16; 7, 169^{b}9–12) and elsewhere (*Top.* 2.11, 115^{b}11–35; *Rh.* 2.24, 1402^{a}3–29).

[49] At *EN* 7.3, 1146^{a}21–7 Aristotle perhaps mentions the Liar. However: (i) The text is dubious: most editors agree with Coraes that the crucial occurrence of 'ψευδόμενος' at 1146^{a}22 should be expunged as a dittograph from 1146^{a}21. (ii) Even if 'ψευδόμενος' were retained, the passage could be speaking (not of the Liar, but) of the treacherous character of all sophistical arguments (cf. Zell (1820), II 258–60). (iii) Even if 'ψευδόμενος' were retained and referred to the Liar, the passage would contribute nothing significant to our understanding of Aristotle's views on the Liar.

[50] Some translators (e.g. Maurus (1668), I 624; O. F. Owen (1899/1900), II 594–5) render 'ἀπειθέω' at 180^{a}36 and 180^{b}1 (not by 'to disobey', but) by 'to disbelieve'. However, 'ἀπειθέω' meaning 'to disbelieve' is attested only in late authors.

T 31 discusses two sophistical refutations dependent on the absolute or qualified use of expressions. The first concerns a man swearing that he will break his oath, the second a man who receives the order 'Disobey me'. T 31 is followed by the passage that could contain Aristotle's discussion of the Liar:

T 32 Similar is the account of the claim that the same man is speaking falsely and is speaking truly at the same time, but since it is not easy to see which of the two renderings one should offer, that he is speaking truly or speaking falsely absolutely, this case appears troublesome. However there is nothing to prevent him[51] from being false absolutely but truthful in some way or with respect to something,[52] and from being truthful with regard to some things but, none the less, not truthful. (180^b2–7)

T 32's sophistical refutation concerns a man who 'is speaking falsely and is speaking truly at the same time' (180^b2–3). The argument leading to the paradoxical conclusion that the same man should be speaking falsely and truly at the same time is not recorded.

Interpretations of T 32. T 32 prompts various reactions.

(i) Some commentators[53] take a sceptical stance: they doubt that the argument on which T 32's sophistical refutation turns can be reconstructed.

(ii) Others[54] think that T 32's sophistical refutation has nothing to do with the Liar: Aristotle is instead describing a pattern of argument which can be used whenever two contrary properties apply merely to a limited extent or with some qualification. Imagine the argument developing within a dialectical debate. The questioner, after drawing the answerer's attention to some object which in different parts displays contrary properties to the same extent, induces him to grant that an assertion where one of those contrary properties is attributed to the object is both true and false. For instance, the questioner shows the answerer a sphere which is half-white

[51] At 180^b5 I read 'κωλύει δ' αὐτὸν οὐδὲν', the text handed down by the main manuscripts, probably read by Sophonias (anon. *in SE* 58, 36), and printed by most editors. Michael of Ephesus ([Alex. Aphr.] *in SE* 171, 5–6) seems to have read 'οὐδὲν δὲ κωλύει τὸν αὐτὸν', which might also be presupposed by the Latin translations of Boethius ('*prohibet autem eundem nichil*') and William of Moerbeke ('*prohibet autem nichil eundem*'). Forster prints 'κωλύει δ' τὸν αὐτὸν οὐδὲν', obviously a misprint for 'κωλύει δὲ τὸν αὐτὸν οὐδὲν'. Wallies reads 'κωλύει δ' οὐδὲν' and transposes 'αὐτὸν' to 180^b7 between 'δὲ" and 'μή' (Ross strangely has 'αὐτὸν' both at 180^b5, between 'κωλύει δ" and 'οὐδὲν', and at 180^b7, between 'δὲ' and 'μή', and provides no explanation). Some translators (e.g. Colli (1955), 710; Zanatta (1995), 233) take 'αὐτὸν' to refer to a discourse: this is unlikely in view of the fact that the subject of 'ψεύδεσθαι' and 'ἀληθεύειν' at 180^b2–3 is not a discourse but a man.

[52] I place the comma after 'πῄ δ' ἀληθῆ ἤ τινος' (180^b6): this is the punctuation printed by most editors. Strache/Wallies instead place the comma between 'πῄ δ' ἀληθῆ' and 'ἤ τινος'. The phrase 'ἀληθής τινος' is difficult: I take the genitive 'τινος' to be an 'ablative genitive' introducing an item with which the person's sincerity is compared (cf. Humbert (1945/60), 280–1).

[53] E.g. Kneale/Kneale (1962), 228.

[54] E.g. [Alex. Aphr.] *in SE* 170, 28–171, 9.

and half-black and then gets him to grant that the assertion 'This sphere is white' is both true and false.

(iii) Other commentators[55] regard T 32's sophistical refutation as an argument that is linked with the 'real' Liar but differs from it in a way that deprives it of its devastating strength (specifically, they take T 32's sophistical refutation to lack the self-referential character of the real Liar). According to these commentators, the questioner focuses the answerer's attention on a man who is false (someone who often lies). The answerer is then required to imagine this man describing himself as false. The answerer is thereby induced to grant that the man is both false (such he is by hypothesis) and truthful (because, in describing himself as false, he speaks truly). Aristotle's solution is to indicate that the answerer did not genuinely contradict himself. For while one of the two incompatible predicates applies to the man absolutely, the other applies with some qualification: 'false' applies absolutely (because the man often lies), 'truthful' with some qualification (because the man speaks truly in describing himself as false). The paradox dissolves in the same way as that of the Indian to whom 'non-white' applies absolutely (because he is black in most of his body), 'white' with some qualification (because he is white in his teeth).[56]

(iv) Finally, some commentators[57] regard T 32's sophistical refutation as a version of the real Liar.

Assessment of the various interpretations. (i) However sound a sceptical approach to the scanty evidence may be, I am disinclined to renounce the attempt to reconstruct T 32's sophistical refutation. I therefore dismiss the sceptical approach.

(ii) The context of T 32's sophistical refutation tells against its first reconstruction. For consider T 31's first sophistical refutation. It probably turns on the following argument. A man swears that he will break his oath. Later he breaks his oath by not performing certain actions he had sworn he would perform: e.g. he breaks his oath by not repaying a debt he had sworn he would repay. But in doing so the man keeps his oath: for he keeps the oath he had taken by swearing that he would break his oath. He therefore keeps and breaks his oath at the same time. In his analysis Aristotle points out that the man keeps one oath: he keeps the oath he had taken by swearing

55 Maurus (1668), I 624; von Kirchmann (1883), 53; Ranulf (1924), 176–9; Spade (1973), 300–6; Zaslawsky (1982), 77–82; (1986), 244, 246–7; Dorion (1995), 385–6; Fait (1998), 139–40. This interpretation was favoured by several medieval writers on fallacies (see Spade (1973), 303–6; (1987), 28–9).

56 Cf. *SE* 5, 167ᵃ7–9.

57 Ockham *in SE* II.X 4, 2–12; Rüstow (1910), 48–53; Bochenski (1951), 101–2; (1962), 152–3; Moline (1969), 398; K. Döring (1972), 108; Montoneri (1984), 98–9; Marrone (1988), 273; Gourinat (2000), 199.

that he would break his oath. But his keeping one oath only warrants that 'keeps his oath' should apply to him with some qualification. In order for 'keeps his oath' to apply absolutely to him, he must keep all the oaths he takes. Thus, in the situation envisaged, it is correct to say that the man breaks his oath, but it is incorrect to say either that he keeps his oath or that he keeps and breaks his oath at the same time. Again, consider T 31's second sophistical refutation. The argument on which it turns probably goes as follows (I add a few details for clarity). A slave receives from his master the order 'Disobey me'. He then disobeys the orders his master subsequently gives him: e.g. his master orders him to repay a certain debt but he fails to do it. But in doing so the slave obeys the order which his master had issued by saying 'Disobey me'. Thus, the slave obeys and disobeys his master at the same time. In his analysis Aristotle points out that the slave obeys one of his master's orders: the order issued by saying 'Disobey me'. But his obeying one of his master's orders only warrants that 'obeys his master' should apply to him with some qualification. In order for 'obeys his master' to apply absolutely to him, he must obey all his master's orders. Thus, in the situation envisaged, it is correct to say that the slave disobeys his master, but it is incorrect to say either that the slave obeys his master or that he obeys and disobeys his master at the same time.[58] Now, the fact that T 32's sophistical refutation is presented immediately after those discussed in T 31, which concern the man who swears that he will break his oath and the man who is ordered 'Disobey me', tells against the first reconstruction: if the first reconstruction of T 32's sophistical refutation were correct, it would be awkward to associate T 32's sophistical refutation with those discussed in T 31. Moreover, T 31's first sophistical refutation strongly suggests that T 32's sophistical refutation should turn around an argument closely connected to the Liar: for one century after Aristotle, Chrysippus seems to discuss the Liar in connection with the argument of the man who swears that he will break his oath.[59]

(iii) This brings us to the second reconstruction of T 32's sophistical refutation: can T 32's sophistical refutation be identified with the easygoing argument envisaged by the second reconstruction, the weak strain of the Liar that lacks self-reference? There is surely a lot going for the second reconstruction. For T 31's two sophistical refutations share a curious characteristic: they are both easygoing arguments, and for each of them there exists a difficult version involving self-reference which is ignored by

[58] Cf. Fait (1998), 140.

[59] Chrysipp. *Log. Invest.*, *PHerc* 307 coll. IX 23–X 6; X 28–31 (cf. Rüstow (1910), 78–9). I shall return to Chrysippus' discussion.

Aristotle. As for T 31's first sophistical refutation, Aristotle does not address the awkward situation of a man who takes an oath by saying 'I swear that I shall break *this* oath'; as for T 31's second sophistical refutation, Aristotle says nothing about the predicament of a man who receives the order 'Disobey *this* order'. Aristotle's silence on the difficult versions of T 31's two sophistical refutations suggests that something similar should be going on with T 32's sophistical refutation – which is precisely what is happening if T 32's sophistical refutation is not the real Liar, but an easygoing argument like the one put forward by the second reconstruction.[60]

However, several considerations suggest that T 32's sophistical refutation should be different from the second reconstruction's easygoing argument.

(iii.i) Aristotle regards T 32's sophistical refutation not only as analogous to those from T 31, but also as harder: it is only about T 32's sophistical refutation that Aristotle says that it 'appears troublesome' (180^{b}5). Now, this is the only passage from *Sophistici Elenchi* containing the adjective 'troublesome' ('δύσκολος').[61] The use of this adjective indicates that T 32's sophistical refutation is special. If T 32's sophistical refutation were an easygoing argument like the one favoured by the second reconstruction, there would be nothing special about it: it would be in the same league as those from T 31. This circumstance provides some evidence for assuming that T 32's sophistical refutation should be not an easygoing argument like the one favoured by the second reconstruction, but the real Liar, which is much harder.[62]

(iii.ii) A passage from Chrysippus' *Logical Investigations* handed down on a badly damaged papyrus seems to discuss the Liar:

T 33[63] Other arguments also tell against the preceding claim [*sc.* the claim that the same man will both keep and break his oath][64] and the claim that they will be speaking falsely and speaking truly at the same time. In all claims of this sort on one occasion there are things said absolutely, on another with something further being expressed together in addition. (*PHerc* 307 col. x 18–25).[65]

60 Cf. Fait (1998), 139–40.

61 In the *Topics* 'δύσκολος' occurs only once, at 8.1, 156^{b}34, where it describes not arguments but human beings: answerers in a dialectical debate who do not play by the game's rules.

62 Cf. Rüstow (1910), 50–1.

63 My translation is based on the text in Marrone (1997), 93.

64 The claim that the same man will both keep and break his oath seems to have been discussed shortly before: cf. the letters 'ομν' at col. x 8, probably a trace of 'ὀμνύειν' ('to swear') (cf. col. IX 30).

65 Chrysippus' attack on those who solve the Liar by claiming that some propositions are both true and false is echoed by the title of one of his lost works on the Liar: *Against those who hold that there are things both false and true* (D.L. 7. 196).

In this passage Chrysippus seems to have in mind Aristotle's discussion in T 32.[66] For:

(iii.ii.i) When he mentions the distinction between 'things said absolutely' and 'things said with something further being expressed together in addition', Chrysippus seems to be addressing the Aristotelian distinction between things 'said absolutely' and things 'said in some way, place, manner, or relation instead of absolutely' (*SE* 25, 180ᵃ23–4).[67] Chrysippus probably uses the monster verb 'to express together in addition' ('συνπαρενφαίνειν', a *hapax*) to indicate that when a linguistic expression is applied not absolutely but with some qualification, the respect justifying its application is an additional factor which is part of the meaning but does not surface in an explicit formulation.

(iii.ii.ii) Chrysippus' phrase 'they will be speaking falsely and speaking truly at the same time [ψεύσεσθαι αὐτοὺς ἅμα καὶ ἀληθεύσειν]' (col. x 20–1)[68] is almost a literal quotation of Aristotle's phrase 'the same man is speaking falsely and is speaking truly at the same time [ψεύδεσθαι τὸν αὐτὸν ἅμα καὶ ἀληθεύειν]' (180ᵇ2–3).[69]

(iii.ii.iii) Chrysippus' phrase 'in all claims of this sort [ἐν πᾶσιν τοῖς τοιούτοις, *sc.* λόγοις]' (col. x 22–3) echoes the phrase 'all arguments of this sort [πάντες οἱ τοιοῦτοι λόγοι]' which Aristotle uses shortly before and immediately after T 32 (at 180ᵃ32 and 180ᵇ8).[70]

Chrysippus, who lived one century after Aristotle, surely had more information available about Aristotle than we do. *If* Chrysippus regarded Aristotle's discussion in T 32 as an attempt to solve the real Liar, T 32 probably was such an attempt.

(iii.iii) Theophrastus wrote a work in three books *On the Liar.*[71] Its content is unknown, but it is at least clear that Theophrastus was aware of the importance of the Liar. We do not know whether Theophrastus addressed the real Liar or some easygoing strain of it. However, in his list of Chrysippus' writings Diogenes Laertius (7. 197) mentions a work (now lost) whose title was *Solution according to the Ancients.* The context of Diogenes Laertius' report suggests that the solution announced by this title was a solution for the real Liar (for the works which in Diogenes Laertius' list come immediately before and immediately after were about solutions for the real Liar). So Chrysippus, who lived one century after Aristotle, probably thought that a certain solution for the real Liar had been formulated so long before as to deserve the label 'solution according

[66] Barnes (1999a), 26–9 shows that Chrysippus could have read Aristotle's logical writings.

[67] Cf. Rüstow (1910), 80; Ebbesen (1981), I 44; Baldassarri (1985/87), II 105.

[68] Cf. col. x 12–13; 15–16. [69] Cf. Marrone (1988), 275. [70] Cf. Rüstow (1910), 80.

[71] Cf. D.L. 5. 49; Rüstow (1910), 54; Graeser (1973), 57; Montoneri (1984), 99; Barnes (1999a), 37–8.

to the ancients'. Later texts often refer to the early Peripatetics as 'the ancients', and it is tempting to think that this later usage originated with Chrysippus.[72] So there is some plausibility in assuming that the solution for the real Liar which Chrysippus describes as 'solution according to the ancients' was endorsed by the early Peripatetics.[73] This provides evidence for thinking that Theophrastus addressed the real Liar. This, in combination with Theophrastus' close association to Aristotle in logic as well as in other fields,[74] makes it plausible to assume that Aristotle himself had some views about the real Liar. But T 32 is the only Aristotelian passage that can be taken to be about the Liar.

(iv) None of the above considerations is decisive. We cannot confidently claim that T 32's sophistical refutation turns on the real Liar and not on some attenuated strain of it (like the one favoured by the second reconstruction), nor can we rule out that the Liar might have evolved between Aristotle and Chrysippus, and that Chrysippus, conscious of this development, might be referring back to the Aristotelian solution of the weak version of the Liar.

Although we cannot confidently claim that T 32's sophistical refutation turns on the real Liar, it is worthwhile assuming that it does. Thus, henceforth I shall assume that T 32's sophistical refutation turns on some version of the real Liar, and then ask, first, what solution Aristotle was offering for it, and, second, what this solution is worth.

Aristotle's solution for the Liar: a tentative reconstruction. T 32's discussion of its sophistical refutation is compressed, and its interpretation must be merely conjectural. I begin with the first half of T 32 (180^b2–5). It is traditionally interpreted as saying that a man who produced an utterance of 'I am speaking falsely' speaks truly with respect to one content of this utterance, falsely with respect to another.[75] Were this interpretation correct, Aristotle's position would be hopeless: what could the two distinct contents of the utterance of 'I am speaking falsely' be?[76] It would be better to avoid saddling Aristotle with so poor a position. Let us then attempt a new interpretation of Aristotle's words.

Any plausible interpretation must take into account Aristotle's claim that 'this case appears troublesome' (180^b5) because 'it is not easy to see which of the two renderings one should offer, that he is speaking truly or

[72] Cf. Brunschwig (1991), 83–7; Barnes (1999a), 32–3.

[73] It is also worthwhile reporting that Chrysippus attacked a solution for the Liar which was based on some kind of 'cut' (τομή) (see D.L. 7. 197). Some commentators (e.g. Rüstow (1910), 65–6; O. Becker (1957b), 51) think that this solution was the one advocated by Aristotle.

[74] Cf. n. 10 of appendix 4. [75] Cf. Calogero (1927), 359; Mignucci (1999b), 65.

[76] Cf. Rüstow (1910), 50; Montoneri (1984), 99; Marrone (1988), 273; Cavini (1993a), 102.

speaking falsely absolutely' (180^b3–5). Now, when in *Sophistici Elenchi* 5 he introduces sophistical refutations dependent on the absolute or qualified use of expressions, Aristotle does say something pertinent to this claim:

T 34 [Sometimes the distinction between an absolute and a qualified use of a linguistic expression escapes notice, as] in those cases where it is not easy to see which of the two should be rendered strictly. Such a situation occurs when the opposites hold to the same extent, for it seems that one should grant that the thing is absolutely both or neither: e.g. if one half is white and the other half black, is it white or black? (167^a15–20)

T 34 is evidently connected with the first half of T 32: T 34 discusses a case where the distinction between the absolute and the qualified use of a linguistic expression is hard to spot, and T 34's description of this case ('It is not easy to see which of the two should be rendered strictly', 167^a16) is, from a linguistic point of view, extremely close to that in the first half of T 32 ('It is not easy to see which of the two renderings one should offer, that he is speaking truly or speaking falsely absolutely', 180^b3–5). One of Aristotle's remarks in T 34 is particularly important for our purpose of interpreting the first half of T 32: it is the remark that in the cases in question 'the opposites hold to the same extent' (167^a17). In T 34's example the opposites are whiteness and blackness, which hold to the same extent of (say) a sphere that is half-white and half-black. Since in the first half of T 32 the opposites in question are speaking-truly and speaking-falsely, Aristotle's position with regard to the Liar is probably that speaking-truly and speaking-falsely hold to the same extent of a man saying 'I am speaking falsely' (or uttering whatever sentence-type the Liar turns on).[77]

What does Aristotle mean when he says that in the cases in question 'the opposites hold to the same extent' (167^a17)? One plausible answer is that in his view the situation where two opposites hold of the same object to the same extent is that where the strongest consideration available in support of one opposite holding is counterpoised by an equally strong consideration in support of the other opposite holding. Consider again the sphere that is half-white and half-black: whiteness and blackness hold of the sphere to the same extent because the strongest consideration available in support of whiteness holding of it (a consideration based on direct observation) is counterpoised by an equally strong consideration in support of blackness holding of it (also based on direct observation). A similar account holds for speaking-truly and speaking-falsely with regard to a man uttering 'I am speaking falsely'. The strongest consideration available in support of speaking-truly holding of this man at *k* is embodied in one half of the

[77] Cf. anon. *in SE* 58, 31–6; Pacius (1597a), 523.

Liar, and is counterpoised by an equally strong consideration in support of speaking-falsely holding of this man at *k*, which is embodied in the other half of the Liar. This is clear in the version of the Liar presented earlier: the first half of that version concludes that speaking-truly holds of the man at *k*, the second half that speaking-falsely holds of him at *k*, and the two halves are equally strong.

In T 34 Aristotle points out that 'when the opposites hold to the same extent, [. . .] it seems that one should grant that the thing is absolutely both or neither' (167^a17–18). Aristotle does not say how the answerer should behave in circumstances of the sort described. Of course, the sophist will entice the answerer to admit that 'the thing is absolutely both'. But what is Aristotle's advice? The most plausible answer is that Aristotle would advise the answerer to say that 'the thing is absolutely neither'. Thus, Aristotle's position is probably that what one should say with regard to a sphere which is half-white and half-black is that it is neither absolutely white nor absolutely black (although it is white in some respect and black in some respect). Similarly, Aristotle's position is probably that what one should say with regard to a man who says 'I am speaking falsely' is that at *k* (a time within some period over which the utterance is produced) neither speaking-truly nor speaking-falsely hold absolutely of him (although they both hold of him in some respect). Aristotle can therefore be plausibly taken to be committed to the view that an utterance of 'I am speaking falsely' is sometimes neither true nor false.

In his discussion of sophistical refutations dependent on the absolute or qualified use of expressions, Aristotle acknowledges many ways in which a linguistic expression may fail to apply absolutely: for he describes these sophistical refutations as dependent 'on something being said strictly or *in some way, place, manner, or relation* instead of absolutely' (180^a23–4). Aristotle does not say in what 'way, place, manner, or relation' speaking-truly and speaking-falsely both hold of a man who says 'I am speaking falsely'. He merely argues that they both hold only in a qualified sense because they hold to the same extent.

The second half of T 32 (180^b5–7) is harder to interpret. It might be (and has been)[78] taken to mean that speaking-falsely holds absolutely of a man who says 'I am speaking falsely' while speaking-truly holds of him merely with some qualification. The line which this interpretation attributes to Aristotle seems hopeless: for the assumption that speaking-falsely holds absolutely of the man whereas speaking-truly holds of him with some qualification seems no more justified than the opposite assumption that

[78] Anon. *in SE* 58, 31–6.

speaking-truly holds absolutely of the man whereas speaking-falsely holds of him with some qualification. We should therefore find an alternative exegesis.

A good starting-point is a feature of the second half of T 32 overlooked by commentators: Aristotle changes the expressions supposed to have an absolute as well as a qualified use. For while in the first half of T 32 the expressions with an absolute and a qualified use are 'to speak truly' ('ἀληθεύειν') and 'to speak falsely' ('ψεύδεσθαι'), in the second half they are 'truthful' and 'false' ('ἀληθής' and 'ψευδής' applied to human beings).[79] Why this change of expression?

Two explanations are possible. First, Aristotle might be comparing the behaviour of 'to speak truly' and 'to speak falsely' with that of 'truthful' and 'false' in order to justify that part of his analysis of the Liar which concerns 'to speak truly' and 'to speak falsely'. More precisely, when he says that nothing prevents the same man from 'being false absolutely but truthful in some respect' (180^b5–6), Aristotle might be justifying his distinction between an absolute and a qualified use of 'to speak truly' and 'to speak falsely', a justification which is needed because such a distinction is far from obvious. The justification would be that since the distinction between an absolute and a qualified use is perfectly natural with 'truthful' and 'false' (it is easy to see that the same person can be truthful in some respect or with regard to certain topics while being, properly speaking, not truthful but false), a parallel distinction between an absolute and a qualified use must apply also to 'to speak truly' and 'to speak falsely' (which are obviously related to 'truthful' and 'false'). Second, Aristotle might be contrasting the real Liar with a similar but more easygoing paradox. Specifically, note that the second half of T 32 (180^b5–7) is introduced by an adversative particle ('however', which translates the elided 'δέ' at 180^b5). Aristotle might thereby be indicating what differentiates the real Liar, whose formulation involves 'to speak truly' and 'to speak falsely', from a similar easygoing paradox formulated by using 'truthful' and 'false'. He might be saying that the two paradoxes differ because while in the real Liar it is not the case that one expression applies absolutely and the other with some qualification, in the easygoing paradox 'false' applies absolutely while 'truthful' applies with some qualification. Aristotle would then be alerting his readers to how different the real Liar is with respect to easygoing arguments like the one attributed to him by the second reconstruction.[80] If this explanation of the

[79] For this use of 'ἀληθής' and its cognates cf. *Metaph.* Δ 29, 1025^a1–13; *EE* 2.3, 1221^a6; 3.4, 1233^b38; 1234^a2.

[80] See the paragraph to which n. 55 above pertains.

change from 'to speak truly' and 'to speak falsely' to 'truthful' and 'false' is correct, then Aristotle was aware that the real Liar is much harder than easygoing arguments like the one envisaged by the second reconstruction, i.e. that the real Liar is 'troublesome'.

How satisfactory is Aristotle's solution? If the interpretation offered in the preceding subsection is correct, Aristotle can be plausibly taken to be committed to the view that an utterance of 'I am speaking falsely' is sometimes neither true nor false. Such a position recalls that of *de Interpretatione* 9, where Aristotle claims that some future-tense singular assertions are sometimes neither true nor false.

Aristotle's solution for the Liar is unsatisfactory because it leaves him exposed to the Strengthened Liar. Consider an utterance *v* of 'This assertion is not true': *v* generates a difficulty similar to that afflicting an utterance of 'I am speaking falsely'. On the one hand, if *v* is not true at a time *j* within some period over which *v* is produced, then at *j* the universal signified by *v*'s predicate (an utterance of 'true') does not hold of the item signified by *v*'s subject (an utterance of 'this assertion'), so that *v* is true at *j*. So, if *v* is not true at *j* it is true at *j*. Hence *v* is true at *j*. On the other hand, if *v* is true at *j*, then at *j* the universal signified by *v*'s predicate does not hold of the item signified by *v*'s subject, so that *v* is not true at *j*. So, if *v* is true at *j* it is not true at *j*. Hence *v* is not true at *j*. Therefore at *j* *v* is true and not true. But the escape route that seemed to work with utterances of 'I am speaking falsely' is unavailable in the case of an utterance *v* of 'This assertion is not true': it does not help to say that at *j* *v* is neither true nor false or that at *j* *v* is neither true nor not true. For, in both cases (both in the case in which at *j* *v* is neither true nor false and in the case in which at *j* *v* is neither true nor not true), *v* is not true at *j*, and, as we have seen, if *v* is not true at *j* it is true at *j*.

However, even if Aristotle's solution for the Liar is unsatisfactory, the direction Aristotle had begun going is not hopeless. For some modern coherent and respectable attempts to solve the Liar make moves that resemble Aristotle's: they treat 'I am speaking falsely' as a case where it is indeterminate which of the predicates 'true' and 'false' applies (in analogy to the well-known cases of vagueness concerning predicates like 'bald' and 'heap').[81] Of course, one cannot say that Aristotle anticipated this modern solution, especially when one recalls that he never explicitly discussed even the well-known cases of vagueness.[82]

[81] Cf. McGee (1991), 4–7. [82] Cf. Moline (1969), 397–8; Fait (1998), 138, 151.

CHAPTER 5

'Vacuous' terms and 'empty' terms[1]

As we saw in chapter 4, Aristotle's theory of truth for assertions can be regarded as a correspondence-as-isomorphism theory of truth: Aristotle takes an assertion's truth to consist in a certain isomorphism obtaining between the assertion and reality. We also saw that Aristotle's correspondence-as-isomorphism theory of truth presents itself in two formats. In the first, the components of reality with respect to which a true assertion's isomorphism holds are objects that correspond to assertions as wholes (one object corresponding to one complete assertion). In the second format, which concerns mainly predicative assertions, the components of reality with respect to which a true predicative assertion's isomorphism holds correspond to parts of the assertion: they are objects, i.e. universals or individuals, signified by the assertion's predicate and subject. A well-known difficulty faced by correspondence-as-isomorphism theories of truth of the second format is the *problem of 'vacuous' terms*. What happens if either the subject or the predicate of an assertion is 'vacuous', i.e. fails to signify an item of the appropriate kind?[2] A correspondence-as-isomorphism theory of truth of the second format loses one of its toeholds.[3]

[1] An earlier version of this chapter appeared as Crivelli (2001).

[2] I apply '(non-)vacuous' to any expression that fails to signify (signifies) an item of the appropriate kind. I reserve '(non-)empty' for any expression that fails to signify (signifies) an *existent* item of the appropriate kind.

Every 'vacuous' expression is 'empty'; the converse holds if there are no non-existent items. I believe that for Aristotle there are no non-existent items, and that therefore for Aristotle an expression is 'vacuous' just in case it is 'empty'. However, the claim that for Aristotle there are no non-existent items needs to be proved (cf. the subsection to which n. 24 below pertains).

Note that an expression can be 'vacuous', and therefore also 'empty', while denoting existent individuals. For instance, if there is no universal walking-white-man (cf. *Int.* 11, 20^{a}15–19), 'walking white man' is 'vacuous' (because there is no item of the appropriate kind for it to signify), and therefore 'empty', but denotes existent individuals (walking white men).

[3] On the problem of 'vacuous' terms cf. Trendelenburg (1876), 78; Brentano (1889), 19, 22 (cf. Srzednicki (1965), 19); Brentano (1915a), 219–20; (1915b), 133–4; (1952), 137–8; Jacobs (1979), 286; Hallett (1988), 8; Fiorentino (2001), 280.

Section 1 contains four arguments for the thesis that Aristotle's reply to the problem of 'vacuous' terms is that in every predicative assertion both the predicate and the subject are 'non-vacuous' in that they signify items of the appropriate kinds. The first three arguments appeal to Aristotle's descriptions of affirmative and negative assertions, the fourth to his treatment of a certain type of anomalou sentence in *de Interpretatione* 8.

Section 2 argues that Aristotle in fact has a position that is even stronger than the one attributed to him in section 1: he thinks that in every predicative assertion both the predicate and the subject are 'non-empty' in that they signify *existent* items of the appropriate kinds.

Section 3 discusses Aristotle's position on utterances that look like predicative assertions whose predicate or subject is 'empty' (e.g. utterances of 'A goatstag is white' or 'A goat is a goatstag'). These utterances are not genuine predicative assertions. Rather, they are composite assertions, i.e. utterances equivalent to utterances constructed from several assertions linked by connective particles. In some cases, what on the surface appears to be a contradictory pair of predicative assertions will really be a pair of composite assertions which are both false.

1 'VACUOUS' SUBJECTS OR PREDICATES

Subjects and predicates are 'non-vacuous'. Aristotle thinks that in every predicative assertion both the predicate and the subject are 'non-vacuous' in that they signify items of the appropriate kinds. Here are four plausible arguments for this thesis.

(i) 'Something *asserted about, or away from,* something'. Aristotle claims both that in every affirmative predicative assertion something is asserted about something, and that in every negative predicative assertion something is asserted away from something.[4] Aristotle formulates these claims with the indefinite pronoun 'something' in an emphatic position: '*Something* is asserted about *something*', '*Something* is asserted away from *something*'. Such formulations strongly suggest that for Aristotle in every affirmative or negative predicative assertion both the predicate and the subject are 'non-vacuous' in that they signify items of the appropriate kinds.[5]

[4] See n. 28 of ch. 2.

[5] Cf. Jacobs (1979), 284–6; (1980), 423–5 (*contra* Simpson (1981), 84–5; Wedin (1990), 136–7).

(ii) Affirmations, denials, joining, and separating. Aristotle thinks that in every affirmative predicative belief one item is joined with one item, and that in every negative predicative belief one item is separated from one item.[6] He also holds that in every affirmative predicative assertion one item is asserted about one item, and that in every negative predicative assertion one item is asserted away from one item. He probably regards the operations of asserting-about and asserting-away-from performed in affirmative and negative predicative assertions as the linguistic counterparts of the mental operations of joining and separating performed in affirmative and negative predicative beliefs. He therefore probably thinks that the operation of asserting-about or asserting-away-from performed in a predicative assertion applies to the same items to which the mental operation of joining or separating applies in the predicative belief expressed by the predicative assertion.[7] But how could something which is not there be joined with, or separated from, something which is not there?[8] Hence Aristotle probably believes that the operations of asserting-about and asserting-away-from are performed on items which are there. But now Aristotle is likely to hold that what is signified by the predicate of a predicative assertion is asserted about or away from what is signified by the subject of that assertion. Hence Aristotle is probably committed to the view that in every predicative assertion both the predicate and the subject signify items that are there.

(iii) Joining and separating performed on inhabitants of the categories. In the last subsection I pointed out that Aristotle can be plausibly credited with the view that the operation of asserting-about or asserting-away-from performed in a predicative assertion applies to the same items to which the mental operation of joining or separating applies in the predicative belief expressed by the predicative assertion. In *Metaphysics* E 4 (1027^{b}29–33) Aristotle says that the items joined or separated by an affirmative or negative predicative belief are inhabitants of the categories.[9] Hence he is probably committed to the view that the operations of asserting-about and asserting-away-from are performed on inhabitants of the categories. But, as I pointed out in the last subsection, Aristotle probably holds that what is signified by the predicate of a predicative assertion is asserted about or away from what is signified by the subject of that assertion. Hence Aristotle is probably committed to the view that in every predicative assertion both

[6] Cf. the subsection to which n. 74 of ch. 1 pertains.
[7] Cf. the subsection to which n. 35 of ch. 2 pertains.
[8] Cf. Miller (1971), 53, 56; Pardey (2000), 17–19.
[9] Cf. the subsection to which n. 54 of ch. 2 pertains.

the predicate and the subject signify inhabitants of the categories. Since he surely believes that the inhabitants of the categories are there, he seems committed to the view that in every predicative assertion both the predicate and the subject signify items that are there.

(iv) De Interpretatione *8*. In *de Interpretatione* 8 Aristotle says:

T 35 A single affirmation or denial signifies a single item about a single item (in case this last item is a universal, it makes no difference whether the affirmation or the denial signifies universally or not). (18ᵃ13–14)

But if a single name is given to two items which do not make up a single one, there is neither a single affirmation nor a single denial.[10] For instance, if somebody were to give the name 'cloak' to horse and man, 'A cloak is white' would be neither a single affirmation nor a single denial:[11] for there is no difference between saying this and 'A horse and a man is white', and saying this does not differ at all from saying 'A horse is white and a man is white'.[12] So if these signify many things and are many, clearly the first also signifies either many things or nothing (for it is not the case that some man is a horse).[13] Hence, in the case of these, too, it is not necessary that one contradictory should be true and the other false. (18ᵃ18–27)

In T 35 Aristotle speaks of a single name given to 'two items which do not make up a single one' (18ᵃ18). To illustrate, he imagines somebody giving 'the name "cloak" to horse and man' (18ᵃ19–20). Then (18ᵃ20–6) he considers the expression 'A cloak is white', which contains the name 'cloak', and he argues that 'A cloak is white' 'signifies either many things or nothing' (18ᵃ25). Is Aristotle thinking of ambiguity? In other words, when Aristotle imagines the name 'cloak' given to horse and man, is he imagining 'cloak' to be ambiguous? When he says that the expression 'A cloak is white' 'signifies either many things or nothing' (18ᵃ25), is he claiming that this expression is either ambiguous or lacking signification? Some commentators[14] answer all

10 I read 'οὐ μία κατάφασις οὐδὲ ἀπόφασις μία' (18ᵃ18–19) with some of the main witnesses, Pacius, Buhle, Bekker, Weise, and Dübner. Minio-Paluello, Waitz, Cooke, and Zadro, following other witnesses, omit 'οὐδὲ ἀπόφασις μία'.

11 I read 'οὐ μία κατάφασις οὐδὲ ἀπόφασις μία' (18ᵃ20–1) with all the main witnesses and most editors. Minio-Paluello and Zadro delete 'οὐδὲ ἀπόφασις μία'.

12 Here (18ᵃ23) I agree with those translators (e.g. Gohlke (1951), 94; Ackrill (1963), 49) who take Aristotle to be mentioning a single conjunctive assertion ('A horse is white and a man is white'). Others (e.g. Weidemann (1994/2002), II, 219) take Aristotle to be mentioning two separate simple assertions ('A horse is white' and 'A man is white').

13 Some (e.g. Colli (1955), 65; Riondato (1957a), 137; Zanatta (1992), 93; Weidemann (1994/2002), II, 221) translate '[. . .] (for it is not the case that there is some man-horse)'.

14 Ammon. *in Int.* 126, 11–14; Boeth. *in Int. Pr. Ed.* 102, 21–4; 103, 12–13; *in Int. Sec. Ed.* 178, 17–23; 181, 25–8; 183, 5; Steph. *in Int.* 33, 19–33; anon. *in Int.* 51, 3–13; Aquinas *in Int.* 162–3 Spiazzi; Ockham *in Int.* I.VI 5, 8–21; Pacius (1597b), 96; (1597a), 77; Maurus (1668), I 70; Steinthal (1863/90), I 245–6;

these questions affirmatively. However, the following considerations show that the negative answer is more plausible.[15]

(iv.i) T 35 does not contain expressions like 'to be said in many ways' or 'homonymy', which Aristotle normally uses in discussing ambiguity.[16]

(iv.ii) When, in T 35, he imagines somebody giving 'the name "cloak" to horse and man' (18^a19–20), Aristotle intends to explain what he meant in speaking of a single name given to 'two items which do not make up a single one' (18^a18). In *de Interpretatione* 11 (20^b13–19) Aristotle returns to the issue of a single name given to many items which do not make up a single one. He produces further examples. Animal, biped, and tame are three items which *do* make up a single one. Although the phrase 'biped tame animal' does in a way signify animal *and* tame *and* biped, one can take it to signify the single item biped–tame–animal consisting of animal, tame, and biped.[17] By contrast, walking, white, and man are three items which *do not* make up a single one. Even if there were a syntactically simple expression – 'whitewalker', say – which signifies walking, white, and man in the same way as the phrase 'walking white man', 'whitewalker' would not signify a single item walking–white–man consisting of walking, white, and man: for there is no such single item. Since the phrase 'walking white man' and the imaginary name 'whitewalker' which is semantically equivalent to it are not ambiguous, the phenomenon Aristotle has in mind when he speaks of a single name given to many items which do not make up a single one cannot be identified with ambiguity.

It is therefore likely that it is not ambiguity that Aristotle has in mind when in T 35 he speaks of a single name given to 'two items which do not make up a single one' (18^a18) and offers as an example the name 'cloak' given to horse and man. What he does have in mind is probably a situation analogous to that arising with plural sentences: as the phrase 'Coriscus and Callias' in the plural sentence 'Coriscus and Callias are at home' signifies two items (the individuals Coriscus and Callias) which do not make up a unity (and ambiguity remains out of the picture), so the expressions 'cloak' (understood in the way suggested by T 35) and 'horse and man' signify two items (the universals horse and man) which do not make up a unity (and

Riondato (1957a), 71; Sainati (1968), 223; Celluprica (1987), 182, 184; Zanatta (1992), 27–8. Boethius (*in Int. Sec. Ed.* 183, 20–1) says that his account of *de Interpretatione* 8 agrees with that of Aspasius, Porphyry, and Alexander.

15 Cf. Ackrill (1963), 126, 131; Irwin (1982), 244; Barnes (1994), 98; Weidemann (1994/2002), 220; Whitaker (1996), 97, 105; Wheeler (1999), 219.

16 Cf. e.g. *Top.* 5.2, 129^b31; *SE* 4, 165^b26.

17 At *APo.* 2.13, 96^b30–5 'biped tame animal' is a possible *definiens* of man. In the *Topics* (5.1, 128^b16–18; 2, 130^a27–8; 3, 132^a6–9; 8, 138^a10–12; 9, 139^a18–20) 'animal by nature tame' expresses a peculiarity of man.

ambiguity, again, remains out of the picture).[18]

Aristotle thinks that the expression 'A cloak is white' can be analysed in two ways. He claims that on its second analysis it 'signifies [. . .] nothing (for it is not the case that some man is a horse)' (18^a25–6).[19] The argument on behalf of this claim can be variously interpreted. On the interpretation which seems to me most plausible (an interpretation I shall not defend here), Aristotle's argument is the following:

[a] There is no universal horse-and-man which is the 'logical product' of the universals horse and man.[20]

[b] If 'A cloak is white' (on its second analysis, whereby it is treated as an indeterminate affirmative predicative assertion) signifies something, then there is a universal horse-and-man which is the 'logical product' of the universals horse and man.

[c] 'A cloak is white' (on its second analysis, whereby it is treated as an indeterminate affirmative predicative assertion) signifies nothing.

Propositions [a] and [b] are premisses. The rationale of [a] is the idea that if there were a universal horse-and-man which was the 'logical product' of the universals horse and man, it would always be predicated of at least one individual which at some time or other exists.[21] But, far from being always so predicated, the universal in question would never be predicated of any individual which at some time or other exists (because no individual ever existed or will exist that is both a horse and a man). The rationale of [b] is the principle of Aristotle's semantics according to which every indeterminate affirmative predicative assertion asserts non-universally that the universal signified by its predicate holds of the universal signified by its subject.[22] For this principle requires that if 'A cloak is white' signifies something when it is regarded as an indeterminate affirmative predicative assertion, then there is a universal signified by its subject 'cloak'. But this universal signified by 'cloak' could only be the universal horse-and-man which is the 'logical product' of the universals horse and man. Conclusion [c] follows from [a] and [b]. A consequence Aristotle 'leaves to the reader' is that on its second analysis, the expression 'A cloak is white' even fails to

[18] Cf. *SE* 17, 175^b41–176^a10. [19] I shall discuss Aristotle's first analysis later.

[20] I am assuming that for Aristotle the compound of horse and man – if there were any such thing – would be the universal horse-and-man which is the 'logical product' of the universals horse and man. This is a plausible assumption: for at *Int.* 11, 20^b15–19, where he offers other examples of compounds which are analogous to the would-be compound of horse and man, Aristotle seems to consider 'logical products' of universals.

[21] Cf. the last subsection of sect. 1 of ch. 2. [22] *Int.* 7, 17^b1–12.

be an assertoric sentence because 'a sentence is a spoken sound significant by convention' (*Int.* 4, 16^b26).[23]

If this interpretation of Aristotle's argument on behalf of his claim that 'A cloak is white' on its second analysis signifies nothing is correct, then Aristotle is probably committed to the view that in every indeterminate affirmative predicative assertion the subject must be 'non-vacuous' in that it signifies some universal: if an utterance looks like an indeterminate affirmative predicative assertion whose would-be subject is 'vacuous' in that it fails to signify a universal, then this utterance is not an indeterminate affirmative predicative assertion because it fails to signify in the way that is appropriate to such assertions.

Aristotle is probably also committed to the further view that if an utterance looks like an indeterminate negative predicative assertion whose would-be subject is 'vacuous', then this utterance is not an indeterminate negative predicative assertion because it fails to signify in the appropriate way: for if the subject's being 'vacuous' causes a would-be indeterminate *affirmative* predicative assertion to signify nothing, it is hard to see how the subject's being 'vacuous' could fail to cause the corresponding would-be indeterminate *negative* predicative assertion to signify nothing. So Aristotle seems committed to a general view about indeterminate predicative assertions: if an utterance looks like an indeterminate predicative assertion whose would-be subject is 'vacuous', then this utterance is not an indeterminate predicative assertion because it fails to signify in the way appropriate to such assertions.

Moreover, Aristotle is unlikely to restrict such a view to indeterminate predicative assertions. That is, Aristotle would probably grant the following: in every general predicative assertion the subject must be 'non-vacuous', and if an utterance looks like a general predicative assertion whose would-be subject is 'vacuous', then this utterance is not a general predicative assertion because it fails to signify in the way appropriate to such assertions.

2 'EMPTY' SUBJECTS OR PREDICATES

'Non-vacuous' vs *'non-empty'*. The previous section's considerations make it plausible to credit Aristotle with the view that in every predicative assertion both the predicate and the subject are 'non-vacuous', i.e. signify items of the appropriate kinds. Does he also believe that in every predicative assertion

[23] Cf. Ackrill (1963), 132; Geach (1963), 17; Irwin (1982), 244–5; Whitaker (1996), 97–8. For the reading cf. n. 96 of ch. 1.

both the predicate and the subject are (not only 'non-vacuous', but also) 'non-empty', i.e. signify *existent* items of the appropriate kinds?

Commentators disagree. In the following subsections I offer four plausible arguments on behalf of the affirmative answer.

(i) 'Everything exists'. Aristotle probably believes that all items are existent items.[24] For:

(i.i) The following passage from *Topics* 4.6 seems a formulation of this view:

T 36 Being and one are predicated of absolutely[25] everything. (127^a33–4)[26]

One might object that T 36's provenance from the *Topics* reduces its evidential value (after all, in the *Topics* Aristotle often presents views he does not endorse). The objection is answered by highlighting that T 36 is echoed by the following cursory remark in *Metaphysics* Γ 2:

T 37 Being is common to everything. (1004^b20)[27]

(i.ii) Aristotle, who has a well worked-out ontology, never states that some items are non-existent. Since this is a somewhat out-of-the-way view, if a philosopher with a well worked-out ontology never states it then one can assume that she or he endorses its contradictory, i.e. that all items are existent.

Now, as we saw in section 1, Aristotle probably holds that in every predicative assertion both the predicate and the subject are 'non-vacuous' in that there are items of the appropriate kinds which they signify. As we have just seen, he also probably holds that all items are existent items. Hence he is probably committed to the view that in every predicative assertion both the predicate and the subject signify existent items of the appropriate kinds, i.e. are 'non-empty'.

(ii) Items within the categorial scheme. As we saw, Aristotle is probably committed to the claim that in every predicative assertion both the predicate and the subject signify inhabitants of the categories.[28] This made it

[24] Cf. Wagner (1961/62), 78; Grice (1988), 178. By contrast, Thom (2002), 298–300 attributes to Aristotle an ontology parallel to Meinong's, according to which some items exist and others do not.

[25] T 36's context makes it clear that 'absolutely' ('ἁπλῶς') modifies 'everything' ('πάντων'), not 'are predicated' ('κατηγορεῖται'): Aristotle means (not that being and one are absolutely-predicated of everything, but) that being and one are predicated of absolutely-everything.

[26] Cf. 4.1, 121^b5–7; 6, 127^a27–8.

[27] The same point is made or implied elsewhere: see *Metaph.* B 3, 998^b20–1; 4, 1001^a19–22; Z 4, 1030^a21; I 2, 1053^b20–1; K 1, 1059^b28–9; 2, 1060^b4–5; Λ 4, 1070^b7–8.

[28] Cf. the subsection to which n. 9 above is appended.

plausible to credit him with the view that there are items of the appropriate kinds signified both by the predicate and by the subject of any predicative assertion. Now, the inhabitants of the categories are existent items.[29] Hence, if Aristotle is committed to the claim that both the predicate and the subject of any predicative assertion signify inhabitants of the categories, he is committed also to the claim that both the predicate and the subject of any predicative assertion signify existent items of the appropriate kinds, i.e. are 'non-empty'.

(iii) De Interpretatione *8*. In T 35 (an excerpt from *de Interpretatione* 8) Aristotle considers the case of a single name given to 'two items which do not make up a single one' (18^a18); he illustrates it by imagining somebody giving 'the name "cloak" to horse and man' (18^a19–20); he considers the expression 'A cloak is white' (18^a20), which he regards as analysable in two ways; and he claims that on its second analysis it 'signifies [. . .] nothing (for it is not the case that some man is a horse)' (18^a25–6). I previously[30] reconstructed Aristotle's argument for his claim that 'A cloak is white', on its second analysis, signifies nothing. Now, if Aristotle allowed some indeterminate assertion to have a subject which is 'empty' because it signifies a non-existent universal, 'A cloak is white' would surely be an example of this case. Then he would not be in a position to claim that 'A cloak is white', on its second analysis, signifies nothing.

(iv) The Square of Opposition. Assume the laws of the Square of Opposition, and assume that every particular predicative assertion is true only when its subject denotes at least one individual that at some time or other exists. Take any quantified predicative assertion, and suppose that at a time *t* its subject denotes no individual that at some time or other exists. Consider a quartet of 'coincident' quantified predicative assertions: a universal affirmative, a universal negative, a particular affirmative, and a particular negative predicative assertion in each of which the subject is a token (an utterance) of the same type as the subject of the original quantified predicative assertion, and, similarly, the predicate is a token (an utterance) of the same type as the predicate of the original quantified predicative assertion.[31] Then at *t* the subjects of the particular predicative assertions denote no individual that at some time or other exists. Then neither particular predicative assertion is

[29] Carson (1996), 21–2, doubts that the items in the categorial scheme should be existent items, but his reasons are unpersuasive.
[30] See the subsection to which n. 10 above is appended.
[31] For 'coincident' see n. 9 of the introduction.

true at *t*. Then, by the Law of Contradictories, both universal predicative assertions are true at *t*. This clashes with the Law of Contraries.[32] Thus, the laws of the Square of Opposition seem to require that in every quantified predicative assertion the subject should always denote at least one individual that at some time or other exists.[33]

Now, if Aristotle believes that in every predicative assertion both the predicate and the subject are 'non-empty', then his theory probably satisfies such a requirement. To see this, assume that for Aristotle in every predicative assertion both the predicate and the subject are 'non-empty', i.e. signify existent universals. Since Aristotle is probably committed to the view that every universal always holds of some individual or other that at some time or other exists,[34] he is probably committed to the view that in every quantified predicative assertion the subject always denotes some individual or other that at some time or other exists – as the laws of the Square of Opposition seem to require.

Objections. Categories 10, 13^b12–33 commits Aristotle to the claim that if Socrates does not exist, then 'Socrates is sick' is false and 'Socrates is not sick' true. Several passages[35] commit him to the claim that certain negative predicative expressions are true of what does not exist. *De Interpretatione* 11, 21^a25–8 commits him to the claim that although Homer does not exist, 'Homer is a poet' is true.

However, these passages do not commit Aristotle to the claim that some true predicative assertion has an 'empty' subject. They only commit him to the claim that the subject of some true singular predicative assertion refers to an object that does not exist *at the time with respect to which the assertion*

[32] For the Law of Contradictories and the Law of Contraries see nn. 15 and 17 of appendix 5 and the portions of the main text they pertain to.

[33] Alternative defences of the laws of the Square of Opposition are available that do not assume that in every quantified predicative assertion the subject should always denote at least one individual that at some time or other exists. These alternative defences, however, face their own difficulties. I cannot address here all the issues raised by the Square of Opposition – for some discussion see Brentano (1909), 61; Bird (1964), 71–82; Church (1965), 418–24; Dapunt (1968); Cavini (1985), 42–3; Crivelli (1989), 79–85; Beaney (1996), 32, 273–5; Mulder (1996), 143–9.

[34] Cf. the last subsection of sect. 1 of ch. 2.

[35] *Int.* 3, 16^b12–15 (cf. 2, 16^a30–3; 10, 19^b5–18; 20^a31–40; *Metaph.* K 9, 1066^a15–16); *Xen.* 4, 978^b15–33; *Metaph.* I 3, 1054^b18–21; *de Ideis* fr. 118, 3 Gigon 378^a23–378^b1 (= Alex. Aphr. *in Metaph.* 80, 16–17); 378^a45–378^b45 (the passage of the *recensio altera* that corresponds to Alex. Aphr. *in Metaph.* 80, 19–81, 2). *APr.* 1.46, 51^b5–52^a14 (cf. *Int.* 10, 19^b19–36) is variously interpreted: on one interpretation (see e.g. Wedin (1978), 188–93; (1990), 142–3) it commits Aristotle to the claim that a negative predicative expression is true of what does not exist; on another (see e.g. Ross (1949), 422–3; Soreth (1973), 403, 404) no such commitment obtains.

is evaluated as true or false.[36] The passages are consistent with the following claim:

[27] In every singular predicative assertion, the subject signifies an individual which at some time or other exists (the time when it exists can be distant both from that at which the assertion is produced and from that with respect to which it is evaluated as true or false).[37] In every singular predicative assertion, the predicate signifies a universal which always exists, i.e. a universal always predicated of at least one individual which at some time or other exists. In every general predicative assertion, both the predicate and the subject signify universals that always exist.[38]

Note how natural this way is of understanding the claim 'In every predicative assertion both the predicate and the subject signify existent items of the appropriate kinds': the claim would be implausibly restrictive if it were to ban from the realm of predicative assertions an utterance of 'Socrates is a philosopher' on the ground that its subject does not signify something that exists at the time when the utterance is produced or at the time with respect to which it is evaluated.[39]

Seeming predicative assertions with an 'empty' predicate or subject. Proposition [27] implies that if an utterance looks like a predicative assertion but its

[36] Cf. Kahn (1976), 325, 326; Pardey (2000), 29–31, 40–1.

[37] The question whether reference can be made to what does not yet exist is debated in modern logic (see e.g. Mayo (1962/68), 282–91), but does not seem to have worried ancient logicians: no difficulty was felt in Apollo's predicting one thousand years in advance that Cypselus would rule Corinth (see Cic. *Fat.* 7.13 with D. Frede (1998), 98).

[38] Aristotle's position might seem inconsistent: what he says about 'Socrates is sick' might seem to require that every affirmation should be false when no item signified by its subject exists, while his discussion about 'Homer is a poet' might seem to require that some affirmation should be true when no item signified by its subject exists. Some commentators (e.g. Oehler (1984), 274) think there is a genuine inconsistency here. However, as other commentators (Barnes (1986), 208–9; van Bennekom (1986), 15; Mignucci (1997a), 61; Thom (2002), 299–300) point out, the inconsistency is merely apparent. Aristotle's remarks about 'Socrates is sick' do not require *every* affirmation to be false when no item signified by its subject exists: affirmations with predicates other than 'sick' (e.g. 'poet') may behave differently. For different explanations of Aristotle's alleged inconsistency see Thompson (1953/68), 55–7; Ackrill (1963), 111; Kirwan (1971/93), 118; Mignucci (1975b), 238–43; Jacobs (1979), 286–95; Wedin (1978), 179–88; Dancy (1986), 66–7; Crivelli (1989), 50–1; Charles (1994), 54–5; Weidemann (1994/2002), 390–1; Carson (1996), 51–70; Goldin (1996), 65–6; Charles (2000), 94.

[39] Two passages are harder to explain away: at *Int.* 11, 21^a32–3 Aristotle seems to imply that 'What does not exist is an object of belief' is true; at *APr.* 1.38, 49^a12–19 and 49^a22–5 he regards 'The goatstag is a non-being; the non-being is known as non-being; hence the goatstag is known as non-being' as a syllogism. However, in both passages Aristotle's examples illustrate points that have nothing to do with the question whether the subject of a predicative assertion can be 'empty': I think that if he were to address these examples in the light of this question, Aristotle would treat them in accordance with the theory I am attributing to him.

would-be subject or would-be predicate is 'empty', then that utterance is not a predicative assertion. Can Aristotle's philosophy of language accommodate such an utterance? For instance, the name 'goatstag' signifies neither an individual which at some time or other exists nor a universal always predicated of at least one individual which at some time or other exists. Proposition [27] then entails that any utterance which looks like a predicative assertion with an utterance of 'goatstag' as subject (e.g. 'A goatstag is white') or predicate (e.g. 'Bucephalus is a goatstag') is not a predicative assertion. Aristotle acknowledges that '"goatstag" signifies something' (*Int.* 1, $16^{a}16$–17).[40] Can his philosophy of language accommodate utterances that look like predicative assertions whose would-be subject or would-be predicate is an utterance of 'goatstag'?

3 ONE ASSERTION *VS* MANY ASSERTIONS

How many assertions does an utterance amount to? Aristotle addresses this question in *de Interpretatione* 5 and 6:

T 38 The first single assertoric sentence is the affirmation, next is the denial;[41] the others are single by virtue of some conjunction. However every assertoric sentence must consist of a verb or an inflexion of a verb: for even the account of man is not yet an assertoric sentence unless 'is' or 'will be' or 'was' or something of this sort is added.[42] But why 'biped walking animal' is something one and not many (for it will certainly not be one through being said all together) – well, to say this belongs to a different inquiry.[43] A single assertoric sentence is either that which reveals a single thing or that which is single in virtue of some conjunction, while many are those which reveal many things and not one or those with no conjunction.[44] (Let names and verbs be merely enunciations because it is impossible to speak like this and to reveal something in such a way as to make an assertion, whether one is answering a question or not but speaking spontaneously.) Of these the one is a simple assertion, i.e. that which asserts something about something or something away from something, the other is compounded of these, i.e.

40 Cf. *APo.* 2.7, $92^{b}5$–8; *Ph.* 4.7, $213^{b}30$–1 (on 'void'). At *APo.* 2.7, $92^{b}29$–30 Aristotle says that 'it is possible to signify things that do not exist'. For the positions taken by the ancient commentators on the signification of 'goatstag' and other similar nouns see Ebbesen (1986), 118.

41 On the priority of affirmations with respect to denials cf. n. 16 of ch. 1 and the corresponding portion of the main text.

42 Cf. *Po.* 20, $1457^{a}24$–7.

43 For the problem of the unity of the *definiens* of a definition cf. *Int.* 11, $20^{b}17$–19; *APo.* 2.6, $92^{a}27$–33. For its solution cf. *Metaph.* Z 11, $1037^{a}18$–20; 12, $1037^{b}8$–$1038^{a}35$; H 3, $1043^{b}23$–$1044^{a}14$; 6, $1045^{a}7$–$1045^{b}24$.

44 Cf. *Int.* 8, $18^{a}13$–27; 11, $20^{b}13$–22; *APo.* 2.10, $93^{b}35$–7; *PA* 1.3, $643^{b}18$; *Metaph.* Z 4, $1030^{b}7$–13; H 6, $1045^{a}12$–14; *Rh.* 3.12, $1413^{b}29$–$1414^{a}1$; *Po.* 20, $1456^{b}38$–$1457^{a}6$; $1457^{a}28$–30; Ammon. *in Int.* 66, 31–67, 19.

> a sentence which is already composite. A simple assertion is a significant spoken sound about whether something holds or does not hold, according to one of the divisions of time; an affirmation is an assertion of something about something, a denial is an assertion of something away from something. (17^a8–26)

In T 38 on two occasions (at 17^a9 and 17^a16) Aristotle mentions assertions that are one 'by virtue of some conjunction'. On the second of these occasions he contrasts assertions that are one 'by virtue of some conjunction' with assertions that are many because they are 'with no conjunction'.

The meaning of 'conjunction'. In T 38 the relevant occurrences of 'conjunction' probably denote connective particles (linguistic expressions like 'and', 'or', etc.).[45] For:

(i) In *Rhetoric* 3.12 Aristotle discusses the styles that are appropriate to different kinds of rhetoric. He says:

T 39 Expressions with no conjunction and involving frequent repetitions are rightly criticised in written style but not in debating style. (1413^b19–21)

> A similar point [*sc.* that one must deliver one's speech in a variegated style] holds for expressions without conjunction, e.g. 'I went, I met, I begged'. For one must act this out and not deliver it with the same tone and character, as if saying only one thing. Moreover, expressions with no conjunction have a peculiarity: they seem to say many things at the same time. For a conjunction makes the many one, so that if it is taken out it is clear that the one will contrariwise be many. It therefore provides amplification: 'I went, I spoke, I implored' (what he said seems to survey many things).[46] (1413^b29–1414^a1)

In T 39 'conjunction' seems to mean 'connective particle':[47] what Aristotle's examples ('I went, I met, I begged' and 'I went, I spoke, I implored') conspicuously lack are connective particles,[48] and it is with regard to linguistic particles that it makes sense to consider the result of taking them out.[49]

45 Cf. Ammon. *in Int.* 66, 31–67, 19; Textor (1870), 25; von Kirchmann (1876), 64; Bywater (1909), 277; Gohlke (1951), 89–90; Morpurgo-Tagliabue (1967), 52; Antiseri (1969), 53–7; Larkin (1971), 26; Kahn (1973b), 151, 156; van Bennekom (1975), 404; Belardi (1977), 263–8; Zadro (1979), 112–13; Thornton (1986), 173–4; Weidemann (1994/2002), 197; Slomkowski (1997), 126. Aristotle applies 'conjunction' to 'and' ('καί', see *Pr.* 19.20, 919^a22–5) and 'or' ('ἤτοι', see *Po.* 20, 1456^b38–1457^a6).

46 Reading 'πολλὰ δοκεῖ ὑπεριδεῖν ὅσα εἶπεν' (1414^a1) with some of the main manuscripts, Cope/Sandys, and Freese (cf. Trenkner (1952/53), 5).

47 This is the view of most translators and commentators (e.g. Maurus (1668), I 808; Steinthal (1863/90), I 265; Cope/Sandys (1877), III 150; Freese (1926), 421; Kennedy (1991), 255–6). Trenkner (1952/53), 4–5 and Blettner (1983), 51 dissent.

48 Cf. 3.19, 1420^b2–3.

49 Cf. *Pr.* 19.20, 919^a22–5.

An aspect of T 39 which is important for present purposes is that it speaks of expressions where 'a conjunction makes the many one' (1413^{b}32–3), and it contrasts such unified expressions with others which are 'with no conjunction' (1413^{b}29 and 1413^{b}31): this obviously recalls what we find in T 38, and therefore supports the suggestion that in T 38 also 'conjunction' should denote connective particles.

(ii) In *Poetics* 20 Aristotle offers two definitions of a conjunction:

T 40 A conjunction is a sound without signification which[50] is not apt to be placed on its own at the beginning of a sentence, e.g. 'μέν', 'ἤτοι', 'δέ'; or a sound without signification which is of such a nature as to make one significant sound out of sounds that are more than one but significant.[51] (1456^{b}38–1457^{a}6)

The first definition is of a syntactic, the second of a semantic character. The second definition fits well with the interpretation of T 38 according to which the relevant occurrences of 'conjunction' in that passage denote connective particles.

One might object that 'conjunction' in T 38 means (not 'connective particle', but) 'connection'.[52] Support for this objection might come from passages where Aristotle offers the *Iliad* as an example of a linguistic expression which is 'single by virtue of some conjunction':[53] the *Iliad*'s unity is not a matter of connective particles linking all the sentences in the poem (a poem of the size of the *Iliad* will surely contain many sequences of sentences not linked by connective particles, an obvious fact which Aristotle could hardly overlook) – rather, the *Iliad*'s unity consists in the fact that the 'action' narrated is unitary.[54] But this is captured by Aristotle's description 'single by virtue of some conjunction' only if, as the objection assumes, 'conjunction' means 'connection'.

[50] Following Margoliouth, I delete 'ἢ οὔτε κωλύει . . . καὶ ἐπὶ τοῦ μέσου' (1456^{b}38–1457^{a}3). For a justification of this expunction see van Bennekom (1975), 400–1.

[51] The phrase 'sounds that are more than one but significant' renders 'πλειόνων μὲν φωνῶν μιᾶς σημαντικῶν δὲ' (1457^{a}4–5): for this construction cf. *Cael.* 1.6, 274^{a}28; 2.14, 296^{a}35–296^{b}1; *Metaph.* A 3, 983^{b}17–18; *Pol.* 3.7, 1279^{a}35; 6.1, 1317^{a}22; Vahlen (1885), 213–14; Rostagni (1927), 81. A. Döring (1890), 365 construes 'μιᾶς' with 'σημαντικῶν', understanding 'μιᾶς ἰδέας' or 'μιᾶς φωνῆς'.

[52] Cf. Gudeman (1934), 353; Pagliaro (1954), 85; Apostle (1980), 104; Zadro (1999), 217; Morgenstern (2001), 279. 'Conjunction' can mean 'connection': see *HA* 10.7, 638^{b}8–9; *PA* 2.6, 652^{a}16–17; 3.7, 670^{a}9. In one passage (*Rh.* 3.5, 1407^{a}26–9) it seems to mean 'connected item' (cf. Belardi (1977), 258–60). The expression 'with no conjunction' is *not* used exclusively to express the absence of connective particles: see *Pr.* 21.17, 929^{a}18; *Rh.* 3.6, 1407^{b}38.

[53] *APo.* 2.10, 93^{b}35–7; *Metaph.* Z 4, 1030^{b}7–13; H 6, 1045^{a}12–14; *Po.* 20, 1457^{a}28–30 (cf. *APo.* 2.7, 92^{b}32).

[54] Cf. Gallavotti (1974), 179; Zadro (1999), 217. On the unity of the *Iliad*'s 'action' see *Po.* 8, 1451^{a}22–30; 26, 1462^{b}7–12.

This objection can be answered. For the evidence it appeals to supports, in fact, the position under attack. A striking characteristic of the *Iliad* is that almost all its sentences are connected by some particle or other (one reason might be that particles make it easier to satisfy the conditions of the metre): Aristotle might well have in mind this characteristic of the *Iliad* when he says that it is 'single by virtue of some conjunction'.[55]

Classification or disambiguation? In T 38 Aristotle discusses how an utterance can coincide with one or more assertions. Two interpretations of his task are possible.

On the first interpretation, in T 38 Aristotle carries out a *classification*.[56] More precisely, Aristotle draws a single classification of utterances based on the number and the complexity of the assertions which a single utterance amounts to. He first introduces two *main* groups: the group comprising utterances that amount to a single assertion and the group comprising utterances that amount to many assertions. Then he subdivides each of these two main groups into two *subordinate* groups: the first subordinate group of the first main group comprises utterances that 'reveal a single thing', its second subordinate group comprises utterances that are 'single by virtue of some conjunction'; the first subordinate group of the second main group comprises utterances that 'reveal many things and not one', its second subordinate group comprises utterances that are 'with no conjunction'.[57]

On the second interpretation, in T 38 Aristotle carries out a *disambiguation*.[58] More precisely, Aristotle distinguishes two senses in which an utterance can be called 'a single assertion' or 'many assertions': a *semantic* sense and a *syntactic* sense. In the semantic sense, an utterance is called 'a single assertion' if it 'reveals a single thing', while it is called 'many assertions' if it reveals 'many things and not one'. In the syntactic sense, an utterance is called 'a single assertion' if it is 'single by virtue of some conjunction', while it is called 'many assertions' if it is 'with no conjunction'.

A difficulty for the first interpretation. The first interpretation sits uneasily with Aristotle's remark at 17^a15–17: 'A single assertoric sentence is either

[55] I owe this point to Annamaria Schiaparelli.

[56] Cf. Ockham *in Int.* I.IV 2, 2–17; 4, 2–13; Maurus (1668), I 66; Textor (1870), 25–6; Ackrill (1963), 125–7; von Fragstein (1967), 64–5; van Bennekom (1975), 404; Zanatta (1992), 183.

[57] According to Maurus (1668), I 66, in T 38 Aristotle distinguishes not four, but three groups of assertions: single *simpliciter*, single *secundum quid*, and multiple. This interpretation is untenable because it presupposes an epexegetical sense of the 'ἢ' at 17^a17, which is unlikely in view of the disjunctive sense of the immediately preceding occurrences of 'ἢ' (17^a15; 17^a16).

[58] Cf. Ammon. *in Int.* 72, 15–22; Boeth. *in Int. Sec. Ed.* 110, 21–111, 12; Aquinas *in Int.* 103 Spiazzi; Pacius (1597a), 70, 77; Weidemann (1994/2002), 195–6; Whitaker (1996), 75–6, 95.

that which reveals a single thing or that which is single by virtue of some conjunction, while many are those which reveal many things and not one or those with no conjunction.' If, as the first interpretation assumes, Aristotle is introducing a single classification of utterances, this remark seems to commit him to the following: the classification's first (second) main group comprises those utterances that amount to a single assertion (many assertions); the first subordinate group of the first main group comprises utterances which reveal a single thing, its second subordinate group covers utterances connected by means of conjunctions; the first subordinate group of the second main group comprises utterances which reveal many things, its second subordinate group covers utterances not connected by means of conjunctions. If the two subordinate groups of the first main group are disjoint (as they should be), then every utterance from the second reveals many things (otherwise it would reveal a single thing and therefore fall within the first subordinate group). But then every utterance from the second subordinate group of the first main group must also be in the first subordinate group of the second main group. Then the second subordinate group of the first main group is included in the first subordinate group of the second main group. Hence the two main groups overlap.[59]

Solution for the first interpretation's difficulty. The first interpretation may solve this difficulty by assuming that the descriptions of the two subdivisions of each main group are elliptical.[60] Specifically, the classification's first main group (which comprises utterances that amount to a single assertion) divides into two subordinate groups: one comprises utterances which *are not overtly made up of further sentences*[61] *and* reveal one thing, the other comprises utterances which *are overtly made up of further sentences and* link them by means of conjunctions. The classification's second main group (which comprises utterances that amount to many assertions) undergoes a parallel division whereby it articulates in two subordinate groups: one comprises utterances which *are not overtly made up of further sentences and* reveal many things, the other comprises utterances which *are overtly made up of further sentences and* do not link them by means of conjunctions. On this account, the second subordinate group of the first main group is (not included in, but) disjoint from the first subordinate group of the second main group:

[59] Cf. Ackrill (1963), 126; van Bennekom (1975), 404; Weidemann (1994/2002), 195.

[60] Cf. Zanatta (1992), 185–6.

[61] An utterance is *overtly made up of further sentences* just in case it has two or more parts which would be regarded as grammatically complete sentences. For instance, an utterance of 'Socrates came and Coriscus came' is overtly made up of further sentences, one of 'Socrates came' and one of 'Socrates and Coriscus came' are not.

every utterance in the second subordinate group of the first main group is overtly made up of further sentences, and therefore does not fall within the first subordinate group of the second main group (which comprises only utterances not overtly made up of further sentences).[62]

A difficulty for the second interpretation. Consider T 38's first sentence: 'The first single assertoric sentence is the affirmation, next is the denial; the others are single by virtue of some conjunction' (17^a8–9). Aristotle is thus contrasting predicative assertions (which in this context coincide with affirmations and denials) with those assertions that are 'single by virtue of some conjunction'. He therefore seems committed to the claim that predicative assertions are not 'single by virtue of some conjunction'. Now, according to the second interpretation, at 17^a15–16 Aristotle characterises utterances to be called 'a single assertion' in the syntactic sense by saying that each of them is 'single by virtue of some conjunction'. He therefore seems committed to the claim that predicative assertions cannot be called 'a single assertion' in the syntactic sense (otherwise, they would be 'single by virtue of some conjunction'). But such a claim is obviously unacceptable for him: he surely thinks that predicative assertions can be called 'a single assertion' in the syntactic sense.[63]

Solution for the second interpretation's difficulty. The second interpretation may solve this difficulty by making two assumptions: (i) what Aristotle means in T 38's first sentence is that single assertions which are not predicative are single *merely* 'by virtue of some conjunction', the implication being that predicative assertions are single not 'by virtue of some conjunction' but by satisfying another *stricter* condition (e.g. containing only one verb); (ii) when, at 17^a15–16, Aristotle characterises utterances to be called 'a single assertion' in the syntactic sense by saying that each of them is 'single by virtue of some conjunction', he means that these utterances satisfy *at least* the condition of being 'single by virtue of some conjunction', the implication being that predicative assertions can be called 'a single assertion' in the syntactic sense because they satisfy the other *stricter* condition.

Assessment of the two interpretations. Here are some considerations bearing on the assessment of the two interpretations.

[62] In Crivelli (2001), 252 I explored the possibility of solving the first interpretation's difficulty by textual emendation.

[63] This difficulty seems to have escaped the commentators' attention.

(i) T 38's language suggests that it is not a disambiguation that is being carried out. It is not simply that T 38 lacks formulae like 'A single assertion is spoken of in many ways': this fact is not decisive because Aristotle does sometimes carry out a disambiguation without using formulae of this sort. Rather, what is important is that at the crucial points Aristotle does not use 'to be spoken of' ('λέγεσθαι', which can also be rendered by 'to be called' or 'to be said'). He says: 'The first single assertoric sentence is the affirmation, next is the denial; the others are single by virtue of some conjunction' (17^a8–9). He does not say: 'A single assertoric sentence is spoken of primarily by being an affirmation, next by being a denial; all other single assertoric sentences are spoken of by virtue of some conjunction.' Again, he says: 'A single assertoric sentence is either that which reveals a single thing or that which is single by virtue of some conjunction, while many are those which reveal many things and not one or those with no conjunction' (17^a15–17). He does not say: 'A single assertoric sentence is spoken of either because it reveals a single thing or because it is single by virtue of some conjunction, while many are those which are spoken of because they reveal many things and not one or because they are with no conjunction.' But in Aristotle an occurrence of 'to be spoken of' is a hallmark of disambiguation. Just consider that 'to be spoken of' occurs at the beginning of each of the thirty chapters of *Metaphysics* Δ, the book dedicated to disambiguation: it is here, if anywhere, that Aristotle could have safely omitted 'to be spoken of' because it could be understood from the context. This consideration favours the first interpretation.

(ii) Suppose that, as the first interpretation assumes, T 38 drew a single classification of utterances by distinguishing, first, two main groups and, then, two subordinate groups within each main group. Then for each of the subordinate groups the chapter would give separate conditions for being a member of it, but for neither main group would the chapter give unitary (non-disjunctive) conditions for membership.[64] No such problem arises if the second interpretation is right. This consideration favours the second interpretation.

(iii) In *Sophistici Elenchi* 6 Aristotle says:

T 41 A single proposition is that which asks a single item about a single item. (169^a11)

Suppose the first interpretation is right: T 38 classifies utterances by distinguishing two main groups and two subordinate groups within each main

[64] Cf. Ackrill (1963), 125–6.

group. Then single propositions as characterised in T 41 correspond to those utterances which in T 38 are described as asserting 'something about something or something away from something' (17^{a}21), which, in turn, probably coincide with the utterances in the first subordinate group of the first main group. Then there is a tension between T 41 and T 38: what, according to T 41, counts as a single proposition constitutes a subclass of what, according to T 38, counts as a single assertion. If, however, as the second interpretation assumes, T 38 is distinguishing a semantic and a syntactic sense in which an utterance can be called 'a single assertion' or 'many assertions', then single propositions as characterised in T 41 can be identified with those utterances which in T 38 are called 'a single assertion' in the semantic sense. Such an identification generates no tension. As in the previous case, this consideration favours the second interpretation.

The above considerations leave the choice between T 38's two interpretations in the balance. However, one further consideration tilts it in favour of the second interpretation. For, were T 38 offering a single classification of utterances, as the first interpretation assumes, it would have set it up by employing two radically different criteria: one is semantic (signifying one thing *vs* signifying many things), the other syntactic (being tantamount to an assertion composed by means of conjunctions *vs* being tantamount to a collection of unconnected assertions).[65] The second interpretation avoids this disturbing consequence: in fact, according to the second interpretation, one reason for distinguishing the two senses in which an utterance can be called 'a single assertion' or 'many assertions' is that the criteria they invoke are so different. Thus, the second interpretation should be preferred: T 38 distinguishes two senses in which an utterance can be called 'a single assertion' or 'many assertions'.[66]

Utterances that can be called 'a single assertion' in the semantic sense reveal a single thing. Aristotle calls both affirmative and negative predicative assertions 'simple assertions'.[67] The following considerations suggest that in Aristotle's view predicative assertions coincide with the utterances that can be called 'a single assertion' in the semantic sense.[68]

(i) At the beginning of T 38, at 17^{a}8–9, Aristotle contrasts those single assertions which are predicative assertions with those single assertions which 'are single by virtue of some conjunction'. Since the latter are the utterances

[65] Cf. Ackrill (1963), 127.
[66] On this point I changed my mind with respect to Crivelli (2001), 252–4.
[67] *Int.* 5, 17^{a}20–1; 17^{a}22–3 (cf. Pl. *Sph.* 262*c*6–7; 262*c*9–10; 263*c*1–3).
[68] Cf. Zanatta (1992), 183; Weidemann (1994/2002), 194; Whitaker (1996), 77, 95.

that can be called 'a single assertion' in the syntactic sense, one feels inclined to identify predicative assertions with those utterances that can be called 'a single assertion' in the semantic sense.

(ii) In the second half of T 38 Aristotle says:

Of these the one is a simple assertion, i.e. that which asserts something about something or something away from something, the other is compounded of these, i.e. a sentence which is already composite. (17^a20–2)

The occurrence of 'of these' at the beginning of the above passage cannot stand for 'of utterances': if it did, Aristotle would be introducing a completely new division of utterances in which predicative assertions are contrasted with all the rest. It is more plausible to assume that the relevant occurrence of 'of these' stands for 'of utterances that can be called "a single assertion" in whatever sense'.

I suspect that for Aristotle utterances that can be called 'a single assertion' in the semantic sense include also some assertions that are not predicative: in particular, I suspect that in his view they include assertions concerning simple objects (which are existential assertions of a special kind).[69] The reason why Aristotle fails to mention these other assertions as cases of utterances that can be called 'a single assertion' in the semantic sense could be that in *de Interpretatione* he focuses on predicative assertions and he tends to forget about simple assertions of other kinds.

Utterances that can be called 'a single assertion' in the syntactic sense comprise not only those utterances that can be called 'a single assertion' in the semantic sense, but also those that are equivalent to utterances constructed from several assertions linked by connective particles. I use 'utterance equivalent to an utterance constructed from several assertions linked by connective particles' to denote *both* utterances constructed from several assertions linked by connective particles *and* utterances that could be reformulated as utterances constructed from several assertions linked by connective particles.[70] Note that in T 35 Aristotle focuses on an utterance of 'A cloak is white' that he regards as equivalent to one of 'A horse is white and a man is white' (I shall discuss Aristotle's argument in a moment).

Aristotle probably holds that a composite assertion 'reveals many things' in that the utterance to which it is equivalent is constructed from several assertions that reveal different things. None the less, a composite assertion amounts to a single assertion because the connective particles of its

[69] Cf. sect. 1 of ch. 3. [70] Cf. Weidemann (1994/2002), 197.

equivalent reformulation somehow link the different things revealed by its component assertions. Aristotle therefore probably has in mind something like the following: every utterance that can be called 'a single assertion' in the semantic sense, i.e. every simple assertion, i.e. every predicative assertion, reveals a single thing in that it introduces only one state of affairs; by contrast, every utterance that can be called 'a single assertion' in the syntactic sense either reveals a single thing (and therefore can be called 'a single assertion' also in the semantic sense) or 'reveals many things' in that it introduces many states of affairs which it somehow links. These links are expressed by the connective particles which surface in the composite assertion to which the utterance that 'reveals many things' is equivalent (for the presence of connective particles brings it about that the whole composite assertion says something about how these states of affairs are related).[71]

Here Aristotle seems to reserve a niche for those composite assertions which were later studied by Peripatetic and Stoic logicians.[72] He seems to regard these composite assertions as truth-evaluable, but he seems to assume that there is no single state of affairs corresponding to any of them. This is in line with his denial of 'negative' states of affairs: as there is no 'negative' state of affairs corresponding to a negative assertion, so there is no 'conjunctive' or 'disjunctive' state of affairs corresponding to a conjunctive or disjunctive assertion. Aristotle's study of these composite assertions was probably prompted by his desire to develop a hint of Plato's in the *Sophist*,[73] where affirmative predicative assertions are described as being the 'smallest' and 'shortest' of assertions – such a description leaves the reader with the curiosity to discover what the 'larger' and 'longer' assertions could be.

Truth-evaluability and different truth-values assigned to contradictories. When Aristotle distinguishes a semantic and a syntactic sense in which an utterance can be called 'a single assertion' or 'many assertions', one of his aims is probably to separate the issue of truth-evaluability from that of the assignment of different truth-values to contradictories. Let me explain. If an

71 Cf. Simons (1988), 111–12.

72 This is the interpretation adopted by all ancient commentators (Ammon. *in Int.* 66, 31–67, 19; 73, 19–74, 14; Boeth. *in Int. Pr. Ed.* 72, 6–10; 75, 9–11; 77, 24–78, 4; *in Int. Sec. Ed.* 96, 28–97, 18; 105, 1–18; 115, 23–116, 6; Steph. *in Int.* 20, 4–10; 20, 16–24; anon. *in Int.* 18, 7–19) and endorsed by many medievals (e.g. Al-Farabi *in Int. Comm. apud* Zimmermann (1981), 46, 47–8; Ockham *in Int.* I.IV 2, 6–16; 4, 9–10; 4, 14–15; 6, 11–14) and some modern writers (Brandis (1862/64), I 437; von Kirchmann (1876), 64; DuLac (1949), 168; Antiseri (1969), 53–7; Weidemann (1994/2002), 197–8; Slomkowski (1997), 126; Damschen (2001), 127). According to other modern commentators (e.g. Lukasiewicz (1957), 131–2; Sainati (1968), 53; D. Frede (1970), 20, 75–6; Patzig (1973), 922; Astroh (1981), 341, 344–5; D. Frede (1985), 77–8; Bobzien (2002), 364), Aristotle never allowed a single assertion to consist of sentences linked by connective particles. In *Metaph.* Γ 4, 1008^{a}4–7 Aristotle ascribes truth to a conjunctive assertion which he describes as consisting of further assertions.

73 262*c*7; 262*c*10; 263*c*3.

utterance can be called 'a single assertion' in any (either semantic or syntactic) sense, then it is truth-evaluable, i.e. it is an utterance with regard to which the question 'Is it true or false?' can be reasonably asked. If instead the utterance can be called 'many assertions' in the syntactic as well as in the semantic sense, then it is not an assertion (in fact, it is a collection of assertions, and a collection of assertions is not an assertion), and therefore it is not truth-evaluable. However, if an utterance can be called 'a single assertion' only in the syntactic sense, but can be called 'many assertions' in the semantic sense, then the utterance, although truth-evaluable, can constitute an exception to the principle that contradictories should be assigned different truth-values. This can be clearly seen in Aristotle's discussion in T 35, which comes back to some of the points made in T 38 (T 35 is an excerpt of chapter 8, while T 38 comprises chapter 5 and the beginning of chapter 6 of *de Interpretatione*).

In T 35 Aristotle considers the case of a single name given to 'two items which do not make up a single one' (18^a18). He illustrates it by imagining somebody giving 'the name "cloak" to horse and man' (18^a19–20). Then (18^a20) he considers an utterance of 'A cloak is white'. He thinks that an utterance of 'A cloak is white' can be analysed in two ways: on its second analysis it 'signifies [. . .] nothing (for it is not the case that some man is a horse)' (18^a25–6);[74] on its first analysis it signifies the same as an utterance of 'A horse and a man is white', which in turn 'does not differ at all from saying "A horse is white and a man is white"' (18^a23). Thus, an utterance of

[a] A cloak is white

on its first analysis signifies the same as an utterance of

[b] A horse and a man is white,

which in turn signifies the same as an utterance of

[c] A horse is white and a man is white.

Aristotle says that utterances of [b] and [c] 'signify many things and are many' (18^a24). Aristotle's reason for saying that an utterance of [c] signifies many things is clear: it is a composite assertion consisting of two further sentences, each of which introduces a different state of affairs. Since an utterance of [c] signifies many things, it can be called 'many assertions' in the semantic sense, i.e. 'it is many'. Since [c] is a paraphrase of [b], an utterance of [b] also signifies many things and is many. From this, and

[74] For the second analysis see the subsection to which n. 10 above pertains.

from the assumption that [b] and [c] are paraphrases of [a], Aristotle infers that an utterance of [a] also signifies many things (18^a25). What he has in mind is probably that an utterance of [a], despite its appearance of being a simple predicative assertion, is really a composite assertion, and signifies many things because it introduces many states of affairs (the state of affairs of a horse being white and that of a man being white). It therefore can be called 'many assertions' in the semantic sense. None the less, it can be called 'a single assertion' in the syntactic sense, and as such it is truth-evaluable. Now consider an utterance of

[d] A cloak is not white.

An utterance of [d] counts, or at least appears to count, as the contradictory of one of [a]. An analysis analogous to the one above shows that this utterance of [d] is equivalent to an utterance of

[e] A horse and a man is not white,

which in turn signifies the same as an utterance of

[f] A horse is not white and a man is not white.

As in the case of the utterance of [a], the utterance of [d], despite its appearance of being a simple predicative assertion, is really a composite assertion, and signifies many things because it introduces many states of affairs. Both the utterance of [a] and that of [d] are truth-evaluable because they both can be called 'a single assertion' in the syntactic sense. However, they can both be false: if every horse is white and no man is, or if no horse is white and every man is, then both utterances are false. Thus, our utterances of [a] and [d] can create an exception (perhaps a merely apparent exception) to the principle that requires assigning different truth-values to contradictories. As Aristotle himself puts it, in this case, 'too,[75] it is not necessary that one contradictory should be true and the other false' (18^a26–7).[76]

Generalisation to all utterances with 'empty' names. In the situation imagined in *de Interpretatione* 8, 'cloak' is an 'empty' name (because it signifies neither an existent universal nor – of course – an individual which at some time

[75] Another case where 'it is not necessary that one contradictory should be true and the other false' is that of indeterminate predicative assertions, already discussed in *de Interpretatione* 7 (17^b29–37, cf. 18^a10–11; 9, 18^a29–33).

[76] Cf. Ackrill (1963), 132; Geach (1963), 18; Whitaker (1996), 100, 105–6, 109, 112; Wheeler (1999), 219. In Crivelli (2001), 262–4 I favoured a different interpretation: that an utterance of [a] and one of [d] should both be neither true nor false. This exegesis, which I now reject, is endorsed by Weidemann (1994/2002), 221–2.

or other exists). Would Aristotle endorse a generalisation of his remarks about an utterance of 'A cloak is white' that applies to every utterance that looks like a predicative assertion whose would-be subject or would-be predicate is 'empty'? Some commentators[77] answer affirmatively. Others[78] instead answer negatively: they think that for Aristotle 'empty' expressions like 'cloak' have a different semantic behaviour from 'empty' expressions like 'goatstag' (because they think that for Aristotle expressions like 'goatstag' have nominal definitions which are fixed by the myths or narratives in which they are introduced, while expressions like 'cloak' lack nominal definitions).

The issue cannot be settled confidently. However, since Aristotle never states that expressions like 'cloak' behave differently from expressions like 'goatstag',[79] there is some likelihood in assuming that Aristotle would endorse a generalisation of his remarks about an utterance of 'A cloak is white' that applies to every utterance that looks like a predicative assertion whose would-be subject or would-be predicate is 'empty'. If this is correct, we can answer the question asked at the end of the preceding section – the question whether Aristotle's philosophy of language can accommodate utterances that look like predicative assertions whose would-be subject or would-be predicate is 'empty'. The answer is affirmative. Aristotle's philosophy of language can accommodate such utterances: it treats them as equivalent to utterances constructed from several assertions linked by connective particles.

Aristotle does not show how every utterance which appears to be a predicative assertion involving an 'empty' name can be analysed as a composite assertion. In fact, had he tried to do this, he would have encountered challenging, perhaps insurmountable, difficulties: just consider how wrong it would be to treat 'Every goatstag is white' as equivalent to 'Every animal is white and everything with a stag's head is white and everything with a goat's body is white'.[80] He probably took his job mainly to be providing a logical account of the basic building-blocks of his logic, i.e. (genuine) predicative assertions, and gave nothing more than a glance to those utterances which appear to be predicative assertions.

A solution for the problems of the Square of Opposition. As I said, the problems that seem to afflict the laws of the Square of Opposition evaporate if in

77 E.g. Bolton (1976), 529; Charles (2000), 91. 78 E.g. Modrak (2001), 25–6, 47–8.

79 When Aristotle says that '"goatstag" signifies something' (*Int.* 1, 16^a16–17, cf. n. 40 above), he is not committing himself to the view that 'goatstag' signifies a single universal: he simply means that 'goatstag' is not devoid of signification.

80 Cf. Geach (1968), 47; Weidemann (1994/2002), 197.

every quantified predicative assertion the subject is 'non-empty'.[81] As for those utterances that seem counter-examples to the laws of the Square of Opposition, they are not real counter-examples.[82] Despite appearances, they are not quantified predicative assertions. They are assertions, and as such are truth-evaluable, but they are composite assertions: as such they fall outside the scope of the laws of the Square of Opposition. The laws of the Square of Opposition govern only those assertions which in Aristotle's view are most basic, i.e. quantified predicative assertions.

Logical form and grammatical form. According to some commentators,[83] an important difference between Aristotle's and Russell's logical views is that while for Aristotle logical form follows closely grammatical form, Russell separates the two. However, if the foregoing reconstruction of Aristotle's ideas about utterances which have the appearance of a predicative assertion whose subject is 'empty' is correct, Aristotle does separate logical form from grammatical form.

Specifically, there is an analogy between Aristotle's treatment of utterances of the aforesaid kind and Russell's treatment of 'ordinary' proper names. The possibility that definite descriptions could be 'empty' prompts Russell to treat them not as 'logically' proper names but as quantifiers (whose logical behaviour is exhibited by paraphrasing the sentences where they occur as wholes). The analogous possibility that 'ordinary' proper names might be 'empty' induces Russell to treat them, too, not as 'logically' proper names but as disguised descriptions, and therefore as disguised quantifiers whose logical behaviour is exhibited by paraphrasing the original sentences as wholes. Aristotle's moves are analogous: when an 'ordinary' common noun is 'empty', he treats the utterance where it occurs as a composite assertion.

'Making many questions into one'. At the beginning of chapter 11 of *de Interpretatione* Aristotle returns to the themes of chapters 5 and 8:

T 42 To affirm or to deny a single item about many, or many about a single one, is not a single affirmation nor a single denial unless the many items make up a single one. I do not speak of 'a single item' if a single name is given but those items do not make up a single one: e.g. a man is perhaps an animal and biped and tame, but these do make up a single item, while white and man and walking do not make up a single item. Hence, if one affirms a single item of these, there will not be a single affirmation, but a single spoken sound

[81] Cf. the paragraph to which n. 34 above is appended.

[82] Cf. Mann (1958), 15; Charles (1994), 53; (1997), 236–7; (2000), 93.

[83] E.g. Rees (1960), 139.

and many affirmations, nor if one affirms these of a single item, but again there will be many affirmations. Therefore, if a dialectical question requires as an answer either the proposition or the other part of the contradictory pair, and a proposition is a part of a single contradictory pair, there will not be a single answer to these (for the question also is not single),[84] not even if it is true. These issues have been discussed in the *Topics*. (20^b13–26)

In T 35 (an excerpt from *de Interpretatione* 8) Aristotle claimed that the universals horse and man do not constitute a single item. I understood him as thereby committing himself to the claim that there is no universal horse-and-man which is the 'logical product' of the universals horse and man, and I took his ground to be that had there been such a universal it would not have always been predicated of some existing individual.[85] Now, in T 42 (the beginning of *de Interpretatione* 11), Aristotle claims that the universals walking, white, and man do not constitute a single item. He can be plausibly understood as thereby committing himself to the claim that there is no universal walking-white-man which is the 'logical product' of the universals walking, white, and man. But his ground for this claim cannot be that the would-be universal walking-white-man would not be always predicated of some existing individual: there exist individuals who are men, white, and walking, and it could well be the case that there always were and always will be some. Aristotle's grounds must be different. One of them is probably that the universals walking, white, and man lack the connectedness exhibited by the items signified by the members of the *definiens* of a definition.[86]

Thus, the universals walking, white, and man do not constitute a single item, so that there is no universal walking-white-man which is the 'logical product' of them. If one introduced a single name – 'whitewalker', say – which signified the universals walking, white, and man in the same way as the phrase 'walking white man' signifies them, and produced an utterance that looked like a predicative assertion where an utterance of that name was contained as subject or predicate, the utterance would be called 'many assertions' in the semantic sense (though it could be called 'a single assertion' in the syntactic sense). As I pointed out earlier,[87] Aristotle cannot be discussing here the issue of ambiguity: for 'walking white man' is an unambiguous expression, so that 'whitewalker' also must be unambiguous (because it is supposed to signify in the same way as 'walking white man').

[84] My punctuation here (20^b25), different from those of the editions I consulted, follows a suggestion of Ammonius (*in Int.* 201, 24–6).

[85] Cf. the portion of the main text to which n. 21 above is appended.

[86] Cf. n. 43 above.

[87] Cf. the paragraph to which n. 17 above is appended.

The last part of T 42 (20^b22–6) connects the previous points with the issue of a questioner in a dialectical debate 'making many questions into one', and declares that this subject was discussed 'in the *Topics*' (20^b26). The issue of a questioner 'making many questions into one' is discussed in the *Topics*[88] and in *Sophistici Elenchi*.[89] In both works Aristotle distinguishes two cases where a questioner 'makes many questions into one'. In the first case, the multiplicity of the questions asked is explicit in that it surfaces in the linguistic expression: e.g. the multiplicity of the questions asked in 'Are Coriscus and Callias at home?' is explicit because it surfaces in the phrase 'Coriscus and Callias'. In the second case, the multiplicity of the questions asked is disguised, and the disguise is provided by ambiguity: e.g. the multiplicity of the questions asked in 'Is a vice a mental state?' is disguised because of the ambiguity of 'vice' (which can signify both a moral condition and a mechanical instrument).

But now T 42's reference to the *Topics* raises two problems: (i) the only disguised multiple questions discussed in the *Topics* and in *Sophistici Elenchi* are those whose disguise is provided by ambiguity, a situation *de Interpretatione* seems to ignore; (ii) the only disguised multiple questions discussed in *de Interpretatione* seem to be those whose disguise involves no ambiguity, a situation the *Topics* and *Sophistici Elenchi* ignore.

I shall discuss these two problems in turn. In particular, I shall tackle the first by arguing that disguised multiple questions whose disguise is provided by ambiguity are discussed in *de Interpretatione*. As for the second problem, I shall argue that the reason why neither the *Topics* nor *Sophistici Elenchi* discuss disguised multiple questions whose disguise involves no ambiguity is that Aristotle had not yet become aware of this possible situation.

Ambiguity. Does the case where the multiplicity of the questions asked *is* disguised behind ambiguity find any collocation in *de Interpretatione*'s schema? Consider an utterance of

[g] A vice is a mental state.

Since the word 'vice' is ambiguous, an utterance of [g] can be taken to make many assertions. These assertions are reciprocally unrelated in that they are not linked either as if by a conjunctive connective or as if by a disjunctive connective. To see this, imagine a dialectical debate about virtue where the answerer endorses [g]: a perverse questioner could attack this answer by saying that mechanical instruments are not mental states. In doing so, the questioner would be treating the utterance of [g] as the 'conjunction of its

88 8.7, 160^a17–34. 89 6, 169^a6–18; 17, 175^b39–176^a18; 30, 181^a36–181^b18.

senses'. Again, imagine a dialectical debate about mechanical instruments which ended up talking about clamps. One can then imagine the answerer saying 'A vice is not a mental state'. Then a perverse questioner could attack this answer by uttering [g]. In doing so, the questioner would be treating the utterance of [g] as the 'disjunction of its senses'. Thus, ambiguous utterances are open both to a conjunctive and to a disjunctive reading – which is because, properly speaking, ambiguous utterances introduce many assertions which are not connected in any way, either conjunctively or disjunctively. This situation suggests that an ambiguous utterance can be regarded as equivalent to many assertions 'with no conjunction' (17^a17), and therefore can be called 'many assertions' not only in the semantic, but also in the syntactic, sense. Thus, after all, ambiguous utterances probably do have a niche in *de Interpretatione*'s schema.

A developmental hypothesis. The *Topics* and *Sophistici Elenchi* present partially conflicting views about a questioner in a dialectical debate 'making many questions into one'. In the *Topics*[90] Aristotle advises the answerer to give a single answer ('Yes' or 'No') to the multiple question just in case that single answer would have seemed true for each of the many questions concealed behind the single but ambiguous interrogative utterance. By contrast, in *Sophistici Elenchi*[91] Aristotle rules that the answerer should never give a single answer to a multiple question, not even if some single answer would have seemed to be true for each of the many questions concealed behind the single but ambiguous interrogative utterance. He points out that this rule conflicts with the advice of certain dialecticians who urge the answerer to give a single answer to the multiple question if that single answer seems true for each of the many questions comprised in the multiple question. These dialecticians remain unnamed, but it is reasonable to assume that Aristotle is politely referring to himself, and hinting that he has changed his mind.[92]

As for the relation between the *Topics* and *Sophistici Elenchi*, Aristotle probably first wrote the eight books of the *Topics* as a complete work, and then added *Sophistici Elenchi* as a ninth book.[93] What Aristotle says near the end of T 42 agrees with the position of *Sophistici Elenchi* rather than that of the *Topics*: for near the end of T 42 (at 20^b25–6) Aristotle urges the answerer in a dialectical debate to avoid giving a single answer to a multiple question even if that single answer would have seemed true for each of the many questions comprised in the multiple question. One can therefore

[90] 8.7, 160^a17–34. [91] 17, 175^b39–176^a18; 30, 181^a36–181^b18.
[92] Cf. Dorion (1995), 30–1, 334; Brunschwig (1999), 87–91.
[93] Cf. Brunschwig (1967), XVIII–XX; Dorion (1995), 25; Brunschwig (1999), 90.

plausibly assume that the reference to the *Topics* at the end of T 42 concerns the later version of the work which included *Sophistici Elenchi*.[94]

I would now like to float a speculative suggestion concerning the relationship between the *Topics*, *Sophistici Elenchi*, and *de Interpretatione* on the issue of a questioner 'making many questions into one'. The suggestion is that there are three stages of Aristotle's reflection on this issue.

In the earliest stage, represented by the version of the *Topics* in eight books, Aristotle considers only apparently single, but really multiple questions which depend on ambiguity, and advises the answerer to offer a single reply if it seems to be true for all of the ambiguous question's senses.

In the intermediate stage, represented by the later version of the *Topics* that includes *Sophistici Elenchi* as a ninth book, Aristotle still considers only apparently single, but really multiple questions which depend on ambiguity, but advises the answerer never to offer a single reply (even if some single answer would have seemed to be true for all of the ambiguous question's senses).

Finally, in the latest stage, represented by *de Interpretatione*, Aristotle considers a larger range of apparently single, but really multiple questions: not only those that depend on ambiguity, but also those that introduce many states of affairs with no ambiguity. Concealed multiple questions that do depend on an ambiguity correspond to those utterances which can be called 'many assertions' both in the semantic and in the syntactic sense; concealed multiple questions that do not depend on an ambiguity correspond to those utterances which can be called 'many assertions' only in the semantic sense, but can be called 'a single assertion' in the syntactic sense. One reason why *de Interpretatione* concentrates on this last group of utterances (concealed multiple questions that do not depend on an ambiguity) is that it constitutes a novelty with respect to the earlier works.

94 Cf. B's scholium on $20^{b}26$ (*apud* Waitz (1844/46), I 42); Pacius (1597a), 92; Bonitz (1870), $98^{a}1$–2, $102^{a}48$–9; Dorion (1995), 24.

PART III

Truth and time

CHAPTER 6

Truth and change

This chapter addresses the relationship of truth to time and change. According to Aristotle, any bearer of truth or falsehood can, at least in principle, be true at one time and false at another. This is somewhat hard to square with his view that the linguistic items that are bearers of truth or falsehood are utterances (expression-tokens). On reflection, however, the position turns out to be consistent: utterances (expression-tokens) can be true at one time and false at another.

Aristotle also claims that if an assertion or a belief is true at one time and false at another, it does not follow that it undergoes a change. This is probably due to the idea that truth (being correspondence to the world) is something like a relative and therefore, like relatives, is involved at most in a 'mere Cambridge change' that does not count as a genuine change. Now, properties involved in a 'mere Cambridge change' are not genuine properties. It follows that truth is not a genuine property.

I DIFFERENT TRUTH-VALUES AT DIFFERENT TIMES

Truth and falsehood at times. Aristotle thinks that the bearers of truth or falsehood are true, or false, at times. He does not formulate this view explicitly: nowhere does he use a sentence like 'States of affairs, beliefs, and assertions are true or false not absolutely, but at times.' Rather, this view is presupposed by the way he speaks about truth and falsehood, which suggests that he would aver the following claim:

[28] An utterance of an instance of the schema 'σ is true at τ' or of 'σ is false at τ' is a proper formulation. An utterance of an instance of the schema 'σ is true' or of 'σ is false' is either improper or elliptical. (The intended instances of these schemata are generated by replacing the occurrences of 'σ' by designations of bearers of truth or falsehood, and the occurrences of 'τ' by designations of times.)

It is worthwhile recalling the often noted[1] fact that Aristotle's view that the bearers of truth or falsehood are true, or false, at times was widely shared in Antiquity – in fact, it remained unchallenged. It is unclear whether the times at which bearers of truth or falsehood are true, or false, are instants or periods. By speaking of 'times' I remain neutral on this issue.

Not only does Aristotle think that the bearers of truth or falsehood are true, or false, at times. He also thinks that some bearer of truth or falsehood is true at one time and false at another.[2] In particular, he thinks this of states of affairs, beliefs, and assertions.[3]

A modern attack on Aristotle's conception of truth and falsehood at times. Some modern commentators[4] attack Aristotle's view that the bearers of truth or falsehood are true, or false, at times. The main ground for this attack is *de Interpretatione* 9, where Aristotle addresses a paradox concerning truth and time: what is primarily responsible for *de Interpretatione* 9's paradox would be, in the eyes of these commentators, Aristotle's mistaken view that the bearers of truth or falsehood are true, or false, at times.

This modern attack is questionable. For modern tense logic rests on the assumption that the bearers of truth or falsehood are true, or false, at times, but modern philosophers do not normally attack tense logic because it relies on this assumption. Of course, this is not a knock-down answer to someone criticising the assumption that the bearers of truth or falsehood are true, or false, at times. But it does seem inappropriate to chastise Aristotle for a thesis that is still assumed by a respected branch of logic.[5]

Utterances with different truth-values at different times. I previously argued that for Aristotle every sentence which is true or false is an utterance (a sentence-token, not a sentence-type).[6] Suppose this is correct. Now,

[1] Prior (1957), 104; Hintikka (1967/73), 62–8, 70–2; M. J. White (1981), 233–4; Mignucci (1985a), 164–9; (1985b), 221–4; von Kutschera (1986), 203; Pardey (2000), 33–6; Goldin (2002), 240–7.

[2] Cf. Maier (1896/1936), I 90–1; Oehler (1962/85), 179–80; Miller (1971), 19; Hintikka (1967/73), 66–7; M. Kneale (1974), 369; Oehler (1984), 222–3; Mignucci (1985b), 219–24; Berti (1992), 87; Liske (1995), 352–3; Seel (2001a), 218.

[3] For states of affairs see *Cat.* 5, 4a34–4b2; 4b8–10; *APo.* 1.6, 74b32–9; *Top.* 8.2, 157b11–16; *de An.* 3.3, 428b4–9; *Metaph.* Δ 29, 1024b17–21; Θ 10, 1051b9–17. For beliefs see *Cat.* 5, 4a23–8; 4a34–4b2; 4b4–13; *APo.* 1.6, 74b32–9; *Top.* 8.2, 157b11–16; *SE* 22, 178b24–9; *de An.* 3.3, 428b4–9; *Metaph.* Z 15, 1039b27–1040a5; Θ 10, 1051b9–17; 1052a4–11. For assertions see *Cat.* 5, 4a23–6; 4a34–4b2; 4b4–13; *SE* 22, 178b24–9; *GC* 2.11, 337b4–5; *de An.* 3.3, 428b7–9; *Metaph.* Γ 8, 1012b24–6; Θ 10, 1051b9–17; K 6, 1063a17–21.

[4] Saunders (1958), 373–4, 377; Scholz (1959), 77; Kneale/Kneale (1962), 51; van Eck (1988), 27–8.

[5] For a defence of the tensed ascription of truth and falsehood see Gale (1961), 379–82; Haack (1974/96), 82–3.

[6] See sect. 3 of ch. 1.

Aristotle thinks that some sentence is true at one time and false at another. Aristotle's views then entail that some utterance is true at one time and false at another. Gabriel Nuchelmans and other commentators[7] commit themselves to the claim that no utterance is true at one time and false at another. So, if Nuchelmans and those who agree with him are right, Aristotle is wrong.

Aristotle might well be wrong. His mistake might derive either from unawareness of the difference between sentence-tokens and sentence-types, or from a failure to think out some of the implications of what he says (some of his claims entailing that the sentences which are true or false should be utterances, others that they should be sentence-types – hence not utterances).

However, an account of the situation that is more charitable to Aristotle ought to be attempted. Perhaps it is Nuchelmans's view that is wrong – perhaps some utterance *is* true at one time and false at another. Here are two suggestions as to how this might be the case.

Suggestion (i). Utterance *u* of 'Socrates is seated' takes three seconds. During these three seconds Socrates stands up. *u* has different truth-values at different times within the three seconds: it is true at t_1 (for t_1 lies within the first of the three seconds, and Socrates is then seated) and false at t_2 (for t_2 lies within the third of the three seconds, and Socrates then is not seated).[8]

Suggestion (i) cannot do: it allows an utterance to have different truth-values only over the relatively short portion of time it occupies, while on reading the passages where Aristotle says that the same bearer of truth or falsehood can have different truth-values at different times one feels that he intends to allow it to have different truth-values over a far longer portion of time.

Suggestion (ii). One morning in May 1992 Jim shouts 'Labour represents the majority of the English nation'. In June 1997 Jim, reflecting on the events of his life in 1992, makes a statement by using the sentence 'That loud remark was false at the time it was made but is true now'. What Jim says in June 1997 is both appropriate and true. Hence, here 'that loud remark' cannot refer to a content avowed by an act of remarking: a content avowed by an act of remarking cannot be appropriately characterised as loud. 'That loud remark' here is most naturally taken to refer to an utterance the production

7 Miller (1971), 47; Nuchelmans (1973), 42–3; K. J. Williams (1978), 70–1; Lucas (1989), 62–3; Bäck (1992), 135.

8 Cf. Waterlow (1982), 135.

of which was the making of a remark: such an utterance can be appropriately characterised as loud. Hence some utterance is true at one time and false at another.[9]

Different truth-values at different times, no change. In *Categories* 5 Aristotle says:

T 43 The same sentence seems to be both true and false. Suppose, for example, that the sentence which says that somebody is sitting is true: after the person has got up, this same sentence will be false. Similarly with belief. Suppose you believe truly that somebody is sitting: after the person has got up, you will believe falsely while having the same belief about that person. (4^a23–8)

However, the sentence and the belief itself remain completely unchanged in every respect, and it is because the object changes that the contrary comes to hold of it. For the sentence which says that somebody is sitting remains the same, and it is because the object has changed that it comes to be true at one time and false at another. Similarly with the belief. (4^a34–4^b2)

Thus Aristotle claims that

[29] A sentence (or a belief) which is true at one time and false at another does not change.[10]

Someone[11] might object to [29] on the ground that a sentence (or a belief) which is true at one time and false at another does change *just because* it is true at one time and false at another. Aristotle does not consider this objection – how would he defend [29] if he were to address it?

Two ancient defences of [29]. The ancient commentators put forward at least two defences of [29].

According to the first defence,[12] the sentences which are true or false are utterances. Consider a situation which one might be inclined to describe by saying that a sentence undergoes a change because it is true at one time and

9 Cf. Waterlow (1982), 135. Evans (1979), 347–52 discusses the view that an utterance can be true at one time and false at another. He regards it as 'such a strange position that it is difficult to believe that anyone has ever held it' (p. 348), and criticises it. His criticism is answered by Percival (1993/94), 198–203.

An event may enjoy a property outside the time during which it occurs: the earthquake was remembered long after it occurred. Uneasiness at the idea of an utterance being true before it occurs can be appeased by adding the restriction that the time when the utterance can be true should be contemporary with, or later than, that during which the utterance occurs.

10 Cf. 4^b4–13. 11 Cf. Mignucci (1985a), 165.

12 Ammon. *in Cat.* 53, 22–4; Phlp. *in Cat.* 82, 19–23; Simp. *in Cat.* 118, 15–16; 118, 18–25; Olymp. *in Cat.* 79, 14–33; Elias *in Cat.* 183, 34–184, 3; anon. *in Cat.* 18, 33–5. The first defence of [29] might originate with Alexander (see Schmidt (1966), 284–5).

false at another. In the situation in question, it is not the case that numerically one and the same sentence (utterance) is true at one time and false at another. Rather, in the situation in question, one sentence (utterance) occurs at one time and is true then, another sentence (utterance) occurs at another time and is false then, and the two sentences (utterances), although not numerically the same, are the same in kind. Hence, the situation would not be described correctly by saying that a sentence undergoes a change because it is true at one time and false at another.

The second defence of [29] is set forth by Dexippus (*in Cat.* 60, 13–23). According to Dexippus, 'a sentence [. . .] receives truth and falsehood not in its own nature, but in the way relatives do (for it is said to be true or false by virtue of its being concordant or discordant with objects)' (60, 13–16). And, as relatives harbour no transformation,[13] so a sentence and a belief 'become false from true not by suffering some affection or being transformed, but remaining unchanged' (60, 18–20).[14]

Would Aristotle adopt either of these two ancient defences?

Assessment of the first ancient defence . . . The first ancient defence of [29] assumes that the sentences which are true or false are utterances. And (as I argued in chapter 1) Aristotle probably thinks that the sentences which are true or false are utterances. Yet two arguments show that this defence is unlikely to be one that Aristotle would adopt.

(i) The part of proposition [29] concerning beliefs is the claim that a belief which is true at one time and false at another does not change. The objection to this is that a belief which is true at one time and false at another does change just because it is true at one time and false at another. The first defence, when so modified as to answer this objection, assumes that beliefs are either utterances or events of some other sort. But Aristotle tends to use 'belief' ('δόξα' or 'ὑπόληψις') for dispositions (or states) of believing, which are neither utterances nor events of any other sort.[15]

(ii) Proposition [29] is appealed to by Aristotle while answering an objection to a claim he makes about substance: the claim about substance

[13] A view notoriously averred by Aristotle: see *Ph.* 3.1, 200b26–201a9; 5.2, 225b11–13 (= *Metaph.* K 12, 1068a11–13); 7.3, 246b10–17; 246b20–247a7; 246b25–6; 247b1–7; 8.1, 251b5–9; *Metaph.* N 1, 1088a29–35 (cf. Pl. *Tht.* 154*b*6–155*c*5). Contrast *Ph.* 1.7, 190a34–5.

[14] It is not clear whether at lines 60, 21–3 Dexippus offers a new argument in defence of Aristotle. Simplicius (*in Cat.* 119, 5–16) suggests essentially the same defence(s) as Dexippus. A defence of [29] similar to Dexippus' has been recently propounded by C. J. F. Williams (1991), 306–7 and Goldin (2002), 242–3.

[15] *Int.* 14, 23a33–4; *APo.* 2.19, 100b5–7; *de An.* 3.3, 428a3–5; *HA* 7.4, 584b6–14; *EN* 6.5, 1140b13–16. Cf. Olymp. *in Cat.* 79, 28–33; Régis (1935), 70–1; Goldin (2002), 244.

(4^a10–21) is that only substances receive contraries while remaining numerically one and the same. The objection to this claim about substance (4^a21–8) is that though sentences (and beliefs) are not substances, still numerically one and the same sentence (or belief) can be true at one time and false at another, and thereby receive contraries. The answer to this objection (4^a28–4^b18) comprises two arguments, both of which rely on [29]. Now, Aristotle does *not* answer the objection by denying what sounds like its central claim, i.e. the claim that numerically one and the same sentence can be true at one time and false at another. Perhaps part of the reason why Aristotle answers the objection in the way he does is that he agrees with it on this point, i.e. he grants that numerically one and the same sentence can be true at one time and false at another. But, if Aristotle adopted the first ancient defence, he could not coherently grant that numerically one and the same sentence can be true at one time and false at another.

. . . and of the second. When he formulates the second defence of [29], Dexippus does not use an expression like 'The true and the false are relatives' or 'Truth and falsehood are relatives'. The expression he uses is 'A sentence receives truth and falsehood in the way relatives do' (60, 15). This suggests that the view he attributes to Aristotle is *not* that truth and falsehood are relatives, but that truth and falsehood are closely linked with relatives in a way that explains their peculiar behaviour with respect to change.

One sees why Dexippus might want to attribute this view to Aristotle. For, according to Aristotle, all relatives satisfy a certain 'linguistic' definition: only 'such items as are said to be just what they are *of* or *than* other items, or in some other way in relation to something else' (*Cat.* 7, 6^a36–7), are relatives. Aristotle claims that the larger,[16] the double, state, condition, perception, knowledge, position, excellence, and defect are relatives and satisfy the foregoing condition:[17] e.g. 'the larger is said just what it is *than* something else, for it is called "larger" *than* something' (6^a38–9). Aristotle also claims that grammatical-knowledge and musical-knowledge do not satisfy the foregoing condition and therefore are not relatives (although they fall under knowledge, which *is* a relative): 'grammatical-knowledge is not called "grammatical-knowledge" *of* something nor musical-knowledge "musical-knowledge" *of* something' (*Cat.* 8, 11^a27–8), and 'grammatical-knowledge is

[16] 'The larger' ('τὸ μεῖζον') can function both as a singular abstract term ('the property of being larger') and as a quantified general concrete term ('whatever is larger'). Aristotle probably wants it to function in both ways: the larger (i.e. the property of being larger) is a relative only if the larger (i.e. whatever is larger) is called 'larger than' something. Cf. *Metaph.* Δ 15, 1021^b6–8; Mignucci (1986), 102–3.

[17] *Cat.* 7, 6^a38–6^b3; 6^b15–16; 10, 11^b24–31.

called "knowledge" *of* something (not "grammatical-knowledge" *of* something) and musical-knowledge "knowledge" *of* something (not "musical-knowledge" *of* something)' (11^{a}29–31).[18] Now, truth and falsehood behave like grammatical-knowledge and musical-knowledge (not like the double or knowledge): what is true is not called 'true' *of* something, and what is false is not called 'false' *of* something.[19] So, Aristotle's 'linguistic' definition of relatives bars truth and falsehood from being relatives. Moreover, in *Sophistici Elenchi* 22 Aristotle commits himself to the view that truth and falsehood are qualities by saying that 'a sentence or a belief being true or false signifies not a "this" [τόδε] but a "such" [τοιόνδε]' (178^{b}27–8) – note that in *Sophistici Elenchi* 22 Aristotle uses 'such' ('τοιόνδε') interchangeably with 'of such a quality' ('ποιόν'), his standard expression for qualified items.[20]

Now: (i) Aristotle claims that a relative can be enjoyed at one time, and lacked at another, by something that does not change; (ii) he claims that a sentence (or a belief) which is true at one time and not true at another does not change; (iii) he imposes on relatives a condition which is not satisfied by truth and falsehood. These facts suggest that if Aristotle were to defend [29], he would take a line similar to that which Dexippus seems to attribute to him: truth is not a relative but is sufficiently similar to relatives to share their peculiar behaviour with respect to change.

2 TRUTH AND RELATIVES

Why does truth not count as an Aristotelian relative? How is truth linked to Aristotelian relatives? I think that these two questions cannot be properly answered by simply pointing out that truth does not satisfy Aristotle's 'linguistic' definition of relatives. I shall try to offer more appropriate answers with the aid of an example.

Take the two-place relation *R* expressed by the formula '*x* is admired by *y*', the property[21] *P* expressed by '*x* is admired', and the property *Q* expressed

[18] Cf. *Top.* 4.4, 124^{b}18–19; 6.8, 146^{a}36–146^{b}2; 146^{b}6–9; *SE* 13, 173^{b}1–3; 31, 181^{b}34–5; *Metaph.* Δ 15, 1021^{b}4–6. Aristotle makes an incompatible claim at *Top.* 4.1, 120^{b}36–121^{a}9.

[19] Aristotle uses 'ἀληθεύεσθαι κατά' + genitive (see *Int.* 12, 21^{b}17; *APr.* 1.37, 49^{a}6–7; etc.), 'ἀληθεύεσθαι ἐπί' + genitive (see *Int.* 13, 22^{b}2), 'ἀληθεύεσθαι περί' + genitive (see *Top.* 7.5, 154^{b}4), and 'ἀληθὴς κατά' + genitive (see *Int.* 11, 20^{b}37–8; 13, 22^{b}23–4; etc.) to say of a predicate (or a universal) that it applies to (or holds of) something. He also uses 'ψευδὴς κατά' + genitive (see *Int.* 13, 22^{b}32–3) to say of an expression that it is disjoint from another expression. But he never applies any of these formulations to assertions, beliefs, or states of affairs.

[20] Cf. 178^{b}37–9 and 179^{a}8–10 (also *Ph.* 3.1, 200^{b}28; *Metaph.* N 2, 1089^{a}18; Goldin (2002), 240–1). The idea that truth and falsehood are qualities goes back to Plato (*Sph.* 262*e*8–9; 263*a*11–263*b*3; *Phl.* 37*b*10–37*c*2).

[21] Here 'property' means 'one-place attribute'.

by 'x is admired by Jim'. P is obtained from R by *existential* saturation: P is the same as the property expressed by the formula 'For some y, x is admired by y' (obtained by applying the *existential* quantifier to a variable in the formula expressing R). Q is obtained from R by *singular* saturation (because the formula expressing Q is obtained by substituting a *singular* term for a variable in the formula expressing R).

First consider an attribution of P, e.g. the attribution made by saying 'Fred is admired'. This might prompt the question 'By whom is the admired admired?', which could be appropriately answered by saying 'The admired is admired by Jim' or 'The admired is admired by Bill'. The predicates of these answers are derived from the formula ('x is admired') which expresses P by dropping the variable and the copula ('x' and 'is') and adding appropriate phrases ('by Jim', 'by Bill'). One might describe the situation by saying that the admired is said to be just what it is 'by' another item. So, P seems to satisfy Aristotle's 'linguistic' definition of relatives.

Consider next an attribution of Q, e.g. the attribution made by saying 'Fred is admired by Jim'. Someone wanting to know about Fred's other admirers might ask: 'By whom is the admired by Jim admired?' Now, the predicates of the appropriate answers to this question cannot be derived from the formula ('x is admired by Jim') which expresses Q by the procedure described above, i.e. by dropping the variable and the copula ('x' and 'is') and adding appropriate phrases ('by Jim', 'by Bill'): this would yield the ungrammatical 'The admired by Jim is admired by Jim by Jim' and 'The admired by Jim is admired by Jim by Bill'. One might describe the situation by saying that the admired by Jim cannot be said to be just what it is 'by' another item, or in some other way in relation to something else. So, Q seems not to satisfy Aristotle's 'linguistic' definition of relatives.

Back to the two questions which are our primary concern. First, why does truth not count as an Aristotelian relative? Because Aristotelian relatives are, like P, properties obtained from a two-place relation by *existential* saturation,[22] while truth is, like Q, a property obtained from a two-place relation by *singular* saturation (for the property truth, expressed by 'x is concordant with the external world',[23] is obtained by singular saturation from the two-place relation S expressed by 'x is concordant with y'). Second, how is truth linked to Aristotelian relatives? The property C expressed by 'x is concordant' is an Aristotelian relative, and truth bears to C the same

[22] This is convincingly argued by Mignucci (1986), 101–5 (cf. Wedin (2000), 22).

[23] For a discussion of how for Aristotle truth amounts to concordance or correspondence with the external world see sect. 1 of ch. 4.

relationship that Q bears to P: as Q and P are obtained by (singular and existential) saturation from the two-place relation R, so truth and C are obtained by (singular and existential) saturation from S.

Aristotle lacks the notion of a two-place relation. Hence, he would not think of Q and P as obtained by saturating the two-place relation R. Rather, he seems to regard the relationship of properties like P to properties like Q as that of a *genus* to what falls under it: P, which *is* an Aristotelian relative, is a *genus* under which Q, which *is not* an Aristotelian relative, falls. The view is reasonable: Q determines P's indeterminateness (which surfaces in the existential quantifier in one of the formulae expressing P). Thus, Aristotle might say that truth (the property expressed by 'x is concordant with the external world') *is not* a relative, but falls under a *genus* (the property C expressed by 'x is concordant' and 'For some y, x is concordant with y') which *is* a relative.[24]

The reason why not only properties like P (which *are* Aristotelian relatives) but also properties like Q (which *are not* Aristotelian relatives) can undergo mere Cambridge change is that they are saturations of two-place relations like R. P undergoes mere Cambridge change if whoever admired Fred stops admiring him, while Q undergoes mere Cambridge change if Jim stops admiring Fred (in either case Fred, who never admires himself, does not change). Truth can similarly undergo mere Cambridge change: a sentence (or belief) s can be true at one time and not true at another without changing because s can at one time be, and at another not be, concordant with the external world by virtue of changes occurring not in s, but only in the external world.[25]

In conclusion, Aristotle might want to say that truth and falsehood are in the same situation as grammatical-knowledge and musical-knowledge: as grammatical-knowledge and musical-knowledge (i) are qualities,[26] (ii) are not relatives,[27] but (iii) are relatives according to their *genera*,[28] so truth and falsehood (i) are qualities,[29] (ii) are not relatives,[30] but (iii) are relatives according to their *genera*.[31]

How genuine a property is truth? In *Metaphysics* N 1 Aristotle says:

[24] Cf. the paragraph to which n. 16 above is appended.

[25] The often repeated claim that events cannot undergo genuine changes (cf. Simons (1987), 134–7) fits well with the idea that utterances, which are events, can undergo mere Cambridge change.

[26] *Cat.* 8, 11^{a}35–6. [27] *Cat.* 8, 11^{a}36. [28] *Cat.* 8, 11^{a}28–9; *Metaph.* Δ 15, 1021^{b}3–6.

[29] Cf. the portion of the main text to which n. 20 above is appended.

[30] Cf. the paragraph to which n. 16 above is appended.

[31] For a different account of the link between truth, relatives, and qualities see Miller (1971), 41–3.

T 44 A sign that a relative is least of all[32] a substance and a being is that only of the relative there are neither generation nor destruction nor change. (1088^a29–31)[33]

As I argued in preceding subsections, for Aristotle truth is closely linked to relatives: he would concede that truth is a relative according to its *genus*, and he says that there is no change with regard to truth and falsehood. Thus, Aristotle would probably apply to truth his general remark about relatives: he would probably grant that truth 'is least of all a substance and a being', i.e. is not a genuine property.[34] Aristotle's ground for this view is probably the intuition that an item cannot possess at one time a genuine property it lacks at another without changing.[35]

Categories 5 indirectly confirms that for Aristotle truth is not a genuine property. One of the theses about substance maintained by Aristotle in *Categories* 5 is that only substances receive contraries while remaining numerically one and the same (4^a10–21). Aristotle considers an objection to this thesis about substance: though sentences (and beliefs) are not substances, still numerically one and the same sentence (or belief) can be true at one time and false at another, and thereby receive contraries (4^a21–8). Aristotle answers this objection by means of two arguments, both of which rely on [29], i.e. the claim that a sentence (or a belief) which is true at one time and false at another does not change. The first argument (4^a28–4^b5) concedes that numerically one and the same sentence (or belief) can receive contraries, i.e. truth and falsehood, but insists that the way in which numerically one and the same substance can receive contraries is different from that in which numerically one and the same sentence (or belief) can: numerically one and the same substance can receive contraries by changing, but it is not the case that numerically one and the same sentence (or belief) can receive contraries by changing ([29] supports this contention). The second argument in Aristotle's answer to the objection (4^b5–18) denies what the first argument had conceded, i.e. it denies that numerically one and the same sentence (or belief) can receive contraries:

T 45 However, this [*sc.* that beliefs and sentences are able to receive contraries] is not true. For it is not because they themselves receive anything that sentences and beliefs are said to be able to receive contraries, but because the affection

32 Morrison (1987), 389–93, 394 convincingly argues that here (1088^a29) 'least of all' ('ἥκισταῦ)ηασ ιτσ στανδαρδ χομπαρατιςε μεανινγ (ΰιντηε λεαστ δεγρεεῦ).

33 Cf. 1088^a22–3; Λ 4, 1070^a33–1070^b10 (where the category of relatives stands for all the categories other than substance because it differs from it most); *EN* 1.4, 1096^a20–2; Wardy (1990), 215.

34 Cf. Brentano (1889), 26; Kraus (1930), 173–4.

35 Aristotle's intuition is shared by several modern philosophers (e.g. Linke (1965), 312–13), but is difficult to motivate.

has come to be about something else. For it is because the object is or is not that the sentence also is said to be true or false, not because it is able itself to receive contraries. For sentences and beliefs are not changed at all by anything, so that they are not able to receive contraries because no affection comes to be[36] in them. A substance, on the other hand, is said to be able to receive contraries because it itself receives contraries. (4^b5–14)

The crucial inference of T 45's argument goes from

[a] Sentences and beliefs are not changed at all by anything (4^b10–11)

to

[b] They [*sc.* sentences and beliefs] are not able to receive contraries (4^b12).

According to its most plausible explanation, this inference goes from

[a′] A sentence (or a belief) that is true at one time and false at another does not thereby change

to

[b′] A sentence (or a belief) which is true at one time and false at another does not thereby receive contraries.

The inference from [a′] to [b′] can be explained as consisting of two subordinate inferences that pass through an intermediate result, which remains unexpressed:

[c] Truth and falsehood are not genuine properties.

The first subordinate inference (from [a′] to [c]) is warranted by those same considerations which back Aristotle's claim that 'a relative is least of all a substance and a being'. As for the second subordinate inference (from [c] to [b′]), if truth and falsehood are not genuine properties, then a sentence (or a belief) which is true at one time and false at another does not thereby receive contraries because there are no contraries for it to receive (contraries are genuine properties).[37]

An apparent inconsistency in Aristotle's ontology. Some commentators[38] feel that T 44 entails an inconsistency in Aristotle's ontology. For T 44 seems to commit Aristotle to the claim that beings are comparable with respect to 'being': relatives 'are' less than quantities and qualities, which in turn

36 I read 'γιγνομένου πάθους' (4^b12–13) with most manuscripts and editors (Minio-Paluello follows n and prints 'γιγνομένου').

37 For a different interpretation of T 45's argument see Goldin (2002), 243–5.

38 E.g. Shields (1999), 260–6.

'are' less than substances. Elsewhere[39] Aristotle claims that objects are not comparable with respect to a predicate that applies homonymously to them: e.g. a flavour and a sound are not comparable with respect to 'sharp' because 'sharp' applies homonymously to them (only in different senses can a flavour and a sound be called 'sharp'). Since beings are comparable with respect to 'being', 'being' does not apply homonymously to beings – contrary to a well-known principle of Aristotle's ontology.

However, on reflection, this inconsistency evaporates. For in T 44 Aristotle says that 'a relative is least of all a substance and a being' (1088^a29–30): he can be plausibly taken to mean that it is in the least degree that relatives 'are' in the substance-sense of 'to be'. Thus, in T 44 the comparison with respect to 'being' is carried out with respect to only one sense of 'being', the substance-sense: relatives 'are' (in the substance-sense) less than quantities and qualities, which in turn 'are' (again in the substance-sense) less than substances. The objection that 'being' in the substance-sense does not apply to qualities, quantities, or relatives carries no weight: Aristotle acknowledges that *a* can be less *F* than *b* when neither *a* nor *b* are *F*.[40]

A 'minimalist' account of truth? Aristotle can be fairly described as committed to the view that truth is not a genuine property. This view recalls modern 'minimalist' theories of truth, which also assert that truth is not a genuine property. Still, there remains an important difference between the view to which Aristotle seems to be committed and modern 'minimalist' theories of truth. For modern 'minimalist' theories of truth are alternatives to the theory of truth as correspondence, and are therefore opposed to it. By contrast, in Aristotle's case the motivation behind the view that truth is not a genuine property is truth's relational character, and this relational character is the essential trait of Aristotle's theory of truth as correspondence.

3 HOW FAR IS TRUTH FROM CHANGE?

A difference between general and singular assertions. Take a singular affirmative assertion *u*, e.g. an utterance of 'Socrates is seated'. At t_1 Socrates is seated. Since the universal seated is the object signified by the predicate of *u* and Socrates is the object signified by the subject of *u*, at t_1 the universal signified by the predicate of *u* is combined with the individual signified by the subject of *u* in such a way as to hold of it. So, *u* is true at t_1. Between t_1 and the later t_2 *u* does not change, but Socrates changes: he stands up.

39 *Top.* 1.15, 107^b13–18; *Ph.* 7.4, 248^b6–249^a8; *Metaph.* I 4, 1055^a6–7; *EN* 8.2, 1155^b13–15.

40 *Top.* 3.6, 119^b17–30; *Rh.* 2.23, 1397^b12–29. There are however oscillations in Aristotle's position on the issue of *a* being less *F* than *b* when neither *a* nor *b* are *F* (cf. Casari (1984), 140–2, 144).

Hence at t_2 the universal signified by the predicate of *u* is not combined with the individual signified by the subject of *u* in such a way as to hold of it. So, *u* is not true at t_2.[41]

Next take a particular affirmative assertion *u*′, e.g. an utterance of 'Some man is seated'. At t_1 Socrates is the only man seated. Since the universal seated is the object signified by the predicate of *u*′ and the universal man is the object signified by the subject of *u*′, at t_1 the universal signified by the predicate of *u*′ is combined with the universal signified by the subject of *u*′ in such a way as not universally to fail to hold of it. So *u*′ is true at t_1. Between t_1 and t_2 *u*′ does not change, but Socrates changes: he stands up. As a consequence of Socrates' change, at t_2 no man is seated. Hence at t_2 the universal signified by the predicate of *u*′ is not combined with the universal signified by the subject of *u*′ in such a way as not universally to fail to hold of it. So *u*′ is not true at t_2.[42]

Between t_1 and t_2 the universals man and seated do not change. For, although seated at t_1 *is*, and at t_2 *is not*, combined with man in such a way as not universally to fail to hold of it, man and seated do not change between t_1 and t_2: all the relevant change occurs in Socrates.[43] Thus, in the case of *u* (a *singular* assertion) the change responsible for the different truth-values at different times occurs in the object (Socrates) signified by the subject. But in the case of *u*′ (a *general* assertion) the change responsible for the different truth-values at different times does not occur in the object (man) signified by the subject (nor, for that matter, in the object signified by the predicate).

Thus: *some* singular assertion has different truth-values at different times without changing because all the relevant change occurs in the object signified by the subject; *no* general assertion has different truth-values at different times without changing because all the relevant change occurs in the object signified by the subject. General assertions are, in a way, at least two steps removed from change. And a general assertion whose subject signifies a universal that ranges only over universals (e.g. an utterance of 'Every biological species is instantiated') is at least three steps removed.

Do states of affairs change? For Aristotle, an affirmative predicative assertion is true when and only when the corresponding state of affairs 'is' in the sense of being true. Hence, if an affirmative predicative assertion is true at t_1 and not true at t_2, the corresponding state of affairs 'is' in the sense of

41 Cf. [17] on pp. 93–4 above. 42 Cf. [17] on pp. 93–4 above.

43 Cf. *Ph.* 4.4, 211ᵃ17–23; 5.1, 224ᵇ4–6; 224ᵇ10–16; *Metaph.* H 5, 1044ᵇ21–9; [Plu.] *Plac.* 899*b*; Simp. *in Cat.* 218, 19–21; G. E. L. Owen (1968a), 110–11.

being true at t_1 and 'is not' in the sense of being false at t_2. Aristotle thinks that the *assertion* can be true at t_1 and not true at t_2 without changing. Does he think that the *state of affairs* can 'be' in the sense of being true at t_1 and 'not be' in the sense of being false at t_2 without changing? Passages relevant to this problem are T 43 and T 45, which can be interpreted in at least two ways.

According to interpretation (i), in T 43 and T 45 'object' denotes those (composite or non-composite) items which are crucial to the truth or falsehood of beliefs and assertions concerning them, and 'is or is not' means '"is" in the sense of being true or "is not" in the sense of being false'. On interpretation (i), T 43 and T 45 commit Aristotle to the claim that a state of affairs, by 'being' in the sense of being true at one time and 'not being' in the sense of being false at another, undergoes a change.[44]

According to interpretation (ii), in T 43 and T 45 'object' indicates an item (an individual, in the case at hand) to which the assertion or belief refers,[45] and 'is or is not' functions as a schematic expression to be expanded as 'is so-and-so or is not so-and-so'.[46] On interpretation (ii), T 43 and T 45 do not commit Aristotle to the claim that a state of affairs, by 'being' in the sense of being true at one time and 'not being' in the sense of being false at another, undergoes a change.

Against interpretation (i) counts the fact that if it is correct, then Aristotle cannot easily escape the awkward consequence that states of affairs should be substances (because he is arguing[47] that only substances receive contraries by changing while remaining numerically one and the same). In favour of interpretation (ii) counts the example with which Aristotle begins the discussion in this section of *Categories* 5 (4^a23–8 < T 43): the change responsible for the assertion or belief that somebody is seated being true at one time and false at another is the getting up, and what gets up is not a state of affairs but the individual to which the assertion or belief refers. Thus, interpretation (ii) has a slight edge over (i).[48] This goes in favour of

[44] Cf. 4^a35–6; 4^a37–4^b1; Mignucci (1985a), 165–6, 168; de Rijk (1987), 33–4; Gaskin (1998), 45; Modrak (2001), 36.

[45] Cf. *Int.* 3, 16^b21–5 (where, contrary to de Rijk (1987), 35, 55 and Gaskin (1998), 45, both Weidemann (1994/2002), 178–87 and Whitaker (1996), 55–8 take 'πρᾶγμα' at 16^b23 to denote the item signified by a verb); 7, 17^a38–9; 12, 21^b27–8 (with Nuchelmans (1973), 36, Hadot (1980), 313, and Gaskin (1998), 45); *APr.* 1.27, 43^b3–5; 43^b11–12; *APo.* 2.5, 91^b14–15; C. J. F. Williams (1991), 307.

[46] Cf. n. 19 of ch. 4.

[47] 4^b2–4 (cf. 4^a35–6; 4^a37–4^b1; 4^b8–9).

[48] Cf. Nuchelmans (1973), 34–5; Graeser (1978), 449–50; (1981), 87. Other Aristotelian passages (*Top.* 8.2, 157^b13; 157^b15–16; *de An.* 3.3, 428^b6; 428^b8–9) also speak of different truth-values at different times in connection with an object (πρᾶγμα) that changes (μεταπίπτειν) or remains unchanged (σώζεσθαι or διαμένειν), but leave it unclear whether the objects that change or remain unchanged

attributing to Aristotle the view that a state of affairs can 'be' in the sense of being true at one time and 'not be' in the sense of being false at another without changing. In fact, the considerations of the preceding subsections suggest that this is the view Aristotle *ought to* adopt: for whatever arguments show that an assertion can be true at one time and false at another without changing should be transferable to states of affairs and thus establish that a state of affairs can 'be' in the sense of being true at one time and 'not be' in the sense of being false at another without changing.

are states of affairs. Aristotle's use of 'μεταπίπτειν' and 'πρᾶγμα' in connection with different truth-values at different times is striking in the light of the technical terminology in Hellenistic philosophy (see e.g. D.L. 7. 65; 76; Simp. *in Ph.* 1299, 36–1300, 11).

CHAPTER 7

Truth and Determinism in de Interpretatione *9*

In chapter 9 of *de Interpretatione* (henceforth '*Int.* 9') Aristotle claims that some future-tense singular assertions[1] are sometimes neither true nor false, and therefore refute Bivalence, the principle stating that every assertion is always either true or false. Aristotle's argument goes as follows:

> If every future-tense singular assertion is always either true or false, then whatever happens was always antecedently bound to happen, i.e. Determinism holds; but it is not the case that whatever happens was always antecedently bound to happen; hence, not every future-tense singular assertion is always either true or false, i.e. some future-tense singular assertions are sometimes neither true nor false.

Int. 9 divides into four parts: the first (18^a28–33) is introductory (it briefly states Aristotle's position); the second (18^a34–18^b25) contains two arguments from Bivalence to Determinism; the third (18^b26–19^a22) argues that Determinism is absurd; the fourth (19^a23–19^b4) contains Aristotle's solution to the problems raised by Bivalence and Determinism.

In section 1 of the present chapter I present the most important modal attributes and theses at play in *Int.* 9: the attribute of necessity as ineluctability (a diachronic modality, with two 'slots for dates'), the thesis of the necessity of the present and the past (the thesis that for whatever obtains at any time it is both then and later necessary to obtain then), and Determinism (the thesis that for whatever obtains at any time it is always antecedently necessary to obtain then). Aristotle endorses the necessity of the present and the past, but rejects Determinism. In section 2 I offer a close textual analysis of *Int.* 9 (I translate and comment on the whole of *Int.* 9). The most important part of this section is that dealing with Aristotle's own solution for the problems raised by Bivalence and Determinism: I defend an interpretation of Aristotle's words that gives him a position that fits well with his view that assertions can, in principle, have different truth-values at

[1] Aristotle concentrates on predicative assertions, but his argument perhaps covers also existential assertions.

different times (the usual interpretation instead lands him with an unstable position). In section 3 I briefly discuss alternative interpretations of *Int.* 9.

1 THE MODAL ATTRIBUTES AND THESES INVOLVED IN *INT.* 9

Necessity as ineluctability. Int. 9's discussion of Determinism employs the attribute of necessity as ineluctability (or inevitability): what is necessary is what is ineluctable (or inevitable), i.e. what nothing can be done about.[2]

The attribute of necessity as ineluctability is a diachronic modality, i.e. a modal attribute with two 'slots for dates'. The key formulations are instances of the schema 'At τ it is necessary that α at τ'', where 'τ' and 'τ'' are to be replaced with designations of times, 'α' with an assertoric sentence-type without dates: e.g. 'At 13.00 of 1 January 1997 it was necessary that the train should reach the station at 13.20 of 1 January 1997'.[3] Such formulations can be deployed to express views involving the attribute of necessity as ineluctability (e.g. 'If the train reached the station at 13.20 of 1 January 1997, then at 13.20 of 1 January 1997 it was necessary that the train should reach the station at 13.20 of 1 January 1997').[4]

The necessity of the present and the past. In several passages Aristotle endorses the thesis of the necessity of the present and the past:

T 46 Nothing that has come to be is an object of choice, e.g. no one chooses to have sacked Troy: for no one deliberates about what has come to be,[5] but

[2] Other passages also seem to employ the attribute of necessity as ineluctability: see *Cael.* 1.12, 283ᵇ8–10; 283ᵇ13–14; *Metaph.* E 3, 1027ᵃ32–1027ᵇ14 (with Gaskin (1995), 97–8); *Rh.* 1.3, 1358ᵇ3–5; 1358ᵇ14–15. On necessity as ineluctability see Peter de Rivo (*apud* Baudry (1950), 75); Lukasiewicz (1930), 155–6; Prior (1953), 322–4; Butler (1955), 268–9; Prior (1955/62), 241, 247–50; Anscombe (1956/68), 23; Lemmon (1956); Grant (1957), 522–7; R. Taylor (1957), 5–15, 22–3; Saunders (1958), 369; Anscombe/Geach (1961), 7; von Fritz (1962), 140; Ackrill (1963), 139; Burrell (1964), 39–41; Hintikka (1964/73a), 164; (1964/73b), 183; Cahn (1967), 25–6, 31; Sainati (1968), 280; Seeskin (1971), 765; McKim (1971/72), 88–91, 107; D. Frede (1972), 160–7; Dickason (1976), 21; Jeffrey (1979), 251–2; M. J. White (1979), 90–1; Sorabji (1980), 105; Spellman (1980), 115–16; Weidemann (1980), 408–10; C. J. F. Williams (1980), 129; M. J. White (1981), 238; Seel (1982a), 244–5; (1982b), 300–1; Waterlow (1982), 11–12; Thomason (1984), 138–9; von Wright (1984c), 76; D. Frede (1985), 72; M. J. White (1985), 17–18; Kirwan (1986), 169–77; von Kutschera (1986), 208–9; Craig (1988), 12–13; van Eck (1988), 20, 24–5; Donini (1989), 8–9; D. Frede (1990), 203; Zagzebski (1991), 15–17; Gaskin (1994), 88–90; Weidemann (1994/2002), 255; Gaskin (1995), 93–4; Mignucci (1996b), 285–7; D. Frede (1998), 96; Enders (1999), 388–91; Bonomi/Zucchi (2001), 10.

[3] Grammar often requires adjusting the otherwise ungrammatical result of a pure and simple substitution (e.g. 'At 13.00 of 1 January 1997 it is necessary that the train reaches the station at 13.20 of 1 January 1997' is ungrammatical).

[4] On diachronic modalities in Aristotle cf. Weidemann (1980), 408–10; Seel (1982b), 297–9; Knuuttila (1993), 31–3; Weidemann (1994/2002), 253–5.

[5] Cf. *EN* 3.5, 1112ᵇ33–1113ᵃ2.

about what will be and is possible, while what has come to be cannot not have come to be. (*EN* 6.2, 1139^{b}5–9)

T 47 Forensic oratory deals with what is and what is not, of which there is more of a demonstration and necessity: for what has come to be is necessary. (*Rh.* 3.17, 1418^{a}4–5)

T 46 states the necessity of the past and the contingency of the future; T 47 presupposes the necessity of the present as well as the past.[6]

The diachronic modality of necessity as ineluctability provides a helpful framework for discussing the necessity of the present and the past. For the thesis of the necessity of the present and the past can be identified with the thesis that for every state of affairs *s* and every time *t*, if *s* obtains (or, respectively, does not obtain) at *t* then at every time *t′* not earlier than *t* it is necessary that *s* should obtain (or, respectively, not obtain) at *t*.

Determinism. The diachronic modality of necessity as ineluctability provides a helpful framework for discussing also Determinism. For Determinism can be identified with the thesis that for every state of affairs *s* and every time *t*, if *s* obtains (or, respectively, does not obtain) at *t* then at every time *t′* earlier than *t* it is necessary that *s* should obtain (or, respectively, not obtain) at *t*.

2 CLOSE TEXTUAL ANALYSIS OF *INT.* 9

The introduction (18^{a}28–33):

T 48 With regard to things that are and things that have come to be, it is then necessary that either the affirmation or the denial should be true or false, and with regard to universals spoken of universally it is necessary that always one should be true and the other false, and with individuals too, as we have said,[7] while with regard to universals not spoken of universally it is not necessary (we discussed these, too).[8] But with regard to individuals that are going to be it is not likewise. (18^{a}28–33)

T 48 draws two contrasts. First, it contrasts past- and present-tense assertions with future-tense singular assertions. Past- and present-tense assertions are said to have, and future-tense singular assertions to lack, a certain property concerning truth and falsehood. What property is it? There are

[6] At *Cael.* 1.12, 283^{b}13–14 Aristotle apparently endorses the necessity of the past but denies that of the present (cf. Sharples (1979), 41; Kirwan (1986), 177–8).

[7] Cf. 7, 17^{b}26–9. [8] Cf. 7, 17^{b}29–37.

two candidates: having always a different truth-value from the contradictory, and being always either true or false. But the first property is ruled out because some past- and present-tense assertions lack it: some indeterminate past- or present-tense assertion sometimes has the same truth-value as its contradictory (e.g. 'A man is white' and 'A man is not white' are both true now).[9] Hence T 48's first contrast is probably the following:

[30] Every past- or present-tense assertion is always either true or false. Not every future-tense singular assertion is always either true or false.

This contrast is not exhaustive: general future-tense assertions fall in neither of its groups. What group should they be attached to? In other words, are they supposed to be always either true or false?[10]

T 48's second contrast is a sub-contrast within the first of the first contrast's two groups. This time the property which makes the difference seems to be that of having always a different truth-value from the contradictory. Thus:

[31] Within the group of past- and present-tense assertions, each of which is always either true or false, some (i.e. singular and quantified assertions) always have a different truth-value from their contradictories (at every time one of the two contradictories is true, the other false), some of the others (i.e. indeterminate assertions) sometimes have the same truth-value as their contradictories (specifically, they are both true).

The first deterministic argument (18^a34–18^b9). The part of *Int.* 9 (18^a34–18^b25) showing that Bivalence entails Determinism contains two deterministic arguments (18^a34–18^b9, 18^b9–16) and a pre-emptive move (18^b16–25) blocking an escape route.

Here is the first deterministic argument:

T 49 For if every affirmation or denial is true or false, it is also necessary for everything either to hold or not to hold. Hence,[11] if someone will affirm that something will be and another will deny precisely this, it is clearly necessary for one of them to be speaking truly, if every affirmation and

[9] Cf. Ackrill (1963), 133–4; Weidemann (1979), 30; Craig (1988), 9–10; Weidemann (1994/2002), 226–7.

[10] Most commentators think they are: see Ammon. *in Int.* 128, 30–129, 35; 138, 28–34; 148, 6–11 (with Mignucci (1998), 54); von Kirchmann (1876), 73–4; DuLac (1949), 166; Wieland (1979), 29; Weidemann (1994/2002), 227. For a dissenting voice see Gaskin (1996), 50.

[11] At 18^a35 I read 'ὑπάρχειν, ὥστε εἰ' with the main manuscripts, Bekker, Waitz, Dübner, Cooke, and Weidemann. Other witnesses have 'ὑπάρχειν· εἰ γὰρ', the reading adopted by Pacius, Buhle, Weise, Minio-Paluello, Zadro, and D. Frede (1970), 85–6. Other attested readings are 'ὑπάρχειν· εἰ δὴ' and 'ὑπάρχειν· εἰ δὲ'.

denial[12] is either true or false (for both will not hold together with regard to such items).[13] For if it is true to say that it is white, or not white, it is necessary for it to be white, or not white, and if it is white, or not white, it was true to affirm, or to deny; and if it does not hold, he is speaking falsely, and if he is speaking falsely, it does not hold. Hence it is necessary that either the affirmation or the denial should be true. Hence nothing[14] is or comes to be, or will be or not be, by chance or however it chances, but everything necessarily and not however it chances (since either he who affirms or he who denies is speaking truly). For things would have come to be just as not have come to be: for what is however it chances is not, nor will be, more thus than not thus. (18^a34–18^b9)

This first deterministic argument has two parts: the first (18^a34–18^b4) concludes that Bivalence's holding for future-tense singular assertions entails that at every time one member of a contradictory pair of future-tense singular assertions is true,[15] the second (18^b5–9) that if at every time one member of a contradictory pair of future-tense singular assertions is true, then whatever will happen is already determined.

The first part of the first deterministic argument (18^a34–18^b4) can be reconstructed by employing conventional symbolism (I omit reference to time because it is inessential at this stage). Begin by assuming Bivalence:

[32] ('α' is true $\vee$ 'α' is false) & ('$\neg\alpha$' is true $\vee$ '$\neg\alpha$' is false) (cf. 18^a37–8)

(here 'α' is a schematic letter to be replaced with singular affirmative assertoric sentence-types). Then assume the following conditionals:

[33] 'α' is true $\rightarrow$ α (cf. 18^a39–18^b1)

[34] '$\neg\alpha$' is true $\rightarrow$ $\neg\alpha$ (cf. 18^a39–18^b1)

[35] α $\rightarrow$ 'α' is true (cf. 18^b1–2)

[12] At 18^a38 I read 'κατάφασις καὶ ἀπόφασις' with some witnesses, Bekker, Dübner, Cooke, and Weidemann. Other witnesses have 'κατάφασις' (printed by Waitz, Minio-Paluello, and Zadro); yet others have 'κατάφασις ἢ ἀπόφασις' (printed by Pacius, Buhle, and Weise).

[13] 'With regard to such items' means 'with regard to individuals', the 'ἐπί'+ dative construction (18^a39) recalling the 'ἐπί'+ genitive construction used five times in T 48 (at 18^a28, 18^a29–30, 18^a31, 18^a31–2, and 18^a33 – cf. 18^b27–8; 19^a35–6; 19^b3–4). Our parenthetical remark can then be paraphrased as follows: 'It is not the case that what is said by someone using a future-tense singular affirmation and what is said by someone who is denying just that hold together'. This justifies the preceding point that 'it is clearly necessary for one [*sc.* exactly one] of them to be speaking truly' (18^a36–7). The intended contrast is with affirmations and denials which are *made non-universally about universals*, which *can* be both true at the same time. Cf. Ammon. *in Int.* 140, 4–10; Steph. *in Int.* 37, 7–10; Ackrill (1963), 135; Weidemann (1979), 30–1; D. Frede (1985), 35, 37; Weidemann (1994/2002), 232, 234, 238.

[14] At 18^b4–5 I read 'ἀληθῆ εἶναι. οὐδὲν': this reading, presupposed by the translations of Boethius and George the Arab, is printed by Minio-Paluello and Zadro. The other witnesses and most editions have 'ἀληθῆ εἶναι ἢ ψευδῆ. οὐδὲν'.

[15] Cf. Craig (1988), 29–30; Weidemann (1994/2002), 232, 236.

[36] $\neg\alpha \rightarrow$ '$\neg\alpha$' is true (cf. 18^b1–2)

[37] $\neg\alpha \rightarrow$ 'α' is false (cf. 18^b3)

[38] 'α' is false $\rightarrow \neg\alpha$ (cf. 18^b3)

Aristotle is consistent only if he does not accept all of [33]–[38]. For Aristotle endorses Excluded Middle (cf. 19^a27–32 < T 53), so he must accept that $\alpha \vee \neg\alpha$. Then, if Aristotle accepts [35] and [37], he must admit that 'α' is true $\vee$ 'α' is false, a form of Bivalence for affirmative assertions which he rejects. So, Aristotle probably does not accept all of [33]–[38], but he only presents them as theses to which the advocate of Bivalence is committed.[16]

Propositions [32]–[38] – actually, a subset of them – entail that in every contradictory pair of singular assertions at least one member is true:

[39] 'α' is true $\vee$ '$\neg\alpha$' is true (cf. 18^a35–7; 18^b4; 18^b7–8).

To derive [39] from [32], [36], and [38], consider that [38] and [36] obviously entail

[40] 'α' is false $\rightarrow$ '$\neg\alpha$' is true.

But now [40] and [32]'s first conjunct trivially entail [39]. Since

[41] $\neg$('α' is true & '$\neg\alpha$' is true) (cf. 18^a38–9)

(because *singular* assertions are involved),

[42] ('α' is true $\vee$ '$\neg\alpha$' is true) & $\neg$('α' is true & '$\neg\alpha$' is true).[17]

The second part of the first deterministic argument (18^b5–9). The first part of the argument established that if Bivalence is true, then in every contradictory pair of singular assertions it is always the case that one member is true. But then the future is already determined. For, on the one hand, if the *affirmative* member 'Tomorrow α' of a contradictory pair of future-tense singular assertions is true today, then today it is ineluctable that one day after today, i.e. tomorrow, it will be the case that α; on the other, if the contradictory pair's *negative* member 'Tomorrow $\neg\alpha$' is true today, then today it is ineluctable that one day after today, i.e. tomorrow, it will be the case that $\neg\alpha$. Hence, either today it is ineluctable that tomorrow it will be the case that α, or today it is ineluctable that tomorrow it will be the case that $\neg\alpha$. The argument can be generalised to cover intervals different from that of one day.[18]

[16] Cf. the subsection to which n. 18 of appendix 6 pertains.

[17] Cf. n. 13 above.

[18] Cf. Weidemann (1994/2002), 240–1.

The second deterministic argument (18^b9–16):

T 50 Moreover, if it is white now, it was true to say earlier that it would be white, so that of any of the things that have come to be it was always true to say that it would be. But if it was always true to say that it is, or that it would be, it was not possible for this not to be, or not to be going to be. But for what it was not possible not to have come to be, it was impossible not to have come to be; and for what it was impossible not to have come to be, it was necessary to have come to be.[19] Hence for all that will be it was necessary that it should have come to be. Hence nothing will be however it chances or by chance: for if by chance, then not necessarily. (18^b9–16)[20]

T 50's deterministic argument is best described in terms of an argument-schema which can, by appropriate substitutions, generate many distinct arguments.[21] In what follows, the schematic letter 'α' can be replaced with any present-tense assertoric sentence-type without dates. The argument's conclusion is that if it is now the case that α, then it has always been necessary that now it should be the case that α. Suppose it is now the case that α. Let t_0 be any past time, and let 'i' name the exact interval between t_0 and now. Given Bivalence, at t_0 an assertion that is an utterance of 'In i it will be the case that α' was either true or false. Since now, i after t_0, it is the case that α, the assertion was not false at t_0. Hence it was then true. Therefore the state of affairs of the assertion's being true obtained at t_0. Hence (by the necessity of the present and the past) at t_0 it was necessary that the state of affairs of the assertion's being true should obtain then. Therefore at t_0 it was necessary that at t_0 it should be the case that i later it would be the case that α. Since i after t_0 is now, at t_0 it was necessary that now it should be the case that α. Since t_0 was arbitrary, we can conclude that it has always been necessary that now it should be the case that α.

The conclusion of T 50's deterministic argument is not yet a formulation of Determinism. One reason why the conclusion of this argument is not yet a formulation of Determinism is that it is restricted to the present: its conclusion is (all appropriate instances of) 'If it is *now* the case that α, then it has always been necessary that *now* it should be the case that α'. This fault can be easily amended by modifying the argument in such a way that it comes to cover all times: the modified argument's conclusion will be (all appropriate instances of) 'For every time t, if at t it is the case that α then

[19] Cf. *Metaph.* Γ 4, 1006^b31–3. [20] T 50's deterministic argument reappears at 18^b33–19^a6.

[21] For similar reconstructions of T 50's deterministic argument see Ockham *in Int.* I.VI 8, 2–12; C. J. F. Williams (1978), 285–7; Sorabji (1980), 91; van Eck (1988), 26–7; Weidemann (1994/2002), 247–8; Sorabji (1998), 7–8. Some commentators (Baylis (1936), 161–2; D. C. Williams (1951), 292; Haack (1974/96), 74–81) think the second deterministic argument commits a fallacy of modal operator shift.

at every time t' earlier than t it is necessary that at t it should be the case that α'. Even this is not yet the thesis with which I identified Determinism ('For every state of affairs *s* and every time *t*, if *s* obtains – or, respectively, does not obtain – at *t* then at every time t' earlier than *t* it is necessary that *s* should obtain – or, respectively, not obtain – at *t*'), but is close enough to it.[22]

The distinctive trait of T 50's deterministic argument is to pass from the past truth of a future-tense assertion to the state of affairs of the assertion's being true obtaining at a past time, and to infer that at this past time it was necessary that this state of affairs should obtain then. This past necessity is then 'transferred' to what the assertion predicts. At 18^b13–14, the inferences that substitute equivalent modal attributes ('it was not possible not to have come to be', 'it was impossible not to have come to be', and 'it was necessary to have come to be') play no important role.

Note that the determinist must claim that whatever is now the case was *always* necessary in the past. The indeterminist can grant that something which is now the case was necessary *at some time or other* in the past: e.g. he can grant that when, a fraction of a second ago, the bullet was very close to its target, it was necessary that it should hit its target.[23]

The pre-emptive move (18^b16–25):

T 51 But neither is it possible to say that neither of the two is true, i.e.[24] that neither it will be nor it will not be. For, first, while the affirmation is false the denial will not be true, and while this is false the affirmation turns out not to be true. Moreover, if it is true to say that it is white and black, it must be the case[25] that they both hold, and if it is true to say that they will hold tomorrow, it must be the case that they will hold[26] tomorrow. But if it will neither be nor not be tomorrow, there will be no 'however it chances', e.g. a sea-battle:[27] for it would be necessary for the sea-battle neither to have come to be nor not to have come to be. (18^b16–25)

22 The deterministic argument I presented in the introduction (pp. 35–6 above), although based on T 50's deterministic argument, departs from it in that it is formulated directly in terms of states of affairs and has Determinism as its conclusion.

23 Cf. Harris (1977/78), 50–1; Kirwan (1986), 172, 186; Donini (1989), 7; Enders (1999), 380.

24 'I.e.' ('οἷον') here introduces a consequence of what precedes.

25 At 18^b21 I read 'μέλαν δεῖ', a reading attested by the ancient translations (with the exception of Boethius') and printed by Minio-Paluello and Zadro. Laur. 72, 15 reads 'μέλαν', the other main manuscripts, Boethius' translation, and Ammonius have 'μέγα δεῖ', the reading adopted by most editors. For 'λευκόν' and 'μέγα' cf. *APr.* 2.4, 57^b4–17.

26 At 18^b22 I read 'ὑπάρξει εἰς αὔριον, ὑπάρξειν' with Pacius, Buhle, Weise, Waitz, Cooke, Ackrill, and Weidemann. Minio-Paluello and Zadro print 'ὑπάρξειν εἰς αὔριον, ὑπάρξει', Bekker and Dübner 'ὑπάρξει εἰς αὔριον, ὑπάρξει'.

27 At *Div. Somn.* 1, 463^b1–3 a sea-battle is an example of something in the fulfilment of which a man has no initiative.

In T 51 the denier of Bivalence forestalls a possible move of an advocate of Bivalence. The advocate of Bivalence might say that neither 'α' nor '¬α' is true (for the sake of simplicity, let the temporal qualifications be dropped), thereby committing himself to the claim that neither α nor ¬α (because otherwise, if either α or ¬α, then, by [35] and [36], which the advocate of Bivalence surely accepts, either 'α' or '¬α' would be true). Such a move would block the first deterministic argument, whose first part established that Bivalence implies that either 'α' or '¬α' is true (cf. above).

The denier of Bivalence takes such a defensive move to have two unacceptable consequences (in drawing these consequences the denier of Bivalence appeals to Bivalence because he is showing what the advocate of Bivalence is committed to).[28]

(i) Given that 'α' is not true, then (by Bivalence) 'α' is false, whence (by [38]) ¬α, whence (by [36]) '¬α' is true. But the advocate of Bivalence is now claiming that '¬α' is not true. Analogously, given that '¬α' is not true, then (by Bivalence) '¬α' is false, whence (by the counterpart of [38] for denials) α, whence (by [35]) 'α' is true. But the advocate of Bivalence is now claiming that 'α' is not true.

(ii) If 'α' and '¬α' both failed to be true now, then (by Bivalence) 'α' and '¬α' would both be false now. Then an argument similar to that of the second part of the first deterministic argument (18^b5–9) would show that it is now necessary (ineluctable) that neither α nor ¬α. So, the advocate of Bivalence would still be landed with a deterministic position (though one of a very peculiar sort).[29]

The position attributed to the advocate of Bivalence, i.e. that neither 'α' nor '¬α' is true, seems something more than a theoretical possibility. The claim that neither the affirmative nor the negative member of a contradictory pair is true entails (by Bivalence, which the advocate of Bivalence of course grants) the claim that both members are false. Elsewhere Aristotle associates this last claim with Anaxagoras. For, according to Aristotle, Anaxagoras' primordial mixture was neither white nor black nor of any other colour, and did not have any property whatsoever, so that no predicate could be truly affirmed or denied of it (the assumption here might be that for a predicate to be truly denied of it, the primordial mixture should have enjoyed some property incompatible with the one signified by

[28] Cf. Judson (1988), 16; Weidemann (1994/2002), 266–8. Some commentators (Anscombe (1956/68), 19; Strang (1960), 452; Hintikka (1964/73a), 167; van Rijen (1989), 105) wrongly claim that in T 51 Aristotle rules out that both members of a contradictory pair of future-tense singular assertions could be neither true nor false.

[29] Cf. Weidemann (1994/2002), 269–70.

that predicate).[30] Aristotle's mention of white and black at $18^{b}21$ might be due not only to his desire to have the incompatibility between white and black mirroring the incompatibility between the predicative expressions of the members of a contradictory pair, but also to his intention to hint at Anaxagoras (several times when he reports on Anaxagoras' primordial mixture Aristotle mentions white and black).[31]

The absurdity of Determinism ($18^{b}26$–$19^{a}22$).

T 52 Thus, the absurdities which result are these[32] and others of the same sort, if of every opposed affirmation and denial, either with regard to universals spoken of universally or with regard to individuals, it is necessary for one to be true and the other false, and[33] that among things that come to be nothing should be however it chances, but everything should be and come to be of necessity,[34] so that there would be no need to deliberate or to take trouble (as if we do this, this will be, while if we fail to do this, this will not be). For nothing prevents someone from having affirmed ten thousand years ago that this would be and someone else having denied it, so that whichever of the two things it was then true to say will be of necessity. But not even this makes a difference, whether someone uttered the contradictory pair or nobody did (for, clearly, this is how objects are even if it is not the case that someone affirmed something[35] and another denied it: for it is not because of the affirming or denying that it will be or fail to be), nor does it matter whether it was ten thousand years ago rather than any other time. Hence, if in the whole of time things were such that one of the two would be true, it was necessary for this to have come to be, and each of the things which have come to be was always in such a condition[36] as to have come to be of necessity. For what someone has truly said would be, it is not possible that it should not have come to be: and what has come to be it was always true to say that it would be.

But if these consequences are impossible – for we see that there is a principle of what will be both from deliberating and from acting, and that in general the possibility of being and not being is present in those things that are not always actual: in these both are possible, to be and not to be,

[30] *Metaph.* Γ 7, $1012^{a}26$–8 (cf. A 8, $989^{b}6$–7; Gaskin (1995), 180; Vuillemin (1996), 139–40).

[31] Cf. *Ph.* 1.4, $187^{b}5$; *Metaph.* A 8, $989^{b}8$–9; Γ 7, $1011^{b}29$–31; Vuillemin (1996), 139–40.

[32] Aristotle is recalling the absurd implication which was shown to follow from the defence against Determinism attempted in T 51: that 'it would be necessary for the sea-battle neither to have come to be nor not to have come to be' ($18^{b}24$–5).

[33] The 'δὲ' at $18^{b}30$ answers the 'μὲν' at $18^{b}26$. Thus, the immediately following 'that among things that come to be [. . .]' corresponds to the initial 'these' and 'others of a similar sort'.

[34] At $18^{b}31$ I place a comma after 'ἀνάγκης' instead of the full stop printed by most editors.

[35] At $18^{b}38$ I read 'καταφήσῃ τι' with some witnesses and most editors. Minio-Paluello and Zadro omit 'τι'.

[36] At $19^{a}3$ I read 'εἶχεν' with most editors. Minio-Paluello and Zadro print 'ἔχειν'.

> and, therefore, to have come to be and not to have come to be. But it is clear to us that many things are like this, e.g. that for this cloak it is possible to be cut up and it will not be cut up, but will wear out before. But not being cut up is equally possible for it: for it would not have been the case that it wore out before if it had not been possible for it not to be cut up. Hence the same holds for the other cases of coming to be, all those which are spoken of according to this type of possibility. It is then[37] clear that not all things are or come to be of necessity, but some are or come to be however it chances, and in no way is the affirmation or the denial more true, whilst with other things one of the two alternatives is or comes to be more and in most cases, while it is none the less possible that the other alternative could have come to be, and the first one not. (18^b26–19^a22)

The assumption from which T 52 claims Determinism follows is not Bivalence, but the principle that in every contradictory pair of singular or quantified assertions one member is true and the other false (at any time). However, with restriction to singular and quantified assertions, Bivalence entails the principle assumed at the beginning of T 52: given Bivalence, exactly one member of a contradictory pair of singular or quantified assertions is true (as the argument at 18^a34–18^b4 showed for the case of singular assertions), and the other is false.

T 52's attack on Determinism raises problems that are not germane to the study of Aristotle's views on truth. I shall therefore leave these problems aside and concentrate on T 52's comments on chance, which are important for understanding Aristotle's views on truth in *Int.* 9.

Aristotle's account of diachronic modalities. Several remarks in *Int.* 9 suggest that Aristotle is operating with a 'statistical' conception of modalities, according to which a state of affairs enjoys a certain modal attribute just in case it obtains with a certain frequency. Specifically, in *Int.* 9 Aristotle seems to be operating with a statistical conception of chance, according to which a state of affairs is a matter of chance just in case it obtains just about as often as it does not.[38]

However, the assumption that Aristotle in *Int.* 9 is operating with a statistical conception of modalities faces objections. According to a first objection, T 52's example rules out a statistical conception of possibility: although this cloak will wear out without being cut up, so that it is never cut up, it is possible for it to be cut up. A second objection points out that, according to *Int.* 9's interpretation developed so far, Aristotle is here

[37] The 'then' ('ἄρα') here (19^a18) answers the 'if' ('εἰ') at the beginning of the paragraph (19^a7) (cf. Weidemann (1994/2002), 277).

[38] 18^b8–9; 19^a9–10; 19^a18–22; 19^a35–9. For the statistical conception of modalities in Aristotle see n. 54 of ch. 1.

operating with diachronic modalities, i.e. modal attributes with two 'slots for dates', whose key formulations are instances of the schemata 'At τ it is necessary that α at τ'', 'At τ it is impossible that α at τ'', etc. However, diachronic modalities have nothing to do with the statistical conception of modalities.

Can one attribute to Aristotle a coherent conception of modalities which accommodates his statistical remarks without being defeated by objections like those raised in the preceding paragraph? Here is one way to do this for chance:

[43] For every time *t* and every non-zero interval *i*, at *t* it is chance whether *i* later it will be the case that α just in case in the infinite course of time up to *i* before *t*, just about half of the times when the total state of the world resembled in relevant respects the total state of the world at *t* were followed *i* later by a time when it was the case that α.[39]

Since there is no clinching evidence for claiming that Aristotle in *Int.* 9 is operating with an attribute of chance like the one described by [43], the suggestion that such an attribute should play a central role in *Int.* 9 remains speculative. As for the other modalities, [43]'s obvious companion is:

[44] For every time *t* and every non-zero interval *i*, at *t* it is necessary (impossible, possible) that *i* later it should be going to be the case that α just in case in the infinite course of time up to *i* before *t*, every (no, some) time when the total state of the world resembled in relevant respects the total state of the world at *t* was followed *i* later by a time when it was the case that α.[40]

Note that [43] and [44] cover only diachronic modalities with a non-zero interval towards the future: they state, for every time *t* and every non-zero interval *i*, necessary and sufficient conditions for it to be chance, necessary, impossible, or possible at *t* that α *i* later. Thus, [44] says nothing about the necessity of the present or the past.

Aristotle's solution (19^a23–19^b4).

T 53 Now, that what is should be whenever it is, and that what is not should not be whenever it is not, is necessary, but it is not necessary that

[39] Cf. M. J. White (1981), 239; Weidemann (1987), 181–2; (1994/2002), 280; Gaskin (1996), 54; Enders (1999), 382–3.

[40] Propositions [43] and [44] at least show that those commentators (e.g. Ackrill (1963), 136; D. Frede (1985), 65; Gaskin (1995), 38) are not obviously right who think that *Int.* 9 cannot accommodate Aristotle's statistical remarks about modalities.

> everything which is should be, nor that what is not should not be: for, that everything which is should be of necessity when it is is not the same as that everything which is should unqualifiedly be of necessity, and similarly with what is not.[41] The same account[42] applies also to the contradictory pair: it is necessary that everything should either be or not be, and either be going to be or not; but it is not necessary[43] to divide and call one or the other necessary. For example, I mean that it is necessary that either there will be a sea-battle tomorrow or there will not be one, but it is not necessary that tomorrow a sea-battle should come to be nor that it should not come to be: however, it is necessary that one should either come to be or not come to be.[44] So, since sentences are true in the same way as the objects, evidently, in the case of those which are in such a condition as to be or come to be[45] however it chances and admit the contrary states,[46] the contradictory pair will necessarily be in the same condition. This happens with those which not always 'are' or not always 'are not':[47] for it is necessary that one of the two members of a contradictory pair concerning these [*sc.* states of affairs which not always 'are' or not always 'are not'] should be true or false, but it is not necessary that this one or this one should be true or false, but it is however it chances, and it is necessary that one of the two should be more true, but not already true or false.[48] Hence, clearly, it is not necessary that of every affirmation and denial that are opposed one should be true and the other false. For with what is things work out differently than with what is not but can be as well as not be – with these it is as we have said. ($19^{a}23$–$19^{b}4$)

T 53 divides into three parts: $19^{a}23$–7, $19^{a}27$–32, and $19^{a}32$–$19^{b}4$. In the following subsections I shall analyse them in turn.

Two claims about necessity. T 53's first part ($19^{a}23$–7) makes two claims. The first is: 'That what is should be whenever it is, and that what is not should

41 Aristotle's distinction here is echoed by Theophrastus: see Alex. Aphr. *in APr.* 36, 25–9 (< Thphr. F 14 Graeser); 156, 26–157, 2 (= Thphr. T 100B Fortenbaugh *et al.* < F 14 Graeser); 141, 1–6 (= Thphr. T 100D Fortenbaugh *et al.* < F 14 Graeser); [Ammon.] *in APr.* 37, 2–4.

42 The Greek words 'ὁ αὐτὸς λόγος' ($19^{a}27$–8), which correspond to the English 'the same account', are absent from one of the main manuscripts (n).

43 I understand 'ἀνάγκη' from $19^{a}28$ and I regard 'θάτερον' and 'ἀναγκαῖον' as objects of 'εἰπεῖν'. Other constructions are possible (see Waitz (1844/46), I 342–3; Weidemann (1994/2002), 293–4).

44 The English present 'to come to be' translates the Greek aorist 'γενέσθαι' ($19^{a}31$–2). Here Aristotle uses the aorist of 'γίγνομαι' merely for its aspectual connotation (cf. Humbert (1945/60), 144–5). The temporal connotation is so absent that Aristotle employs the aorist despite the fact that one would expect a future.

45 Here ($19^{a}34$) the words 'be or come to be' are supplied from $19^{a}10$–11 and $19^{a}18$–19.

46 At $19^{a}34$ I take 'τὰ ἐναντία' as the object of 'ἐνδέχεσθαι': a similar construction occurs at *Metaph.* Θ 10, $1051^{b}11$. Some translators instead regard 'τὰ ἐναντία' as the subject of 'ἐνδέχεσθαι' (see e.g. Weidemann (1994/2002), 15).

47 Here ($19^{a}36$) I read 'τοῖς μὴ ἀεὶ οὖσιν ἢ μὴ ἀεὶ μὴ οὖσιν', which is the reading handed down by most witnesses and printed by all the editions I consulted. One of the main manuscripts (A), however, reads 'τοῖς μὴ ἀεὶ οὖσιν', and Laur. 72, 15 has 'τοῖς μὴ ἀεὶ οὐκ οὖσιν'.

48 Here ($19^{a}39$) I read 'ψευδῆ. ὥστε', which is the reading handed down by most witnesses and printed by all editors. A and Laur. 72, 3 read 'ψευδῆ εἶναι. ὥστε'.

not be whenever it is not, is necessary' (19^a23–4). The best interpretation is achieved by understanding the crucial occurrences of 'to be' in the veridical sense and regarding them as predicated of states of affairs. This makes the first claim of T 53's first part equivalent to:

[45] For every state of affairs *s* and every time *t*, if *s* obtains at *t* then at *t* it is necessary that *s* should obtain at *t*. For every state of affairs *s* and every time *t*, if *s* does not obtain at *t* then at *t* it is necessary that *s* should not obtain at *t*.

Proposition [45] states the 'necessity of the present'. The necessity at play is ineluctability: if Socrates' being seated obtains at noon on 1 January 399 BC, then at noon on 1 January 399 BC it is necessary (ineluctable) that Socrates' being seated should obtain at noon on 1 January 399 BC (for at noon on 1 January 399 BC nothing can be done about its being the case that at noon on 1 January 399 BC Socrates is seated); similarly, if Socrates' being seated does not obtain at noon on 1 January 399 BC, then at noon on 1 January 399 BC it is necessary (ineluctable) that Socrates' being seated should not obtain at noon on 1 January 399 BC.[49]

The second claim of T 53's first part is: 'It is not necessary that everything which is should be, nor that what is not should not be' (19^a24–5). This second claim is obscure. A clue for its interpretation is provided by Aristotle's own explanation of how it differs from the first claim: 'For, that everything which is should be of necessity when it is is not the same as that everything which is should unqualifiedly be of necessity, and similarly with what is not' (19^a25–7). Since Aristotle sometimes uses 'unqualifiedly' ('ἁπλῶς', 19^a26) to mean 'without restriction to any specific time',[50] the second claim of T 53's first part can be plausibly regarded as equivalent to:

[46] It is not the case that for every state of affairs *s* and every time *t*, if *s* obtains at *t* then it is always necessary that *s* should obtain at *t*. It is not the case that for every state of affairs *s* and every time *t*, if *s* does not obtain at *t* then it is always necessary that *s* should not obtain at *t*.

The necessity at play in [46] is again ineluctability: it is not the case that if Socrates' being seated obtains at noon on 1 January 399 BC, then it is always necessary (ineluctable) that Socrates' being seated should obtain at noon on 1 January 399 BC; similarly, it is not the case that if Socrates' being

[49] Cf. Seel (1982a), 244; Waterlow (1982), 89; Weidemann (1994/2002), 254, 284; Gaskin (1995), 47–8; Enders (1999), 384–8.

[50] Cf. Bonitz (1870), 77^a19–21, cf. Hintikka (1964/73a), 158–9; von Wright (1979), 245, 250; Waterlow (1982), 90; Weidemann (1994/2002), 283–4; Enders (1999), 391–3.

seated does not obtain at noon on 1 January 399 BC, then it is always necessary (ineluctable) that Socrates' being seated should not obtain at noon on 1 January 399 BC. Thus, the second claim of T 53's first part is almost a repetition of the denial of Determinism defended in the chapter's preceding section (18^b26–19^a22 = T 52): to say that not everything is always – in particular, antecedently – necessary is to say that not everything is predetermined.[51]

By asserting [45] and [46], Aristotle warns that upholding the necessity of the present does not commit one to Determinism.[52]

The validity of Excluded Middle. In T 53's second part (19^a27–32) Aristotle makes three claims:

[47] For every state of affairs *s* and every time *t*, at *t* it is necessary that either *s* should obtain at *t* or *s* should not obtain at *t*.

[48] For every state of affairs *s*, every time *t*, and every non-zero interval *i*, at *t* it is necessary that *i* later *s* should either obtain or not obtain.

[49] It is not the case that for every state of affairs *s*, every time *t*, and every non-zero interval *i*, either at *t* it is necessary that *i* later *s* should obtain or at *t* it is necessary that *i* later *s* should not obtain.

The necessity at play in [47], [48], and [49] is still ineluctability.[53]

By asserting [47] and [48] Aristotle endorses Excluded Middle: he does not want to be regarded as giving Excluded Middle up because he rejects Bivalence. By asserting [49] Aristotle makes it clear that his defence of Excluded Middle does not commit him to Determinism. He warns that one should not make the fallacious inference which we would characterise as a distribution of the necessity operator over the disjunction: for every state of affairs and every interval, it is always necessary that after that interval the state of affairs should either obtain or not obtain; however, it is not the case that for every state of affairs and every interval it is always the case that either it is necessary for the state of affairs to obtain after that interval or it is necessary for it not to obtain after that interval. For instance, it is now necessary that tomorrow a sea-battle should either take place or not take

[51] Cf. Kirwan (1986), 172.

[52] Cf. Strang (1960), 458; Waterlow (1982), 16–28, 89–90; van Rijen (1989), 127–8; Weidemann (1994/2002), 284–5; Gaskin (1995), 94–6; Enders (1999), 391–3. For different interpretations of the second claim of T 53's first part see D. Frede (1970), 65–6; (1972), 153; von Fritz (1972), 248; M. J. White (1980), 291–3; Seel (1982a), 244–5; von Wright (1984c), 72–3; D. Frede (1985), 72–3; M. J. White (1985), 64; Craig (1988), 51; van Eck (1988), 24–5; Donini (1989), 8–9; Strobach (1998), 115.

[53] Cf. Seel (1982a), 380; Weidemann (1994/2002), 293; Enders (1999), 394.

place, but it is not the case that either it is now necessary that a sea-battle should take place tomorrow or it is now necessary that a sea-battle should not take place tomorrow.

The fallacy of division. The fallacious inference from Excluded Middle to Determinism, an inference which we would characterise as a distribution of the necessity operator over the disjunction, is described by Aristotle at 19^{a}29 as involving some sort of 'dividing'. What he means can be plausibly reconstructed by considering his remarks in *Sophistici Elenchi* concerning sophistical refutations that depend on a division.[54] A sophistical refutation dependent on division occurs whenever in a dialectical debate a sentence is understood differently by the answerer who grants it and by the questioner who derives from it the contradictory of the answerer's original thesis, and the questioner's way to understand the sentence can be described as a division (thus, the *appearance* of a refutation depends on the questioner's *dividing*).[55] Here is the most illuminating passage:

T 54 Dependent upon combination are those like, e.g. 'to have the possibility to walk while sitting' and 'to write while not writing'. For it does not mean the same if one divides or combines when one says that it is possible to walk while sitting.[56] And this, 'to write while not writing', also behaves in the same way if one combines it, for it means that one has the following possibility: to write while not writing. But if one does not combine, it means that while he is not writing he has the possibility to write. (*SE* 4, 166^{a}23–30)[57]

In T 54 Aristotle uses the verbs 'to combine' and 'to divide' to describe different readings of a sentence containing a modal operator. These readings depend on the scope assigned to the modal operator.[58] Consider Aristotle's first example: 'It is possible to walk while sitting'. One 'combines' if one understands 'It is possible to walk while sitting' in such a way that the *whole* phrase 'walk while sitting' falls within the scope of the modal operator 'it is possible to': 'It is possible to (walk while sitting)'. One instead 'divides' if one understands 'It is possible to walk while sitting' in such a way that only a *part* of the phrase 'walk while sitting' falls within the scope of the modal operator 'it is possible to': 'While sitting it is possible to walk'. So,

[54] For the connection of *Int.* 9, 19^{a}29 to the discussion in *Sophistici Elenchi* see Prior (1953), 324; Brandt (1965), 94–5; Fine (1984a), 31; Bäck (1992), 141–2.

[55] For Aristotle's conception of sophistical refutations see the subsection to which n. 43 of ch. 4 is appended.

[56] At 166^{a}26–7 I follow Wallies, Forster, and Ross in omitting the words 'καὶ μὴ γράφοντα γράφειν', attested by the main manuscripts with several variants. Earlier editors retain them.

[57] Cf. *Cael.* 1.12, 281^{b}2–14.

[58] Cf. Zaslawsky (1986), 242; Schiaparelli (1999a), 161; (1999b), 58–9.

by using the verb 'to combine' ('to divide') Aristotle probably means that the person to whom it applies takes the whole (a part) of an expression as falling within the scope of an operator. Since in T 54 Aristotle uses 'to combine' and 'to divide' to describe these different readings which (as we would put it) depend on assigning a large or a narrow scope to a modal operator, it is plausible to assume that when in T 53 he says that 'it is not necessary to divide', he means that one need not give a narrow scope to the modal operator.

How are the first two parts of T 53 related? At the beginning of the second part of T 53, before asserting [47], [48], and [49], Aristotle says: 'The same account applies also to the contradictory pair' (19^a27–8). He means that the account he just offered in T 53's first part is relevant to the claims he makes in the second part, in particular to [49]. This is because were one to miss the points made in T 53's first part, one would have some inclination to erroneously endorse the claim denied by [49]. To see this, suppose one were to miss the second point made in T 53, i.e. suppose one were to endorse the claims which [46] denies. By endorsing the claims which [46] denies, one would be accepting, on the one hand, that for every state of affairs *s* and every time *t*, if *s* obtains at *t* then it is always necessary that *s* should obtain at *t*, and, on the other hand, that for every state of affairs *s* and every time *t*, if *s* does not obtain at *t* then it is always necessary that *s* should not obtain at *t*. Let *s* be a state of affairs, let *t* be a time, and let *i* be a non-zero interval. Let t' be a time *i* after *t*. One should accept that either *s* obtains at t' or *s* does not obtain at t' (cf. [47]). From this result one can then infer that either it is always necessary that *s* should obtain at t' or it is always necessary that *s* should not obtain at t'. It follows that either at *t* it is necessary that *s* should obtain at t' or at *t* it is necessary that *s* should not obtain at t'. Hence either at *t* it is necessary that *i* later *s* should obtain or at *t* it is necessary that *i* later *s* should not obtain. By generalising in the appropriate way (because *s*, *t*, and *i* were arbitrary), one can conclude that for every state of affairs *s*, every time *t*, and every non-zero interval *i*, either at *t* it is necessary that *i* later *s* should obtain or at *t* it is necessary that *i* later *s* should not obtain – the claim which [49] denies.[59]

The 'equimodality' of the truth of assertions and states of affairs. At the beginning of the third part of T 53 Aristotle says:

[59] Different commentators explain differently Aristotle's remark 'The same account applies also to the contradictory pair' (19^a27–8): see e.g. Rescher (1968), 189; D. Frede (1970), 67–9; Lowe (1980), 57–8; D. Frede (1985), 74; van Eck (1988), 31–2; Donini (1989), 9–11; Weidemann (1994/2002), 287–93; Gaskin (1995), 45.

Sentences are true in the same way as the objects. (19^a33 = T 5)

Since elsewhere Aristotle uses 'object' to denote states of affairs, of which he says that they can be true,[60] at 19^a33 he can be plausibly taken to be using again 'object' to denote states of affairs.[61] Aristotle's claim at 19^a33 can therefore be plausibly taken to be that the modality with which a present-tense affirmative assertion is true is the same as the modality with which the corresponding state of affairs is true, or – as I often say – obtains:[62]

[50] For every time *t* and every non-zero interval *i*, at *t* it is necessary that (impossible that, chance whether) a present-tense affirmative assertion should be true *i* later just in case at *t* it is necessary that (impossible that, chance whether) the state of affairs corresponding to the assertion should obtain *i* later.

Aristotle believes that there are no 'negative' states of affairs corresponding to negative assertions (e.g. he believes that there is no 'negative' state of affairs like the diagonal's not being incommensurable corresponding to a negative assertion that is an utterance of 'The diagonal is not incommensurable').[63] He is therefore likely to believe that there are no 'future-tense' states of affairs corresponding to future-tense assertions (e.g. he is likely to believe that there is no 'future-tense' state of affairs of a sea-battle occurring in 24 hours corresponding to a future-tense assertion that is an utterance of 'In 24 hours a sea-battle will take place'). If there are no 'negative' or 'future-tense' states of affairs, the 'equimodality' of the truth of assertions and states of affairs can hold only for present-tense affirmative assertions. It is for this reason that [50] mentions only present-tense affirmative assertions.

Proposition [50] has an obvious counterpart that concerns present-tense negative assertions:

[51] For every time *t* and every non-zero interval *i*, at *t* it is necessary that (impossible that, chance whether) a present-tense negative assertion should be true *i* later just in case at *t* it is necessary that (impossible that, chance whether) the state of affairs corresponding to the assertion should not obtain *i* later.

60 See n. 1 of ch. 1.

61 Cf. Talanga (1986), 78; de Rijk (1987), 40; van Eck (1988), 24; Gaskin (1995), 89. Weidemann (1994/2002), 295–7 argues that since elsewhere in *de Interpretatione* Aristotle never uses 'object' for items of which he says that they can be true, the Greek sentence at 19^a33 should be so understood as to avoid committing Aristotle to such a usage. But in other works Aristotle does use 'object' for items of which he says that they can be true, so Weidemann's worry seems unjustified.

62 Cf. Kullmann (1994/95), 297–8; Gaskin (1995), 89. D. Frede (1970), 28, criticises this interpretation of 19^a33, but her grounds are unconvincing.

63 Cf. the subsection to which n. 15 of ch. 1 is appended.

Although Aristotle does not explicitly state [51], he can be plausibly taken to endorse it.

In the specific case of the modality of chance, Aristotle's claim of 'equimodality' allows a simplified formulation:

[52] For every time *t* and every non-zero interval *i*, at *t* it is chance whether a present-tense assertion will be true *i* later just in case at *t* it is chance whether the state of affairs corresponding to the assertion will obtain *i* later.

The failure of Bivalence. In the final bit of the third part of T 53 Aristotle draws his conclusions with regard to Bivalence:

T 55 [a] It is necessary that one of the two members of a contradictory pair concerning these [*sc.* states of affairs which not always 'are' or not always 'are not'] should be true or false, [b] but it is not necessary that[64] this one or this one should be true or false,[65] [c] but it is however it chances, and [d] it is necessary that[66] one of the two should be more true, [e] but not already true or false. [f] Hence, clearly, it is not necessary that of every affirmation and denial that are opposed one should be true and the other false. [g] For with what is things work out differently than with what is not but can be as well as not be – with these it is as we have said. (19^a36–19^b4 < T 53)

The attributes of necessity and chance at play in T 55 are, as in many other crucial points of *Int.* 9, diachronic: they are most accurately expressed by instances of the schemata 'At τ it is necessary that α at τ′' and 'At τ it is chance whether α at τ′' (with 'τ' and 'τ′' to be replaced with designations of times, 'α' with an assertoric sentence-type without dates).

T 55 is puzzling: clause [a] seems to commit Aristotle to Bivalence, while Aristotle should be denying Bivalence. At least two interpretations of T 55 are possible which solve this difficulty. The best way to expound these two interpretations is to display how they paraphrase each of the clauses that constitute T 55.

64 The 'μὲν' at 19^a36 is answered by the 'μέντοι' at 19^a38. Since the 'μὲν' at 19^a36 is closely linked to the 'ἀνάγκη' at 19^a36, an occurrence of 'ἀνάγκη' should be understood between the 'οὐ' at 19^a37 and the immediately following 'μέντοι' at 19^a38. Hence the rendering of the Greek clauses that correspond to [a] and [b] by (respectively) 'It is necessary that . . .' and 'But it is not necessary that . . .'. Cf. 'ἀνάγκη μὲν [. . .] οὐ μέντοι [. . .] ἀναγκαῖον' at 19^a30–1.

65 Alternative translation: '[a] It is necessary that either member of a contradictory pair concerning these should be either true or false, [b] but it is not necessary that it should be this [*sc.* true] or this [*sc.* false]'. On this alternative translation see D. Frede (1970), 71; Bosley (1977), 32–3; D. Frede (1985), 76; van Eck (1988), 24.

66 Since the Greek clause that corresponds to [d] is an accusative with infinitive, it is most probably still governed by the 'ἀνάγκη' at 19^a36: hence, in my translation, the words 'it is necessary that' at the beginning of clause [d].

Interpretation A. According to the first interpretation of T 55 (henceforth 'interpretation *A*'), clause [a] says that at time *t* it is necessary that of the two members of a given contradictory pair of future-tense singular assertions concerning a time t' later than *t*, one should be true at t' and the other false at t'. In clause [a] the operator 'it is necessary that . . .' affirms *necessitas consequentis*: it indicates (not that something follows necessarily from previous results, but) that something obtains necessarily. For instance, let *t* be noon on 1 January 399 BC, let t' be noon on 2 January 399 BC, let *u* be an utterance of 'In 24 hours a sea-battle will take place' produced at noon on 1 January 399 BC, and let *v* be an utterance of 'In 24 hours no sea-battle will take place' also produced at noon on 1 January 399 BC. Then *u* and *v* are members of a contradictory pair and they both concern noon on 2 January 399 BC. Clause [a] commits Aristotle to the claim that at noon on 1 January 399 BC it is necessary that either *u* should be true at noon on 2 January 399 BC and *v* false then, or *u* should be false at noon on 2 January 399 BC and *v* true then. Clause [a] does not commit Aristotle to Bivalence because it does not say that at *t* it is necessary that of the two members of the given contradictory pair of future-tense singular assertions concerning the later time t', one should be true at *t* and the other false at *t*.[67]

Clause [b] says that despite [a], at *t* it is not necessary that the affirmative member of the given contradictory pair of future-tense singular assertions concerning t' should be true at t', nor is it at *t* necessary that the negative member of that contradictory pair should be true at t'. Thus, in clause [b] the operator 'it is not necessary that . . .' denies *necessitas consequentis*. Going back to the last paragraph's example, clause [b] commits Aristotle to the claim that at noon on 1 January 399 BC it is not necessary that *u* should be true at noon on 2 January 399 BC, and, similarly, at noon on 1 January 399 BC it is not necessary that *v* should be true at noon on 2 January 399 BC.

Clause [c] strengthens [b]'s denial of necessity by saying that for each of the two members of the given contradictory pair of future-tense singular assertions concerning the later time t', at *t* it is chance whether it will be true at t'. Going back to the example of the last two paragraphs, clause [c] commits Aristotle to the claim that at noon on 1 January 399 BC it is chance whether *u* will be true at noon on 2 January 399 BC, and, similarly, at noon on 1 January 399 BC it is chance whether *v* will be true at noon on 2 January 399 BC.

[67] For this interpretation of clause [a] see Ackrill (1963), 142; Ihrig (1965), 227; Haack (1974/96), 77; Seel (1982a), 379–80; Weidemann (1994/2002), 297–8; Liske (1995), 354; Kretzmann (1998), 26.

Clauses [d] and [e] consider the case where a certain outcome is antecedently likely to occur. The necessity operator 'it is necessary that . . .' at the beginning of clause [d] affirms *necessitas consequentiae*: it indicates (not that something obtains necessarily, but) that something follows necessarily from previous results. Clause [e] falls within the scope of this necessity operator. Hence clauses [d] and [e] introduce two necessary consequences of previous results: the first necessary consequence, stated in the second half of clause [d], is that in some cases at t one member of the given contradictory pair of future-tense singular assertions concerning the later time t' is more likely to be true at t' than the other; the second necessary consequence, stated in clause [e], is that despite [d], at t neither member of the given contradictory pair of future-tense singular assertions concerning the later time t' is 'already' true or false ('already' has its usual temporal meaning), i.e. at t both members of the contradictory pair are neither true nor false. For instance, let t be noon on 1 January 399 BC, let t' be noon on 2 January 399 BC, and let w and y be utterances of 'In 24 hours Socrates will be sober' and 'In 24 hours Socrates will not be sober' produced at noon on 1 January 399 BC. Then w and y are members of a contradictory pair and they both concern noon on 2 January 399 BC. In accordance with clause [d], at noon on 1 January 399 BC the likelihood of w being true at noon on 2 January 399 BC is greater than that of y being true at noon on 2 January 399 BC. Clause [e] commits Aristotle to the claim that despite this, at noon on 1 January 399 BC neither w nor y is 'already' true or false.

Clause [f] states the conclusion Aristotle was aiming for: with some contradictory pairs of future-tense assertions, sometimes it is not the case that one member is true and the other false. This is because with some contradictory pairs of future-tense assertions, sometimes both members are neither true nor false.

Clause [g] emphasises that the principle requiring that it should always be the case that one contradictory assertion is true and the other false has exceptions with regard not to the present ('what is') but to what lies in the future ('what is not', i.e. 'what is not yet') and is contingent ('can be as well as not be').

A problem for interpretation A. According to interpretation *A*, Aristotle concentrates on certain future-tense singular assertions that are temporally determinate, i.e. speak about specific times, and he claims that they are neither true nor false at the times when they are uttered but become either true or false at the times they speak about. On this conception, the truth-value of one of these future-tense singular assertions, though dependent on time insofar as it is only at a time that the assertion has it, is independent of time insofar as it cannot, even in principle, be different at different times. For, according to the conception in question, once the time the assertion speaks about has come, the assertion is either true or false, and whatever it is then it remains forever afterwards.[68]

Now, several Aristotelian passages indicate that Aristotle would endorse the following claim about present-tense singular assertions, truth-values, and time:

[h] A present-tense singular assertion is temporally indeterminate, i.e. does not speak about any specific time. It therefore can, at least in principle, be true at one time and false at another.[69]

Aristotle's endorsement of [h] strongly suggests that he would aver the following similar claim about future-tense singular assertions, truth-values, and time:

[i] A future-tense singular assertion is temporally indeterminate. It therefore can, at least in principle, be true at one time and false at another.

Claim[i] conflicts with the theory attributed to Aristotle by interpretation *A*.[70]

Defence of interpretation A. Some advocates of interpretation *A* assume that Aristotle is confused about the bearers of truth or falsehood.[71] However, I feel uneasy at saddling Aristotle with a confusion about such a fundamental issue.

A more promising defence of interpretation *A* assumes that Aristotle endorses neither [h] nor [i] because he thinks that there is an important distinction between kinds of singular assertions: singular assertions which do not contain utterances of pseudo-dates (like 'now' or 'tomorrow') comply with [h] and [i] (they are temporally indeterminate, and can, at least in principle, be true at one time and false at another), singular assertions which do contain utterances of pseudo-dates behave differently – they are temporally determinate and cannot, even in principle, be true at one time and false at another. What can be said for this defence?

[68] Cf. Jordan (1963), 12; Hintikka (1964/73a), 151; Ihrig (1965), 219; Hintikka/Remes/Knuuttila (1977), 31–2; Weidemann (1994/2002), 300–1.

[69] Cf. the subsection to which n. 1 of ch. 6 appended.

[70] Cf. Sorabji (1980), 100; (1998), 8; Mignucci (1998), 62.

[71] Cf. Weidemann (1994/2002), 300–1, 308, 325.

(i) It credits Aristotle with a sound intuition: according to many modern logicians and linguists, utterances of pseudo-dates behave differently from verbal tenses and must be treated as temporally rigid designators.[72]

(ii) In *Categories* 4 Aristotle says:

T 56 Each of the things said with no interweaving signifies either a substance or a quantity or a qualified item or a relative or where or when or being-in-a-posture or having or doing or being affected. (1^b25–7)[73]

Aristotle then offers examples: man and horse are substances, white and grammatical are qualified items, yesterday and last-year are items in the category of time. On the plausible assumption that for Aristotle items in the categorial scheme can be signified by parts of sentences, Aristotle is committed to the view that as an utterance of 'man' within an assertion signifies a substance (the universal man) and an utterance of 'white' signifies a qualified item (the universal white), so utterances of 'yesterday' or 'last year' within assertions signify items in the category of time. This makes it plausible to assume that an utterance of 'tomorrow' within an assertion should signify the portion of time which is the day after that when the utterance is produced. Then an assertion containing an utterance of 'tomorrow' is temporally determinate and cannot, even in principle, be true at one time and false at another.

(iii) In *Topics* 5.3 (131^b5–18) Aristotle distinguishes what is *always* peculiar to something from what is peculiar to it *at a certain moment*. Suppose that in a dialectical debate one is requested to indicate a peculiarity of x: if one answers by mentioning a y that is peculiar to x at that moment but fails to specify that it is at that moment that y is peculiar to x, then one's reply is objectionable; if instead one answers by mentioning a y that is peculiar to x at that moment and points out that it is at that moment that y is peculiar to x, then one's reply is fine.[74] For instance, if one indicates what is peculiar to Socrates by saying

[j] What is peculiar to Socrates is being seated next to Alcibiades

then one's reply is objectionable; if instead one says

[k] What is now peculiar to Socrates is being seated next to Alcibiades

then one's reply is fine. What makes a difference is the presence of an utterance of 'now'. Aristotle's analysis presupposes that an utterance of 'now' adds something to the mere utterance of a present-tense verb-phrase to which it is attached. Moreover, what Aristotle has in mind might be that

72 Cf. Landman (1991), 134–5; K. Taylor (1998), 269–82.

73 Cf. *APo.* 1.22, 83^b13–15.

74 Cf. 1.5, 102^a22–8; 102^b20–6; 5.1, 128^b16–21; 129^a26–30.

the difference here is that while [j] can pass from being true now to being false later, [k] cannot.[75]

(iv) At the end of *de Interpretatione* 1 Aristotle says that 'goatstag' is neither true nor false 'unless "to be" or "not to be" is added, either simply or with reference to time' (16ᵃ17–18). According to some commentators,[76] the phrase 'either simply or with reference to time' distinguishes assertions which lack from assertions which contain utterances of pseudo-dates.[77]

Regrettably, the above considerations do not prove that Aristotle drew the distinction attributed to him by the defence of interpretation *A*. The problem remains that in no passage does Aristotle explicitly draw this distinction.[78]

Interpretation B. An alternative interpretation of T 55 is available – call it 'interpretation *B*'. Before expounding interpretation *B*'s clause-by-clause paraphrase of T 55, let me sketch the philosophical intuition behind it. The rejection of Bivalence need not assume that future-tense singular assertions are temporally determinate. Consider an utterance *u* of 'In 24 hours a sea-battle will take place'. Understand *u* as temporally indeterminate, i.e. as not speaking about any specific time (there is no more reason for taking *u* to be about the time 24 hours after when it is produced than there is for taking an utterance of 'A sea-battle is taking place' to be about the time when it is produced). One can also assume that for every time *t*, *u* is true (false) at *t* just in case at *t* the state of the world is such that a (no) sea-battle will take place 24 hours later. If one is not a determinist, one will claim that sometimes the state of the world is neither such that a sea-battle will take place 24 hours later nor such that no sea-battle will take place 24 hours later. One will then be led to admit that there are times when *u* is neither true nor false. This amounts to a rejection of Bivalence. This rejection of Bivalence, however, is based on understanding *u* as temporally indeterminate. Interpretation *B* assumes that for Aristotle all assertions are temporally indeterminate, and can, at least in principle, have different truth-values at different times.

Clause-by-clause paraphrase. The first half of T 55 (clauses [a]–[c]) concentrates on states of affairs whose obtaining is antecedently a matter of chance.

[75] Cf. Remes (1977), 42–3. [76] Boeth. *in Int. Sec. Ed.* 51, 30–52, 6; Ammon. *in Int.* 29, 12–17.

[77] For the various interpretations of the passage see Boeth. *in Int. Sec. Ed.* 51, 2–52, 9; Montanari (1984/88), II 76–7; Kneepkens (1994), 162–7.

[78] It is worthwhile recalling that certain unnamed (but probably Stoic) opponents of Alexander's in *de Fato* (10. 177, 7–9) seem to regard the proposition (ἀξίωμα) expressed by an utterance of 'A sea-battle will take place tomorrow' as temporally indeterminate.

Consider a state of affairs *s* (e.g. the state of affairs of a sea-battle taking place), a non-zero interval *i* (e.g. the interval of 24 hours), and a time *t* such that in the infinite course of time up to *i* before *t*, just about half of the times when the universe resembled in relevant respects the universe at *t* were followed *i* later by a time when *s* obtained. In such a situation, at *t* it is chance whether *i* later *s* will obtain. Consider also a contradictory pair of present-tense singular assertions *p* and *q*, where *p* affirms, and *q* denies, that *s* is obtaining (e.g. let *p* and *q* be utterances of 'A sea-battle is taking place' and 'No sea-battle is taking place'), and consider the contradictory pair of future-tense singular assertions *u* and *v*, where *u* asserts that *s* will obtain *i* later and *v* asserts that *i* later *s* will not obtain (e.g. let *u* and *v* be utterances of 'In 24 hours a sea-battle will take place' and 'In 24 hours no sea-battle will take place').

In the situation described, at *t* it is necessary that *i* later either the present-tense affirmation *p* will be true and its denial *q* false, or *p* will be false and *q* true. This is what clause [a] claims: 'It is necessary that one of the two members of a contradictory pair concerning these [*sc.* states of affairs which not always "are" or not always "are not"] should be true or false.' Note that the members of the contradictory pair in question are present-tense singular assertions: those present-tense singular assertions whose later truth-value is crucial to the present truth-value of the future-tense singular assertions which will refute Bivalence. In clause [a] the operator 'it is necessary that . . .' affirms *necessitas consequentis*: it indicates (not that something follows necessarily from previous results, but) that something obtains necessarily. Clause [a] does not commit Aristotle to Bivalence because it speaks about present-tense assertions, while it is future-tense assertions which in Aristotle's view will refute Bivalence.

However, at *t* it is not necessary that *i* later the present-tense affirmation *p* should be true and its denial *q* false, and, analogously, at *t* it is not necessary that *i* later *p* should be false and *q* true. This is what clause [b] claims: 'But it is not necessary that this one or this one should be true or false'. Here 'it is not necessary that . . .' denies *necessitas consequentis.*

In fact, at *t* it is chance whether *i* later the present-tense affirmation *p* will be true and its denial *q* false, and, analogously, at *t* it is chance whether *i* later *p* will be false and *q* true. This is what clause [c] claims: 'But it is however it chances'.

Clauses [d] and [e] go on to consider states of affairs that are antecedently likely to obtain. Consider a state of affairs *s′* (e.g. the state of affairs of Socrates' being sober), a non-zero interval *i* (e.g. the interval of 24 hours), and a time *t* such that in the infinite course of time up to *i* before *t*, most but not all of the times when the universe resembled in relevant respects the universe at *t* were followed *i* later by a time when *s′* obtained. In such circumstances, at *t* it is likely that *i* later *s′* will obtain. Consider also a contradictory pair of present-tense singular assertions *r* and *o*, where *r* affirms, and *o* denies, that *s′* is obtaining (e.g. let *r* and *o* be utterances of 'Socrates is sober' and 'Socrates is not sober'), and a contradictory pair of future-tense singular assertions *w* and *y*, where *w* asserts that *s′* will obtain *i* later and *y* asserts that *i* later *s′* will not obtain (e.g. let *w* and *y* be utterances of 'In 24 hours Socrates will be sober' and 'In 24 hours Socrates will not be sober').

In such a situation, at *t* it is necessary that at *t* the case in which *i* later the present-tense affirmation *r* is true should be more likely than that in which *i* later the present-tense denial *o* is true. This is what clause [d] says by asserting that 'it is necessary that one of the two should be more true'. Here the necessity operator 'it is necessary that . . .' affirms *necessitas consequentis* and governs only clause [d] (clause [e] falls outside its scope).

Still, from what is stated by clause [d] it does not follow that at *t* it is necessary that *i* later the present-tense affirmation *r* should be true and the present-tense denial *o* false. This is what clause [e] claims: 'But not already true or false'. Here 'already' has not a temporal, but a logical sense:[79] it means 'thereby'. After 'already' an occurrence of the necessity operator 'it is necessary that . . .' must be understood.[80] The necessity denied by 'But <it is> not already <necessary that it should be> true or false' is *necessitas consequentis*. 'True' here is supposed to apply to whichever member of the contradictory pair is likely to be true, 'false' to the other member. Clause [e] is therefore to be paraphrased by 'It does not follow that it is necessary that the member of the contradictory pair which is likely to be true should be true and that the member which is likely to be false should be false'. The claims concerning present-tense assertions made by clauses [d] and [e] recall those made at the end of T 52 with regard to states of affairs: 'With other things one of the two alternatives is or comes to be more and in most

[79] Cf. Bonitz (1870), 314^{a}10–17; Anscombe (1956/68), 25; Ackrill (1963), 141; Bosley (1977), 34; Sorabji (1980), 95; Fine (1984a), 35, 45; Judson (1988), 17. For 'ἤδη' ('already') used in a logical sense see *Int.* 1, 16^{a}8; *APo.* 1.1, 71^{a}23; *Ph.* 1.4, 187^{a}36; *Metaph.* Δ 5, 1015^{b}13; 21, 1022^{b}19; *EN* 5.3, 1130^{a}2; 10, 1136^{a}2; 6.10, 1142^{b}14; 10.6, 1177^{a}6.

[80] The particles in the Greek text suggest an understood 'ἀνάγκη' after 'ἤδη' at 19^{a}39. For the 'μὲν' at 19^{a}38 is answered by the 'οὐ μέντοι' at 19^{a}39, and this recalls the 'μὲν' at 19^{a}36 answered by the 'οὐ μέντοι' at 19^{a}37–8. But the 'μὲν' at 19^{a}36 and the 'οὐ μέντοι' at 19^{a}37–8 introduce the contrast between what is and what is not ἀνάγκη (cf. n. 64 above).

cases, while it is nonetheless possible that the other alternative could have come to be, and the first one not' (19^a20–2).[81]

The foregoing has a crucial consequence. Consider again *u*, an assertion to the effect that the state of affairs *s* will obtain *i* later, and *p*, an assertion to the effect that *s* is obtaining. *u*, which is a future-tense inflection of the present-tense affirmation *p*, is neither true nor false at *t*: since at *t* it is not necessary that *i* later *p* should be true, *u* is not true at *t*; analogously, since at *t* it is not necessary that *i* later *p* should be false, *u* is not false at *t*. This is because at *t* the universe as it has evolved until then is such as to require the truth (or, respectively, falsehood) of *u* just in case in whatever possible way it evolves after *t*, *i* after *t* the universe is such as to require the truth (or, respectively, falsehood) of *p*:[82] if in some possible developments after *t* the universe *i* after *t* is such as to require the truth of *p* whereas in other possible developments after *t* the universe *i* after *t* is such as to require the falsehood of *p*, then at *t* the universe is not such as to require either the truth or the falsehood of *u* (in such a case, the universe as it is at *t* simply leaves the truth or falsehood of *u* at *t* unsettled – at *t* the universe neither matches nor disagrees with *u*). This is tantamount to saying that *u* is true (or, respectively, false) at *t* just in case at *t* it is necessary that *i* later *p* should be true (or, respectively, false). Therefore Bivalence fails. Aristotle does not spell out this crucial consequence. However, clause [f] states the consequence of this consequence which is most important in the context of *de Interpretatione* as a whole: that with certain contradictory pairs of future-tense assertions sometimes it is not the case that one member is true and the other false (at *t* it is not the case that *u* is true and *v* false, nor is it at *t* the case that *u* is false and *v* true).

Clause [g] emphasises that the principle that in every contradictory pair it is always the case that one member is true and the other false has exceptions with regard not to the present but to what lies in the future and is contingent.

A problem for interpretation B. According to interpretation *B*, in T 55 Aristotle reaches the conclusion that certain future-tense assertions are now neither true nor false by discussing the future truth or falsehood of present-tense assertions. This procedure seems awkward: why should claims about the present truth or falsehood of future-tense assertions be based on a discussion of the future truth or falsehood of present-tense assertions?

[81] Cf. Judson (1988), 17–18.

[82] In some passages (*Int.* 9, 18^b9–11; 19^a4–6; *GC* 2.11, 337^b3–7) Aristotle explicitly links the truth at a time of a future-tense assertion with the later truth of the present-tense assertion from which it is inflected.

Defence of interpretation B. At the beginning of T 55 Aristotle mentions states of affairs that 'not always "are" or not always "are not"' (19^a36), i.e. states of affairs that 'are in such a condition as to be or come to be however it chances and admit the contrary states' (19^a34). Since the aim of T 55 is to establish that certain future-tense assertions are now neither true nor false, Aristotle is probably assuming that some future-tense assertions which now are neither true nor false concern states of affairs whose obtaining is a matter of chance. Since in *Int.* 9 the modality of chance, like the other modalities, is diachronic, i.e. is a modal attribute with two 'slots for dates', it can be plausibly assumed that for Aristotle certain future-tense assertions which now are neither true nor false concern states of affairs for which now it is chance whether they will obtain later.

Shortly before T 55 Aristotle makes a claim about the 'equimodality' of the truth of assertions and states of affairs. In a previous subsection[83] I argued that part of this claim is that for every time *t* and every non-zero interval *i*, at *t* it is chance whether a present-tense assertion will be true *i* later just in case at *t* it is chance whether the state of affairs corresponding to that assertion will obtain *i* later (cf. [52] above). This makes it plausible to assume that Aristotle wants to introduce certain present-tense assertions for which it is now chance whether they will be true later, and link them with the future-tense assertions which now are neither true nor false and concern states of affairs for which it is now chance whether they will obtain later. The present-tense assertions in question are those to which the states of affairs correspond which the future-tense assertions which now are neither true nor false concern. They are the present-tense assertions from which the future-tense assertions which now are neither true nor false are inflected.

The reason why Aristotle's claims about the present truth or falsehood of future-tense assertions are based on a discussion of the future truth or falsehood of present-tense assertions is probably that Aristotle thinks that the future-tense assertions which now are neither true nor false concern states of affairs for which it is now chance whether they will obtain later, and he can link this modality of chance for states of affairs with the truth-values of assertions only by means of the 'equimodality' of the truth of assertions and states of affairs, 'equimodality' which, however, concerns present-tense assertions.

Assessment of T 55's two interpretations. Interpretation *A* seems to saddle Aristotle with an inconsistent position about assertions, truth, and time. The

[83] See the subsection to which n. 60 above is appended.

best possible defence of interpretation *A* fails because it requires attributing to Aristotle distinctions for which the textual evidence is slim. Interpretation *B* avoids saddling Aristotle with an inconsistent position about assertions, truth, and time. Interpretation *B* faces its own problem, which, however, can be solved. Hence, interpretation *B* is more likely than interpretation *A*.

Aristotle's rejection of Bivalence. Interpretation *A* requires that for Aristotle an utterance produced today of 'A sea-battle will take place in 24 hours' should remain without truth-value at most until tomorrow. In general, according to interpretation *A*, although Aristotle rejects Bivalence, he is none the less committed to a thesis which is close (though not identical) to Bivalence, i.e. that every assertion sooner or later is either true or false.

By contrast, interpretation *B* requires that for Aristotle an utterance produced today of 'A sea-battle will take place in 24 hours' could remain without truth-value for ever: it is not the case that tomorrow this utterance is bound to become true or false (tomorrow it will be true, or false, only if the conditions of the universe tomorrow will be such as to necessitate, or exclude, a sea-battle taking place the day after tomorrow). In general, according to interpretation *B*, Aristotle is committed to avoiding endorsing the previously mentioned thesis which is close to Bivalence, i.e. the thesis that every assertion sooner or later is either true or false.

Therefore, although interpretation *A* attributes to Aristotle a rejection of Bivalence no less than interpretation *B*, the rejection of Bivalence attributed to Aristotle by interpretation *B* is more 'serious' than the one attributed to him by interpretation *A*.

3 ALTERNATIVE INTERPRETATIONS

Realism and anti-realism. My interpretation of *Int.* 9 is a version of what is sometimes called an *anti-realist* interpretation. What distinguishes anti-realist interpretations is crediting Aristotle with a rejection of Bivalence.[84]

[84] Anti-realist interpretations (often called 'traditional interpretations' or 'standard interpretations') were avowed by some Peripatetics (see Simp. *in Cat.* 407, 6–13, a controversial witness on which cf. Weidemann (1994/2002), 303; Kretzmann (1998), 24–5; Mignucci (1998), 75–6; Gaskin (2000), 230–1), some Stoics (see Boeth. *in Int. Sec. Ed.* 208, 1–7; Simp. *in Cat.* 406, 34–407, 5 – cf. Mates (1953/61), 28–9; Mignucci (1989), 52; Weidemann (1994/2002), 305–6; Gaskin (1995), 86; Mignucci (1996b), 283; Kretzmann (1998), 24–5), and the middle-Platonist Nicostratus (see Simp. *in Cat.* 406, 12–16, cf. Mignucci (1996b), 305; (1998), 75, 85). It is not clear whether Ammonius and Boethius favoured

However, *Int.* 9 has been interpreted in different ways too. Discussing all these interpretations is beyond the scope of this study.[85] I restrict myself to examining briefly *realist* interpretations, which constitute the most authoritative alternative to my favoured exegesis.

According to realist interpretations, in *Int.* 9 Aristotle does not reject Bivalence. Rather, he distinguishes ways in which tensed assertions have whatever truth-value they have: all past- and present-tense assertions have their truth-values *necessarily*, some future-tense singular assertions have them *contingently*. Aristotle then addresses some deterministic arguments which, if sound, would prove Determinism, and therefore demolish his position: future-tense singular assertions also would have their truth-values necessarily. He then argues that Determinism is absurd and criticises the deterministic arguments: they are fallacious because they give modal operators a narrow scope in contexts requiring a wide scope.

The anti-realist interpretation is more plausible than the realist.

(i) The anti-realist interpretation fits chapter 9 well within *de Interpretatione* as a whole. For chapters 7 and 8 discuss exceptions to the principle that in every contradictory pair it is always the case that one member is true and the other false. Chapter 7's exception is indeterminate assertions: sometimes both members of a contradictory pair of indeterminate assertions are true. Chapter 8's exception is utterances which seem simple assertions but really are composite assertions. On the anti-realist interpretation, chapter 9 presents another exception to the same principle: sometimes both members of a contradictory pair of future-tense singular assertions are neither true nor false, so it is not then the case that one is true and the other false. Realist interpretations lack an equally smooth account of chapter 9's position within *de Interpretatione*.

(ii) Realist interpretations have an unnatural reading of the chapter's introduction (18^a28–33) and conclusion (19^a39–19^b4): Albrecht Becker, who favours a realist interpretation, regards both passages as

an anti-realist interpretation (Gaskin (1995), 146–84 and Weidemann (1994/2002), 305–8 affirm they did, Mignucci (1996b), Skarica (1997), 184, and Mignucci (1998) deny it). Epicurus rejected Bivalence to block an argument for fatalism (see Cic. *Fat.* 9.18; 10.21; 16.37–8; *Ac.* II 30.97; *Nat. Deor.* I 25.70), but it is unclear whether he had in mind *Int.* 9 (cf. D. Frede (1985), 79; Weidemann (1994/2002), 319; Bobzien (1998), 75–86). For anti-realist interpretations in Antiquity see Lukasiewicz (1922), 125; (1930), 176–8; Sorabji (1980), 93; Weidemann (1994/2002), 303–8, 319; Mignucci (1996b), 305–10; (1998), 75, 85; Sorabji (1998), 3, 13.

85 For a discussion of the interpretations of *Int.* 9 see Dickason (1976), 11–19; Celluprica (1977); Weidemann (1994/2002), 302–28; Gaskin (1995), 12–192; Grossato (1999).

spurious.[86] Other commentators[87] unearth the theses predicted by a realist interpretation in the chapter's introduction and conclusion. For instance, in their view the introduction's initial remark, 'With regard to things that are and things that have come to be, it is [. . .] necessary that either the affirmation or the denial should be true or false' (18^a28–9), means 'With regard to things that are and things that have come to be, every affirmation or denial is either necessarily true or necessarily false'. This seems to be bending Aristotle's words to fit what one dreams to find in them.

(iii) Realist interpretations saddle Aristotle with a disappointing analysis of the deterministic arguments: dismissing them by claiming that they trade on the scope of modal operators is hardly satisfactory.[88] Moreover, realist interpretations credit Aristotle with the view that whenever a past- or present-tense assertion is true, it is necessarily true. Does this after all not saddle Aristotle with Determinism? If tomorrow a sea-battle will take place, then '"A sea-battle will take place tomorrow" is true now' is true now, and therefore necessarily true now, whence it is now necessary that a sea-battle should take place tomorrow. The realist solution of this difficulty is to class '"A sea-battle will take place tomorrow" is true now' with future- rather than present-tense assertions: despite the present-tense verb 'is true', the assertion is 'about the future'. (I shall not address here the difficult question of what it is for an assertion to be 'about the future'.) What embarrasses realist interpretations is that they take Aristotle to be silent about this issue.[89]

Evidence that Aristotle endorsed Bivalence. The anti-realist interpretation also faces a difficulty: outside *Int.* 9 Aristotle seems to endorse Bivalence. Here is the evidence.

(i) In *Categories* 4 Aristotle endorses Bivalence for all affirmations and denials:

T 57 Every affirmation and denial[90] appears to be true or false, but none of the things said with no interweaving is either true or false, e.g. 'man', 'white', 'runs', 'wins'. (2^a7–10)

[86] See A. Becker (1936), 74.

[87] E.g. Rescher (1963b), 44, 49; Spellman (1980), 121–2; Judson (1988), 9, 18–21.

[88] Cf. Judson (1988), 32–3.

[89] Cf. Ackrill (1963), 139–40; Prior (1967c), 1; Spellman (1980), 122–3; Kirwan (1986), 187; von Kutschera (1986), 209, 213; Craig (1988), 28–9; Bäck (1992), 144–5; Gaskin (1994), 91–3.

[90] At 2^a8 I read 'κατάφασις καὶ ἀπόφασις': this reading is attested by some of the main manuscripts and printed by Bekker, Dübner, and Cooke. Other manuscripts have 'κατάφασις ἢ ἀπόφασις' (printed by Pacius, Buhle, and Weise). Waitz, Minio-Paluello, and Bodéüs follow other witnesses and print 'κατάφασις'.

(ii) According to *Categories* 10 (13^a37–13^b3 and 13^b27–35), in a contradictory pair it is always the case that one member is true and the other false. Since for every affirmation or denial there is a contradictory opposite (cf. *Int.* 6, 17^a31–3), this entails that every affirmation or denial is always either true or false.

(iii) In *de Interpretatione* 10 (20^a31–6) Aristotle says that indefinite names (e.g. 'non-man') and indefinite verbs (e.g. 'does not run') might seem to be denials lacking a verb or a name, 'but they are not, for a denial must always be true or false, whilst he who says "non-man" – without adding anything else – has no more said something true or false, indeed rather less so, than he who says "man"' (20^a33–6). Here Aristotle seems to postulate that every denial is always either true or false.

(iv) In *de Anima* 3.6, 430^b26–7 (< T 24) Aristotle endorses Bivalence for all affirmations.[91]

(v) In *Metaphysics* Γ Aristotle avers a semantic version of Excluded Middle according to which 'it is necessary that either member of the contradictory pair should be true' (8, 1012^b10–11).[92] Thus, if an affirmation is not true at *t*, then its contradictory denial is true at *t*. Then, by the definition of truth, the object of which the denial claims that it 'is not' in the sense of being false, at *t* 'is not' in the sense of being false. Then the object of which the original affirmation claims that it 'is' in the sense of being true, at *t* 'is not' in the sense of being false. Then, by the definition of falsehood, the original affirmation is false at *t*. Thus, if an affirmation is not true at *t* then it is false at *t*. Hence, an affirmation is either true or false at *t*. A parallel argument goes through for denials. Then Aristotle is committed to Bivalence.

The anti-realist interpretation can be defended in two ways. (i) The first defence assumes that wherever Aristotle seems to endorse Bivalence, he is really only claiming that every present-tense assertion is always either true or false. Some support for this line comes from the circumstance that there is a case for attributing to Aristotle the view that only present-tense assertions are, strictly, 'assertions', while past- and future-tense assertions are 'assertions' merely in a secondary sense: for in *de Interpretatione* 3 (16^b16–18) Aristotle says that only certain present indicative forms of a verb are 'verbs' ('ῥήματα'), while a verb's past and future forms are not 'verbs'

[91] Cf. 3.3, 427^b20–1; 6, 430^b4–5.

[92] Cf. *APr.* 1.13, 32^a27–8; 46, 51^b32–3; *APo.* 1.1, 71^a14; *Top.* 6.6, 143^b15–16; *Metaph.* Γ 7, 1012^a26–7; 1012^a28; 8, 1012^a31–3; 1012^b3–4. Aristotle uses also several other formulations of Excluded Middle. On these formulations and their mutual relations see D. Frede (1970), 77–8; (1985), 79–80; Cavini (1998), 5–7.

but 'inflections of a verb' ('πτώσεις ῥήματος').[93] If he believes that only present-tense assertions are, strictly, 'assertions', those remarks that appear to commit him to Bivalence could in fact commit him only to the weaker claim that every present-tense assertion is always either true or false.

(ii) The second defence of *Int.* 9's anti-realist interpretation assumes that Aristotle changed his mind about Bivalence. Many commentators[94] now agree that most of *de Interpretatione* is an early work of Aristotle's. Chapter 9 could be a late addition to an early draft of *de Interpretatione*, and the denial of Bivalence could be a late development of Aristotle's thought.[95] This hypothesis has some independent support.

(ii.i) Chapter 9 could well have been added later to answer a Megarian objection which was not yet around when the rest of the treatise was originally written.[96]

(ii.ii) Chapter 9 is isolated within *de Interpretatione*: no other passage in the work refers to or presupposes it.

(ii.iii) In *de Interpretatione* 6 Aristotle claims that 'for every affirmation there is a denial opposed to it, and for every denial an affirmation' (17^a32–3). He defends this claim by saying:

T 58 Since it is possible to assert that what holds does not hold, that what does not hold holds, that what holds holds, and that what does not hold does not hold, and similarly for times outside the present, whatever one affirmed it is possible to deny, and whatever one denied it is possible to affirm. (17^a26–31)

T 58's consequent claims that it is possible to contradict. T 58's antecedent briefly discusses the truth and the falsehood of affirmations and denials: such a discussion is relevant because a sophistical argument that it is impossible to contradict was based on the assumption that it is impossible to speak falsely.[97] The first part of T 58's antecedent focuses on the truth and the

[93] Cf. 5, 17^a10. Elsewhere (*Int.* 10, 19^b13–14; *Po.* 20, 1457^a14–23) Aristotle seems to contradict this by claiming or implying that the past and the future forms of a verb count as 'verbs'.

[94] E.g. Bochenski (1951), 23; Düring (1961), 287; Ackrill (1963), 69; Düring (1966), 49; Sainati (1968), 203–4; Blanché/Dubucs (1970/96), 28–9; Dickason (1976), 11; Sorabji (1980), 106–7; Graham (1987), 115; Brakas (1988), 5; Zanatta (1992), 8–10; Weidemann (1994/2002), 47–51; D. Frede (1998), 88. Other commentators (e.g. Maier (1899), 40–1, 44, 72; A. Mansion (1913/45), 10; Riondato (1957a), 7; Schuhl (1960), 34; Adorno (1961), 291, 398; von Fritz (1962), 147, 148; Brandt (1965), 5–10; Magris (1977), 114–15, 122–6, 129; Montanari (1984/88), I 18, 142, II 63) regard *de Interpretatione* as a late work.

[95] Cf. Maier (1899), 28, 34; A. Becker (1936), 74; Blanché/Dubucs (1970/96), 42; D. Frede (1970), 11, 81; von Fritz (1972), 243; Astroh (1981), 335, 337; D. Frede (1985), 81–2; von Kutschera (1986), 214, 216. Sainati (1968), 240–2 thinks that *Int.* 9 is later than the preceding eight chapters, but still early.

[96] Cf. Celluprica (1977), 37–9.

[97] Cf. Vollrath (1959), 24–5; Ackrill (1963), 128; Capozzi (1974), 320, 332; Weidemann (1994/2002), 200; Galluzzo (1997/98), 53. According to Aristotle, Antisthenes claimed both that it is impossible to contradict and that it is impossible to speak falsely (see *Top.* 1.11, 104^b19–21; *Metaph.* Δ 29, 1024^b32–4, cf. Pl. *Euthd.* 285*d*7–286*b*6; Isocr. *Hel.* 1; Procl. *in Cra.* 37 12, 18–23).

falsehood of present-tense assertions, while its second part suggests that past- and future-tense assertions should behave with regard to truth and falsehood in the same way as present-tense assertions. In general, nothing in *de Interpretatione*'s first eight chapters suggests that there might be some difference between past-, present-, and future-tense assertions in connection with truth and falsehood. Thus, when chapter 9 contrasts past- and present-tense assertions with future-tense assertions, this contrast comes as a surprise.[98]

(ii.iv) Although most of *de Interpretatione* was probably written at a rather early stage of Aristotle's life, the treatise at various points mentions works of Aristotle which are probably later.[99] Thus, the treatise probably underwent some late revision.

(ii.v) Another passage from *de Interpretatione* is regarded by some commentators[100] as a later addition: chapter 13's discussion of potentiality and actuality (at 23^a21–6) presupposes ideas which are developed in the *Metaphysics* and which commentators are disinclined to attribute to the early stage of Aristotle's thought to which the main bulk of *de Interpretatione* should belong.

It might be objected that one passage of *de Interpretatione* itself (10, 20^a31–6, discussed above) seems to commit Aristotle to Bivalence. However, even if this passage were to commit Aristotle to Bivalence, the commitment would be nothing more than an implication of an aside: it might well be the case that when Aristotle added chapter 9 to the main bulk of *de Interpretatione* he failed to notice the implication of this aside and its inconsistency with the additional chapter's rejection of Bivalence.[101]

98 Cf. Sainati (1968), 240–1.

99 Chapter 1, 16^a8–9 refers to *de Anima*. Chapter 5, 17^a14–15 might be understood as referring to *Metaphysics* Z and H, which are probably late works (cf. Magris (1977), 124). Chapter 10, 19^b31 refers to the *Prior Analytics*, whose analysis of sentences is often regarded as more mature than the one offered in *de Interpretatione* 1–6. Chapter 11, 20^b26 refers to the *Topics*, which, however, were probably written either before or at the same time as *de Interpretatione*. At 4, 17^a5–6 the study of certain non-assertoric sentences is dismissed as more appropriate to rhetoric and poetics, or to the *Rhetoric* and the *Poetics* (cf. Brandt (1965), 6). No other work of Aristotle's refers to *de Interpretatione*.

100 Ackrill (1963), 153; Magris (1977), 124–5; Graham (1987), 99–100; Wildberg (1989), 195; Weidemann (1994/2002), 457.

101 Other solutions are less plausible. Sorabji (1980), 95 suggests that according to an anti-realist interpretation 'Aristotle does not regard himself as rejecting Bivalence, but only as qualifying it with a "yet"'. Whatever the merits of this suggestion, it is not viable on the interpretation of *Int.* 9 I defended in the last section. Gaskin (1995), 180 thinks that in some of the above 'contexts "true or false" can, without undue strain, be read as "true, false, or true-or-false"' (where 'true-or-false' expresses a third truth-value besides the standard truth and falsehood). I feel some 'undue strain' in the suggested reading: were Aristotle to recognise a third truth-value, it would be misleading of him to claim that every assertion has one of these three truth-values by saying something like 'Every assertion is true or false'.

External evidence supporting anti-realist interpretations. At the beginning of *de Generatione et Corruptione* 2.11 Aristotle says:

T 59 Since in the case of things that change continuously [. . .] we encounter that which is successively and comes to be this after this with no intermission, we must investigate whether there is anything it will be of necessity, or there is nothing of this sort, but it may fail to come to be all things. For it is clear that there are some [*sc.* things it may fail to come to be], and this is why 'will be' and 'is about to'[102] are different. For what it is true to say that it will be, this it must at some time be true to say that it is, whilst what it is now true to say that it is about to be, there is nothing to prevent that it should not come to be it – for a man who is about to go for a walk could well not go for a walk. (337^a34–337^b7)[103]

In T 59's first part Aristotle considers two alternatives: are some of the states a thing comes to be in necessary, i.e. necessitated by antecedent circumstances, or are all these states contingent, i.e. not necessitated by antecedent circumstances? Aristotle then goes on to argue that at least some of the states a thing comes to be in are contingent. His argument is of a 'semantic' character. It appeals to the difference between the truth conditions for assertions whose predicative expression is a future-tense verb and those of assertions whose predicative expression is a phrase consisting of 'is about to' followed by an infinitive. The argument relies on two assumptions. The first is that if an assertion whose predicative expression is a future-tense verb is true at *t*, then at *t* it is necessary that the corresponding present-tense assertion should be true later,[104] and this in turn obviously entails that at *t* it is necessary that the universal signified by the predicative expression should later hold of the object signified by the subject. The second assumption is that if an assertion whose predicative expression is a phrase consisting of 'is about to' followed by an infinitive is true at *t*, it does not follow that at *t* it is necessary that the corresponding present-tense assertion should be true later, whence it does not follow that at *t* it is necessary that the universal signified by the predicative expression should later hold of the object signified by the subject.[105] The existence of assertions

102 Here (337^b4) I read 'μέλλει', a conjecture by Joachim (partly supported by Phlp. *in GC* 302, 25 and 306, 12). All manuscripts have 'μέλλον', the reading printed by Bekker, Weise, Dübner, Forster, and Mugler.

103 Cf. *Div. Somn.* 2, 463^b28–31.

104 I regard the relevant occurrences in T 59 of 'will be' ('ἔσται' at 337^b4) and 'is' ('ἐστίν' at 337^b5) as place-holders for verbs in the future and in the present tense (Aristotle's own example, at 337^b7, does not contain forms of 'to be').

105 Aristotle's remarks about assertions whose predicative expression is constructed around a 'μέλλει' + infinitive phrase match the findings of modern studies of Greek grammar: see e.g. Goodwin (1889), 20; Humbert (1945/60), 154, 168–9. In T 59, the relevant occurrences of forms of the English 'to be about to' translate occurrences of forms of the Greek 'μέλλειν'.

of the second kind, i.e. assertions whose predicative expression consists of 'is about to' followed by an infinitive, is due to some of the states a thing comes to be in being contingent.

What is important, for present purposes, is the first assumption: that if an assertion whose predicative expression is a verb in the future tense is true at *t*, then at *t* it is necessary that the corresponding present-tense assertion should be true later. Anti-realist interpretations find a similar assumption in *Int.* 9.[106]

[106] Cf. Phlp. *in GC* 302, 34–303, 5; D. Frede (1970), 22–3; Seel (1982a), 243–4; C. J. F. Williams (1982), 197–8; D. Frede (1985), 41–2; Craig (1988), 13–16; Kullmann (1994/95), 300–3.

APPENDIX I

Metaph. Θ *10, 1051^{b}1: the text*

The evidence. At 1051^{b}1 the main witnesses present a variety of readings: A^b and (probably) ps.-Alexander (*in Metaph.* 598, 1–2) have 'κυριώτατα ὂν'; the first hand of E has 'κυριώτατον εἶ'; J and the second hand of E have 'κυριώτατα εἶ'; William of Moerbeke's translation presupposes 'κυριώτατα ἦ'.

Brandis, Bekker, Weise, Schwegler, Bonitz, Dübner, Christ, and Jaeger print 'κυριώτατα ὂν'. Ross (followed by Tredennick and various commentators)[1] excises 'κυριώτατα ὂν' (he also contemplates the possibility of transposing it after 'τὸ μὲν' at 1051^{a}34). Jaeger suspects a lacuna between 'κυριώτατα ὄν' and 'ἀληθὲς ἢ ψεῦδος': he suggests 'κυριώτατα ὂν <ἡ οὐσία, λείπεται δὲ ἐπισκοπεῖν τὸ ὂν> ἀληθὲς ἢ ψεῦδος'.

An inconsistency? Many editors and commentators[2] find the reading 'κυριώτατα ὂν' of A^b at 1051^{b}1 hard to accept because in *Metaphysics* E 4 (= T 7), at 1027^{b}31, Aristotle says that what 'is' in the sense of being true 'is a different thing that "is" from the things that "are" in the strict sense [κυρίως]': were the reading 'κυριώτατα ὂν' genuine, in *Metaphysics* Θ 10 Aristotle would be committing himself to the incompatible claim that what 'is' in the sense of being true is what 'is' in the strictest sense. The fact that E 4, at 1027^{b}28–9, contains a forward reference to Θ 10 makes it particularly implausible to assume that Aristotle should entertain such incompatible views about what 'is' in the sense of being true. Moreover in *de Anima* 2.1, at 412^{b}8–9, Aristotle says that actuality is what is meant when 'unity and being are spoken of in the strict sense [κυρίως]'.[3] On the other hand, one feels uneasy at ironing the inconsistency away by emending the text.

1 E.g. Oehler (1962/85), 179; Bormann (1982), 3.
2 Jaeger (1912), 51; Ross (1924), II 274–5; Oehler (1962/85), 179; von Fragstein (1967), 145; Berti (1990), 111–13.
3 Cf. Berti (2000), 6.

Solution (i). Jaeger[4] tries to resolve the alleged inconsistency between E 4 and Θ 10 by taking 'κυριώτατα' to mean something like 'in the most common or widespread sense'.[5] So: in E 4 Aristotle would be saying that 'being' in the sense of being true is different from 'being' in the strict sense; in Θ 10 he would be saying that 'being' in the sense of being true is 'being' in the most common or widespread sense (because it is the 'being' involved in every predication). The inconsistency between E 4 and Θ 10 would then be merely apparent.

Solution (i) is unconvincing: when in the course of a discussion of the various senses of an expression Aristotle uses a sentence like 'This is what the expression means κυριώτατα', 'κυριώτατα' normally means (not 'in the most common or widespread sense', but) 'in the most proper or strictest sense'.[6]

Solution (ii). Heidegger[7] tries to resolve the alleged inconsistency between E 4 and Θ 10 by assuming that they address different topics. In his view, E 4 concerns the 'being' in the sense of being true which is a property of thoughts, i.e. of mental items like beliefs; Θ 10 instead concerns the 'being' in the sense of being true which is a property of objects. Aristotle could consistently say, on the one hand, that the 'being' in the sense of being true which is a property of thoughts is different from 'being' in the strict sense, and, on the other, that the 'being' in the sense of being true which is a property of objects is 'being' in the strictest sense.[8]

I think that some claims made by Heidegger in his attempt to resolve the alleged inconsistency between E 4 and Θ 10 are true and important: he is right in claiming that E 4 and Θ 10 are about different properties, and, specifically, that E 4 is about a property of thoughts while Θ 10 is about a property of objects.[9] However, I also think that Heidegger's solution cannot stay as it stands. For it requires that this change of properties should not be reflected in any change in terminology: Aristotle would be using the same word, 'true', to express both the property that holds of thoughts and the

[4] See Jaeger (1912), 51–2, cf. Wilpert (1940), 9; Owens (1951/78), 411–12; Tugendhat (1966b), 408; Berti (1990), 111–13; Pritzl (1998), 178; Berti (2000), 6–7.

[5] At *Metaph.* Θ 1, 1045^{b}36 Aristotle perhaps uses 'μάλιστα κυρίως' to mean 'in the most common or widespread sense'.

[6] Cf. Ross (1924), II 275; Heidegger (1930), 83–5. Jaeger himself later abandoned solution (i): for in his 1957 edition of the *Metaphysics* he resorted to textual emendation (cf. the paragraph to which n. 1 above is appended).

[7] See Heidegger (1926), 168, 305–6; (1930), 87–91.

[8] Elsewhere (in his (1924/25), 187–8) Heidegger insists that the 'being' in the sense of being true discussed in E 4 is a property of objects.

[9] Cf. the subsection to which n. 70 of ch. 1 is appended.

property that holds of objects. This would be poor practice, particularly in view of the fact that the passages exhibiting the two uses are supposed to be reciprocally connected (for in E 4, at 1027b28–9, Aristotle promises to discuss later certain questions concerning what 'is' in the sense of being true and what 'is not' in the sense of being false,[10] and Θ 10 seems his fulfilment of this promise).

Solution (iii). Other commentators[11] have a better solution for the alleged inconsistency between E 4 and Θ 10. The words 'κυριώτατα ὂν ἀληθὲς ἢ ψεῦδος' must constitute a single clause ('being in the strictest sense true or false'): the adverb 'κυριώτατα' can be construed only with 'ὂν', and 'ὂν' must be construed with the phrase 'ἀληθὲς ἢ ψεῦδος' (which would otherwise remain unconnected to its context). Since 'τὸ μὲν' at 1051a34 corresponds to 'τὸ δὲ' at 1051a35 and to 'τὸ δὲ' at 1051b1, the clause 'κυριώτατα ὂν ἀληθὲς ἢ ψεῦδος' explains the third sense in which what 'is' and what 'is not' are spoken of (in the immediately preceding portion of text this role is played by the clauses 'κατὰ τὰ σχήματα τῶν κατηγοριῶν' and 'κατὰ δύναμιν ἢ ἐνέργειαν τούτων ἢ τἀναντία'). So at 1051a34–1051b2 Aristotle is saying that what 'is' and what 'is not' are spoken of, in a first sense, with reference to the categories, in a second sense, with reference to the potentiality or the actuality of the categories or to their opposites, and, in a third sense, 'by *being* in the strictest sense *true or false*'. Hence in Θ 10 there is no question of '*being* in the strictest sense': the text only speaks of '*being* in the strictest sense *true or false*'. Since Θ 10 does not contain the claim that 'being' in the sense of being true is 'being' in the strictest sense, the alleged inconsistency between E 4 and Θ 10 evaporates.

Objection: since what is being offered is a classification of the uses of 'to be' or 'being', the adverb 'κυριώτατα' ('in the strictest sense') is most naturally understood as introducing the strictest sense of 'to be' or 'being'.[12] Answer: since Θ 10 discusses truth and falsehood, it is just as natural to understand 'κυριώτατα' ('in the strictest sense') as introducing the strictest sense in which something can be called true or false.[13]

Solution (iii) seems adequate. Hence I adopt the reading 'κυριώτατα ὂν' and understand the words 'κυριώτατα ὂν ἀληθὲς ἢ ψεῦδος' as a single

[10] Cf. n. 67 of ch. 1.

[11] Brandis (1835/66), II.II.1 519–20; Prantl (1855), 185; Grote (1880), 618; Ross (1908), *ad loc.*; (1924), II 275; Deninger (1961), 140–1; Tricot (1966), II 522; Russo (1973/82), 273; Seidl (1989/91), II 491; Burnyeat *et al.* (1984), 156; Salmeri (1996), 243, 306.

[12] Cf. Burnyeat *et al.* (1984), 156.

[13] For an explanation of why Aristotle introduces the idea of the strictest sense in which something can be called true or false cf. the subsection to which n. 42 of ch. 1 is appended.

clause ('by being in the strictest sense true or false') explaining the third sense in which what 'is' and what 'is not' are spoken of.

No reason for claiming that the notion of truth or the veridical sense of 'to be' have a privileged status. Contrary to what Heidegger and other commentators think,[14] the reading 'κυριώτατα ὂν' constitutes no evidence for crediting Aristotle with the idea that the notion of truth provides a privileged insight into that of being. Similarly, *pace* Kahn,[15] the reading in question provides no support for the contention that in Greek the veridical sense of 'to be' is fundamental.

[14] Heidegger (1925/26), 174, 178, 190–3 (cf. (1930), 82–3); Volkmann-Schluck (1979), 281–2.
[15] Kahn (1966), 250 (cf. Pritzl (1998), 178).

APPENDIX 2

Metaph. Θ *10, 1051^{b}2–3: the text*

The evidence. At 1051^{b}2–3 various readings are available. E and J have

[a] τοῦτο δ' ἐπὶ τῶν πραγμάτων ἐστὶ τὸ συγκεῖσθαι ἢ διῃρῆσθαι.

This reading, also presupposed by William of Moerbeke's translation, is printed by some early editors (the Aldine edition, Brandis, and Weise).

A^b has instead

[b] τοῦτο δὴ ἔτι τῶν πραγμάτων ἐστὶ τῷ συγκεῖσθαι ἢ διῃρῆσθαι.

No editor prints this.

Most modern editors (Bekker, Schwegler, Bonitz, Dübner, Christ, Ross, Tredennick, and Jaeger) print

[c] τοῦτο δ' ἐπὶ τῶν πραγμάτων ἐστὶ τῷ συγκεῖσθαι ἢ διῃρῆσθαι,

a text obtained by combining readings [a] and [b].

Evaluation. Reading [b] makes no sense and must be discarded. Reading [a] has the edge on [c] because of the parallel with 1051^{b}11–13, 1051^{b}19–20, and 1051^{b}33–5. I therefore opt for reading [a].

APPENDIX 3

Int. *7, 17^{b}16–18: the text*[1]

The evidence. At 17^{b}16–20 Aristotle discusses contradictory pairs where one member is a universal predicative assertion. Here is the text handed down by the main manuscripts and printed by the majority of recent editors (Bekker, Waitz, Dübner, Cooke, Minio-Paluello, and Zadro):

T 60 ἀντικεῖσθαι μὲν οὖν κατάφασιν ἀπο- 17^b
φάσει λέγω ἀντιφατικῶς τὴν τὸ καθόλου σημαίνουσαν τῷ αὐτῷ ὅτι οὐ καθόλου, οἷον πᾶς ἄνθρωπος λευκός-οὐ πᾶς ἄνθρωπος λευκός, οὐδεὶς ἄνθρωπος λευκός-ἔστι τις ἄνθρωπος λευκός.[2]

Ammonius (*in Int.* 109, 24–5) reports that according to Porphyry at 17^{b}17 some manuscripts instead of 'ἀντιφατικῶς' read 'ἀποφαντικῶς' (some manuscripts of Ammonius have 'ἀποφατικῶς', the reading we find also in some manuscripts of *de Interpretatione*, e.g. in Laur. 72, 17).[3] In n 'τῷ' (17^{b}17) is added above the line. Bekker claims that at 17^{b}17–18 B reads 'τὴν τὸ καθόλου σημαίνουσαν τῇ τὸ οὐ καθόλου', but he is wrong: B's reading is the same as that of the other main manuscripts.[4] (Was this reading attested in some other manuscript?) At 17^{b}18 Laur. 72, 4 omits the first 'οὐ'. In Vat. Palat. Gr. 74 a later hand added 'τῇ τὸ αὐτὸ' above 'τῷ αὐτῷ'.[5] In Oxon. New College C. 225 (fourteenth century, f. 29r) a variant on the standard text at 17^{b}17–18 is reported: 'τὴν τὸ καθόλου σημαίνουσαν ὅτι καθόλου τῇ τὸ αὐτὸ ὅτι οὐ καθόλου' ('τὴν τὸ καθόλου σημαίνουσαν ὅτι καθόλου τῇ' is in the margin, 'τῇ τὸ αὐτὸ' is above 'τῷ αὐτῷ': the 'τῇ' at the end of the phrase in the margin is obviously picked up by the 'τῇ' at the beginning of the phrase above 'τῷ αὐτῷ'). It remains unclear whether this variant is a reader's conjecture (the hand that wrote it seems different

[1] Cf. the subsection to which n. 46 of ch. 2 is appended. [2] Cf. *Int.* 14, 24^{b}1–6.
[3] Cf. the variants to 'ἀντιφατικῶς' at *Int.* 14, 24^{b}5.
[4] Cf. Waitz (1857), 726; Weidemann (1985), 52.
[5] Cf. Weidemann (1985), 53; Weidemann (1994/2002), 214.

from that which copied the main text) or a record of some manuscript's reading.[6]

Some manuscripts of Boethius' Latin translation of *de Interpretatione* report the following rendering of 17^b16–18: '*Opponi autem adfirmationem negationi dico contradictorie quae universaliter significat ei quae non universaliter*'. The reading presupposed by this translation is 'ἀντικεῖσθαι μὲν οὖν κατάφασιν ἀποφάσει λέγω ἀντιφατικῶς τὴν τὸ καθόλου σημαίνουσαν τῇ τὸ οὐ καθόλου'.[7] (This is the reading which Bekker falsely claims to find in B.)

Two problems of literal interpretation. The literal interpretation of the initial part of T 60 at 17^b16–18 poses two problems. The first concerns the phrase 'τῷ αὐτῷ' at 17^b17–18: it is at best an extremely compressed formula.[8] The second problem concerns the phrase 'ὅτι οὐ καθόλου' at 17^b18: there is nothing with which this phrase can be construed. (One is inclined to construe 'ὅτι οὐ καθόλου' with 'ἀποφάσει' at 17^b16–17, but there is not enough of a connection between the two expressions for such a construction to be possible. Things would pan out if, for instance, at an appropriate point there were a 'τῇ [*sc.* σημαινούσῃ]' to pick up 'ἀποφάσει' just as 'τὴν σημαίνουσαν' picks up 'κατάφασιν'.)[9] These problems suggest that the initial part of T 60 at 17^b16–18 is corrupt.

Emendations. The problems of literal interpretation posed by the initial part of T 60 at 17^b16–18 instigate emendation.

6 In many manuscripts some gloss can be found above the words 'τῷ αὐτῷ' (17^b17–18): 'ὑποκειμ(έν)ῳ' (B, Laur. 71, 35, and Vat. Barberin. Gr. 87, in all cases a later hand); 'τῷ ὑποκειμ(έν)ῳ' (Laur. 72, 4 and Laur. 87, 16, in both cases a later hand); 'κατηγορουμέ(νῳ)' (Laur. 72, 12, a later hand); 'ἢ τῷ αὐτῷ ὑποκειμ(έν)ῳ κ(αὶ) κατηγορουμ(έν)ῳ' (Marc. 211, the first hand); 'ὑποκειμ(έν)ῳ κ(αὶ) κατηγορουμ(έν)ῳ' (A, a later hand). In Laur. 72, 5 a later hand adds the words 'κατάφασιν καὶ ἀπόφασιν τὴν πᾶς ἢ τὴν οὐδείς' above the phrase 'τὸ καθόλου σημαίνουσαν' (17^b17). In Vat. Barberin. Gr. 87 a later hand adds 'πρότασιν' above 'σημαίνουσαν' (17^b17).

7 Cf. Buhle (1792/1800), II 71; Waitz (1844/46), I.XXII. Other manuscripts of Boethius' Latin translation report a different rendering of 17^b16–18: '*Opponi autem adfirmationem negationi dico contradictorie quae universale significat eidem, quoniam non universaliter*'. This second rendering of 17^b16–18 presupposes the reading of the main manuscripts. The two different renderings of 17^b16–18 are also attested by different manuscripts for the lemma of Boethius' *First Commentary on Aristotle's* de Interpretatione, but the second rendering only is attested for the lemma of Boethius' *Second Commentary on Aristotle's* de Interpretatione. According to Conybeare (1892), 33, 98 some manuscripts of the Armenian version of *de Interpretatione* presuppose a Greek text lacking 'ὅτι', and perhaps presuppose 'τὸ οὐ καθόλου'.

8 Cf. Buhle (1792/1800), II 71.

9 The word order does not allow 'τῷ αὐτῷ ὅτι οὐ καθόλου' at 17^b17–18 to be understood as a single phrase: 'by virtue of the claim of non-universality itself' could translate 'αὐτῷ τῷ ὅτι οὐ καθόλου', not 'τῷ αὐτῷ ὅτι οὐ καθόλου'.

At 17^{b}17–18 Pacius reads 'τὴν τὸ καθόλου σημαίνουσαν <τῇ> τὸ αὐτὸ ὅτι οὐ καθόλου'.[10]

Du Val (recently followed by Weidemann) reads 'τὴν τὸ καθόλου <ὅτι καθόλου> σημαίνουσαν <τῇ> τὸ αὐτὸ ὅτι οὐ καθόλου'.[11]

Buhle (followed by Weise) adopts the reading presupposed by the rendering of the passage handed down by some manuscripts of Boethius' Latin translation of *de Interpretatione*: 'τὴν τὸ καθόλου σημαίνουσαν τῇ τὸ οὐ καθόλου'.

Two apparent incongruities. There seem to be two incongruities in Aristotle's account of contradictory pairs where one member is a universal predicative assertion. They both concern the relation between the general characterisation (in the initial part of T 60 at 17^{b}16–18) of contradictory pairs where one member is a universal predicative assertion, on the one hand, and the two contradictory pairs introduced (in the final part of T 60 at 17^{b}18–20) to clarify that general characterisation on the other:

(i) The general characterisation of contradictory pairs where one member is a universal predicative assertion is formulated in the initial part of T 60 at 17^{b}16–18. The literal interpretation of this portion of text poses problems which suggest that what Aristotle wrote underwent some corruption (cf. the penultimate subsection). Therefore it is not clear what is Aristotle's general characterisation of contradictory pairs where one member is a universal predicative assertion. According to one interpretation, Aristotle is claiming that in every such contradictory pair one member asserts something non-universally of the same universal of which the other member asserts something universally. Suppose Aristotle claims this. In T 20 Aristotle claimed, on the one hand, that something can be asserted universally of a universal by producing a universal predicative assertion (e.g. 'Every man is white' or 'No man is white'), and, on the other, that something can be asserted non-universally of a universal by producing an *indeterminate* predicative assertion (e.g. 'A man is white' or 'A man is not white').[12] Therefore one expects that when he illustrates his general characterisation of contradictory pairs where one member is a universal predicative assertion, Aristotle should produce one or more contradictory pairs each

[10] Pacius (1597b), 94; (1623), 107. This is just like the corrector of Vat. Palat. Gr. 74, on which Pacius might depend.

[11] Du Val (1629), 40; Weidemann (1985), 51–5; (1994/2002), 88, 214–15 (cf. Trendelenburg (1836/92), 76; Crivelli (1996), 152). Word order apart, this emendation is the same as the reading recorded by Oxon. New College C. 225.

[12] Cf. proposition [15] on p. 91 above.

of which consists of a universal predicative assertion and an *indeterminate* predicative assertion (e.g. 'Every man is white' – 'A man is not white' or 'No man is white' – 'A man is white'). However, when he illustrates his general characterisation (in the final part of T 60 at 17^{b}18–20), Aristotle produces two contradictory pairs each of which consists of a universal predicative assertion and a *particular* predicative assertion ('Every man is white' – 'Not every man is white' and 'No man is white' – 'Some man is white').[13]

(ii) In his general characterisation (in the initial part of T 60 at 17^{b}16–18) of contradictory pairs where one member is a universal predicative assertion, Aristotle seems to say that a predicative assertion which is *universal* and *affirmative* is contradictorily opposed to a negative assertion. When (in the final part of T 60 at 17^{b}18–20) he illustrates his general characterisation, Aristotle produces not only a contradictory pair ('Every man is white' – 'Not every man is white') consisting of a universal affirmative and a particular negative predicative assertion, but also one ('No man is white' – 'Some man is white') consisting of a *universal negative* and a *particular affirmative* predicative assertion, i.e. a contradictory pair no member of which is a *universal affirmative* predicative assertion.

There are at least three ways of rescuing the consistency of Aristotle's account of contradictory pairs where one member is a universal predicative assertion. Each of these three rescues endeavours to show that the two foregoing apparent incongruities in Aristotle's account are *merely* apparent.

The first rescue dissolves the first apparent incongruity in Aristotle's account by attributing to him an extended conception of asserting non-universally: not only an *indeterminate* predicative assertion, but also a *particular* predicative assertion asserts something non-universally of a universal, and the way in which a particular predicative assertion (e.g. 'Some man is white' or 'Not every man is white') asserts something non-universally of a universal is *different* from the way in which any 'coincident' indeterminate predicative assertion ('A man is white' or 'A man is not white')[14] asserts something non-universally of a universal (particular and indeterminate predicative assertions all assert something non-universally of a universal merely because they fail to assert something universally of it – only universal predicative assertions assert universally).[15] If Aristotle holds this view, then there is no incongruity if, on the one hand, in giving a general characterisation of contradictory pairs where one member is a universal predicative assertion, he

[13] Cf. Riondato (1957a), 55–6; Whitaker (1996), 88. [14] For 'coincident' see n. 9 of the introduction.
[15] Cf. Maier (1896/1936), I 158–9; Riondato (1957b), 29; Zanatta (1992), 33–4.

claims that in every such contradictory pair one member asserts something non-universally of the same universal of which the other member asserts something universally, and, on the other hand, in illustrating that general characterisation, he produces two contradictory pairs each of which consists of a universal predicative assertion and a *particular* (rather than an *indeterminate*) predicative assertion.

The first rescue can dissolve the second apparent incongruity in Aristotle's account by assuming that Aristotle is expressing himself succinctly:[16] he formulates the general characterisation only for contradictory pairs of predicative assertions where one member is universal affirmative and the other particular negative, and 'leaves it to the reader' to formulate the general characterisation for contradictory pairs of the other type.

The first rescue fails. In T 20, at 17^b8–10, Aristotle illustrates what it is to assert something non-universally of a universal by mentioning two indeterminate predicative assertions ('A man is white' and 'A man is not white'): he does not mention any particular predicative assertion, nor any assertion of any other sort. This suggests that for Aristotle, there is an especially close link between indeterminate predicative assertions and asserting something non-universally of a universal, so close that it can be ruled out that a particular predicative assertion could assert something non-universally of a universal and do this in a way that is *different* from that in which any 'coincident' indeterminate predicative assertion asserts something non-universally of a universal. This difficulty, combined with the uneasy treatment of the second apparent incongruity, suggests that the first rescue of the consistency of Aristotle's account of contradictory pairs where one member is a universal predicative assertion fails.

The second rescue handles the first apparent incongruity in Aristotle's account by attributing to him a view similar to that attributed to him by the first rescue: not only an *indeterminate* predicative assertion, but also a *particular* predicative assertion asserts something non-universally of a universal, and the way in which a particular predicative assertion asserts something non-universally of a universal is *the same* as that in which any 'coincident' indeterminate predicative assertion asserts something non-universally of a universal. (The second rescue is unlike the first in that, according to the second rescue, Aristotle believes that a particular predicative assertion asserts something non-universally of a universal in *the same* way as any

[16] Cf. Weidemann (1985), 55–6.

'coincident' indeterminate predicative assertion, while, according to the first rescue, Aristotle believes that the way in which a particular predicative assertion asserts something non-universally of a universal is *different* from the way in which any 'coincident' indeterminate predicative assertion performs such an operation.) If Aristotle holds this view, then there is no incongruity if, on the one hand, in giving a general characterisation of contradictory pairs where one member is a universal predicative assertion, he claims that in every such contradictory pair one member asserts something non-universally of the same universal of which the other member asserts something universally, and, on the other hand, in illustrating that general characterisation, he produces two contradictory pairs each of which consists of a universal predicative assertion and a *particular* (rather than an *indeterminate*) predicative assertion.

Here is some independent evidence supporting the second rescue. If in the *Prior Analytics* Aristotle believes that every indeterminate predicative assertion is logically equivalent to any 'coincident' particular predicative assertion, then most passages from that work[17] where Aristotle mentions or uses indeterminate predicative assertions are coherent.[18] Hence, in the *Prior Analytics* Aristotle probably believes that every indeterminate predicative assertion is logically equivalent to any 'coincident' particular predicative assertion.[19] But one would expect Aristotle to believe this if, as the second rescue assumes, he thinks that a particular predicative assertion asserts something non-universally of a universal in the same way as any 'coincident' indeterminate predicative assertion.

Note, however, that this independent evidence on behalf of the second rescue is weak. For, if in the *Prior Analytics* Aristotle believes, on the one hand, that every indeterminate predicative assertion logically entails any 'coincident' particular predicative assertion, and, on the other, that

17 1.1, $24^{a}17$; $24^{a}19$–22; 2, $25^{a}5$; 4, $26^{a}28$–30; $26^{a}32$–3; $26^{a}36$–9; $26^{b}21$–4; 5, $27^{b}36$–8; 6, $29^{a}6$–9; 7, $29^{a}19$–29; 14, $33^{a}37$–8; 15, $35^{b}14$–15; 16, $36^{b}12$–13; 17, $37^{b}13$–16; 18, $38^{a}10$–11; 19, $38^{b}35$–7; 20, $39^{b}2$–3; 21, $40^{a}1$–2.

18 In one passage (*APr.* 1.27, $43^{b}11$–15, cf. *Int.* 7, $17^{b}7$–8) Aristotle seems to claim that indeterminate predicative assertions can be understood as equivalent to universal predicative assertions. However, elsewhere (*Int.* 7, $17^{b}34$–7) he says that the indeterminate predicative assertion 'A man is not white' and the universal predicative assertion 'No man is white' appear to have the same meaning but really 'neither mean the same nor hold necessarily together'. His view is probably that speakers sometimes use an indeterminate predicative assertion to convey what would be appropriately expressed by a universal predicative assertion (cf. Averroes *in Int. apud* Butterworth (1983), 139; Zadro (1974), 409–10).

19 Cf. Ammon. *in Int.* 100, 21–2; 110, 23–6; 111, 10–17; Boeth. *in Int. Pr. Ed.* 87, 2–88, 3; Steph. *in Int.* 31, 11–12; Waitz (1844/46), I 369; Ross (1923), 29; Kneale/Kneale (1962), 55; Ackrill (1963), 129; G. E. L. Owen (1965), 86–7; Brunschwig (1967), 163; Rose (1968), 13; Sainati (1968), 228, 234; Brunschwig (1969), 9, 13; Soreth (1973), 421; Thom (1981), 19; Cavini (1985), 30–2.

not every particular predicative assertion logically entails any 'coincident' indeterminate predicative assertion – on this alternative hypothesis, too, most passages from the *Prior Analytics* where Aristotle mentions or uses indeterminate predicative assertions turn out to be coherent.[20] But, on this alternative hypothesis, it is unlikely that Aristotle should believe that a particular predicative assertion asserts something non-universally of a universal in the same way as a 'coincident' indeterminate predicative assertion.[21]

The second rescue raises two questions: (i) What is it, according to Aristotle, for a universal *p* to be asserted non-universally to hold (not to hold) of a universal *s*? (ii) Why does Aristotle initially characterise what it is to assert non-universally by introducing indeterminate predicative assertions and then unexpectedly introduce particular predicative assertions, if he thinks that an indeterminate predicative assertion asserts something non-universally of a universal in the same way as a 'coincident' particular predicative assertion?

(i) In T 20 Aristotle, on the one hand, associates asserting *universally* with predicative assertions whose subject is preceded by a *universal* quantifier ('every' or 'no'), and, on the other, associates asserting *non-universally* with predicative assertions whose subject is preceded by *no* quantifier (the Greek sentences which are translated in English by 'A man is white', 'A man is not white', etc. contain no expression corresponding to the English indefinite pronoun 'a'). The association of asserting universally with predicative assertions whose subject is preceded by a universal quantifier indicates that according to Aristotle for a universal *p* to be asserted universally to hold (not to hold) of a universal *s* is for *p* to be asserted to hold (not to hold) of items of which *s* holds with the additional specification that it is of *all* of the items of which *s* holds that *p* holds (does not hold). Analogously, the association of asserting non-universally with predicative assertions whose subject is preceded by no quantifier strongly suggests that according to Aristotle for a universal *p* to be asserted non-universally to hold (not to hold) of a universal *s* is for *p* to be asserted to hold (not to hold) of items of which *s* holds *without* any additional specification as to how many the

[20] Cf. Whitaker (1996), 86.

[21] Aristotle applies 'ἀδιόριστος' ('indeterminate') not only to indeterminate but also to particular predicative assertions (see *APr.* 1.4, 26^b14–15; 6, 28^b28–9; *Top.* 3.6, 120^a6–31, reading 'εἰ τινὰ ἔφησεν' at 120^a7 with Brunschwig). However, the sense in which 'ἀδιόριστος' applies to indeterminate predicative assertions must be different from that in which it applies to particular predicative assertions (cf. Brunschwig (1969), 13, 19). For 'ἀδιόριστος', when applied to indeterminate predicative assertions, contrasts with 'διωρισμένος' ('determinate'), which applies to particular predicative assertions (see *APr.* 1.4, 26^b21–4). Hence 'ἀδιόριστος', when applied to indeterminate predicative assertions, probably expresses the absence of quantifying particles. Obviously 'ἀδιόριστος' does not apply in this sense to particular predicative assertions, which do contain quantifying particles.

items of which *s* holds are of which *p* holds (does not hold), i.e. without an additional specification that it is of one or two or twenty or all of the items of which *s* holds that *p* holds (does not hold). Therefore Aristotle probably thinks that for a universal *p* to be asserted non-universally to hold (not to hold) of a universal *s* is for *p* to be asserted to hold (not to hold) of at least one of the items of which *s* holds, the possibility being left open that *p* could hold of many or even of all of the items of which *s* holds.

(ii) Aristotle initially characterises asserting non-universally by introducing indeterminate predicative assertions because such a characterisation clarifies what asserting non-universally is, and he subsequently uses the notion thus clarified to explain particular predicative assertions, in which he was most interested from the start. Perhaps Aristotle initially does not associate asserting non-universally with particular predicative assertions, whose subject is preceded by a *particular* quantifier ('some' or 'not every'), because the particular quantifier 'some' lends itself to be (mistakenly) interpreted as expressing unique instantiation, or even as being a vague proper name (one might be inclined to make the mistake of taking 'Some man is white' as meaning that there is exactly one man who is white, or even as referring in a vague way to Socrates).

The second rescue fails. The second rescue shares one defect with the first: it deals uneasily with the second apparent incongruity. But it encounters a further difficulty which speaks specifically against it.[22] If the second rescue is correct, then Aristotle is committed to the claim that asserting non-universally that white holds of man is contradictorily opposed *both* to asserting universally that white does not hold of man (because the particular affirmative predicative assertion 'Some man is white' is contradictorily opposed to the universal negative predicative assertion 'No man is white') *and* to asserting non-universally that white does not hold of man (because the indeterminate affirmative predicative assertion 'A man is white' is contradictorily opposed to the indeterminate negative predicative assertion 'A man is not white'). This claim seems incompatible with Aristotle's other claim that 'a single affirmation is contradictorily opposed to a single denial' (7, 18^a8–9)[23] – note that according to the second rescue Aristotle believes that a particular predicative assertion 'Some man is white' asserts something non-universally of the universal man in *the same* way as a 'coincident' indeterminate predicative assertion 'A man is white'. Therefore the second rescue also fails.

[22] Cf. Whitaker (1996), 86–7. [23] Cf. 17^b38–9; 10, 20^b3–4.

The third rescue differs radically from the first two with respect to the reconstruction of Aristotle's general characterisation of contradictory pairs where one member is a universal predicative assertion. According to the third rescue, in his general characterisation of contradictory pairs where one member is a universal predicative assertion Aristotle makes two claims. First, he claims that every *universal* predicative assertion *affirms universality*: it affirms that it is universally that the universal signified by the predicate holds, or does not hold, of the universal signified by the subject. Second, he claims that the contradictory opposite of any universal predicative assertion – i.e. every *particular* predicative assertion – *denies universality*: it denies that it is universally that the universal signified by the predicate holds, or does not hold, of the universal signified by the subject.[24]

How does the third rescue of the consistency of Aristotle's account of contradictory pairs where one member is a universal predicative assertion dissolve the first apparent incongruity in that account? According to the third rescue, in his general characterisation of contradictory pairs where one member is a universal predicative assertion Aristotle does *not* claim that in every such contradictory pair one member asserts something non-universally of the same universal of which the other member asserts something universally. Therefore, according to the third rescue, there is no incongruity when (in the final part of T 60 at 17^b18–20) Aristotle illustrates his general characterisation by producing two contradictory pairs each of which consists of a universal predicative assertion and a *particular* predicative assertion (rather than by producing one or more contradictory pairs each of which consists of a universal predicative assertion and an *indeterminate* predicative assertion – indeterminate predicative assertions having been associated with asserting non-universally in T 20).

As for the second apparent incongruity, the third rescue handles it well. For, according to the third rescue, Aristotle is claiming that every *universal* predicative assertion *affirms* universality (it affirms that it is universally that the universal signified by the predicate holds, or does not hold, of the universal signified by the subject): hence, for Aristotle, every universal predicative assertion is in a way affirmative. Moreover, according to the third rescue, Aristotle is also claiming that the contradictory opposite of any universal predicative assertion – i.e. every *particular* predicative assertion – *denies* universality (it denies that it is universally that the universal signified by the predicate holds, or does not hold, of the universal signified

[24] Cf. Viano (1955), 30–2; Riondato (1957a), 55; Morpurgo-Tagliabue (1971), 49; von Fritz (1972), 243; Weidemann (1985), 55; (1994/2002), 214–15; Crivelli (1996), 152–3; Whitaker (1996), 86–9; Hafemann (1999), 112, 114, 136; Pardey (2000), 21–4.

by the subject): hence, for Aristotle, every particular predicative assertion is in a way negative. This is why in his general characterisation of contradictory pairs where one member is a universal predicative assertion Aristotle says that a predicative assertion which is universal and affirmative is contradictorily opposed to a negative assertion, and then, when he comes to illustrating this general characterisation, he produces not only a contradictory pair consisting of a universal affirmative and a particular negative predicative assertion ('Every man is white' – 'Not every man is white'), but also a contradictory pair consisting of a universal negative and a particular affirmative predicative assertion ('No man is white' – 'Some man is white'): he regards the universal negative predicative assertion as affirmative because it affirms universality (it affirms that it is universally that the universal white fails to hold of the universal man), and he regards the particular affirmative predicative assertion as negative because it denies universality (it denies that it is universally that the universal white fails to hold of the universal man).

Three further considerations suggest that the third rescue should be the correct one.

First, the theory of quantification which the third rescue attributes to Aristotle fits with the account of contradictories and modality in chapters 12 and 13 of *de Interpretatione*. In these chapters Aristotle claims, on the one hand, that the modal operators ('it is possible', 'it is contingent', etc.) modify the copula of a predicative sentence, and, on the other, that in the denial of a modally qualified predicative sentence the negative particle attaches (not to the copula, but) to the modal operator: e.g. the denial of 'It is possible that Socrates is white' is (not 'It is possible that Socrates is not white', but) 'It is not possible that Socrates is white'. The analysis of contradictories and quantification which most closely corresponds to this account of contradictories and modality is that according to which, on the one hand, the universal quantifier modifies the copula of a predicative sentence, and, on the other, in the denial of a universally quantified predicative sentence the negative particle attaches (not to the copula, but) to the universal quantifier: e.g. the denial of 'It is universal that man is white' is (not 'It is universal that man is not white', but) 'It is not universal that man is white'. Clearly, such an account of contradictories and quantification is close to views attributed to Aristotle by the third rescue.[25]

Second, the third rescue fits well with the way in which Aristotle in *de Interpretatione* speaks about contradictory pairs. For, several times in

[25] Cf. Rose (1968), 14; Cavini (1985), 15–16.

de Interpretatione[26] Aristotle (i) describes those contradictory pairs whose members are a universal affirmative (negative) and a particular negative (affirmative) predicative assertion as if in such contradictory pairs the contradiction turned on the act of asserting something universally of a universal, (ii) contrasts these contradictory pairs with those whose members are indeterminate (affirmative and negative) predicative assertions, and (iii) describes the latter contradictory pairs as if they were about universals of which something is asserted non-universally. This manner of speaking can be accommodated by the third rescue. For, according to the third rescue, when Aristotle describes those contradictory pairs whose members are a universal affirmative (negative) and a particular negative (affirmative) predicative assertion as if in such contradictory pairs the contradiction turned on the act of asserting something universally of a universal, what he has in mind is that in such contradictory pairs the contradiction turns on whether it is universally that one universal holds (or does not hold) of one universal: universality is affirmed by every universal predicative assertion (affirmative as well as negative), denied by every particular predicative assertion (negative as well as affirmative).[27]

Third, in *Prior Analytics* 1.1 (24^b28–30) Aristotle defines the expressions 'being predicated of every' ('κατὰ παντὸς κατηγορεῖσθαι') and 'being predicated of no' ('κατὰ μηδενὸς κατηγορεῖσθαι').[28] He does not define 'being predicated of some' and 'not being predicated of every'. Why does he not define these last two expressions? Perhaps one reason is that he avows

[53] The notion expressed by 'being predicated of some' ('not being predicated of every') is nothing but the 'denial' of that expressed by 'being predicated of no' ('being predicated of every').

Aristotle's avowal of [53] would provide further support for the third rescue: the conception of quantified predicative assertions presupposed by [53] is essentially the same as the one attributed to Aristotle by the third rescue.[29]

In conclusion, the third rescue of the consistency of Aristotle's account of contradictory pairs where one member is a universal predicative assertion

[26] 7, 17^b26–37; 9, 18^a28–33; 18^b27–9; 10, 20^a3–14. [27] Cf. Whitaker (1996), 88.

[28] Cf. 24^a14–15; 4, 25^b39–40; 26^a24; 26^a27; *APo.* 1.4, 73^a28–34.

[29] Aristotle defines 'being predicated of every' and 'being predicated of no' to show that first-figure syllogisms are 'complete', i.e. that no addition is needed for it to become manifest that the conclusion follows necessarily from the premisses (cf. 1, 24^b22–4; 4, 25^b32–40; 26^a17–28). This, however, does not explain why Aristotle should omit defining 'being predicated of some' and 'not being predicated of every': some 'complete' first-figure syllogisms (cf. 4, 26^a17–28) have premisses that involve being predicated of some and not being predicated of every.

is more plausible than the first two. Can one read into $17^{b}16$–18 the claims attributed to Aristotle by the third rescue?

How do the possible readings fit with the third rescue?

(i) Consider the text of $17^{b}16$–18 handed down by the main manuscripts:

[a] ἀντικεῖσθαι μὲν οὖν κατάφασιν ἀποφάσει λέγω ἀντιφατικῶς τὴν τὸ καθόλου σημαίνουσαν τῷ αὐτῷ ὅτι οὐ καθόλου.

The claims which the third rescue attributes to Aristotle cannot be plausibly read into [a].

(ii) Consider the text of $17^{b}16$–18 presupposed by the rendering of the passage handed down by some manuscripts of Boethius' Latin translation of *de Interpretatione*:

[b] ἀντικεῖσθαι μὲν οὖν κατάφασιν ἀποφάσει λέγω ἀντιφατικῶς τὴν τὸ καθόλου σημαίνουσαν τῇ τὸ οὐ καθόλου.

In *de Interpretatione* before $17^{b}16$ we encounter two uses of the word 'καθόλου': as a common noun denoting universals and as an adverb.[30] It is therefore extremely likely that in [b] 'καθόλου' should be used either as a common noun denoting universals or as an adverb (I am assuming that in its two occurrences in [b] 'καθόλου' is used in the same way). The first alternative is implausible because it commits Aristotle to the bizarre claim that in a contradictory pair of the sort under discussion the affirmative member signifies (refers to?) a universal while the negative member signifies (refers to?) something that is not a universal. Hence it can be plausibly inferred that in [b] 'καθόλου' is used as an adverb. Therefore in [b] the first occurrence of 'καθόλου' and the occurrence of 'οὐ καθόλου' are probably instances of adverbial phrases. It follows that instances of some verb-phrase must be understood for them to modify. These understood instances can be plausibly taken to be occurrences of 'ὑπάρχειν ἢ μὴ ὑπάρχειν'. For:

(ii.i) At $17^{b}2$–3 Aristotle uses 'ἀποφαίνεσθαι ὡς ὑπάρχει τι ἢ μή [. . .] τινί'. This suggests that [b] should be describing affirmations and denials as signifying the ὑπάρχειν ἢ μὴ ὑπάρχειν of something to something.

(ii.ii) In his discussion of contradictory opposition at $17^{a}26$–30 (< T 58) Aristotle says that an affirmative predicative assertion asserts something as holding ('ὡς ὑπάρχον') while a negative predicative assertion asserts

[30] For 'καθόλου' as a common noun denoting universals see 7, $17^{a}38$; $17^{a}39$; $17^{b}1$; $17^{b}2$; $17^{b}4$; $17^{b}5$; $17^{b}7$; $17^{b}9$; $17^{b}10$; $17^{b}11$; $17^{b}12$; $17^{b}13$; $17^{b}15$. For 'καθόλου' as an adverb see 7, $17^{b}3$; $17^{b}5$–6; $17^{b}7$; $17^{b}9$; $17^{b}12$; $17^{b}13$; $17^{b}15$.

something as not holding (‘ὡς μὴ ὑπάρχον’).[31] Moreover, at $17^{a}22$–3 Aristotle describes a simple assertion as ‘a significant spoken sound about whether something holds or does not hold [ὑπάρχει τι ἢ μὴ ὑπάρχει]’. These occurrences of forms of ‘ὑπάρχειν’ and ‘μὴ ὑπάρχειν’ parallel those I am suggesting we understand in [b]’s elliptical formulation.

(ii.iii) Forms of ‘ὑπάρχειν καθόλου’ occur elsewhere in Aristotle’s works.[32] This provides a partial parallel for my suggested reconstruction of [b]’s elliptical formulation.

If the suggestion that the understood instances of a verb-phrase in [b]’s elliptical formulation should be occurrences of ‘ὑπάρχειν ἢ μὴ ὑπάρχειν’ is correct, reading [b] should be rendered by:

[b′] I say that an affirmation signifying the <holding, or failing to hold,> universally is contradictorily opposed to a denial signifying the not <holding, or failing to hold,> universally.

Translation [b′], in turn, should be understood as a compressed formulation of

[b″] I say that an affirmation signifying that a universal *p* universally holds, or fails to hold, of a universal *s* is contradictorily opposed to a denial signifying that *p* does not universally hold, or fail to hold, of *s*.

The claims which the third rescue attributes to Aristotle can be read in [b″], and therefore in [b] too.

(iii) Consider the reading of $17^{b}16$–18 recorded by Oxon. New College C. 225:

[c] ἀντικεῖσθαι μὲν οὖν κατάφασιν ἀποφάσει λέγω ἀντιφατικῶς τὴν τὸ καθόλου σημαίνουσαν ὅτι καθόλου τῇ τὸ αὐτὸ ὅτι οὐ καθόλου.[33]

In [c] two occurrences of ‘ὑπάρχει ἢ μὴ ὑπάρχει’ must be understood from the context. [c] should therefore be rendered by:

[c′] I say that an affirmation signifying that a universal <holds, or fails to hold,> universally is contradictorily opposed to a denial signifying that that same universal does not <hold, or fail to hold,> universally.

The claims which the third rescue attributes to Aristotle can be read in [c′], and therefore in [c].

(iv) A possible emendation (which, to the best of my knowledge, has not yet been suggested) is:

[31] Cf. *Top.* 2.1, $109^{a}29$–30. [32] See n. 2 of appendix 4.

[33] Reading [c] is equivalent to the one favoured by Du Val and Weidemann (cf. n. 11 above).

[d] ἀντικεῖσθαι μὲν οὖν κατάφασιν ἀποφάσει λέγω ἀντιφατικῶς τὴν τὸ καθόλου σημαίνουσαν τῷ αὐτῷ <ὑπάρχειν ἢ μὴ ὑπάρχειν τὸ αὐτὸ τῇ> ὅτι οὐ καθόλου.[34]

Perhaps [a] (i.e. the text of $17^{b}16$–18 handed down by the main MSS) came about because the words 'ὑπάρχειν ἢ μὴ ὑπάρχειν τὸ αὐτὸ τῇ' dropped out from [d]. In support of the emendation at hand, consider that these words might have easily dropped out from [d]: some scribe after copying 'τῷ αὐτῷ' might have resumed copying after 'τὸ αὐτὸ τῇ'. Moreover, 'ὑπάρχειν ἢ μὴ ὑπάρχειν τὸ αὐτὸ τῇ' consists of 28 letters: many lines of the papyrus *PBerol* inv. 5002 (fifth century AD, containing *APo.* $71^{b}19$–$72^{a}38$) consist of exactly 28 letters. Thus, the words 'ὑπάρχειν ἢ μὴ ὑπάρχειν τὸ αὐτὸ τῇ' might have constituted a papyrus line which was entirely skipped by a scribe. In the papyrus at hand the *iota mutum* is written: this makes the palaeographical similarity between 'τῷ αὐτῷ' and 'τὸ αὐτὸ τῇ' even greater. Note that on the suggested emendation [a] was generated by only one mistake from Aristotle's original text. [d] can be rendered by:

[d′] I say that an affirmation signifying that one item universally holds, or fails to hold, of one item is contradictorily opposed to a denial signifying that that same item does not universally hold, or fail to hold, of that same item.

The claims which the third rescue attributes to Aristotle can be read in [d′], and therefore in [d].

(v) Alternatively, the original text at $17^{b}16$–18 could have been

[e] ἀντικεῖσθαι μὲν οὖν κατάφασιν ἀποφάσει λέγω ἀντιφατικῶς τὴν τὸ καθόλου σημαίνουσαν τῷ αὐτῷ <τὸ αὐτὸ τῇ> ὅτι οὐ καθόλου,

and [a] might have come about because the words 'τὸ αὐτὸ τῇ' dropped out from [e]. The error this alternative emendation presupposes a scribe

34 In [d] 'σημαίνουσαν τὸ' + infinitive is followed by 'σημαινούσῃ ὅτι' ('σημαινούσῃ' is understood). A similar asymmetry occurs at *Int.* 10, $20^{a}16$–17, where only the second member of a pair of contrary predicative assertions is described by using 'σημαίνουσα ὅτι' + finite verb form.

In [d] 'ὑπάρχειν ἢ μὴ ὑπάρχειν' *follows* the dative case ('τῷ αὐτῷ') with which it is construed, and *precedes* its subject. At *APr.* 1.5, $27^{a}34$ Aristotle uses the sentence 'οὐδενὶ τῷ M ὑπάρξει τὸ N', where 'ὑπάρξει' *follows* the dative case ('οὐδενὶ τῷ M') with which it is construed, and *precedes* its subject (cf. *APo.* 1.15, $79^{a}41$–$79^{b}1$).

According to C (followed by Bekker, Weise, Waitz, Dübner, and Tredennick) at *APr.* 1.15, $35^{b}3$–4 Aristotle describes a premiss of a syllogism by saying that it 'σημαίνῃ τὸ ὑπάρχειν ἢ μὴ ὑπάρχειν'. (Ross excises 'ἢ μὴ ὑπάρχειν'.) This parallels [d]'s 'τὸ [. . .] σημαίνουσαν [. . .] ὑπάρχειν ἢ μὴ ὑπάρχειν'.

to have made is one that can be easily committed. If [e] was the original text at 17^b16–18, then Aristotle expected the reader to supply 'ὑπάρχειν ἢ μὴ ὑπάρχειν' from the context.[35] Reading [e] can be rendered in the same way as [d].

Reading [b] is attested in the tradition (although it is not widely attested, it is there). Moreover, the claims which the third rescue attributes to Aristotle can be read in [b]. Reading [b] is therefore the best reading for 17^b16–18.

[35] In the *Analytics* (*APr.* 1.5, 27^a7–8; 27^a10–1; 2.10, 60^b20–2; *APo.* 1.15, 79^a41–79^b1) Aristotle employs elliptical constructions for which some form of 'ὑπάρχειν' must be supplied from the context.

APPENDIX 4

The two-place relations in Aristotle's definition of truth[1]

The two-place relations involved in the truth conditions for quantified assertions. An important feature of [17], the definition of truth for predicative assertions I attribute to Aristotle, is that the truth conditions for (those utterances which are) quantified predicative assertions involve two-place relations (the combination of universally holding, the division of universally failing to hold, the combination of not universally failing to hold, and the division of not universally holding) obtaining between the universals signified by the predicates and the subjects of the assertions. These two-place relations are to some extent reflected in views formulated in the logical writings of Aristotle himself and of some of his pupils.

(i) The expression 'to hold universally'. In some passages[2] Aristotle uses the expression 'to hold universally' ('καθόλου ὑπάρχειν') to express a relation which is at least close to the combination of universally holding. This fits well with the part of [17] which concerns universal affirmative predicative assertions.

(ii) Universal affirmative predicative assertions and being a part of a whole. At the beginning of the *Prior Analytics* Aristotle says that he intends to determine 'what it is for this to be, or not to be, in this taken as a whole [ἐν ὅλῳ εἶναι ἢ μὴ εἶναι τόδε τῷδε]' (1.1, $24^{a}13$–14). Aristotle probably wants to describe what universal affirmations and denials say. But the expression he uses, i.e.

[a] ἐν ὅλῳ εἶναι ἢ μὴ εἶναι τόδε τῷδε,[3]

[1] Cf. the subsection to which n. 52 of ch. 2 is appended.

[2] *APr.* 1.24, $41^{b}6$; $41^{b}22$–3; 2.4, $57^{a}34$; *APo.* 1.4, $74^{a}1$; 5, $74^{a}5$; $74^{a}24$–5; 2.13, $96^{a}26$. Cf. the use of 'ἐπὶ πλέον ὑπάρχειν' at *APo.* 2.13, $96^{a}25$–7; $96^{a}29$–30; $96^{a}33$–4; $96^{b}8$; $96^{b}9$–10; 17, $99^{a}31$–2.

[3] Cf. *APr.* 1.4, $25^{b}33$–4; *APo.* 2.15, $79^{a}40$–1; $79^{b}6$–7.

is problematic. For in [a] 'ὅλῳ' seems to have to be understood differently depending on whether it is taken with 'εἶναι' or with 'μὴ εἶναι'. When 'ὅλῳ' is taken with 'εἶναι', it yields the phrase

[b] ἐν ὅλῳ εἶναι τόδε τῷδε,[4]

which, on its most natural (and traditional) interpretation, is paraphrased by

[c] This is in this as in a whole of which it is a part.[5]

Interpretation [c] is a reasonable description of what universal affirmative predicative assertions assert. However, when 'ὅλῳ' is taken with 'μὴ εἶναι', one gets

[d] ἐν ὅλῳ μὴ εἶναι τόδε τῷδε.[6]

Now, if 'ὅλῳ' in [d] were understood in the same way as in [b], [d] ought to be paraphrased by

[e] This is not in this as in a whole of which it is a part.

But [e] cannot be the correct paraphrase of [d] because [e] cannot describe what is asserted by a universal negative predicative assertion – [e] can at most describe what is asserted by a *particular* negative predicative assertion. The most plausible guess is that 'ὅλῳ' in [d] ought to be so understood as to allow [d] to be paraphrased by

[f] This is completely not in this.

Therefore [c] is probably Aristotle's description of what is asserted by a universal affirmative predicative assertion: a universal affirmative predicative assertion asserts that one universal (signified by the assertion's predicate) is related to another universal (signified by the assertion's subject) as a

[4] Cf. *APr.* 1.1, 24^{b}26–7; 4, 25^{b}32–3; 2.1, 53^{a}21–3; *APo.* 1.15, 79^{a}36–7; 79^{a}38; 79^{b}2; 79^{b}5; 79^{b}10; 79^{b}12–13; 79^{b}15; 79^{b}17; 16, 79^{b}38.

[5] Cf. *APr.* 1.4, 25^{b}32–7; 2.1, 53^{a}21–4; *Ph.* 4.3, 210^{a}14–18; Alex. Aphr. *in APr.* 25, 2–9; Trendelenburg (1836/92), 94–5; Waitz (1844/46), I 375; Ross (1949), 301; Patzig (1968), 91; Cosenza (1987), 28–31; Patterson (1995), 19–21. According to Mignucci (1969), 182, [b] should be understood as equivalent to

[c′] This subject holds of this predicate universally

with 'ἐν ὅλῳ' taken as an adverb (parallel to 'ἐν μέρει' and used like 'καθόλου' at *APr.* 1.23, 40^{b}23–5; 32, 47^{a}13; 2.6, 58^{b}28–30; 20, 66^{b}16) and 'τῷδε' as a dative of property. Such an interpretation is implausible in the light of *APr.* 1.4, 25^{b}32–7 and 2.1, 53^{a}21–4, where Aristotle switches between instances of 'τὸ *x* ἐν ὅλῳ τῷ *y*' and the corresponding instances of 'τὸ *x* ἐν τῷ *y*'. Cosenza (1987), 28–31 also shows that Mignucci's interpretation of [b] as equivalent to [c′] clashes with Aristotle's usage at *APo.* 1.15, 79^{a}36–40. Mignucci (1975a), 336–7 retracts this interpretation.

[6] Cf. *APo.* 1.15, 79^{a}39.

whole to one of its parts. This suggests that Aristotle associates universal affirmative predicative assertions with something like the combination of universally holding.[7] Analogously, [f] is probably Aristotle's description of what is asserted by a universal negative predicative assertion: a universal negative predicative assertion asserts that one universal (signified by the assertion's predicate) is related to another universal (signified by the assertion's subject) in such a way as to be completely not in it, i.e. in such a way as to be 'outside' it. This suggests that Aristotle associates universal negative predicative assertions with something like the division of universally failing to hold.[8]

(iii) Theophrastus and Eudemus on universal negative predicative assertions. Aristotle's pupils Theophrastus and Eudemus in their (now lost) *Analytics* linked universal negative predicative assertions with something like the division of universally failing to hold. Such an account of universal negative predicative assertions allowed Theophrastus and Eudemus to construct a proof of the conversion of universal negative predicative assertions which is simpler than the one given by Aristotle in the *Prior Analytics* (1.2, 25^a14–17).[9] Since Theophrastus' work as a logician is in many respects an expansion on Aristotle's,[10] Theophrastus perhaps knew that the account of universal negative predicative assertions presupposed by his proof was approved by Aristotle. Such an approval would fit well with the part of [17] which concerns universal negative predicative assertions.

(iv) Particular predicative assertions and parts. Aristotle's use of 'ἐν μέρει' and 'κατὰ μέρος' ('particular') to describe particular predicative assertions[11] suggests that he regarded a particular affirmative predicative assertion as asserting that the universal signified by its predicate includes at least *part* of the universal signified by its subject ('μέρος' in Greek means 'part').[12] Such a view about particular affirmative predicative assertions is tantamount to

7 See also the use of 'περιέχω' at *APr.* 1.27, 43^b23; 43^b29–30. Cf. Miller (1971), 29–32; Cosenza (1983); Patterson (1995), 19–22, 37.

8 Cf. Miller (1971), 29–32.

9 Cf. Alex. Aphr. *in APr.* 31, 4–10; 34, 13–15; 124, 18–21; 132, 24–32; 220, 12–16; *On the Conversion of Propositions apud* Badawi (1971), 65; Ammon. *in Int.* 108, 29–30; 185, 14–18; *in APr.* 4, 12–14; [Ammon.] *in APr.* 44, 1–4; 58, 19–23; 60, 21–2; Phlp. *in APr.* 48, 11–18; 74, 17–20; 74, 24–6; 124, 12–16; 129, 13–18; 198, 10–11; 201, 19–21; Bochenski (1947), 54–6; Graeser (1973), 75; Mignucci (1999a), 24–38. Authors who questioned the axiom that only syllogisms in the first figure are complete also linked universal negative predicative assertions with something like the division of universally failing to hold: see *Schol. in Arist.* 157^a13–24; Them. *apud* Badawi (1987), 186.

10 Cf. Boeth. *in Int. Sec. Ed.* 12, 3–16; Barnes (1999b), 78; Mignucci (1999a), 21–4; Bobzien (2000), 102.

11 *APr.* 1.1, 24^a17; 2, 25^a10; 25^a20; etc.

12 At *APr.* 1.4, 26^a17 Aristotle says: 'If one of the terms is related universally [καθόλου] to another and the other term is related partially [ἐν μέρει] [. . .]'. Cf. Cosenza (1987), 38–9; Mignucci (1997a), 69.

the view that a particular affirmative predicative assertion asserts that the universal signified by its predicate bears to the universal signified by its subject something like the combination of not universally failing to hold.[13] This fits well with the part of [17] which concerns particular affirmative predicative assertions.

(v) Aristotle's jargon for particular negative predicative assertions. Aristotle's use of 'ὑπερτείνειν' ('to exceed'),[14] 'ἔξω ἐπεκτείνειν' ('to extend outside'),[15] and 'ἔξω ὑπάρχειν' ('to hold outside')[16] suggests that in his view a particular negative predicative assertion says that one universal (signified by the assertion's subject) extends outside, or exceeds, another universal (signified by the assertion's predicate). Thus, Aristotle probably associates particular negative predicative assertions with something like the division of not universally holding. This fits well with the part of [17] which concerns particular negative predicative assertions.

(vi) Particular negative predicative assertions and proofs of invalidity by counter-example. Two of the proofs of invalidity by counter-example[17] suggest that Aristotle thinks that a particular negative predicative assertion is true just in case some part of the universal signified by its subject holds of none of the items of which the universal signified by its predicate holds. This view fits well with the idea that particular negative predicative assertions are linked with the division of not universally holding.

[13] At *APr.* 1.28, 43^b43–44^a2 Aristotle says that to establish that *A* holds of some *B* one must find an *X* of all of which both *A* and *B* hold. This suggests that Aristotle might be associating particular affirmative predicative assertions with something like the relation of not universally failing to hold (cf. Thom (1981), 73–5). Cf. the use of 'ἐπαλλάττω' at *APo.* 1.15, 79^b7–8; 79^b11; *GA* 2.1, 733^a27; 4.4, 770^b6; 6, 774^b17.

[14] *APr.* 1.14, 33^a39–40; 2.23, 68^b24; 27, 70^b34; *APo.* 1.22, 84^a25.

[15] *APo.* 2.13, 96^a24–5.

[16] *APo.* 2.13, 96^a30–1.

[17] *APr.* 1.4, 26^a39–26^b14.

APPENDIX 5

Aristotle's theory of truth for predicative assertions: formal presentation[1]

Alphabet. Let me first give the alphabet of the formal language in which the formal presentation of Aristotle's theory of truth is formulated.

[54] The logical symbols of the alphabet are:
two parentheses: '(' and ')';
one propositional connective of one argument: '$\neg$';
four propositional connectives of two arguments: '&', '$\vee$', '$\rightarrow$', and '$\leftrightarrow$';
two quantifiers: '$\forall$' and '$\exists$';
one two-place relation constant: '$=$'.

These logical symbols are understood in the usual way.

[55] The descriptive symbols of the alphabet include:
eleven one-place relation constants: 'V', 'S_n', 'S_a', 'S_e', 'S_i', 'S_o', 'S_y', 'S_d', 'U', 'I', and 'X';
six two-place relation constants: 'T', 'H', 'K', 'D', 'C_h', and 'C_k';
thirteen three-place relation constants: 'C_u', 'D_u', 'C_p', 'D_p', 'C_s', 'D_s', 'P', 'J_u', 'S_u', 'J_p', 'S_p', 'J_s', and 'S_s';
infinitely many individual variables: 'x', 'y', 'z', 'u', 'v', 'w', 't', 's', 'x_0', 'x_1', 'x_2', . . .;
infinitely many individual parameters: 'a', 'b', 'c', 'd', . . . , 'p', 'q', 'a_0', 'a_1', 'a_2', . . .;
infinitely many one-place relation parameters: 'R_0^1', 'R_1^1', 'R_2^1', . . .;
infinitely many two-place relation parameters: 'R_0^2', 'R_1^2', 'R_2^2', . . .;

⋮

The meanings of the relation constants are best explained by considering them in context:

[56] Every instance of every schema in the following left-hand side column has the same meaning as the corresponding instance of the schema on the same line in the following right-hand side column:

[1] Cf. the subsection to which n. 52 of ch. 2 is appended.

'$V\alpha$'	'α is an utterance'[2]
'$S_n\alpha$'	'α is a present-tense predicative assertion'[3]
'$S_a\alpha$'	'α is a universal affirmative present-tense predicative assertion'
'$S_e\alpha$'	'α is a universal negative present-tense predicative assertion'
'$S_i\alpha$'	'α is a particular affirmative present-tense predicative assertion'
'$S_o\alpha$'	'α is a particular negative present-tense predicative assertion'[4]
'$S_y\alpha$'	'α is a singular affirmative present-tense predicative assertion'
'$S_d\alpha$'	'α is a singular negative present-tense predicative assertion'[5]
'$U\alpha$'	'α is a universal'
'$I\alpha$'	'α is an individual'
'$X\alpha$'	'α is a time'[6]
'$T\alpha\beta$'	'α is true at β'
'$H\alpha\beta$'	'α is signified by the part of β that constitutes its subject'[7]
'$K\alpha\beta$'	'α is signified by the part of β that constitutes its predicate'[8]
'$D\alpha\beta$'	'α is other than β'[9]
'$C_h\alpha\beta$'	'the part of α that constitutes its subject and the part of β that constitutes its subject are tokens of the same type'
'$C_k\alpha\beta$'	'the part of α that constitutes its predicate and the part of β that constitutes its predicate are tokens of the same type'[10]
'$C_u\alpha\beta\gamma$'	'at γ α is combined with β in such a way as universally to hold of it'
'$D_u\alpha\beta\gamma$'	'at γ α is divided from β in such a way as universally to fail to hold of it'
'$C_p\alpha\beta\gamma$'	'at γ α is combined with β in such a way as not universally to fail to hold of it'
'$D_p\alpha\beta\gamma$'	'at γ α is divided from β in such a way as not universally to hold of it'
'$C_s\alpha\beta\gamma$'	'at γ α is combined with β in such a way as to hold of it'

2 '*V*' is an abbreviation of the Latin '*vox*', which in the present context should be taken to mean 'utterance'.

3 The subscript '*n*' is an abbreviation of 'now'.

4 The subscripts '*a*', '*e*', '*i*', and '*o*' are the traditional symbols for (respectively) universal affirmative, universal negative, particular affirmative, and particular negative predicative assertions.

5 The subscripts '*y*' and '*d*' are abbreviations of 'yes' and 'denial'.

6 '*X*' is an abbreviation of the Greek 'χρόνος' ('time').

7 '*H*' is an abbreviation of the Greek 'ὑποκείμενον', which in the present context should be taken to mean 'ontological subject', i.e. 'object signified by the grammatical subject'.

8 '*K*' is an abbreviation of the Greek 'κατηγορούμενον', which in the present context should be taken to mean 'ontological predicate', i.e. 'object signified by the grammatical predicate'.

9 '*D*' is an abbreviation of 'distinct'.

10 'C_h' and 'C_k' stand for 'common subject' and 'common predicate'.

'$D_s\alpha\beta\gamma$'	'at γ α is divided from β in such a way as to hold outside it'
'$P\alpha\beta\gamma$'	'at γ α is predicated of β'
'$J_u\alpha\beta\gamma$'	'α is asserted by γ to be combined with β in such a way as universally to hold of it'
'$S_u\alpha\beta\gamma$'	'α is asserted by γ to be divided from β in such a way as universally to fail to hold of it'
'$J_p\alpha\beta\gamma$'	'α is asserted by γ to be combined with β in such a way as not universally to fail to hold of it'
'$S_p\alpha\beta\gamma$'	'α is asserted by γ to be divided from β in such a way as not universally to hold of it'
'$J_s\alpha\beta\gamma$'	'α is asserted by γ to be combined with β in such a way as to hold of it'
'$S_s\alpha\beta\gamma$'	'α is asserted by γ to be divided from β in such a way as to hold outside it'

Formulae. Formulae are formed in the standard way. The usual conventions for economising on parentheses are adopted (the conjunctive and the disjunctive connective, '&' and '$\vee$', are taken to have more binding power than the conditional and the biconditional connective, '$\rightarrow$' and '$\leftrightarrow$').

The definition of truth relies on nine assumptions:

[57] $\forall x\,(S_n x \rightarrow Vx)$.

[58] $\forall x\,(S_n x \leftrightarrow S_a x \vee S_e x \vee S_i x \vee S_o x \vee S_y x \vee S_d x)$.

[59] $\forall x\,((S_a x \rightarrow \neg(S_e x \vee S_i x \vee S_o x \vee S_y x \vee S_d x))\ \&\ (S_e x \rightarrow \neg(S_i x \vee S_o x \vee S_y x \vee S_d x))\ \&\ (S_i x \rightarrow \neg(S_o x \vee S_y x \vee S_d x))\ \&\ (S_o x \rightarrow \neg(S_y x \vee S_d x))\ \&\ (S_y x \rightarrow \neg S_d x))$.

[60] $\forall x\,(S_n x \rightarrow \exists y\,(Kyx\ \&\ \forall z\,(Kzx \rightarrow z = y)\ \&\ Uy))$.

[61] $\forall x\,(S_a x \vee S_e x \vee S_i x \vee S_o x \rightarrow \exists y\,(Hyx\ \&\ \forall z\,(Hzx \rightarrow z = y)\ \&\ Uy))$.

[62] $\forall x\,(S_y x \vee S_d x \rightarrow \exists y\,(Hyx\ \&\ \forall z\,(Hzx \rightarrow z = y)\ \&\ Iy))$.

[63] $\forall x \forall y\,(S_n x\ \&\ S_n y\ \&\ C_h xy \rightarrow \exists z\,(Hzx\ \&\ Hzy))$.

[64] $\forall x \forall y\,(S_n x\ \&\ S_n y\ \&\ C_k xy \rightarrow \exists z\,(Kzx\ \&\ Kzy))$.

[65] $\forall x\,(S_n x \rightarrow (S_a x \leftrightarrow \exists y\,\exists z\,(Kyx\ \&\ Hzx\ \&\ J_u yzx))\ \&\ (S_e x \leftrightarrow \exists y\,\exists z\,(Kyx\ \&\ Hzx\ \&\ S_u yzx))\ \&\ (S_i x \leftrightarrow \exists y\,\exists z\,(Kyx\ \&\ Hzx\ \&\ J_p yzx))\ \&\ (S_o x \leftrightarrow \exists y\,\exists z\,(Kyx\ \&\ Hzx\ \&\ S_p yzx))\ \&\ (S_y x \leftrightarrow \exists y\,\exists z\,(Kyx\ \&\ Hzx\ \&\ J_s yzx))\ \&\ (S_d x \leftrightarrow \exists y\,\exists z\,(Kyx\ \&\ Hzx\ \&\ S_s yzx)))$.

Here is the definition:

[66] $\forall x\,(S_a x \rightarrow \forall t\,(Xt \rightarrow (Txt \leftrightarrow \exists y\,\exists z\,(Kyx\ \&\ Hzx\ \&\ C_u yzt))))$.

[67] $\forall x\,(S_e x \rightarrow \forall t\,(Xt \rightarrow (Txt \leftrightarrow \exists y\,\exists z\,(Kyx\ \&\ Hzx\ \&\ D_u yzt))))$.

[68] $\forall x\,(S_i x \rightarrow \forall t\,(Xt \rightarrow (Txt \leftrightarrow \exists y\,\exists z\,(Kyx\ \&\ Hzx\ \&\ C_p yzt))))$.

[69] $\forall x\,(S_o x \rightarrow \forall t\,(Xt \rightarrow (Txt \leftrightarrow \exists y\,\exists z\,(Kyx\ \&\ Hzx\ \&\ D_p yzt))))$.

[70] $\forall x\,(S_y x \rightarrow \forall t\,(Xt \rightarrow (Txt \leftrightarrow \exists y\,\exists z\,(Kyx\ \&\ Hzx\ \&\ C_s yzt))))$.

[71] $\forall x\,(S_d x \rightarrow \forall t\,(Xt \rightarrow (Txt \leftrightarrow \exists y\,\exists z\,(Kyx\ \&\ Hzx\ \&\ D_s yzt))))$.

Propositions [66]–[71] appeal to six relations of combination and division: C_u (the *combination of universally holding*), D_u (the *division of universally failing to hold*), C_p (the *combination of not universally failing to hold*), D_p (the *division of not universally holding*), C_s (the *combination of holding*), and D_s (the *division of holding outside*). They are defined as follows:

[72] $\forall x\,\forall y\,\forall t\,(C_u xyt \leftrightarrow \forall z\,(Iz\ \&\ Pyzt \rightarrow Pxzt))$.

[73] $\forall x\,\forall y\,\forall t\,(D_u xyt \leftrightarrow \forall z\,(Iz\ \&\ Pyzt \rightarrow \forall u\,(Iu\ \&\ Pxut \rightarrow Dzu)))$.

[74] $\forall x\,\forall y\,\forall t\,(C_p xyt \leftrightarrow \exists z\,(Iz\ \&\ Pyzt\ \&\ Pxzt))$.

[75] $\forall x\,\forall y\,\forall t\,(D_p xyt \leftrightarrow \exists z\,(Iz\ \&\ Pyzt\ \&\ \forall u\,(Iu\ \&\ Pxut \rightarrow Dzu)))$.

[76] $\forall x\,\forall y\,\forall t\,(C_s xyt \leftrightarrow Pxyt)$.

[77] $\forall x\,\forall y\,\forall t\,(D_s xyt \leftrightarrow \forall z\,(Iz\ \&\ Pxzt \rightarrow Dyz))$.

Some additional clauses are necessary to pin down the foregoing:

[78] $\forall x\,\forall y\,\forall z\,\forall t\,(Pxyt\ \&\ Pyzt \rightarrow Pxzt)$.

[79] $\exists t\,Xt$.

[80] $\forall x\,(Ux \leftrightarrow \exists y\,\exists z\,\exists t\,\exists s\,(Pxyt\ \&\ Pxzs\ \&\ Dyz))$.[11]

[81] $\forall x\,(Ix \leftrightarrow \neg Ux)$.[12]

[82] $\forall x\,(Ux \rightarrow \forall t\,(Xt \rightarrow \exists y\,(Iy\ \&\ Pxyt)))$.[13]

[83] $\forall x\,\forall y\,(S_n x\ \&\ S_n y \rightarrow (C_h xy \rightarrow C_h yx)\ \&\ (C_k xy \rightarrow C_k yx))$.

[84] $\forall x\,\forall y\,(Dxy \leftrightarrow \neg x = y)$.

[11] Cf. [10] on p. 80 above and the subsection to which it belongs.
[12] Cf. [11] on p. 80 above and the subsection to which it belongs.
[13] Cf. the subsection to which n. 6 of ch. 2 is appended.

A few remarks are in order.

Remark (i): alternative truth conditions for quantified predicative assertions. The truth conditions for quantified present-tense predicative assertions given by [66]–[69] are such that some quantified present-tense predicative assertion can be true at one time and false at another. These truth conditions correspond to a temporally 'specific' reading of quantified present-tense predicative assertions. Alternative truth conditions are available which do not allow quantified present-tense predicative assertions to have different truth-values at different times, and correspond to a temporally 'unqualified' reading of these assertions.[14] I shall not offer a formal presentation of these alternative truth conditions – the task would not present any particular difficulties.

Remark (ii): the Square of Opposition. Here are some trivial consequences of the foregoing definitions and assumptions:

[85] $\forall x\, \forall y\, \forall t\, (C_u xyt \leftrightarrow \neg D_p xyt)$.

[86] $\forall x\, \forall y\, \forall t\, (D_u xyt \leftrightarrow \neg C_p xyt)$.

[87] $\forall x\, \forall y\, \forall t\, (Ux\ \&\ Uy\ \&\ Xt \rightarrow \neg(C_u xyt\ \&\ D_u xyt))$.

[88] $\forall x\, \forall y\, \forall t\, (Ux\ \&\ Uy\ \&\ Xt \rightarrow (C_u xyt \rightarrow C_p xyt)\ \&\ (D_u xyt \rightarrow D_p xyt))$.

[89] $\forall x\, \forall y\, \forall t\, (Ux\ \&\ Uy\ \&\ Xt \rightarrow C_p xyt \vee D_p xyt)$.

The proofs of [85] and [86] rely only on definitions [72]–[75] and [84]. For instance, consider the proof of [85]. Assume $C_u abc$. Then (by [72]) $\forall z\, (Iz\ \&\ Pbzc \rightarrow Pazc)$. Suppose $D_p abc$. Then (by [75]) $\exists z\, (Iz\ \&\ Pbzc\ \&\ \forall u\, (Iu\ \&\ Pauc \rightarrow Dzu))$. Let then d be such that $Id\ \&\ Pbdc\ \&\ \forall u\, (Iu\ \&\ Pauc \rightarrow Ddu)$. Then $Padc$. Then Ddd. Then (by [84]) $\neg d = d$, which is absurd. Then $\neg D_p abc$. So $C_u abc \rightarrow \neg D_p abc$. Vice versa, assume $\neg D_p abc$. Let e be such that $Ie\ \&\ Pbec$. Suppose that $\neg Paec$. Let f be such that $If\ \&\ Pafc$. Suppose $e = f$. Then $Paec$, contrary to the hypothesis. Then $\neg e = f$. Then (by [84]) Def. But f was arbitrary. Then $\forall u\, (Iu\ \&\ Pauc \rightarrow Deu)$. Then $\exists z\, (Iz\ \&\ Pbzc\ \&\ \forall u\, (Iu\ \&\ Pauc \rightarrow Dzu))$. Then (by [75]) $D_p abc$, contrary to the assumption. Then $Paec$. But e was arbitrary. Then $\forall z\, (Iz\ \&\ Pbzc \rightarrow Pazc)$. Then (by [72]) $C_u abc$. So $\neg D_p abc \rightarrow C_u abc$. Then $C_u abc \leftrightarrow \neg D_p abc$. But a, b, and c were arbitrary. Then $\forall x\, \forall y\, \forall t\, (C_u xyt \leftrightarrow \neg D_p xyt)$, i.e. [85] holds. The proof of [86] is equally simple.

[14] For Aristotle's distinction between temporally 'specific' and 'unqualified' readings of quantified present-tense predicative assertions see *APr.* 1.15, 34^b7–18 (cf. *APo.* 1.4, 73^a28–34; 8, 75^b21–30; 2.12, 96^a15; *GC* 1.3, 317^b5–13; Hintikka (1957), 68–9).

The proofs of [87], [88], and [89] rely (not only on definitions [72]–[75] and [84], but also) on assumption [82]: [87], [88], and [89] hold because every universal is always predicated of at least one individual. I omit them because they are trivial.

From [58], [60], [61], [63], [64], [66]–[69], and [85]–[89] it follows (trivially) that the laws of the Square of Opposition are valid:

[90] *Law of Contradictories.* A universal affirmative (negative) present-tense predicative assertion is true when and only when any 'coincident' particular negative (affirmative) present-tense predicative assertion is not true:[15] $\forall x\, \forall y\, (((S_a x \,\&\, S_o y) \vee (S_e x \,\&\, S_i y)) \,\&\, C_k xy \,\&\, C_h xy \rightarrow \forall t\, (Xt \rightarrow (Txt \leftrightarrow \neg Tyt)))$.[16]

[91] *Law of Contraries.* A universal affirmative and a 'coincident' universal negative present-tense predicative assertion are never both true:[17] $\forall x\, \forall y\, (S_a x \,\&\, S_e y \,\&\, C_k xy \,\&\, C_h xy \rightarrow \forall t\, (Xt \rightarrow \neg(Txt \,\&\, Tyt)))$.

[92] *Law of Subalternation.* When a universal affirmative (negative) present-tense predicative assertion is true, any 'coincident' particular affirmative (negative) present-tense predicative assertion is also true:[18] $\forall x\, \forall y\, (((S_a x \,\&\, S_i y) \vee (S_e x \,\&\, S_o y)) \,\&\, C_k xy \,\&\, C_h xy \,\& \rightarrow \forall t\, (Xt \rightarrow (Txt \rightarrow Tyt)))$.

[93] *Law of Subcontraries.* For any particular affirmative and any 'coincident' particular negative present-tense predicative assertion, it is always the case that at least one of them is true:[19] $\forall x\, \forall y\, (S_i x \,\&\, S_o y \,\&\, C_k xy \,\&\, C_h xy \rightarrow \forall t\, (Xt \rightarrow (Txt \vee Tyt))$.

Remark (iii): contradictory opposition of singular predicative assertions. Here is the principle governing the ontological relations of combination and division relevant to singular present-tense predicative assertions:

[94] $\forall x\, \forall y\, \forall t\, (Iy \rightarrow (C_s xyt \leftrightarrow \neg D_s xyt))$.

[15] *Int.* 7, 17^b26–7; 9, 18^a28–33; *Top.* 2.3, 110^a32–7; 3.6, 120^a8–14; 120^a20–4.

[16] For 'coincident' see n. 9 of the introduction.

[17] *Int.* 7, 17^b20–4; 10, 20^a16–18; 14, 24^b6–7; *APr.* 2.15, 63^b23–8; *Top.* 2.1, 109^a5–6; 2, 109^b23–5.

[18] *Top.* 2.1, 108^b34–109^a6; 3.6, 119^a34–6; 120^a14–20 (cf. Slomkowski (1997), 121–4). The Laws of Conversion for universal and particular affirmations (see *APr.* 1.2, 25^a7–12), joined with some straightforward existential assumptions about predicative assertions, entail the Law of Subalternation for affirmations (cf. Pozzi (1974), 46; Crivelli (1989), 74).

[19] Aristotle never formulates the Law of Subcontraries (cf. Blanché/Dubucs (1970/96), 41): he only says that a particular affirmative and a 'coincident' particular negative predicative assertion can both be true (see *Int.* 7, 17^b24–6; 10, 20^a16–20; *Top.* 3.6, 120^a12–14).

Proposition [94] yields the principle that governs contradictory singular present-tense predicative assertions:

[95] $\forall x \forall y (S_y x \,\&\, S_d y \,\&\, C_k xy \,\&\, C_b xy \rightarrow \forall t (Xt \rightarrow (Txt \leftrightarrow \neg Tyt)))$.

The proofs of [94] and [95] are trivial.

Remark (iv): predicative assertions classified. The thesis only partly captured by [58] and [59] is that the genus present-tense-predicative-assertion (a universal) divides into the six species (universals) universal-affirmative-present-tense-predicative-assertion, universal-negative-present-tense-predicative-assertion, particular-affirmative-present-tense-predicative-assertion, particular-negative-present-tense-predicative-assertion, singular-affirmative-present-tense-predicative-assertion, and singular-negative-present-tense-predicative-assertion (each of these species has many individuals as members, and these individuals are present-tense predicative assertions – utterances, expression-tokens). One might add one layer by postulating that each of the six species divides into many subspecies (universals) which are sentence-types (e.g. the species universal-affirmative-present-tense-predicative-assertion would divide into the many subspecies which are the sentence-types 'Every man is an animal', 'Every man is tall', 'Every dog is barking', etc.). (Propositions [58] and [59] do not attempt to formulate this.)

Remark (v): what is the domain of quantification? Throughout the present account of Aristotle's theory of truth I have assumed that every quantified present-tense predicative assertion quantifies over the individuals (rather than over both the universals and the individuals) which the universal signified by its subject is predicated of.[20] There are three reasons for attributing this thesis to Aristotle.

(i) The thesis agrees best with the most natural reading of quantified present-tense predicative assertions: e.g. 'Some animal is hiding in that corner' is most naturally understood as saying that some individual which the universal animal is predicated of is hiding in that corner (it can hardly be understood as saying that some individual or universal which the universal animal is predicated of is hiding in that corner).

(ii) A remark in *Posterior Analytics* 1.4 *suggests* that universal predicative assertions quantify over individuals: '[. . .] if animal holds of every man, then if it is true to call *this one* a man, it is true to call him an animal

[20] Cf. Apelt (1891b), 138; Sainati (1968), 227; Miller (1971), 30–1.

too' (73^a30–1). (The reason why this remark merely *suggests* that universal predicative assertions quantify over individuals is that it would be true even if universal predicative assertions were to quantify over universals as well as individuals.)[21]

However, Mario Mignucci makes a good case for attributing to Aristotle alternative truth conditions, according to which every quantified predicative assertion quantifies over both the universals and the individuals of which the universal signified by its subject is predicated.[22] It would not be difficult to implement these alternative truth conditions, but I will not undertake the task here.

21 Cf. Mignucci (1997b), 138.

22 See Mignucci (1997a), 68–70; (1997b), 138–9; (2000), 13–15 (cf. Church (1965), 418).

APPENDIX 6

The failure of Bivalence for future-tense assertions: formal presentation

Is Aristotle coherent? Aristotle's position in *Int.* 9 has been taken to be incoherent.[1] For Aristotle accepts Excluded Middle (which involves endorsing every instance of '$\alpha \vee \neg\alpha$') but denies Bivalence (which involves denying that at every time every assertion is either true or false). It is hard to see how this could be coherent – but the following formal semantic theory shows that it is.[2]

Expanded semantic theory. Appendix 5 contained a formal presentation of a semantic theory for a fragment of natural language that includes some present-tense predicative assertions. Here, in appendix 6, this semantic theory is expanded. The expanded semantic theory covers a slightly larger fragment of natural language, a fragment including not only some present-tense predicative assertions, but also some past- and future-tense predicative assertions, some 'tomorrow'-assertions (i.e. predicative assertions that begin with an utterance of the phrase 'tomorrow it will be the case that'), and some negative and disjunctive assertions.

[1] Cf. Cic. *Fat.* 16. 37–8 (an attack on some Epicureans whose position resembles Aristotle's); D. C. Williams (1951), 289–90; Quine (1953), 19; D. C. Williams (1954), 253; Bradley (1959/68), 237–8; Strang (1960), 454; Kneale/Kneale (1962), 46–8; Hintikka (1964/73a), 148, 163, 166–7; von Kutschera (1986), 215.

[2] A formal model for *Int.* 9's theory of truth was offered at the beginning of the twentieth century by Jan Lukasiewicz (see his (1918); (1922), 125–6; (1930), 175–6 – cf. Prior (1953), 317; (1955/62), 240–4; (1957), 25–6, 85–6; (1967d), 1–3; Patzig (1973), 921, 927). Lukasiewicz postulated three truth-values for assertions: truth, falsehood, and an 'indeterminate' value. He then described truth-tables for the standard connectives. Lukasiewicz's three-valued logic, whatever its logical merits, cannot work as an exegesis of *Int.* 9 because it fails to validate Excluded Middle (cf. Sugihara (1954); King-Farlow (1958/59), 36; Haack (1974/96), 84–5; Knabenschuh de Porta (1997), 203–4, 208). Lukasiewicz's truth-tables can be so modified as to validate Excluded Middle, but these modifications have other unacceptable consequences. Late in his life, Lukasiewicz abandoned his interpretation in terms of three-valued logic in favour of one in terms of four-valued logic (see his (1957), 166–80). A four-valued logic is implausible as an interpretation of *Int.* 9, which does not distinguish two ways of being neither true nor false.

Expansion of the alphabet. The alphabet of the semantic theory presented in appendix 5, described in [54] and [55], must be expanded. Here are the symbols to be added:

[96] The descriptive symbols of the alphabet include:
eight one-place relation constants: 'S', 'S_b', 'S_f', 'S_t', 'S_c', 'S_v', 'M', and 'B';
ten two-place relation constants: '∈', 'I_b', 'I_f', 'I_t', 'I_c', 'O', 'W', '<', 'T^*', and 'F^*';
two three-place relation constants: 'I_v' and 'C'.

As before, the meanings of the relation constants are explained by considering them in context:

[97] Every instance of every schema in the following left-hand side column has the same meaning as the corresponding instance of the schema on the same line in the following right-hand side column:

'$S\alpha$'	'α is an assertion'
'$S_b\alpha$'	'α is a past-tense predicative assertion'
'$S_f\alpha$'	'α is a future-tense predicative assertion'
'$S_t\alpha$'	'α is a "tomorrow"-assertion'
'$S_c\alpha$'	'α is a negative assertion'
'$S_v\alpha$'	'α is a disjunctive assertion'[3]
'$M\alpha$'	'α is a set'[4]
'$B\alpha$'	'α is a branch'
'∈αβ'	'α is an element of β'
'$I_b\alpha\beta$'	'α consists of an utterance of "it has been the case that" followed by β'
'$I_f\alpha\beta$'	'α consists of an utterance of "it will be the case that" followed by β'
'$I_t\alpha\beta$'	'α consists of an utterance of "tomorrow it will be the case that" followed by β'
'$I_c\alpha\beta$'	'α consists of an utterance of "it is not the case that" followed by β'
'$O\alpha\beta$'	'α is a token of the same type as β'[5]
'$W\alpha\beta$'	'β lies within the day after the day within which α lies'[6]
'<αβ'	'α precedes β'

[3] The subscripts '*b*', '*f*', '*t*', '*c*', and '*v*' stand for 'before', 'future', 'tomorrow', 'contradictory', and '*vel*' (the Latin word for 'or').
[4] '*M*' is an abbreviation of the German '*Menge*' ('set').
[5] '*O*' stands for 'occurrence of the same type as'.
[6] '*W*' stands for 'within the day after the day within which'.

'$T^*\alpha\beta$' 'α is true at β'
'$F^*\alpha\beta$' 'α is false at β'
'$I_v\alpha\beta\gamma$' 'α consists of an utterance of "either", followed by β, followed by an utterance of "or", followed by γ'[7]
'$C\alpha\beta\gamma$' 'α is correct at β on γ'

For the sake of readability, expressions of set-theoretical membership and temporal order are written in the usual way: every instance of the schema '$\alpha \in \beta$' stands for the corresponding instance of the schema '$\in\alpha\,\beta$', and every instance of the schema '$\alpha < \beta$' stands for the corresponding instance of the schema '$<\alpha\beta$'.

Note the new symbol, 'T^*', for truth. We already have a symbol, 'T', for the property of truth that applies to present-tense predicative assertions.[8] The present expanded semantic theory concerns not only present-tense predicative assertions, but also assertions of other kinds. The property of truth that applies to all assertions (not only to present-tense predicative assertions) is different from the property of truth that applies only to present-tense predicative assertions, and must be defined differently. For this reason a new symbol for truth is needed. However, as far as present-tense predicative assertions are concerned, the property of truth signified by the new symbol 'T^*' has the same extension as the one signified by the old symbol 'T'.[9]

Kinds of assertions. There are six kinds of assertions: present-tense, past-tense, future-tense, 'tomorrow'-, negative, and disjunctive assertions. Their main characteristics are spelled out by the following principles:

[98] $\forall x\,(Sx \rightarrow Vx)$.

[99] $\forall x\,(S_b x \leftrightarrow \exists y\,(S_n y \,\&\, I_b xy))$.

[100] $\forall x\,(S_f x \leftrightarrow \exists y\,(S_n y \,\&\, I_f xy))$.

[101] $\forall x\,(S_t x \leftrightarrow \exists y\,(S_n y \,\&\, I_t xy))$.

[102] $\forall x\,(S_c x \leftrightarrow \exists y\,((S_n y \vee S_b y \vee S_f y \vee S_t y) \,\&\, I_c xy))$.

[103] $\forall x\,(S_v x \leftrightarrow \exists y\,\exists z\,((S_n y \vee S_b y \vee S_f y \vee S_t y \vee S_c y) \,\&\, (S_n z \vee S_b z \vee S_f z \vee S_t z \vee S_c z) \,\&\, I_v xyz))$.

[104] $\forall x\,((S_n x \rightarrow \neg(S_b x \vee S_f x \vee S_t x \vee S_c x \vee S_v x)) \,\&\, (S_b x \rightarrow \neg(S_f x \vee S_t x \vee S_c x \vee S_v x)) \,\&\, (S_f x \rightarrow \neg(S_t x \vee S_c x \vee S_v x)) \,\&\, (S_t x \rightarrow \neg(S_c x \vee S_v x)) \,\&\, (S_c x \rightarrow \neg S_v x))$.

[7] The 'I' in 'I_b', 'I_f', 'I_t', 'I_c', and 'I_v' is an abbreviation of 'inflected from'.
[8] Cf. [55] and [56] above. [9] Cf. [140] below.

[105] $\forall x\,(Sx \leftrightarrow S_n x \vee S_b x \vee S_f x \vee S_t x \vee S_c x \vee S_v x)$.

The foregoing principles allow only a restricted range of assertions: e.g. the only disjunctive assertions permitted are those whose disjuncts are either present- or past- or future-tense or 'tomorrow'- or negative assertions. The principles could be so modified as to allow assertions of other kinds (e.g. disjunctive assertions whose disjuncts are further disjunctive assertions), but I am not presently interested in constructing a semantic theory that covers a large fraction of natural language.

Inflection of predicates vs *inflection of whole assertions*. Propositions [99] and [100] take tense inflection to be performed on complete assertions. For instance, the past-tense assertion 'It has been the case that some man is pale' is obtained by adding an utterance of 'it has been the case that . . .' to the whole present-tense assertion 'Some man is pale'. This is not the only way one can conceive of tense inflection. An alternative is to regard tense inflection as performed on verb-phrases. According to this alternative conception, a past-tense assertion like 'Some man was pale' is composed of utterances of 'some man' and of the past-tense verb-phrase 'was pale', which in turn is obtained by inflecting the present-tense verb-phrase 'is pale'. In fact, some remarks from *de Interpretatione* 3 suggest that this alternative conception of tense inflection is closer to Aristotle's view of the matter:

T 61 Similarly, 'recovered' and 'will recover' are not verbs but cases of verbs. They differ from the verb in that it additionally signifies the present time, they the time outside the present. (16^b16–18)

The difference between the two conceptions of tense inflection reflects on truth conditions. On the truth conditions associated with the first conception, the past-tense assertion 'It has been the case that some dark man is pale' never is true (because no time is preceded by a time when 'Some dark man is pale' is true). On the truth conditions associated with the second conception, the past-tense assertion 'Some dark man was pale' is sometimes true because its predicate, an utterance of the past-tense verb-phrase 'was pale', is true of some dark man (pale men do tan).[10]

I opt for the first conception of tense inflection because it is more amenable to logical treatment. Moreover, as far as singular past- or future-tense assertions whose subjects are proper names are concerned, the truth conditions associated with the two conceptions are equivalent: 'It has been the case that Socrates is pale' is true when and only when 'Socrates was pale' is. But *Int.* 9 focuses on singular future-tense predicative assertions.

[10] Cf. Ockham *in Int.* I.VI 10, 23–4; 10, 26–8.

Tokens of the same type. A part of the expanded semantic theory to be presented relies on the two-place relation of being-a-token-of-the-same-type-as. This relation is defined case by case:

[106] $\forall x \forall y (S_n x \,\&\, Vy \rightarrow (Oxy \leftrightarrow ((S_a x \,\&\, S_a y) \vee (S_e x \,\&\, S_e y) \vee (S_i x \,\&\, S_i y) \vee (S_o x \,\&\, S_o y) \vee (S_y x \,\&\, S_y y) \vee (S_d x \,\&\, S_d y)) \,\&\, C_k xy \,\&\, C_h xy))$.

[107] $\forall x \forall y \forall z (S_n y \,\&\, I_b xy \,\&\, Vz \rightarrow (Oxz \leftrightarrow \exists u (S_n u \,\&\, I_b zu \,\&\, Oyu)))$.

[108] $\forall x \forall y \forall z (S_n y \,\&\, I_f xy \,\&\, Vz \rightarrow (Oxz \leftrightarrow \exists u (S_n u \,\&\, I_f zu \,\&\, Oyu)))$.

[109] $\forall x \forall y \forall z (S_n y \,\&\, I_t xy \,\&\, Vz \rightarrow (Oxz \leftrightarrow \exists u (S_n u \,\&\, I_t zu \,\&\, Oyu)))$.

[110] $\forall x \forall y \forall z ((S_n y \vee S_b y \vee S_f y \vee S_t y) \,\&\, I_c xy \,\&\, Vz \rightarrow (Oxz \leftrightarrow \exists u ((S_n u \vee S_b u \vee S_f u \vee S_t u) \,\&\, I_c zu \,\&\, Oyu)))$.

[111] $\forall x \forall y \forall z \forall u ((S_n y \vee S_b y \vee S_f y \vee S_t y \vee S_c y) \,\&\, (S_n z \vee S_b z \vee S_f z \vee S_t z \vee S_c z) \,\&\, I_v xyz \,\&\, Vu \rightarrow (Oxu \leftrightarrow \exists v \exists w ((S_n v \vee S_b v \vee S_f v \vee S_t v \vee S_c v) \,\&\, (S_n w \vee S_b w \vee S_f w \vee S_t w \vee S_c w) \,\&\, I_v uvw \,\&\, Oyv \,\&\, Ozw)))$.

The tree of time. The central ontological idea of the semantic theory outlined in these pages is that of a *tree*. A tree (which represents the totality of time) is based on the two-place relation $<$ (which represents the relation of preceding) holding between times. $<$ arranges times in a tree-like structure. One can thereby distinguish two directions: the 'backwards' direction (towards the root), the direction of the past by moving in which one encounters earlier times, and the 'forward' direction (away from the root), the direction of the future by moving in which one encounters later times.

For each point of a tree, there is only one backwards route (towards the past). However, a point of the tree may have many alternative forward routes (towards the future). In the case of the tree of time, this crucial feature represents the idea that while the past is unique and determined, the future is open, i.e. can take many different courses. With regard to the openness of the future, it is important to be clear that the multiple alternative forward routes do not represent mere epistemic alternatives: it is not the case that the multiplicity of the forward routes represents our ignorance of what the future will be like. Rather, the multiplicity of the forward routes represents the fact that various alternative future evolutions are possible. Another important feature is that none of the many forward routes is privileged in the sense that it represents the future which will be realised: all forward routes are on a par. Times are conceived of as intimately tied to the possible world-states obtaining in them: for this reason we speak of different future possible times rather than of possible future events or states at the same time.[11]

The properties of the tree of time reduce to those of its ordering relation $<$. This relation, which obtains only between times, is asymmetric and transitive (and is therefore a strict partial order), has no 'beginning' and no 'end', and is connected (for any two times there is a further time preceding both). The property that characterises the tree-structure is that any two distinct times that are followed by one and the same time are linked by $<$. Here is the full formulation:

[112] $\forall t\, \forall s\, (t < s \rightarrow Xt\, \&\, Xs)$.

[113] $\forall t\, \forall s\, (t < s \rightarrow \neg s < t)$.

[114] $\forall t\, \forall s\, \forall u\, (t < s\, \&\, s < u \rightarrow t < u)$.

[115] $\forall t\, \forall s\, \forall u\, (t < u\, \&\, s < u \rightarrow t < s \vee t = s \vee s < t)$.

[116] $\forall t\, \forall s\, (Xt\, \&\, Xs \rightarrow \exists u\, (u < t\, \&\, u < s))$.

Set theory. The expanded semantic theory to be presented relies on a minimal amount of set theory:

[117] $\forall x\, \exists y\, (My\, \&\, \forall z\, (z \in y \leftrightarrow z = x))$.

[118] $\forall x\, \forall y\, (Mx\, \&\, My \rightarrow \exists z\, (Mz\, \&\, \forall u\, (u \in z \leftrightarrow u \in x \vee u \in y)))$.

[119] $\forall x\, (Mx\, \&\, \forall t\, (t \in x \rightarrow Xt)\, \&\, \forall t\, \forall s\, (t \in x\, \&\, s \in x \rightarrow t < s \vee t = s \vee s < t) \rightarrow \exists u\, (Mu\, \&\, \forall t\, (t \in u \rightarrow Xt)\, \&\, \forall t\, \forall s\, (t \in u\, \&\, s \in u \rightarrow t < s \vee t = s \vee s < t)\, \&\, \forall y\, (My\, \&\, \forall t\, (t \in y \rightarrow Xt)\, \&\, \forall t\, \forall s\, (t \in y\, \&\, s \in y \rightarrow t < s \vee t = s \vee s < t)\, \&\, \forall t\, (t \in u \rightarrow t \in y) \rightarrow u = y)\, \&\, \forall t\, (t \in x \rightarrow t \in u)))$.

Proposition [117] assumes that for every object there is its singleton, i.e. the set whose only element is that object. Proposition [118] assumes that for any two sets there is their union, i.e. the set whose elements are precisely the elements of those two sets. Proposition [119] makes instead a rather strong assumption: that every linearly ordered set of times can be extended to a maximal linearly ordered set of times. This assumption can be regarded as

[11] For the representation of time as a tree cf. McCall (1966), 280–1; Prior (1967a), 126–7; Rescher (1968), 209–15; Thomason (1970), 265; Boudot (1973), 454–8; von Wright (1974), 162–6; Code (1976), 184; McArthur (1976), 37–41; M. J. White (1980), 288; Thomason (1984), 141–2; Yourgrau (1985), 549–50; Lucas (1989), 99–102, 135–9; Landman (1991), 101–3; Weidemann (1994/2002), 251–4, 285; León (1996), 385–6, 388–9; Mignucci (1996b), 291–2; Strobach (1998), 106–8.

an instance of the Maximal Chain Principle, which is equivalent to Zorn's Lemma.[12]

Branches through the tree of time. A *branch* is a maximal linearly ordered set of times:

[120] $\forall x\,(Bx \leftrightarrow Mx \,\&\, \forall t\,(t \in x \rightarrow Xt) \,\&\, \forall t\,\forall s\,(t \in x \,\&\, s \in x \rightarrow t < s \vee t = s \vee s < t) \,\&\, \forall y\,(My \,\&\, \forall t\,(t \in y \rightarrow Xt) \,\&\, \forall t\,\forall s\,(t \in y \,\&\, s \in y \rightarrow t < s \vee t = s \vee s < t) \,\&\, \forall t\,(t \in x \rightarrow t \in y) \rightarrow x = y))$.

Every element of a branch is a time:

[121] $\forall x\,\forall t\,(Bx \,\&\, t \in x \rightarrow Xt)$.

The proof is trivial.

Whatever precedes an element of a branch is also an element of that branch:

[122] $\forall x\,\forall t\,\forall s\,(Bx \,\&\, t \in x \,\&\, s < t \rightarrow s \in x)$.

This is a well-known result of the theory of trees, and I restrict myself to sketching the proof. Let *a*, *b*, and *c* be such that *a* is a branch, *b* is an element of it, and *c* precedes *b*. Let *d* be the union of *a* with the singleton of *c*. *d* can be shown to be a linearly ordered set of times. Since *a* is a subset of *d* and (being a branch) is a maximal linearly ordered set of times, *a* must be identical to *d*. Since *c* is an element of *d*, it is also an element of *a*.

Every time lies on some branch or other:

[123] $\forall t\,(Xt \rightarrow \exists x\,(Bx \,\&\, t \in x))$.

I again restrict myself to sketching the (trivial) proof. Let *a* be a time. Let *b* be the singleton of *a*. Obviously, *b* is a linearly ordered set of times. By [119], *b* can be extended to a maximal linearly ordered set of times *c*. Then *c* is a branch and *a* is an element of it.

The day after. One straightforward assumption is that every time that lies within the day after a given time is preceded by that given time:

[124] $\forall t\,\forall s\,(Wts \rightarrow t < s)$.

Another assumption is that on every branch every time is followed by a time within the day that follows its day – in short, no branch has a 'last day':

[125] $\forall x\,\forall t\,(Bx \,\&\, t \in x \rightarrow \exists s\,(s \in x \,\&\, Wts))$.

[12] Cf. Landman (1991), 115–17.

Correctness is relative to times as well as to their possible futures. Consider a time t with several 'forward routes' stemming from it, i.e. several alternative possible futures. How can a future-tense assertion (i.e. an utterance of an instance of 'It will be the case that α' or 'Tomorrow it will be the case that α') be evaluated at t? One might lack adequate grounds for such an evaluation: it might be the case that at t the assertion is correct on one of its several possible futures but not on another. The best one can then do is to evaluate the assertion as correct, or not correct, at t *relatively to* one of its several possible futures. For such a reason the notion of correctness is here regarded as relative not only to a time t, but also to a possible future of t, i.e. as relative to t as well as to a branch of which t is an element (a possible future of t determines a complete branch because t's past is unique).[13]

Correctness at a time on a branch. Present-tense predicative assertions are correct at a time on a branch just in case they are 'true' at that time according to appendix 5's definition of truth:

[126] $\forall x\,(S_n x \rightarrow \forall s\,\forall t\,(Bs\ \&\ t \in s \rightarrow (Cxts \leftrightarrow Txt)))$.

A past-tense (future-tense) predicative assertion is correct at a time on a branch just in case the present-tense predicative assertion of which it is a past (future) inflection is correct at some earlier (later) time on the same branch.[14] Analogously, a 'tomorrow'-assertion is correct at a time t on a branch just in case the present-tense predicative assertion of which it is a 'tomorrow'-inflection is correct on the same branch at some time that lies within the day after the day in which t lies.

[127] $\forall x\,\forall y\,(S_n y\ \&\ I_b xy \rightarrow \forall s\,\forall t\,(Bs\ \&\ t \in s \rightarrow (Cxts \leftrightarrow \exists u\,(u \in s\ \&\ u < t\ \&\ Cyus))))$.

[128] $\forall x\,\forall y\,(S_n y\ \&\ I_f xy \rightarrow \forall s\,\forall t\,(Bs\ \&\ t \in s \rightarrow (Cxts \leftrightarrow \exists u\,(u \in s\ \&\ t < u\ \&\ Cyus))))$.

[129] $\forall x\,\forall y\,(S_n y\ \&\ I_t xy \rightarrow \forall s\,\forall t\,(Bs\ \&\ t \in s \rightarrow (Cxts \leftrightarrow \exists u\,(u \in s\ \&\ Wtu\ \&\ Cyus))))$.

A negative (disjunctive) assertion is correct at a time on a branch just in case the assertion of which it is the negation is not correct (at least one of its disjuncts is correct) at that time on that branch:

[130] $\forall x\,\forall y\,((S_n y \vee S_b y \vee S_f y \vee S_t y)\ \&\ I_c xy \rightarrow \forall s\,\forall t\,(Bs\ \&\ t \in s \rightarrow (Cxts \leftrightarrow \neg Cyts)))$.

[13] Cf. Prior (1967a), 122–7; Thomason (1970), 268–70; (1984), 133–4; Weidemann (1994/2002), 256.
[14] Cf. n. 82 of ch. 7.

[131] $\forall x\, \forall y\, \forall z\, ((S_n y \vee S_b y \vee S_f y \vee S_t y \vee S_c y)\ \&\ (S_n z \vee S_b z \vee S_f z \vee S_t z \vee S_c z)\ \&\ I_v xyz \rightarrow \forall s\, \forall t\, (Bs\ \&\ t \in s \rightarrow (Cxts \leftrightarrow Cyts \vee Czts)))$.

Tokens of the same type are either both or neither correct at the same time on the same branch. The first result in this area concerns present-tense predicative assertions:

[132] $\forall x\, \forall y\, (S_n x\ \&\ S_n y\ \&\ Oxy \rightarrow \forall s\, \forall t\, (Bs\ \&\ t \in s \rightarrow (Cxts \leftrightarrow Cyts)))$.

Let a and b be such that $S_n a\ \&\ S_n b\ \&\ Oab$. Since $S_n b$, Vb (by [57]). Then $S_n a\ \&\ Vb\ \&\ Oab$, so that (by [106]) $((S_a a\ \&\ S_a b) \vee (S_e a\ \&\ S_e b) \vee (S_i a\ \&\ S_i b) \vee (S_o a\ \&\ S_o b) \vee (S_y a\ \&\ S_y b) \vee (S_d a\ \&\ S_d b))\ \&\ C_k ab\ \&\ C_h ab$. Since $S_n a\ \&\ S_n b\ \&\ C_k ab$, $\exists z\, (Kza\ \&\ Kzb)$ (by [64]): let then c be such that $Kca\ \&\ Kcb$. Similarly, since $S_n a\ \&\ S_n b\ \&\ C_h ab$, $\exists z\, (Hza\ \&\ Hzb)$ (by [63]): let then d be such that $Hda\ \&\ Hdb$. Let e and f be such that $Be\ \&\ f \in e$. Then Xf (by [121]). Since $(S_a a\ \&\ S_a b) \vee (S_e a\ \&\ S_e b) \vee (S_i a\ \&\ S_i b) \vee (S_o a\ \&\ S_o b) \vee (S_y a\ \&\ S_y b) \vee (S_d a\ \&\ S_d b)$, distinguish six cases corresponding to these six disjuncts.

(1) $S_a a\ \&\ S_a b$. Since $S_n a$, $\exists y\, (Kya\ \&\ \forall z\, (Kza \rightarrow z = y)\ \&\ Uy)$ (by [60]): let then g be such that $Kga\ \&\ \forall z\, (Kza \rightarrow z = g)\ \&\ Ug$. Since $S_a a$, $\exists y\, (Hya\ \&\ \forall z\, (Hza \rightarrow z = y)\ \&\ Uy)$ (by [61]): let then h be such that $Hha\ \&\ \forall z\, (Hza \rightarrow z = h)\ \&\ Uh$. Analogously, since $S_n b$, $\exists y\, (Kyb\ \&\ \forall z\, (Kzb \rightarrow z = y)\ \&\ Uy)$ (by [60]): let then i be such that $Kib\ \&\ \forall z\, (Kzb \rightarrow z = i)\ \&\ Ui$. Since $S_a b$, $\exists y\, (Hyb\ \&\ \forall z\, (Hzb \rightarrow z = y)\ \&\ Uy)$ (by [61]): let then j be such that $Hjb\ \&\ \forall z\, (Hzb \rightarrow z = j)\ \&\ Uj$. Since $S_n a$, $\forall s\, \forall t\, (Bs\ \&\ t \in s \rightarrow (Cats \leftrightarrow Tat))$ (by [126]), so that $Cafe \leftrightarrow Taf$. Similarly, since $S_n b$, $\forall s\, \forall t\, (Bs\ \&\ t \in s \rightarrow (Cbts \leftrightarrow Tbt))$ (again by [126]), so that $Cbfe \leftrightarrow Tbf$. Since $S_a a$, $\forall t\, (Xt \rightarrow (Tat \leftrightarrow \exists y\, \exists z\, (Kya\ \&\ Hza\ \&\ C_u yzt)))$ (by [66]). Since Xf, $Taf \leftrightarrow \exists y\, \exists z\, (Kya\ \&\ Hza\ \&\ C_u yzf)$. Analogously, since $S_a b$, $\forall t\, (Xt \rightarrow (Tbt \leftrightarrow \exists y\, \exists z\, (Kyb\ \&\ Hzb\ \&\ C_u yzt)))$ (again by [66]). Since Xf, $Tbf \leftrightarrow \exists y\, \exists z\, (Kyb\ \&\ Hzb\ \&\ C_u yzf)$. Suppose $Cafe$. Then Taf. Then $\exists y\, \exists z\, (Kya\ \&\ Hza\ \&\ C_u yzf)$. Let then k and l be such that $Kka\ \&\ Hla\ \&\ C_u klf$. Since $Kka\ \&\ Kca\ \&\ \forall z\, (Kza \rightarrow z = g)$, $k = g\ \&\ c = g$, so that $k = c$; since $Hla\ \&\ Hda\ \&\ \forall z\, (Hza \rightarrow z = h)$, $l = h\ \&\ d = h$, so that $l = d$. Since $C_u klf\ \&\ k = c\ \&\ l = d$, $C_u cdf$. Then $Kcb\ \&\ Hdb\ \&\ C_u cdf$, so that $\exists y\, \exists z\, (Kyb\ \&\ Hzb\ \&\ C_u yzf)$. Then Tbf, so that $Cbfe$. Thus: $Cafe \rightarrow Cbfe$. Vice versa, suppose $Cbfe$. Then Tbf. Then $\exists y\, \exists z\, (Kyb\ \&\ Hzb\ \&\ C_u yzf)$. Let then m and n be such that $Kmb\ \&\ Hnb\ \&\ C_u mnf$. Since $Kmb\ \&\ Kcb\ \&\ \forall z\, (Kzb \rightarrow z = i)$, $m = i\ \&\ c = i$, so that $m = c$; since $Hnb\ \&\ Hdb\ \&\ \forall z\, (Hzb \rightarrow z = j)$, $n = j\ \&\ d = j$, so that $n = d$. Since $C_u mnf\ \&\ m = c\ \&\ n = d$, $C_u cdf$. Then $Kca\ \&\ Hda\ \&\ C_u cdf$, so that $\exists y\, \exists z\, (Kya\ \&\ Hza\ \&\ C_u yzf)$. Then Taf, so that $Cafe$. Thus: $Cbfe \rightarrow Cafe$. Hence $Cafe \leftrightarrow Cbfe$.

The remaining cases (2)–(6) are treated similarly: in each of them we have $Cafe \leftrightarrow Cbfe$. Thus, in all cases, $Cafe \leftrightarrow Cbfe$. But e and f were arbitrary. Then $\forall s\, \forall t\, (Bs\ \&\ t \in s \rightarrow (Cats \leftrightarrow Cbts))$. But a and b were arbitrary. Then $\forall x\, \forall y\, (S_n x\ \&\ S_n y\ \&\ Oxy \rightarrow \forall s\, \forall t\, (Bs\ \&\ t \in s \rightarrow (Cxts \leftrightarrow Cyts)))$.

More results of the same type can be proved on the basis of [132]:

[133] $\forall x\, \forall y\, (S_b x\ \&\ S_b y\ \&\ Oxy \rightarrow \forall s\, \forall t\, (Bs\ \&\ t \in s \rightarrow (Cxts \leftrightarrow Cyts)))$.

[134] $\forall x\, \forall y\, (S_f x\ \&\ S_f y\ \&\ Oxy \rightarrow \forall s\, \forall t\, (Bs\ \&\ t \in s \rightarrow (Cxts \leftrightarrow Cyts)))$.

[135] $\forall x\, \forall y\, (S_t x\ \&\ S_t y\ \&\ Oxy \rightarrow \forall s\, \forall t\, (Bs\ \&\ t \in s \rightarrow (Cxts \leftrightarrow Cyts)))$.

[136] $\forall x\, \forall y\, (S_c x\ \&\ S_c y\ \&\ Oxy \rightarrow \forall s\, \forall t\, (Bs\ \&\ t \in s \rightarrow (Cxts \leftrightarrow Cyts)))$.

[137] $\forall x\, \forall y\, (S_v x\ \&\ S_v y\ \&\ Oxy \rightarrow \forall s\, \forall t\, (Bs\ \&\ t \in s \rightarrow (Cxts \leftrightarrow Cyts)))$.

Truth-value gaps: (i) quasi-formal considerations:

(1) We want to think of the truth of an assertion as being determined *exclusively* by a time. We shall thereby speak of an assertion *a* as being true at a time *t*. Analogously, we want to think of the falsehood of an assertion as being determined exclusively by a time. We shall thereby speak of *a* as being false at *t*.

(2) In a preceding subsection it was made clear that *t* is not in general enough to evaluate a future-tense assertion as true or false: a possible future of *t* (i.e. one of the possibly many 'forward routes' stemming from *t*) may need to be taken into account. Say that a valuation of *a based on t* is a valuation of *a* carried out with reference to *t* and, moreover, one possible future of *t*.

(3) We want to think that whether *a* is true at *t* depends on the valuations of *a* which are based on *t* (i.e. those valuations of *a* each of which is carried out with reference to *t* and, moreover, one possible future of *t*). Analogously, we want to think that whether *a* is false at *t* depends on the valuations of *a* which are based on *t*.

(4) As far as the valuations of *a* based on *t* are concerned, what is determined exclusively by *t* is only what is *common* to *all* valuations of *a* based on *t*. Hence, as far as the valuations of *a* based on *t* are concerned, what is determined exclusively by *t* can only be either that *a* is correct at *t* on *every* possible future of *t*, or else that *a* is correct at *t* on *no* possible future of *t*.

These points suggest (i) that *a* should be *true* at *t* if *a* is correct at *t* on *every* possible future of *t*; (ii) that *a* should be *false* at *t* if *a* is correct at *t* on *no* possible future of *t*; and (iii) that *a* should be *neither true nor false, i.e., indeterminate*, at *t* if *a* is correct at *t* on *some but not all* possible futures of *t*.[15]

Truth-value gaps: (ii) intuitive considerations. It is worthwhile reflecting on the intuitions behind the last subsection's quasi-formal considerations. Think of *t* as the present moment, and think of the forward routes stemming from *t* as the possible futures of *t*: the past of *t* is unique, but its future branches out into several alternatives – this is how the world now really is.

By requiring that the truth or falsehood of an assertion *a* should be determined exclusively by *t*,[16] we are requiring that the truth or falsehood of *a* should be determined by how the world is at present. At present the world is such as to be unique in the direction of the past, but branching out into alternative possible futures. Up to now the world has been, and is, going in precisely one way, but from now onwards it could go in several ways. If *a* is a future-tense assertion, then how the world is at present can determine *a* as true (false) only if *a* is correct on every (no) possible future development. Otherwise (i.e. if *a* is correct on some possible future developments but not on others), how the world is at present is unable to determine *a* as true, and is also unable to determine *a* as false. In such circumstances, at present *a* is neither true nor false, i.e. is indeterminate.[17]

Truth-value gaps: (iii) truth does not enjoy the disquotational property. Clearly, the indeterminacy of truth-value of *a* at the present moment (whose past is unique whereas its future branches out into several possible evolutions) is compatible with *a*'s turning out to be correct 'on the actual evolution (whatever that may be) of the present'. Hence, *a*'s truth now is not entailed by *a*'s turning out to be correct 'on the actual evolution (whatever that may be) of the present'. The converse entailment holds trivially: if *a* is true now, it is correct on every possible evolution of the present, and is therefore correct 'on the actual evolution (whatever that may be) of the present'. In this sense, asserting that *a* is true now is something stronger than asserting *a*: it might be the case that by asserting *a*, one commits oneself (merely) to *a*'s turning out to be correct 'on the actual evolution (whatever that

15 Cf. van Fraassen (1966), 487, 494; Prior (1967a), 136; Thomason (1970), 272–3; Seeskin (1971), 770–3; Haack (1974/96), 85–6, 90; M. J. White (1980), 288–91; Thomason (1984), 144–6; Bencivenga *et al.* (1986/91), 40–5; Sayward (1989), 129; Gaskin (1994), 85; Weidemann (1994/2002), 320; Williamson (1994), 144, 156–7; Vuillemin (1996), 160–1; Hafemann (1999), 129.

16 Cf. point (1) of the preceding subsection.

17 Cf. Hildebrand (1884), VI; Prior (1953), 322–3; Lenz (1957), 773–4; Ackrill (1963), 140–1; Hintikka (1964/73a), 172–3; McCall (1966), 275–6; Patzig (1973), 923; von Wright (1974), 166–7; Dickason (1976), 20–2; Wolf (1979), 114, 417; Weidemann (1980), 420; M. J. White (1981), 236, 240; Seel (1982a), 241; M. J. White (1985), 66–7; Craig (1988), 23, 58; D. Frede (1990), 202; Weidemann (1994/2002), 257–8; Inciarte (1999), 146–7.

may be) of the present', but does not commit oneself to *a*'s being true now (because – the speaker thinks – the present branches out into several possible evolutions, and *a* is correct on some but not all of these possible evolutions). Thus, the direction 'from fact to truth' of the equivalence that constitutes the disquotational property of truth can fail.[18]

Truth-value gaps: (iv) objections and answers. One might object: 'If the claims made in the preceding subsections are correct, truth lacks the disquotational property; but truth enjoys the disquotational property;[19] hence some of the claims made in the preceding subsections are not correct.' The objection could be rubbed in: consider a man who one day makes a prediction by uttering the sentence 'A sea-battle will take place tomorrow'. The day after, a sea-battle actually takes place. If the preceding subsections' claims are correct, this man cannot say 'The remark I made yesterday was true'.

This objection can be answered by assuming that there are several notions of truth, and that the claims made in the preceding subsections concern only one of these notions of truth – a 'loaded' notion of truth. In particular, the last subsection's claim about the lack of the disquotational property concerns only this 'loaded' notion of truth. Obviously, this claim about the 'loaded' notion of truth is consistent with the claim that other notions of truth enjoy the disquotational property. The idea here is that apart from the 'loaded' notion of truth, there is also a 'plain' notion of truth: while the 'loaded' notion of truth lacks the disquotational property, the 'plain' notion enjoys it.[20]

But what guarantees that the 'loaded' notion of truth should be a notion of truth at all? Does not its lack of the disquotational property show that it is not a notion of truth? This development of the objection can be answered by means of two arguments.

(iv.i) One of our most deeply entrenched (albeit hazy) intuitions about truth is that for an assertion or a belief to be true is to 'match' or 'correspond to' the world. Now, the notion discussed in the preceding subsections is that of an assertion corresponding to as much of the world as there is at a given time. Hence, the notion discussed in the preceding subsections is a notion of truth.

(iv.ii) The notion discussed in the preceding subsections matches certain tensed uses of the phrase '. . . is true'. If at time *t* it is not yet certain whether

[18] Cf. McCall (1966), 274–5; Gaskin (1994), 87; (1995), 85.

[19] Cf. Tarski (1933), 187–8; Williamson (1994), 162; K. Taylor (1998), 116.

[20] Cf. Peter de Rivo *apud* Baudry (1950), 94–5, 97–9, 221–3; Albritton (1957), 30, 33; McCall (1966), 270–3, 274–7; von Wright (1974), 174–7; (1984b), 5–10; Weidemann (1994/2002), 255–61; Mignucci (1996b), 295–6.

at the later time t' it will be the case that α, at t one can react to a statement to the effect that at t' it will be the case that α by saying 'That is not yet true'. Situations of this kind arise when one reacts to the worry that an as yet uncertain future calamity could come about: e.g. Jim is on the verge of bankruptcy and asserts that he is going to lose all his money, but Fred, who optimistically thinks that matters might be mended, answers by saying 'That is not yet true'.[21] Moreover, if at t it is not yet certain whether at the later time t' it will be the case that α but at t'', later than t but still earlier than t', it becomes certain that at t' it will be the case that α, at t'' one can react to a statement to the effect that at t' it will be the case that α by saying 'That is now true' or 'That has become true'. Situations of this sort can arise when what one feared might fail to come about becomes certain to be going to happen: e.g. Jim has been believing for a long time that he was going to obtain his share of the inheritance, but only after the legal uncertainties have been sorted out can his lawyer (who had previously been reacting to Jim's remarks by expressing doubt) say 'Your belief is at last true'. The fact that the notion discussed in the preceding subsections corresponds to these uses of '. . . is true' suggests that it is a notion of truth. According to this argument, the 'loaded' notion of truth corresponds to some tensed uses of '. . . is true' while the 'plain' notion corresponds to other (tensed or tenseless) uses of that phrase.[22]

The 'loaded' and the 'plain' notions of truth seem to be connected with two different ways of regarding the world's history. The 'loaded' notion is connected to a viewpoint 'inside' the world's history, at a certain stage of it at which the past is uniquely determined while the future branches out in several possible alternatives: according to the 'loaded' notion of truth, an assertion is true at a certain time just in case it corresponds to the world at the stage it has reached at that time. The 'plain' notion of truth is connected with a viewpoint 'outside' the world's history, which is 'given' in its totality: according to the 'plain' notion, an assertion is true just in case it corresponds to the whole world's history.[23] Note that the viewpoint corresponding to the 'loaded' notion of truth, i.e. the viewpoint 'inside' the world's history, is likely to be that of an agent for whom it is important to regard the future as at least partially 'open'.

A further possible objection is that the 'loaded' notion of truth can be ignored because the 'plain' notion of truth is more important. However, this objection makes a dubious move: even granting that the 'plain' notion

[21] Cf. McCall (1966), 273.
[22] On the uses of '. . . is true' corresponding to the 'loaded' notion of truth see von Wright (1974), 175.
[23] Cf. Peter de Rivo *apud* Baudry (1950), 94–5, 97–9; Burrell (1964), 47–50; Hartshorne (1965), 58; McCall (1966), 270–3, 274, 279–81; Jeffrey (1979), 253; M. J. White (1981), 232–5.

of truth is more important, it does not follow that the 'loaded' notion can be ignored. In natural language the tensed uses of '... is true' that introduce the 'loaded' notion are common: why should one ignore them? Codifying the rules that govern their behaviour seems a worthwhile enterprise.

Truth-value gaps: (v) formalities. Let me now state rigorously the principles which in the preceding subsections were only vaguely characterised:

[138] $\forall x \, \forall t \, (Sx \,\&\, Xt \rightarrow (T^{*}xt \leftrightarrow \forall s \, (Bs \,\&\, t \in s \rightarrow Cxts)))$.

[139] $\forall x \, \forall t \, (Sx \,\&\, Xt \rightarrow (F^{*}xt \leftrightarrow \forall s \, (Bs \,\&\, t \in s \rightarrow \neg Cxts)))$.

The two properties of truth coincide on present-tense predicative assertions:

[140] $\forall x \, \forall t \, (S_n x \,\&\, Xt \rightarrow (Txt \leftrightarrow T^{*}xt))$.

Let a and b be such that $S_n a \,\&\, Xb$. Since $S_n a$, $\forall s \, \forall t \, (Bs \,\&\, t \in s \rightarrow (Cats \leftrightarrow Tat))$ (by [126]) and Sa (by [105]). Since $Sa \,\&\, Xb$, $T^{*}ab \leftrightarrow \forall s \, (Bs \,\&\, b \in s \rightarrow Cabs)$ (by [138]).

Suppose that Tab. Let c be such that $Bc \,\&\, b \in c$. Since $\forall s \, \forall t \, (Bs \,\&\, t \in s \rightarrow (Cats \leftrightarrow Tat))$, $Cabc \leftrightarrow Tab$. Then $Cabc$. But c was arbitrary. Then $\forall s \, (Bs \,\&\, b \in s \rightarrow Cabs)$. Hence $T^{*}ab$. Thus $Tab \rightarrow T^{*}ab$. Vice versa, suppose that $T^{*}ab$. Then $\forall s \, (Bs \,\&\, b \in s \rightarrow Cabs)$. Since Xb, $\exists x \, (Bx \,\&\, b \in x)$ (by [123]). Let then d be such that $Bd \,\&\, b \in d$. Then $Cabd$ and $Cabd \leftrightarrow Tab$. Then Tab. Thus $T^{*}ab \rightarrow Tab$. Hence $Tab \leftrightarrow T^{*}ab$. But a and b were arbitrary. Then $\forall x \, \forall t \, (S_n x \,\&\, Xt \rightarrow (Txt \leftrightarrow T^{*}xt))$, i.e. [140] holds.

Bivalence fails for 'tomorrow'-assertions. Consider the tree of time partially illustrated by the following diagram:

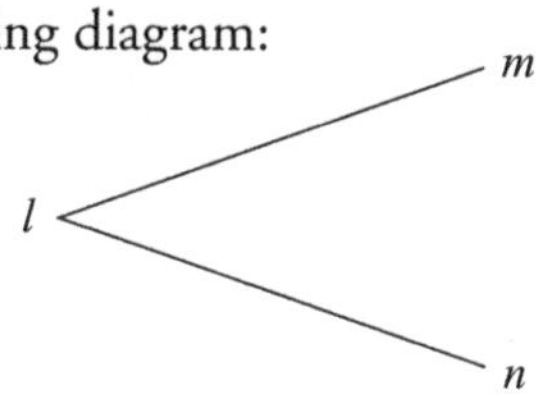

Part of the information encoded by this diagram is that $Xl \,\&\, Xm \,\&\, Xn \,\&\, Dlm \,\&\, Dln \,\&\, Dmn$ (i.e. l, m, and n are distinct times) $\&\, l < m \,\&\, l < n$.

Let j and k be such that $Bj \,\&\, l \in j \,\&\, m \in j \,\&\, Bk \,\&\, l \in k \,\&\, n \in k$ (i.e. j is a branch through l and m, and k is a branch through l and n).

Let Wlm (i.e. m lies within the day after the day within which l lies).

Let c and d be such that $Pcdm \,\&\, \forall t \, (t \in k \rightarrow \neg Pcdt)$ (i.e. c is predicated of d at m, but at no time on branch k is c predicated of d).

Let a and b be such that $S_y b \,\&\, I_t ab \,\&\, Kcb \,\&\, Hdb$ (i.e. a is a 'tomorrow'-assertion constructed from the singular affirmative present-tense predicative assertion b, c is signified by the predicate of b, and d is signified by the subject of b). Since $S_y b$, $S_n b$ (by [58]). Then $S_n b$ & $I_t ab$, so that $\exists y\ (S_n y$ & $I_t ay)$. Then (by [101]) $S_t a$, so that (by [105]) Sa.

Since $S_y b$, $\exists y\ (Hyb$ & $\forall z\ (Hzb \rightarrow z = y)$ & $Iy)$ (by [62]). Let then e be such that Heb & $\forall z\ (Hzb \rightarrow z = e)$ & Ie. Since $S_n b$, $\exists y\ (Kyb$ & $\forall z\ (Kzb \rightarrow z = y)$ & $Uy)$ (by [60]). Let then f be such that Kfb & $\forall z\ (Kzb \rightarrow z = f)$ & Uf.

Suppose T^*al. Since Sa & Xl, $T^*al \leftrightarrow \forall s\ (Bs$ & $l \in s \rightarrow Cals)$ (by [138]). Then $\forall s\ (Bs$ & $l \in s \rightarrow Cals)$. Since Bk & $l \in k$, $Calk$. Since $S_n b$ & $I_t ab$, $\forall s\ \forall t\ (Bs$ & $t \in s \rightarrow (Cats \leftrightarrow \exists u\ (u \in s$ & Wtu & $Cbus)))$ (by [129]). Since Bk & $l \in k$, $Calk \leftrightarrow \exists u\ (u \in k$ & Wlu & $Cbuk)$. Then $\exists u\ (u \in k$ & Wlu & $Cbuk)$. Let then g be such that $g \in k$ & Wlg & $Cbgk$. Since $S_n b$, $\forall s\ \forall t\ (Bs$ & $t \in s \rightarrow (Cbts \leftrightarrow Tbt))$ (by [126]). Since Bk & $g \in k$, $Cbgk \leftrightarrow Tbg$. Hence Tbg. Since Bk & $g \in k$, Xg (by [121]). Since $S_y b$ and Xg, $Tbg \leftrightarrow \exists y\ \exists z\ (Kyb$ & Hzb & $C_s yzg)$ (by [70]). Hence $\exists y\ \exists z\ (Kyb$ & Hzb & $C_s yzg)$. Let then h and i be such that Khb & Hib & $C_s hig$. Since Khb & Kcb & $\forall z\ (Kzb \rightarrow z = f)$, $h = f$ & $c = f$, so that $h = c$; similarly, since Hib & Hdb & $\forall z\ (Hzb \rightarrow z = e)$, $i = e$ & $d = e$, so that $i = d$. Since $C_s hig$ & $h = c$ & $i = d$, $C_s cdg$. Then (by [76]) $Pcdg$. Since $g \in k$ & $\forall t\ (t \in k \rightarrow \neg Pcdt)$, $\neg Pcdg$, which yields a contradiction. Hence $\neg T^*al$.

Suppose F^*al. Since Sa & Xl, $F^*al \leftrightarrow \forall s\ (Bs$ & $l \in s \rightarrow \neg Cals)$ (by [139]). Then $\forall s\ (Bs$ & $l \in s \rightarrow \neg Cals)$. Since Bj & $l \in j$, $\neg Calj$. Since $Pcdm$, $C_s cdm$ (by [76]). Then Kcb & Hdb & $C_s cdm$, so that $\exists y\ \exists z\ (Kyb$ & Hzb & $C_s yzm)$. Since $S_y b$ and Xm, $Tbm \leftrightarrow \exists y\ \exists z\ (Kyb$ & Hzb & $C_s yzm)$ (by [70]). Hence Tbm. Since $S_n b$, $\forall s\ \forall t\ (Bs$ & $t \in s \rightarrow (Cbts \leftrightarrow Tbt))$ (by [126]). Since Bj & $m \in j$, $Cbmj \leftrightarrow Tbm$. Hence $Cbmj$. Since $m \in j$ & Wlm & $Cbmj$, $\exists u\ (u \in j$ & Wlu & $Cbuj)$. Since $S_n b$ & $I_t ab$, $\forall s\ \forall t\ (Bs$ & $t \in s \rightarrow (Cats \leftrightarrow \exists u\ (u \in s$ & Wtu & $Cbus)))$ (by [129]). Since Bj & $l \in j$, $Calj \leftrightarrow \exists u\ (u \in j$ & Wlu & $Cbuj)$. Then $Calj$, which contradicts a previous result. Hence $\neg F^*al$.

Thus: $S_t a$ & Xl & $\neg T^*al$ & $\neg F^*al$. In other words, Bivalence fails for some 'tomorrow'-assertion.

A similar argument, based on the same diagram, establishes that Bivalence fails for some future-tense predicative assertion: take a and b to be such that $S_y b$ & $I_f ab$ & Kcb & Hdb, and establish that $S_f a$ & Xl & $\neg T^*al$ & $\neg F^*al$.

Excluded Middle is valid: (i) general considerations. In what sense does *Int.* 9 endorse Excluded Middle? Surely *not* in the sense of claiming that every disjunctive assertion with contradictory disjuncts is always true, or necessarily true. Again, *not* in the sense of claiming, with regard to certain disjunctive assertions with contradictory disjuncts, that they are always true, or necessarily true – e.g. Aristotle does not claim that utterances of 'A sea-battle will take place tomorrow or a sea-battle will not take place tomorrow' are always true, or necessarily true. In general, *Int.* 9's endorsement of Excluded Middle does not involve *mentioning* disjunctive assertions with contradictory disjuncts.

Int. 9's endorsement of Excluded Middle involves *using* some disjunctive assertion whose disjuncts are future inflections of contradictory assertions to state that something is necessary. Here is what Aristotle says:

> It is necessary that everything should either be or not be, and either be going to be or not [. . .]. For example, I mean that it is necessary that either there will be a sea-battle tomorrow or there will not be one, but it is not necessary that tomorrow a sea-battle should come to be nor that it should not come to be: however, it is necessary that one should either come to be or not come to be. (19^a28–32 < T53)

Hence, to establish the coherence of *Int.* 9, *it is not necessary* to show that every disjunctive assertion with contradictory disjuncts is always true, or that every disjunctive assertion whose disjuncts are future inflections of contradictory assertions is always true.[24] However, showing that every disjunctive assertion of the kinds described is always true *suffices* to establish the coherence of *Int.* 9. For, if every such disjunctive assertion is always true, then in particular it is true before any given time. Then, on the basis of the deterministic argument whose validity he accepts, Aristotle is justified in using the disjunctive assertion to state antecedent necessity (ineluctability). For instance, if an utterance of 'Tomorrow a sea-battle will take place or tomorrow a sea-battle will not take place' is true now, Aristotle is justified in saying that it is now necessary that either tomorrow a sea-battle will take place or tomorrow a sea-battle will not take place. The present semantic theory can show that every disjunctive assertion of the kinds described is always true.

Excluded Middle is valid: (ii) formulation with 'internal negation'. Aristotle does not recognise 'external negation', i.e. an operator 'it is not the case that . . .' whose utterances attach to complete sentences.[25] Hence, although the present semantic theory does have 'external negation', appealing to it would hardly count as a vindication of Aristotle. However, in the present

[24] Cf. Linsky (1954), 250–1; D. Frede (1970), 75–6; Sorabji (1980), 94; D. Frede (1985), 77; Weidemann (1994/2002), 319.

[25] However he does sometimes use 'external negation': see *Int.* 11, 20^b35–6.

semantic theory it can be shown that every disjunction whose disjuncts are 'tomorrow'-assertions inflected from contradictory present-tense predicative assertions is always true (this includes utterances of 'Tomorrow a sea-battle will take place or tomorrow a sea-battle will not take place'). Here are the precise formulation and the proof:

[141] $\forall x \forall y \forall z \forall u \forall v\, (I_v xyz\ \&\ I_t yu\ \&\ I_t zv\ \&\ ((S_a u\ \&\ S_o v) \vee (S_e u\ \&\ S_i v) \vee (S_i u\ \&\ S_e v) \vee (S_o u\ \&\ S_a v) \vee (S_y u\ \&\ S_d v) \vee (S_d u\ \&\ S_y v))\ \&\ C_k uv\ \&\ C_h uv \rightarrow \forall t\, (Xt \rightarrow T^* xt))$.

Let a, b, c, d, and e be such that $I_v abc\ \&\ I_t bd\ \&\ I_t ce\ \&\ ((S_a d\ \&\ S_o e) \vee (S_e d\ \&\ S_i e) \vee (S_i d\ \&\ S_e e) \vee (S_o d\ \&\ S_a e) \vee (S_y d\ \&\ S_d e) \vee (S_d d\ \&\ S_y e))\ \&\ C_k de\ \&\ C_h de$. Since $(S_a d\ \&\ S_o e) \vee (S_e d\ \&\ S_i e) \vee (S_i d\ \&\ S_e e) \vee (S_o d\ \&\ S_a e) \vee (S_y d\ \&\ S_d e) \vee (S_d d\ \&\ S_y e)$, it follows that $(S_a d \vee S_e d \vee S_i d \vee S_o d \vee S_y d \vee S_d d)\ \&\ (S_a e \vee S_e e \vee S_i e \vee S_o e \vee S_y e \vee S_d e)$. Then $S_n d\ \&\ S_n e$ (by [58]). Then $S_n d\ \&\ I_t bd$, so that $\exists y\, (S_n y\ \&\ I_t by)$, whence $S_t b$ (by [101]). Similarly, we have $S_n e\ \&\ I_t ce$, so that $\exists y\, (S_n y\ \&\ I_t cy)$, whence $S_t c$ (again by [101]). Then $(S_n b \vee S_b b \vee S_f b \vee S_t b \vee S_c b)\ \&\ (S_n c \vee S_b c \vee S_f c \vee S_t c \vee S_c c)\ \&\ I_v abc$, so that $\exists y \exists z\, ((S_n y \vee S_b y \vee S_f y \vee S_t y \vee S_c y)\ \&\ (S_n z \vee S_b z \vee S_f z \vee S_t z \vee S_c z)\ \&\ I_v ayz)$. Then (by [103]) $S_v a$. Then (by [105]) Sa. Since $S_n d\ \&\ S_n e\ \&\ C_k de\ \&\ C_h de$, $C_k ed\ \&\ C_h ed$ (by [83]).

Let Xf. Let g be such that $Bg\ \&\ f \in g$. Then $\exists s\, (s \in g\ \&\ Wfs)$ (by [125]). Let then h be such that $h \in g\ \&\ Wfh$. Since $Bg\ \&\ h \in g$, Xh (by [121]). Distinguish two cases.

(1) Suppose that $Cehg$. Then $h \in g\ \&\ Wfh\ \&\ Cehg$, so that $\exists u\, (u \in g\ \&\ Wfu\ \&\ Ceug)$. Since $S_n e\ \&\ I_t ce$, $\forall s \forall t\, (Bs\ \&\ t \in s \rightarrow (Ccts \leftrightarrow \exists u\, (u \in s\ \&\ Wtu\ \&\ Ceus)))$ (by [129]). Since $Bg\ \&\ f \in g$, $Ccfg \leftrightarrow \exists u\, (u \in g\ \&\ Wfu\ \&\ Ceug)$. Hence $Ccfg$, so that $Cbfg \vee Ccfg$.

(2) Suppose that $\neg Cehg$. Since $S_n e$, $\forall s \forall t\, (Bs\ \&\ t \in s \rightarrow (Cets \leftrightarrow Tet))$ (by [126]). Since $Bg\ \&\ h \in g$, $Cehg \leftrightarrow Teh$. Hence $\neg Teh$. Since $(S_a d\ \&\ S_o e) \vee (S_e d\ \&\ S_i e) \vee (S_i d\ \&\ S_e e) \vee (S_o d\ \&\ S_a e) \vee (S_y d\ \&\ S_d e) \vee (S_d d\ \&\ S_y e)$, distinguish four subordinate cases. (2.1) If $(S_a d\ \&\ S_o e) \vee (S_e d\ \&\ S_i e)$, then $((S_a d\ \&\ S_o e) \vee (S_e d\ \&\ S_i e))\ \&\ C_k de\ \&\ C_h de$. Then (by [90]) $\forall t\, (Xt \rightarrow (Tdt \leftrightarrow \neg Tet))$. Since Xh, $Tdh \leftrightarrow \neg Teh$. Hence Tdh. (2.2) If $(S_i d\ \&\ S_e e) \vee (S_o d\ \&\ S_a e)$, then $((S_a e\ \&\ S_o d) \vee (S_e e\ \&\ S_i d))\ \&\ C_k ed\ \&\ C_h ed$. Then (again by [90]) $\forall t\, (Xt \rightarrow (Tet \leftrightarrow \neg Tdt))$. Since Xh, $Teh \leftrightarrow \neg Tdh$. Then $\neg\neg Tdh$, whence Tdh. (2.3) If $S_y d\ \&\ S_d e$, then $S_y d\ \&\ S_d e\ \&\ C_k de\ \&\ C_h de$. Then (by [95]) $\forall t\, (Xt \rightarrow (Tdt \leftrightarrow \neg Tet))$. Since Xh, $Tdh \leftrightarrow \neg Teh$. Hence Tdh. (2.4) If $S_d d\ \&\ S_y e$, then $S_y e\ \&\ S_d d\ \&\ C_k ed\ \&\ C_h ed$. Then (again by [95]) $\forall t\, (Xt \rightarrow (Tet \leftrightarrow \neg Tdt))$. Since Xh, $Teh \leftrightarrow \neg Tdh$. Then $\neg\neg Tdh$, whence Tdh. Thus, in

each of the four subordinate cases, Tdh. Since $S_n d$, $\forall s\, \forall t\, (Bs\ \&\ t \in s \rightarrow (Cdts \leftrightarrow Tdt))$ (by [126]). Since $Bg\ \&\ h \in g$, $Cdhg \leftrightarrow Tdh$. Hence $Cdhg$. Then $h \in g\ \&\ Wfh\ \&\ Cdhg$, so that $\exists u\, (u \in g\ \&\ Wfu\ \&\ Cdug)$. Since $S_n d\ \&\ I_t bd$, $\forall s\, \forall t\, (Bs\ \&\ t \in s \rightarrow (Cbts \leftrightarrow \exists u\, (u \in s\ \&\ Wtu\ \&\ Cdus)))$ (by [129]). Since $Bg\ \&\ f \in g$, $Cbfg \leftrightarrow \exists u\, (u \in g\ \&\ Wfu\ \&\ Cdug)$. Hence $Cbfg$, so that $Cbfg \vee Ccfg$.

Thus, in all cases, $Cbfg \vee Ccfg$. Since $(S_n b \vee S_b b \vee S_f b \vee S_t b \vee S_c b)\ \&\ (S_n c \vee S_b c \vee S_f c \vee S_t c \vee S_c c)\ \&\ I_v abc$, it follows (by [131]) that $\forall s\, \forall t\, (Bs\ \&\ t \in s \rightarrow (Cats \leftrightarrow Cbts \vee Ccts))$. Since $Bg\ \&\ f \in g$, $Cafg \leftrightarrow Cbfg \vee Ccfg$. Hence $Cafg$. But g was arbitrary. Then $\forall s\, (Bs\ \&\ f \in s \rightarrow Cafs)$. Since $Sa\ \&\ Xf$, $T^*af \leftrightarrow \forall s\, (Bs\ \&\ f \in s \rightarrow Cafs)$ (by [138]). Then T^*af. But f was arbitrary. Then $\forall t\, (Xt \rightarrow T^*at)$. But a, b, c, d, and e were arbitrary. Then $\forall x\, \forall y\, \forall z\, \forall u\, \forall v\, (I_v xyz\ \&\ I_t yu\ \&\ I_t zv\ \&\ ((S_a u\ \&\ S_o v) \vee (S_e u\ \&\ S_i v) \vee (S_i u\ \&\ S_e v) \vee (S_o u\ \&\ S_a v) \vee (S_y u\ \&\ S_d v) \vee (S_d u\ \&\ S_y v))\ \&\ C_k uv\ \&\ C_h uv \rightarrow \forall t\, (Xt \rightarrow T^*xt))$, i.e. [141] holds.

Similarly, every disjunction whose disjuncts are future-tense predicative assertions inflected from contradictory present-tense predicative assertions is always true:

[142] $\forall x\, \forall y\, \forall z\, \forall u\, \forall v\, (I_v xyz\ \&\ I_f yu\ \&\ I_f zv\ \&\ ((S_a u\ \&\ S_o v) \vee (S_e u\ \&\ S_i v) \vee (S_i u\ \&\ S_e v) \vee (S_o u\ \&\ S_a v) \vee (S_y u\ \&\ S_d v) \vee (S_d u\ \&\ S_y v))\ \&\ C_k uv\ \&\ C_h uv \rightarrow \forall t\, (Xt \rightarrow T^*xt))$.

The proof of [142] resembles that of [141].

Excluded Middle is valid: (iii) formulation with 'external negation'. Since Aristotle does not recognise 'external negation', proving the validity of Excluded Middle for assertions formulated with 'external negation' goes beyond the range of tasks which Aristotle can be taken to set for himself. It is, none the less, worthwhile stating such a result:

[143] $\forall x\, \forall y\, \forall z\, \forall u\, ((S_n y \vee S_b y \vee S_f y \vee S_t y)\ \&\ (S_n u \vee S_b u \vee S_f u \vee S_t u)\ \&\ Oyu\ \&\ I_c zu\ \&\ I_v xyz \rightarrow \forall t\, (Xt \rightarrow T^*xt))$.

The proof, which is straightforward, is omitted.

References

AA. VV. 1936, *Actes du Congrès International de Philosophie Scientifique (Sorbonne, Paris, 1935)*, VI, Paris.
AA. VV. 1953, *Actes du XIème Congrès International de Philosophie, Bruxelles, 20–26 Août 1953*, Amsterdam and Louvain.
AA. VV. 1960, *Atti del XII Congresso Internazionale di Filosofia (Venezia, 12–18 Settembre 1958)*, XI, Florence.
AA. VV. 1975, *Scritti in onore di † Carlo Diano*, Bologna.
AA. VV. 1985, *Sapienza antica. Studi in onore di Domenico Pesce*, Milan.
AA. VV. 1986, *Philosophie du langage et grammaire dans l'antiquité*, Brussels.
AA. VV. 1988, *Proceedings of the XVIII International Congress of Papyrology*, I, Athens.
Abbagnano, N. 1971, *Dizionario di Filosofia*, 2nd edn, Turin.
Abrusci, V. M., Casari, E., and Mugnai, M. (eds.) 1983, *Atti del Convegno Internazionale di Storia della Logica, San Gimignano, 4–8 dicembre 1982*, Bologna.
Ackrill, J. L. 1972, 'Aristotle on "Good" and the Categories' = Ackrill (1997), 201–11.
— 1997, *Essays on Plato and Aristotle*, Oxford.
Ackrill, J. L. (trans. and comm.) 1963, Aristotle, *Categories and De Interpretatione*, Oxford.
ACPA = *Proceedings of the American Catholic Philosophical Association.*
Adorno, F. 1961, *La filosofia antica*, I, Milan.
AGPh = *Archiv für Geschichte der Philosophie.*
Alberti, A. (ed.) 1990, *Logica, mente e persona. Studi sulla filosofia antica*, Florence.
— (ed.) 1994, *Realtà e ragione. Studi di filosofia antica*, Florence.
Albritton, R. A. 1957, 'Present Truth and Future Contingency', *PR* 66: 29–46.
Algra, K. A. A., Barnes, J., Mansfeld, J., and Schofield, M. (eds.) 1999, *The Cambridge History of Hellenistic Philosophy*, Cambridge.
Algra, K. A. A., van der Horst, P. W., and Runia, D. T. (eds.) 1996, *Polyhistor: Studies . . . Presented to Jaap Mansfeld . . .*, Leiden, New York, and Cologne.
Angelelli, I. and Cerezo, M. (eds.) 1996, *Studies on the History of Logic: Proceedings of the III Symposium on the History of Logic*, Berlin and New York.
Anscombe, G. E. M. 1956/68, 'Aristotle and the Sea Battle: De Interpretatione, Chapter IX' = Moravcsik (1968), 15–33.
Anscombe, G. E. M. and Geach, P. T. 1961, *Three Philosophers*, Oxford.

Antiseri, D. (trans. and comm.) 1969, Aristotele, *De Interpretatione*, Bergamo.
Anton, J. P. 1992, 'On the Meaning of Kategoria in Aristotle's Categories' = Preus/Anton (1992), 1–18.
AP = *Ancient Philosophy*.
Apelt, O. 1891a, *Beiträge zur Geschichte der griechischen Philosophie*, Leipzig.
— 1891b, 'Die Kategorieenlehre des Aristoteles' = Apelt (1891a), 101–216.
Apostle, H. G. (trans. and comm.) 1966, Aristotle, *Metaphysics*, Bloomington, Ind. and London.
— (trans. and comm.) 1980, Aristotle, *Categories and Propositions (De Interpretatione)*, Grinnell, Ia.
— (trans. and comm.) 1981, Aristotle, *On the Soul*, Grinnell, Ia.
Arens, H. 1984, *Aristotle's Theory of Language and its Tradition: Texts from 500 to 1750*, Amsterdam and Philadelphia.
Astroh, M. 1981, 'Apophansis und Kontingenz. Zum neunten Kapitel der Schrift Peri Hermeneias', *Tijdschrift voor Filosofie* 43: 328–62.
Aubenque, P. 1962/83, *Le problème de l'être chez Aristote. Essai sur la problématique aristotélicienne*, 5th edn, Paris.
— 1979a, 'La pensée du simple dans la Métaphysique (Z 17 et Θ 10)' = Aubenque (1979b), 69–80.
Aubenque, P. (ed.) 1979b, *Etudes sur la* Métaphysique *d'Aristote – Actes du VIe Symposium Aristotelicum*, Paris.
— (ed.) 1980, *Concepts et catégories dans la pensée antique*, Paris.
Austin, J. L. 1950, 'Truth' = Blackburn/Simmons (1999), 149–61.
Avgelis, N. and Peonidis, F. (eds.) 1998, *Aristotle on Logic, Language and Science*, Thessaloniki.
BACAP = *Proceedings of the Boston Area Colloquium in Ancient Philosophy*.
Bäck, A. T. 1992, 'Sailing through the Sea Battle', *AP* 12: 133–51.
— 2000, *Aristotle's Theory of Predication*, Leiden, Boston, and Cologne.
Badawi, A. 1971, *Commentaires sur Aristote perdus en Grec*, Beirut.
— 1987, *La transmission de la philosophie grecque au monde arabe*, 2nd edn, Paris.
Baldassarri, M. (ed., trans., and comm.) 1985/87, *La logica stoica. Testimonianze e frammenti*, Como.
Bambrough, R. (ed.) 1965, *New Essays on Plato and Aristotle*, London and New York.
Bar-Hillel, Y. (ed.) 1965, *Logic, Methodology and Philosophy of Science: Proceedings of the 1964 International Congress*, Amsterdam.
Barnes, J. 1986, 'Peripatetic Negations', *OSAP* 4: 201–14.
— 1993, 'Meaning, Saying and Thinking' = Döring/Ebert (1993), 47–61.
— 1995a, 'Metaphysics' = Barnes (1995b), 66–108.
— 1996, 'Grammar on Aristotle's Terms' = Frede/Striker (1996), 175–202.
— 1999a, 'Aristotle and Stoic Logic' = Ierodiakonou (1999), 23–53.
— 1999b, 'Logic: 1 The Peripatetics' = Algra/Barnes/Mansfeld/Schofield (1999), 77–83.
Barnes, J. (ed.) 1995b, *The Cambridge Companion to Aristotle*, Cambridge.
Barnes, J. (trans. and comm.) 1994, Aristotle, *Posterior Analytics*, 2nd edn, Oxford.

Bärthlein, K. 1972, *Die Transzendentalienlehre der alten Ontologie*, 1, Berlin and New York.
Battegazzore, A. M. (ed.) 1993, *Dimostrazione, argomentazione dialettica e argomentazione retorica nel pensiero antico. Atti del Convegno di Filosofia (Bocca di Magra, 18–22 marzo 1990)*, Genoa.
Baudry, L. 1950, *La querelle des futurs contingents (Louvain 1465–1475). Textes inédits*, Paris.
Baylis, C. A. 1936, 'Are Some Propositions neither True nor False?', *Philosophy of Science* 3: 156–66.
Beaney, M. 1996, *Frege: Making Sense*, London.
Becker, A. 1936, 'Bestreitet Aristoteles die Gültigkeit des "Tertium non datur" für Zukunftsaussagen? (Zum 9. Kapitel der Aristotelischen Hermeneutik)' = AA. VV. (1936), 69–74.
Becker, O. 1957a, *Zwei Untersuchungen zur antiken Logik*, Wiesbaden.
— 1957b, 'Chrysippos über den "Lügner"' = O. Becker (1957a), 50–2.
Bekker, I. and Gigon, O. (eds.) 1960/87, Aristotelis *Opera*, 2nd ed., Berlin.
Belardi, W. 1977, 'Semantica di σύνδεσμος e di ἀσύνδετος in Aristotele', *Rivista di filologia e di istruzione classica* 105: 257–73.
Bencivenga, E., Lambert, K., and van Fraassen, B. C. 1986/91, *Logic, Bivalence, and Denotation*, 2nd edn, Atascadero, Calif.
Benson, H. H. 1988, 'Universals as Sortals in the *Categories*', *Pacific Philosophical Quarterly* 69: 282–306.
Ben-Zeev, A. 1984, 'Aristotle on Perceptual Truth and Falsity', *Apeiron* 18: 118–25.
Berti, E. 1978, 'The Intellection of "Indivisibles" according to Aristotle, de Anima III 6' = Lloyd/Owen (1978), 141–63.
— 1983a, 'La fonction de Métaph. Alpha Elatton dans la philosophie d'Aristote' = Moraux/Wiesner (1983), 260–94.
— 1983b, 'Quelques remarques sur la conception aristotélicienne du non-être', *RPA* 1: 115–42.
— 1990, 'Heidegger e il concetto aristotelico di verità' = Brague/Courtine (1990), 97–120.
— 1992, *Aristotele nel Novecento*, Rome and Bari.
— 1993, 'Intellezione e dialettica in Aristotele, *Metaph.* IX 10' = Battegazzore (1993), 21–36.
— 1994, 'Encore sur l'intellection des "indivisibles" selon Aristote, *De anima* III 6' = Alberti (1994), 123–36.
— 1996a, 'Encore sur l'intellection des "indivisibles" selon Aristote, *De anima* III 6' = Romeyer Dherbey/Viano (1996), 391–404.
— 1996b, 'La logica dell'argomentazione filosofica tra Aristotele e Ryle' = Guetti/Pujia (1996), 59–68.
— 2000, 'I luoghi della verità secondo Aristotele. Un confronto con Heidegger' = Melchiorre (2000), 3–27.
Berti, E. (ed.) 1981, *Aristotle on Science: The 'Posterior Analytics' – Proceedings of the Eighth Symposium Aristotelicum Held in Padua from September 7 to 15, 1978*, Padua.

— (ed.) 1997, *Guida ad Aristotele*, Rome and Bari.
Besoli, S. 1985, 'Percezione, verità e giudizio: luoghi dell'intuizionismo aristotelico' = Besoli (2002), 9–54.
— 2002, *Esistenza, verità e giudizio. Percorsi di critica e fenomenologia della conoscenza*, Macerata.
BICS = *Bulletin of the Institute of Classical Studies*.
Bird, O. 1964, *Syllogistic and Its Extensions*, Englewood Cliffs, NJ.
Birondo, N. 2001, 'Aristotle on Illusory Perception: Phantasia without Phantasmata', *AP* 21: 57–71.
Blackburn, S. and Simmons, K. (eds.) 1999, *Truth*, Oxford.
Blanché, R. and Dubucs, J. 1970/96, *La logique et son histoire*, Paris.
Blank, D. (trans. and comm.) 1996, Ammonius, *On Aristotle On Interpretation 1–8*, London.
Blank, D. and Kretzmann, N. (eds., trans., and comm.) 1998, *On Determinism: Ammonius* On Aristotle On Interpretation 9 *with Boethius* On Aristotle On Interpretation 9 *First and Second Commentaries*, London.
Blettner, E. 1983, 'One Made Many and Many Made One: The Role of Asyndeton in Aristotle's Rhetoric', *Philosophy and Rhetoric* 16: 49–54.
Block, I. 1961, 'Truth and Error in Aristotle's Theory of Sense Perception', *PQ* 11: 1–9.
Bobzien, S. 1998, *Determinism and Freedom in Stoic Philosophy*, Oxford.
— 2000, 'Wholly Hypothetical Syllogisms', *Phronesis* 45: 87–137.
— 2002, 'The Development of *Modus Ponens* in Antiquity: From Aristotle to the 2nd Century AD', *Phronesis* 47: 359–94.
Bochenski, I. M. 1947, *La logique de Théophraste*, Fribourg en Suisse.
— 1951, *Ancient Formal Logic*, Amsterdam.
— 1962, *Formale Logik*, 2nd edn, Freiburg and Munich.
Bodéüs, R. (trans. and comm.) 1993, Aristote, *De l'âme*, Paris.
Bodéüs, R. (ed. and comm.) 2001, Aristote, *[Catégories]*, Paris.
Boehner, P., Moody, E. A., Gál, G., Gambatese, A., and Brown, S. (eds.) 1978, William of Ockham, *Expositionis in Libros Artis Logicae Prooemium, Expositio in Librum Porphyrii de Predicabilibus, Expositio in Librum Praedicamentorum Aristotelis, Expositio in Librum Perihermeneias Aristotelis, Tractatus de Praedestinatione et de Praescientia Dei respectu Futurorum Contingentium*, St Bonaventure, NY.
Bolton, R. 1976, 'Essentialism and Semantic Theory in Aristotle: *Posterior Analytics*, II, 7–10', *PR* 85: 514–44.
Bonitz, H. 1842, *Observationes criticae in Aristotelis libros metaphysicos*, Berlin.
— 1862/67, *Aristotelische Studien*, repr., Hildesheim 1969.
— 1870, *Index Aristotelicus*, repr., Graz 1955.
Bonitz, H. (ed. and comm.) 1848/49, Aristotelis *Metaphysica*, Bonn.
Bonitz, H. (trans.) 1890, Aristoteles, *Metaphysik*, repr., Munich 1966.
Bonomi, A. and Zucchi, A. 2001, *Tempo e linguaggio. Introduzione alla semantica del tempo e dell'aspetto verbale*, Milan.

Bormann, K. 1982, 'Wahrheitsbegriff und νοῦς-Lehre bei Aristoteles und einigen seiner Kommentatoren', *Miscellanea Mediaevalia* 12: 1–24.
Bosley, R. 1977, 'In Support of an Interpretation of *On Int.* 9', *Ajatus* 37: 29–40.
Bostock, D. (trans. and comm.) 1994, Aristotle, *Metaphysics: Books Z and H*, Oxford.
Bottani, A., Carrara, M., and Giaretta, P. (eds.) 2002, *Individuals, Essence and Identity: Themes of Analytic Metaphysics*, Dordrecht, Boston, and London.
Boudot, M. 1973, 'Temps, nécessité et prédétermination', *Les Études Philosophiques* n.n.: 435–73.
Bradley, R. D. 1959/68, 'Must the Future Be What It Is Going to Be?' = Gale (1968), 232–51.
Brague, R. and Courtine, F. (eds.) 1990, *Herméneutique et ontologie. Mélanges en hommage à Pierre Aubenque*, Paris.
Brakas, G. 1988, *Aristotle's Concept of the Universal*, Hildesheim, Zurich, and New York.
Brandis, C. A. 1835/66, *Handbuch der Geschichte der griechisch-römischen Philosophie*, Berlin.
— 1862/64, *Geschichte der Entwicklungen der griechischen Philosophie und ihrer Nachwirkungen im römischen Reiche*, repr., Hildesheim and New York 1981.
Brandis, C. A. (ed.) 1823, Aristotelis et Theophrasti *Metaphysica*, Berlin.
Brandt, R. 1965, *Die Aristotelische Urteilslehre. Untersuchungen zur 'Hermeneutik'*, Marburg.
Brentano, F. 1862, *Von der mannigfachen Bedeutung des Seienden nach Aristoteles*, repr., Darmstadt 1960.
— 1874/1925, *Psychologie vom empirischen Standpunkt*, ed. by O. Kraus, repr., Hamburg 1955 and 1959.
— 1889, 'Über den Begriff der Wahrheit' = Brentano (1930), 3–29.
— 1909, 'De Interpretatione' = Brentano (1986), 59–65.
— 1914a, 'Über die Entstehung der irrigen Lehre von den entia irrealia' = Brentano (1930), 162–4.
— 1914b, 'Zur Frage der Existenz der Inhalte und von der adaequatio rei et intellectus' = Brentano (1930), 121–30.
— 1915a, Letter to O. Kraus dated 9 January, 1915, partly quoted in Brentano (1930), 219–20.
— 1915b, 'Über den Sinn des Satzes: veritas est adaequatio rei et intellectus' = Brentano (1930), 131–6.
— 1930, *Wahrheit und Evidenz*, ed. by O. Kraus, repr., Hamburg 1974.
— 1952, *Grundlegung und Aufbau der Ethik*, ed. by F. Mayer-Hillebrand, Bern.
— 1986, *Über Aristoteles*, ed. by R. George, Hamburg.
— n.d., 'Aristoteles' Lehre von der mannigfachen Bedeutung des Seienden' = Brentano (1986), 190–7.
Brown, L. 1994, 'The Verb "To Be" in Greek Philosophy: Some Remarks' = Everson (1994), 212–36.
Brunschwig, J. 1969, 'La proposition particulière et les preuves de non-concluance chez Aristote', *Cahiers pour l'Analyse* 10: 3–26.

— 1979, 'La forme, prédicat de la matière?' = Aubenque (1979b), 131–66.
— 1991, 'On a Book-Title by Chrysipppus: "On the Fact that the Ancients Admitted Dialectic along with Demonstrations"', *OSAP* suppl. vol.: 81–95.
— 1999, 'Homonymie et contradiction dans la dialectique aristotélicienne' = Büttgen/Diebler/Rashed (1999), 81–101.
Brunschwig, J. (ed., trans., and comm.) 1967, Aristote, *Topiques*, I, Paris.
Buhle, I. T. (ed., trans., and comm.) 1792/1800, Aristotelis *Opera Omnia Graece*..., Biponti.
Bullinger, A. 1882, *Aristoteles' Nus-Lehre (De an. III, c. 4–8 incl.)*, Dillingen.
Burnyeat, M. 2002, '*De Anima* II 5', *Phronesis* 47: 28–90.
Burnyeat, M. *et al.* 1984, *Notes on Eta and Theta of Aristotle's Metaphysics*, Oxford.
Burrell, D. 1964, 'Aristotle and "Future Contingencies"', *Philosophical Studies* (Ireland) 13: 37–52.
Bussemaker, C., Dübner, F., and Heitz, A. (eds. and trans.) 1848/74, Aristotelis *Opera Omnia Graece et Latine*, Paris.
Butler, R. J. 1955, 'Aristotle's Sea Fight and Three-Valued Logic', *PR* 64: 264–74.
Butterworth, C. E. (trans. and comm.) 1983, Averroes, *Middle Commentaries on Aristotle's Categories and De Interpretatione*, Princeton.
Büttgen, P., Diebler, S., and Rashed, M. (eds.) 1999, *Théories de la phrase et de la proposition de Platon à Averroès*, Paris.
Bywater, I. 1913, 'Aristotelia V', *The Journal of Philology* 32: 107–22.
Bywater, I. (ed. and comm.) 1909, Aristotle, *On the Art of Poetry*, Oxford.
Cahn, S. M. 1967, *Fate, Logic, and Time*, New Haven and London.
Calogero, G. 1927, 'Una nuova concezione della logica prearistotelica' = Calogero (1984), 349–62.
— 1927/68, *I fondamenti della logica aristotelica*, 2nd edn, Florence.
— 1984, *Scritti minori di filosofia antica*, Naples.
Capozzi, G. 1974, *Giudizio, prova e verità. I principi della scienza nell'analitica di Aristotele*, Naples.
Carson, D. S. 1996, *Being and Truth: Elements of Aristotle's Philosophy of Language*, diss. (Duke University).
Casari, E. 1984, 'Note sulla logica aristotelica della comparazione', *Sileno* 10: 131–46.
Cashdollar, S. 1973, 'Aristotle's Account of Incidental Perception', *Phronesis* 18: 156–75.
Cassin, B. 1996, 'Enquête sur le *logos* dans le *De anima*' = Romeyer Dherbey/Viano (1996), 257–93.
Cassirer, H. 1932, *Aristoteles' Schrift 'Von der Seele' und ihre Stellung innerhalb der aristotelischen Philosophie*, Tübingen.
Caston, V. 1996, 'Why Aristotle Needs Imagination', *Phronesis* 41: 20–55.
— 1998a, 'Aristotle and the Problem of Intentionality', *Philosophy and Phenomenological Research* 58: 249–98.
— 1998b, 'Commentary on Kurt Pritzl: Aristotle on the Conditions of Thought', *BACAP* 14: 202–12.
Caston, V. and Graham, D. W. (eds.) 2002, *Presocratic Philosophy: Essays in Honour of Alexander Mourelatos*, Aldershot.

Cathala, M.-R. and Spiazzi, R. M. (eds.) 1950, S. Thomae Aquinatis *in Duodecim Libros Metaphysicorum Aristotelis Expositio*, Turin and Rome.
Cavini, W. 1985, 'La negazione di frase nella logica greca' = Cavini/Donnini Macciò/Funghi/Manetti (1985), 7–126.
— 1993a, 'Chrysippus on Speaking Truly and the Liar' = Döring/Ebert (1993), 85–109.
— 1993b, 'Aristotele e i modi del paradosso' = Battegazzore (1993), 61–81.
— 1998, 'Arguing from a Definition: Aristotle on Truth and the Excluded Middle' = Avgelis/Peonidis (1998), 5–15.
Cavini, W., Donnini Macciò, M. C., Funghi, M. S., and Manetti, D. 1985, *Studi su papiri greci di logica e medicina*, Florence.
Celluprica, V. 1977, *Il capitolo 9 del 'De interpretatione' di Aristotele. Rassegna di studi: 1930–1973*, Bologna.
— 1987, 'Logica e semantica nella teoria aristotelica della predicazione', *Phronesis* 32: 166–87.
Charles, D. 1994, 'Aristotle on Names and Their Signification' = Everson (1994), 37–73.
— 1997, 'Method and Argument in the Study of Aristotle: A Critical Notice of *The Cambridge Companion to Aristotle*', *OSAP* 15: 231–57.
— 2000, *Aristotle on Meaning and Essence*, Oxford.
— 2002, 'Some Comments on Prof. Enrico Berti's "Being and Essence in Contemporary Interpretations of Aristotle"' = Bottani/Carrara/Giaretta (2002), 109–26.
Chisholm, R. M. 1966, *Theory of Knowledge*, Englewood Cliffs, NJ.
Chisholm, R. M. and Haller, R. (eds.) 1978, *Die Philosophie Franz Brentanos: Beiträge zur Brentano-Konferenz (Graz, 4.–8. September 1977)*, Amsterdam.
Christ, W. (ed.) 1906, Aristotelis *Metaphysica*, 2nd edn, Leipzig.
Church, A. 1965, 'The History of the Question of Existential Import of Categorical Propositions' = Bar-Hillel (1965), 417–24.
Cleary, J. J. 1988, *Aristotle on the Many Senses of Priority*, Carbondale and Edwardsville.
Code, A. 1976, 'Aristotle's Response to Quine's Objections to Modal Logic', *Journal of Philosophical Logic* 5: 159–86.
Colli, G. (trans. and comm.) 1955, Aristotele, *Organon*, Turin.
Conybeare, F. C. 1892, *Anecdota Oxoniensia: A Collation with the Ancient Armenian Versions of the Greek Text of Aristotle's Categories, de Interpretatione, de Mundo, de Virtutibus et Vitiis, and of Porphyry's Introduction*, Oxford.
Cooke, H. P. and Tredennick, H. (eds. and trans.) 1938, Aristotle, *The Categories, On Interpretation, Prior Analytics*, Cambridge, Mass. and London.
Cope, E. M. and Sandys, J. E. (eds. and comm.) 1877, *The Rhetoric of* Aristotle, Cambridge.
Corsi, G., Mangione, C., and Mugnai, M. (eds.) 1989, *Atti del Convegno Internazionale di Storia della Logica. Le teorie delle modalità (San Gimignano, 5–8 dicembre 1987)*, Bologna.

Cosenza, P. 1983, 'Procedimenti di trasformazione nella sillogistica di Aristotele' = Abrusci/Casari/Mugnai (1983), 223–8.
— 1987, *Logica formale e antiformalismo (da Aristotele a Descartes)*, Naples.
Craig, W. L. 1988, *The Problem of Divine Foreknowledge and Future Contingency from Aristotle to Suarez*, Leiden, New York, Copenhagen, and Cologne.
Cresswell, M. J. 1971, 'Essence and Existence in Plato and Aristotle', *Theoria* 37: 91–113.
Crivelli, P. 1989, 'Presupposti esistenziali della negazione in Aristotele', *Annali del Dipartimento di Filosofia – Università di Firenze* 5: 45–90.
— 1990, 'Il "Sofista" di Platone. Non essere, negazione e falsità', *Atti e memorie dell'Accademia Toscana di Scienze e Lettere 'La Colombaria'* 55: 9–104.
— 1996, 'Notes on Aristotle's Conception of Truth' = Funghi (1996), 147–59.
— 1999, 'Aristotle on the Truth of Utterances', *OSAP* 17: 37–56.
— 2001, 'Empty Terms in Aristotle's Logic', *BACAP* 17: 237–69, 282–4.
— 2002, 'Sameness in Aristotle's *Topics*' = Bottani/Carrara/Giaretta (2002), 239–45.
Damschen, G. 2001, 'Aristoteles, "Analytica Posteriora" A 2, 72a8–9: "Der eine Teil einer Aussage"', *Hermes* 129: 125–8.
Dancy, R. M. 1986, 'Aristotle and Existence' = Knuuttila/Hintikka (1986), 49–80.
Dapunt, I. 1968, 'Zwei Typen von Systemen der traditionellen Logik', *AGPh* 50: 275–81.
David, M. 1994, *Correspondence and Disquotation: An Essay on the Nature of Truth*, New York and Oxford.
Davidson, D. 1996, 'The Folly of Trying to Define Truth', *JP* 93: 263–78.
Décarie, V. 1961, *L'objet de la métaphysique selon Aristote*, Montreal and Paris.
De Corte, M. 1934, *La doctrine de l'intelligence chez Aristote*, Paris.
de Koninck, T. 1990, 'La noêsis et l'indivisible selon Aristote' = Mattéi (1990), 215–28.
del Punta, F. (ed.) 1979, William of Ockham, *Expositio super Libros Elenchorum*, St Bonaventure, NY.
Demoss, D. and Devereux, D. T. 1988, 'Essence, Existence, and Nominal Definition in Aristotle's Posterior Analytics II 8–10', *Phronesis* 33: 133–54.
Deninger, J. G. 1961, *'Wahres Sein' in der Philosophie des Aristoteles*, Meisenheim am Glan.
Denyer, N. 1991, *Language, Thought and Falsehood in Ancient Greek Philosophy*, London and New York.
de Rijk, L. M. 1952, *The Place of the Categories of Being in Aristotle's Philosophy*, Assen.
— 1987, 'The Anatomy of the Proposition: Logos and Pragma in Plato and Aristotle' = de Rijk/Braakhuis (1987), 27–61.
— 1996, 'On Aristotle's Semantics in de Interpretatione 1–4' = Algra *et al.* (1996), 115–34.
— 2002, *Aristotle: Semantics and Ontology*, Leiden, Boston, and Cologne.
de Rijk, L. M. and Braakhuis, H. A. G. (eds.) 1987, *Logos and Pragma: Essays on the Philosophy of Language in Honour of Professor Gabriel Nuchelmans*, Nijmegen.

Detel, W. 1998, 'Aristotle's *Posterior Analytics* and the Path to the Principles' = Avgelis/Peonidis (1998), 155–81.

Devereux, D. T. 1992, 'Inherence and Primary Substance in Aristotle's *Categories*', *AP* 12: 113–31.

Diamond, C. and Teichmann, J. (eds.) 1979, *Intention and Intentionality: Essays in Honour of G. E. M. Anscombe*, Ithaca.

Dickason, A. 1976, 'Aristotle, the Sea Fight, and the Cloud', *JHP* 14: 11–22.

Dilthey, W. 1883, *Einleitung in die Geisteswissenschaften. Versuch einer Grundlegung für das Studium der Gesellschaft und der Geschichte*, 1, 7th edn, Stuttgart and Göttingen 1959.

Dod, B. G. (ed.) 1975, Aristoteles, *de Sophisticis Elenchis*, trans. by Boethius, James of Venice, and William of Moerbeke, Leiden and Brussels.

Donini, P. L. 1989, *Ethos. Aristotele e il determinismo*, Alessandria.

Döring, A. 1890, 'Die aristotelischen Definitionen von σύνδεσμος und ἄρθρον, Poetik c. 20', *AGPh* 3: 363–9.

Döring, K. 1972, *Die Megariker. Kommentierte Sammlung der Testimonien*, Amsterdam.

Döring, K. and Ebert, T. (eds.) 1993, *Dialektiker und Stoiker: Zur Logik der Stoa und ihrer Vorläufer*, Stuttgart.

Dorion, L.-A. (trans. and comm.) 1995, Aristote, *Les réfutations sophistiques*, Paris.

DuLac, H. 1949, 'The *Peri Hermeneias*: Its Place in Logic and Its Order', *Laval théologique et philosophique* 5: 161–9.

Duminil, M.-P. and Jaulin, A. (trans. and comm.) 1991, Aristote, *Metaphysiques. Livre Delta*, Toulouse.

Düring, I. 1961, *Aristotle's Protrepticus: An Attempt at Reconstruction*, Stockholm, Göteborg, and Uppsala.

— 1966, *Aristoteles. Darstellung und Interpretation seines Denkens*, Heidelberg.

Düring, I. and Owen, G. E. L. (eds.) 1960, *Aristotle and Plato in the Mid-Fourth Century: Papers of the Symposium Aristotelicum Held at Oxford in August 1957*, Göteborg.

Du Val, G. (ed. and comm.) 1629, Aristotelis *Opera Omnia Quae Exstant Graece et Latine . . .* , Paris.

Ebbesen, S. 1981, *Commentators and Commentaries on Aristotle's Sophistici Elenchi*, Leiden.

— 1986, 'The Chimera's Diary' = Knuuttila/Hintikka (1986), 115–42.

Edel, A. 1982, *Aristotle and His Philosophy*, Chapel Hill, NC.

Edwards, P. (ed.) 1967, *The Encyclopedia of Philosophy*, New York and London.

Enders, M. 1999, *Wahrheit und Notwendigkeit. Die Theorie der Wahrheit bei Anselm von Canterbury im Gesamtzusammenhang seines Denkens und unter besonderer Berücksichtigung seiner antiken Quellen (Aristoteles, Cicero, Augustinus, Boethius)*, Leiden, Boston, and Cologne.

Engel, P. 2002, *Truth*, Chesham.

Engelhardt, P. M. 1953, *Die Wahrheit in der Einheit und Entzweiung*, diss. (Univ. of Freiburg i. Br.).

Engmann, J. 1976, 'Imagination and Truth in Aristotle', *JHP* 14: 259–65.

Evans, G. 1979, 'Does Tense Logic Rest upon a Mistake?' = Evans (1985), 343–63.
— 1985, *Collected Papers*, Oxford.
Everson, S. (ed.) 1994, *Language*, Cambridge.
— 1995, 'Proper Sensibles and Καθ' Αὑτά Causes', *Phronesis* 40: 265–92.
— 1997, *Aristotle on Perception*, Oxford.
Fait, P. 1996, 'Il linguaggio e l'abaco (Aristotele, *Soph. El.* 1, 165a6–17)' = Funghi (1996), 181–90.
— 1998, 'L'éristique mise en formules', *Dialogue* 37: 131–54.
Fattal, M. 1996, 'L'intellection des indivisibles dans le *De anima* (III, 6) d'Aristote. Lectures arabes et modernes' = Romeyer Dherbey/Viano (1996), 423–40.
Faust, A. 1931/32, *Der Möglichkeitsgedanke. Systemgeschichtliche Untersuchungen*, repr., New York and London 1987.
Field, H. 1972, 'Tarski's Theory of Truth', *JP* 69: 347–75.
Fine, G. 1980, 'The One over Many', *PR* 89: 197–240.
— 1984a, 'Truth and Necessity in De Interpretatione 9', *History of Philosophy Quarterly* 1: 23–47.
— 1984b, 'Separation', *OSAP* 2: 31–87.
— 1985, 'Separation: A Reply to Morrison', *OSAP* 3: 159–65.
— 1993, *On Ideas: Aristotle's Criticism of Plato's Theory of Forms*, Oxford.
Fiorentino, F. 2001, 'Il problema della verità in Aristotele', *Sapienza* 54: 257–302.
Fleischer, M. 1984, *Wahrheit und Wahrheitsgrund: Zum Wahrheitsproblem und zu seiner Geschichte*, Berlin and New York.
Fonseca, P. 1577/89, *Commentarii in Metaphysicorum Aristotelis Stagiritae Libros*, rev. edn, Cologne 1615/24, repr., Hildesheim 1964.
Förster, A. (ed.) 1912, Aristotelis *de Anima Libri III*, Budapest.
Forster, E. S. and Furley, D. J. (eds. and trans.) 1955, Aristotle, *On Sophistical Refutations, On Coming-To-Be and Passing-Away, On the Cosmos*, Cambridge, Mass. and London.
Fortenbaugh, W. W., Huby, P. M., Sharples, R. W., and Gutas, D. (eds. and trans.) 1993, Theophrastus of Eresus, *Sources for His Life, Writings, Thought and Influence*, Leiden, New York, and Cologne.
Fox, J. F. 1987, 'Truthmaker', *Australasian Journal of Philosophy* 65: 189–207.
Fraser, K. 2002, 'Demonstrative Science and the Science of Being *qua* Being', *OSAP* 22: 43–82.
Frede, D. 1970, *Aristoteles und die 'Seeschlacht'. Das Problem der Contingentia Futura in De Interpretatione 9*, Göttingen.
— 1972, 'Omne quod est quando est necesse est esse', *AGPh* 54: 153–67.
— 1985, 'The Sea-Battle Reconsidered: A Defence of the Traditional Interpretation', *OSAP* 3: 31–87.
— 1990, 'Fatalism and Future Truth', *BACAP* 6: 195–227.
— 1998, 'Logik, Sprache und die Offenheit der Zukunft in der Antike: Bemerkungen zu zwei neuen Forschungsbeiträgen', *ZPhF* 52: 84–104.
Frede, M. 1967, *Prädikation und Existenzaussage: Platons Gebrauch von '. . . ist . . .' und '. . . ist nicht . . .' im Sophistes*, Göttingen.
— 1978, 'Individuals in Aristotle' = M. Frede (1987), 49–71, 367.

— 1981, 'Categories in Aristotle' = M. Frede (1987), 29–48, 367.
— 1987, *Essays in Ancient Philosophy*, Oxford.
Frede, M. and Patzig, G. 1988, *Aristoteles 'Metaphysik Z': Text, Übersetzung und Kommentar*, Munich.
Frede, M. and Striker, G. (eds.) 1996, *Rationality in Greek Thought*, Oxford.
Freese, J. H. (ed. and trans.) 1926, Aristotle, *The 'Art' of Rhetoric*, London and New York.
Freeland, C. 1992, 'Aristotle on the Sense of Touch' = Nussbaum/Oksenberg Rorty (1992/95), 227–48.
Frege, G. 1918/19, 'Die Verneinung', *Beiträge zur Philosophie des deutschen Idealismus* 1: 143–57.
Funghi, M. S. (ed.) 1996, *ΟΔΟΙ ΔΙΖΗΣΙΟΣ–Le vie della ricerca. Studi in onore di Francesco Adorno*, Florence.
Gabbay, D. and Guenthner, F. (eds.) 1983/89, *Handbook of Philosophical Logic*, Dordrecht, Boston, and Lancaster.
Gagnebin, C. (ed.) 1981, *Métaphysique, histoire de la philosophie. Recueil d'études offert à F. Brunner*, Neuchâtel.
Gale, R. M. 1961, 'Endorsing Predictions', *PR* 70: 376–85.
Gale, R. M. (ed.) 1968, *The Philosophy of Time: A Collection of Essays*, London and Melbourne.
Gallavotti, C. (ed., trans., and comm.) 1974, Aristotele, *Dell'arte poetica*, n.p.
Galluzzo, G. 1997/98, *Il concetto di verità nei primi scritti di S. Agostino*, diss. (University of Pisa).
— 2000, 'Il tema della verità dell'*Expositio Libri Peryermenias* di Tommaso d'Aquino', *Documenti e studi sulla tradizione filosofica medievale* 11: 217–57.
Gaskin, R. 1994, 'Fatalism, Foreknowledge and the Reality of the Future', *The Modern Schoolman* 81: 83–113.
— 1995, *The Sea Battle and the Master Argument: Aristotle and Diodorus Cronus on the Metaphysics of the Future*, Berlin and New York.
— 1996, 'Sea Battles, Worn-out Cloaks, and Other Matters of Interpretation: Weidemann on Aristotle's Peri Hermeneias', *AGPh* 78: 48–59.
— 1998, 'Simplicius on the Meaning of Sentences: A Commentary on In Cat. 396, 30–397, 28', *Phronesis* 43: 42–62.
Gaskin, R. (trans. and comm.) 2000, Simplicius, *On Aristotle Categories 9–15*, London.
Geach, P. T. 1963, 'Aristotle on Conjunctive Propositions' = Geach (1972), 13–27.
— 1968, 'History of the Corruptions of Logic' = Geach (1972), 44–61.
— 1972, *Logic Matters*, repr., Berkeley and Los Angeles 1980.
Geyser, G. J. A. M. 1917, *Die Erkenntnistheorie des Aristoteles*, repr., Aalen 1980.
Gigon, O. and Fischer, M. W. (eds.) 1988, *Antike Rechts- und Sozialphilosophie*, Frankfurt a. M., Bern, New York, and Paris.
Gobbo, E. 1997, 'La concezione "diretta" dell' ἔλεγχος negli *Analitici primi* e nelle *Confutazioni sofistiche*', *Elenchos* 18: 311–57.
Gohlke, P. (trans. and comm.) 1951, Aristoteles, *Kategorien und Hermeneutik*, Paderborn.

— (trans. and comm.) 1961, Aristoteles, *Metaphysik*, 2nd edn, Paderborn.
Goldin, O. 1996, *Explaining an Eclipse: Aristotle's* Posterior Analytics *2.1–10*, Ann Arbor.
— 2002, 'To Tell the Truth: *Dissoi Logoi* 4 and Aristotle's Responses' = Caston/Graham (2002), 233–49.
Gómez-Lobo, A. 1980, 'The So-Called Question of Existence in Aristotle, An. Post. 2. 1–2', *RM* 34: 71–89.
Goodwin, W. W. 1889, *Syntax of the Moods and Tenses of the Greek Verb*, repr., Bristol 1998.
Gourinat, J.-B. 2000, *La dialectique des stoïciens*, Paris.
Graeser, A. 1977, 'On Language, Thought, and Reality in Ancient Greek Philosophy', *Dialectica* 31: 359–88.
— 1978, 'Sprache und Ontologie bei Aristoteles', *Freiburger Zeitschrift für Philosophie und Theologie* 25: 443–55.
— 1981, 'Aristotle and Aquinas on Being as Being True' = Gagnebin (1981), 85–97.
— 1983a, 'Aspekte der Ontologie in der Kategorienschrift' = Moraux/Wiesner (1983), 30–56.
— 1983b, *Die Philosophie der Antike 2: Sophistik und Sokratik, Plato und Aristoteles*, Munich.
Graeser, A. (ed. and comm.) 1973, *Die logischen Fragmente des Theophrast*, Berlin and New York.
Graham, D. W. 1987, *Aristotle's Two Systems*, Oxford.
Grant, C. K. 1957, 'Certainty, Necessity and Aristotle's Sea Battle', *Mind* 66: 522–31.
Grayeff, F. 1974, *Aristotle and His School: An Inquiry into the History of the Peripatos with a Commentary on* Metaphysics *Z, H, Λ and Θ*, London.
Grice, P. 1988, 'Aristotle on the Multiplicity of Being', *Pacific Philosophical Quarterly* 69: 175–200.
Grossato, A. 1999, 'La critica del capitolo 9 del *De interpretatione* di Aristotele mediante la logica formale moderna' = Zadro (1999), 397–443.
Grote, G. 1880, *Aristotle*, ed. by A. Bain and G. C. Robertson, 2nd edn, London.
Gudeman, A. (ed. and comm.) 1934, Aristoteles, ΠΕΡΙ ΠΟΙΗΤΙΚΗΣ, Berlin.
Guetti, C. and Pujia, R. (eds.) 1996, *Atti del convegno 'Momenti di Storia della Logica e di Storia della Filosofia', Roma, 9–11 novembre 1994*, Rome.
Günther, H.-C. and Rengakos, A. (eds.) 1997, *Beiträge zur antiken Philosophie. Festschrift für Wolfgang Kullman*, Stuttgart.
Haack, S. 1974/96, *Deviant Logic, Fuzzy Logic: Beyond the Formalism*, 2nd edn, Chicago and London.
Hadot, P. 1980, 'Sur divers sens du mot pragma dans la tradition philosophique grecque' = Aubenque (1980), 309–19.
Hafemann, B. 1998, *Aristoteles' Transzendentaler Realismus. Inhalt und Umfang erster Prinzipien in der 'Metaphysik'*, Berlin and New York.
— 1999, 'Indefinite Aussagen und das kontingent Zukünftige: Akzidenzien allgemeiner Gegenstände und graduelle Wahrheit in Aristoteles' *De Interpretatione* 7 und 9', *Philosophiegeschichte und logische Analyse* 2: 109–37.
Hallett, G. L. 1988, *Language and Truth*, New Haven and London.

Halper, E. C. 1989, *One and Many in Aristotle's Metaphysics: The Central Books*, Columbus, Ohio.
Hamblin, C. L. 1970, *Fallacies*, London.
Hamlyn, D. W. 1962, 'The Correspondence Theory of Truth', *PQ* 12: 193–205.
Hamlyn, D. W. (trans. and comm.) 1968/93, Aristotle, *De Anima: Books II and III (with Passages from Book I)*, 2nd edn (with contributions by C. Shields), Oxford.
Harris, L. D. 1977/78, 'Solving the "Naval Battle"', *PAS* n.s., 78: 45–61.
Hartshorne, C. 1965, 'The Meaning of "Is Going to Be"', *Mind* 74: 46–58.
Harvey, P. J. 1975, *Aristotle on Truth with Respect to Incomposites*, diss. (University of Michigan).
— 1978, 'Aristotle on Truth and Falsity in *De Anima* 3. 6', *JHP* 16: 219–20.
Heidegger, M. 1924/25, *Platon. Sophistes*, ed. by I. Schüssler, Frankfurt a. M. 1992.
— 1925/26, *Logik: Die Frage nach der Wahrheit*, ed. by W. Biemel, 2nd edn, Frankfurt a. M. 1995.
— 1926, *Die Grundbegriffe der antiken Philosophie*, ed. by F.-K. Bust, Frankfurt a. M. 1993.
— 1927, *Sein und Zeit*, 10th edn, Tübingen 1963.
— 1930, *Vom Wesen der menschlichen Freiheit. Einleitung in die Philosophie*, ed. by H. Tietjen, Frankfurt a. M. 1982.
— 1930/31, 'Platons Lehre von der Wahrheit' = Heidegger (1967), 109–44.
— 1946, 'Brief über den "Humanismus"' = Heidegger (1967), 145–94.
— 1967, *Wegmarken*, Frankfurt a. M.
Heinaman, R. 1981, 'Non-substantial Individuals in the Categories', *Phronesis* 26: 295–307.
Henle, P., Kallen, H. M., and Langer, S. K. (eds.) 1951, *Structure, Method, and Meaning: Essays in Honor of Henry M. Sheffer*, New York.
Hennigfeld, J. 1994, *Geschichte der Sprachphilosophie. Antike und Mittelalter*, Berlin and New York.
Herbertz, R. 1913, *Das Wahrheitsproblem in der griechischen Philosophie*, Berlin.
Hicks, R. D. (ed., trans., and comm.) 1907, Aristotle, *De Anima*, Cambridge.
Hildebrand, H. 1884, *Aristoteles' Stellung zum Determinismus und Indeterminismus*, diss. (University of Leipzig).
Hintikka, J. 1957, 'Necessity, Universality and Time in Aristotle', *Ajatus* 20: 65–90.
— 1964/73a, 'The Once and Future Sea Fight: Aristotle's Discussion of Future Contingents in *De Interpretatione* IX' = Hintikka (1973), 147–78.
— 1964/73b, 'Aristotle and the "Master Argument" of Diodorus' = Hintikka (1973), 179–213.
— 1967/73, 'Time, Truth, and Knowledge in Aristotle and Other Greek Philosophers' = Hintikka (1973), 62–92.
— 1973, *Time and Necessity: Studies in Aristotle's Theory of Modality*, Oxford.
— 1986, 'The Varieties of Being in Aristotle' = Knuuttila/Hintikka (1986), 81–114.
— 1999, 'On Aristotle's Notion of Existence', *RM* 52: 779–805.
Hintikka, J., Remes, U., and Knuuttila, S. 1977, *Aristotle on Modality and Determinism*, Amsterdam.

Hitchcock, D. 2000, 'Fallacies and Formal Logic in Aristotle', *HPL* 21: 207–21.
Hiz, H. (ed.) 1978, *Questions*, Dordrecht.
Hope, R. (trans.) 1952, Aristotle, *Metaphysics*, repr., Ann Arbor, Mich. 1994.
Horn, H.-J. 1994, *Studien zum dritten Buch der aristotelischen Schrift De anima*, Göttingen.
HPL = History and Philosophy of Logic.
Hughes, R. I. G. (ed.) 1993, *A Philosophical Companion to First-Order Logic*, Indianapolis, Ind. and Cambridge, Mass.
Humbert, J. 1945/60, *Syntaxe grecque*, 3rd edn, Paris.
Ierodiakonou, K. (ed.) 1999, *Topics in Stoic Philosophy*, Oxford.
Ihrig, A. H. 1965, 'Remarks on Logical Necessity and Future Contingencies', *Mind* 74: 215–28.
Inciarte, F. 1999, 'Aristotle and Aquinas: The Principle of Excluded Middle', *Philosophiegeschichte und logische Analyse* 2: 139–48.
Irmscher, J. and Müller, R. (eds.) 1983, *Aristoteles als Wissenschaftstheoretiker*, Berlin.
Irwin, T. H. 1977, *Plato's Moral Theory: The Early and Middle Dialogues*, Oxford.
— 1982, 'Aristotle's Concept of Signification' = Schofield/Craven Nussbaum (1982), 241–66.
— 1988, *Aristotle's First Principles*, Oxford.
Isnardi Parente, M. (ed., trans., and comm.) 1980, Speusippo, *Frammenti*, Naples.
Jacobs, W. 1979, 'Aristotle and Non-Referring Subjects', *Phronesis* 24: 282–300.
— 1980, 'The Existential Presuppositions of Aristotle's Logic', *Philosophical Studies* 37: 419–28.
Jaeger, W. W. 1911, 'Emendationum aristotelearum specimen' = Jaeger (1960), 1–38.
— 1912, *Studien zur Entstehungsgeschichte der Metaphysik des Aristoteles*, Berlin.
— 1923, *Aristoteles: Grundlegung einer Geschichte seiner Entwicklung*, Berlin.
— 1960, *Scripta minora*, 1, Rome.
Jaeger, W. W. (ed.) 1957, Aristotelis *Metaphysica*, Oxford.
Jeffrey, R. C. 1979, 'Coming True' = Diamond/Teichmann (1979), 251–60.
JHP = Journal of the History of Philosophy.
Joachim, H. H. 1906, *The Nature of Truth*, Oxford.
— 1948, *Logical Studies*, Oxford.
Joachim, H. H. (ed. and comm.) 1926, Aristotle, *On Coming-to-Be & Passing-Away*, Oxford.
Jordan, Z. 1963, 'Logical Determinism', *NDJFL* 4: 1–38.
JP = The Journal of Philosophy.
JSL = The Journal of Symbolic Logic.
Judson, L. 1988, 'La bataille navale d'aujourd'hui: *De Interpretatione* 9', *RPA* 6: 5–37.
Kahn, C. H. 1966, 'The Greek Verb "To Be" and the Concept of Being', *Foundations of Language* 2: 245–65.
— 1973a, *The Verb 'Be' in Ancient Greek*, Dordrecht and Boston.
— 1973b, 'On the Terminology for Copula and Existence' = Stern/Hourani/Brown (1973), 141–58.

— 1973c, 'On the Theory of the Verb "To Be"' = Munitz (1973), 1–20.
— 1976, 'Why Existence does not Emerge as a Distinct Concept in Greek Philosophy', *AGPh* 58: 323–34.
— 1978, 'Questions and Categories: Aristotle's Doctrine of Categories in the Light of Modern Research' = Hiz (1978), 227–78.
— 1985, 'On the Intended Interpretation of Aristotle's Metaphysics' = Wiesner (1985), 311–38.
Kal, V. 1988, *On Intuition and Discursive Reasoning in Aristotle*, Leiden, New York, Copenhagen, and Cologne.
Kapp, E. 1942, *Greek Foundations of Traditional Logic*, New York.
Keeler, L. 1932, 'Aristotle on the Problem of Error', *Gregorianum* 13: 241–60.
Kennedy, G. A. (trans. and comm.) 1991, Aristotle, *On Rhetoric: A Theory of Civic Discourse*, New York and Oxford.
Kenny, A. 1967, 'The Argument from Illusion in Aristotle's Metaphysics (Γ, 1009–10)', *Mind* 76: 184–97.
Kessler, M. 1976, *Aristoteles' Lehre von der Einheit der Definition*, Munich.
Ketchum, R. J. 1998, 'Being and Existence in Greek Ontology', *AGPh* 80: 321–32.
King-Farlow, J. 1958/59, 'Sea-Fights without Tears', *Analysis* 19: 36–42.
Kirkham, R. L. 1992, *Theories of Truth: A Critical Introduction*, Cambridge, Mass. and London.
Kirwan, C. 1986, 'Aristotle on the Necessity of the Present', *OSAP* 4: 167–87.
Kirwan, C. (trans. and comm.) 1971/93, Aristotle, *Metaphysics: Books Γ, Δ, and E*, 2nd edn, Oxford.
Knabenschuh de Porta, S. 1997, 'Über die Contingentia Futura und ihre epistemologischen Implikationen' = Öffenberger/Vigo (1997), 189–240.
Kneale, M. 1974, rev. of Hintikka (1973), *PQ* 24: 369–70.
Kneale, W. C. and Kneale, M. 1962, *The Development of Logic*, Oxford.
Kneepkens, C. H. 1994, 'From Eternal to Perpetual Truths: A Note on the Mediaeval History of Aristotle, *De interpretatione*, Ch. 1, 16a18', *Vivarium* 32: 161–85.
Knuuttila, S. 1993, *Modalities in Medieval Philosophy*, London and New York.
Knuuttila, S. and Hintikka, J. (eds.) 1986, *The Logic of Being: Historical Studies*, Dordrecht.
Kraus, O. 1930, introduction and notes to Brentano (1930).
Kreiser, L. 1983, 'Aristotelischer und Nicht-Aristotelischer Wahrheitsbegriff' = Irmscher/Müller (1983), 96–9.
Krell, D. F. 1975, 'On the Manifold Meaning of *Aletheia*: Brentano, Aristotle, Heidegger', *Research in Phenomenology* 5: 77–94.
Kretzmann, N. 1998, 'Boethius and the Truth about Tomorrow's Sea Battle' = Blank/Kretzmann (1998), 24–52.
Kretzmann, N., Kenny, A., and Pinborg, J. (eds.) 1982, *The Cambridge History of Later Medieval Philosophy*, Cambridge.
Kullmann, W. 1994/95, 'Einige Gedanken zur Entwicklung deterministischer Lehren bei den Griechen und zu Aristoteles, De interpretatione 9', *Wiener Studien* 107/108: 291–306.
Landman, F. 1991, *Structures for Semantics*, Dordrecht, Boston, and London.

Lang, P. 1911, *De Speusippi Academici scriptis*, repr., Hildesheim 1965.
Larkin, M. T. 1971, *Language in the Philosophy of Aristotle*, The Hague and Paris.
Lask, E. 1912, *Die Lehre vom Urteil* = Lask (1923), 283–463.
— 1923, *Gesammelte Schriften*, ed. by E. Herrigel, II, Tübingen.
Leal Carretero, F. M. 1983, *Der aristotelische Wahrheitsbegriff und die Aufgabe der Semantik*, diss. (University of Cologne).
Ledda, G. 1990, 'Verità e poesia nella *Poetica* di Aristotele', *Annali del Dipartimento di Filosofia – Università di Firenze* 6: 3–57.
Lemmon, E. J. 1956, rev. of Anscombe (1956/68), *JSL* 21: 388–9.
Lenz, J. W. 1957, 'Looking Back at the "Sea Fight Tomorrow"', *JP* 54: 773–4.
León, J. C. 1996, 'Indeterminism and Future Contingency in Non-Classical Logics' = Angelelli/Cerezo (1996), 383–95.
Leszl, W. 1970, *Logic and Metaphysics in Aristotle: Aristotle's Treatment of Types of Equivocity and Its Relevance to His Metaphysical Theories*, Padua.
— 1971, 'Metodi di analisi nella filosofia di Aristotele', *Rivista di filosofia* 62: 325–53.
— 1975, *Aristotle's Conception of Ontology*, Padua.
Lewinsohn, W. 1911, 'Zur Lehre von Urteil und Verneinung bei Aristoteles', *AGPh* 24: 197–217.
Lewis, F. A. 1991, *Substance and Predication in Aristotle*, Cambridge.
Linke, P. F. 1924, 'Die Existentialtheorie der Wahrheit und der Psychologismus der Geltungslogik', *Kant-Studien* 29: 395–415.
— 1965, 'Die Unhaltbarkeit des aristotelischen Wahrheitsbegriffs – und die Folgen', *ZPhF* 19: 306–19.
Linsky, L. 1954, 'Professor Donald Williams on Aristotle', *PR* 63: 250–2.
Liske, M.-T. 1985, *Aristoteles und der aristotelische Essentialismus: Individuum, Art, Gattung*, Freiburg and Munich.
— 1988, 'Das veritative "ist" und der logische Atomismus in Platons *Theaitetos*', *AGPh* 70: 147–66.
— 1995, 'In welcher Weise hängen Modalbegriffe und Zeitbegriffe bei Aristoteles zusammen?', *ZPhF* 49: 351–77.
Lloyd, A. C. 1981, *Form and Universal in Aristotle*, Liverpool.
Lloyd, G. E. R. and Owen, G. E. L. (eds.) 1978, *Aristotle on Mind and the Senses: Proceedings of the Seventh Symposium Aristotelicum*, Cambridge.
Long, A. A. 1981, 'Aristotle and the History of Greek Scepticism' = O'Meara (1981), 79–106.
Loux, M. J. 1991, *Primary* Ousia*: An Essay on Aristotle's* Metaphysics *Z and H*, Ithaca and London.
Lowe, M. F. 1980, 'Aristotle on the Sea-Battle: A Clarification', *Analysis* 40: 55–9.
LSJ = Liddell, H. G., Scott, R., and Jones, H. S., *A Greek-English Lexicon*, 9th edn with a revised supplement, Oxford 1996.
Lucas, J. R. 1989, *The Future: An Essay on God, Temporality, and Truth*, Oxford.
Lugarini, L. 1955, 'Il problema delle categorie in Aristotele', *Acme* 8: 3–107.
Lukasiewicz, J. 1910a, *Über den Satz des Widerspruchs bei Aristoteles*, trans. by J. Barski, Hildesheim, Zürich, and New York 1993.

— 1910b, 'Über den Satz des Widerspruchs bei Aristoteles', *Bulletin international de l'Académie des Sciences de Cracovie, Classe de Philosophie et d'Histoire* n.n.: 15–38.
— 1918, 'On Three-Valued Logic' = Lukasiewicz (1970), 87–8.
— 1922, 'On Determinism' = Lukasiewicz (1970), 110–28.
— 1930, 'Philosophical Remarks on Many-Valued Systems of Propositional Logic' = Lukasiewicz (1970), 153–78.
— 1957, *Aristotle's Syllogistic from the Standpoint of Modern Formal Logic*, 2nd edn, Oxford.
— 1970, *Selected Works*, ed. by L. Borkowski, Amsterdam, London, and Warsaw.
Luther, W. 1966, 'Wahrheit, Licht und Erkenntnis in der griechischen Philosophie bis Demokrit. Ein Beitrag zur Erforschung des Zusammenhangs von Sprache und philosophischem Denken', *Archiv für Begriffsgeschichte* 10: 1–240.
Magris, A. 1977, 'Aristotele e i Megarici. Contributo alla storia del determinismo antico', *Atti dell'Accademia delle Scienze di Torino* 111: 113–33.
Maier, H. 1896/1936, *Die Syllogistik des Aristoteles*, 2nd edn, repr., Hildesheim 1969.
— 1899, 'Die Echtheit der Aristotelischen Hermeneutik', *AGPh* 13: 23–72.
Manetti, G. (ed.) 1996, *Knowledge through Signs: Ancient Semiotic Theories and Practices*, Brussels.
Mann, J. A. 1958, *Existential Import and the Aristotelian Syllogistic*, Washington, D.C.
Mansion, A. 1913/45, *Introduction à la physique aristotélicienne*, 2nd edn, Louvain.
Mansion, S. 1946/76, *Le jugement d'existence chez Aristote*, 2nd edn, Louvain.
Mansion, S. (ed.) 1961, *Aristote et les problèmes de méthode. Communications présentées au Symposium Aristotelicum tenu à Louvain du 24 août au 1er septembre 1960*, Louvain and Paris.
Margoliouth, D. S. (ed., trans., and comm.) 1911, *The Poetics of Aristotle*, London.
Marrone, L. 1988, 'Il Mentitore nel *PHerc*. 307 (Questioni logiche di Crisippo)' = AA. VV. (1988), 271–6.
— 1997, 'Le *Questioni logiche* di Crisippo (*PHerc 307*)', *Cronache Ercolanesi* 27: 83–100.
Marx, W. 1977, *Introduction to Aristotle's Theory of Being as Being*, trans. by R. M. Schine, The Hague.
Mates, B. 1953/61, *Stoic Logic*, 2nd edn, Berkeley and Los Angeles.
Mattéi, J.-F. (ed.) 1990, *La naissance de la raison en Grèce (Actes du Congrès de Nice, mai 1987)*, Paris.
Matthen, M. 1983, 'Greek Ontology and the "Is" of Truth', *Phronesis* 28: 113–35.
— 1984, 'Aristotle's Semantics and a Puzzle Concerning Change' = Pelletier/King-Farlow (1984), 21–40.
Matthews, G. B. 1995, 'Aristotle on Existence', *BICS* 42: 233–8.
Maurus, S. (trans. and comm.) 1668, Aristotelis *Opera quae Extant Omnia . . .*, repr., Paris 1885–86.
Mayo, B. 1962/68, 'The Open Future' = Gale (1968), 275–91.
McArthur, R. P. 1976, *Tense Logic*, Dordrecht and Boston.
McCall, S. 1966, 'Temporal Flux', *American Philosophical Quarterly* 3: 270–81.

McGee, V. 1991, *Truth, Vagueness, and Paradox: An Essay on the Logic of Truth*, Indianapolis, Ind. and Cambridge, Mass.
McKim, V. R. 1971/72, 'Fatalism and the Future: Aristotle's Way Out', *RM* 25: 80–111.
McKirahan, R. D., Jr 1992, *Principles and Proofs: Aristotle's Theory of Demonstrative Science*, Princeton.
Melchiorre, V. (ed.) 2000, *I luoghi del comprendere*, Milan.
Merlan, P. 1953, *From Platonism to Neoplatonism*, The Hague.
Michelis, D. F. 1886, *Aristotelis περὶ Ἑρμηνείας Librum pro Restituendo Totius Philosophiae Fundamento* . . . , Heidelberg.
Mignucci, M. 1975a, *L'argomentazione dimostrativa in Aristotele. Commento agli Analitici secondi*, Padua.
— 1975b, 'In margine al concetto aristotelico di esistenza' = AA. VV. (1975), 227–61.
— 1985a, 'Temporalità e verità nella filosofia greca' = AA. VV. (1985), 163–91.
— 1985b, 'Logic and Omniscience: Alexander of Aphrodisias and Proclus', *OSAP* 3: 219–46.
— 1986, 'Aristotle's Definitions of Relatives in Cat. 7', *Phronesis* 31: 101–27.
— 1989, 'Truth and Modality in Late Antiquity: Boethius on Future Contingent Propositions' = Corsi/Mangione/Mugnai (1989), 47–78.
— 1994, 'Truth and Thought in the *De anima*' = Alberti (1994), 137–55.
— 1996a, 'Vérité et pensée dans le *De anima*' = Romeyer Dherbey/Viano (1996), 405–22.
— 1996b, 'Ammonius on Future Contingent Propositions' = Frede/Striker (1996), 279–310.
— 1997a, 'Logica' = Berti (1997), 47–101.
— 1997b, 'Remarks on Aristotle's Theory of Predication' = Günther/Rengakos (1997), 135–51.
— 1998, 'Ammonius' Sea Battle' = Blank/Kretzmann (1998), 53–86.
— 1999a, 'La critica di Teofrasto alla logica aristotelica' = Natali/Maso (1999), 21–39.
— 1999b, 'The Liar Paradox and the Stoics' = Ierodiakonou (1999), 54–70.
Mignucci, M. (trans. and comm.) 1969, Aristotele, *Gli Analitici Primi*, Naples.
Miller, F. D., Jr 1971, *Aristotle's Account of Being and Truth*, diss. (University of Washington).
Minio-Paluello, L. (ed.) 1949, Aristotelis *Categoriae et Liber de Interpretatione*, Oxford.
Modrak, D. K. W. 1987, *Aristotle: The Power of Perception*, Chicago and London.
— 2001, *Aristotle's Theory of Language and Meaning*, Cambridge.
Moline, J. 1969, 'Aristotle, Eubulides and the Sorites', *Mind* 78: 393–407.
Montanari, E. 1984/88, *La sezione linguistica del* Peri Hermeneias *di Aristotele*, Florence.
Montoneri, M. 1984, *I Megarici. Studio storico-critico e traduzione delle testimonianze antiche*, Catania.
Moore, G. E. 1953, *Some Main Problems of Philosophy*, London.

Moraux, P. and Wiesner, J. (eds.) 1983, *Zweifelhaftes im Corpus Aristotelicum: Studien zu einigen Dubia – Akten des 9. Symposium Aristotelicum (Berlin, 7.–16. September 1981)*, Berlin and New York.

Moravcsik, J. M. E. (ed.) 1968, *Aristotle: A Collection of Critical Essays*, London and Melbourne.

Moreau, J. 1961, 'Aristote et la vérité antéprédicative' = S. Mansion (1961), 21–33.

Morgenstern, A. 2001, 'Commentary on Crivelli', *BACAP* 17: 270–84.

Morpurgo-Tagliabue, G. 1967, *Linguistica e stilistica di Aristotele*, Rome.

— 1971, 'Asserzione ed esistenza nella logica di Aristotele', *Filosofia* 22: 29–60.

Morrison, D. 1985, 'Separation in Aristotle's Metaphysics', *OSAP* 3: 125–57.

— 1987, 'The Evidence for Degrees of Being in Aristotle', *Classical Quarterly* 37: 382–401.

— 1992, 'The Taxonomical Interpretation of Aristotle's Categories: A Criticism' = Preus/Anton (1992), 19–46.

Movia, G. (trans. and comm.) 1979, Aristotele, *L'anima*, Naples.

— (trans. and comm.) 1996, Aristotele, *L'anima*, Milan.

Muckle, J. T. 1933, 'Isaac Israeli's Definition of Truth', *Archives d'Histoire Doctrinale et Litteraire du Moyen-Age* 8: 5–8.

Mugler, C. (ed. and trans.) 1966, Aristote, *De la génération et de la corruption*, Paris.

Mulder, D. H. 1996, 'The Existential Assumptions of Traditional Logic', *HPL* 17: 141–54.

Munitz, M. K. (ed.) 1973, *Logic and Ontology*, New York.

Natali, C. and Maso, S. (eds.) 1999, *Antiaristotelismo*, Amsterdam.

Natorp, P. 1888, 'Ueber Aristoteles' Metaphysik K 1–8, 1065a26', *AGPh* 1: 178–93.

NDJFL = *Notre Dame Journal of Formal Logic.*

Neale, S. 2001, *Facing Facts*, Oxford.

Negro, G. 1996/97, 'Alcune note sul *vero* in Aristotele. L' ἀλήθεια come isomorfismo di essere e conoscere', *Atti dell'Istituto Veneto di Scienze, Lettere ed Arti – Classe di Scienze Morali, Lettere ed Arti* 155: 335–57.

Nuchelmans, G. 1973, *Theories of the Proposition: Ancient and Medieval Conceptions of the Bearers of Truth and Falsity*, Amsterdam and London.

Nussbaum, M. C. and Oksenberg Rorty, A. (eds.) 1992/95, *Essays on Aristotle's* De anima, 2nd edn, Oxford.

O'Brien, D. 1978, 'Aristote et la catégorie de quantité: divisions de la quantité', *Les études philosophiques* n.n.: 25–40.

Oehler, K. 1962/85, *Die Lehre vom noetischen und dianoetischen Denken bei Platon und Aristoteles. Ein Beitrag zur Erforschung der Geschichte des Bewusstseinsproblems in der Antike*, 2nd edn, Hamburg.

Oehler, K. (trans. and comm.) 1984, Aristoteles, *Kategorien*, Darmstadt.

Öffenberger, N. and Vigo, A. G. (eds.) 1997, *Südamerikanische Beiträge zur modernen Deutung der Aristotelischen Logik*, Hildesheim, Zürich, and New York.

O'Meara, D. J. (ed.) 1981, *Studies in Aristotle*, Washington D.C.

OSAP = *Oxford Studies in Ancient Philosophy.*

Owen, G. E. L. 1960, 'Logic and Metaphysics in Some Earlier Works of Aristotle' = Düring/Owen (1960), 163–90.

— 1965, 'Aristotle on the Snares of Ontology' = Bambrough (1965), 69–95.
— 1966, 'The Platonism of Aristotle', *Proceedings of the British Academy* 51: 125–50.
— 1968a, 'Dialectic and Eristic in the Treatment of the Forms' = G. E. L. Owen (1968b), 103–25.
— 1978/79, 'Particular and General', *PAS* n.s., 79: 1–21.
Owen, G. E. L. (ed.) 1968b, *Aristotle on Dialectic: the Topics – Papers of the Third Symposium Aristotelicum*, Oxford.
Owen, O. F. (trans. and comm.) 1899/1900, Aristotle, *The Organon or Logical Treatises*, London.
Owens, J. 1951/78, *The Doctrine of Being in the Aristotelian 'Metaphysics': A Study in the Greek Background of Mediaeval Thought*, 3rd edn, Toronto.
Pacius, J. 1597a, *In Porphyrii Isagogen et Aristotelis Organum Commentarius Analyticus*, repr., Hildesheim 1966.
Pacius, J. (ed., trans., and comm.) 1597b, Aristotelis . . . *Organum* . . . , 2nd edn, repr., Hildesheim 1967.
— 1611, Aristotelis *de Anima* . . . , Hannover.
— 1623, Aristotelis . . . *Organum* . . . , repr., Frankfurt a. M. 1967.
Pagliaro, A. 1954, 'Il capitolo linguistico della "Poetica" di Aristotele' = Pagliaro (1956/63), 77–151.
— 1956/63, *Nuovi saggi di critica semantica*, 2nd edn, Messina and Florence.
Pardey, U. 2000, 'Verneinen als Absprechen bei Aristoteles oder: Muss man Aristoteles durch die Russellsche Brille lesen?', *Bochumer Philosophisches Jahrbuch für Antike und Mittelalter* 5: 17–42.
PAS = *Proceedings of the Aristotelian Society.*
Patrizi, F. (trans.) 1583, Pseudo-Johannis Philoponi *Expositiones in Omnes XIV Aristotelis Libros Metaphysicos*, repr., with an intr. by C. Lohr, Stuttgart and Bad Cannstatt 1991.
Patterson, R. 1995, *Aristotle's Modal Logic: Essence and Entailment in the Organon*, Cambridge, New York, and Melbourne.
Patzig, G. 1968, *Aristotle's Theory of the Syllogism: A Logico-Philosophical Study of Book A of the* Prior Analytics, English ed., trans. by J. Barnes, Dordrecht.
— 1973, 'Aristotle, Lukasiewicz and the Origins of Many-Valued Logic' = Suppes *et al.* (1973), 921–9.
Pelletier, F. J. and King-Farlow, J. (eds.) 1984, *New Essays on Aristotle*, Calgary.
Percival, P. 1993/94, 'Absolute Truth', *PAS* n.s., 94: 189–213.
Pirotta, A. M. (ed.) 1925, S. Thomae Aquinatis *in Aristotelis Librum De Anima Commentarium*, Turin.
Popper, K. R. 1934/59/75, *The Logic of Scientific Discovery*, English trans., 8th impression, London.
Pozzi, L. 1974, *Studi di logica antica e medievale*, Padua.
PQ = *The Philosophical Quarterly.*
PR = *The Philosophical Review.*
Prantl, C. 1855, *Geschichte der Logik im Abenlande*, I, repr., Hildesheim, Zurich, and New York 1997.
Preus, A. and Anton, J. P. (eds.) 1992, *Essays in Ancient Greek Philosophy*, V, Albany.

Prior, A. N. 1953, 'Three-Valued Logic and Future Contingents', *PQ* 3: 317–26.
— 1955/62, *Formal Logic*, 2nd edn, Oxford.
— 1957, *Time and Modality*, Oxford.
— 1967a, *Past, Present and Future*, Oxford.
— 1967b, 'Correspondence Theory of Truth' = Edwards (1967), II 223–32.
— 1967c, 'Logic, Many-Valued' = Edwards (1967), V 1–5.
Pritzl, K. 1984, 'The Cognition of Indivisibles and the Argument of De Anima 3.4–8', *ACPA* 58: 140–50.
— 1993, 'Ways of Truth and Ways of Opinion in Aristotle', *ACPA* 67: 241–52.
— 1998, 'Being True in Aristotle's Thinking', *BACAP* 14: 177–201, 212.
Quine, W. V. 1953, 'On a Supposed Antinomy' = Quine (1976), 19–21.
— 1976, *The Ways of Paradox and Other Essays*, 2nd edn, Cambridge, Mass. and London.
— 1986, *Philosophy of Logic*, 2nd edn, Cambridge, Mass. and London.
Ranulf, S. 1924, *Der eleatische Satz vom Widerspruch*, Copenhagen, Christiania, London, and Berlin.
Reale, G. 1961/67, *Il concetto di filosofia prima e l'unità della Metafisica di Aristotele*, 3rd edn, Milan.
Reale, G. (trans. and comm.) 1968/93, Aristotele, *Metafisica*, 2nd edn, Milan.
Rees, D. A. 1960, 'Language, Logic and Reality in Aristotle and Russell' = AA. VV. (1960), 137–43.
Régis, L.-M. 1935, *L'opinion selon Aristote*, Paris and Ottawa.
Remes, U. 1977, 'Aristotle's Sea-Fight Discussion against its Background in the Topics', *Ajatus* 37: 41–7.
Rescher, N. 1963a, *Studies in the History of Arabic Logic*, Pittsburgh.
— 1963b, 'An Interpretation of Aristotle's Doctrine of Future Contingency and Excluded Middle' = Rescher (1963a), 43–54.
— 1968, 'Truth and Necessity in Temporal Perspective' = Gale (1968), 183–220.
Ringbom, M. 1972, 'Thoughts and Facts: An Aristotelian Problem', *Ajatus* 34: 7–25.
Riondato, E. 1957a, *La teoria aristotelica dell'enunciazione*, Padua.
Riondato, E. (trans. and comm.) 1957b, Aristotele, *De interpretatione*, Padua.
RM = *The Review of Metaphysics*.
Rodier, G. (ed., trans., and comm.) 1900, Aristote, *Traité de lâme*, Paris.
Roeper, G. 1852, 'Zu Aristoteles de anima', *Philologus* 7: 324, 768.
Rolfes, E. (trans. and comm.) 1904/28, Aristoteles, *Metaphysik*, 3rd edn, Leipzig.
Romeyer Dherbey, G. and Viano, C. (eds.) 1996, *Corps et âme. Sur le* De anima *d'Aristote*, Paris.
Rose, L. E. 1968, *Aristotle's Syllogistic*, Springfield, Ill.
Rosen, S. H. 1961, 'Thought and Touch: A Note on Aristotle's De Anima', *Phronesis* 6: 127–37.
Ross, W. D. 1923, *Aristotle*, 6th edn, London and New York 1995.
Ross, W. D. (ed. and comm.) 1924, Aristotle, *Metaphysics*, repr., Oxford 1975.
— (ed. and comm.) 1949, Aristotle, *Prior and Posterior Analytics*, Oxford.
— (ed.) 1956, Aristotelis *de Anima*, Oxford.

— (ed.) 1958, Aristotelis *Topica et Sophistici Elenchi*, Oxford.
— (ed. and comm.) 1961, Aristotle, *De Anima*, Oxford.
Ross, W. D. (trans.) 1908, Aristotle, *Metaphysica*, Oxford.
Rostagni, A. (ed. and comm.) 1927, *La Poetica di* Aristotele, Turin.
RPA = Revue de Philosophie Ancienne.
Russell, B. 1912, *The Problems of Philosophy*, repr., Oxford and New York 1991.
Russo, A. (trans.) 1973/82, Aristotele, *Metafisica*, 2nd edn, Rome and Bari.
Rüstow, A. 1910, *Der Lügner. Theorie, Geschichte und Auflösung*, repr., New York and London 1987.
Sadun Bordoni, G. 1994, *Linguaggio e realtà in Aristotele*, Rome and Bari.
Sainati, V. 1968, *Storia dell' 'Organon' aristotelico*, 1, Florence.
Salmeri, G. (trans. and comm.) 1996, Aristotele, *Discorsi sull'esistenza. Libri 7-8-9 della* Metafisica, Cinisello Balsamo.
Saunders, J. T. 1958, 'A Sea Fight Tomorrow?', *PR* 67: 367–78.
Sayward, C. 1989, 'Does the Law of Excluded Middle Require Bivalence?', *Erkenntnis* 31: 129–37.
Scarpat, G. 1950, *Il discorso e le sue parti in Aristotele*, Arona.
Schiaparelli, A. 1999a, 'L'ambiguità in Aristotele e in Galeno' = Natali/Maso (1999), 143–66.
— 1999b, 'L'influenza della Retorica di Aristotele in età imperiale. L'importanza di essere chiaramente ambigui', *Méthexis* 12: 53–75.
Schmidt, E. G. 1966, 'Alexander von Aphrodisias in einem altarmenischen Kategorien-Kommentar', *Philologus* 110: 277–86.
Schmitz, H. 1985, *Die Ideenlehre des Aristoteles*, 1.11, Bonn.
Schofield, M. and Craven Nussbaum, M. (eds.) 1982, *Language and Logos: Studies in Ancient Greek Philosophy Presented to G. E. L. Owen*, Cambridge.
Scholz, H. 1959, *Abriss der Geschichte der Logik*, 2nd edn, Freiburg and Munich.
Schuhl, P. M. 1960, *Le dominateur et les possibles*, Paris.
Schulz, G. 1993, *Veritas est Adaequatio Intellectus et Rei: Untersuchungen zur Wahrheitslehre des Thomas von Aquin und zur Kritik Kants an einem überlieferten Wahrheitsbegriff*, Leiden, New York, and Cologne.
Schwegler, A. (ed., trans., and comm.) 1847/48, Aristoteles, *Die Metaphysik*, repr., Frankfurt a. M. 1968.
Scott, T. K. (trans.) 1966, John Buridan, *Sophisms on Meaning and Truth*, New York.
Scott, T. K. (ed.) 1977, J. Buridanus, *Sophismata*, Stuttgart and Bad Cannstat.
Sedley, D. 1996, 'Aristotle's de Interpretatione and Ancient Semantics' = G. Manetti (1996), 87–108.
Seel, G. 1982a, *Die aristotelische Modaltheorie*, Berlin and New York.
— 1982b, 'Diodore domine-t-il-Aristote?', *Revue de Métaphysique et de Morale* 87: 293–313.
— 2001a, 'Ammonius' Semantics of the Assertoric Sentence' = Seel (2001b), 213–33.
Seel, G. (ed.) 2001b, *Ammonius and the Seabattle: Texts, Commentary, and Essays*, Berlin and New York.

Seeskin, K. R. 1971, 'Many-Valued Logic and Future Contingencies', *Logique et Analyse* 14: 759–73.
Segalerba, G. 2001, *Note su Ousia*, 1, Pisa.
Seidl, H. 1971, *Der Begriff des Intellekts (νοῦς) bei Aristoteles im philosophischen Zusammenhang seiner Hauptschriften*, Meisenheim am Glan.
Seidl, H. (trans. and comm.) 1989/91, Aristoteles' *Metaphysik*, 3rd edn, Hamburg.
Sepich, J. R. 1953, 'La noción de verdad en el libro IX capitulo 10 de la Metafisica de Aristóteles' = AA. VV. (1953), XII 107–8.
Sharples, R. W. 1979, '"If What Is Earlier, then Of Necessity What Is Later"? Some Ancient Discussions of Aristotle, *De Generatione et Corruptione* 2.11', *BICS* 26: 27–44.
Shields, C. 1999, *Order in Multiplicity: Homonymy in the Philosophy of Aristotle*, Oxford.
Sillitti, G. 1966, 'I "Fondamenti della logica aristotelica" e la critica di Emanuele Severino' = Calogero (1927/68), 313–25.
— 1968, 'Il non ente tra Platone e Aristotele', *La cultura* 6: 474–88.
Simons, P. 1987, *Parts: A Study in Ontology*, Oxford.
— 1988, 'Aristotle's Concept of State of Affairs' = Gigon/Fischer (1988), 97–112.
Simpson, P. 1981, 'Aristotle's Theory of Assertions: A Reply to William Jacobs', *Phronesis* 26: 84–7.
Siwek, P. (ed., trans., and comm.) 1965, Aristotelis *Tractatus de Anima Graece et Latine*, Rome.
Skarica, M. 1997, 'Anmerkungen zum Kommentar von Boethius zu *De Interpretatione* 9 von Aristoteles' = Öffenberger/Vigo (1997), 182–8.
Slomkowski, P. 1997, *Aristotle's* Topics, Leiden, New York, and Cologne.
Smith, R. (trans. and comm.) 1989, Aristotle, *Prior Analytics*, Indianapolis, Ind. and Cambridge, Mass.
— (trans. and comm.) 1997, Aristotle, *Topics: Books I and VIII with Excerpts from Related Texts*, Oxford.
Sommers, F. 1969/70, 'On Concepts of Truth in Natural Languages', *RM* 23: 259–86.
Sorabji, R. 1980, *Necessity, Cause and Blame: Perspectives on Aristotle's Theory*, London.
— 1981, 'Definitions: Why Necessary, and in What Way?' = Berti (1981), 205–44.
— 1982, 'Myths about Non-Propositional Thought' = Schofield/Craven Nussbaum (1982), 295–314.
— 1983, *Time, Creation and the Continuum: Theories in Antiquity and the Early Middle Ages*, London.
— 1988, *Matter, Space and Motion: Theories in Antiquity and Their Sequel*, London.
— 1992, 'Intentionality and Physiological Processes: Aristotle's Theory of Sense-Perception' = Nussbaum/Oksenberg Rorty (1992/95), 195–225.
— 1996, 'Rationality' = Frede/Striker (1996), 311–34.
— 1998, 'The Three Deterministic Arguments Opposed by Ammonius' = Blank/Kretzmann (1998), 3–15.

Soreth, M. 1973, 'Zum infiniten Prädikat im zehnten Kapitel der aristotelischen Hermeneutik' = Stern/Hourani/Brown (1973), 389–424.
Spade, P. V. 1973, 'The Origins of the Mediaeval *Insolubilia* Literature', *Franciscan Studies* 33: 292–309.
— 1982, 'Insolubilia' = Kretzmann/Kenny/Pinborg (1982), 246–53.
— 1987, 'Five Early Theories in the Mediaeval *Insolubilia*-Literature', *Vivarium* 25: 24–46.
Spellman, L. 1980, '*DI* 9: An Exegetical Stalemate', *Apeiron* 14: 115–24.
Spiazzi, R. M. (ed.) 1964, S. Thomae Aquinatis *in Aristotelis Libros Peri Hermeneias et Posteriorum Analyticorum Expositio*, 2nd edn, Turin.
Srzednicki, J. 1965, *Franz Brentano's Analysis of Truth*, The Hague.
Steinthal, H. 1863/90, *Geschichte der Sprachwissenschaft bei den Griechen und Römern mit besonderer Rücksicht auf die Logik*, 2nd edn, repr., Hildesheim, Zurich, and New York 2001.
Stenzel, J. 1931, *Metaphysik des Altertums*, Munich and Berlin.
Stern, S. M., Hourani, A., and Brown, V. (eds.) 1973, *Islamic Philosophy and the Classical Tradition: Essays Presented by His Friends and Pupils to Richard Walzer*, Columbia, SC.
Stough, C. L. 1972, 'Language and Ontology in Aristotle's *Categories*', *JHP* 10: 261–72.
Strache, I. and Wallies, M. (eds.) 1923, Aristotelis *Topica cum Libro de Sophisticis Elenchis*, Leipzig.
Strang, C. 1960, 'Aristotle and the Sea Battle', *Mind* 69: 447–65.
Strawson, P. F. 1950, 'Truth' = Blackburn/Simmons (1999), 162–82.
Strobach, N. 1998, 'Logik für die Seeschlacht – mögliche Spielzüge', *ZPhF* 52: 105–19.
Suarez, F. 1597, *Disputationes Metaphysicae*, repr., Hildesheim, Zurich, and New York 1998.
Sugihara, T. 1954, rev. of Prior (1953), *JSL* 19: 294.
Sullivan, M. 1970, 'What Was True or False in the *Old Logic*?', *JP* 67: 788–800.
Suppes, P., Henkin, L., Joja, A., and Moisil, G. C. (eds.) 1973, *Logic, Methodology and Philosophy of Science IV: Proceedings of the Fourth International Congress for Logic, Methodology and Philosophy of Science, Bucharest, 1971*, Amsterdam, London, and New York.
Szaif, J. 1998, *Platons Begriff der Wahrheit*, 3rd edn, Freiburg and Munich.
Szaniawski, K. (ed.) 1989, *The Vienna Circle and the Lvov-Warsaw School*, Dordrecht, Boston, and London.
Talanga, J. 1986, *Zukunftsurteile und Fatum: Eine Untersuchung über Aristoteles'* De interpretatione 9 *und Ciceros* De fato, *mit einem Überblick über die spätantiken Heimarmene-Lehren*, Bonn.
Tarski, A. 1933, 'The Concept of Truth in Formalized Languages' = Tarski (1956/83), 152–278.
— 1944, 'The Semantic Conception of Truth and the Foundations of Semantics' = Blackburn/Simmons (1999), 115–43.

— 1956/83, *Logic, Semantics, Metamathematics: Papers from 1923 to 1938*, trans. by J. H. Woodger, 2nd edn, ed. by J. Corcoran, Indianapolis, Ind.
— 1969, 'Truth and Proof' = Hughes (1993), 101–25.
Taylor, K. 1998, *Truth and Meaning: An Introduction to the Philosophy of Language*, Oxford.
Taylor, R. 1957, 'The Problem of Future Contingencies', *PR* 66: 1–28.
Textor, A. 1870, *De Hermeniae Aristoteleae capitibus I–XI*, diss., Berlin.
Theiler, W. (trans. and comm.) 1959, Aristoteles, *Über die Seele*, Darmstadt.
Thom, P. 1981, *The Syllogism*, Munich.
— 2002, 'On the Pervasiveness of Being' = Caston/Graham (2002), 293–301.
Thomason, R. H. 1970, 'Indeterminist Time and Truth-Value Gaps', *Theoria* 36: 264–81.
— 1984, 'Combinations of Tense and Modality' = Gabbay/Guenthner (1983/89), II 135–65.
Thompson, M. 1953/68, 'On Aristotle's Square of Opposition' = Moravcsik (1968), 51–72.
Thornton, A. M. 1986, 'Λόγος-phrase et λόγος-texte chez Platon et Aristote' = AA. VV. (1986), 165–79.
Thorp, J. 2001, '"Being in the Strictest Sense": Aristotle on Truth, Reality and Existence', unpublished typescript.
Torstrik, A. (ed. and comm.) 1862, Aristotelis *de Anima Libri III*, Berlin.
Tredennick, H. (ed. and trans.) 1933, Aristotle, *The Metaphysics*, Cambridge, Mass. and London.
Trendelenburg, F. A. 1836/92, *Elementa Logices Aristoteleae*, 9th edn, Berlin.
— 1846, *Geschichte der Kategorienlehre*, Berlin.
— 1876, *Elemente der aristotelischen Logik*, 3rd edn, repr., Munich 1967.
Trendelenburg, F. A. (ed. and comm.) 1833, Aristotelis *de Anima Libri Tres*, Jena.
— (ed. and comm.) 1877, Aristotelis *de Anima Libri Tres*, 2nd edn, Berlin.
Trenkner, S. 1952/53, 'Aristotle, *Rhetoric* III, 12, 4', *Proceedings of the Cambridge Philological Society* n.s., 2: 3–6.
Tricot, J. (trans. and comm.) 1966, Aristote, *La métaphysique*, 2nd edn, Paris.
Trundle, R. 1981, '*De Interpretatione IX*: The Problem of Future Truth or of Infinite Past Truth?', *The Modern Schoolman* 59: 49–55.
Tugendhat, E. 1956/88, *TI KATA TINOΣ: Eine Untersuchung zu Struktur und Ursprung aristotelischer Grundbegriffe*, 4th edn, Freiburg and Munich.
— 1966a, 'Der Wahrheitsbegriff bei Aristoteles' = Tugendhat (1992), 251–60.
— 1966b, rev. of Oehler (1962/85) = Tugendhat (1992), 402–13.
— 1992, *Philosophische Aufsätze*, Frankfurt a. M.
Ueberweg, F. 1868, *System der Logik und Geschichte der logischen Lehren*, 3rd edn, Bonn.
Upton, T. V. 1988, 'Aristotle on Existence: Escaping the Snares of Ontology?', *The New Scholasticism* 62: 373–99.
— 1991, 'The If-It-Is Question in Aristotle', *AP* 11: 315–30.

Vahlen, I. 1872, 'Über eine Stelle in Aristoteles' Schrift von der Seele', *Sitzungberichte der Wiener Akademie – Phil.-Hist. Cl.* 71: 419–34.

Vahlen, I. (ed. and comm.) 1885, Aristotelis *de Arte Poetica Liber*, 3rd edn, repr., Hildesheim 1964.

van Bennekom, R. 1975, 'The Definitions of Σύνδεσμος and Ἄρθρον in Aristotle, *Poetics* Ch. 20', *Mnemosyne* 28: 399–411.

— 1986, 'Aristotle and the Copula', *JHP* 24: 1–18.

van Eck, J. A. 1988, 'Another Interpretation of Aristotle's De Interpretatione IX: A Support for the So-Called Second Oldest or "Mediaeval" Interpretation', *Vivarium* 26: 19–38.

van Fraassen, B. C. 1966, 'Singular Terms, Truth-Value Gaps, and Free Logic', *JP* 63: 481–95.

van Raalte, M. (trans. and comm.) 1993, Theophrastus, *Metaphysics*, Leiden, New York, and Cologne.

van Rijen, J. 1989, *Aspects of Aristotle's Logic of Modalities*, Dordrecht, Boston, and London.

Vasiliou, I. 1996, 'Perception, Knowledge, and the Sceptic in Aristotle', *OSAP* 14: 83–131.

Verbeke, G. (ed.) 1966, Jean Philopon, *Commentaire sur le De anima d'Aristote*, trans. by William of Moerbeke, Louvain and Paris.

Viano, C. A. 1955, *La logica di Aristotele*, Turin.

Viano, C. A. (trans. and comm.) 1974, Aristotele, *La metafisica*, Turin.

Vigo, A. G. 1994, 'Wahrheit, Logos und Praxis. Die Transformation der aristotelischen Wahrheitskonzeption durch Heidegger', *Internationale Zeitschrift für Philosophie* 1: 73–95.

— 1997, 'Der theoretische Wahrheitsbegriff bei Aristoteles. Versuch einer systematischen Rekonstruktion' = Öffenberger/Vigo (1997), 1–48.

Volkmann-Schluck, K.-H. 1979, *Die Metaphysik des Aristoteles*, Frankfurt a. M.

Vollrath, G. E. 1959, *Studien zur Kategorienlehre des Aristoteles*, diss. (University of Cologne).

von Fragstein, A. 1967, *Die Diairesis bei Aristoteles*, Amsterdam.

von Fritz, K. 1962, rev. of Schuhl (1960), *Gnomon* 34: 138–52.

— 1972, rev. of D. Frede (1970), *Gnomon* 44: 241–50.

von Ivánka, E. 1932, 'Die Behandlung der Metaphysik in Jaegers "Aristoteles"', *Scholastik* 7: 1–29.

von Kirchmann, J. H. 1876, *Erläuterungen zu den Kategorien und den Hermeneutiken des Aristoteles*, Leipzig.

— 1883, *Erläuterungen zu Aristoteles' Sophistischen Widerlegungen*, Leipzig.

von Kutschera, F. 1986, 'Zwei modallogische Argumente für den Determinismus: Aristoteles und Diodor', *Erkenntnis* 24: 203–17.

von Wright, G. H. 1974, 'Determinismus, Wahrheit und Zeitlichkeit. Ein Beitrag zum Problem der zukünftigen kontingenten Wahrheiten', *Studia Leibnitiana* 6: 161–78.

— 1979, 'Time, Truth and Necessity' = Diamond/Teichmann (1979), 237–50.

— 1984a, *Truth, Knowledge, and Modality*, Oxford.
— 1984b, 'Determinism and Future Truth' = von Wright (1984a), 1–13.
— 1984c, '"Omne quod est quando est necesse est esse"' = von Wright (1984a), 72–85.
Vuillemin, J. 1996, *Necessity or Contingency: The Master Argument*, Stanford.
Vuillemin-Diem, G. (ed.) 1995, Aristoteles, *Metaphysica*, trans. by William of Moerbeke, Leiden, New York, and Cologne.
Wagner, H. 1961/62, 'Über das Aristotelische πολλαχῶς λέγεται τὸ ὄν', *Kant-Studien* 53: 75–91.
Waitz, T. 1857, 'Varianten zu Aristoteles Organon', *Philologus* 12: 726–34.
Waitz, T. (ed. and comm.) 1844/46, Aristoteles, *Organon Graece*, Leipzig.
Wallace, E. (ed., trans., and comm.) 1882, *Aristotle's Psychology*, Cambridge.
Wardy, R. 1990, *The Chain of Change: A Study of Aristotle's* Physics *VII*, Cambridge.
Warrington, J. (trans.) 1956, Aristotle, *Metaphysics*, London and New York.
Waterlow, S. 1982, *Passage and Possibility: A Study of Aristotle's Modal Concepts*, Oxford.
Wedin, M. V. 1978, 'Aristotle on the Existential Import of Singular Sentences', *Phronesis* 23: 179–96.
— 1988, *Mind and Imagination in Aristotle*, New Haven and London.
— 1990, 'Negation and Quantification in Aristotle', *HPL* 11: 131–50.
— 2000, *Aristotle's Theory of Substance: The* Categories *and* Metaphysics *Zeta*, Oxford.
Weidemann, H. 1979, 'Möglichkeit und Wahrheit. Oskar Beckers modale Grundfigur und das Aristotelische Bivalenzprinzip', *AGPh* 61: 22–36.
— 1980, 'Überlegungen zu einer temporalen Modalanalyse', *ZPhF* 34: 405–22.
— 1985, 'Textkritische Bemerkungen zum siebten Kapitel der aristotelischen "Hermeneutik". Int. 7, 17b12–16/16–20' = Wiesner (1985), 45–56.
— 1987, 'Möglichkeit und Wahrscheinlichkeit bei Aristoteles', *Studia Philosophica (Jahrbuch der Schweizerischen Philosophischen Gesellschaft)* 46: 171–89.
Weidemann, H. (trans. and comm.) 1994/2002, Aristoteles, *Peri Hermeneias*, 2nd edn, Berlin.
Weingartner, P. 1978, 'Brentano's Criticism of the Correspondence Theory of Truth and of the Principle "Ens et Verum Convertuntur"' = Chisholm/Haller (1978), 183–95.
Weise, C. H. (ed.) 1843, Aristotelis *Opera Omnia Quae Extant* . . . , Leipzig.
Wheeler, M. 1999, 'Semantics in Aristotle's *Organon*', *JHP* 37: 191–226.
Whitaker, C. W. A. 1996, *Aristotle's* De Interpretatione*: Contradiction and Dialectic*, Oxford.
White, A. R. 1970, *Truth*, London and Basingstoke.
White, M. J. 1979, 'Aristotle and Temporally Relative Modalities', *Analysis* 39: 88–93.
— 1980, 'Necessity and Unactualized Possibilities in Aristotle', *Philosophical Studies* 38: 287–98.
— 1981, 'Fatalism and Causal Determinism: An Aristotelian Essay', *PQ* 31: 231–41.

— 1985, *Agency and Integrality: Philosophical Themes in the Ancient Discussions of Determinism and Responsibility*, Dordrecht, Boston, Lancaster, and Tokyo.
Wieland, W. 1962, *Die aristotelische Physik. Untersuchungen über die Grundlegung der Naturwissenschaft und die sprachlichen Bedingungen der Prinzipienforschung bei Aristoteles*, Göttingen.
— 1972, 'Zeitliche Kausalstrukturen in der aristotelischen Logik', *AGPh* 54: 229–37.
— 1979, 'Aristoteles und die Seeschlacht. Zur Struktur prognostischer Aussagen', *Berichte zur Wissenschaftsgeschichte* 2: 25–33.
Wiesner, J. (ed.) 1985, *Aristoteles – Werk und Wirkung. Paul Moraux gewidmet*, I, Berlin and New York.
Wildberg, C. 1989, 'Two Systems in Aristotle?', *OSAP* 7: 193–202.
Williams, C. J. F. 1976, *What is Truth?*, Cambridge.
— 1978, 'True Tomorrow, Never True Today', *PQ* 28: 285–99.
— 1980, 'What Is, Necessarily Is, When It Is', *Analysis* 40: 127–31.
— 1981, *What is Existence?*, Oxford.
— 1991, 'Aristotle and Copernican Revolutions', *Phronesis* 36: 305–12.
Williams, C. J. F. (trans. and comm.) 1982, Aristotle, *De Generatione et Corruptione*, Oxford.
Williams, D. C. 1951, 'The Sea Fight Tomorrow' = Henle/Kallen/Langer (1951), 282–306.
— 1954, 'Professor Linsky on Aristotle', *PR* 63: 253–5.
Williams, K. J. 1978, 'Aristotle's Theory of Truth', *Prudentia* 10: 67–76.
Williamson, T. 1994, *Vagueness*, London and New York.
Wilpert, P. 1940, 'Zum aristotelischen Wahrheitsbegriff', *Philosophisches Jahrbuch der Görres-Gesellschaft* 53: 3–16.
— 1949, *Zwei aristotelische Frühschriften über die Ideenlehre*, Regensburg.
Wlodarczyk, M. 2000, 'Aristotelian Dialectic and the Discovery of Truth', *OSAP* 18: 153–210.
Wolenski, J. and Simons, P. 1989, 'De Veritate: Austro-Polish Contributions to the Theory of Truth from Brentano to Tarski' = Szaniawski (1989), 391–442.
Wolf, U. 1979, *Möglichkeit und Notwendigkeit bei Aristoteles und heute*, Munich.
Wolff, F. 1999, 'Proposition, être et vérité. Aristote ou Antisthène? (À propos de *Métaphysique* Δ, 29)' = Büttgen/Diebler/Rashed (1999), 43–63.
Xenakis, J. 1957, 'Aristotle on Truth-Value', *The New Scholasticism* 31: 538–47.
Yourgrau, P. 1985, 'On the Logic of Indeterminist Time', *JP* 82: 548–59.
Zadro, A. 1979, *Tempo ed enunciati nel 'de interpretatione' di Aristotele*, Padua.
Zadro, A. (trans. and comm.) 1974, Aristotele, *I topici*, Naples.
— (ed., trans., and comm.) 1999, Aristotele, *De interpretatione*, Naples.
Zagzebski, L. T. 1991, *The Dilemma of Freedom and Foreknowledge*, New York and Oxford.
Zanatta, M. (trans. and comm.) 1992, Aristotele, *Della interpretazione*, Milan.
— 1995, Aristotele, *Le confutazioni sofistiche*, Milan.
Zaslawsky, D. 1982, *Analyse de l'être. Essai de philosophie analytique*, Paris.

— 1986, 'Paradoxes linguistiques: A propos de Λέξις chez Aristote' = AA. VV. (1986), 239–61.
Zell, C. (ed., trans., and comm.) 1820, Aristotelis *Ethicorum Nicomacheorum Libri Decem*, Heidelberg.
Zeller, E. 1921, *Die Philosophie der Griechen in ihrer geschichtlichen Entwicklung*, II.II, 5th edn, Hildesheim 1963.
Zimmermann, F. W. (trans. and comm.) 1981, Alfarabi, *Commentary and Treatise on Aristotle's* de Interpretatione, Oxford.
ZPhF = *Zeitschrift für philosophische Forschung*.

Index of names

Abbagnano, N., 131n
Ackrill, J. L., 50n, 63n, 84n, 85n, 100n, 123n, 131n, 155n, 156n, 158n, 162n, 166n, 167n, 169n, 170n, 174n, 199n, 201n, 202n, 205n, 209n, 217n, 223n, 228n, 230n, 231n, 244n, 276n
Adorno, F., 131n, 230n
Albritton, R. A., 277n
Alexander of Aphrodisias, 72n, 156n, 186n, 221n
Al-Farabi, 172n
Ammonius, 45, 205n, 226n, 239
Anaxagoras, 206, 207
Anscombe, G. E. M., 123n, 199n, 206n, 223n
Antiseri, D., 164n, 172n
Antisthenes, 230n
Anton, J. P., 97n
Apelt, O., 97n, 264n
Apollo, 162n
Apostle, H. G., 58n, 96n, 114n, 165n
Aquinas, Thomas, 59n, 63n, 64n, 66n, 69n, 71n, 82n, 87n, 88n, 96n, 98n, 107n, 117n, 131n, 155n, 166n
Arens, H., 83n
Aspasius, 156n
Astroh, M., 172n, 230n
Aubenque, P., 114n, 117n, 123n, 131n
Austin, J. L., 72n
Averroes, 244n

Bäck, A. T., 48n, 52n, 72n, 123n, 185n, 213n, 228n
Badawi, A., 256n
Baldassarri, M., 146n
Barnes, J., 55n, 72n, 79n, 84n, 100n, 116n, 123n, 146n, 147n, 156n, 162n, 256n
Bärthlein, K., 103n, 133n
Baudry, L., 87n, 131n, 199n, 277n, 278n
Baylis, C. A., 204n
Beaney, M., 161n
Becker, A., 227, 228n, 230n
Becker, O., 147n
Bekker, I., 62n, 74n, 89n, 101n, 155n, 201n, 202n, 205n, 228n, 232n, 234, 238, 239, 252n
Belardi, W., 164n, 165n
Bencivenga, E., 276n
Benson, H. H., 79n
Ben-Zeev, A., 109n
Berti, E., 52n, 64n, 86n, 97n, 101n, 107n, 114n, 115, 115n, 117n, 118n, 119n, 131n, 132n, 140n, 184n, 234n, 235n
Besoli, S., 114n
Bird, O., 161n
Birondo, N., 109n
Blanché, R., 230n, 263n
Blank, D., 86n
Blettner, E., 164n
Block, I., 109n, 110n
Bobzien, S., 133n, 172n, 227n, 256n
Bochenski, I. M., 72n, 143n, 230n, 256n
Bodéüs, R., 73n, 102n, 228n
Boethius, 142n, 156n, 202n, 205n, 226n, 240, 240n, 241, 250
Bolton, R., 100n, 116n, 175n
Bonitz, H., 58n, 59n, 62n, 63n, 64n, 89n, 98n, 101n, 102n, 107n, 114n, 117n, 123n, 131n, 138n, 180n, 211n, 223n, 234, 238
Bonomi, A., 199n
Bormann, K., 131n, 234n
Bosley, R., 216n, 223n
Bostock, D., 100n, 123n
Boudot, M., 271n
Bradley, R. D., 266n
Brakas, G., 79n, 88n, 114n, 230n
Brandis, C. A., 63n, 114n, 172n, 234, 236n, 238
Brandt, R., 64n, 69n, 82n, 83n, 84n, 131n, 213n, 230n, 231n
Brentano, F., 52n, 57n, 64n, 70n, 79n, 84n, 98n, 104n, 113n, 114n, 117n, 131n, 133n, 136n, 152n, 161n, 192n
Brown, L., 123n
Brunschwig, J., 107n, 122n, 147n, 179n, 244n, 245n
Buhle, I. T., 89n, 155n, 201n, 202n, 205n, 228n, 240n, 241

Bullinger, A., 102n
Buridan, John, 72n, 95n
Burnyeat, M., 52n, 83n, 107n, 109n, 117n, 118n, 236n
Burrell, D., 131n, 199n, 278n
Butler, R. J., 199n
Butterworth, C. E., 244n
Bywater, I., 53n, 164n

Cahn, S. M., 131n, 199n
Calogero, G., 100n, 101n, 102n, 104n, 114n, 131n, 147n
Capozzi, G., 131n, 230n
Carson, D. S., 160n, 162n
Casari, E., 194n
Cashdollar, S., 102n, 109n, 110n
Cassin, B., 109n
Cassirer, H., 101n
Caston, V., 83n, 109n
Cathala, M.-R., 59n, 63n, 64n, 66n, 69n, 96n, 98n, 107n, 117n
Cavini, W., 51n, 70n, 132n, 139n, 140n, 147n, 161n, 229n, 244n, 248n
Celluprica, V., 100n, 156n, 227n, 230n
Charles, D., 100n, 107n, 109n, 110n, 123n, 162n, 175n, 176n
Chisholm, R. M., 130n
Christ, W., 62n, 63n, 64n, 101n, 234, 238
Chrysippus, 144, 144n, 145, 145n, 146, 146n, 147, 147n
Church, A., 161n, 265n
Cleary, J. J., 96n
Code, A., 271n
Colli, G., 74n, 89n, 142n, 155n
Conybeare, F. C., 240n
Cooke, H. P., 74n, 89n, 131n, 155n, 201n, 202n, 205n, 228n, 239
Cope, E. M., 164n
Coraes, A., 141n
Corinth, 162n
Cosenza, P., 255n, 256n
Craig, W. L., 131n, 199n, 201n, 202n, 212n, 228n, 233n, 276n
Cresswell, M. J., 123n
Crivelli, P., 52n, 55n, 115n, 131n, 137n, 138n, 152n, 161n, 162n, 168n, 170n, 174n, 241n, 247n, 263n
Cypselus, 162n

Damschen, G., 172n
Dancy, R. M., 123n, 162n
Dapunt, I., 161n
David, M., 130n
Davidson, D., 131n, 133n, 134n
Décarie, V., 117n, 123n
De Corte, M., 106n, 107n, 114n
de Koninck, T., 72n
Demoss, D., 100n, 132n
Deninger, J. G., 236n
Denyer, N., 111n
de Rijk, L. M., 47n, 49n, 50n, 52n, 55n, 58n, 59n, 64n, 69n, 98n, 103n, 105n, 114n, 121n, 131n, 196n, 215n
de Rivo, Peter, *see* Peter de Rivo
Detel, W., 114n
Devereux, D. T., 79n, 100n, 132n
Dexippus, 187, 187n, 188, 189
Dickason, A., 131n, 138n, 199n, 227n, 230n, 276n
Dilthey, W., 114n, 131n
Diogenes Laertius, 146
Donini, P. L., 131n, 138n, 199n, 205n, 212n, 214n
Döring, A., 165n
Döring, K., 143n
Dorion, L.-A., 107n, 143n, 179n, 180n
Dübner, F., 63n, 74n, 89n, 155n, 201n, 202n, 205n, 228n, 232n, 234, 238, 239, 252n
Dubucs, J., 230n, 263n
DuLac, H., 86n, 100n, 172n, 201n
Duminil, M.-P., 48n
Düring, I., 120n, 230n
Du Val, G., 241, 241n, 251n

Ebbesen, S., 146n, 163n
Edel, A., 131n
Enders, M., 131n, 199n, 205n, 209n, 211n, 212n
Engel, P., 131n
Engelhardt, P. M., 101n, 114n, 117n, 131n
Engmann, J., 114n
Epicurus, 226n
Eudemus, 256
Evans, G., 186n
Everson, S., 109n

Fait, P., 88n, 143n, 144n, 145n, 151n
Fattal, M., 104n, 107n, 109n
Faust, A., 117n
Field, H., 72n
Fine, G., 79n, 80n, 81n, 213n, 223n
Fiorentino, F., 64n, 88n, 114n, 131n, 138n, 152n
Fleischer, M., 65n, 86n, 114n, 131n
Fonseca, P., 107n, 114n
Förster, A., 71n
Forster, E. S., 142n, 213n, 232n
Fortenbaugh, W. W., 210n
Fox, J. F., 133n
Fraser, K., 114n
Frede, D., 87n, 100n, 131n, 162n, 172n, 199n, 201n, 202n, 209n, 212n, 214n, 215n, 216n, 227n, 229n, 230n, 233n, 276n, 281n
Frede, M., 79n, 80n, 97n, 114n, 123n, 133n

Freese, J. H., 164n
Freeland, C., 106n
Frege, G., 70n

Gale, R. M., 184n
Gallavotti, C., 165n
Galluzzo, G., 52n, 93n, 111n, 114n, 131n, 230n
Gaskin, R., 50n, 87n, 105n, 196n, 199n, 207n, 209n, 211n, 212n, 214n, 215n, 226n, 227n, 228n, 231n, 276n, 277n
Geach, P. T., 123n, 130n, 158n, 174n, 175n, 199n
George the Arab, 202n
Geyser, G. J. A. M., 69n, 70n, 83n, 131n
Gobbo, E., 140n
Gohlke, P., 53n, 64n, 155n, 164n
Goldin, O., 72n, 100n, 132n, 138n, 162n, 184n, 187n, 189n, 193n
Gómez-Lobo, A., 100n
Goodwin, W. W., 233n
Gourinat, J.-B., 143n
Graeser, A., 47n, 52n, 53n, 66n, 79n, 98n, 131n, 132n, 146n, 196n, 210n, 256n
Graham, D. W., 122n, 230n, 231n
Grant, C. K., 199n
Grayeff, F., 55n, 58n, 107n, 114n, 117n, 123n
Grice, P., 114n, 123n, 159n
Grossato, A., 227n
Grote, G., 100n, 107n, 114n, 236n
Gudeman, A., 165n

Haack, S., 184n, 204n, 217n, 266n, 276n
Hadot, P., 196n
Hafemann, B., 56n, 79n, 88n, 131n, 134n, 247n, 276n
Hallett, G. L., 131n, 137n, 152n
Halper, E. C., 53n, 64n, 66n, 131n
Hamblin, C. L., 107n
Hamlyn, D. W., 64n, 71n, 102n, 105n, 107n, 114n
Harris, L. D., 205n
Hartshorne, C., 278n
Harvey, P. J., 47n, 64n
Hayduck, M., 64n, 71n
Heidegger, M., 64n, 66n, 71n, 87n, 98n, 101n, 114n, 132n, 235, 235n, 237, 237n
Heinaman, R., 73n
Hennigfeld, J., 50n
Herbertz, R., 131n
Hicks, R. D., 71n, 114n
Hildebrand, H., 276n
Hintikka, J., 100n, 114n, 123n, 133n, 184n, 199n, 206n, 211n, 219n, 262n, 266n, 276n
Hitchcock, D., 140n
Hope, R., 47n, 58n
Horn, H.-J., 71n, 102n
Humbert, J., 142n, 210n, 233n

Ihrig, A. H., 217n, 219n
Inciarte, F., 276n
Irwin, T. H., 79n, 80n, 81n, 109n, 131n, 156n, 158n
Isnardi Parente, M., 106n

Jacobs, W., 152n, 153n, 162n
Jaeger, W. W., 53n, 62n, 63n, 64n, 69n, 101n, 113n, 114n, 117n, 131n, 234, 234n, 235, 235n, 238
Jaulin, A., 48n
Jeffrey, R. C., 199n, 278n
Joachim, H. H., 55n, 106n, 114n, 131n, 137n, 232n
Jordan, Z., 219n
Judson, L., 206n, 223n, 224n, 228n

Kahn, C. H., 100n, 114n, 123n, 133n, 162n, 164n, 237, 237n
Kal, V., 114n, 117n
Kapp, E., 84n
Keeler, L., 48n, 70n, 83n, 107n, 114n, 131n
Kennedy, G. A., 164n
Kenny, A., 109n
Kessler, M., 68n, 83n, 107n, 117n
Ketchum, R. J., 48n
King-Farlow, J., 266n
Kirkham, R. L., 130n, 134n
Kirwan, C., 47n, 52n, 55n, 57n, 68n, 70n, 83n, 96n, 97n, 98n, 132n, 133n, 162n, 199n, 200n, 205n, 212n, 228n
Knabenschuh de Porta, S., 131n, 133n, 134n, 266n
Kneale, M., 72n, 142n, 184n, 244n, 266n
Kneale, W. C., 72n, 142n, 184n, 244n, 266n
Kneepkens, C. H., 221n
Knuuttila, S., 199n, 219n
Kraus, O., 192n
Kreiser, L., 131n, 137n
Krell, D. F., 104n, 131n, 132n
Kretzmann, N., 217n, 226n
Kullmann, W., 215n, 233n

Landman, F., 220n, 271n, 272n
Lang, P., 106n
Larkin, M. T., 164n
Lask, E., 47n, 50n
Leal Carretero, F. M., 132n, 133n
Ledda, G., 132n, 133n
Lemmon, E. J., 199n
Lenz, J. W., 131n, 276n
León, J. C., 271n
Leszl, W., 64n, 98n, 114n, 121n, 122n, 123n, 124n
Lewinsohn, W., 52n, 114n
Lewis, F. A., 121n, 122n
Linke, P. F., 57n, 131n, 192n
Linsky, L., 281n
Liske, M.-T., 61n, 117n, 121n, 184n, 217n

Lloyd, A. C., 79n
Long, A. A., 109n
Loux, M. J., 114n, 123n
Lowe, M. F., 214n
Lucas, J. R., 185n, 271n
Lugarini, L., 52n
Lukasiewicz, J., 52n, 131n, 172n, 199n, 227n, 266n
Luther, W., 64n, 66n, 87n, 114n, 131n, 132n, 137n

Magris, A., 230n, 231n
Maier, H., 58n, 65n, 70n, 71n, 83n, 96n, 98n, 100n, 101n, 102n, 106n, 107n, 114n, 117n, 131n, 184n, 230n, 242n
Mann, J. A., 176n
Mansion, A., 230n
Mansion, S., 96n, 116n, 131n
Margoliouth, D. S., 165n
Marrone, L., 143n, 145n, 146n, 147n
Marx, W., 114n, 117n, 131n
Mates, B., 226n
Matthen, M., 48n, 52n, 55n, 84n, 89n
Matthews, G. B., 123n, 124n
Maurus, S., 52n, 71n, 107n, 115, 115n, 141n, 143n, 155n, 164n, 166n
Mayo, B., 162n
McArthur, R. P., 271n
McCall, S., 271n, 276n, 277n, 278n
McGee, V., 151n
McKim, V. R., 131n, 199n
McKirahan, R. D., Jr., 100n
Meinong, A., 159n
Merlan, P., 117n
Michelis, D. F., 87n
Mignucci, M., 52n, 70n, 100n, 114n, 116n, 117n, 119n, 133n, 147n, 162n, 184n, 186n, 188n, 190n, 196n, 199n, 201n, 219n, 226n, 227n, 255n, 256n, 265, 265n, 271n, 277n
Miller, F. D., 70n, 72n, 75n, 83n, 93n, 100n, 154n, 184n, 185n, 191n, 255n, 256n, 264n
Minio-Paluello, L., 74n, 89n, 155n, 193n, 201n, 202n, 205n, 207n, 228n, 239
Modrak, D. K. W., 47n, 57n, 63n, 64n, 79n, 108n, 110n, 114n, 131n, 134n, 138n, 175n, 196n
Moline, J., 143n, 151n
Montanari, E., 64n, 74n, 221n, 230n
Montoneri, M., 143n, 146n, 147n
Moore, G. E., 130n
Moreau, J., 110n, 131n
Morgenstern, A., 165n
Morpurgo-Tagliabue, G., 88n, 131n, 164n, 247n
Morrison, D., 80n, 97n, 192n
Movia, G., 71n, 107n, 110n
Muckle, J. T., 137n
Mugler, C., 232n
Mulder, D. H., 161n

Natorp, P., 98n
Neale, S., 47n, 130n
Negro, G., 63n, 114n, 131n
Nicostratus, 226n
Nuchelmans, G., 56n, 72n, 87n, 88n, 105n, 185, 185n, 196n

O'Brien, D., 73n
Ockham, William of, 143n, 155n, 166n, 172n, 204n, 269n
Oehler, K., 50n, 51n, 56n, 58n, 59n, 64n, 71n, 80n, 96n, 102n, 107n, 111n, 114n, 117n, 120n, 121n, 131n, 133n, 136n, 162n, 184n, 234n
Owen, G. E. L., 96n, 97n, 100n, 114n, 122n, 123n, 125n, 195n, 244n
Owen, O. F., 141n
Owens, J., 96n, 98n, 114n, 117n, 235n

Pacius, J., 74n, 82n, 84n, 86n, 87n, 89n, 102n, 107n, 114n, 148n, 155n, 166n, 180n, 201n, 202n, 205n, 228n, 241, 241n
Pagliaro, A., 82n, 165n
Pardey, U., 154n, 162n, 184n, 247n
Patterson, R., 97n, 255n
Patzig, G., 114n, 123n, 131n, 172n, 255n, 266n, 276n
Percival, P., 186n
Peter de Rivo, 87n, 199n, 277n, 278n
Pirotta, A. M., 71n, 107n, 131n
Plato, 68, 88n, 138, 172, 189n
Popper, K. R., 131n
Porphyry, 156n, 239
Pozzi, L., 263n
Prantl, C., 236n
Prior, A. N., 100n, 130n, 133n, 184n, 199n, 213n, 228n, 266n, 271n, 273n, 276n
Pritzl, K., 63n, 64n, 69n, 114n, 117n, 130n, 131n, 235n, 237n
Protagoras, 138

Quine, W. V., 72n, 266n

Ranulf, S., 143n
Reale, G., 64n, 66n, 96n, 98n, 114n, 117n, 131n
Rees, D. A., 176n
Régis, L.-M., 63n, 187n
Remes, U., 219n, 221n
Rescher, N., 214n, 228n, 271n
Ringbom, M., 83n, 130n
Riondato, E., 155n, 156n, 230n, 242n, 247n
Rodier, G., 71n, 102n
Roeper, G., 102n
Rolfes, E., 51n, 58n, 117n
Rose, L. E., 244n, 248n
Rosen, S. H., 106n

Ross, W. D., 52n, 53n, 58n, 62n, 63n, 64n, 70n, 71n, 72n, 79n, 83n, 96n, 98n, 100n, 101n, 102n, 106n, 107n, 112n, 114n, 116n, 117n, 122n, 123n, 131n, 142n, 161n, 213n, 234, 234n, 235n, 236n, 238, 244n, 252n, 255n
Rostagni, A., 165n
Russell, B., 130n, 176
Russo, A., 236n
Rüstow, A., 143n, 144n, 145n, 146n, 147n

Sadun Bordoni, G., 47n, 83n, 104n
Sainati, V., 131n, 156n, 172n, 199n, 230n, 231n, 244n, 264n
Salmeri, G., 236n
Sandys, J. E., 164n
Saunders, J. T., 131n, 184n, 199n
Sayward, C., 276n
Scarpat, G., 70n, 131n
Schiaparelli, A., 166n, 213n
Schmidt, E. G., 72n, 186n
Schmitz, H., 47n, 52n, 65n
Scholz, H., 184n
Schuhl, P. M., 230n
Schulz, G., 137n
Schwegler, A., 62n, 64n, 98n, 101n, 117n, 234, 238
Scott, T. K., 72n, 95n
Sedley, D., 82n
Seel, G., 72n, 131n, 184n, 199n, 211n, 212n, 217n, 233n, 276n
Seeskin, K. R., 199n, 276n
Segalerba, G., 83n
Seidl, H., 57n, 58n, 64n, 66n, 83n, 107n, 114n, 117n, 119n, 236n
Sepich, J. R., 52n
Sharples, R. W., 200n
Shields, C., 123n, 193n
Sillitti, G., 64n, 97n, 104n
Simons, P., 47n, 50n, 131n, 132n, 133n, 134n, 136n, 172n, 191n
Simplicius, 187n
Simpson, P., 153n
Siwek, P., 72n
Skarica, M., 226n
Slomkowski, P., 164n, 172n, 263n
Smith, R., 61n, 84n, 97n, 114n
Sommers, F., 130n, 133n
Sophonias, 142n
Sorabji, R., 64n, 109n, 111n, 115, 115n, 117n, 199n, 204n, 219n, 223n, 227n, 230n, 231n, 281n
Soreth, M., 161n, 244n
Spade, P. V., 72n, 143n
Spellman, L., 199n, 228n
Spiazzi, R. M., 59n, 63n, 64n, 66n, 69n, 82n, 87n, 88n, 96n, 98n, 107n, 117n, 131n, 155n, 166n
Srzednicki, J., 131n, 133n, 136n, 152n
Steinthal, H., 83n, 131n, 155n, 164n
Stenzel, J., 114n
Stephanus, 87n
Stough, C. L., 97n
Strache, I., 142n
Strang, C., 206n, 212n, 266n
Strawson, P. F., 72n
Strobach, N., 212n, 271n
Suarez, F., 107n, 117n
Sugihara, T., 266n
Sullivan, M., 72n, 73n
Szaif, J., 52n, 55n, 114n, 131n, 132n, 136n

Talanga, J., 215n
Tarski, A., 130n, 131n, 277n
Taylor, K., 131n, 220n, 277n
Taylor, R., 199n
Textor, A., 86n, 87n, 164n, 166n
Theiler, W., 102n
Themistius, 256n
Theophrastus, 146, 147, 210n, 256
Thom, P., 100n, 159n, 162n, 244n, 257n
Thomason, R. H., 199n, 271n, 273n, 276n
Thompson, M., 162n
Thornton, A. M., 164n
Thorp, J., 48n, 52n, 66n
Torstrik, A., 71n, 88n, 102n, 112n, 114n
Tredennick, H., 53n, 58n, 62n, 101n, 131n, 234, 238, 252n
Trendelenburg, F. A., 71n, 79n, 83n, 88n, 102n, 131n, 138n, 152n, 241n, 255n
Trenkner, S., 164n
Tricot, J., 51n, 64n, 107n, 236n
Trundle, R., 60n
Tugendhat, E., 52n, 55n, 63n, 65n, 69n, 114n, 133n, 235n

Ueberweg, F., 131n
Upton, T. V., 79n, 100n, 123n

Vahlen, I., 102n, 165n
van Bennekom, R., 100n, 124n, 162n, 164n, 165n, 166n, 167n
van Eck, J. A., 184n, 199n, 204n, 212n, 214n, 215n, 216n
van Fraassen, B. C., 276n
van Raalte, M., 106n
van Rijen, J., 206n, 212n
Vasiliou, I., 109n, 110n
Verbeke, G., 71n
Viano, C. A., 79n, 98n, 131n, 247n
Vigo, A. G., 57n, 61n, 64n, 69n, 71n, 82n, 88n, 89n, 96n, 98n, 107n, 111n, 114n, 119n, 131n, 132n, 134n

Volkmann-Schluck, K.-H., 59n, 64n, 107n, 114n, 117n, 131n, 237n
Vollrath, G. E., 65n, 71n, 88n, 230n
von Fragstein, A., 101n, 107n, 114n, 117n, 166n, 234n
von Fritz, K., 199n, 212n, 230n, 247n
von Ivánka, E., 104n, 123n
von Kirchmann, J. H., 143n, 164n, 172n, 201n
von Kutschera, F., 184n, 199n, 228n, 230n, 266n
von Wright, G. H., 199n, 211n, 212n, 271n, 276n, 277n, 278n
Vuillemin, J., 207n, 276n

Wagner, H., 97n, 159n
Waitz, T., 73n, 74n, 82n, 88n, 89n, 107n, 155n, 180n, 201n, 202n, 205n, 210n, 228n, 239, 239n, 240n, 244n, 252n, 255n
Wallace, E., 71n, 114n
Wallies, M., 142n, 213n
Wardy, R., 192n
Warrington, J., 58n
Waterlow, S., 72n, 185n, 186n, 199n, 211n, 212n
Wedin, M. V., 115n, 116n, 153n, 161n, 162n, 190n
Weidemann, H., 47n, 74n, 82n, 83n, 84n, 86n, 89n, 100n, 155n, 156n, 162n, 164n, 166n, 167n, 170n, 171n, 172n, 174n, 175n, 196n, 199n, 201n, 202n, 203n, 204n, 205n, 206n, 208n, 209n, 210n, 211n, 212n, 214n, 215n, 217n, 219n, 226n, 227n, 230n, 231n, 239n, 241, 241n, 243n, 247n, 251n, 271n, 273n, 276n, 277n, 281n
Weingartner, P., 133n, 137n
Weise, C. H., 74n, 89n, 155n, 201n, 202n, 205n, 228n, 232n, 234, 238, 241, 252n
Wheeler, M., 88n, 156n, 174n
Whitaker, C. W. A., 47n, 52n, 55n, 75n, 82n, 83n, 88n, 100n, 106n, 114n, 123n, 156n, 158n, 166n, 170n, 174n, 196n, 242n, 245n, 246n, 247n, 249n
White, A. R., 72n, 73n
White, M. J., 131n, 184n, 199n, 209n, 212n, 271n, 276n, 278n
Wieland, W., 66n, 75n, 201n
Wildberg, C., 231n
William of Moerbeke, 58n, 63n, 101n, 142n, 234, 238
Williams, C. J. F., 123n, 133n, 187n, 196n, 199n, 204n, 233n
Williams, D. C., 204n, 266n
Williams, K. J., 131n, 134n, 185n
Williamson, T., 276n, 277n
Wilpert, P., 47n, 59n, 64n, 70n, 71n, 98n, 103n, 114n, 117n, 138n, 235n
Wlodarczyk, M., 63n
Wolenski, J., 131n, 132n, 133n, 134n, 136n
Wolf, U., 52n, 53n, 55n, 59n, 117n, 276n
Wolff, F., 47n, 52n, 115n, 131n, 132n, 134n

Xenakis, J., 86n, 133n

Yourgrau, P., 271n

Zadro, A., 74n, 89n, 155n, 164n, 165n, 201n, 202n, 205n, 207n, 239, 244n
Zagzebski, L. T., 199n
Zanatta, M., 83n, 85n, 142n, 155n, 156n, 166n, 167n, 170n, 230n, 242n
Zaslawsky, D., 100n, 143n, 213n
Zell, C., 141n
Zeller, E., 97n
Zimmermann, F. W., 172n
Zucchi, A., 199n

Index of subjects

ambiguity, 155–7, 178–9
anti-realism, *see* realism and anti-realism
asserting-about and asserting-away-from, 87–9, 154–5
assertions, 7–8, 86–9, 134–5
  affirmative and negative, 8, 10, 11–12
  are utterances, 72–5
  existential, *see* existentials
  indeterminate and quantified, 11, 12, 26, 90–2, 157–8
  predicative, 10, 12
  simple and composite, 8, 170–6
  single and multiple, 163–80
  singular and general, 11, 89–90, 92
  temporally determinate and temporally indeterminate, 218–21
  universal and particular, 11
assertoric sentences, *see* assertions

bearers of truth or falsehood, 3
  objects, 3–22
  perceptions, 3
  sentences, 3, 7–8, 72–5, 86–7
  statements, 72n
  thoughts, 3, 8, 62
'being' said in many senses, 62, 193–4
  see also uses of 'to be'
beliefs, 8, 46, 54–6
  affirmative and negative, 8, 11–12
  existential, *see* existentials
  indeterminate and quantified, 11, 12
  predicative, 10–11, 12
  simple and composite, 8
  singular and general, 11, 13–14
  universal and particular, 11, 13
Bivalence, 31, 37, 86–7, 198, 202, 228–33, 266
  and Determinism, 198–9

categories, 16–18, 114
'coincident' predicative assertions, 26, 160

combination and division, 4–5, 12–13, 15, 92–5, 136–7, 254–7, 261–2
  see also fallacy of division
composite and non-composite objects, 3–6, 48–9, 105
  see also non-composite substances
concepts, 85–6
conjunctions, 164–6
contradictories, *see* Law of Contradictories
contraries, *see* Law of Contraries
copula, 10–11
corporeal and incorporeal substances, 6, 20, 105
correspondence theory of truth, 129–38
criterion of truth, 9

definition of truth, 9, 56–7, 132–5, 260–2
definitions, 110–12, 115–16
Determinism, 34, 198, 200, 204–5, 211–12
deterministic arguments, 201–5, 228
diachronic modalities, 199, 208–9, 216
division, *see* combination and division
domain of quantification, 264–5

'empty' and 'non-empty' terms, 25–6, 152–3, 158–63
enunciation, 112
Epicureans, 226n, 266n
'equimodality', 214–15
essences, 6, 105
Excluded Middle, 36, 37–8, 132, 134, 203, 212–13, 229, 266, 280–3
existence, 159
existentials, 18–20, 99–125
  concerning composite items, 99–100
  concerning material substances, 121–5
  concerning simple items, 99
  distinguished from predications, 100–21

facts, 47–8, 130
fallacy of division, 213–14

'goatstag', 84

ignorance, 106
immaterial substances, *see* material and immaterial substances
incidental error, 106–12
incorporeal substances, *see* corporeal and incorporeal substances
ineluctability, *see* necessity, as ineluctability
isomorphism between assertions and reality, 23–4, 131–7

joining and separating, 67–71, 82–6, 87–9, 154–5

knowledge and truth, 138

Law of Contradictories, 26, 161, 263
Law of Contraries, 26, 161, 263
Law of Subalternation, 263
Law of Subcontraries, 263
Liar, 31–4, 139–51
  Aristotle's solution, 32–3, 140
  Strengthened Liar, 151
  version addressed by Aristotle, 31–2

material and immaterial substances, 5, 121–3
Megarians, 95n, 230
middle-Platonists, 226n
'minimalist' theories of truth, 194
modal attributes, 20–1, 34, 60–1, 199, 208–9, 248

necessitas consequentiae, 218
necessitas consequentis, 217, 222
necessity, 21, 34
  as ineluctability, 34, 198, 199, 200, 211
  of the present and the past, 34–5, 198, 199–200, 211–12
non-composite substances, 116–21
  see also composite and non-composite objects
non-propositional truth, 114–15

objects, *see* bearers of truth or falsehood

perceptions of special objects, 107–10
Peripatetics, 147, 172, 226n
predicate, 10–11
predicative expression, 10–11
propositional attitudes, 21–2

realism and anti-realism, 226–33
refutations, 140
  see also sophistical refutations
relational properties, 30–1, 189–91
relatives, 188–94

sentences, *see* bearers of truth or falsehood
separating, *see* joining and separating
signification, 2–3
simple objects, *see* composite and non-composite objects
sophistical refutations, 140–1
  dependent on the absolute or qualified use of expressions, 141
speaking-truly and speaking-falsely, 31–2, 139
Square of Opposition, 26–7, 160–1, 175–6, 262–3
  see also Law of Contradictories, Law of Contraries, Law of Subalternation, and Law of Subcontraries
states of affairs, 3–5, 12, 45–62, 130–1, 172, 195–7, 215
statistical modalities, 20–1, 208–9
Stoics, 95n, 172, 221n, 226n
Strengthened Liar, *see* Liar
subject, 10–11

thoughts, *see* bearers of truth or falsehood
time, *see* tree of time
touch, 106, 111
tree of time, 270–1
truth conditions, 12–20, 93–5
truth
  and 'mere Cambridge change', 30–1, 183, 186–9, 194–5
  and relatives, 183, 188–94
  and time, 28–31, 38, 57–60, 183–6
  of singular predications, existence, and time, 27–8, 161–2
truth-value gaps, 275–9

universals, 1–2, 77, 78–81, 177
  and being, 113–14
  dependent on individuals, 2, 80, 157, 177
  everlasting, 2, 80–1, 157
  realism, 1–2
uses of 'to be', 132–3
utterances, 28, 72

'vacuous' and 'non-vacuous' terms, 152–8
vagueness, 151

'when and only when', 2n

Index of passages

ALEXANDER OF APHRODISIAS

COMMENTARY ON ARISTOTLE'S METAPHYSICS

80, 7–81, 22: 71n
80, 16–17: 161n
80, 19–81, 2: 161n
89, 2–6: 138n
98, 19–20: 80n
339, 18–20: 132n
431, 15–432, 4: 47n
456, 31: 62n
457, 20–1: 62n
457, 22: 62n
457, 25–6: 62n
457, 27: 62n
457, 36–458, 1: 63n, 64n
457, 38–9: 62n
458, 4–5: 62n
458, 7–9: 96n
458, 8–9: 63n
458, 10–15: 64n
458, 18–19: 98n
598, 1–2: 234
598, 10–41: 59n
598, 23–7: 59n
599, 27: 101n
600, 16–17: 107n
600, 25–7: 117n, 120n
600, 34: 101n

COMMENTARY ON THE FIRST BOOK OF ARISTOTLE'S PRIOR ANALYTICS

25, 2–9: 255n
31, 4–10: 256n
34, 13–15: 256n
36, 25–9: 210n
124, 18–21: 256n
132, 24–32: 256n
141, 1–6: 210n
156, 26–157, 2: 210n
220, 12–16: 256n

COMMENTARY ON ARISTOTLE'S TOPICS

188, 19–28: 139n

DE FATO

10 177, 7–9: 221n

PSEUDO-ALEXANDER OF APHRODISIAS (PROBABLY MICHAEL OF EPHESUS)

COMMENTARY ON ARISTOTLE'S SOPHISTICI ELENCHI

170, 28–171, 9: 142n
171, 5–6: 142n

AMMONIUS

COMMENTARY ON ARISTOTLE'S CATEGORIES

53, 22–4: 72n, 186n
60, 10–12: 72n

COMMENTARY ON ARISTOTLE'S DE INTERPRETATIONE

17, 29–30: 45
20, 32–21, 16: 131n

26, 12–22: 83n
26, 23–27, 8: 82n
27, 27–28, 1: 64n
27, 28–33: 114n
28, 29–31: 83n
29, 12–17: 221n
29, 18–26: 83n
29, 23–6: 83n
64, 29–30: 86n
66, 10–19: 87n
66, 31–67, 19: 163n, 164n, 172n
72, 15–22: 166n
73, 19–74, 14: 172n
100, 21–2: 244n
108, 29–30: 256n
109, 24–5: 239
110, 23–6: 244n
111, 10–17: 244n
126, 11–14: 155n
128, 30–129, 35: 201n
138, 28–34: 201n
140, 4–10: 202n
148, 6–11: 201n
185, 14–18: 256n
201, 24–6: 177n

COMMENTARY ON THE FIRST BOOK OF ARISTOTLE'S PRIOR ANALYTICS

4, 12–14: 256n
23, 2–4: 82n

PSEUDO-AMMONIUS

COMMENTARY ON ARISTOTLE'S PRIOR ANALYTICS

37, 2–4: 210n
44, 1–4: 256n
58, 19–23: 256n
60, 21–2: 256n

ANONYMOUS

COMMENTARY ON ARISTOTLE'S CATEGORIES

18, 33–5: 72n, 186n

ANONYMOUS

COMMENTARY ON ARISTOTLE'S DE INTERPRETATIONE

16, 20–17, 3: 86n
17, 3–5: 87n
18, 7–19: 172n
51, 3–13: 155n

ANONYMOUS (PROBABLY SOPHONIAS)

COMMENTARY ON ARISTOTLE'S SOPHISTICI ELENCHI

58, 31–6: 148n, 149n
58, 36: 142n

ANONYMOUS

DISSOI LOGOI

4.2: 138n

ARISTOTLE

CATEGORIES

2 1^a24–5: 80n
1^b6–9: 80n
4 1
1^b25–7: 220
2^a4–10: 82n
2^a7–10: 228
2^a8: 228n
5 1, 192
2^a14–19: 72n
2^b29–30: 72n
3^b21–2: 89n
4^a10–21: 188, 192
4^a21–4^b19: 73
4^a21–8: 188, 192
4^a22: 73n
4^a23–8: 184n, 186, 196
4^a23–6: 45n, 184n
4^a26–8: 45n
4^a28–4^b18: 188
4^a28–4^b5: 192
4^a34–4^b2: 56n, 184n, 186
4^a35–6: 196n
4^a37–4^b1: 196n
4^b2–4: 196n
4^b4–13: 184n, 186n
4^b5–18: 192
4^b5–14: 193

4^{b}6–13: 56n
4^{b}8–10: 45n, 56, 184n
4^{b}8–9: 196n
4^{b}10–11: 193
4^{b}11: 73n
4^{b}12–13: 193n
4^{b}12: 193
6 73
4^{b}23: 73n
4^{b}32–7: 73n
4^{b}32: 73n
5^{a}33–6: 73
5^{a}38–5^{b}10: 107n
7 123n
6^{a}36–7: 188
6^{a}38–6^{b}3: 188n
6^{a}38–9: 188
6^{b}15–16: 188n
8^{a}32: 123n
8^{a}34–5: 123n
8^{a}39: 123n
8 11^{a}27–8: 188
11^{a}28–9: 191n
11^{a}29–31: 189
11^{a}35–6: 191n
11^{a}36: 191n
11^{a}37–8: 114n
10 1
11^{b}15–16: 114n
11^{b}24–31: 188n
12^{b}5–16: 45n
12^{b}6–15: 50n
13^{a}37–13^{b}3: 229
13^{a}37–13^{b}1: 50n
13^{b}10–11: 82n
13^{b}12–33: 161
13^{b}27–35: 229
11 14^{a}7–10: 80n
14^{a}10–14: 45n
12 1
14^{a}29–35: 96n
14^{b}11–22: 45n, 56n, 104
14^{b}11–13: 104
14^{b}14–22: 45n
14^{b}14–18: 104
14^{b}15: 104
14^{b}18–19: 105
14^{b}19–21: 104
14^{b}19–20: 105
14^{b}21–2: 105

DE INTERPRETATIONE

1–9 1
1–6 231n
1 77, 85, 88n
16^{a}3–4: 88n
16^{a}6–7: 88n
16^{a}7: 88n
16^{a}8–9: 231n
16^{a}8: 223n
16^{a}9–18: 45n, 67n, 82, 92
16^{a}10: 82
16^{a}12–13: 85
16^{a}13: 83
16^{a}14: 82, 83
16^{a}15: 84
16^{a}16–18: 82n, 113
16^{a}16–17: 163, 175n
16^{a}17–18: 84, 221
2 16^{a}19: 86n
16^{a}27–9: 86n
16^{a}30–3: 161n
3 16^{b}6–8: 74
16^{b}7: 74n
16^{b}8–18: 74n
16^{b}12–15: 71n, 161n
16^{b}16–18: 229, 269
16^{b}19–22: 74
16^{b}21–5: 196n
16^{b}23: 196n
4 16^{b}26–30: 112n
16^{b}26–8: 82n
16^{b}26–7: 74
16^{b}26: 74n, 86n, 158
16^{b}27: 102n
16^{b}28–30: 84n
17^{a}1–5: 45n, 86
17^{a}1–2: 74n
17^{a}2–3: 74, 86
17^{a}5–6: 231n
5–6 17^{a}8–26: 164
5 89, 173, 176
17^{a}8–9: 50n, 86, 135n, 168, 169, 170
17^{a}9: 164
17^{a}10: 230n
17^{a}11–12: 84n, 86n
17^{a}14–15: 231n
17^{a}15–17: 166, 169
17^{a}15–16: 135n, 168
17^{a}15: 166n
17^{a}16: 164, 166n
17^{a}17–20: 82n
17^{a}17–19: 112n
17^{a}17: 102n, 166n, 179
17^{a}20–2: 171
17^{a}20–1: 86n, 170n
17^{a}21: 170
17^{a}22–3: 170n, 251

6 173
17^{a}25–37: 92n
17^{a}25–6: 86
17^{a}26–31: 230
17^{a}26–30: 133n, 250
17^{a}26–9: 132n
17^{a}31–3: 229
17^{a}32–3: 230
17^{a}34–5: 70n
7 77, 89, 95, 227
17^{a}38–17^{b}12: 89
17^{a}38–17^{b}1: 79, 90
17^{a}38–9: 196n
17^{a}38: 89n, 250n
17^{a}39: 250n
17^{b}1–12: 90, 157n
17^{b}1: 250n
17^{b}2–3: 250
17^{b}2: 250n
17^{b}3–4: 90n
17^{b}3: 89n, 250n
17^{b}4: 89n, 250n
17^{b}5–6: 90n, 250n
17^{b}5: 250n
17^{b}7–8: 244n
17^{b}7: 90n, 250n
17^{b}8–10: 243
17^{b}9: 90n, 250n
17^{b}10: 250n
17^{b}11–12: 90n
17^{b}11: 89n, 92n, 250n
17^{b}12: 250n
17^{b}13: 250n
17^{b}15: 250n
17^{b}16–20: 91, 239
17^{b}16–18: 91n, 239, 240, 240n, 241, 242, 250, 251, 252, 253
17^{b}16–17: 240
17^{b}16: 250
17^{b}17–18: 239, 240, 240n, 241
17^{b}17: 239, 240n
17^{b}18–20: 95, 241, 242, 247
17^{b}18: 239, 240
17^{b}20–4: 263n
17^{b}24–6: 263n
17^{b}26–37: 249n
17^{b}26–9: 200
17^{b}26–7: 263n
17^{b}29–37: 174n, 200n
17^{b}34–7: 244n
17^{b}38–18^{a}7: 92
17^{b}38–18^{a}4: 86n
17^{b}38–9: 246n
18^{a}1: 92n
18^{a}2–7: 95
18^{a}6–7: 92n
18^{a}8–9: 246
18^{a}10–11: 174n
8 153, 156n, 155–8, 160, 173, 174, 176, 227
18^{a}13–27: 163n
18^{a}13–14: 70n, 155
18^{a}14–17: 95
18^{a}18–27: 155
18^{a}18–19: 155n
18^{a}18: 155, 156, 160, 173
18^{a}19–20: 155, 156, 160, 173
18^{a}20–6: 155
18^{a}20–1: 155n
18^{a}20: 160, 173
18^{a}23: 155n, 173
18^{a}24: 173
18^{a}25–6: 157, 160, 173
18^{a}25: 155, 174
18^{a}26–7: 174
9 34, 151, 184, 198, 199, 200, 208, 209, 209n, 216, 225, 226, 227, 227n, 228, 230, 230n, 231, 231n, 233, 266, 266n, 269, 280
18^{a}28–33: 198, 200, 227, 249n, 263n
18^{a}28: 202n
18^{a}29–33: 174n
18^{a}29–30: 202n
18^{a}31–2: 202n
18^{a}31: 202n
18^{a}33: 202n
18^{a}34–18^{b}25: 198, 201
18^{a}34–18^{b}9: 201, 202
18^{a}34–18^{b}4: 202
18^{a}35–7: 75n, 203
18^{a}35: 201n
18^{a}36–7: 202n
18^{a}37–8: 202
18^{a}38–9: 203
18^{a}38: 202n
18^{a}39–18^{b}3: 133n
18^{a}39–18^{b}1: 202
18^{a}39: 202n
18^{b}1–2: 202, 203
18^{b}3: 203
18^{b}4–5: 202n
18^{b}4: 203
18^{b}5–9: 202, 203, 206
18^{b}7–8: 75n, 203
18^{b}8–9: 208n
18^{b}9–16: 201, 204
18^{b}9–11: 224n

18^{b}13–14: 205
18^{b}16–25: 201, 205
18^{b}21: 205n, 207
18^{b}22: 205n
18^{b}24–5: 207n
18^{b}26–19^{a}22: 198, 207, 208, 212
18^{b}26: 207n
18^{b}27–9: 249n
18^{b}27–8: 202n
18^{b}30: 207n
18^{b}31: 207n
18^{b}33–19^{a}6: 204n
18^{b}38–9: 56n
18^{b}38: 207n
19^{a}3: 207n
19^{a}4–6: 224n
19^{a}4: 75n
19^{a}7–22: 63n
19^{a}7: 208n
19^{a}9–10: 208n
19^{a}10–11: 210n
19^{a}15–16: 45n
19^{a}18–22: 208n
19^{a}18–19: 210n
19^{a}18: 208n
19^{a}20–2: 224
19^{a}22: 132n
19^{a}23–19^{b}4: 198, 209, 210
19^{a}23–7: 210
19^{a}23–4: 211
19^{a}24–5: 211
19^{a}25–7: 211
19^{a}26: 211
19^{a}27–32: 203, 210, 212
19^{a}27–8: 210n, 214, 214n
19^{a}28–32: 281
19^{a}28: 210n
19^{a}29: 213, 213n
19^{a}30–1: 216n
19^{a}31–2: 210n
19^{a}32–19^{b}4: 210
19^{a}33: 45n, 56, 138n, 215, 215n
19^{a}34: 210n, 225
19^{a}35–9: 208n
19^{a}35–6: 202n
19^{a}36–19^{b}4: 216
19^{a}36: 210n, 216n, 223n, 225
19^{a}37–8: 223n
19^{a}37: 216n
19^{a}38: 216n, 223n
19^{a}39–19^{b}4: 227
19^{a}39: 210n, 223n
19^{b}3–4: 202n
10 19^{b}5–18: 161n
19^{b}13–14: 230n
19^{b}14–31: 100n
19^{b}19–36: 161n
19^{b}24–6: 84n
19^{b}29–30: 84n
19^{b}31: 231n
19^{b}32: 90n
20^{a}3–14: 249n
20^{a}9–10: 90n
20^{a}12–14: 90n
20^{a}13–14: 89n
20^{a}15–19: 152n
20^{a}16–20: 263n
20^{a}16–18: 263n
20^{a}16–17: 252n
20^{a}31–40: 161n
20^{a}31–6: 229, 231
20^{a}33–6: 229
20^{a}35–6: 84n
20^{a}36: 75n
20^{b}3–4: 246n
11 176
20^{b}13–26: 177
20^{b}13–22: 163n
20^{b}13–19: 156
20^{b}13: 70n
20^{b}15–19: 157n
20^{b}17–19: 163n
20^{b}22–6: 178
20^{b}25–6: 179
20^{b}25: 177n
20^{b}26: 178, 180n, 231n
20^{b}35–6: 281n
20^{b}37–8: 189n
21^{a}18–33: 100n
21^{a}25–8: 161
21^{a}32–3: 162n
12–13 248
12 21^{b}17: 189n
21^{b}19–20: 70n
21^{b}19: 102n
21^{b}21–2: 84n
21^{b}26–33: 84n
21^{b}27–8: 196n
13 22^{b}2: 189n
22^{b}23–4: 189n
22^{b}32–3: 189n
23^{a}21–6: 231
14 23^{a}33–4: 187n
23^{a}38: 45n
23^{a}40–23^{b}1: 133n
23^{b}4–6: 133n
23^{b}7–13: 133n

23^{b}7–8: 133n
23^{b}33–24^{a}3: 133n
24^{b}1–6: 239n
24^{b}1–2: 55n
24^{b}5: 239n
24^{b}6–7: 263n
24^{b}8: 75n

PRIOR ANALYTICS

1.1 24^{a}13–14: 254
24^{a}14–15: 249n
24^{a}16–22: 91n
24^{a}16–17: 70n
24^{a}17: 244n, 256n
24^{a}19–22: 244n
24^{a}29: 70n
24^{b}16–18: 84n
24^{b}22–4: 249n
24^{b}26–7: 255n
24^{b}28–30: 249
1.2 25^{a}5: 91n, 244n
25^{a}7–12: 263n
25^{a}10: 256n
25^{a}14–17: 256
25^{a}20: 256n
1.4 25^{b}32–40: 249n
25^{b}32–7: 255n
25^{b}32–3: 255n
25^{b}33–4: 254n
25^{b}39–40: 249n
26^{a}17–28: 249n
26^{a}17: 256n
26^{a}24: 249n
26^{a}27: 249n
26^{a}28–30: 91n, 244n
26^{a}32–3: 91n, 244n
26^{a}36–9: 244n
26^{a}39–26^{b}14: 257n
26^{a}39: 91n
26^{b}14–20: 89n
26^{b}14–15: 245n
26^{b}21–4: 244n, 245n
26^{b}23–4: 91n
1.5 27^{a}7–8: 253n
27^{a}10–11: 253n
27^{a}34: 252n
27^{b}36–8: 244n
27^{b}38: 91n
1.6 28^{b}28–9: 245n
29^{a}6–9: 244n
29^{a}8: 91n
1.7 29^{a}19–29: 244n
29^{a}27–8: 91n
1.13 32^{a}27–8: 229n
1.14 33^{a}37–8: 244n
33^{a}37: 91n
33^{a}39–40: 257n
1.15 34^{b}7–18: 262n
35^{b}3–4: 252n
35^{b}14–15: 244n
35^{b}15: 91n
1.16 36^{b}12–13: 244n
36^{b}12: 91n
1.17 37^{b}13–16: 244n
1.18 38^{a}10–11: 91n, 244n
1.19 38^{b}35–7: 244n
38^{b}36: 91n
1.20 39^{b}2–3: 244n
39^{b}2: 91n
1.21 40^{a}1–2: 244n
40^{a}1: 91n
1.23 40^{b}23–5: 255n
1.24 41^{b}6: 254n
41^{b}22–3: 254n
1.27 43^{a}25–32: 79n
43^{a}29–30: 114n
43^{a}32–6: 80n
43^{a}33–6: 108n
43^{a}36–7: 114n
43^{a}39–40: 80n
43^{b}3–5: 196n
43^{b}11–15: 244n
43^{b}11–12: 196n
43^{b}14: 91n
43^{b}23: 255n
43^{b}29–30: 255n
1.28 43^{b}43–44^{a}2: 257n
1.30 46^{a}14–15: 86n
1.32 47^{a}13: 255n
47^{b}3: 86n
1.37 49^{a}6–9: 97n
49^{a}6–7: 189n
1.38 49^{a}12–19: 162n
49^{a}22–5: 162n
49^{a}27–8: 100n
49^{a}37–8: 100n
1.46 51^{b}5–52^{a}14: 161n
51^{b}32–3: 229n
2.1 53^{a}21–4: 255n
53^{a}21–3: 255n
2.4 57^{a}34: 254n
57^{b}4–17: 205n
2.6 58^{b}28–30: 255n
2.10 60^{b}20–2: 253n
2.15 63^{b}23–8: 263n
63^{b}35–8: 70n
64^{a}13–15: 86n
64^{b}9–10: 138
64^{b}10: 130n

2.19 66^{a}26: 89n
2.20 66^{b}11: 140n
66^{b}16: 255n
2.23 68^{b}24: 257n
2.27 70^{b}30–1: 89n
70^{b}34: 257n

POSTERIOR ANALYTICS

1.1 71^{a}12–14: 133n
71^{a}14–15: 82n
71^{a}14: 229n
71^{a}15–16: 132n
71^{a}23–4: 79n
71^{a}23: 223n
71^{a}26–7: 100n
1.2 71^{b}19–72^{a}38: 252
71^{b}25–6: 133n
72^{a}8–9: 70n
72^{a}13–14: 86n
72^{a}20–1: 116n
1.4 73^{a}28–34: 249n, 262n
73^{a}30–1: 264
74^{a}1: 254n
1.5 74^{a}5: 254n
74^{a}24–5: 254n
75^{a}16: 130n
1.6 74^{b}32–9: 184n
75^{a}27: 75n
1.8 75^{b}21–30: 262n
1.10 76^{b}6: 100n
76^{b}15–16: 132n
76^{b}19: 132n
76^{b}20: 132n
76^{b}36–8: 106n
1.11 77^{a}5–9: 79n
1.14 79^{a}24–9: 116
1.15 79^{a}36–40: 255n
79^{a}36–7: 255n
79^{a}38: 255n
79^{a}39: 255n
79^{a}40–1: 254n
79^{a}41–79^{b}1: 252n, 253n
79^{b}2: 255n
79^{b}5: 255n
79^{b}6–7: 254n
79^{b}7–8: 257n
79^{b}10: 255n
79^{b}11: 257n
79^{b}12–13: 255n
79^{b}15: 255n
79^{b}17: 255n
1.16 79^{b}38: 255n
1.19 81^{b}24–9: 107n
1.22 83^{a}1–23: 107n
83^{a}1–2: 75n
83^{a}18–23: 97n
83^{b}12–17: 114n
83^{b}13–15: 220n
84^{a}25: 257n
1.24 85^{b}15–18: 79n, 81
85^{b}17–18: 81
1.25 86^{b}33–6: 50n
1.32 88^{a}19–20: 45n
88^{b}1–3: 114n
88^{b}1–2: 113n
1.33 88^{b}32–89^{a}3: 45n
88^{b}32–3: 45n
89^{a}2–3: 45n
2.1 89^{b}23–35: 100n
89^{b}24: 130n
89^{b}33–5: 112n
89^{b}33: 100n
2.2 89^{b}36–90^{a}23: 100n, 112n
89^{b}39: 100n
90^{a}2: 100n
90^{a}3–5: 100n
90^{a}9–11: 100n
90^{a}12: 122n
90^{a}31–4: 112n
90^{a}32–4: 100n
2.3 90^{b}1–7: 116
90^{b}33–8: 116n
90^{b}33–4: 70n
2.4 91^{a}14–15: 116
91^{a}15–16: 116n
2.5 91^{b}14–15: 196n
2.6 92^{a}27–33: 163n
2.7 92^{b}5–8: 163n
92^{b}14: 113n
92^{b}26–8: 132n
92^{b}29–30: 163n
92^{b}32: 165n
2.8 93^{a}16–20: 100n
2.10 93^{b}29–32: 132n
93^{b}35–7: 70n, 163n, 165n
93^{b}36: 102n
2.11 94^{b}32: 102n
95^{a}1: 102n
2.12 96^{a}15: 262n
2.13 96^{a}24–5: 257n
96^{a}25–7: 254n
96^{a}26: 254n
96^{a}29–30: 254n
96^{a}30–1: 257n
96^{a}32–4: 116, 254n
96^{b}8: 254n
96^{b}9–10: 254n
96^{b}19–20: 114n

96^{b}30–5: 156n
97^{b}26–7: 116
2.16 98^{a}36–7: 102n
2.17 99^{a}31–2: 254n
2.19 100^{b}5–8: 45n
100^{b}5–7: 45n, 187n
100^{b}6: 75n

TOPICS

1.1 100^{b}23–5: 140n
101^{a}1–4: 140n
1.4 101^{b}11–25: 115
101^{b}21–2: 111n
1.5 101^{b}39: 111n
102^{a}5–17: 115n
102^{a}22–8: 220n
102^{b}20–6: 220n
1.7 103^{a}23–39: 115n
1.8 103^{b}7–9: 116
103^{b}9–10: 111n
1.9 103^{b}20–39: 97n
103^{b}27–37: 119n
1.11 104^{b}19–21: 231n
1.15 107^{a}3–12: 63n
107^{b}13–18: 194n
1.17 108^{a}11: 106n
2.1 108^{b}34–109^{a}6: 263n
109^{a}5–6: 263n
109^{a}29–30: 133n, 251n
2.2 109^{b}23–5: 263n
2.3 110^{a}32–7: 263n
110^{b}17–25: 107n
110^{b}24–5: 107n
2.4 111^{a}14–20: 45n
111^{b}12–16: 132n
111^{b}17–23: 133n
2.6 112^{b}1–20: 60n
2.11 115^{b}11–35: 100n, 141n
3.6 119^{a}34–6: 263n
119^{b}17–30: 194n
120^{a}6–31: 245n
120^{a}6–8: 91n
120^{a}7: 245n
120^{a}8–14: 263n
120^{a}12–14: 263n
120^{a}14–20: 263n
120^{a}20–4: 263n
4.1 120^{b}36–121^{a}9: 189n
121^{b}5–7: 159n
4.2 123^{a}15–19: 45n
4.4 124^{b}18–19: 189n
4.6 127^{a}27–8: 159n
127^{a}33–4: 159
5.1 128^{b}16–21: 220n
128^{b}16–18: 156n
129^{a}26–30: 220n
5.2 129^{b}31: 156n
130^{a}27–8: 156n
5.3 131^{b}5–18: 220
132^{a}6–9: 156n
5.4 133^{b}33–6: 123n
5.8 138^{a}10–12: 156n
5.9 139^{a}18–20: 156n
6.6 143^{b}15–16: 229n
6.8 146^{a}36–146^{b}2: 189n
146^{b}6–9: 189n
7.3 153^{a}15–16: 111n
7.5 154^{a}31–2: 111n
154^{a}36–154^{b}2: 116n
154^{b}4: 189n
8.1 156^{b}34: 145n
8.2 157^{b}11–16: 184n
157^{b}13: 196n
157^{b}15–16: 196n
8.7 160^{a}17–34: 178n, 179n
8.12 162^{b}3–22: 45n
162^{b}3–5: 140n

SOPHISTICI ELENCHI

1 164^{a}20–1: 140n
165^{a}2–3: 140
165^{a}6–8: 88n
4 165^{b}25: 141n
165^{b}26: 156n
165^{b}30: 141n
166^{a}6: 141n
166^{a}23–30: 213
166^{a}26–7: 213n
166^{b}22–3: 141n
5 166^{b}28–36: 107n
166^{b}37–167^{a}20: 141n
166^{b}37–167^{a}6: 100n
166^{b}38: 100n
167^{a}7–9: 143n
167^{a}15–20: 148
167^{a}16: 148
167^{a}17: 148
167^{a}17–18: 149
168^{a}9–11: 133n
6 168^{a}36–7: 140n
168^{a}40–168^{b}2: 107n
168^{b}11–16: 141n
169^{a}6–18: 178n
169^{a}7–8: 70n
169^{a}10–11: 70n
169^{a}11: 169
169^{a}14: 70n

7 169b9–12: 141n
8 169b18–23: 140n
169b27–8: 140n
9 170b1–2: 140n
10 171a1–5: 140n
171a4–5: 140n
171a5–7: 140n
11 171b7–11: 140n
171b18–19: 140n
13 173b1–3: 189n
17 175b39–176a18: 178n, 179n
175b41–176a10: 157n
18 176b29–33: 45n
176b31–3: 140n
22 189
178b24–9: 45n, 184n
178b27–8: 189
178b37–9: 79n, 189n
179a8–10: 79n, 189n
25 1, 32, 141
180a23–4: 141, 146, 149
180a32: 146
180a34–180b7: 31
180a34–180b2: 141
180a36–8: 100n
180a36: 141n
180b1: 141n
180b2–7: 142
180b2–5: 75n, 147
180b2–3: 142, 142n, 146
180b3–5: 148
180b5–7: 149, 150
180b5–6: 150
180b5: 142n, 145, 147, 150
180b6: 142n
180b7: 142n
180b8: 146
30 181a36–181b18: 178n, 179n
181a39: 70n
181b23–4: 70n
31 181b34–5: 189n
32 182a10: 75n

PHYSICS

1.1 184a21–6: 71n
1.3 186b9–10: 100n
187a5–6: 100n
1.4 187a36: 223n
187b5: 207n
1.6 189a14: 114n
189b23–4: 114n
1.7 122
190a34–5: 187n
190b10–17: 122n
190b24–7: 120n
1.8 191a25: 103n
1.9 192a31–2: 120n
2.3 194b23–6: 120n
195b3–4: 107n
2.5 196b10–21: 60n
3.1 200b26–201a9: 187n
200b28: 189n
4.3 210a14–18: 255n
4.4 211a17–23: 195n
4.7 213b30–1: 163n
4.12 222a3–9: 45n
5.1 224a21–3: 107n
224b4–6: 195n
224b10–16: 195n
225a20–6: 97n
5.2 225b11–13: 187n
5.4 227b4–6: 114n
7.1 242b35: 114n
7.3 246b10–17: 187n
246b20–247a7: 187n
246b25–6: 187n
247b1–7: 187n
7.4 248b6–249a8: 194n
8.1 251b5–9: 187n
8.7 260b16–19: 96n
8.8 263a17: 130n
263a18: 103n
8.9 265a22–4: 96n

DE CAELO

1.5 271b6: 103n
271b9: 103n
1.6 274a28: 165n
1.12 281b2–14: 213n
281b8–14: 133n
283b8–10: 199n
283b13–14: 199n, 200n
2.3 286a25–6: 50n
2.14 296a35–296b1: 165n
3.1 298b13: 103n

DE GENERATIONE ET CORRUPTIONE

1.3 317b5–13: 262n
317b8–11: 80n
317b31–3: 80n
318b25: 123n
1.4 320a2–5: 122n

1.8 $325^{a}18$: 130n
2.9 $335^{a}33$–$335^{b}4$: 60n
2.11 $337^{a}34$–$337^{b}7$: 232
$337^{b}3$–7: 224n
$337^{b}4$–5: 184n
$337^{b}4$: 232n
$337^{b}5$: 232n
$337^{b}7$: 232n
$337^{b}33$–$338^{a}3$: 60n
$338^{b}5$–19: 81n

DE ANIMA

1.1 $402^{a}22$–5: 114n
$402^{b}7$–8: 80n
$402^{b}16$–21: 119n
1.2 $404^{a}27$–31: 45n
1.3 $407^{a}6$–10: 63n
$407^{a}8$–9: 69n
1.5 $410^{a}18$–21: 114n
$410^{a}25$–6: 106n
2.1 $412^{a}6$–9: 117n
$412^{a}6$: 114n
$412^{a}9$: 120n
$412^{a}16$–19: 122n
$412^{b}8$–9: 234
2.3 $414^{b}6$–11: 108n
2.4 $415^{a}22$–$415^{b}7$: 81n
$415^{b}12$–14: 123n
2.6 $418^{a}7$–25: 108
$418^{a}8$–25: 108n, 109n
$418^{a}9$–14: 108n
$418^{a}9$–11: 108n
$418^{a}11$–16: 45n, 109n
$418^{a}15$: 109
$418^{a}16$–20: 108n
$418^{a}17$–18: 108n
$418^{a}24$–5: 108n
2.9 $421^{a}9$–26: 109n
$421^{a}19$–26: 106n
2.10 $422^{b}5$–10: 109n
3.1 $425^{a}13$–$425^{b}11$: 108n
$425^{a}15$–16: 108n
$425^{a}27$–30: 108n
$425^{a}30$–$425^{b}4$: 109n
$425^{b}4$–11: 108n
3.3 $427^{a}17$–29: 106n
$427^{a}26$–$427^{b}6$: 138
$427^{b}4$: 106n
$427^{b}11$–14: 45n
$427^{b}11$–12: 109n
$427^{b}20$–1: 45n, 229n
$427^{b}27$–9: 71n
$428^{a}1$–4: 45n
$428^{a}3$–5: 45n, 187n
$428^{a}3$–4: 45n
$428^{a}11$: 45n, 109n
$428^{a}12$: 45n
$428^{a}16$–18: 45n
$428^{a}17$–18: 45n
$428^{a}19$: 45n
$428^{b}2$–9: 45n
$428^{b}4$–9: 184n
$428^{b}6$: 196n
$428^{b}7$–9: 184n
$428^{b}8$–9: 196n
$428^{b}10$–17: 45n
$428^{b}18$–30: 45n, 108n
$428^{b}18$–19: 109n
$428^{b}19$–25: 109n
$428^{b}21$: 109
$428^{b}25$–30: 109n
3.4 $429^{a}13$–18: 106n
$429^{a}18$–27: 107n
$429^{a}23$–$429^{b}5$: 106n
$429^{a}29$–$429^{b}5$: 109n
$429^{b}10$–12: 119n
3.5 $430^{a}10$–11: 120n
$430^{a}14$–25: 106n
3.6 1, 64, 71, 99, 114, 115
$430^{a}26$–$430^{b}6$: 63n
$430^{a}26$–$430^{b}3$: 70n, 84n, 102
$430^{a}26$: 71, 103, 117n
$430^{b}1$–3: 133n
$430^{b}2$–3: 71n, 102n
$430^{b}3$–4: 71
$430^{b}3$: 84n
$430^{b}4$–5: 229n
$430^{b}6$–26: 105n
$430^{b}26$–31: 45n, 64, 102, 107
$430^{b}26$–7: 70n, 102n, 229
$430^{b}27$–31: 105n
$430^{b}27$–8: 115
$430^{b}28$: 102, 107
$430^{b}29$–31: 108n, 109n
$430^{b}29$–30: 45n
$430^{b}29$: 109n
$430^{b}30$–1: 107, 107n
3.7 $431^{a}8$–17: 61n
$431^{a}8$: 102n, 106n
$431^{a}14$–16: 55n
$431^{a}16$–17: 71n
$431^{b}2$: 71n
$431^{b}6$–10: 71n
$431^{b}10$–12: 63n
3.8 $431^{b}26$–$432^{a}3$: 106n
$432^{a}1$–3: 106n
$432^{a}7$–14: 71n
$432^{a}10$–12: 45n, 70n, 84n
3.10 $433^{a}26$: 45n

DE SENSU

1 437^{a}14: 88n
4 442^{b}4–10: 108n, 110n
442^{b}8–10: 45n, 109n

DE MEMORIA

1 450^{a}9–12: 108n

DE SOMNO ET VIGILIA

2 455^{a}12–15: 108n

DE INSOMNIIS

1 458^{b}4–6: 108n
458^{b}31–3: 108n, 109n
2 459^{b}5–23: 109n

DE DIVINATIONE PER SOMNIA

1 463^{b}1–3: 205n
2 463^{b}28–31: 232n

DE LONGAEVITATE

3 465^{b}12–14: 80n

HISTORIA ANIMALIUM

7.4 584^{b}6–14: 187n
10.7 638^{b}8–9: 165n

DE PARTIBUS ANIMALIUM

1.1 639^{b}23–4: 60n
640^{b}23–8: 122n
1.3 643^{b}18: 163n
1.4 644^{a}27–8: 79n, 80
1.5 645^{a}36–645^{b}2: 107n
2.2 648^{b}12–17: 109n
2.6 652^{a}16–17: 165n
3.7 670^{a}9: 165n

DE GENERATIONE ANIMALIUM

2.1 731^{b}28–30: 123n
731^{b}35–732^{a}1: 81
733^{a}27: 257n
3.10 760^{a}35–760^{b}1: 81n
4.4 770^{b}6: 257n
4.6 774^{b}17: 257n
5.1 779^{b}12–780^{a}25: 109n

PROBLEMS

19.20 919^{a}22–5: 164n
21.17 929^{a}18: 165n
31.7 958^{a}24–7: 109n
31.11 958^{b}11–15: 109n

DE XENOPHANE

4 978^{b}15–33: 161n

METAPHYSICS

A1 981^{a}18–20: 107n
A3 983^{b}3: 103n
983^{b}17–18: 165n
984^{a}18: 130n
A6 987^{a}29–987^{b}7: 81n
A7 988^{a}20: 103n
A8 989^{b}6–7: 207n
989^{b}8–9: 207n
α 1 993^{a}30: 103n
993^{b}9–11: 106n
993^{b}17: 103n
993 ^{b}19–31: 103n
993^{b}19–21: 63n
B1 995^{b}35: 122n
B2 996^{b}21: 118n
997^{b}20: 118n
B3 998^{b}20–1: 159n
998^{b}22: 113n
B4 999^{a}33–4: 122n
999^{b}33–1000^{a}1: 79n
1001^{a}19–22: 159n
1001^{a}23: 120n
1001^{a}27: 120n
1001^{a}30: 120n
B6 1002^{b}21: 118n
Γ 229
Γ2 1003^{b}26–7: 113
1003^{b}30: 118n
1004^{b}4: 118n
1004^{b}20: 159
Γ3 1005^{b}28–9: 61
Γ4 1005^{b}35–1006^{a}1: 133n
1006^{a}21–2: 74n
1006^{b}18–22: 133n
1006^{b}31–3: 204n
1008^{a}4–7: 172n

Γ5 1009b12–33: 138n
1010b1–26: 109n
1010b2–3: 45n
1010b14–26: 45n, 108n, 109n
Γ6 1011a25–1011b1: 109n
1011b19–20: 86n
Γ7 1
1011b24: 70n, 134
1011b25–7: 132
1011b29–31: 207n
1012a2–5: 65n, 70n
1012a2–3: 55n
1012a3: 132n
1012a21–4: 132n
1012a26–8: 207n
1012a26–7: 229n
1012a28: 229n
Γ8 1012a31–3: 229n
1012b3–4: 229n
1012b7–11: 132
1012b8–9: 132n
1012b10–11: 229
1012b11: 132n
1012b24–6: 184n
Δ 169
Δ2 1013a24–6: 120n
1014a7–8: 107n
Δ4 1014b30: 118n
Δ5 1015b13: 223n
Δ6 1016a33–4: 111n
1016b1–3: 45n, 119n
1016b31–5: 114n
1017a6: 111n
Δ7 1
1017a7–1017b9: 51n
1017a30: 118n
1017a31–5: 45n
1017b6: 118n
Δ8 1017b14–16: 123n
1017b21–2: 111n
Δ9 1018a1–4: 79n
Δ11 1018b30–6: 96n
1019a1–4: 96n
1019a2–4: 104n
Δ12 1019a26: 118n
Δ15 1021a25–6: 51n
1021b3–6: 191n
1021b4–6: 189n
1021b6–8: 188n
Δ21 1022b19: 223n
Δ26 1023b29–32: 79n, 80n
Δ28 1024b9–16: 114n
Δ29 1, 46, 50, 57n
1024b17–26: 57n
1024b17–21: 45n, 46, 184n
1024b18–19: 49, 52
1024b19–20: 47, 48
1024b20: 47, 48
1024b21–4: 138n
1024b22–4: 133n
1024b24–5: 47
1024b26–1025a1: 57n
1024b32–4: 231n
1025a1–13: 57n, 150n
E1 62
1025b3–4: 62
E2 62
1026a33–1026b2: 51n, 62
1026a37: 63n
1026b27–30: 60n
E3 62
1027a29–30: 121n
1027a32–1027b14: 199n
E4 1, 46, 62, 63, 64, 64n, 65, 66, 67, 68, 68n, 70, 77, 82, 83, 97n, 235, 235n, 236
1027b17–1028a4: 63
1027b17–19: 51n
1027b19–26: 63n
1027b19: 62n
1027b20–3: 67
1027b23: 68
1027b24–5: 69
1027b25–9: 64n
1027b25–7: 63, 65
1027b27–8: 45n, 64, 65n, 103n, 105n, 117n
1027b28–9: 63, 234, 236
1027b29–1028a4: 95
1027b29–33: 154
1027b29–31: 67
1027b29: 46n, 64n, 103n
1027b31–3: 67
1027b31: 46n, 64n, 96, 103n, 234
1027b32: 63n
1027b33: 63n
1027b34–1028a1: 62n
1028a2: 98
Z 81, 231n
Z1 1028a10–14: 51n
1028a22: 118n
1028a30–1: 100n
1028a31–1028b2: 98n
1028a31–6: 96n
1028a31–4: 80n, 96n
Z2 1028b8–13: 122n
Z3 1028b36–1029a7: 117n
1028b36–1029a5: 122n
1029a2–3: 122n
1029a3–5: 122n
1029a23–4: 122n

Z4 1030^{a}17–27: 119n
1030^{a}21: 159n
1030^{a}25–6: 100n
1030^{b}7–13: 163n, 165n
Z5 1030^{b}20–1: 107n
1031^{a}12: 111n
Z7 1032^{a}12–14: 120n
1032^{a}13–25: 122n
1033^{a}19–22: 120n
Z8 1033^{a}24–1033^{b}19: 121n
1033^{a}25–6: 120n
1033^{b}1–3: 120n
1033^{b}8–9: 120n
Z9 1034^{b}7–16: 121n
Z10 1035^{a}1–2: 117n
1035^{a}17–21: 122n
1035^{a}28–30: 121n
1035^{b}34–1036^{a}1: 81n
1036^{a}2–9: 81n
Z11 1036^{a}28–9: 81n
1037^{a}18–20: 163n
Z12 1037^{b}8–1038^{a}35: 163n
1037^{b}18–21: 116n
Z13 1038^{b}4–6: 122n
1038^{b}5–6: 122n
1038^{b}11–12: 79n
1038^{b}16: 79n
1038^{b}27–8: 96n
Z15 1039^{b}20–7: 121n
1039^{b}27–1040^{a}7: 81n
1039^{b}27–1040^{a}5: 184n
Z16 1040^{b}25–6: 79n
1040^{b}26–7: 80
1040^{b}33–4: 120n
Z17 123n
1041^{a}9–10: 123n
1041^{a}10–1041^{b}11: 123
1041^{a}27–8: 123n
1041^{b}8–9: 123n
1041^{b}9–11: 123n
1041^{b}27–8: 123n
1041^{b}27: 118n
H 231n
H1 1042^{a}17: 111n
1042^{a}26–31: 121n, 122n
1042^{a}32–1042^{b}3: 122n
1042^{b}1: 118n
H2 1042^{b}15–1043^{a}14: 123
1042^{b}32–3: 123n
1043^{a}2–4: 123n
1043^{a}4–7: 122n
1043^{a}5–6: 122n
H3 1043^{a}30: 117n
1043^{b}14–16: 121n
1043^{b}23–1044^{a}14: 163n
1043^{b}28–32: 116n
H4 1044^{b}8–12: 122
H5 1044^{b}21–9: 195n
1044^{b}21–4: 121n
H6 1045^{a}7–1045^{b}24: 163n
1045^{a}12–14: 163n, 165n
Θ1 1045^{b}32–4: 51n
1045^{b}36: 235n
1046^{a}25–6: 118n
Θ2 1046^{b}13–15: 86n
Θ3 1046^{b}32: 118n
1046^{b}35–6: 118n
1047^{a}22: 118n
Θ4 1047^{b}12–14: 45n
Θ7 1049^{a}27–36: 122n
1049^{a}34–1049^{b}2: 122n
Θ8 1049^{b}4–1050^{b}6: 98n
1049^{b}12–14: 96n
1050^{a}16: 118n
1050^{a}33: 118n
1050^{b}8–34: 51n
Θ10 1, 46, 50, 52, 54, 58, 62, 63, 64, 64n, 65, 65n, 66, 67, 83, 85, 99, 104, 105, 114, 115, 121, 123n, 134, 234, 235, 236
1051^{a}34–1051^{b}17: 50, 100, 103
1051^{a}34–1051^{b}9: 51, 64, 66, 67
1051^{a}34–1051^{b}6: 45n, 56
1051^{a}34–1051^{b}5: 54
1051^{a}34–1051^{b}3: 52
1051^{a}34–1051^{b}2: 51, 54, 236
1051^{a}34–5: 97n
1051^{a}34: 234, 236
1051^{a}35–1051^{b}1: 51n
1051^{a}35: 51n, 236
1051^{b}1–3: 65
1051^{b}1–2: 57
1051^{b}1: 51n, 234, 236
1051^{b}2–3: 51, 52, 54, 238
1051^{b}3–5: 54
1051^{b}3: 55
1051^{b}4–5: 130n
1051^{b}5–6: 56
1051^{b}5: 51n, 58n
1051^{b}6–9: 56, 57, 61
1051^{b}6: 56, 58n
1051^{b}9–17: 53n, 59, 60n, 184n
1051^{b}9–10: 60
1051^{b}10–11: 60
1051^{b}10: 60
1051^{b}11–13: 51, 58n, 59, 59n, 238
1051^{b}11: 58n, 210n
1051^{b}13–14: 45n
1051^{b}13: 58n

1051^{b}17–1052^{a}4: 50, 64, 101, 102, 103
1051^{b}17–23: 53
1051^{b}17: 59n, 102
1051^{b}18–21: 45n
1051^{b}19–20: 52, 238
1051^{b}20–1: 53
1051^{b}20: 53n
1051^{b}22–33: 45n
1051^{b}23–4: 101n
1051^{b}23: 101n
1051^{b}24: 106, 112
1051^{b}25–6: 102, 105n, 106, 110, 117
1051^{b}25: 102n, 106n
1051^{b}26–8: 117
1051^{b}26–7: 118, 119
1051^{b}26: 106, 107, 107n, 110
1051^{b}27: 101n, 105n, 116
1051^{b}28–30: 101n, 120
1051^{b}29: 120, 120n
1051^{b}30–3: 110
1051^{b}30–2: 105n
1051^{b}30–1: 120
1051^{b}31: 101n
1051^{b}32–3: 101n, 119
1051^{b}32: 101n, 106n
1051^{b}33–1052^{a}1: 103
1051^{b}33–5: 52, 238
1051^{b}33: 101n
1051^{b}35–1052^{a}1: 46n, 101n
1052^{a}1–4: 45n, 106n
1052^{a}1: 106, 112
1052^{a}2–4: 106n
1052^{a}2: 106n
1052^{a}4–11: 50, 184n
1052^{a}4–7: 113
I1 1052^{a}17–19: 107n
1052^{a}29–31: 45n
1052^{b}18–19: 114n
1053^{a}31–5: 138n
1053^{a}35–6: 138n
I2 1053^{b}20–1: 159n
1053^{b}22–4: 114n
1053^{b}26: 118n
1054^{a}1: 118n
1054^{a}16–17: 113n
I4 1054^{b}18–21: 161n
1054^{b}27–31: 114n
1055^{a}6–7: 194n
I6 1056^{b}3: 118n
1057^{a}11–12: 138n
I7 1057^{a}26: 118n
K1 1059^{b}28–9: 159n
1059^{b}33–4: 113n
K2 1060^{b}4–5: 159n
1060^{b}20–2: 80n
K6 1062^{b}12–14: 138n
1062^{b}19: 138n
1062^{b}35–1063^{a}10: 109n
1063^{a}4: 138n
1063^{a}17–21: 184n
K8 1064^{b}30–1065^{a}6: 60n
1065^{a}21–4: 98n
1065^{a}21–3: 70n
K9 1066^{a}15–16: 161n
1066^{a}34: 118n
K11 1067^{b}25–30: 97n
K12 1068^{a}11–13: 187n
Λ 119
Λ1 1069^{b}3–20: 122n
Λ2 1069^{b}17: 118n
1069^{b}26–8: 51n, 97n
Λ3 1069^{b}35–1070^{a}4: 121n
1070^{a}15–17: 121n
1070^{a}28–9: 118n
Λ4 1070^{a}33–1070^{b}10: 192n
1070^{b}7–8: 159n
Λ5 1071^{a}8–11: 120n
1071^{a}23–4: 72n
1071^{a}24–6: 114n
Λ6 1071^{b}17–20: 120n
Λ7 1072^{a}25–6: 120n
1072^{b}8: 120n
1072^{b}20–1: 106n
Λ9 1075^{a}5–10: 45n
Λ10 1075^{a}38–1075^{b}1: 120n
1075^{b}34–7: 120n
M2 1077^{b}2–4: 96n
1077^{b}8–9: 122n
M4 1078^{b}12–17: 81n
M6 1080^{a}29: 118n
1080^{b}23: 118n
M9 1085^{a}7: 118n
1085^{b}27: 118n
1086^{a}31–1086^{b}11: 80n
M10 1087^{a}19–20: 108n
1087^{a}20–1: 72n
N1 1087^{b}36: 118n
1088^{a}17–18: 107n
1088^{a}22–3: 192n
1088^{a}29–35: 187n
1088^{a}29–31: 192
1088^{a}29–30: 194
1088^{a}29: 192n
N2 1089^{a}3: 120n
1089^{a}15–19: 97n
1089^{a}18: 189n
1089^{a}26–8: 51n
1089^{a}26–7: 97n

NICOMACHEAN ETHICS

1.4 1096a20–2: 192n
1096a25–34: 63n
1096a34–1096b5: 120n
1096b28–9: 106n
1.7 1098b1: 130n
3.4 1111b31–4: 45n
1111b33–4: 63n
1112a5–7: 63n
3.5 1112a21–3: 45n
1112b33–1113a2: 199n
3.6 1113a25–31: 109n
4.8 1124b6: 45n
4.13 1127a28–30: 63n
5.3 1130a2: 223n
5.10 1136a2: 223n
6.2 1139a21–2: 61
1139a21: 55n
1139a26–31: 40
1139a27–9: 63n
1139b5–9: 200
1139b12–13: 63n
6.3 1139b15–18: 45n, 55n
1139b19–24: 81n
1139b22–4: 60n, 81n
6.5 1140b13–16: 187n
6.6 1141a3–8: 45n
6.10 1142b8–11: 63n
1142b10: 45n
1142b11: 45n
1142b13–14: 55n
1142b14: 223n
6.12 1143b5: 106n
7.3 1146a21–7: 141n
1146a21: 141n
1146a22: 141n
7.10 1151b3–4: 45n
8.2 1155b13–15: 194n
9.4 1166a4–5: 123n
9.7 1168a5–7: 123n
10.2 1173b20–5: 109n
10.6 1177a6: 223n

MAGNA MORALIA

1.1 1182a29: 103n
1.34 1196b35–6: 63n

EUDEMIAN ETHICS

1.4 1215b2: 103n
1.8 1217b1–16: 80n
1217b8–16: 96n
1217b25–1218a1: 63n
1217b33–5: 113n
1218a4–5: 96n
1218a11: 120n
2.3 1221a6: 150n
2.4 1221b29–30: 63n
2.10 1226a1–4: 45n
3.4 1233b38: 150n
1234a2: 150n

POLITICS

3.7 1279a35: 165n
3.10 1281a27: 132n
6.1 1317a22: 165n

RHETORIC

1.1 1354a27–8: 45n
1355a21–2: 63n
1355a37: 63n
1.3 1358b3–5: 199n
1358b14–15: 199n
1.7 1364b7–10: 45n
1364b9: 103n
2.21 1394a22–5: 87
2.23 1397b12–29: 194n
2.24 1400b34–5: 140n
1402a2–4: 100n
1402a3–29: 141n
3.2 1404b26–7: 74n
3.5 1407a26–9: 165n
3.6 1407b38: 165n
3.12 1413b19–21: 164
1413b29–1414a1: 163n, 164
1413b29: 165
1413b31: 165
1413b32–3: 165
1414a1: 164n
3.17 1418a4–5: 200
3.19 1420b2–3: 164n

POETICS

8 1451a22–30: 165n
19 1456b8–13: 86n
20 1456b38–1457a6: 163n, 164n, 165
1456b38–1457a3: 165n
1457a4–5: 165n
1457a14–23: 230n
1457a14–18: 74n
1457a23–4: 74n
1457a24–7: 163n
1457a28–30: 163n, 165n

25 $1460^{b}8$–11: 138n
$1460^{b}32$–$1461^{a}4$: 138n
26 $1462^{b}7$–12: 165n

PROTREPTICUS

fr. 73 Gigon $302^{b}36$–8: 45n
$304^{a}20$: 103n
$304^{b}13$: 103n
$305^{b}25$–$306^{a}2$: 63n
$306^{b}7$: 45n
$306^{b}8$: 45n
$306^{b}12$: 45n
$310^{a}27$: 103n
$310^{b}14$: 103n
$310^{b}20$: 103n
$311^{b}39$–40: 123n
$312^{a}36$: 45n

DE IDEIS

fr. 118, 3 Gigon $378^{a}8$–$379^{a}3$: 71n
$378^{a}23$–$378^{b}1$: 161n
$378^{a}45$–$378^{b}45$: 161n
$382^{a}24$–31: 138n
fr. 119 Gigon $384^{a}12$–15: 80n

ON OPPOSITES

fr. 625 Gigon $726^{b}9$–19: 106n

PSEUDO-ARISTOTLE

DIVISIONS

30 49, 20–2: 45n
31 50, 8–10: 45n
50, 8–9: 138n

RHETORIC TO ALEXANDER

12 $1430^{a}40$–$1430^{b}1$: 87

ASCLEPIUS

COMMENTARY ON ARISTOTLE'S METAPHYSICS

6, 20–1: 117n
373, 32: 62n
374, 1–4: 69n
374, 7–8: 64n
374, 12–16: 96n
374, 18–21: 98n

BOETHIUS

COMMENTARY ON ARISTOTLE'S DE INTERPRETATIONE, *FIRST EDITION*

43, 11–14: 82n
72, 6–10: 172n
75, 9–11: 172n
77, 15–24: 88n
77, 24–78, 4: 172n
78, 24–79, 6: 88n
87, 2–88, 3: 244n
102, 21–4: 155n
103, 12–13: 155n
110, 16–18: 130n

COMMENTARY ON ARISTOTLE'S DE INTERPRETATIONE, *SECOND EDITION*

12, 3–16: 256n
48, 21–49, 23: 82n, 84n
50, 1–51, 3: 85n
51, 2–52, 9: 221n
51, 30–52, 6: 221
96, 28–97, 18: 172n
105, 1–18: 172n
110, 21–111, 12: 166n
115, 23–116, 6: 172n
118, 5–16: 88n
122, 27–123, 22: 88n
178, 17–23: 155n
181, 25–8: 155n
183, 5: 155n
183, 20–1: 156n
208, 1–7: 226n

CHRYSIPPUS

LOGICAL INVESTIGATIONS (PHERC *307*)

IX 23–X 6: 144n
IX 30: 145n
X 8: 145n
X 12–13: 146n

x 15–16: 146n
x 18–25: 145
x 20–1: 146
x 22–3: 146
x 28–31: 144n

CICERO

ACADEMICA

II 30 97: 227n

DE FATO

7 13: 162n
9 18: 227n
10 21: 227n
16 37–8: 227n, 266n

DE NATURA DEORUM

I 25 70: 227n

DEXIPPUS

COMMENTARY ON ARISTOTLE'S CATEGORIES

60, 13–23: 187
60, 13–16: 187
60, 15: 188
60, 18–20: 187
60, 21–3: 187n

DIOGENES LAERTIUS

LIVES AND OPINIONS OF EMINENT PHILOSOPHERS

5. 49: 146n
7. 65: 197n
7. 73–4: 95n
7. 76: 197n
7. 196: 145n
7. 197: 146, 147n

ELIAS

COMMENTARY ON ARISTOTLE'S CATEGORIES

183, 34–184, 3: 72n, 186n

IAMBLICHUS

PROTREPTICUS

34, 17–18: 45n
38, 2: 103n
39, 9: 103n
42, 5–23: 63n
44, 5–6: 45n
44, 5: 45n
44, 9: 45n
54, 4: 103n
55, 2: 103n
55, 7: 103n
58, 11: 123n
59, 13–14: 45n

ISOCRATES

HELENAE ENCOMIUM

1: 231n

OLYMPIODORUS

COMMENTARY ON ARISTOTLE'S CATEGORIES

79, 14–33: 72n, 186n
79, 28–33: 187n

PHILOPONUS

COMMENTARY ON ARISTOTLE'S CATEGORIES

82, 19–23: 186n
82, 19–20: 72n

COMMENTARY ON ARISTOTLE'S DE ANIMA (HAYDUCK)

544, 21–545, 5: 64n
546, 8–9: 71n

548, 11–20: 71n
553, 30–554, 2: 110n
557, 1–6: 110n
557, 9–10: 107n

COMMENTARY ON ARISTOTLE'S DE ANIMA (VERBEKE)

70, 90–71, 99: 71n
88, 66–78: 110n
88, 68–72: 109n

COMMENTARY ON ARISTOTLE'S DE GENERATIONE ET CORRUPTIONE

302, 25: 232n
302, 34–303, 5: 233n
306, 12: 232n

COMMENTARY ON ARISTOTLE'S POSTERIOR ANALYTICS

35, 2–13: 116n
37, 7–13: 116n

COMMENTARY ON ARISTOTLE'S PRIOR ANALYTICS

48, 11–18: 256n
74, 17–20: 256n
74, 24–6: 256n
124, 12–16: 256n
129, 13–18: 256n
198, 10–11: 256n
201, 19–21: 256n

PSEUDO-PHILOPONUS

COMMENTARY ON ARISTOTLE'S METAPHYSICS

39va: 107n

PLATO

CRATYLUS

385*b*7–8: 138n
385*b*7: 138n
385*b*8: 138n

EUTHYDEMUS

284*c*9–284*d*2: 138
284*d*5: 138n
285*d*7–286*b*6: 231n

LAWS

XII 965*b*4: 106n
969*b*6: 106n

PARMENIDES

161*e*4–5: 138n

PHAEDO

79*d*6: 106n

PHAEDRUS

273*a*4: 106n

PHILEBUS

37*b*10–37*c*2: 189n

REPUBLIC

V 477*b*10–11: 138n
478*a*6: 138n
VI 509*b*8–10: 120n

SOPHIST

240*d*9–241*a*2: 132n
253*c*2–3: 68n
256*b*2–3: 68n
257*b*1–257*c*4: 68n
262*a*3–5: 88n
262*a*6–8: 88n
262*b*5–6: 88n
262*b*9–262*c*1: 88n
262*c*6–7: 170n
262*c*7: 172n
262*c*9–10: 170n
262*c*10: 172n
262*c*12–13: 88n
262*e*8–9: 189n
262*e*11–263*b*13: 133n

263*a*11–263*b*3: 189n
263*b*4–10: 132n
263*b*4–5: 138n
263*b*4: 138n
263*c*1–3: 170n
263*c*3: 172n

SYMPOSIUM

212*a*4–5: 106n

THEAETETUS

154*b*6–155*c*5: 187n
186*d*3–4: 106n
190*c*6–7: 106n
190*d*9–10: 106n
194*c*1–3: 63n
202*b*5–6: 106n
209*a*8: 106n

TIMAEUS

37*a*6: 106n
52*b*2: 106n

PLOTINUS

ENNEADS

1, 1, 9, 12–14: 106n
5, 3, 10, 43: 106n
5, 3, 17, 24–7: 106n

PSEUDO-PLUTARCH

PLACITA PHILOSOPHORUM

899*b*: 195n

PROCLUS

COMMENTARY ON THE FIRST BOOK OF EUCLID'S ELEMENTS

179, 18: 106n

COMMENTARY ON PLATO'S CRATYLUS

37 12, 18–23: 231n

SCHOLIA IN ARISTOTELEM

157[a]13–24: 256n

SEXTUS EMPIRICUS

AGAINST THE PROFESSORS

8. 265: 95n
8. 428: 95n

OUTLINES OF PYRRHONISM

2. 110–12: 95n

SIMPLICIUS

COMMENTARY ON ARISTOTLE'S CATEGORIES

118, 15–16: 186n
118, 18–25: 186n
118, 19–25: 72n
119, 5–16: 187n
218, 19–21: 195n
390, 19–25: 106n
406, 12–16: 226n
406, 34–407, 5: 226n
407, 6–13: 226n

COMMENTARY ON ARISTOTLE'S DE ANIMA

250, 37–40: 71n

COMMENTARY ON ARISTOTLE'S PHYSICS

1299, 36–1300, 11: 197n

SPEUSIPPUS

FRAGMENTS (ACCORDING TO LANG'S ORDERING)

30: 106n

FRAGMENTS (ACCORDING TO ISNARDI'S ORDERING)

35: 106n

STEPHANUS

COMMENTARY ON ARISTOTLE'S DE INTERPRETATIONE

6, 22–5: 82n
18, 26–35: 87n
20, 4–10: 172n
20, 16–24: 172n
31, 11–12: 244n
33, 19–33: 155n
37, 7–10: 202n

THEMISTIUS

COMMENTARY ON ARISTOTLE'S DE ANIMA

109, 33–110, 1: 71n

THEOPHRASTUS

METAPHYSICS

9^b13–16: 106n

FRAGMENTS (ACCORDING TO THE ORDERING OF FORTENBAUGH *ET AL.*)

T100B: 210n
T100D: 210n

FRAGMENTS (ACCORDING TO THE ORDERING OF GRAESER)

F 14: 210n

Lightning Source UK Ltd.
Milton Keynes UK
UKHW011923040819
347408UK00001B/20/P

9 780521 036474